BOURBON ISLAND 1730

BOURBON ISLAND 1730

By Appollo & Lewis Trondheim
Art by Lewis Trondheim

Translated by Alexis Siegel

First Second
New York & London

Disclaimer:
Bourbon Island 1730 is not intended to be a historical account.
It is a fictional narrative, freely inspired by historical events.

THE BIRDS

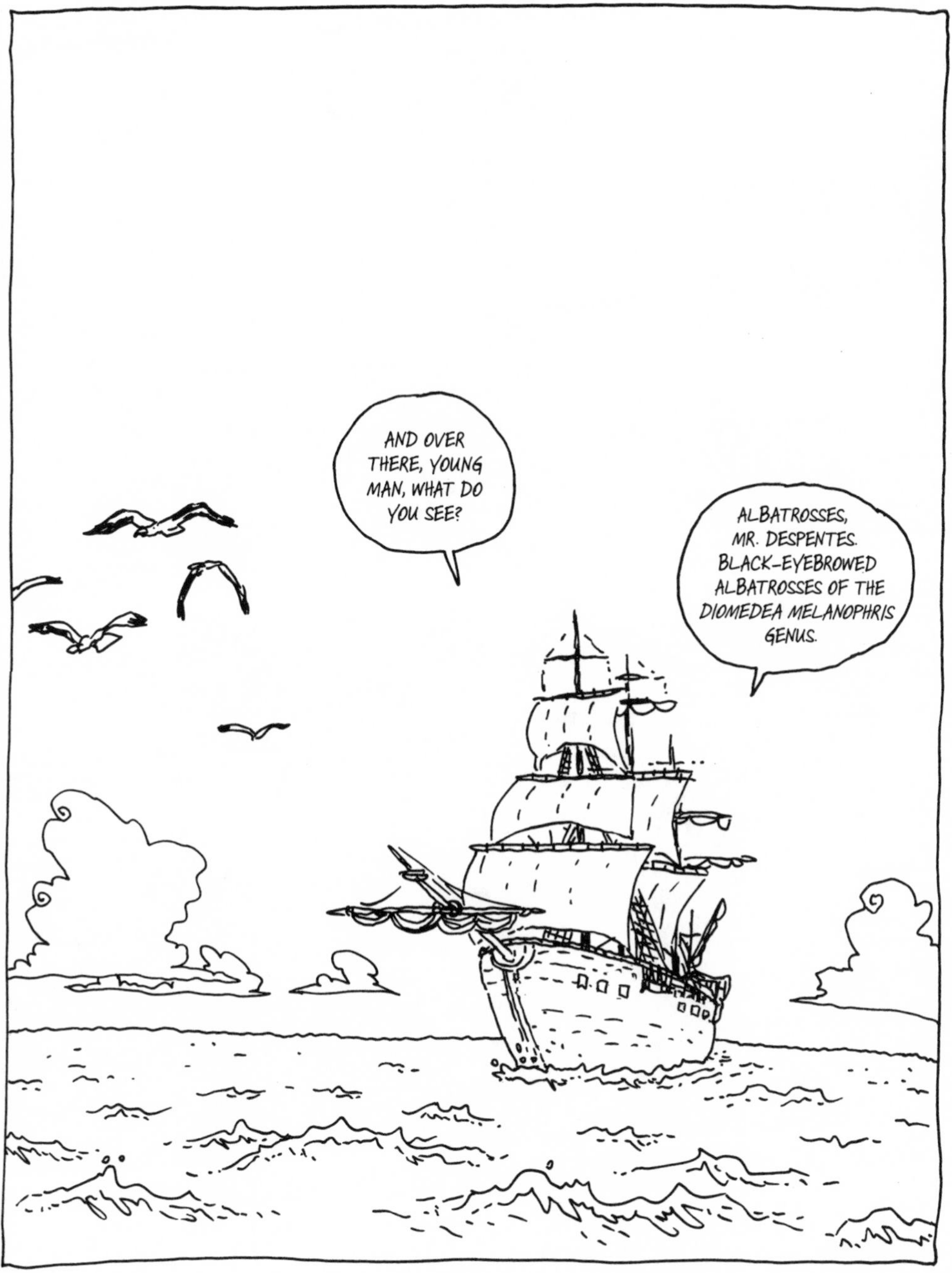
AND OVER THERE, YOUNG MAN, WHAT DO YOU SEE?
ALBATROSSES, MR. DESPENTES. BLACK-EYEBROWED ALBATROSSES OF THE DIOMEDEA MELANOPHRIS GENUS.

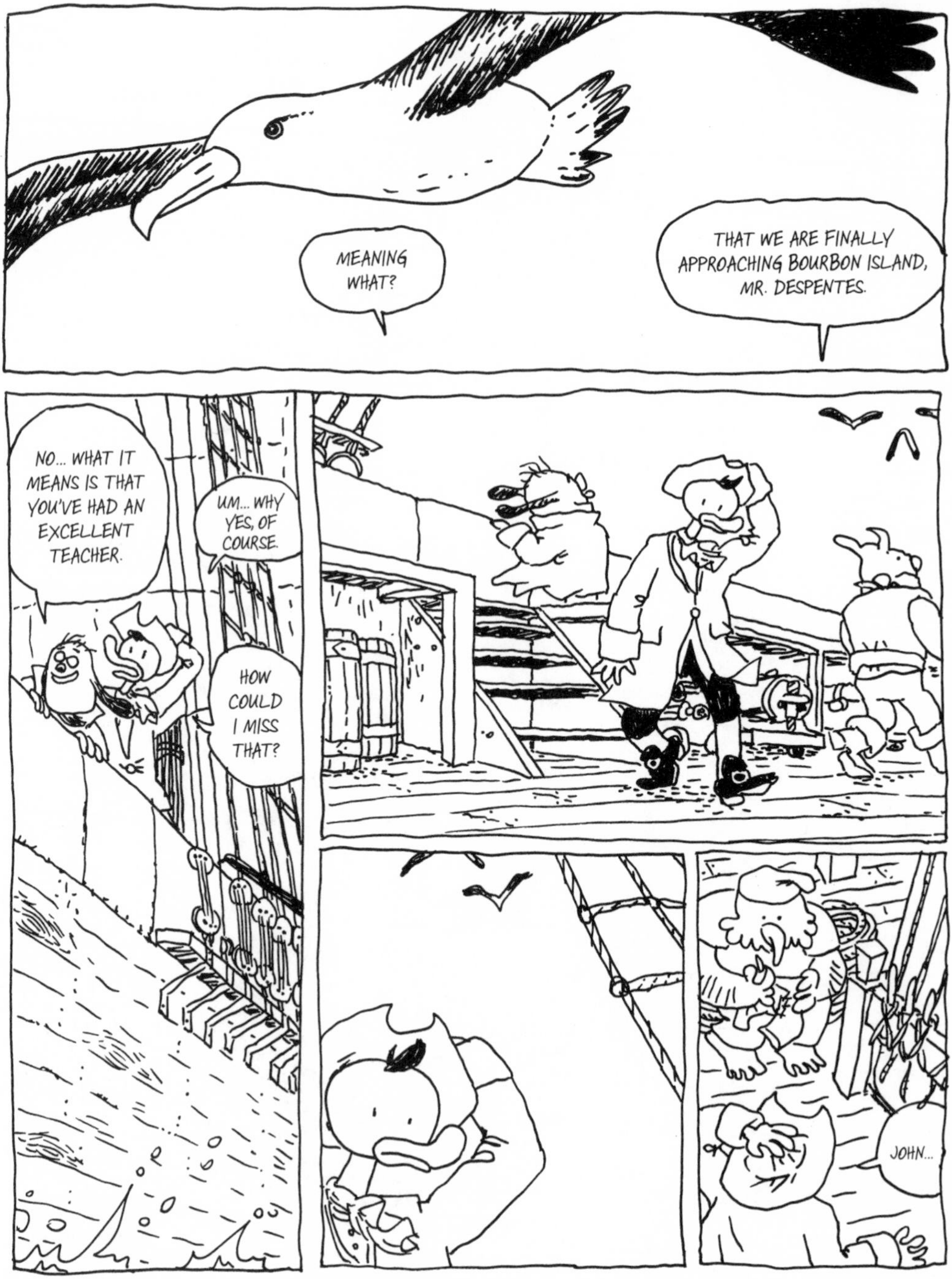
MEANING WHAT?
THAT WE ARE FINALLY APPROACHING BOURBON ISLAND, MR. DESPENTES.
NO... WHAT IT MEANS IS THAT YOU'VE HAD AN EXCELLENT TEACHER.
UM... WHY YES, OF COURSE.
HOW COULD I MISS THAT?
JOHN...

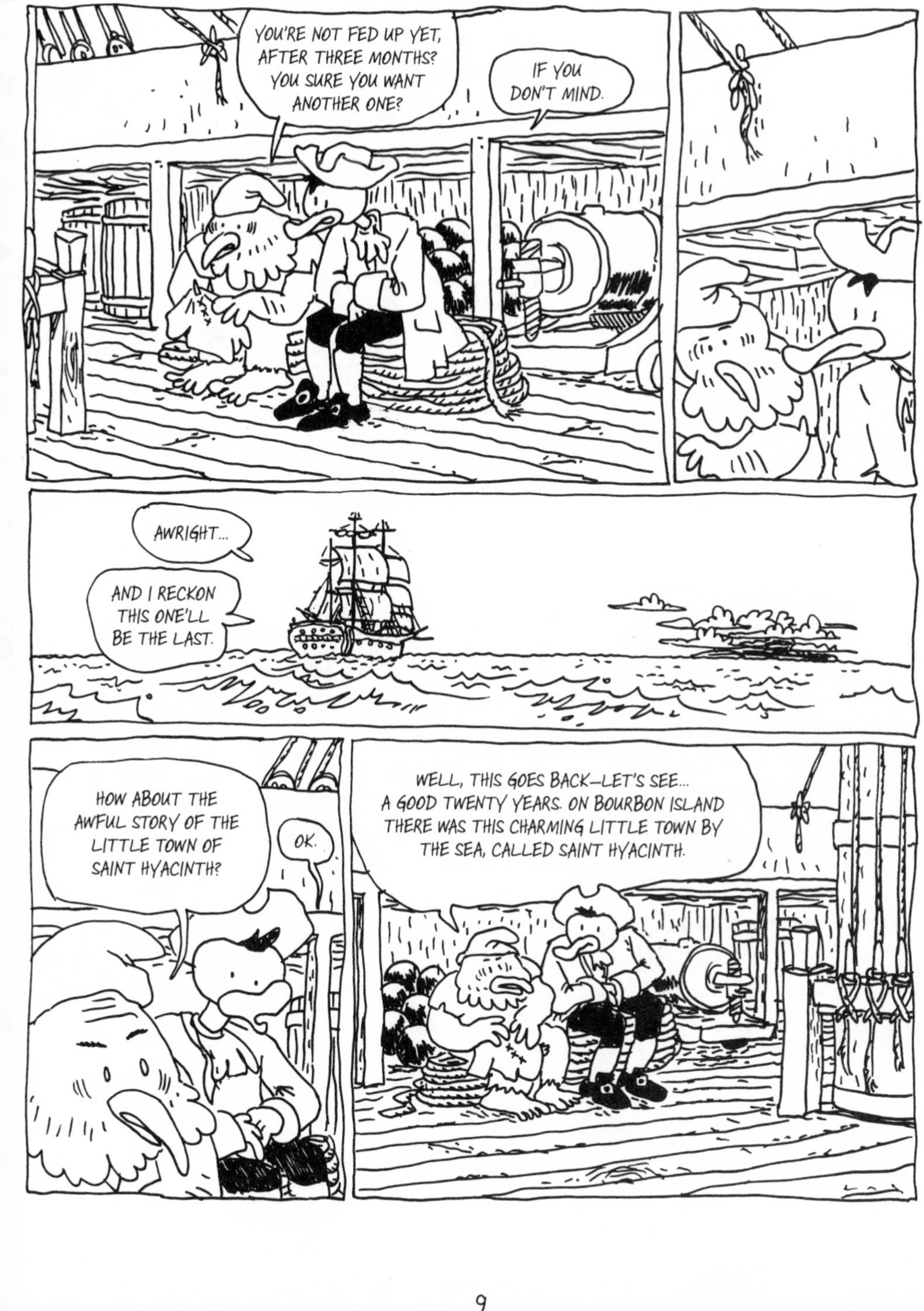
YOU'RE NOT FED UP YET, AFTER THREE MONTHS? YOU SURE YOU WANT ANOTHER ONE?
IF YOU DON'T MIND.
AWRIGHT...
AND I RECKON THIS ONE'LL BE THE LAST.
HOW ABOUT THE AWFUL STORY OF THE LITTLE TOWN OF SAINT HYACINTH?
OK.
WELL, THIS GOES BACK—LET'S SEE... A GOOD TWENTY YEARS. ON BOURBON ISLAND THERE WAS THIS CHARMING LITTLE TOWN BY THE SEA, CALLED SAINT HYACINTH.

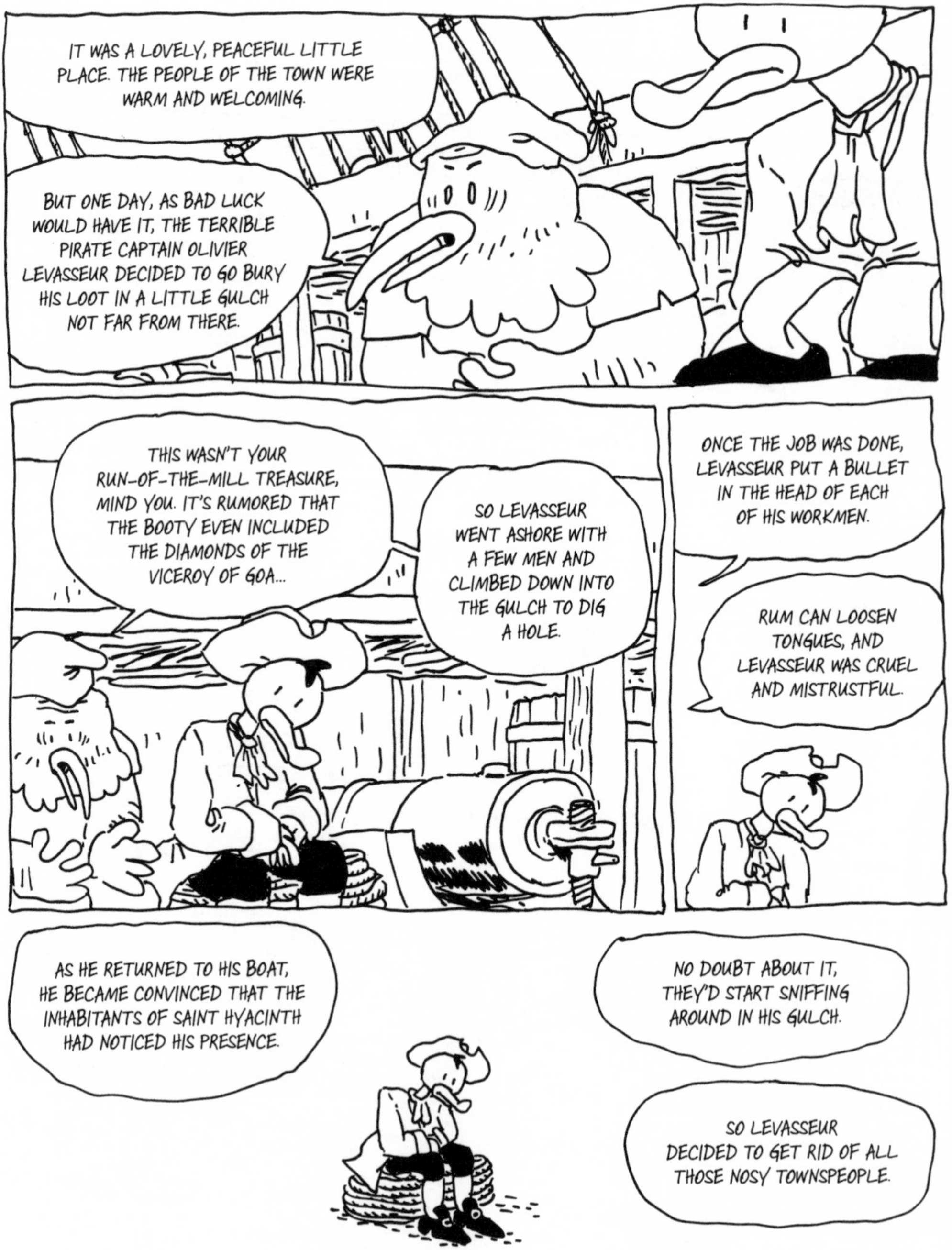
IT WAS A LOVELY, PEACEFUL LITTLE PLACE. THE PEOPLE OF THE TOWN WERE WARM AND WELCOMING.
BUT ONE DAY, AS BAD LUCK WOULD HAVE IT, THE TERRIBLE PIRATE CAPTAIN OLIVIER LEVASSEUR DECIDED TO GO BURY HIS LOOT IN A LITTLE GULCH NOT FAR FROM THERE.
THIS WASN'T YOUR RUN-OF-THE-MILL TREASURE, MIND YOU. IT'S RUMORED THAT THE BOOTY EVEN INCLUDED THE DIAMONDS OF THE VICEROY OF GOA...
SO LEVASSEUR WENT ASHORE WITH A FEW MEN AND CLIMBED DOWN INTO THE GULCH TO DIG A HOLE.
ONCE THE JOB WAS DONE, LEVASSEUR PUT A BULLET IN THE HEAD OF EACH OF HIS WORKMEN.
RUM CAN LOOSEN TONGUES, AND LEVASSEUR WAS CRUEL AND MISTRUSTFUL.
AS HE RETURNED TO HIS BOAT, HE BECAME CONVINCED THAT THE INHABITANTS OF SAINT HYACINTH HAD NOTICED HIS PRESENCE.
NO DOUBT ABOUT IT, THEY'D START SNIFFING AROUND IN HIS GULCH.
SO LEVASSEUR DECIDED TO GET RID OF ALL THOSE NOSY TOWNSPEOPLE.

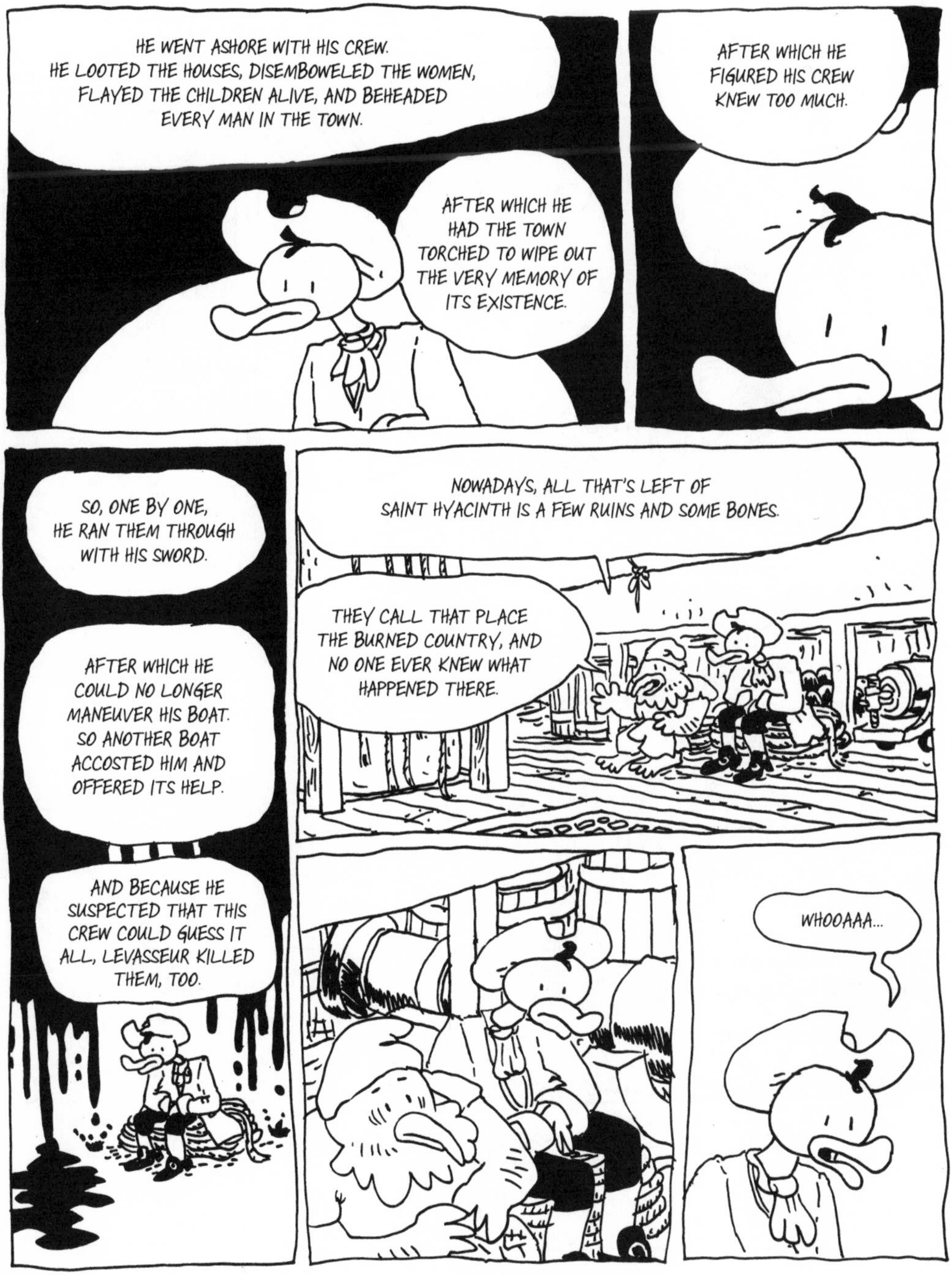
HE WENT ASHORE WITH HIS CREW. HE LOOTED THE HOUSES, DISEMBOWELED THE WOMEN, FLAYED THE CHILDREN ALIVE, AND BEHEADED EVERY MAN IN THE TOWN.
AFTER WHICH HE HAD THE TOWN TORCHED TO WIPE OUT THE VERY MEMORY OF ITS EXISTENCE.
AFTER WHICH HE FIGURED HIS CREW KNEW TOO MUCH.
SO, ONE BY ONE, HE RAN THEM THROUGH WITH HIS SWORD.
AFTER WHICH HE COULD NO LONGER MANEUVER HIS BOAT. SO ANOTHER BOAT ACCOSTED HIM AND OFFERED ITS HELP.
AND BECAUSE HE SUSPECTED THAT THIS CREW COULD GUESS IT ALL, LEVASSEUR KILLED THEM, TOO.
NOWADAYS, ALL THAT'S LEFT OF SAINT HYACINTH IS A FEW RUINS AND SOME BONES.
THEY CALL THAT PLACE THE BURNED COUNTRY, AND NO ONE EVER KNEW WHAT HAPPENED THERE.
WHOOAAA...

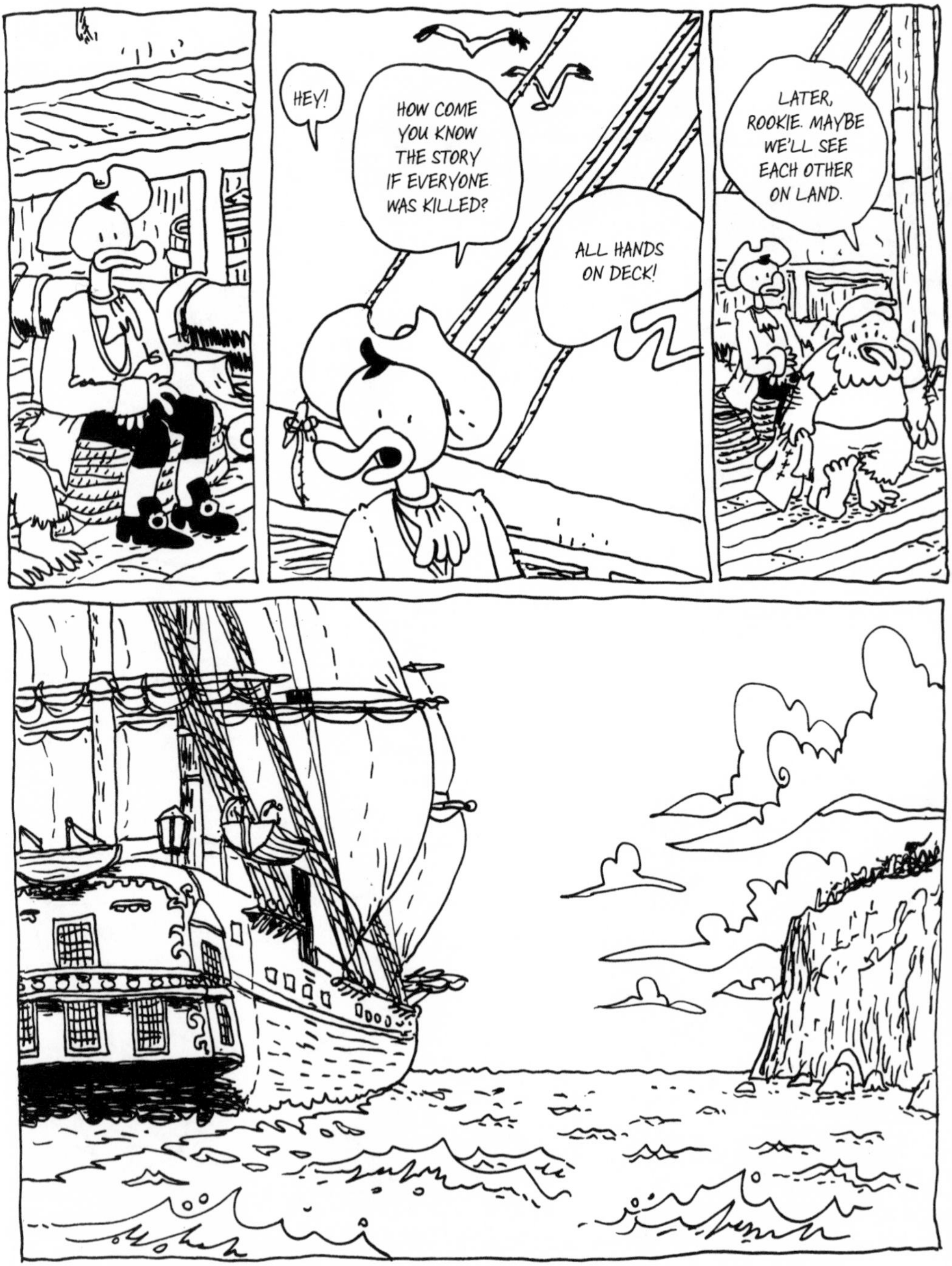
HEY!
HOW COME YOU KNOW THE STORY IF EVERYONE WAS KILLED?
ALL HANDS ON DECK!
LATER, ROOKIE. MAYBE WE'LL SEE EACH OTHER ON LAND.

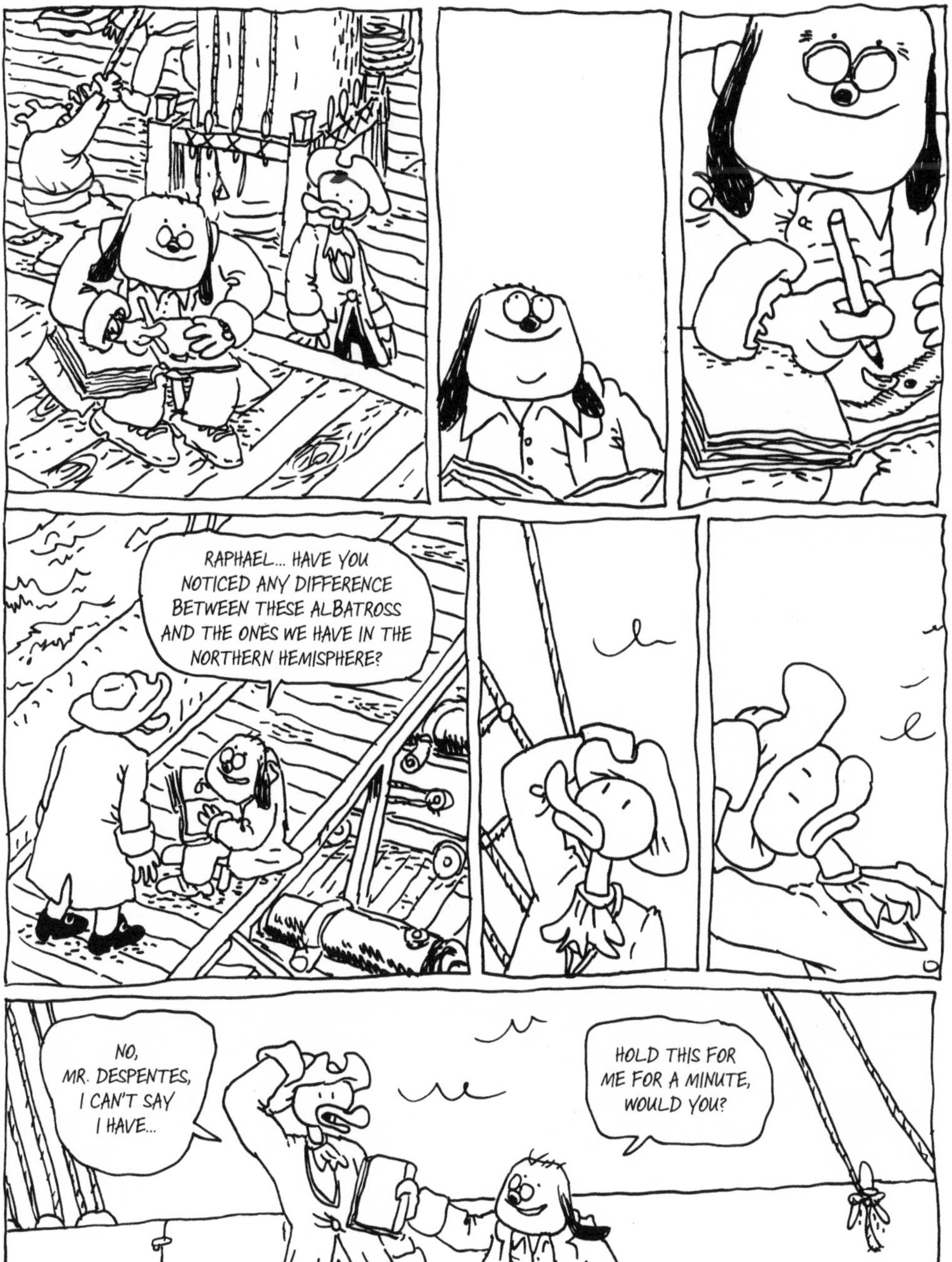
RAPHAEL... HAVE YOU NOTICED ANY DIFFERENCE BETWEEN THESE ALBATROSS AND THE ONES WE HAVE IN THE NORTHERN HEMISPHERE?
NO, MR. DESPENTES, I CAN'T SAY I HAVE...
HOLD THIS FOR ME FOR A MINUTE, WOULD YOU?

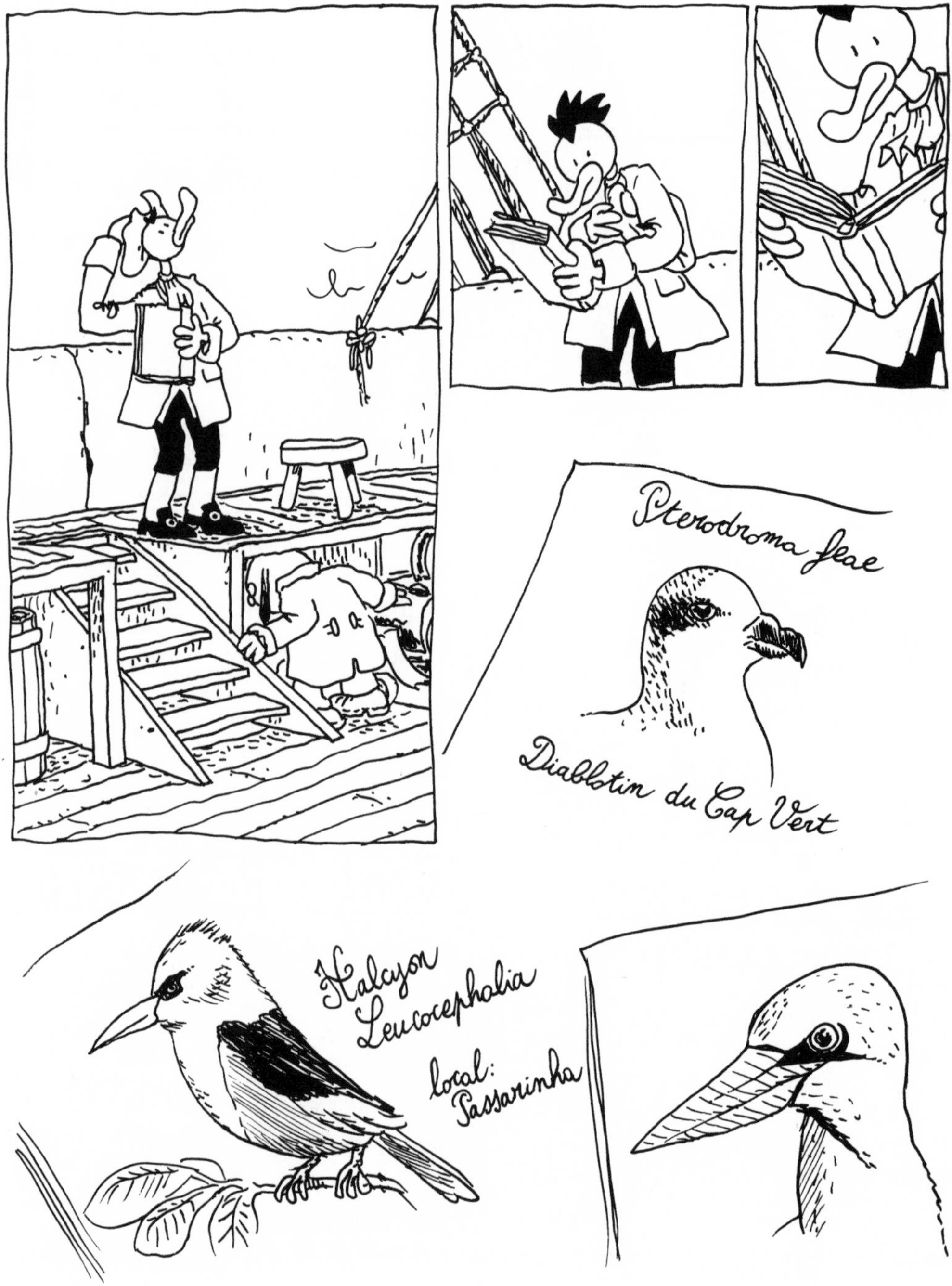
Pterodroma feae
Diablotin du Cap Vert
Halcyon Leucocephalia
local: Passarinha

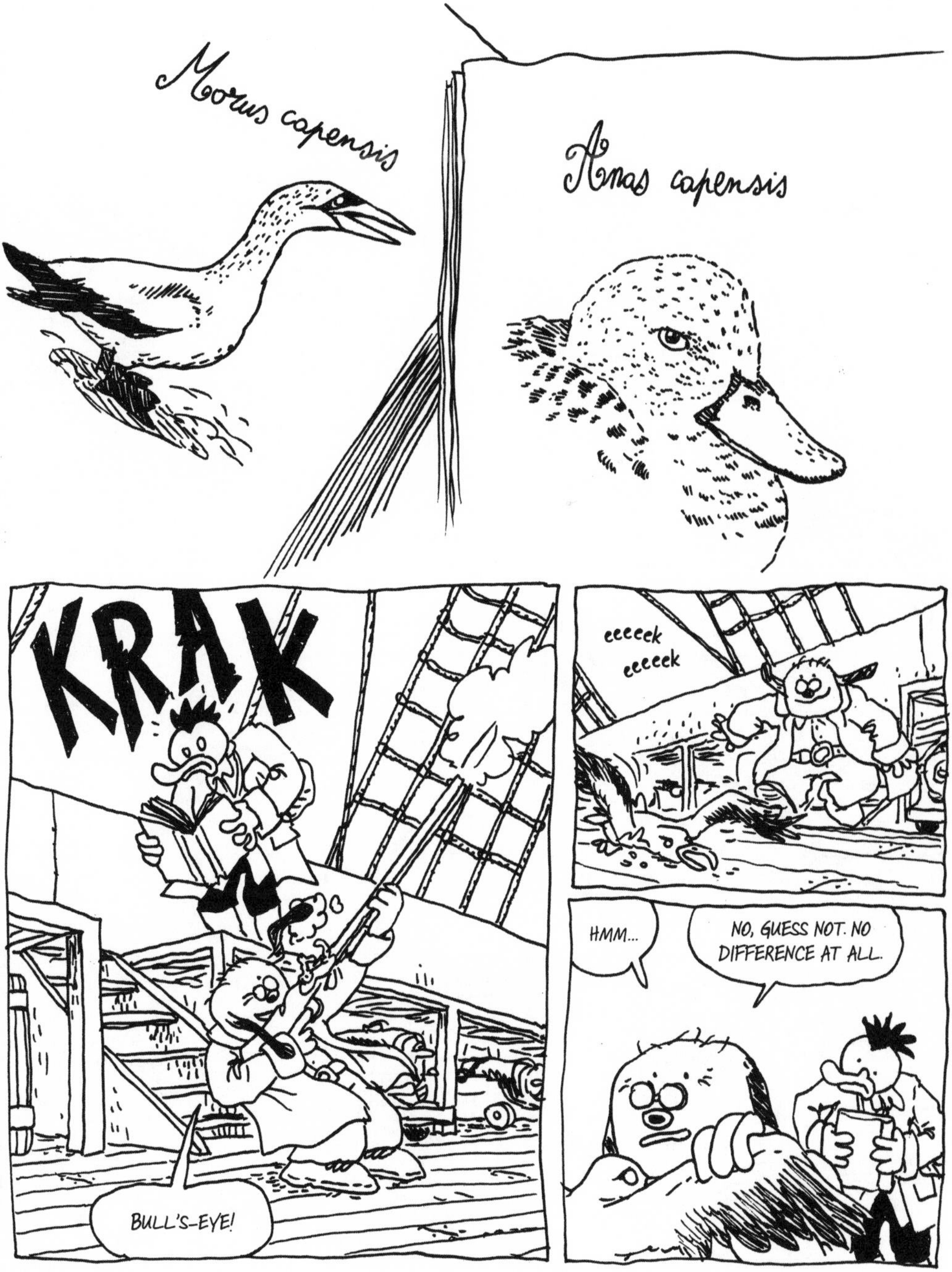
Morus capensis
Anas capensis
KRAK
BULL'S-EYE!
eeeeek
eeeeek
HMM...
NO, GUESS NOT. NO DIFFERENCE AT ALL.

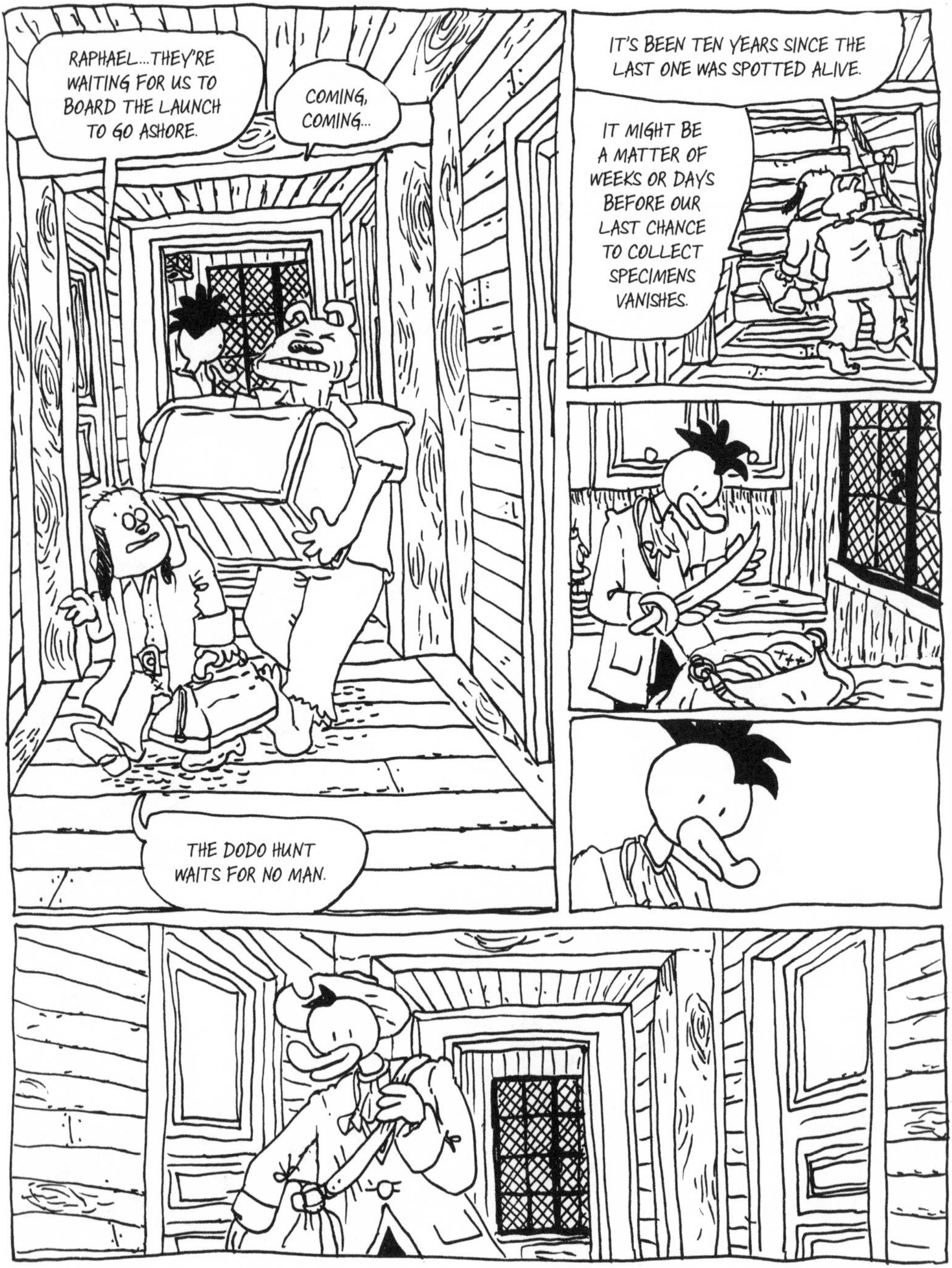
RAPHAEL...THEY'RE WAITING FOR US TO BOARD THE LAUNCH TO GO ASHORE.
COMING, COMING...
THE DODO HUNT WAITS FOR NO MAN.
IT'S BEEN TEN YEARS SINCE THE LAST ONE WAS SPOTTED ALIVE.
IT MIGHT BE A MATTER OF WEEKS OR DAYS BEFORE OUR LAST CHANCE TO COLLECT SPECIMENS VANISHES.

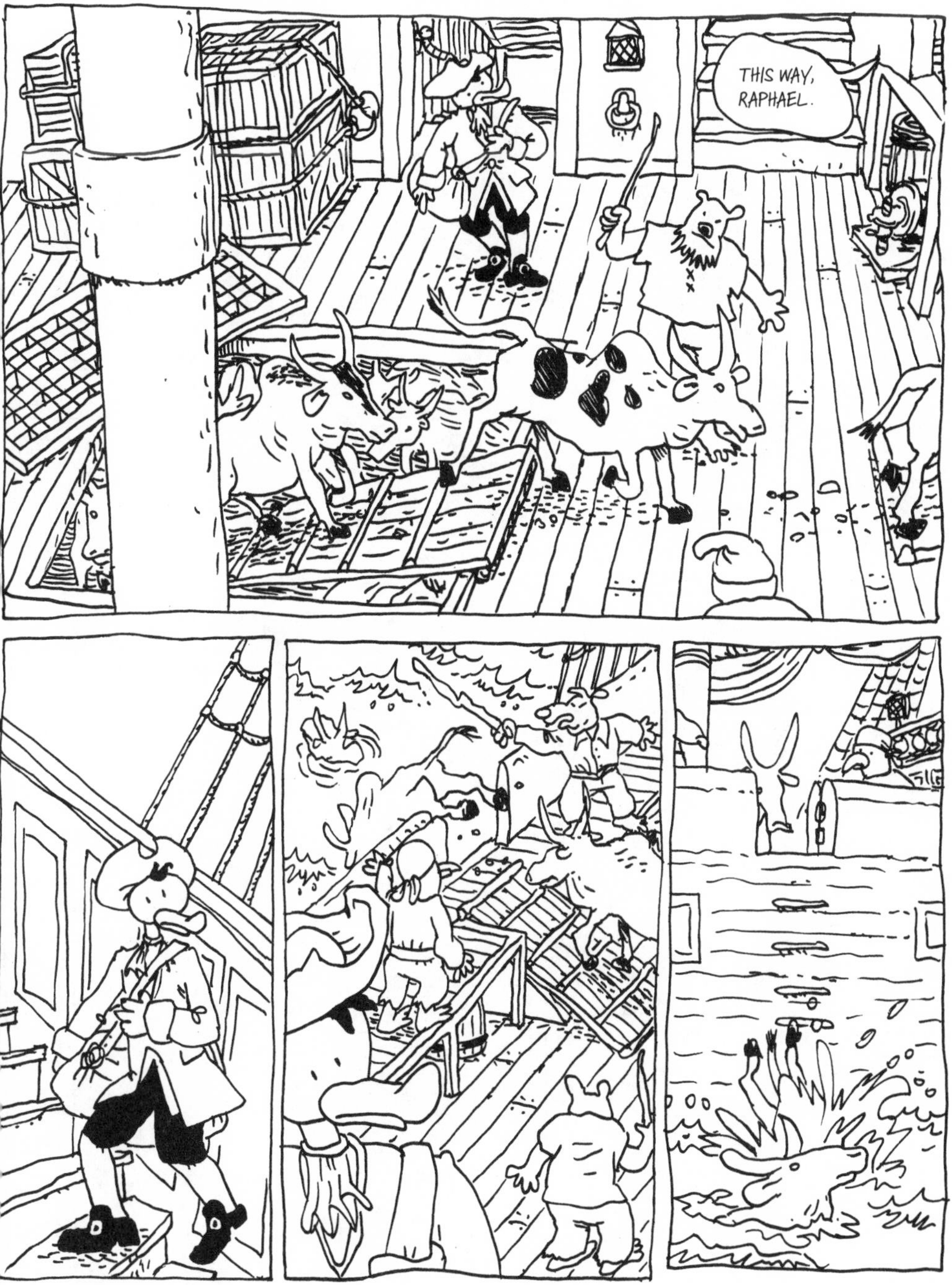
THIS WAY, RAPHAEL.

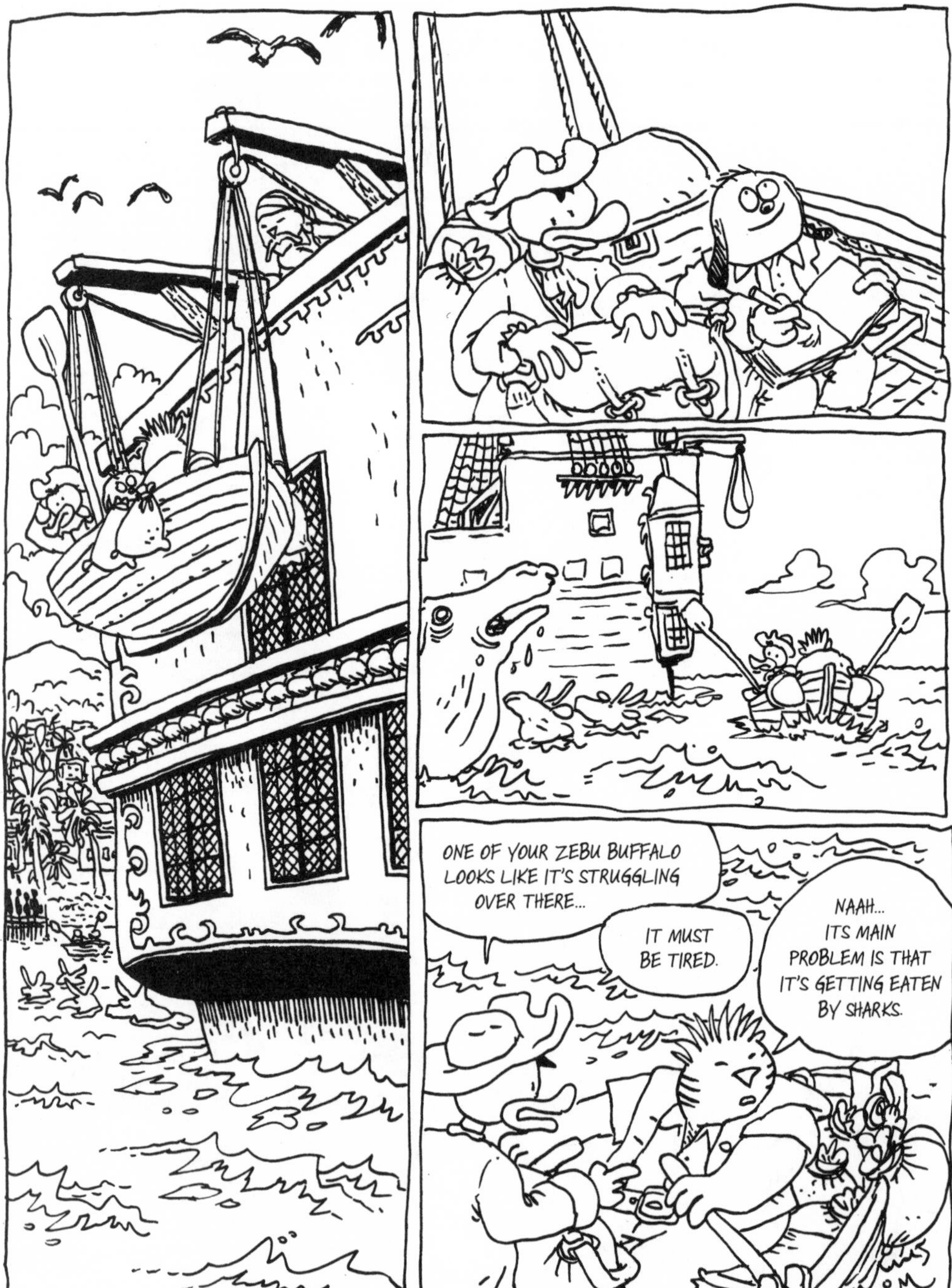
ONE OF YOUR ZEBU BUFFALO LOOKS LIKE IT'S STRUGGLING OVER THERE...
IT MUST BE TIRED.
NAAH... ITS MAIN PROBLEM IS THAT IT'S GETTING EATEN BY SHARKS.

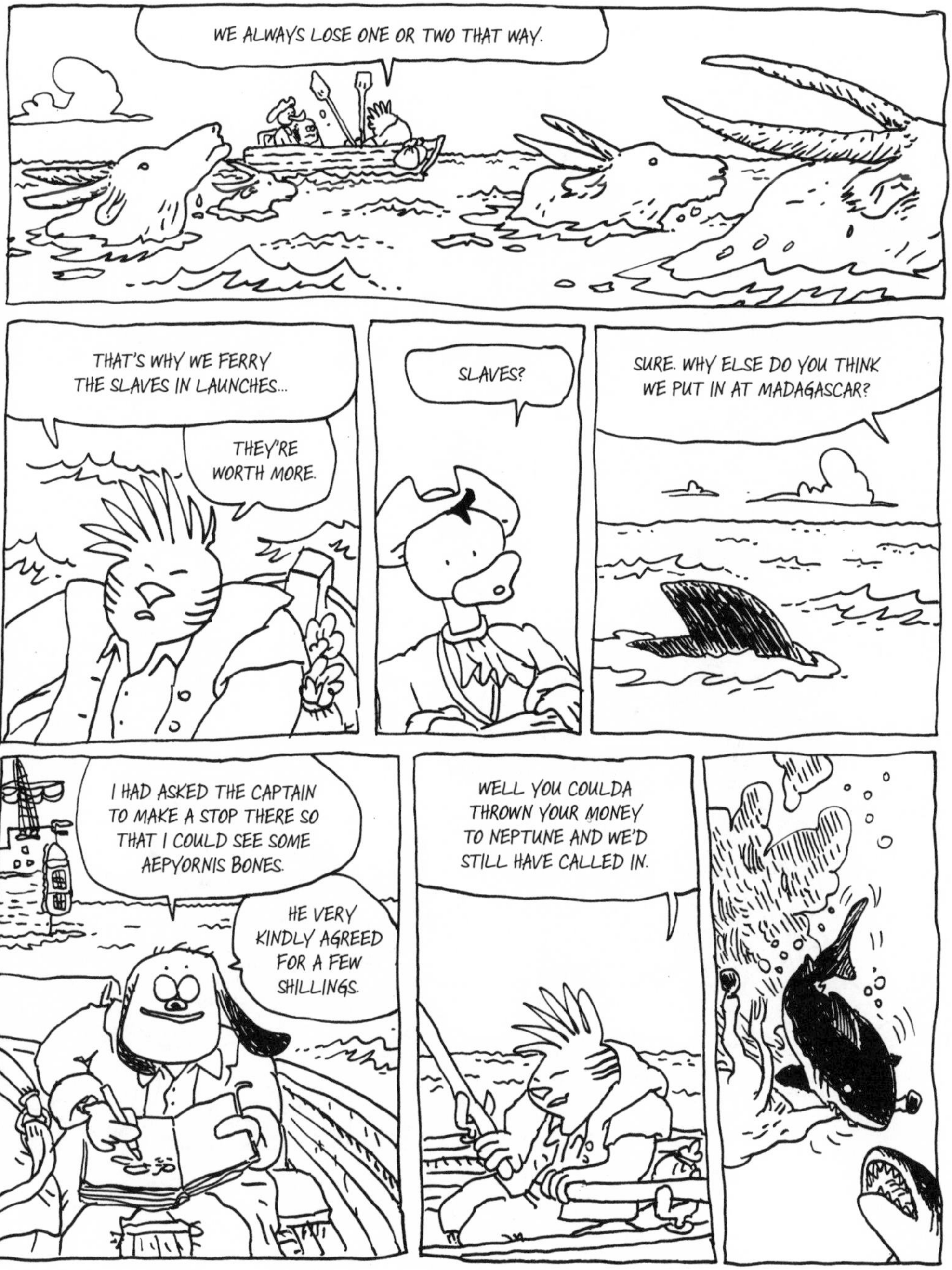
WE ALWAYS LOSE ONE OR TWO THAT WAY.
THAT'S WHY WE FERRY THE SLAVES IN LAUNCHES...
THEY'RE WORTH MORE.
SLAVES?
SURE. WHY ELSE DO YOU THINK WE PUT IN AT MADAGASCAR?
I HAD ASKED THE CAPTAIN TO MAKE A STOP THERE SO THAT I COULD SEE SOME AEPYORNIS BONES.
HE VERY KINDLY AGREED FOR A FEW SHILLINGS.
WELL YOU COULDA THROWN YOUR MONEY TO NEPTUNE AND WE'D STILL HAVE CALLED IN.

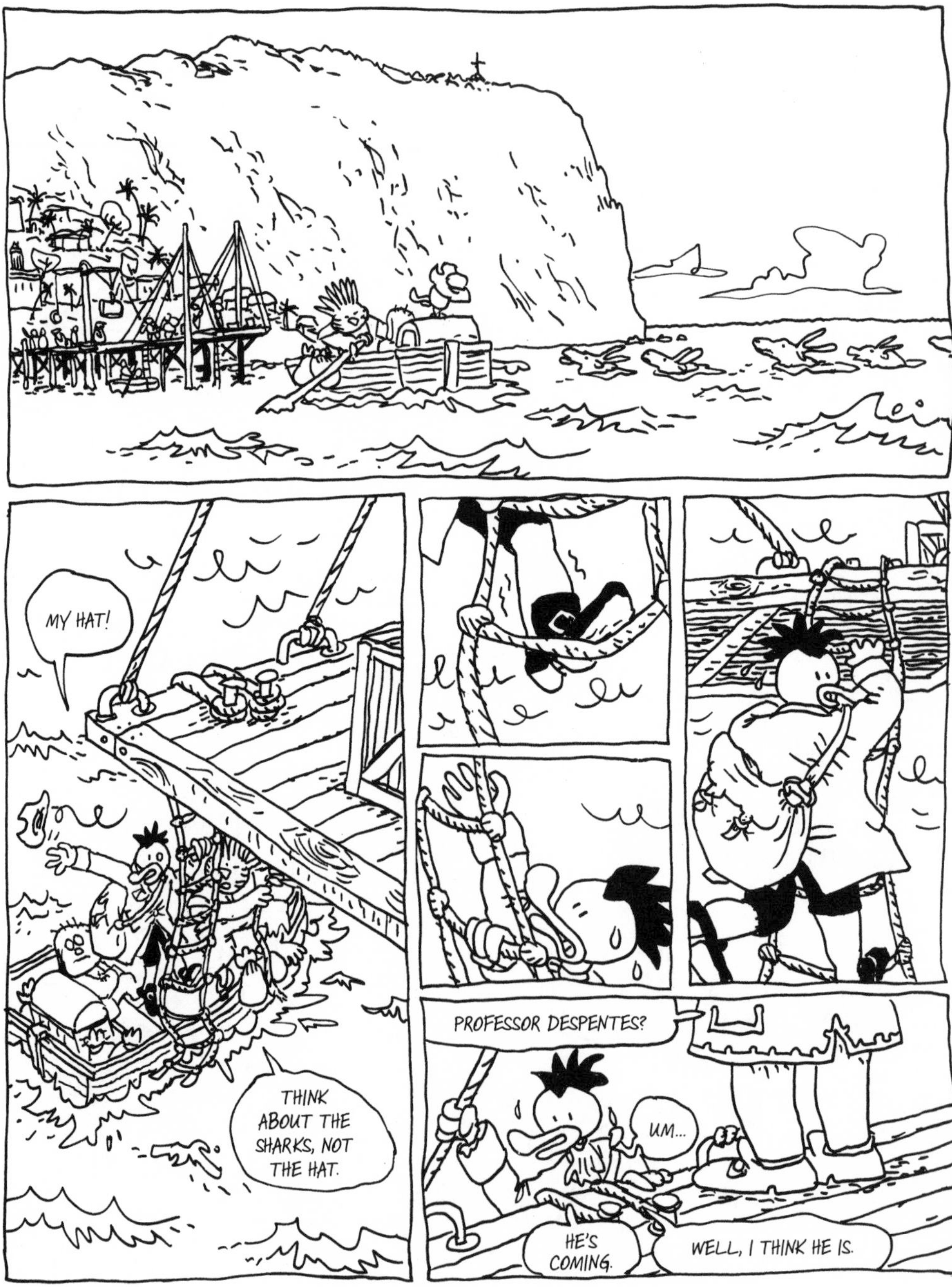
MY HAT!
THINK ABOUT THE SHARKS, NOT THE HAT.
PROFESSOR DESPENTES?
UM...
HE'S COMING.
WELL, I THINK HE IS.

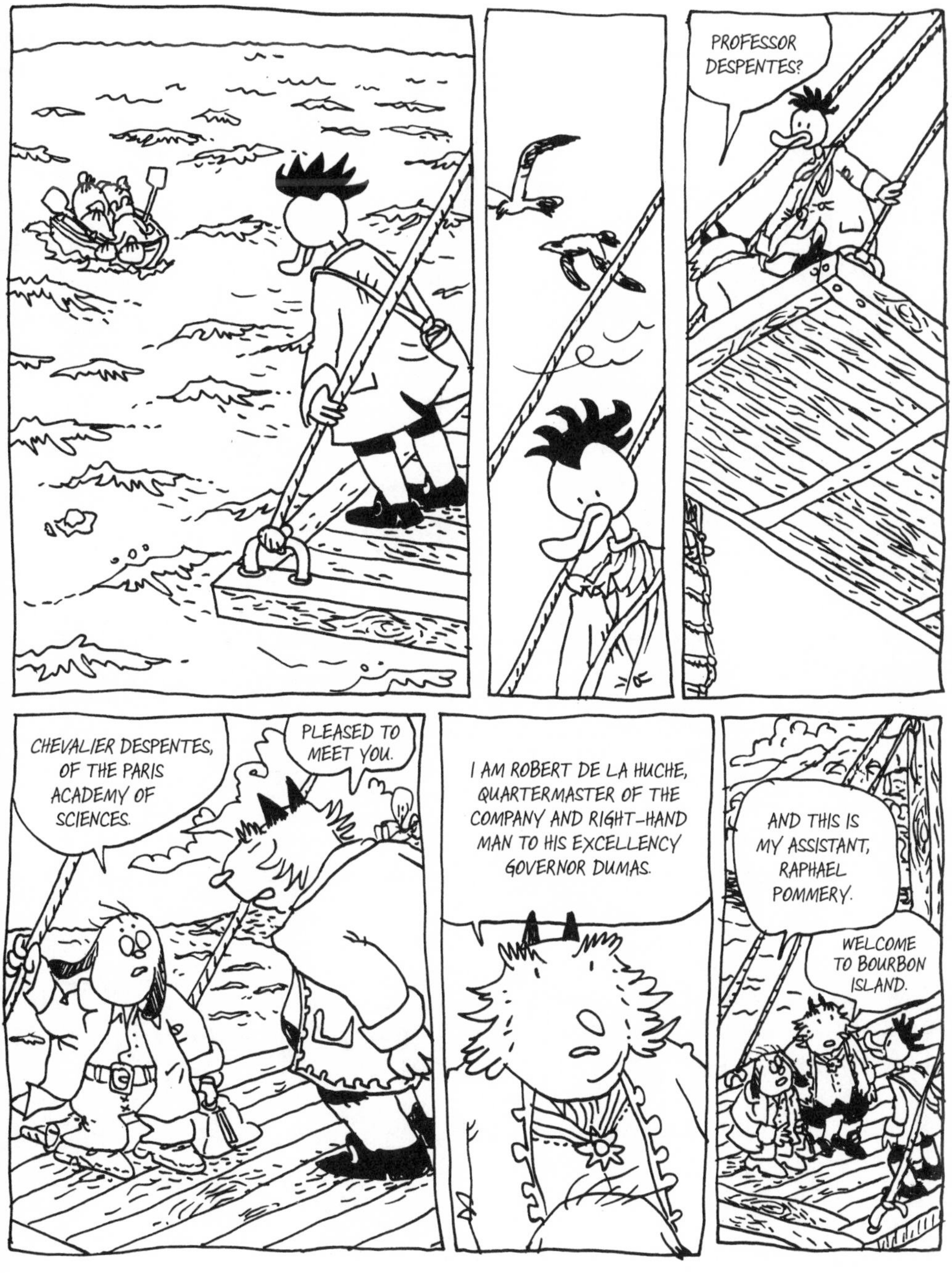
PROFESSOR DESPENTES?
CHEVALIER DESPENTES, OF THE PARIS ACADEMY OF SCIENCES.
PLEASED TO MEET YOU.
I AM ROBERT DE LA HUCHE, QUARTERMASTER OF THE COMPANY AND RIGHT-HAND MAN TO HIS EXCELLENCY GOVERNOR DUMAS.
AND THIS IS MY ASSISTANT, RAPHAEL POMMERY.
WELCOME TO BOURBON ISLAND.

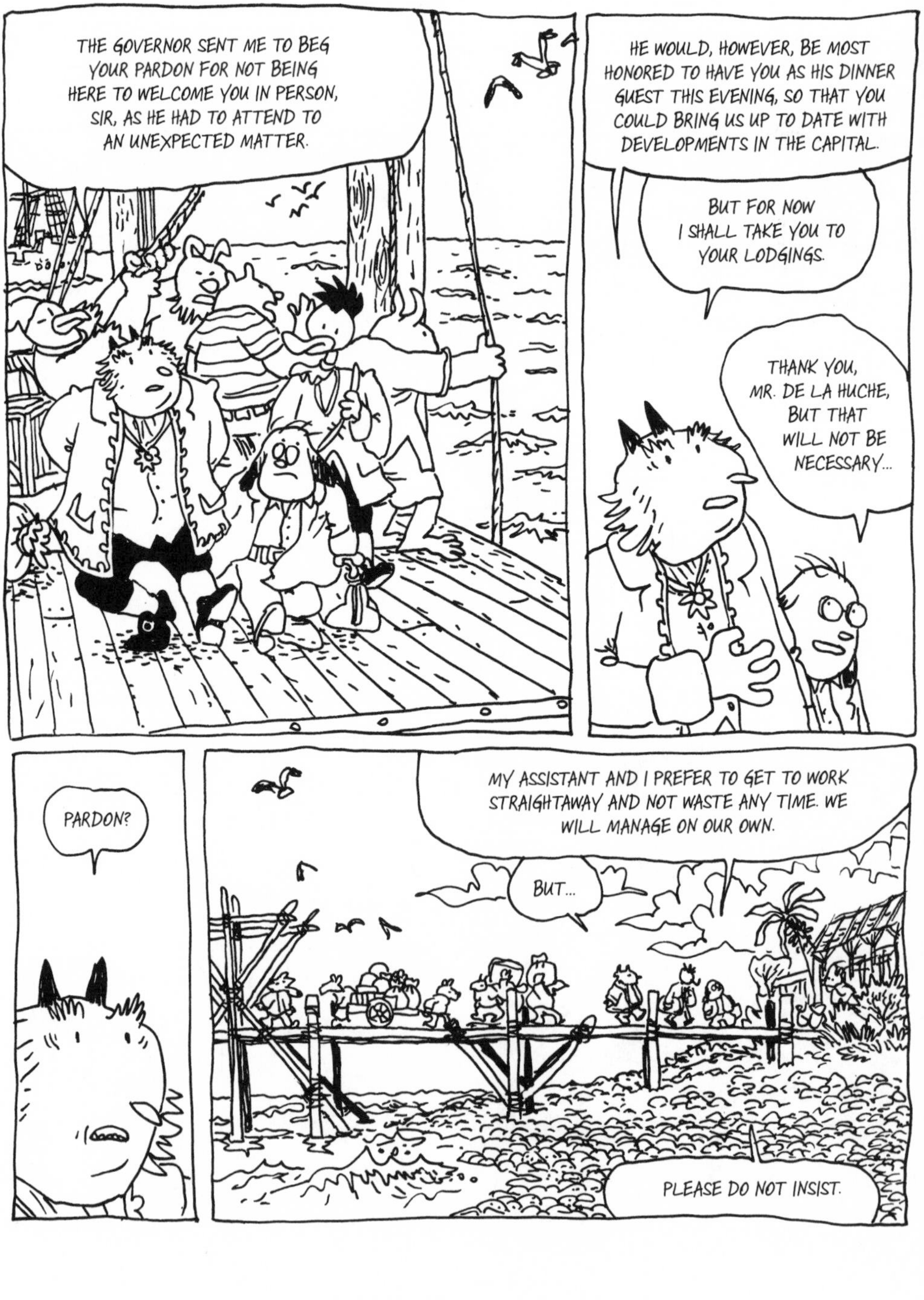
THE GOVERNOR SENT ME TO BEG YOUR PARDON FOR NOT BEING HERE TO WELCOME YOU IN PERSON, SIR, AS HE HAD TO ATTEND TO AN UNEXPECTED MATTER.
HE WOULD, HOWEVER, BE MOST HONORED TO HAVE YOU AS HIS DINNER GUEST THIS EVENING, SO THAT YOU COULD BRING US UP TO DATE WITH DEVELOPMENTS IN THE CAPITAL.
BUT FOR NOW I SHALL TAKE YOU TO YOUR LODGINGS.
THANK YOU, MR. DE LA HUCHE, BUT THAT WILL NOT BE NECESSARY...
PARDON?
MY ASSISTANT AND I PREFER TO GET TO WORK STRAIGHTAWAY AND NOT WASTE ANY TIME. WE WILL MANAGE ON OUR OWN.
BUT...
PLEASE DO NOT INSIST.

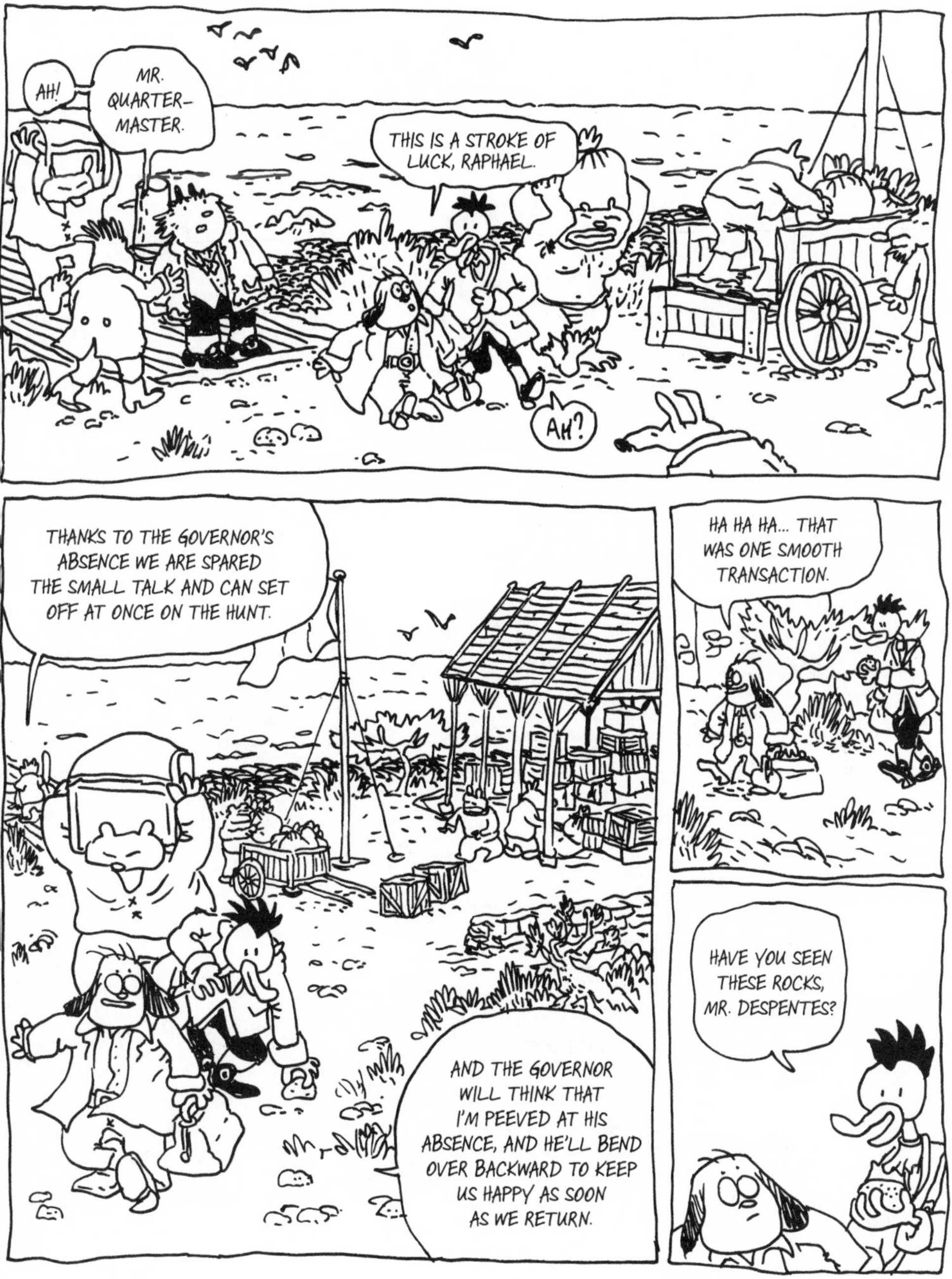
AH!
MR. QUARTER-MASTER.
THIS IS A STROKE OF LUCK, RAPHAEL.
AH?
THANKS TO THE GOVERNOR'S ABSENCE WE ARE SPARED THE SMALL TALK AND CAN SET OFF AT ONCE ON THE HUNT.
AND THE GOVERNOR WILL THINK THAT I'M PEEVED AT HIS ABSENCE, AND HE'LL BEND OVER BACKWARD TO KEEP US HAPPY AS SOON AS WE RETURN.
HA HA HA... THAT WAS ONE SMOOTH TRANSACTION.
HAVE YOU SEEN THESE ROCKS, MR. DESPENTES?

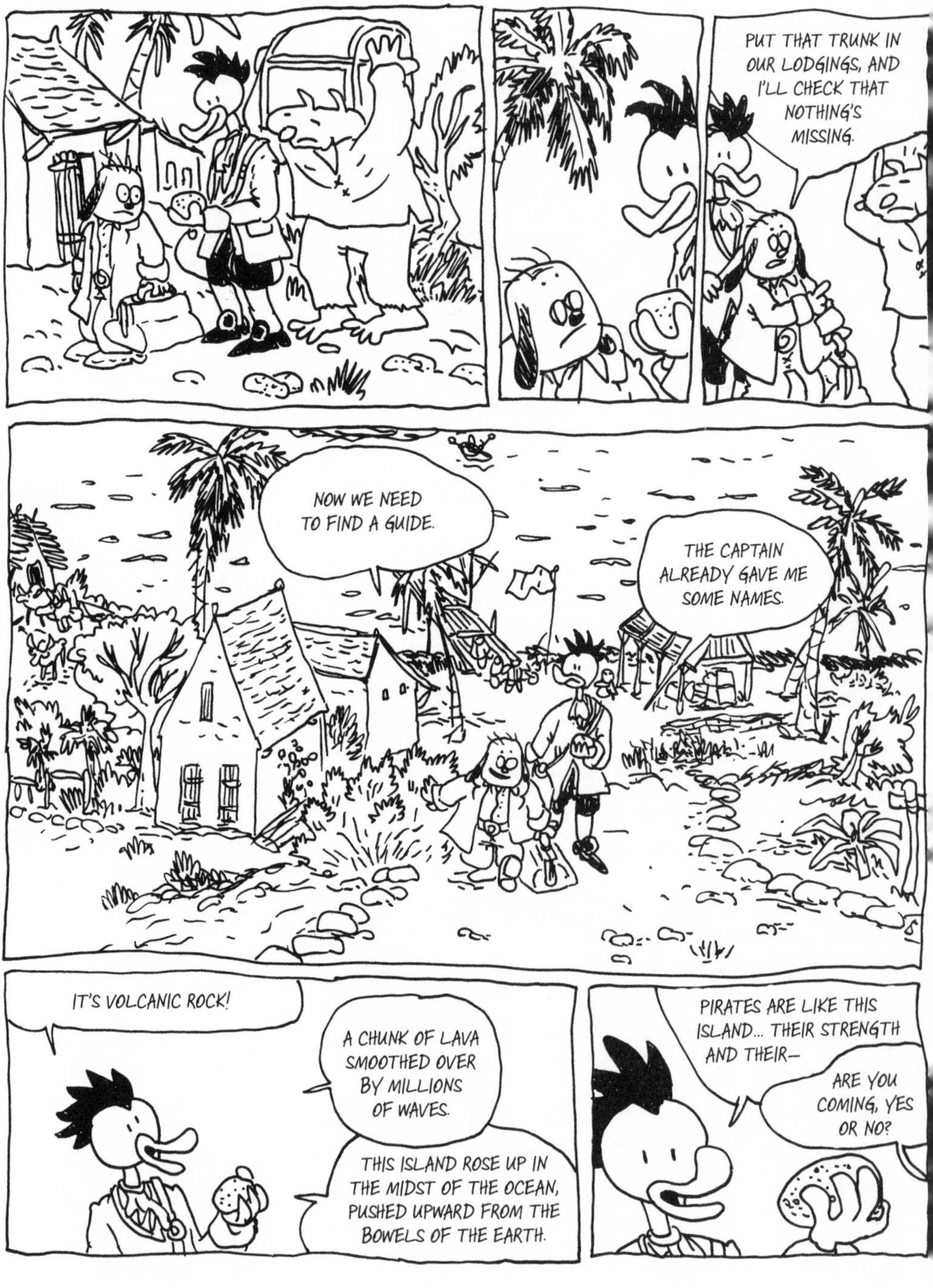
PUT THAT TRUNK IN OUR LODGINGS, AND I'LL CHECK THAT NOTHING'S MISSING.
NOW WE NEED TO FIND A GUIDE.
THE CAPTAIN ALREADY GAVE ME SOME NAMES.
IT'S VOLCANIC ROCK!
A CHUNK OF LAVA SMOOTHED OVER BY MILLIONS OF WAVES.
THIS ISLAND ROSE UP IN THE MIDST OF THE OCEAN, PUSHED UPWARD FROM THE BOWELS OF THE EARTH.
PIRATES ARE LIKE THIS ISLAND... THEIR STRENGTH AND THEIR—
ARE YOU COMING, YES OR NO?

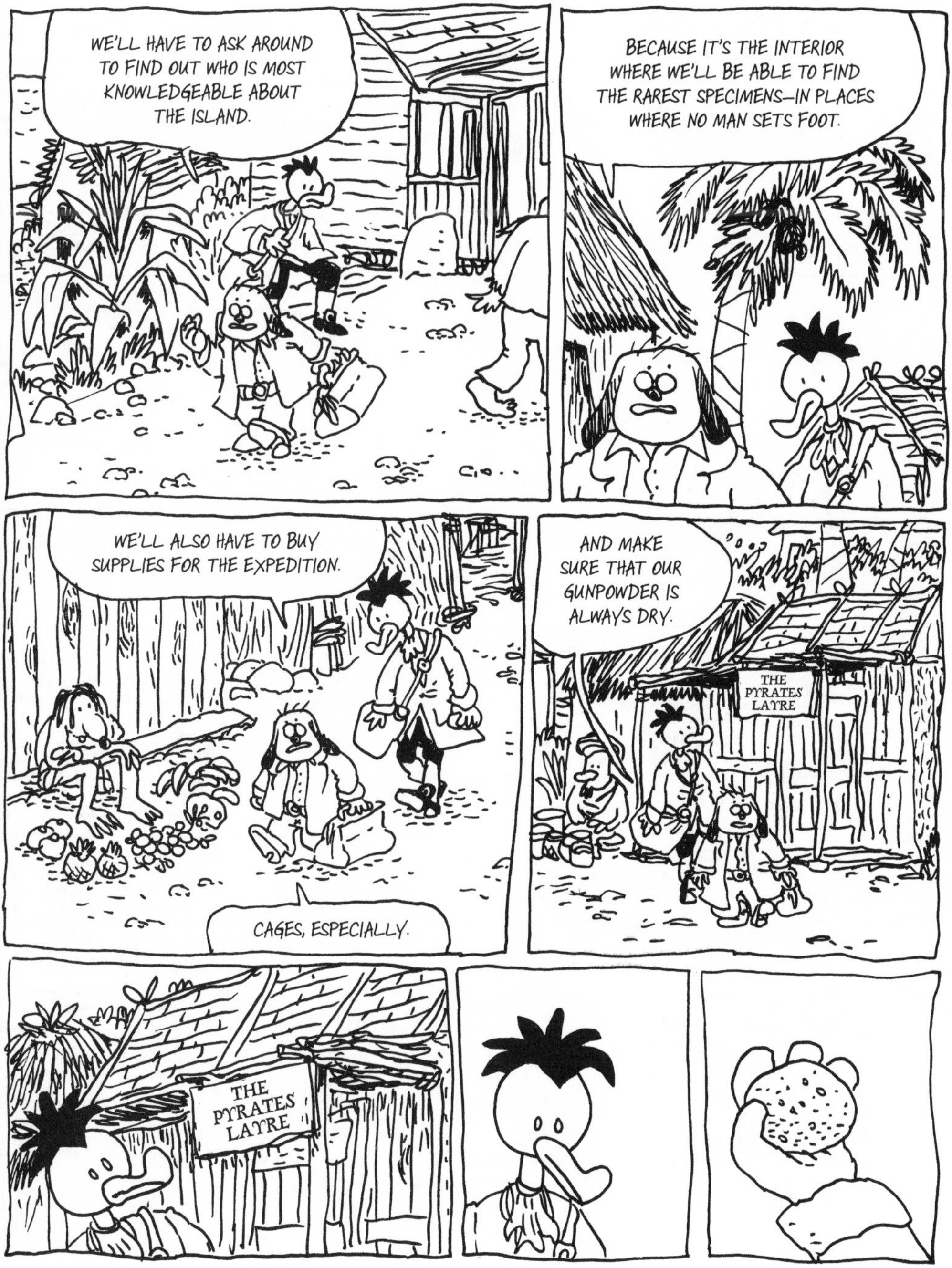
WE'LL HAVE TO ASK AROUND TO FIND OUT WHO IS MOST KNOWLEDGEABLE ABOUT THE ISLAND.
BECAUSE IT'S THE INTERIOR WHERE WE'LL BE ABLE TO FIND THE RAREST SPECIMENS—IN PLACES WHERE NO MAN SETS FOOT.
WE'LL ALSO HAVE TO BUY SUPPLIES FOR THE EXPEDITION.
CAGES, ESPECIALLY.
AND MAKE SURE THAT OUR GUNPOWDER IS ALWAYS DRY.
THE PYRATES LAYRE
THE PYRATES LAYRE

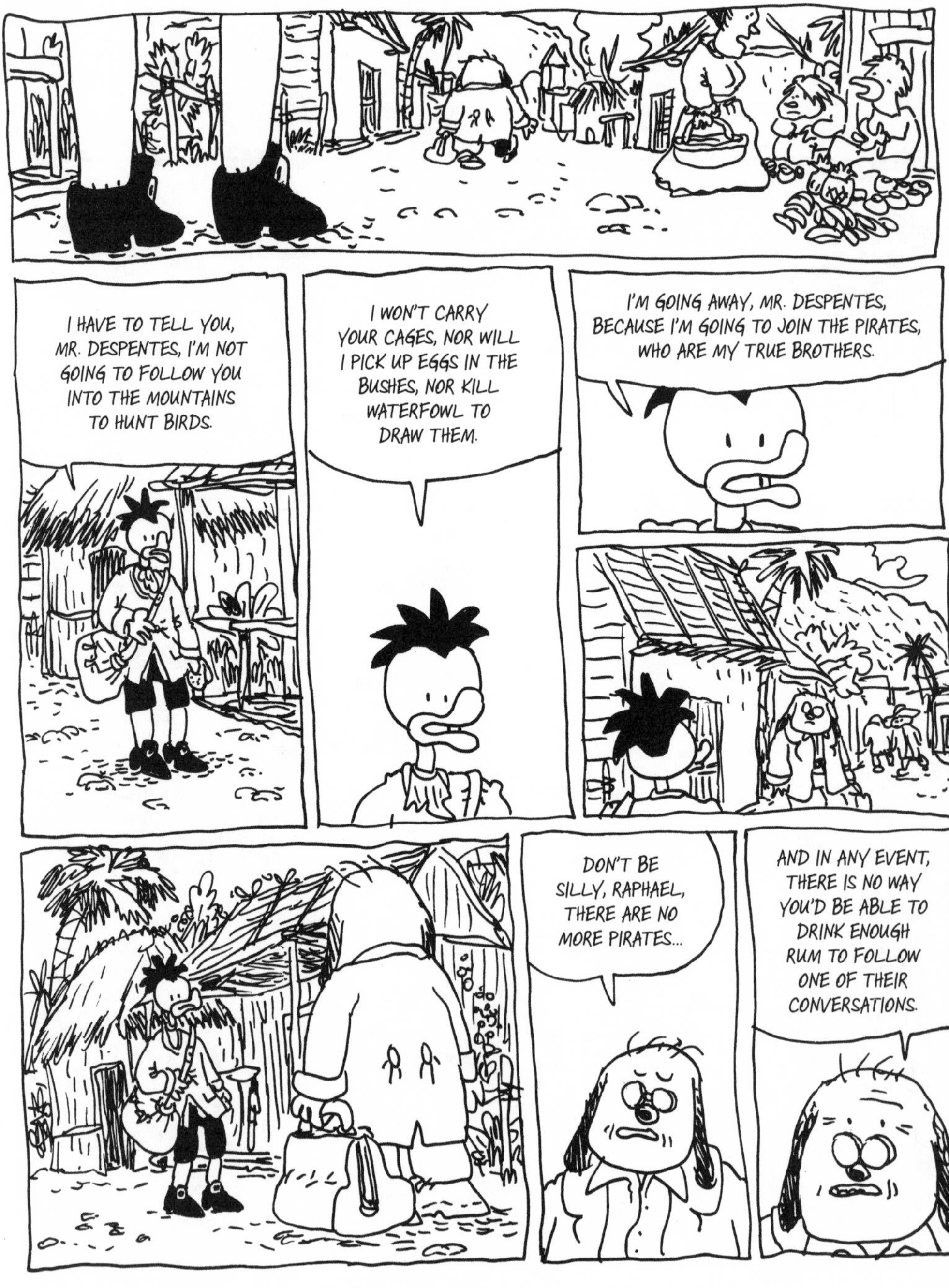
I HAVE TO TELL YOU, MR. DESPENTES, I'M NOT GOING TO FOLLOW YOU INTO THE MOUNTAINS TO HUNT BIRDS.
I WON'T CARRY YOUR CAGES, NOR WILL I PICK UP EGGS IN THE BUSHES, NOR KILL WATERFOWL TO DRAW THEM.
I'M GOING AWAY, MR. DESPENTES, BECAUSE I'M GOING TO JOIN THE PIRATES, WHO ARE MY TRUE BROTHERS.
DON'T BE SILLY, RAPHAEL, THERE ARE NO MORE PIRATES...
AND IN ANY EVENT, THERE IS NO WAY YOU'D BE ABLE TO DRINK ENOUGH RUM TO FOLLOW ONE OF THEIR CONVERSATIONS.

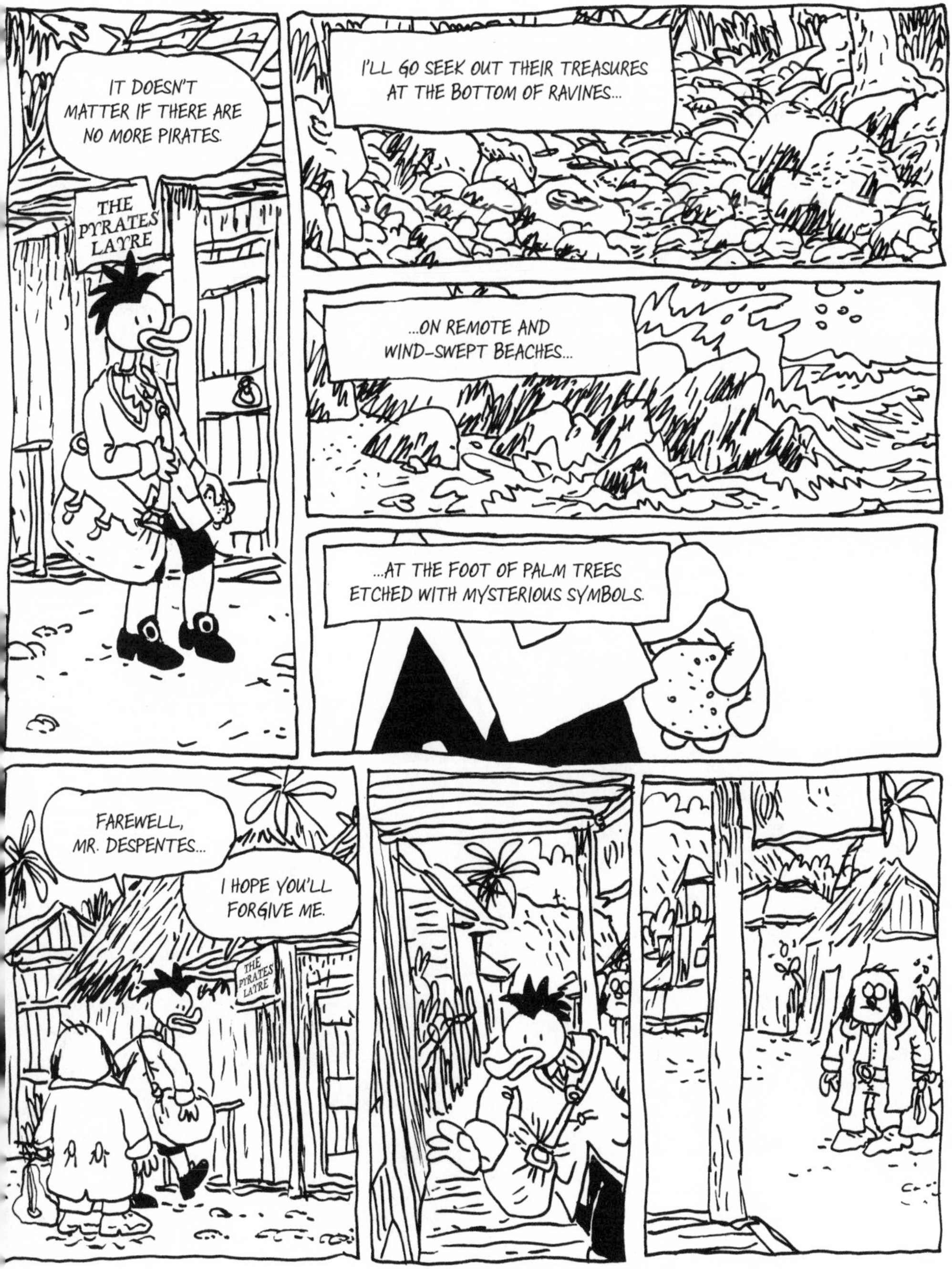

IT DOESN'T MATTER IF THERE ARE NO MORE PIRATES.
THE PYRATES LAYRE
I'LL GO SEEK OUT THEIR TREASURES AT THE BOTTOM OF RAVINES...
...ON REMOTE AND WIND-SWEPT BEACHES...
...AT THE FOOT OF PALM TREES ETCHED WITH MYSTERIOUS SYMBOLS.
FAREWELL, MR. DESPENTES...
I HOPE YOU'LL FORGIVE ME.
THE PYRATES LAYRE

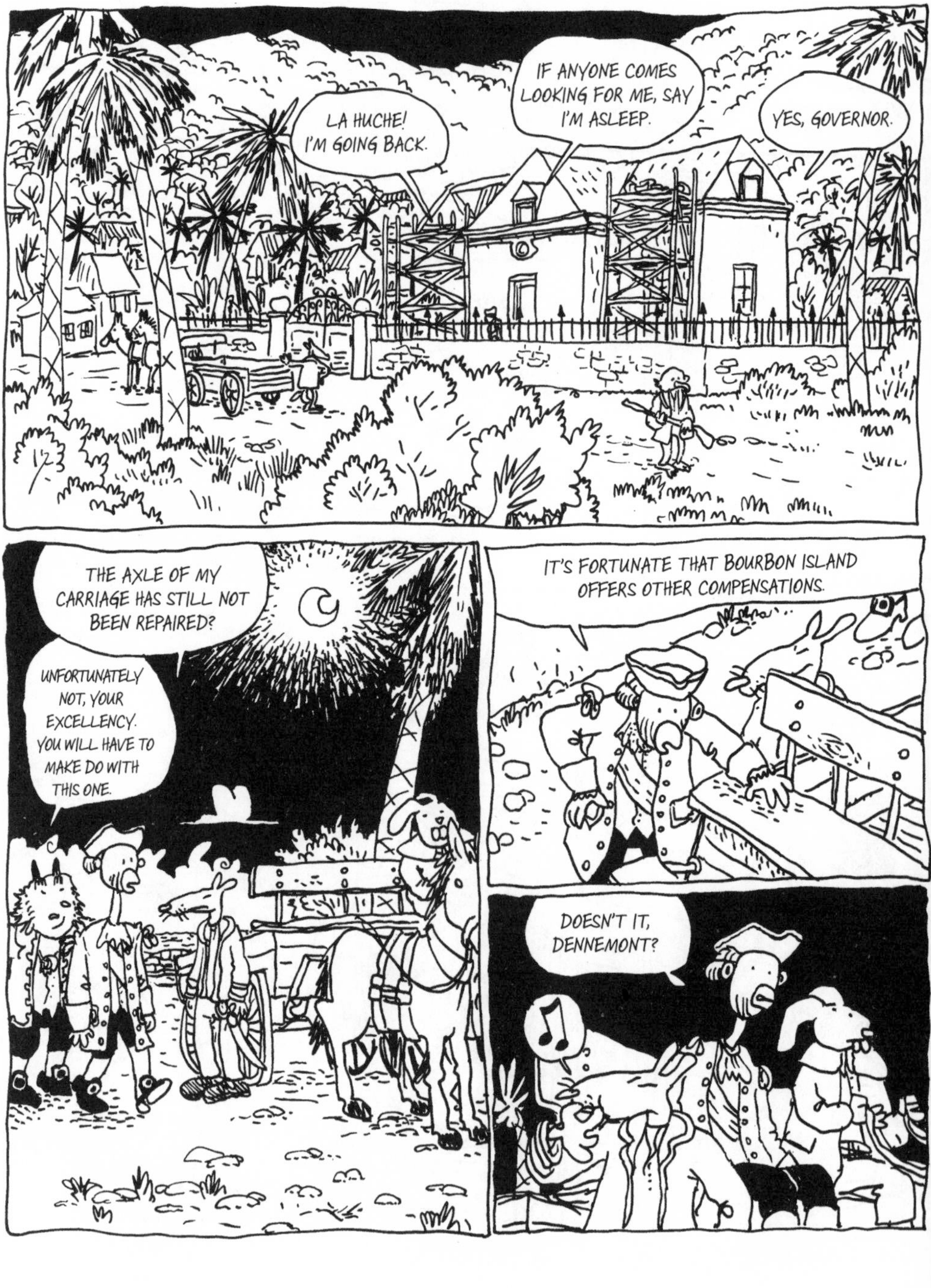
LA HUCHE! I'M GOING BACK.
IF ANYONE COMES LOOKING FOR ME, SAY I'M ASLEEP.
YES, GOVERNOR.
THE AXLE OF MY CARRIAGE HAS STILL NOT BEEN REPAIRED?
UNFORTUNATELY NOT, YOUR EXCELLENCY. YOU WILL HAVE TO MAKE DO WITH THIS ONE.
IT'S FORTUNATE THAT BOURBON ISLAND OFFERS OTHER COMPENSATIONS.
DOESN'T IT, DENNEMONT?

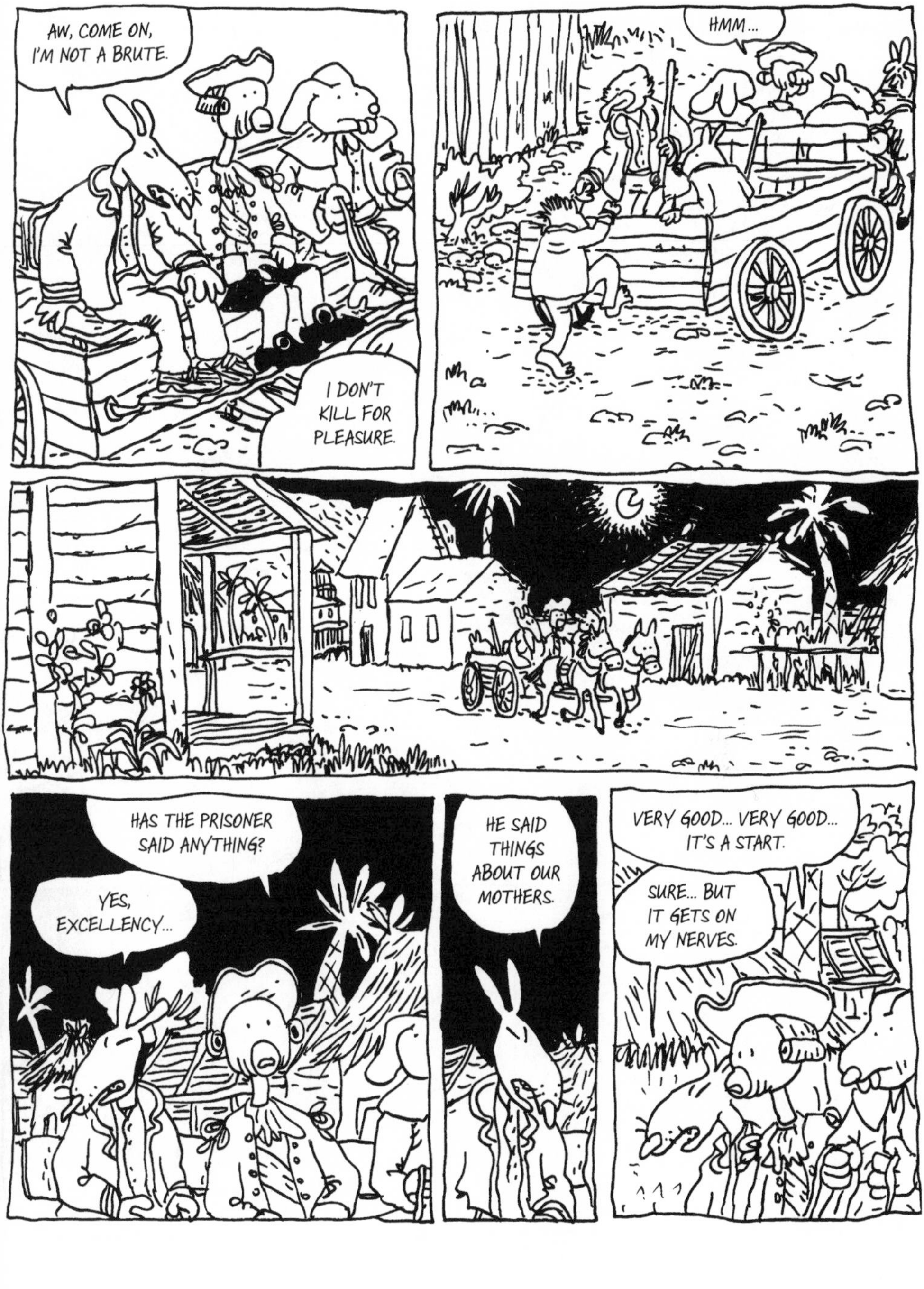
AW, COME ON, I'M NOT A BRUTE.
I DON'T KILL FOR PLEASURE.
HMM...
HAS THE PRISONER SAID ANYTHING?
YES, EXCELLENCY...
HE SAID THINGS ABOUT OUR MOTHERS.
VERY GOOD... VERY GOOD... IT'S A START.
SURE... BUT IT GETS ON MY NERVES.

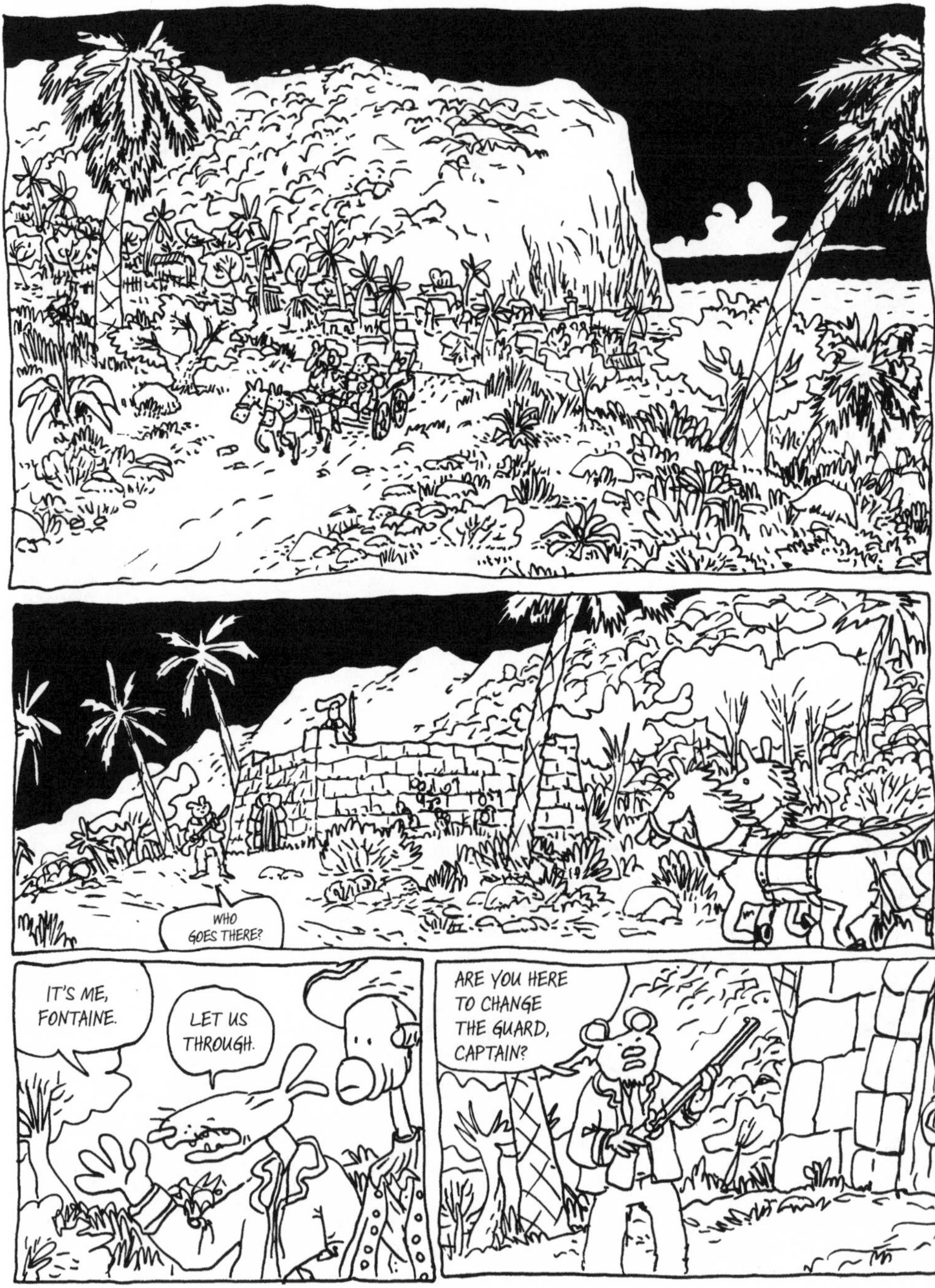
WHO GOES THERE?
IT'S ME, FONTAINE.
LET US THROUGH.
ARE YOU HERE TO CHANGE THE GUARD, CAPTAIN?

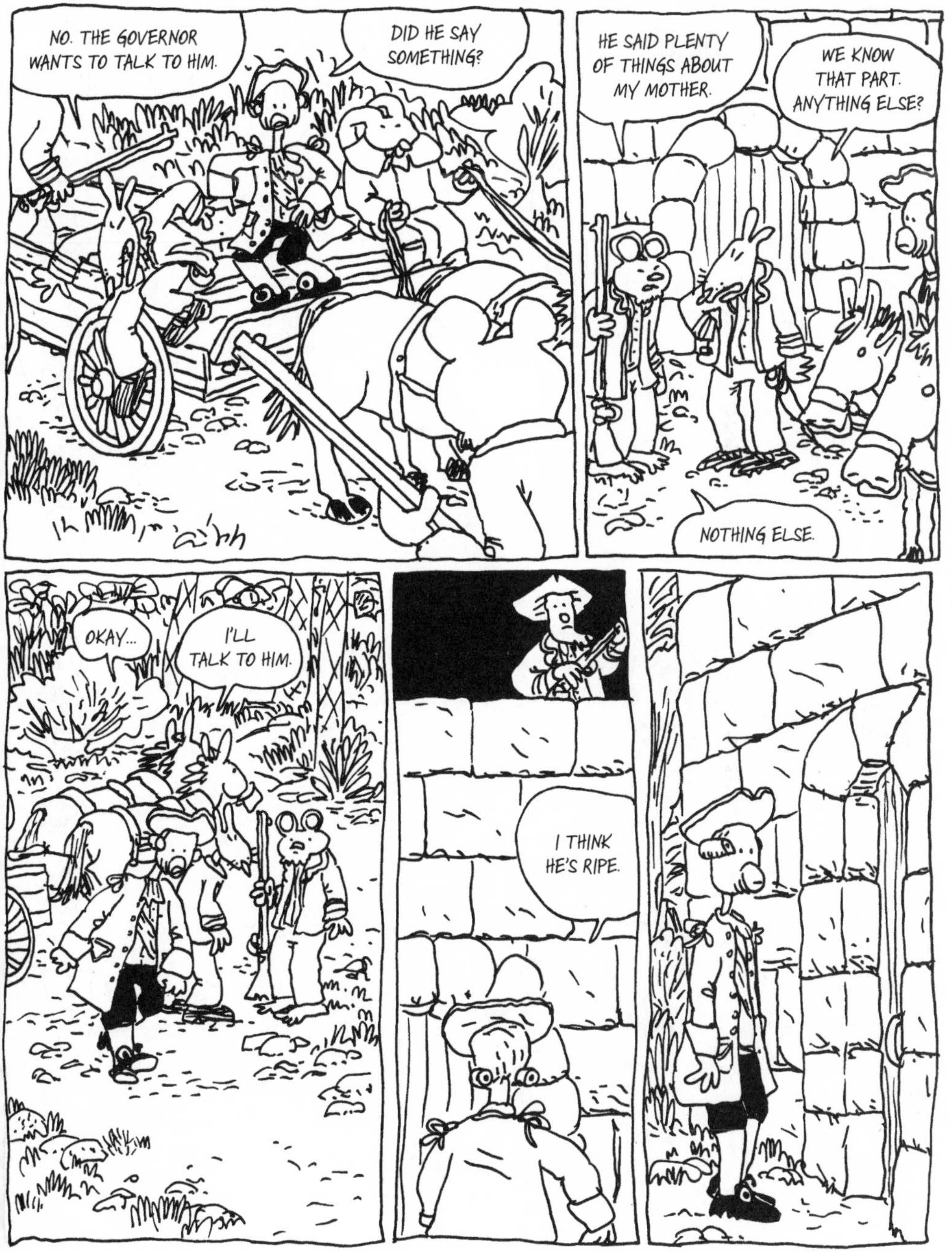
NO. THE GOVERNOR WANTS TO TALK TO HIM.
DID HE SAY SOMETHING?
HE SAID PLENTY OF THINGS ABOUT MY MOTHER.
WE KNOW THAT PART. ANYTHING ELSE?
NOTHING ELSE.
OKAY...
I'LL TALK TO HIM.
I THINK HE'S RIPE.

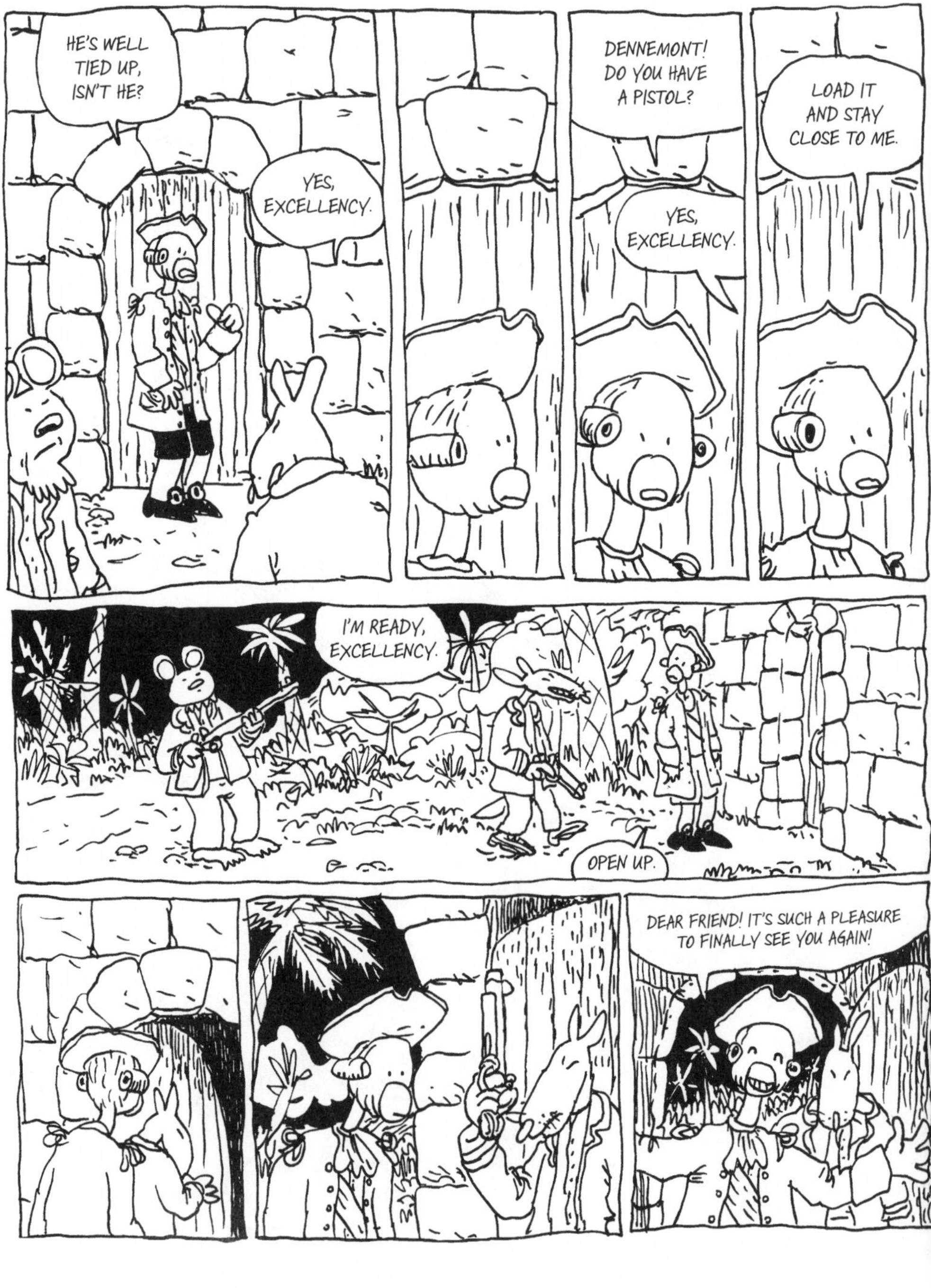
HE'S WELL TIED UP, ISN'T HE?
YES, EXCELLENCY.
DENNEMONT! DO YOU HAVE A PISTOL?
YES, EXCELLENCY.
LOAD IT AND STAY CLOSE TO ME.
I'M READY, EXCELLENCY.
OPEN UP.
DEAR FRIEND! IT'S SUCH A PLEASURE TO FINALLY SEE YOU AGAIN!

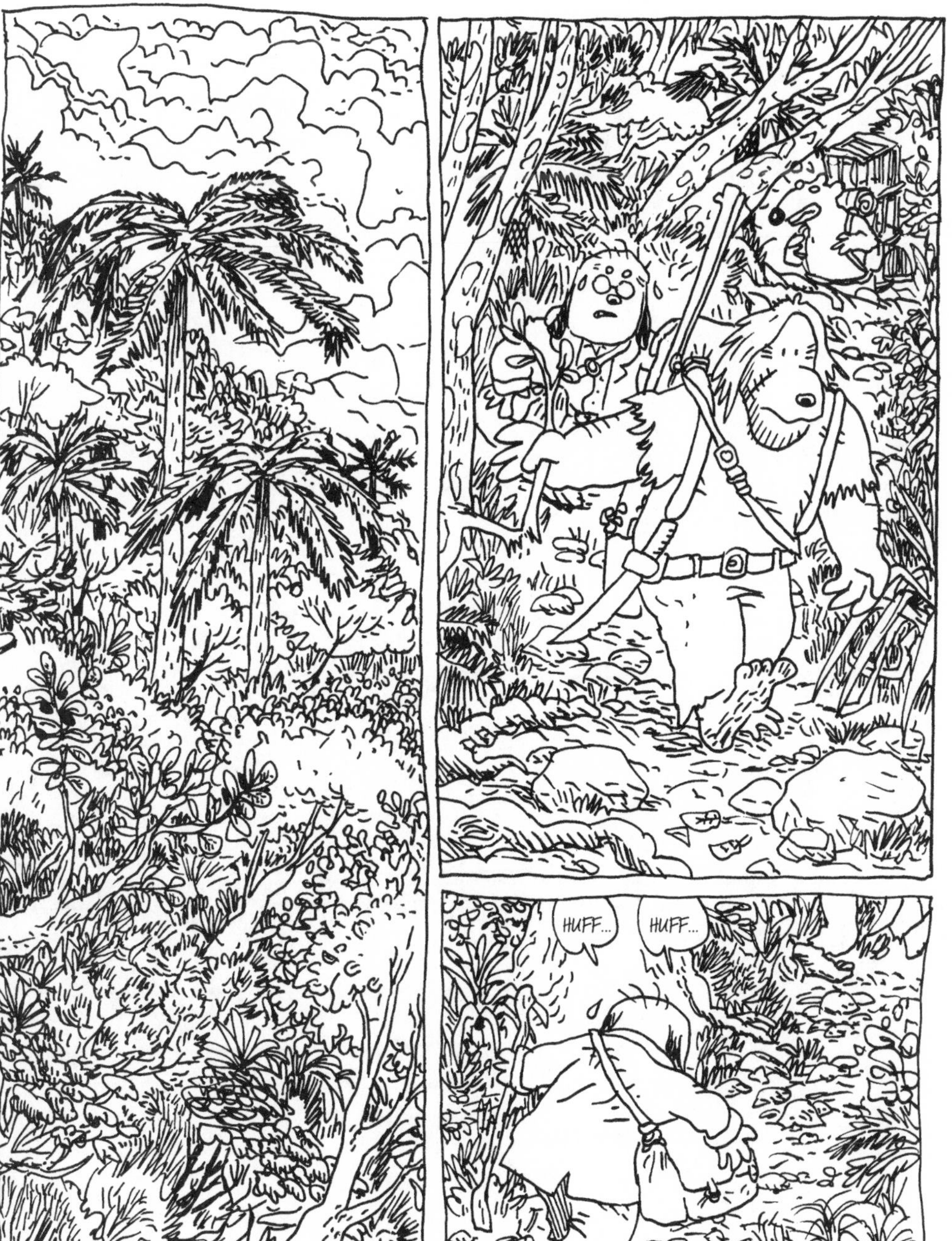
HUFF...
HUFF...

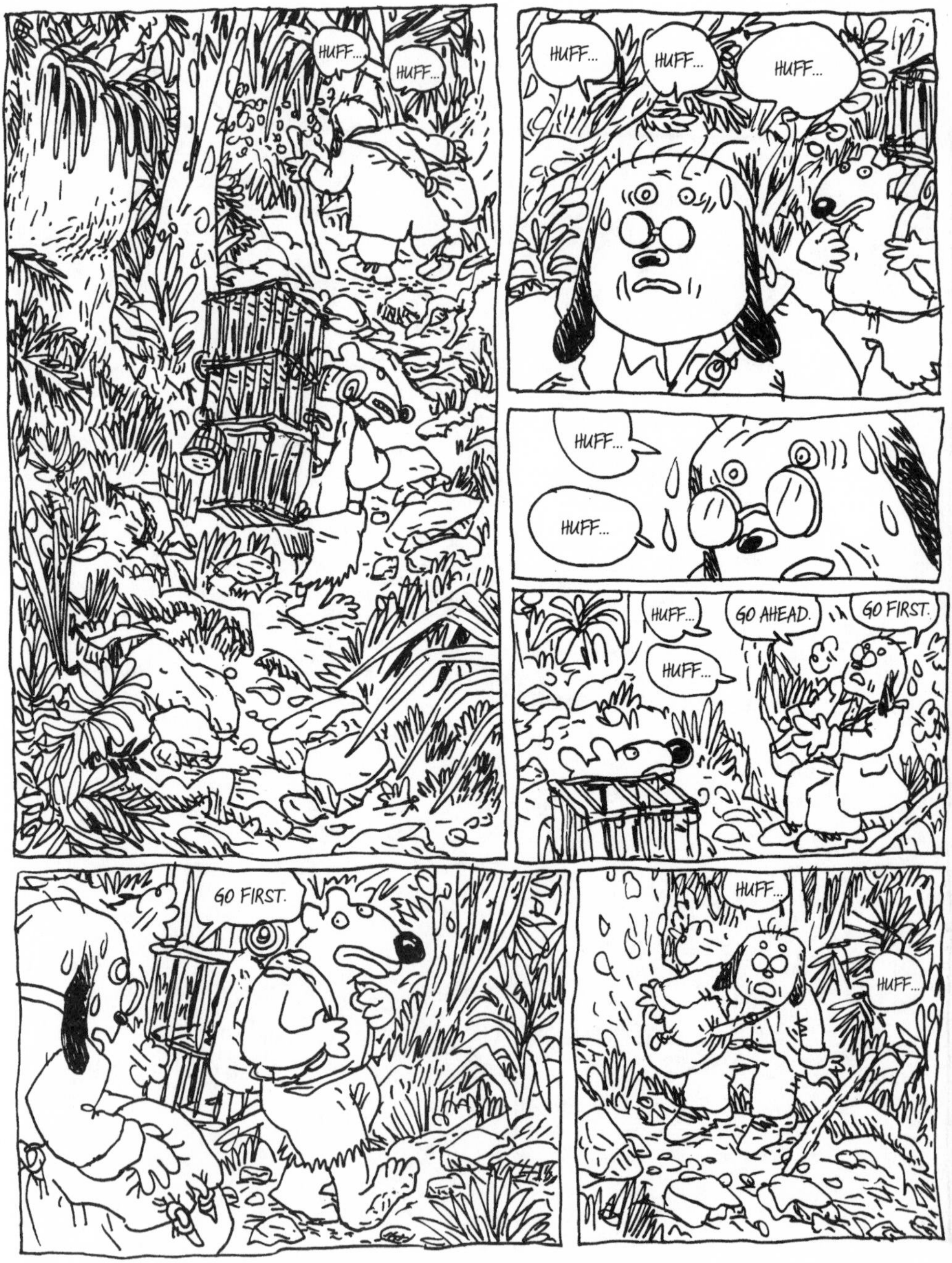
HUFF...
HUFF...
HUFF...
HUFF...
HUFF...
HUFF...
HUFF...
HUFF...
GO AHEAD.
GO FIRST.
HUFF...
GO FIRST.
HUFF...
HUFF...

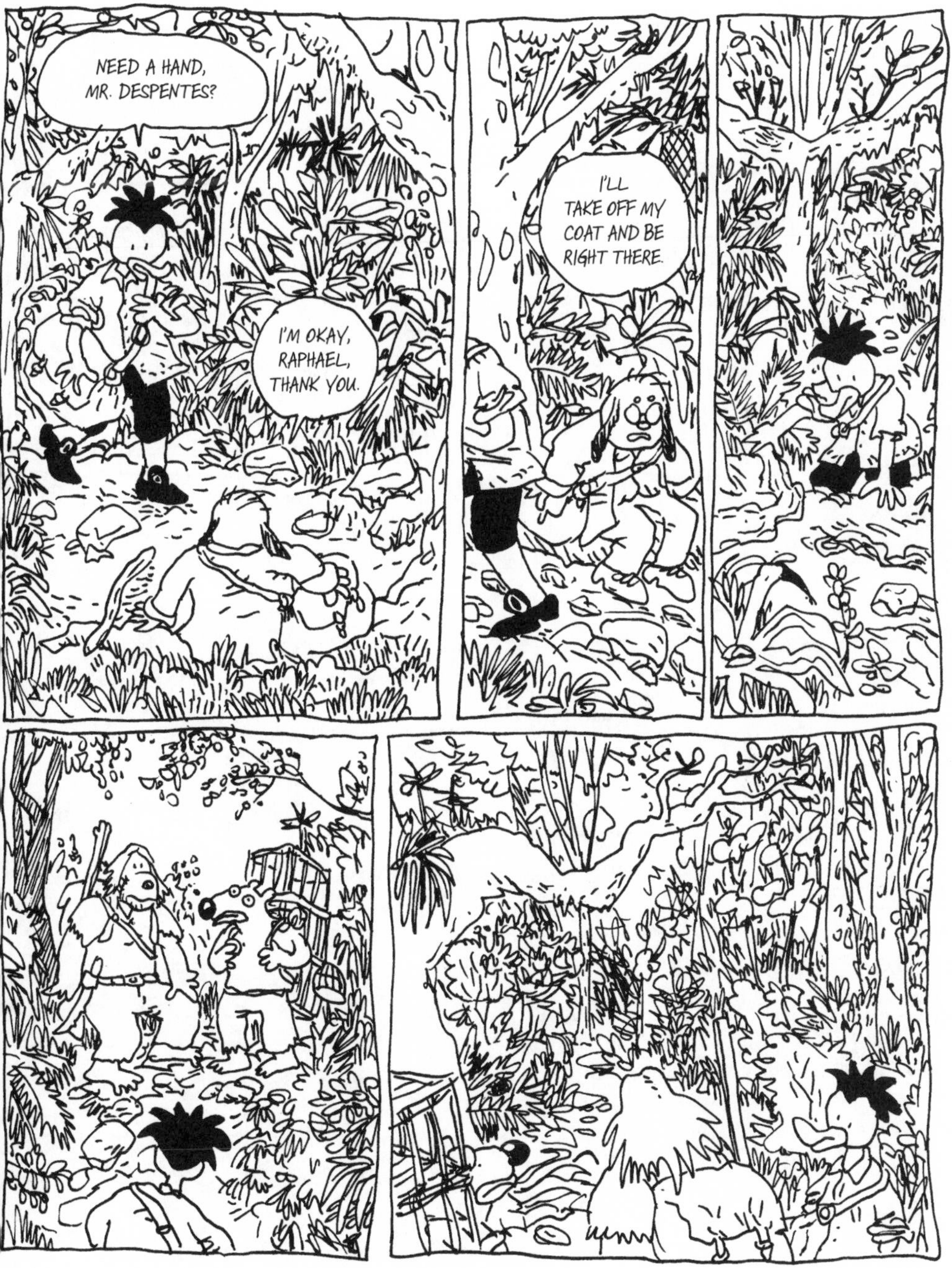
NEED A HAND, MR. DESPENTES?
I'M OKAY, RAPHAEL, THANK YOU.
I'LL TAKE OFF MY COAT AND BE RIGHT THERE.

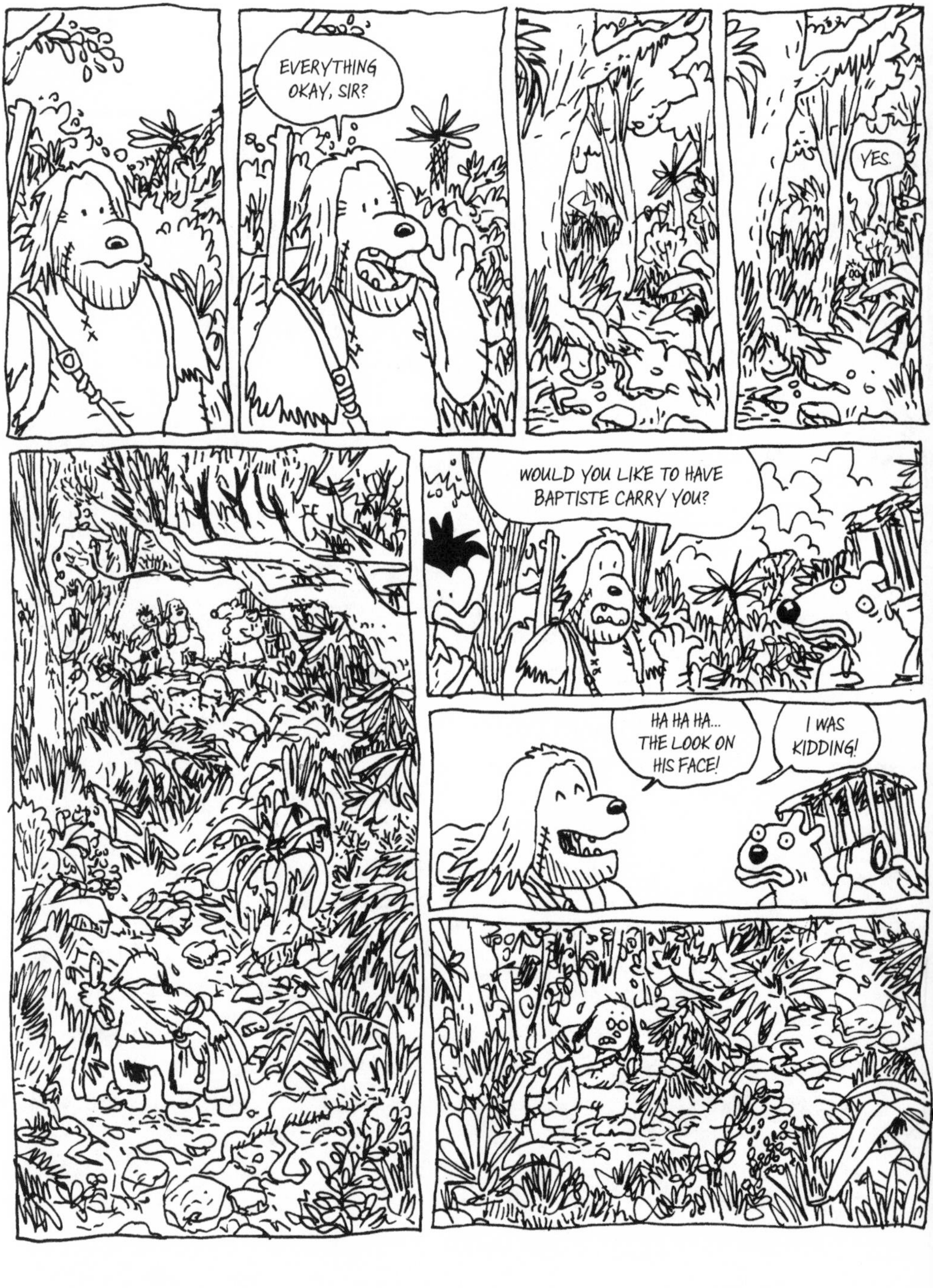
EVERYTHING OKAY, SIR?
YES.
WOULD YOU LIKE TO HAVE BAPTISTE CARRY YOU?
HA HA HA... THE LOOK ON HIS FACE!
I WAS KIDDING!

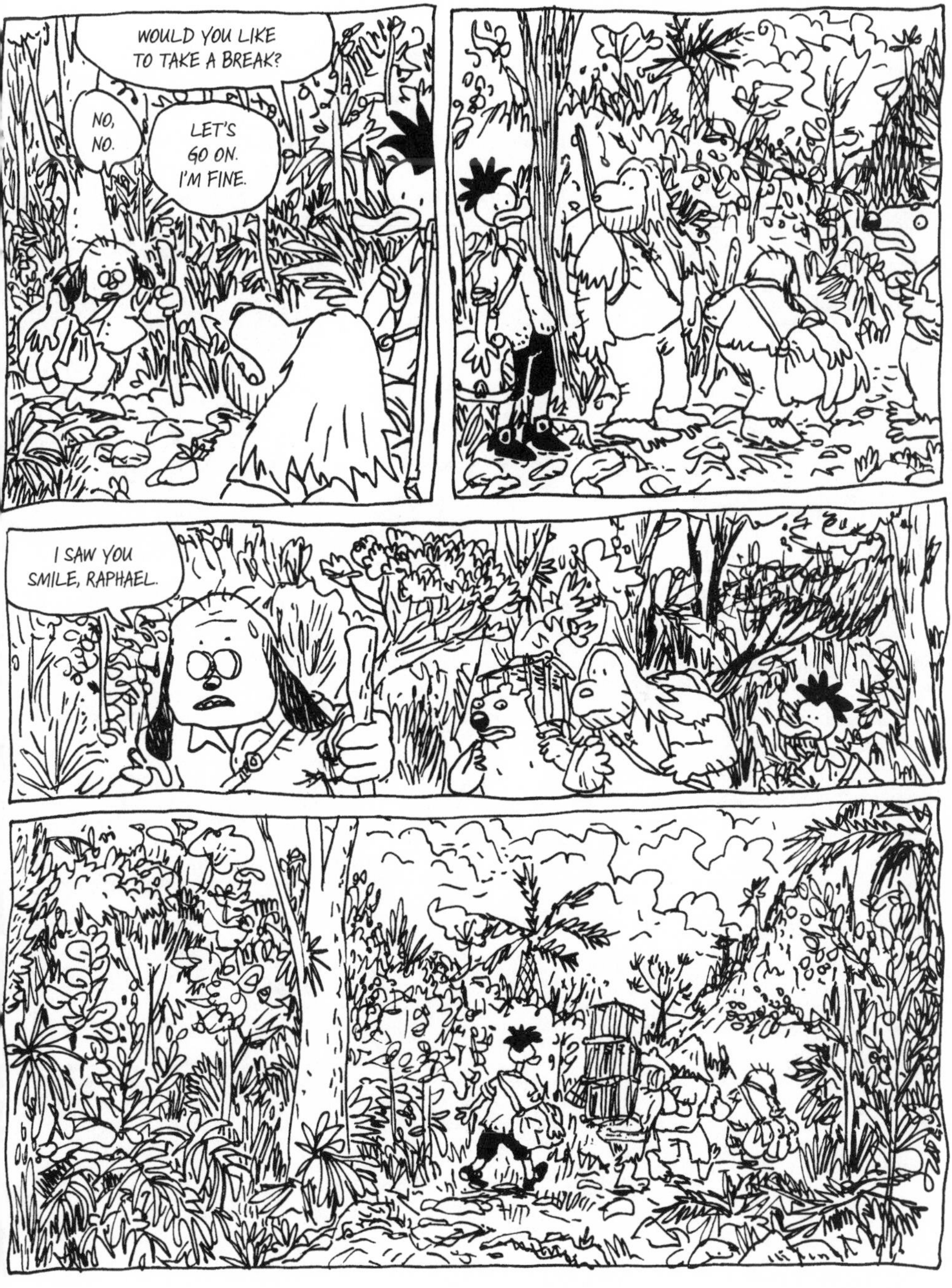
WOULD YOU LIKE TO TAKE A BREAK?
NO, NO.
LET'S GO ON. I'M FINE.
I SAW YOU SMILE, RAPHAEL.

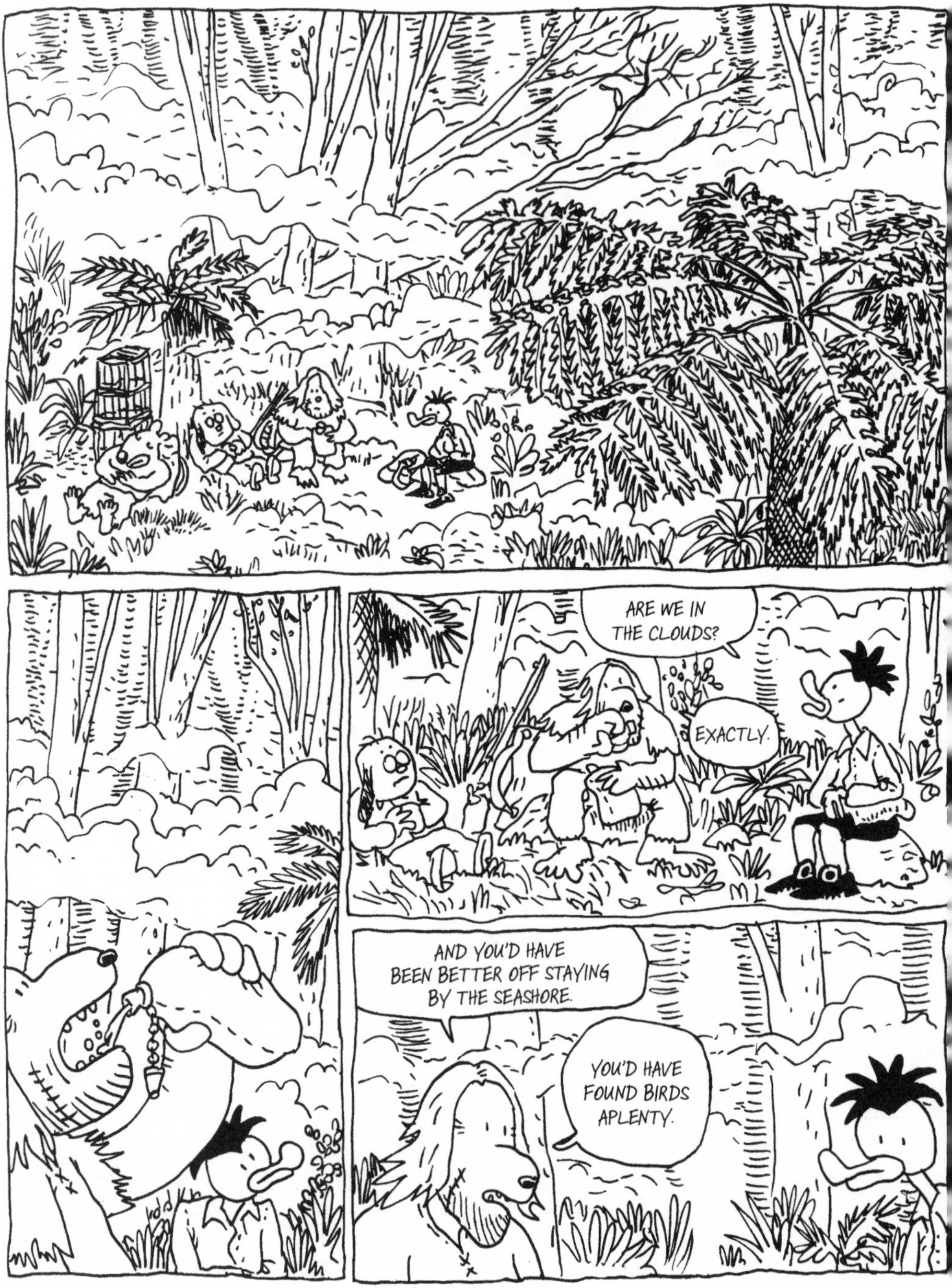
ARE WE IN THE CLOUDS?
EXACTLY.
AND YOU'D HAVE BEEN BETTER OFF STAYING BY THE SEASHORE.
YOU'D HAVE FOUND BIRDS APLENTY.

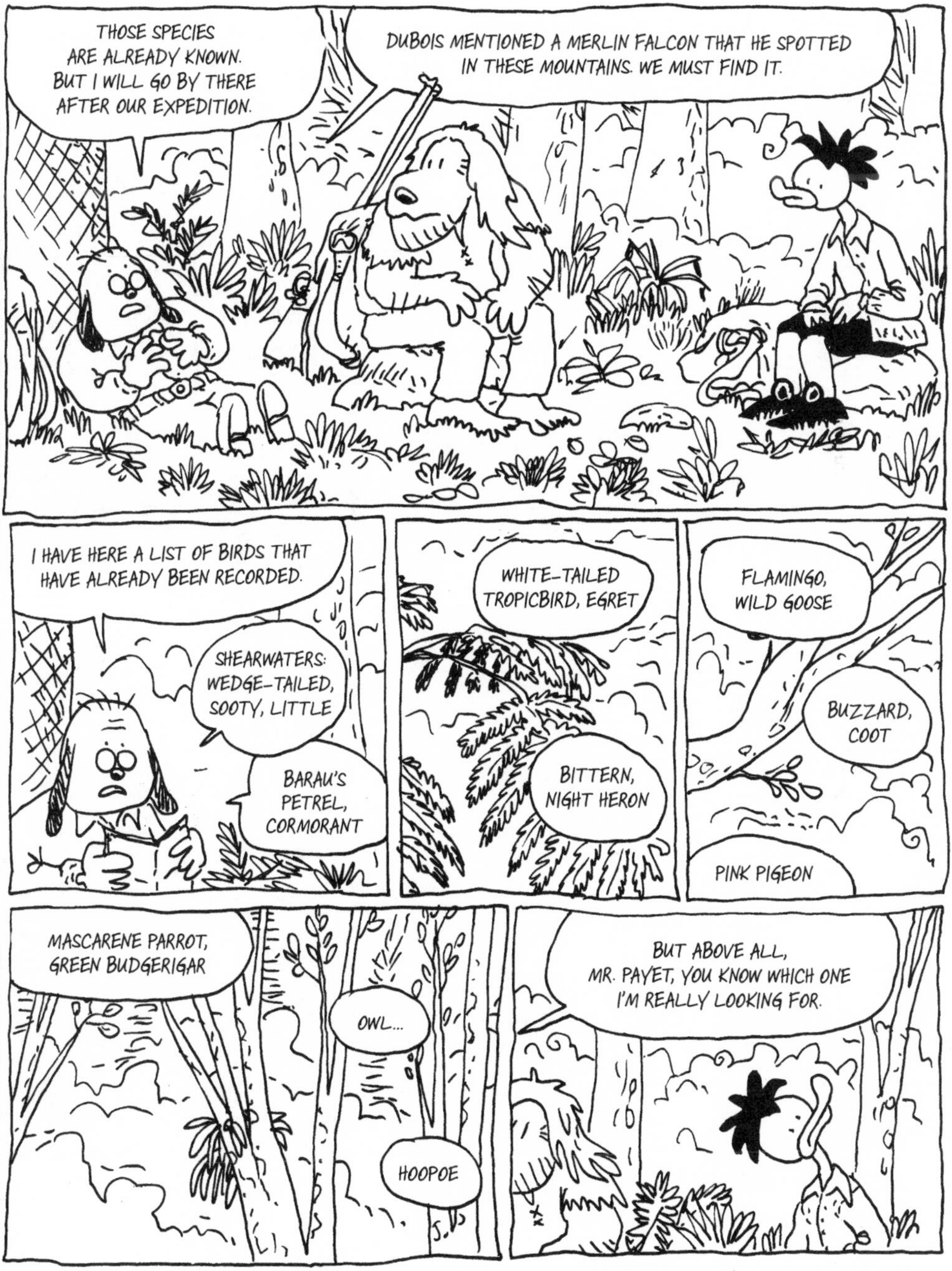
THOSE SPECIES ARE ALREADY KNOWN. BUT I WILL GO BY THERE AFTER OUR EXPEDITION.
DUBOIS MENTIONED A MERLIN FALCON THAT HE SPOTTED IN THESE MOUNTAINS. WE MUST FIND IT.
I HAVE HERE A LIST OF BIRDS THAT HAVE ALREADY BEEN RECORDED.
SHEARWATERS: WEDGE-TAILED, SOOTY, LITTLE
BARAU'S PETREL, CORMORANT
WHITE-TAILED TROPICBIRD, EGRET
BITTERN, NIGHT HERON
FLAMINGO, WILD GOOSE
BUZZARD, COOT
PINK PIGEON
MASCARENE PARROT, GREEN BUDGERIGAR
OWL...
HOOPOE
BUT ABOVE ALL, MR. PAYET, YOU KNOW WHICH ONE I'M REALLY LOOKING FOR.

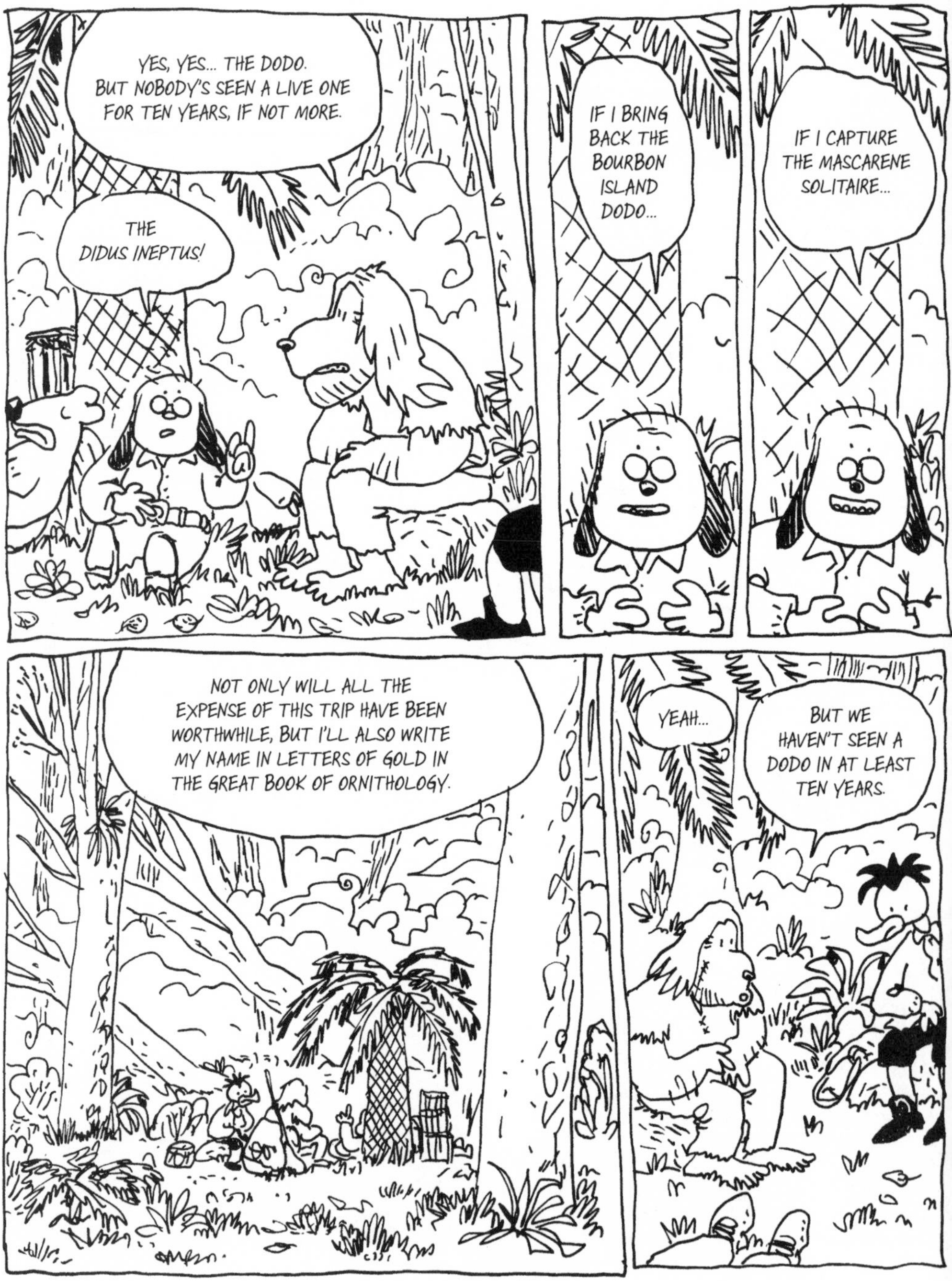
YES, YES... THE DODO.
BUT NOBODY'S SEEN A LIVE ONE
FOR TEN YEARS, IF NOT MORE.
THE DIDUS INEPTUS!
IF I BRING BACK THE BOURBON ISLAND DODO...
IF I CAPTURE THE MASCARENE SOLITAIRE...
NOT ONLY WILL ALL THE EXPENSE OF THIS TRIP HAVE BEEN WORTHWHILE, BUT I'LL ALSO WRITE MY NAME IN LETTERS OF GOLD IN THE GREAT BOOK OF ORNITHOLOGY.
YEAH...
BUT WE HAVEN'T SEEN A DODO IN AT LEAST TEN YEARS.

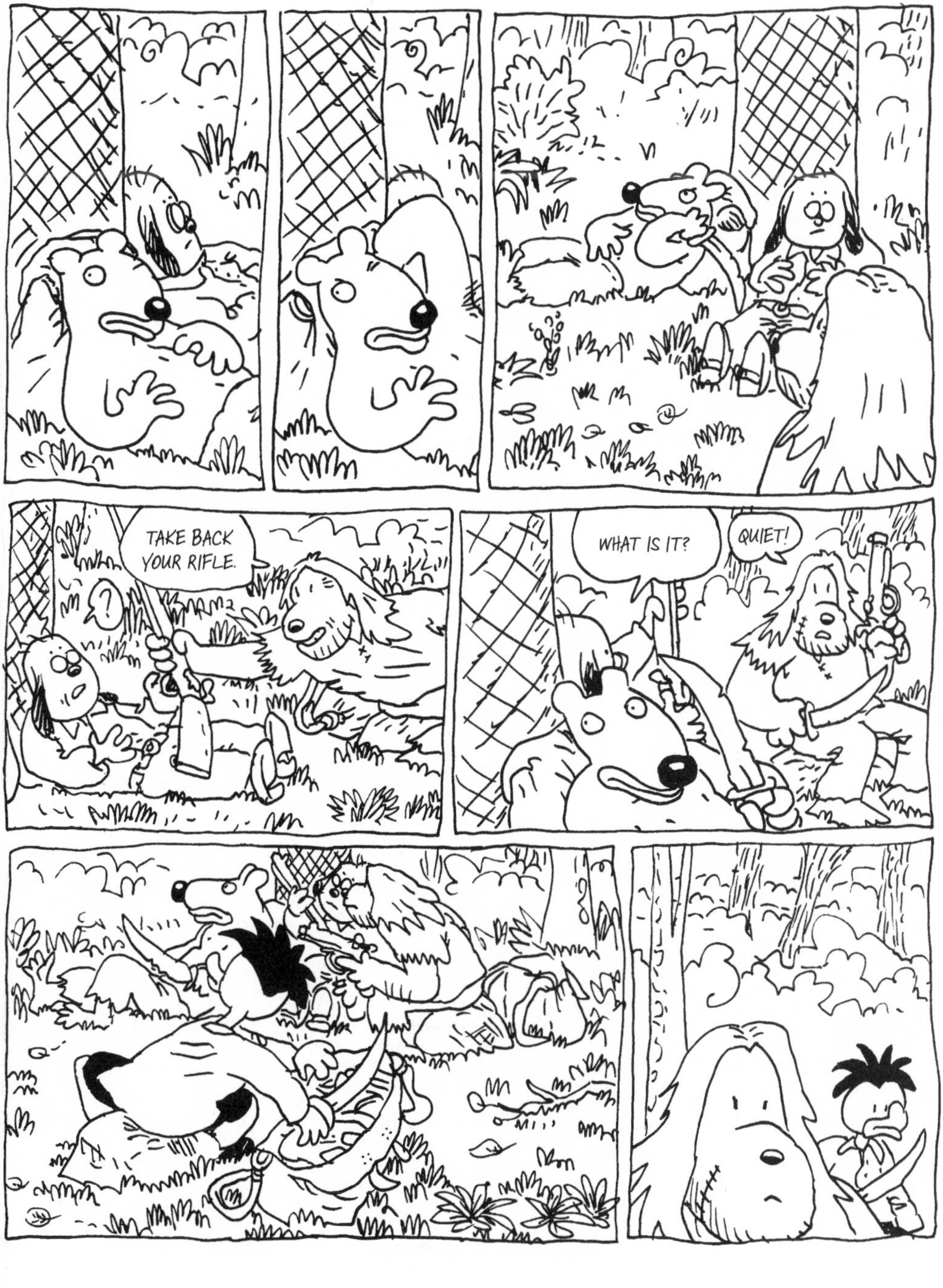
TAKE BACK YOUR RIFLE.
?
WHAT IS IT?
QUIET!

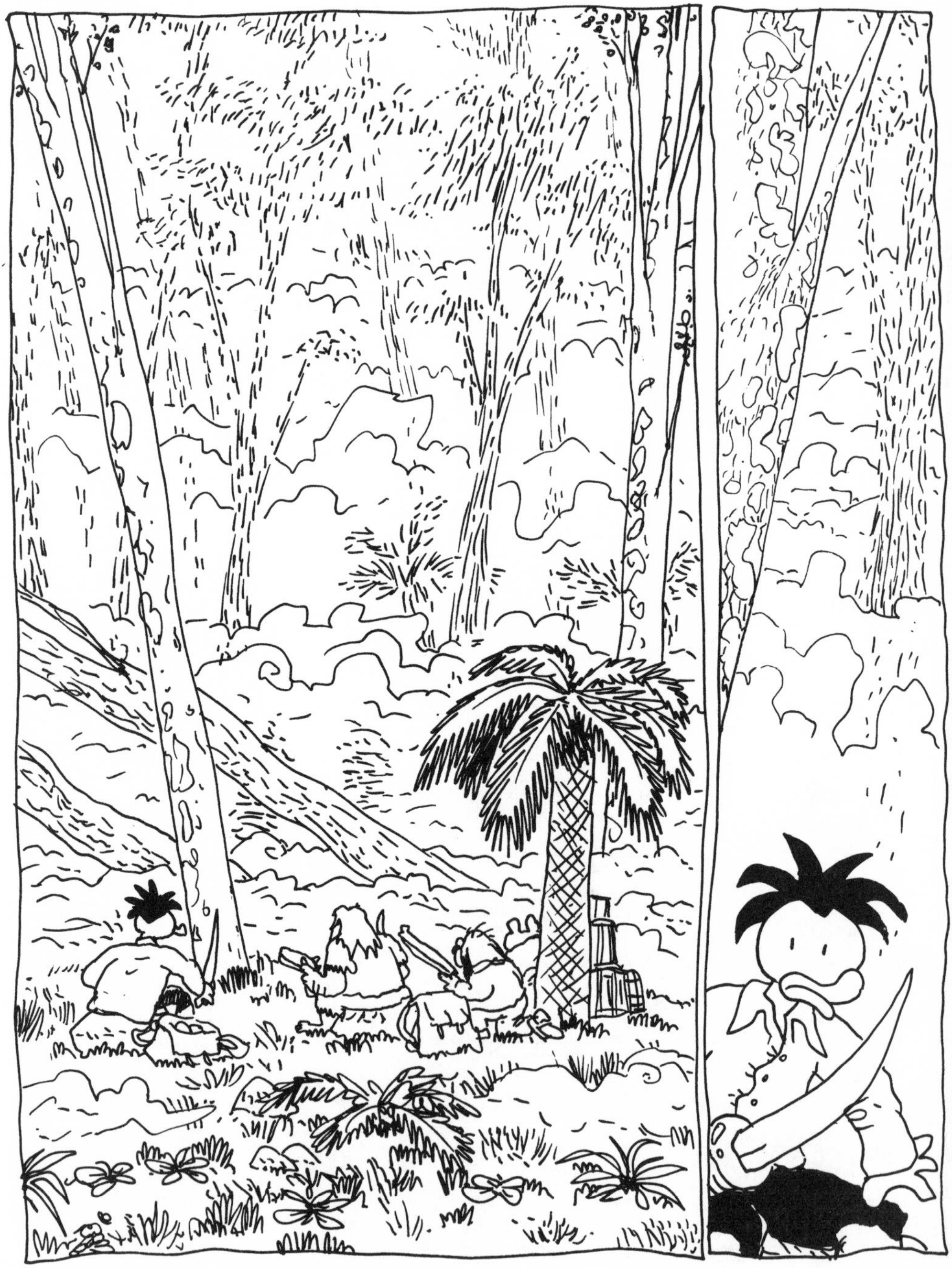

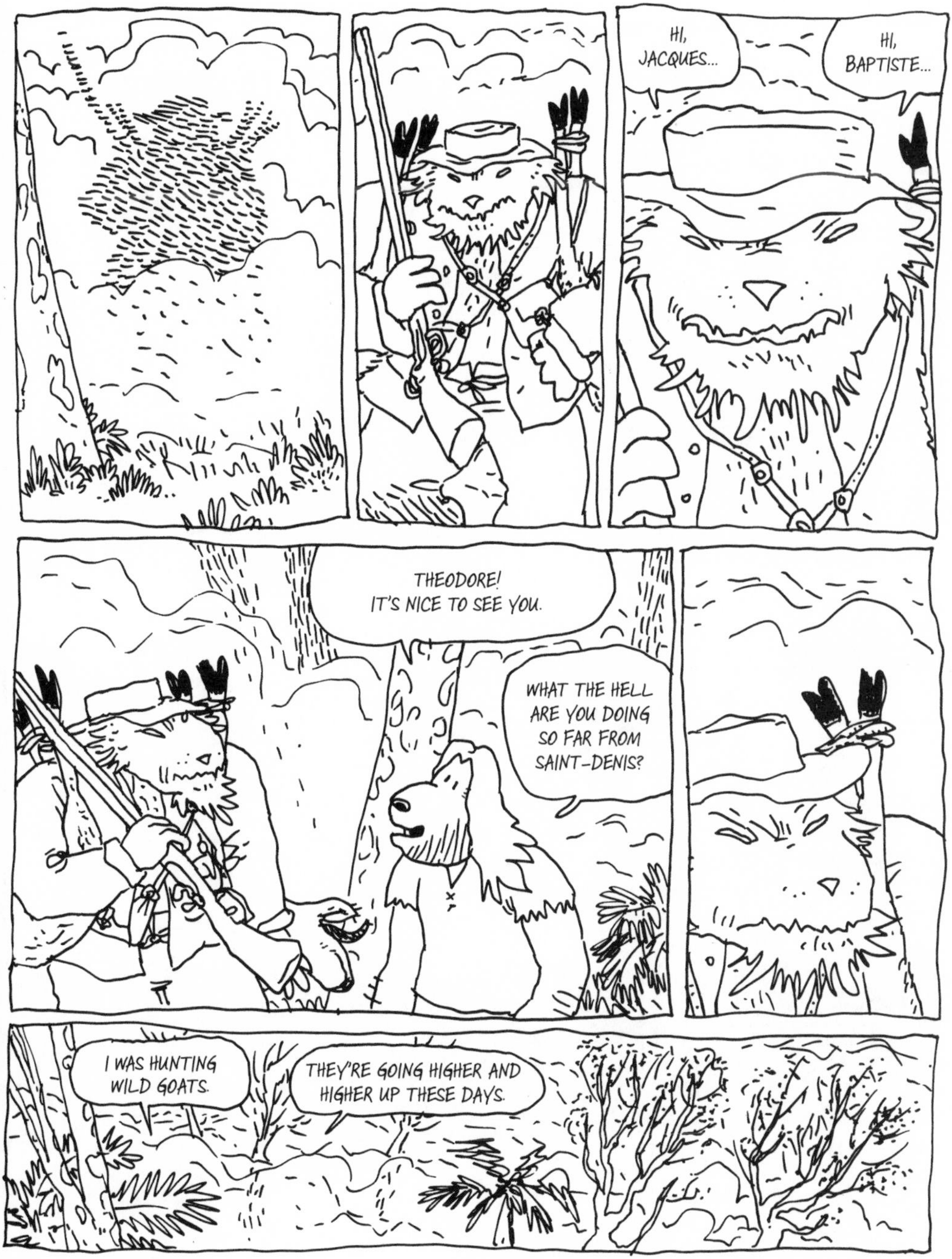
HI, JACQUES...
HI, BAPTISTE...
THEODORE! IT'S NICE TO SEE YOU.
WHAT THE HELL ARE YOU DOING SO FAR FROM SAINT-DENIS?
I WAS HUNTING WILD GOATS.
THEY'RE GOING HIGHER AND HIGHER UP THESE DAYS.

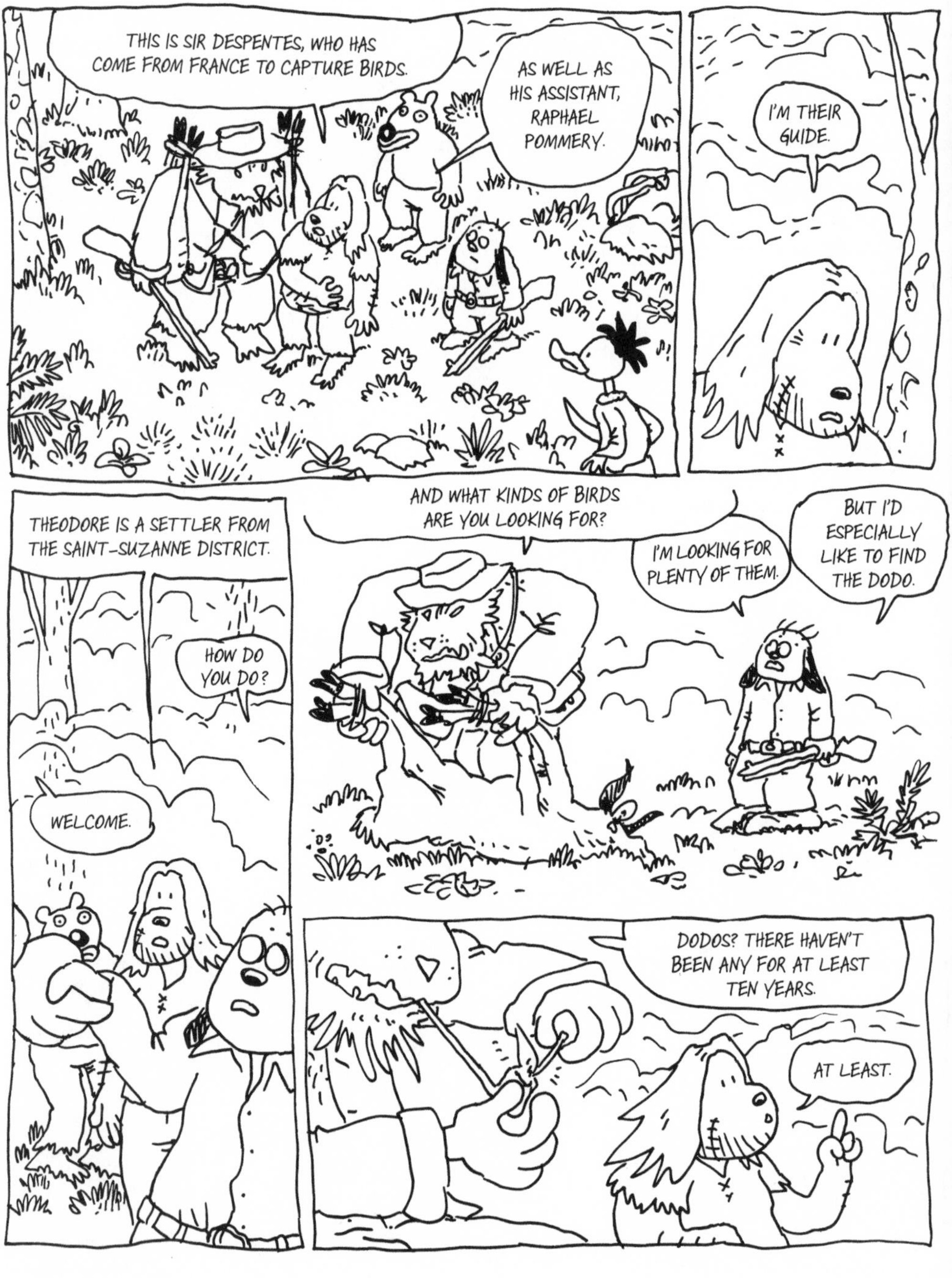
THIS IS SIR DESPENTES, WHO HAS COME FROM FRANCE TO CAPTURE BIRDS.
AS WELL AS HIS ASSISTANT, RAPHAEL POMMERY.
I'M THEIR GUIDE.
THEODORE IS A SETTLER FROM THE SAINT-SUZANNE DISTRICT.
HOW DO YOU DO?
WELCOME.
AND WHAT KINDS OF BIRDS ARE YOU LOOKING FOR?
I'M LOOKING FOR PLENTY OF THEM.
BUT I'D ESPECIALLY LIKE TO FIND THE DODO.
DODOS? THERE HAVEN'T BEEN ANY FOR AT LEAST TEN YEARS.
AT LEAST.

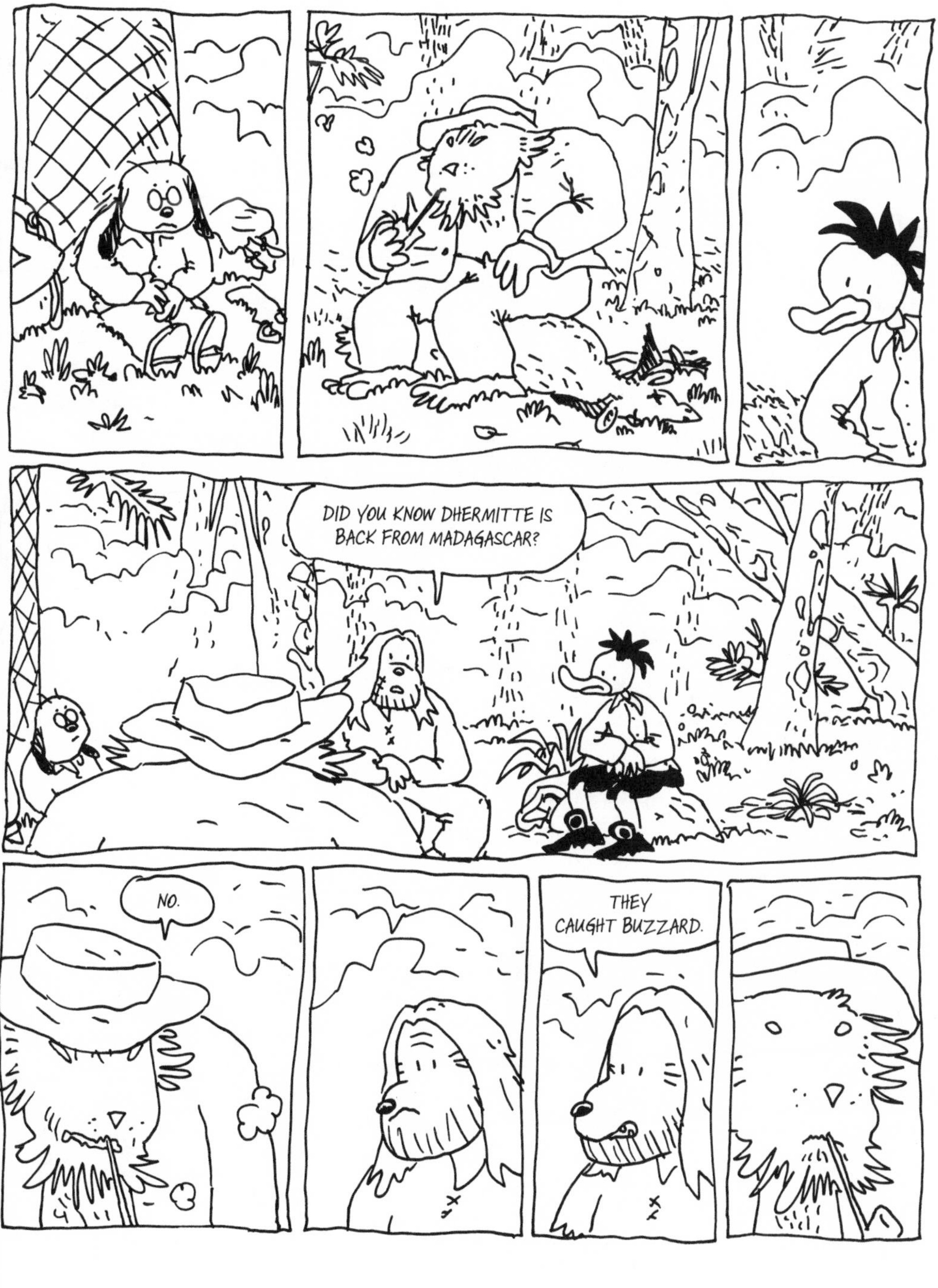
DID YOU KNOW DHERMITTE IS BACK FROM MADAGASCAR?
NO.
THEY CAUGHT BUZZARD.

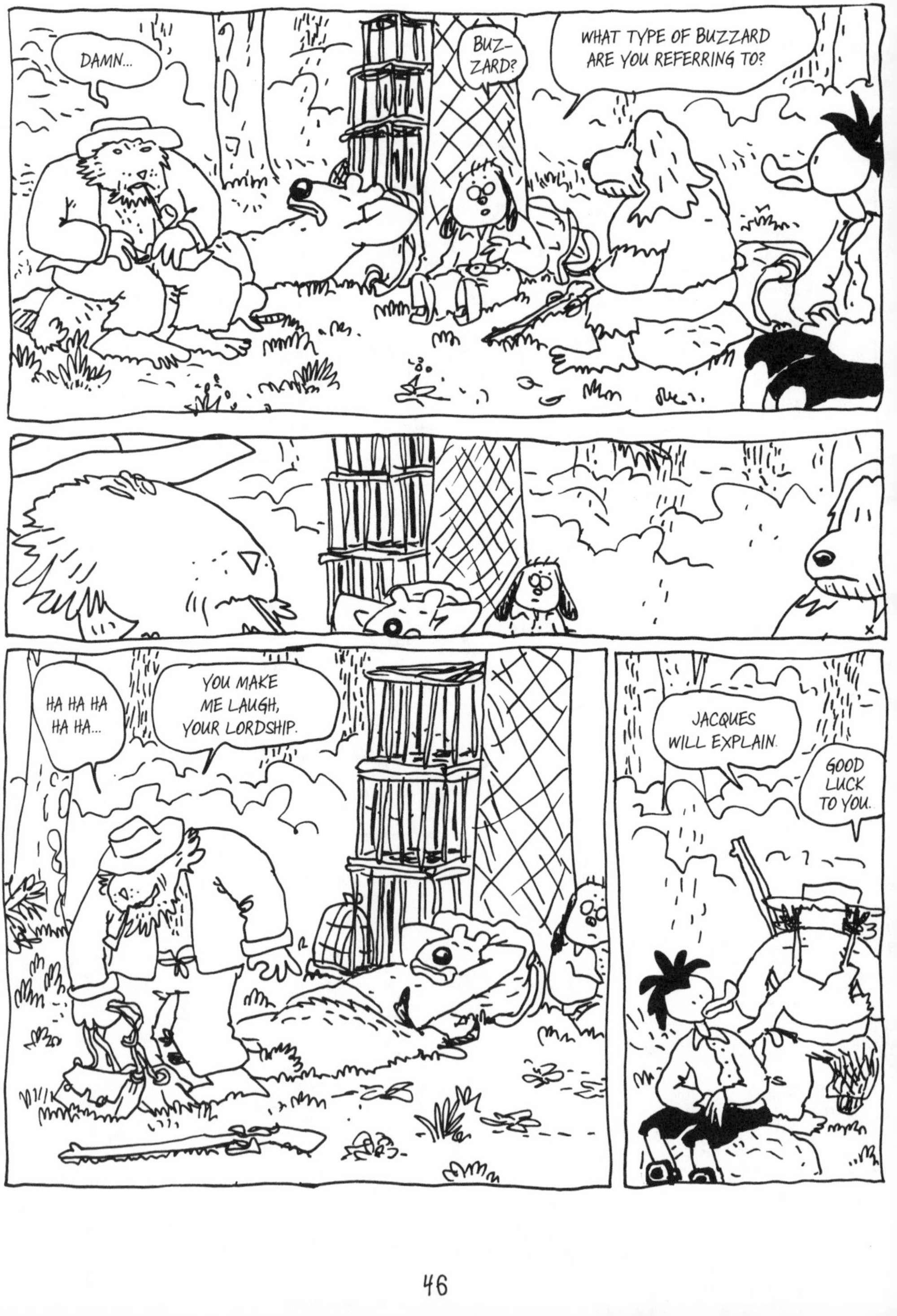
DAMN...
BUZ-ZARD?
WHAT TYPE OF BUZZARD ARE YOU REFERRING TO?
HA HA HA HA HA...
YOU MAKE ME LAUGH, YOUR LORDSHIP.
JACQUES WILL EXPLAIN.
GOOD LUCK TO YOU.

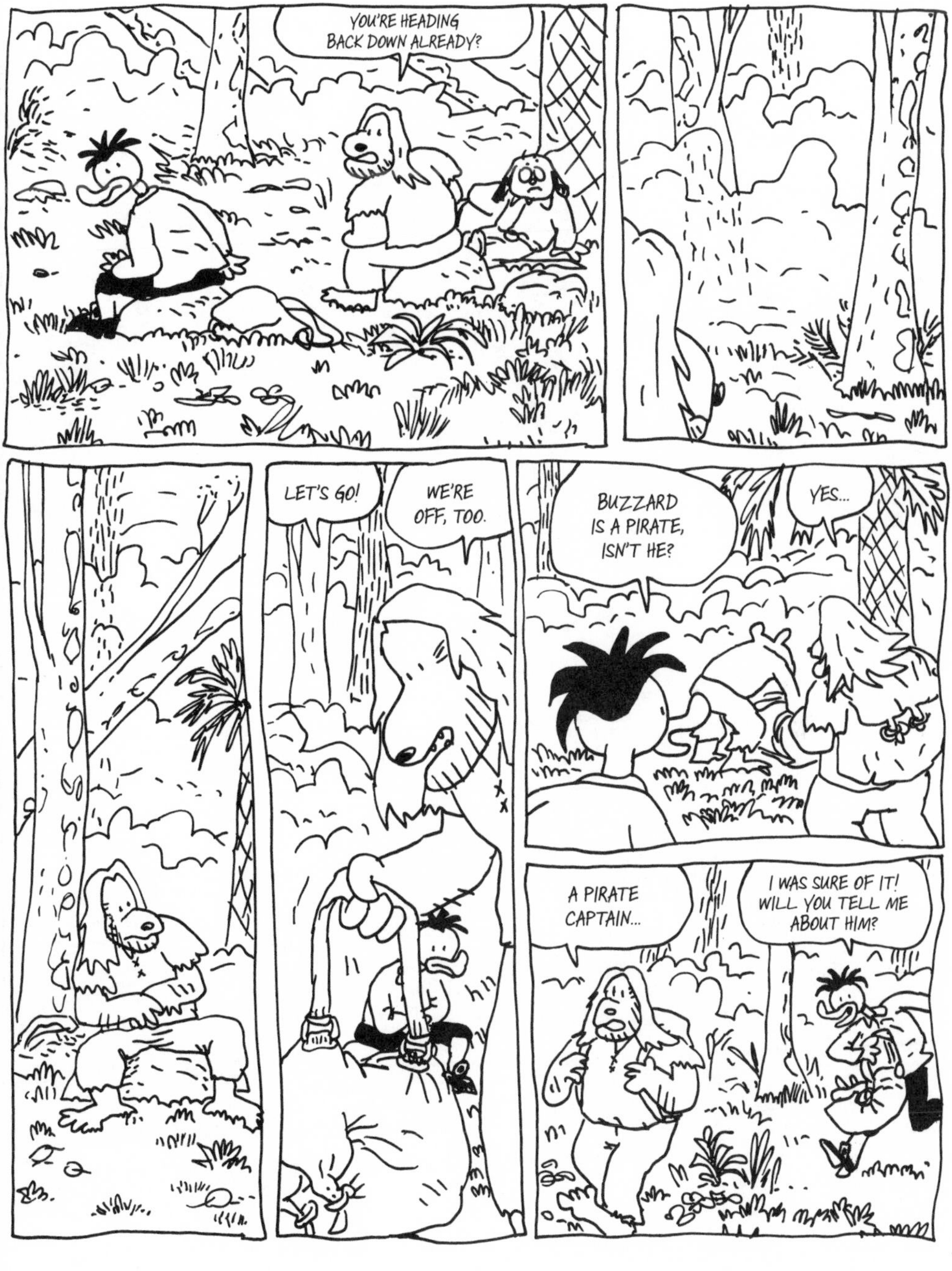
YOU'RE HEADING BACK DOWN ALREADY?
LET'S GO!
WE'RE OFF, TOO.
BUZZARD IS A PIRATE, ISN'T HE?
YES...
A PIRATE CAPTAIN...
I WAS SURE OF IT! WILL YOU TELL ME ABOUT HIM?

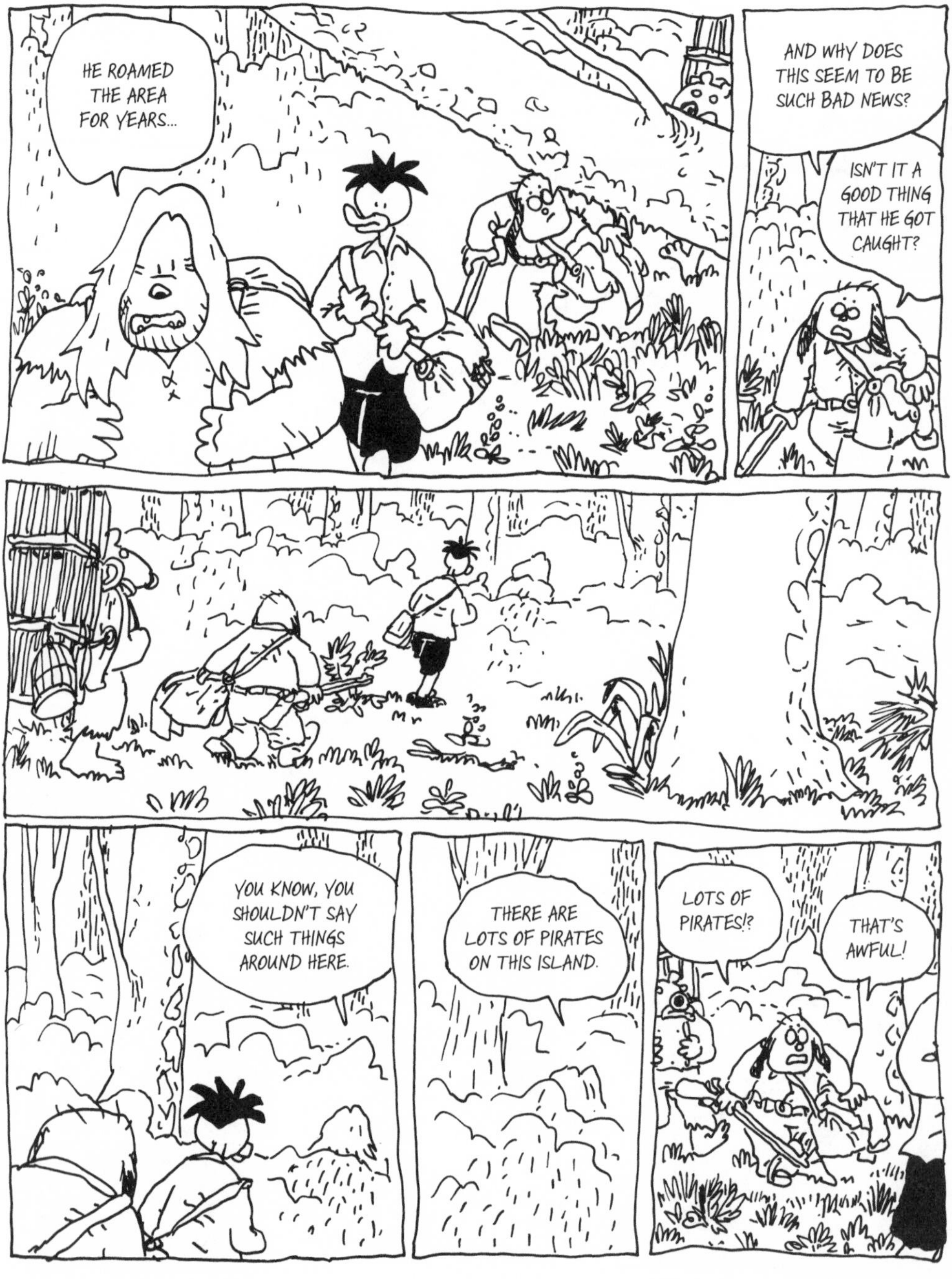
HE ROAMED THE AREA FOR YEARS...
AND WHY DOES THIS SEEM TO BE SUCH BAD NEWS?
ISN'T IT A GOOD THING THAT HE GOT CAUGHT?
YOU KNOW, YOU SHOULDN'T SAY SUCH THINGS AROUND HERE.
THERE ARE LOTS OF PIRATES ON THIS ISLAND.
LOTS OF PIRATES!?
THAT'S AWFUL!

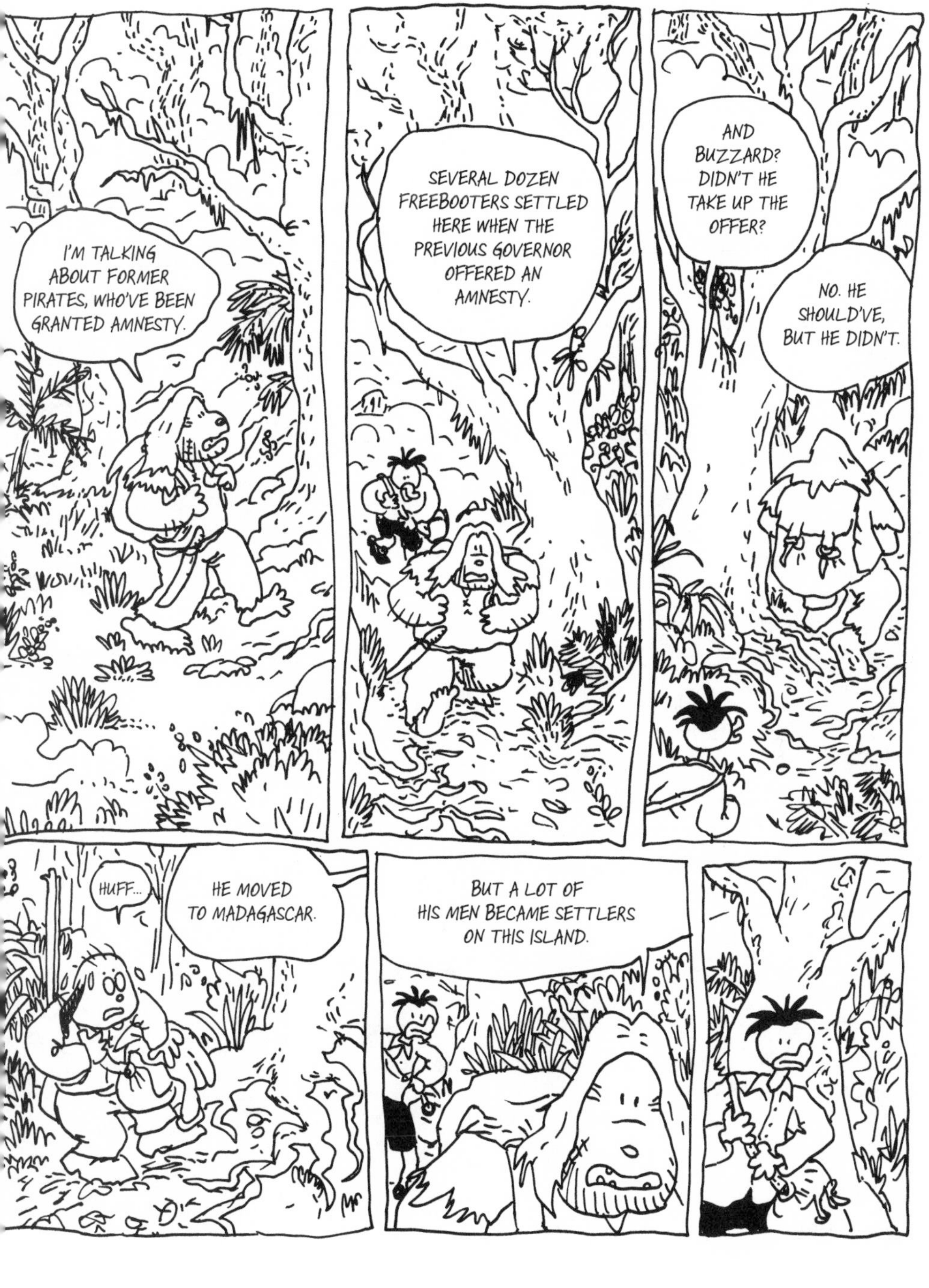
I'M TALKING ABOUT FORMER PIRATES, WHO'VE BEEN GRANTED AMNESTY.
SEVERAL DOZEN FREEBOOTERS SETTLED HERE WHEN THE PREVIOUS GOVERNOR OFFERED AN AMNESTY.
AND BUZZARD? DIDN'T HE TAKE UP THE OFFER?
NO. HE SHOULD'VE, BUT HE DIDN'T.
HUFF...
HE MOVED TO MADAGASCAR.
BUT A LOT OF HIS MEN BECAME SETTLERS ON THIS ISLAND.

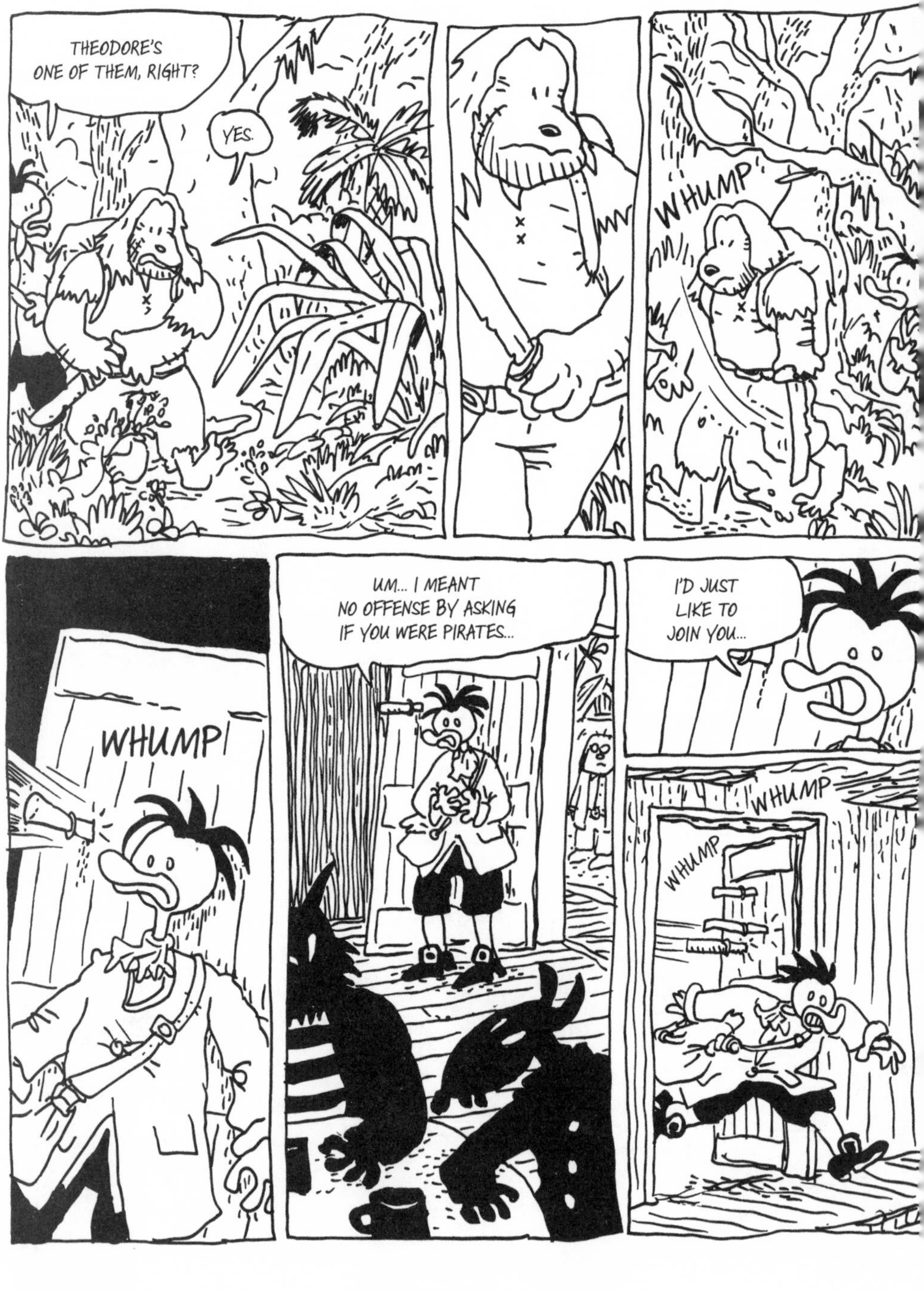
THEODORE'S ONE OF THEM, RIGHT?
YES.
WHUMP
WHUMP
UM... I MEANT NO OFFENSE BY ASKING IF YOU WERE PIRATES...
I'D JUST LIKE TO JOIN YOU...
WHUMP
WHUMP

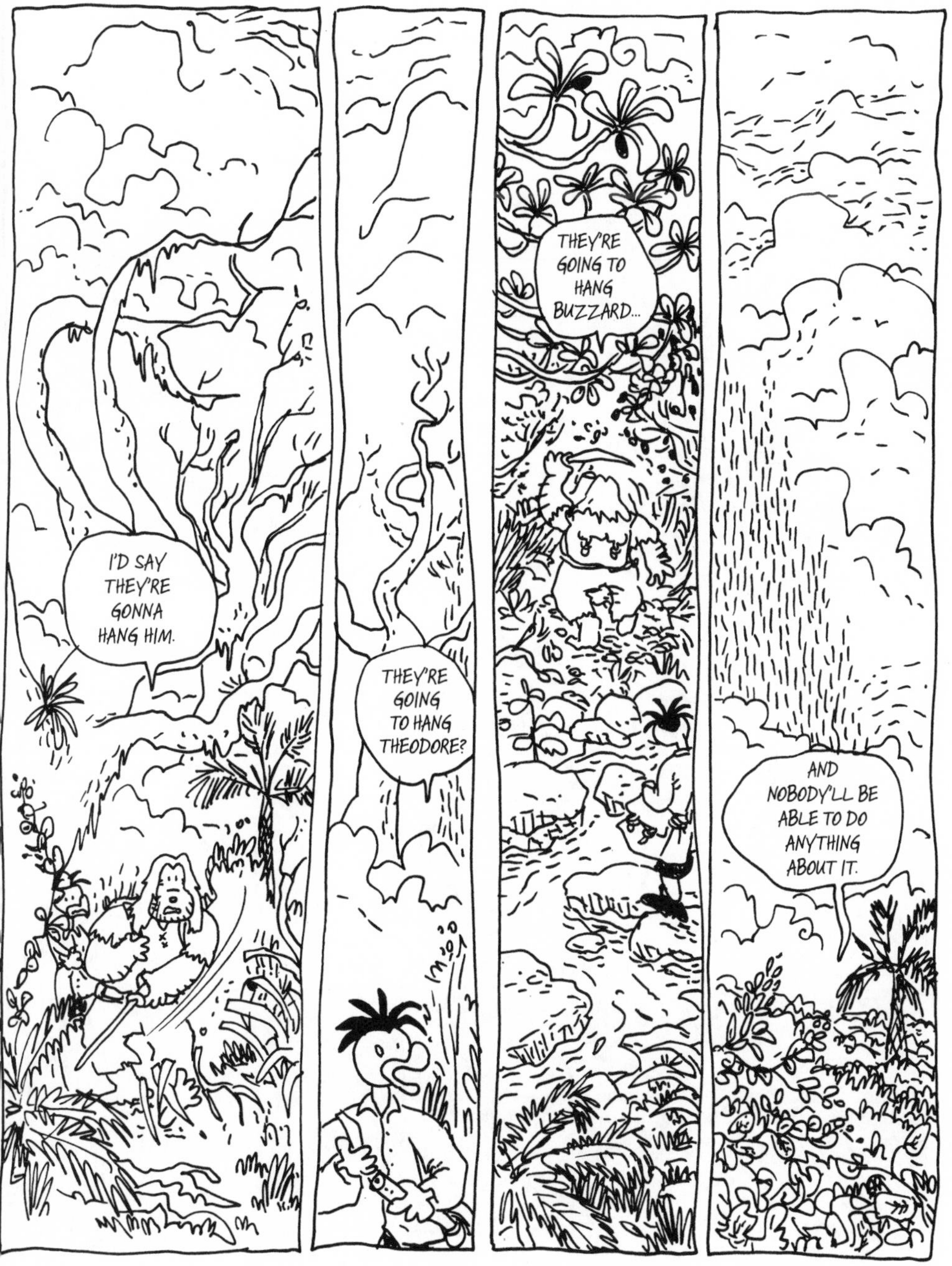
I'D SAY THEY'RE GONNA HANG HIM.
THEY'RE GOING TO HANG THEODORE?
THEY'RE GOING TO HANG BUZZARD...
AND NOBODY'LL BE ABLE TO DO ANYTHING ABOUT IT.

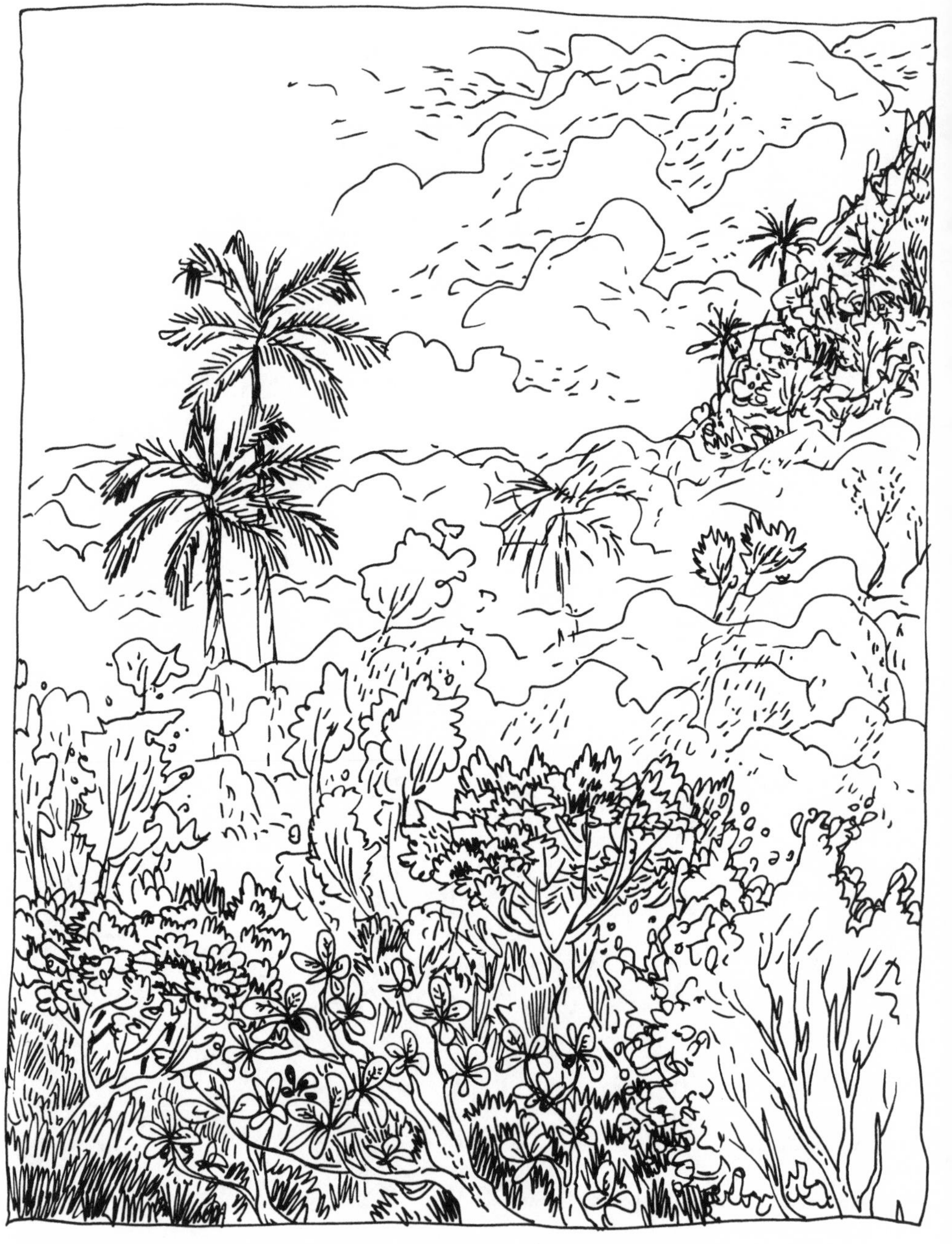

THE MAROONS

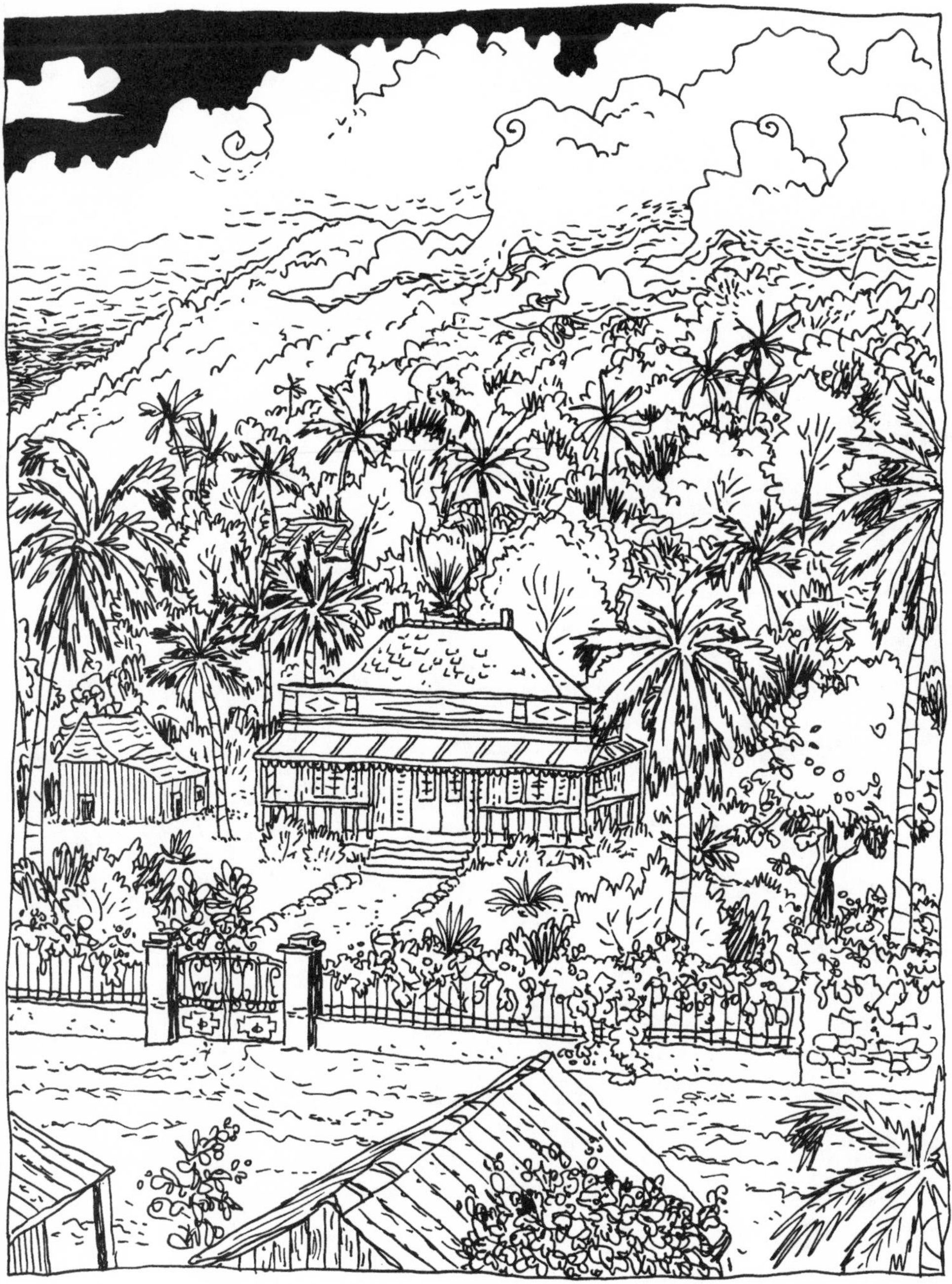

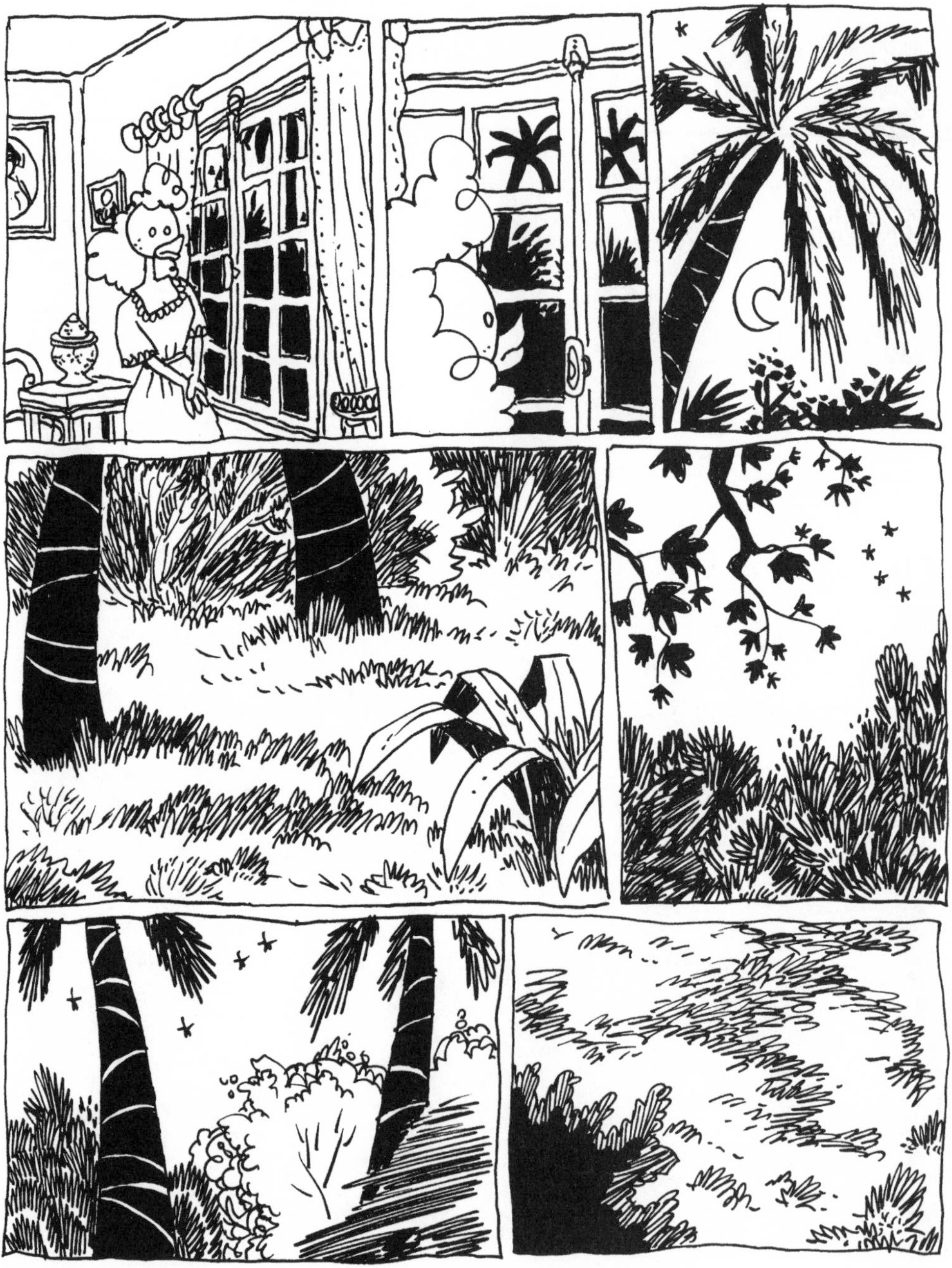

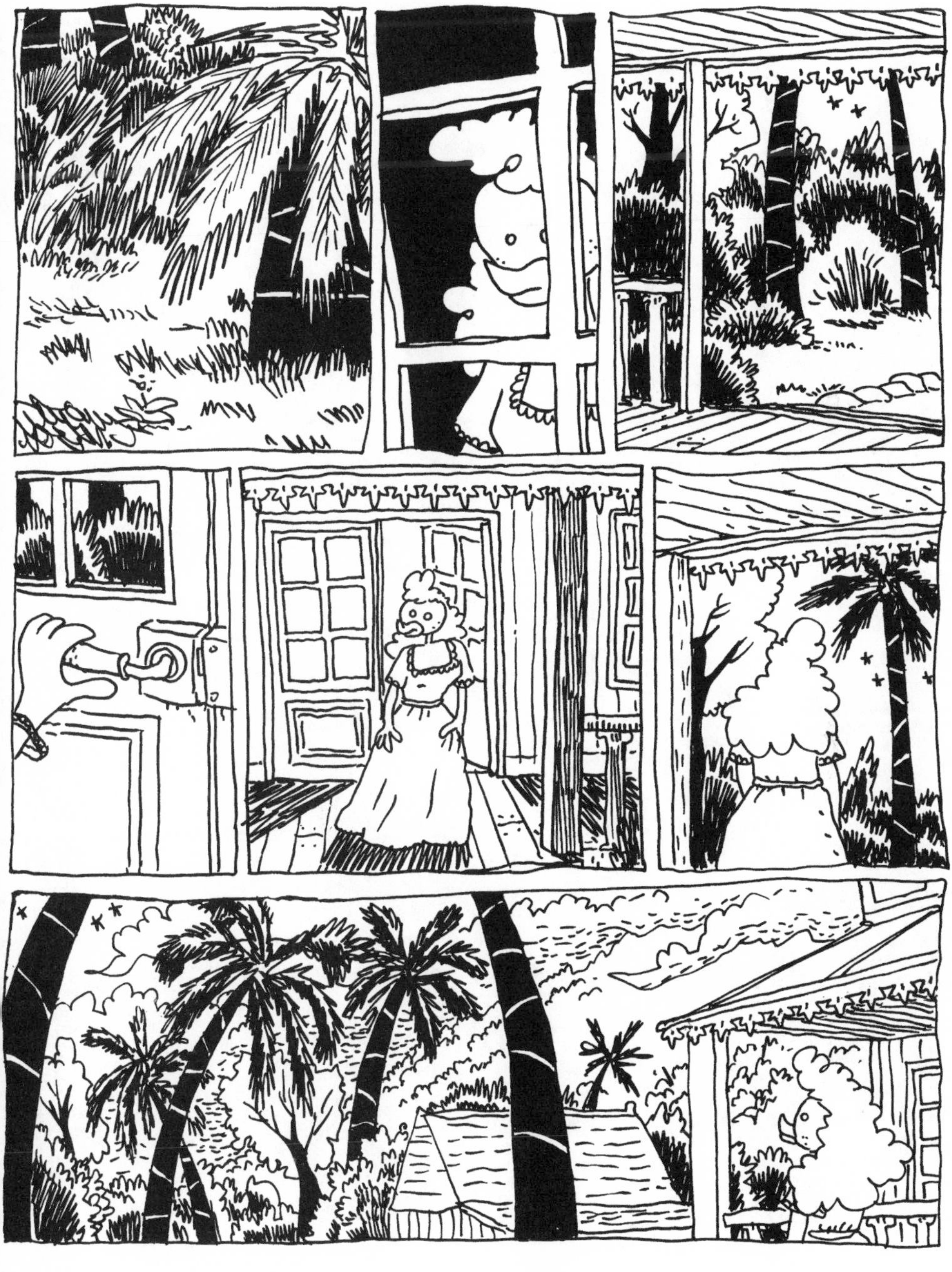

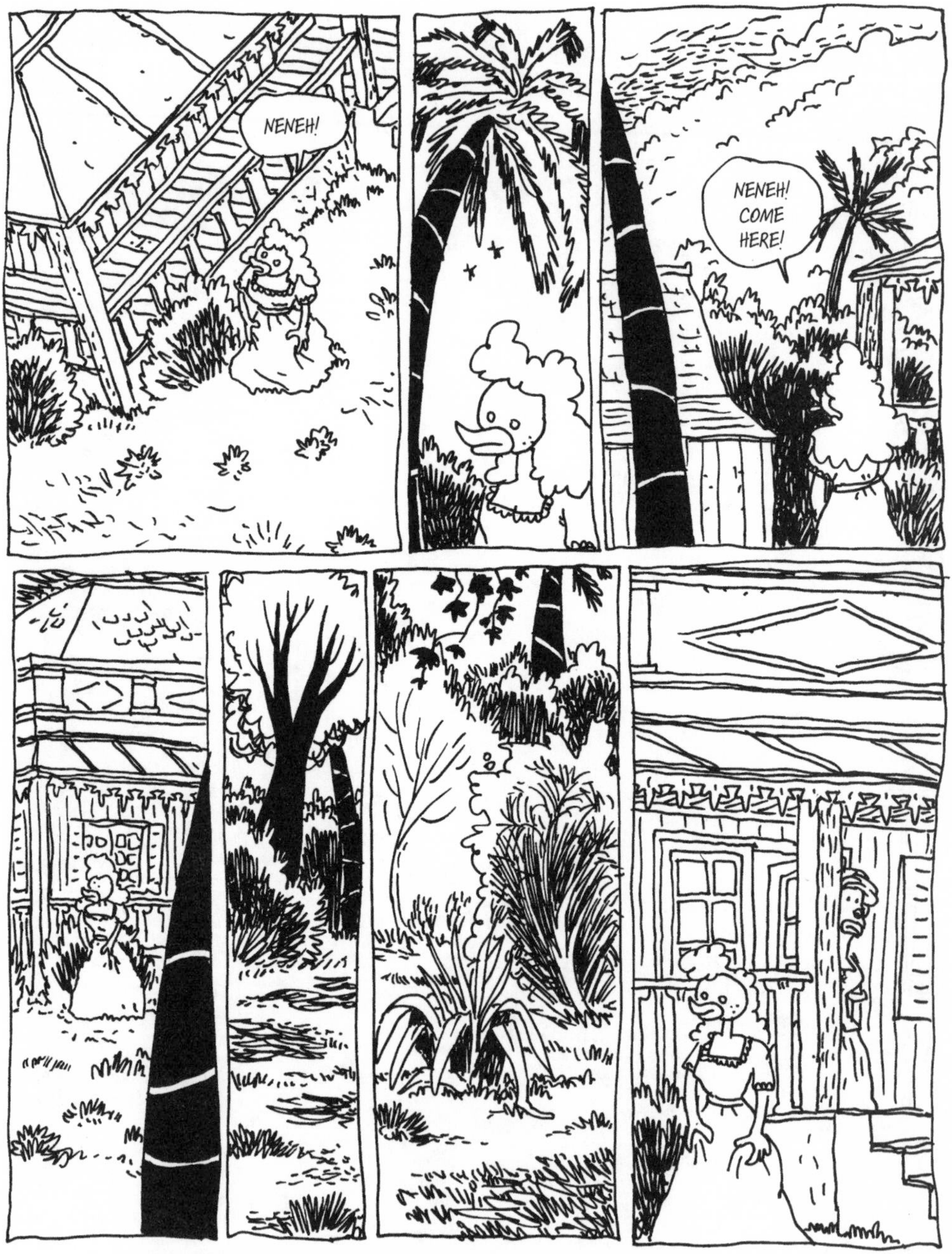
NENEH!
NENEH! COME HERE!

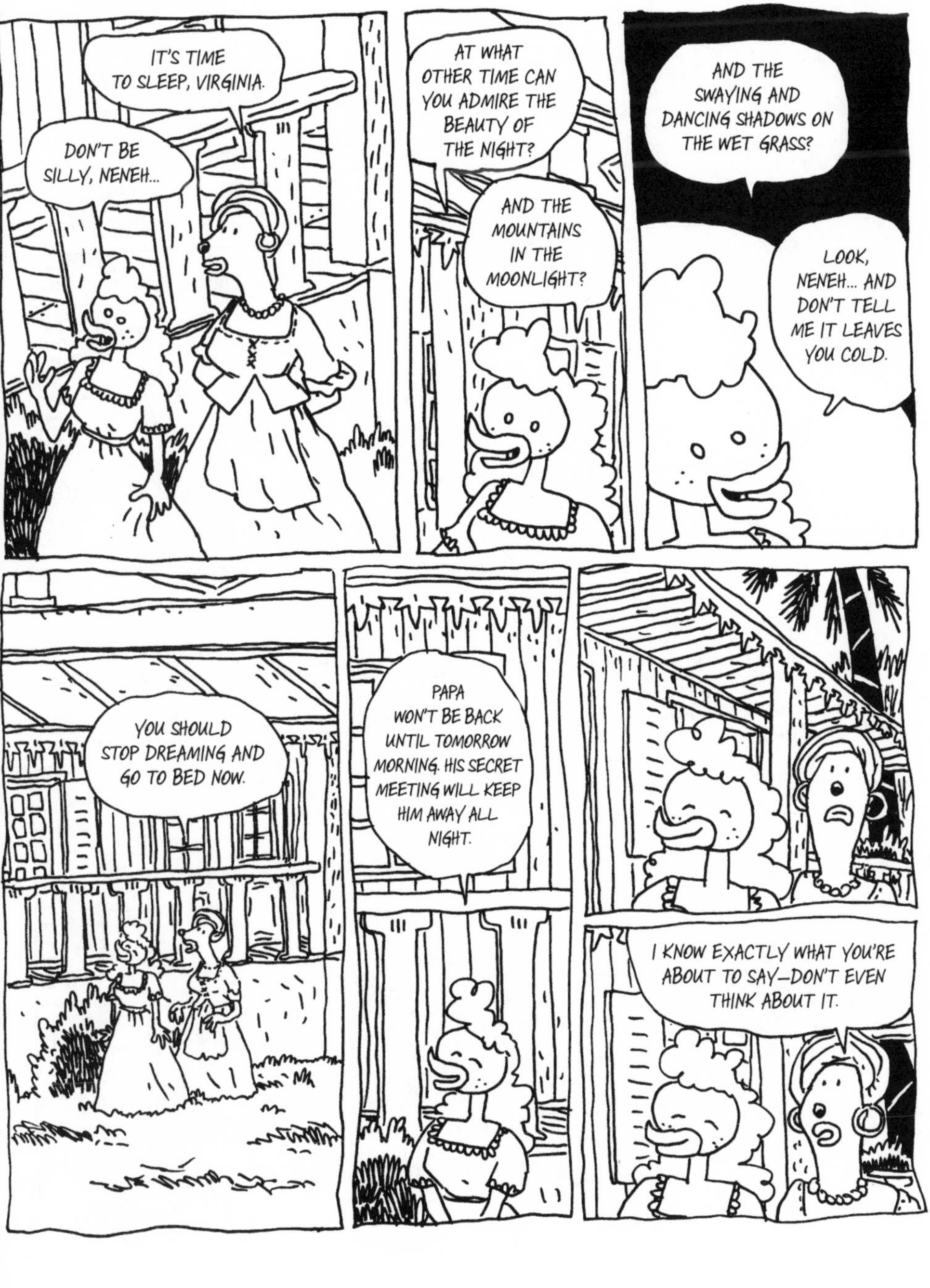
IT'S TIME TO SLEEP, VIRGINIA.
DON'T BE SILLY, NENEH...
AT WHAT OTHER TIME CAN YOU ADMIRE THE BEAUTY OF THE NIGHT?
AND THE MOUNTAINS IN THE MOONLIGHT?
AND THE SWAYING AND DANCING SHADOWS ON THE WET GRASS?
LOOK, NENEH... AND DON'T TELL ME IT LEAVES YOU COLD.
YOU SHOULD STOP DREAMING AND GO TO BED NOW.
PAPA WON'T BE BACK UNTIL TOMORROW MORNING. HIS SECRET MEETING WILL KEEP HIM AWAY ALL NIGHT.
I KNOW EXACTLY WHAT YOU'RE ABOUT TO SAY—DON'T EVEN THINK ABOUT IT.

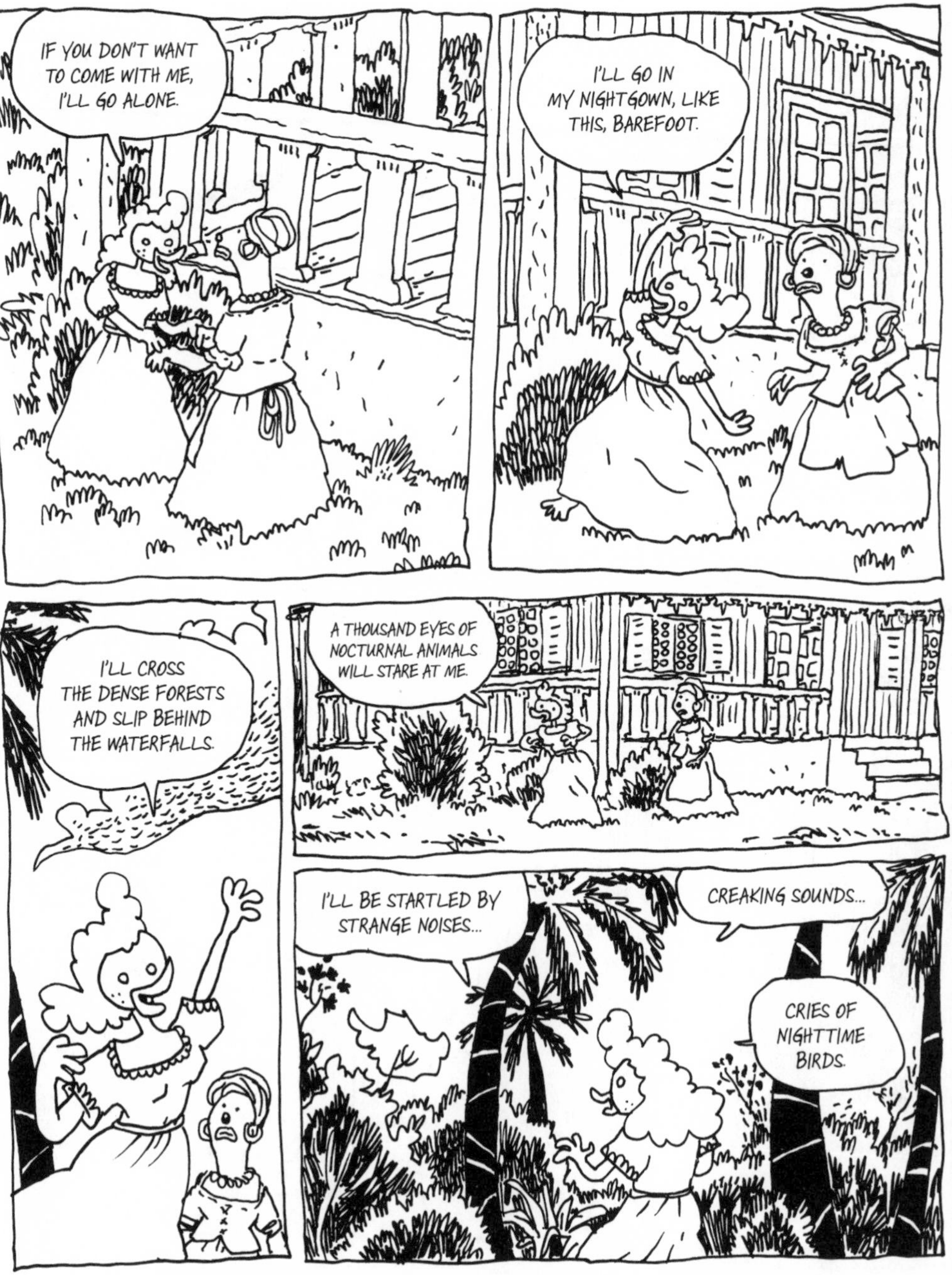
IF YOU DON'T WANT TO COME WITH ME, I'LL GO ALONE.
I'LL GO IN MY NIGHTGOWN, LIKE THIS, BAREFOOT.
I'LL CROSS THE DENSE FORESTS AND SLIP BEHIND THE WATERFALLS.
A THOUSAND EYES OF NOCTURNAL ANIMALS WILL STARE AT ME.
I'LL BE STARTLED BY STRANGE NOISES...
CREAKING SOUNDS...
CRIES OF NIGHTTIME BIRDS.

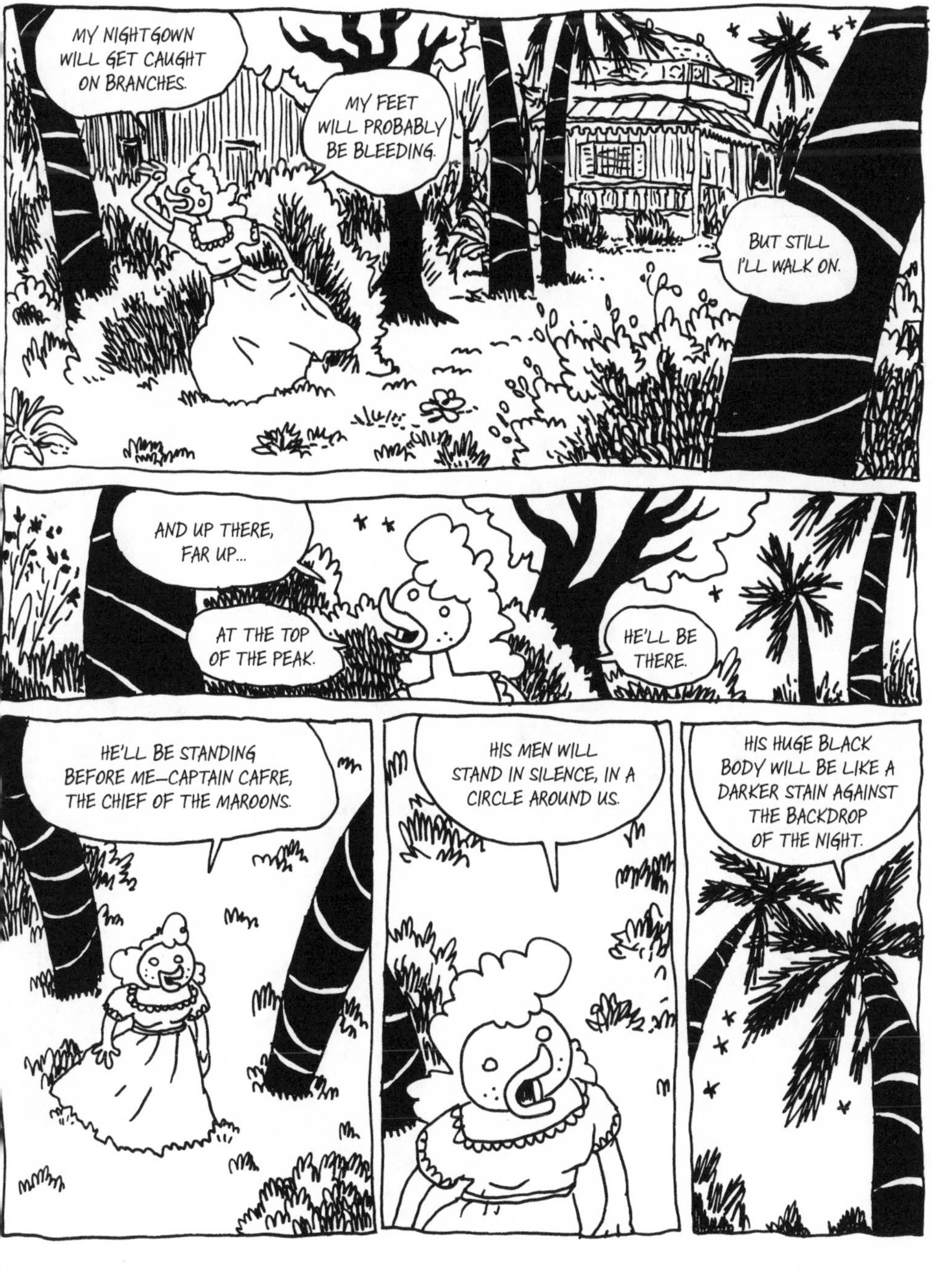

MY NIGHTGOWN WILL GET CAUGHT ON BRANCHES.
MY FEET WILL PROBABLY BE BLEEDING.
BUT STILL I'LL WALK ON.
AND UP THERE, FAR UP...
AT THE TOP OF THE PEAK.
HE'LL BE THERE.
HE'LL BE STANDING BEFORE ME—CAPTAIN CAFRE, THE CHIEF OF THE MAROONS.
HIS MEN WILL STAND IN SILENCE, IN A CIRCLE AROUND US.
HIS HUGE BLACK BODY WILL BE LIKE A DARKER STAIN AGAINST THE BACKDROP OF THE NIGHT.

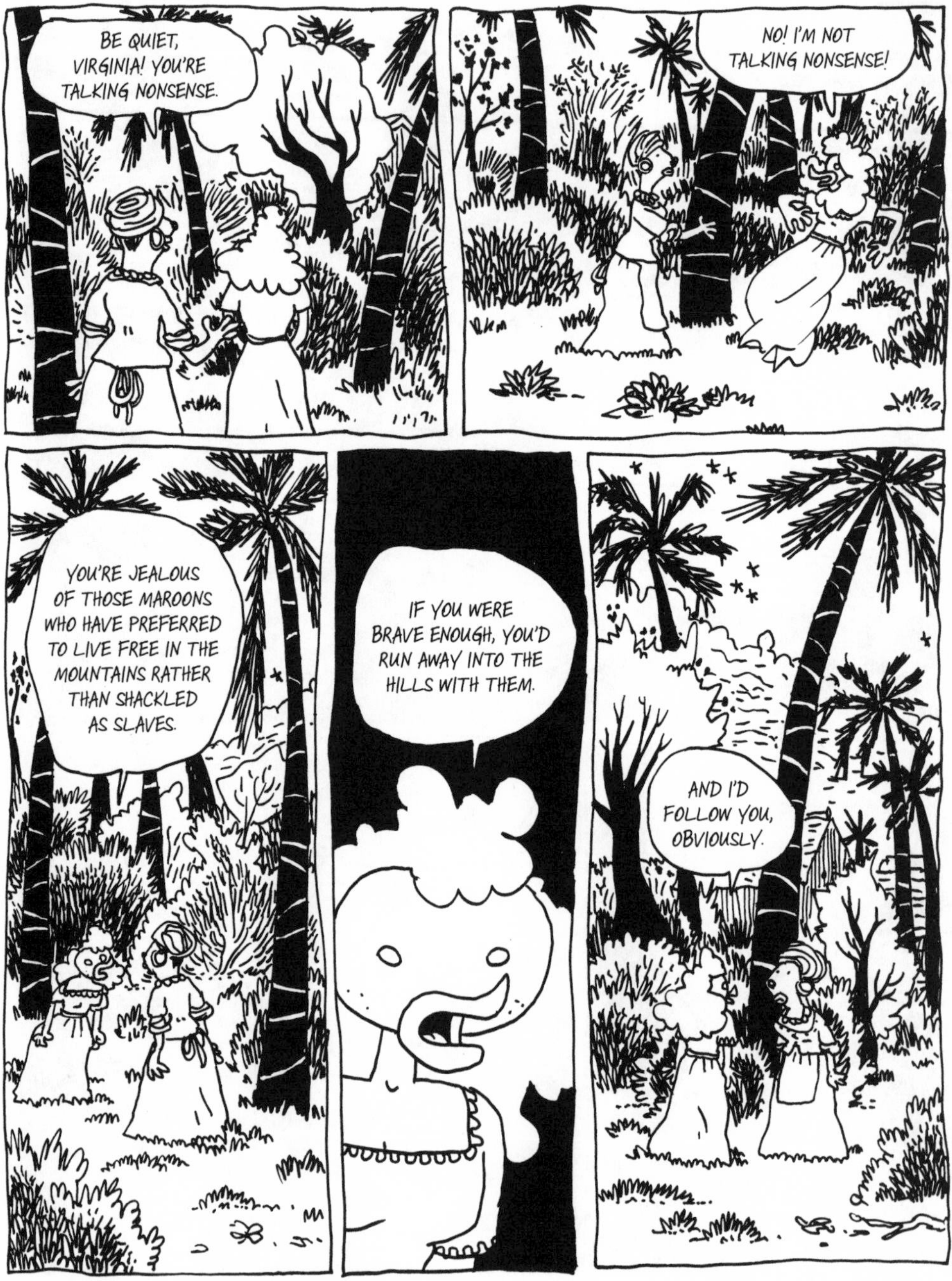
BE QUIET, VIRGINIA! YOU'RE TALKING NONSENSE.
NO! I'M NOT TALKING NONSENSE!
YOU'RE JEALOUS OF THOSE MAROONS WHO HAVE PREFERRED TO LIVE FREE IN THE MOUNTAINS RATHER THAN SHACKLED AS SLAVES.
IF YOU WERE BRAVE ENOUGH, YOU'D RUN AWAY INTO THE HILLS WITH THEM.
AND I'D FOLLOW YOU, OBVIOUSLY.

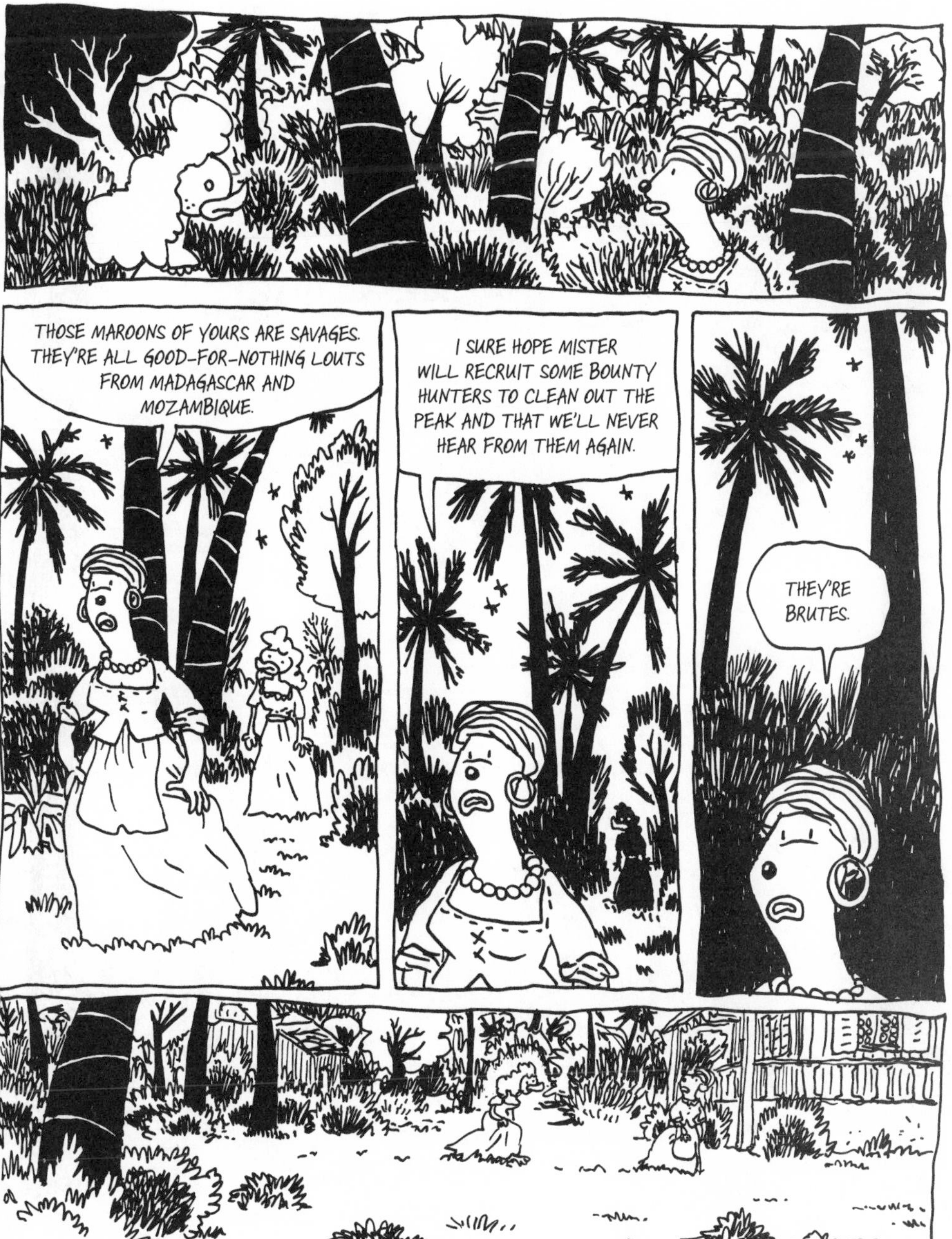
THOSE MAROONS OF YOURS ARE SAVAGES. THEY'RE ALL GOOD-FOR-NOTHING LOUTS FROM MADAGASCAR AND MOZAMBIQUE.
I SURE HOPE MISTER WILL RECRUIT SOME BOUNTY HUNTERS TO CLEAN OUT THE PEAK AND THAT WE'LL NEVER HEAR FROM THEM AGAIN.
THEY'RE BRUTES.

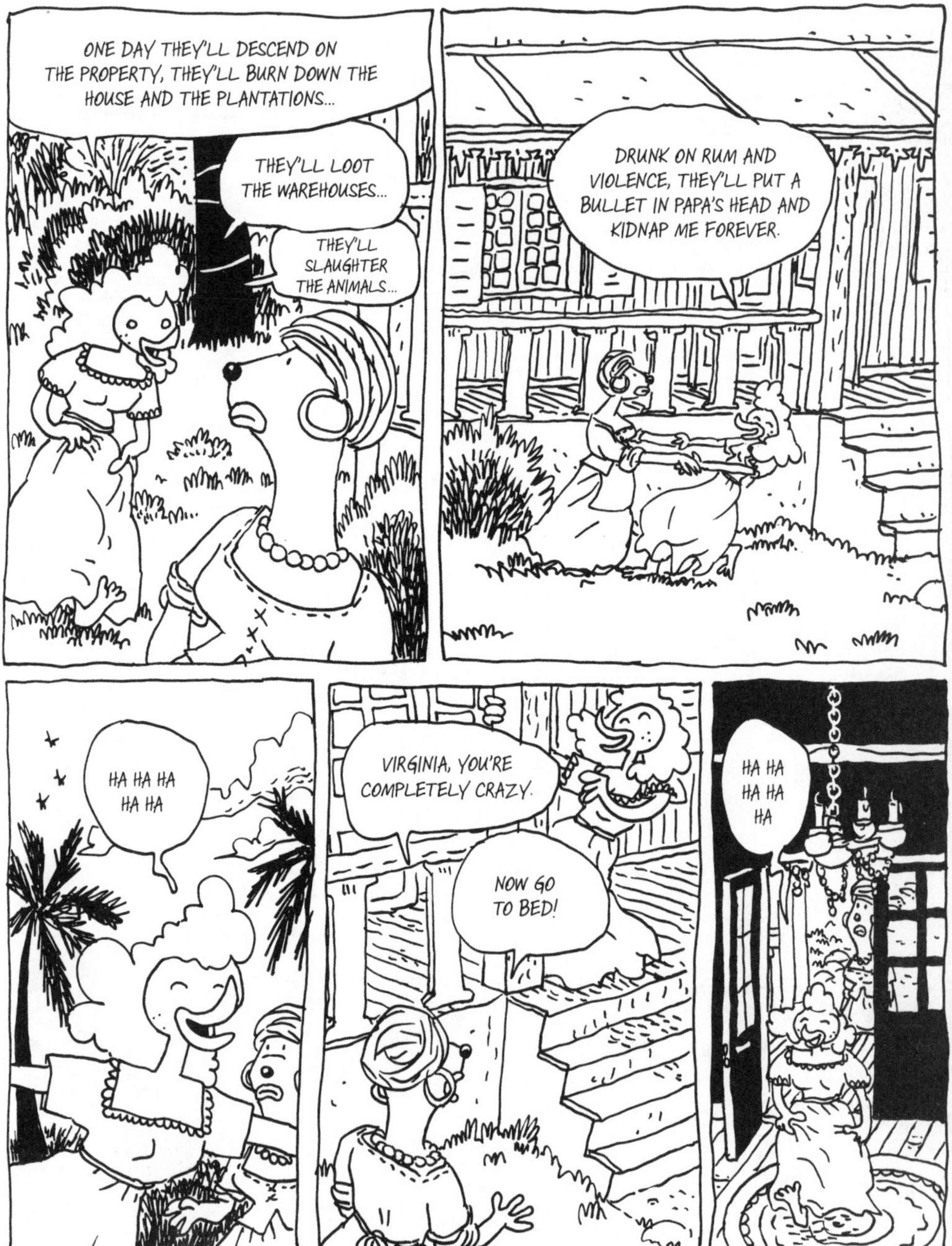
ONE DAY THEY'LL DESCEND ON THE PROPERTY, THEY'LL BURN DOWN THE HOUSE AND THE PLANTATIONS...
THEY'LL LOOT THE WAREHOUSES...
THEY'LL SLAUGHTER THE ANIMALS...
DRUNK ON RUM AND VIOLENCE, THEY'LL PUT A BULLET IN PAPA'S HEAD AND KIDNAP ME FOREVER.
HA HA HA HA HA
VIRGINIA, YOU'RE COMPLETELY CRAZY.
NOW GO TO BED!
HA HA HA HA HA

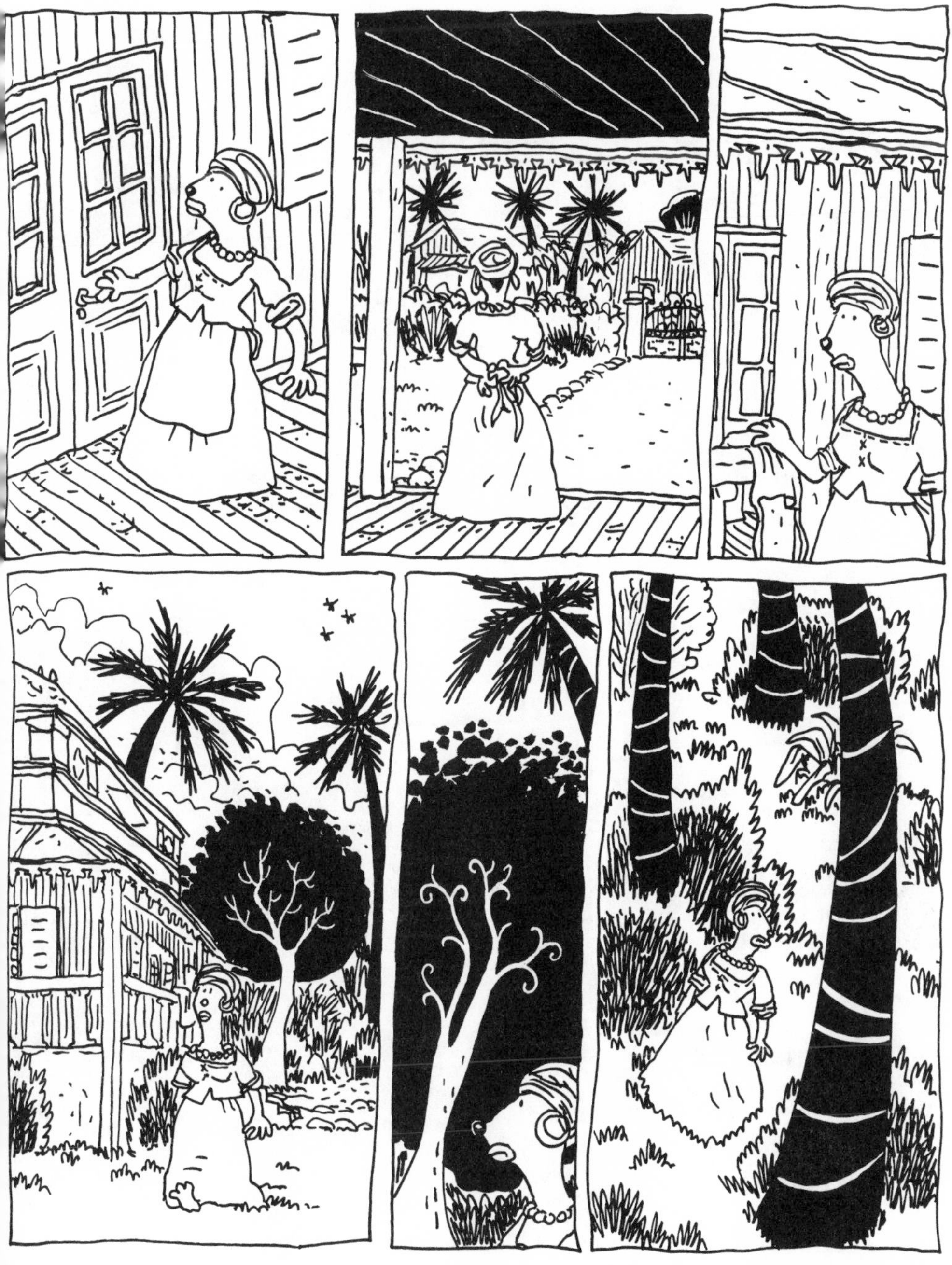

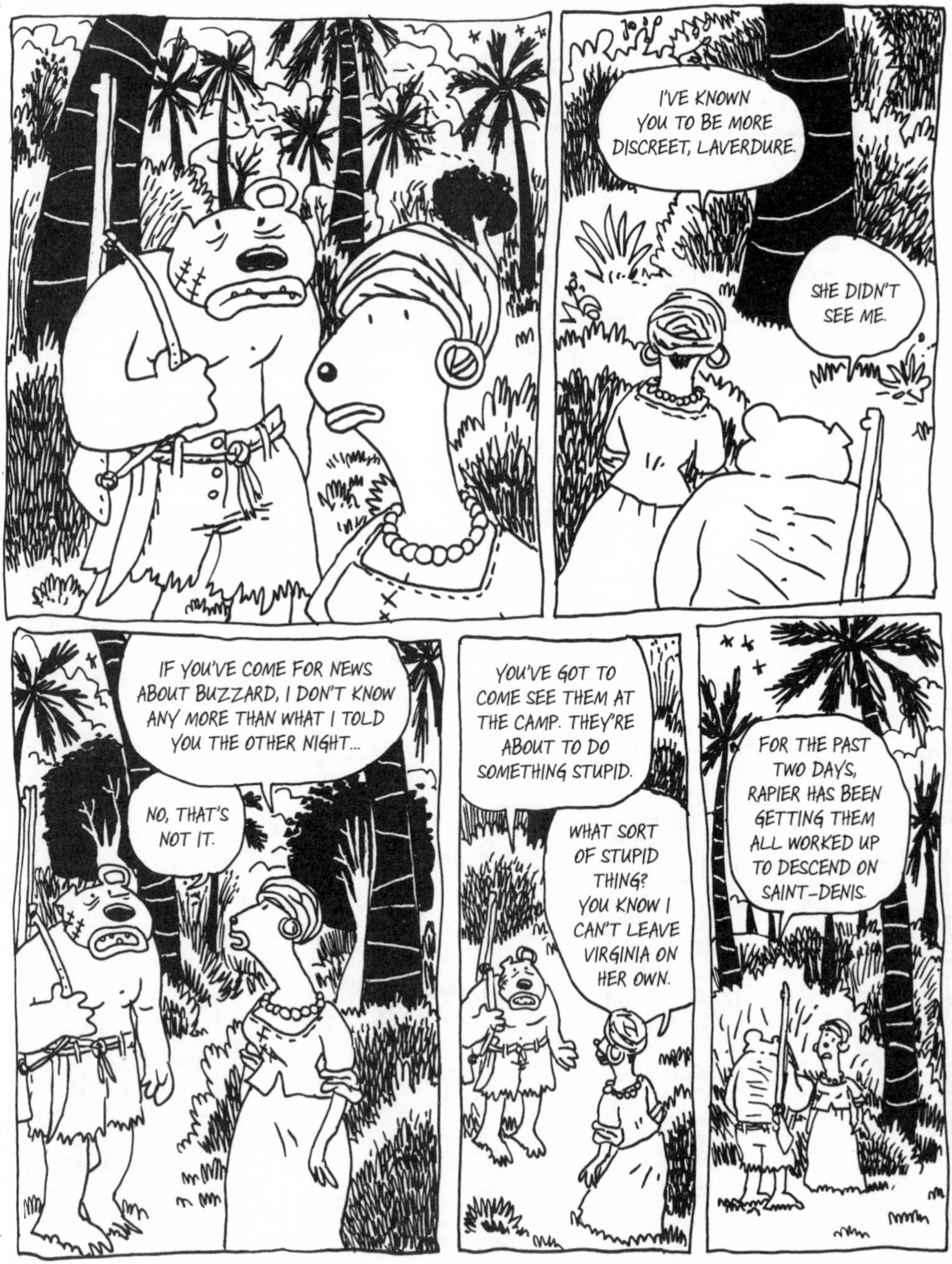

I'VE KNOWN YOU TO BE MORE DISCREET, LAVERDURE.
SHE DIDN'T SEE ME.
IF YOU'VE COME FOR NEWS ABOUT BUZZARD, I DON'T KNOW ANY MORE THAN WHAT I TOLD YOU THE OTHER NIGHT...
NO, THAT'S NOT IT.
YOU'VE GOT TO COME SEE THEM AT THE CAMP. THEY'RE ABOUT TO DO SOMETHING STUPID.
WHAT SORT OF STUPID THING? YOU KNOW I CAN'T LEAVE VIRGINIA ON HER OWN.
FOR THE PAST TWO DAYS, RAPIER HAS BEEN GETTING THEM ALL WORKED UP TO DESCEND ON SAINT-DENIS.

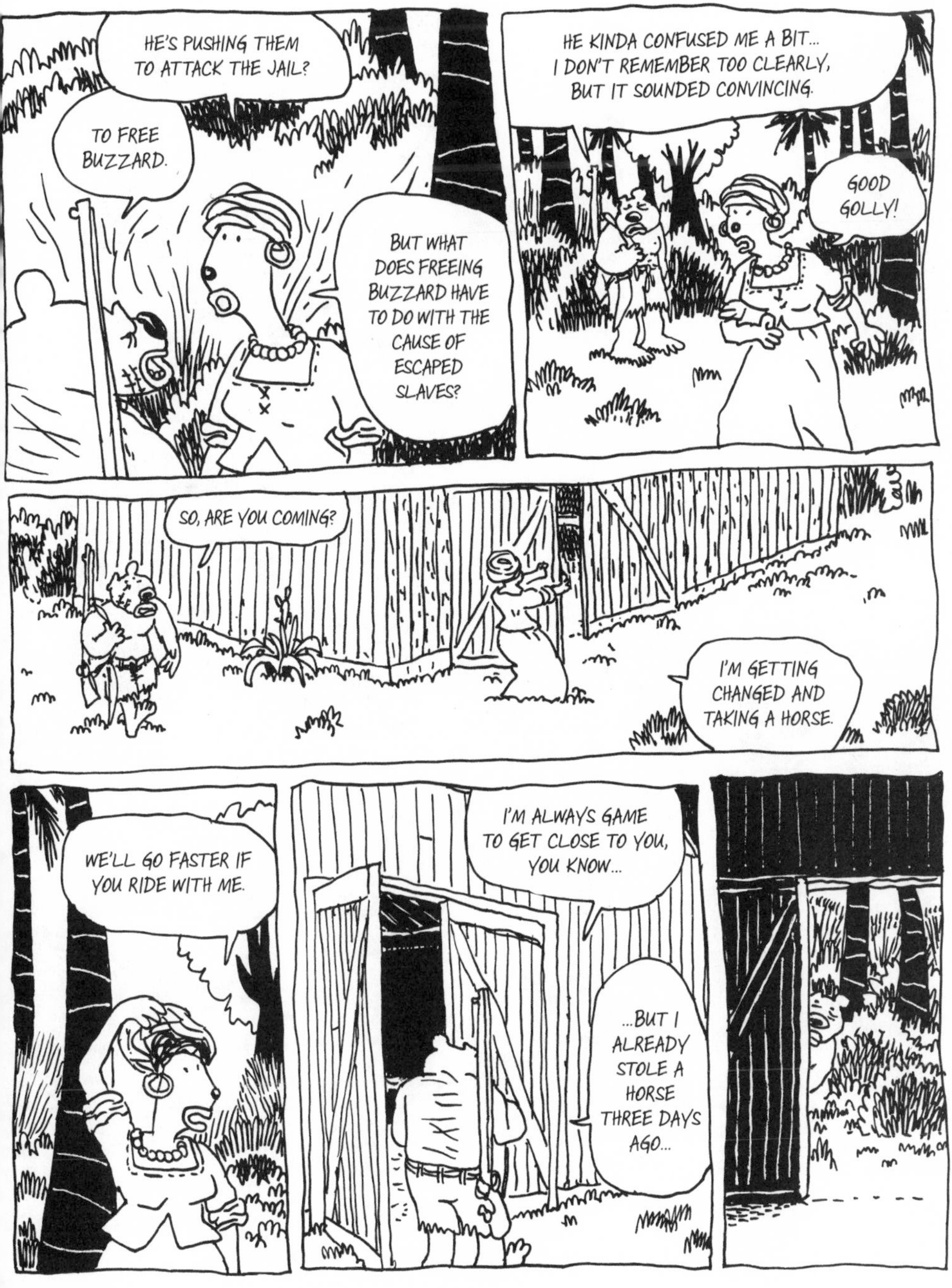
HE'S PUSHING THEM TO ATTACK THE JAIL?
TO FREE BUZZARD.
BUT WHAT DOES FREEING BUZZARD HAVE TO DO WITH THE CAUSE OF ESCAPED SLAVES?
HE KINDA CONFUSED ME A BIT... I DON'T REMEMBER TOO CLEARLY, BUT IT SOUNDED CONVINCING.
GOOD GOLLY!
SO, ARE YOU COMING?
I'M GETTING CHANGED AND TAKING A HORSE.
WE'LL GO FASTER IF YOU RIDE WITH ME.
I'M ALWAYS GAME TO GET CLOSE TO YOU, YOU KNOW...
...BUT I ALREADY STOLE A HORSE THREE DAYS AGO...

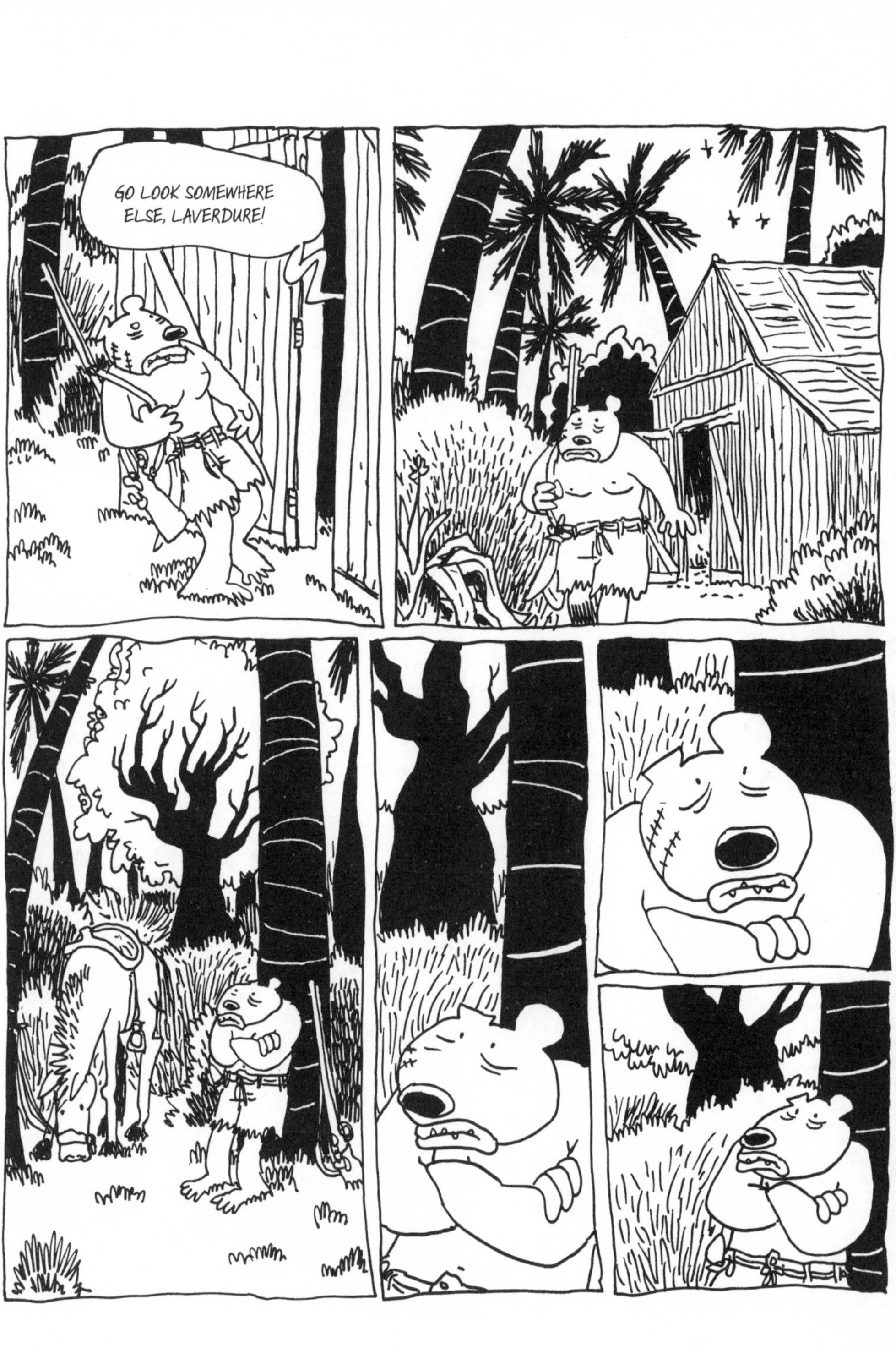
GO LOOK SOMEWHERE ELSE, LAVERDURE!

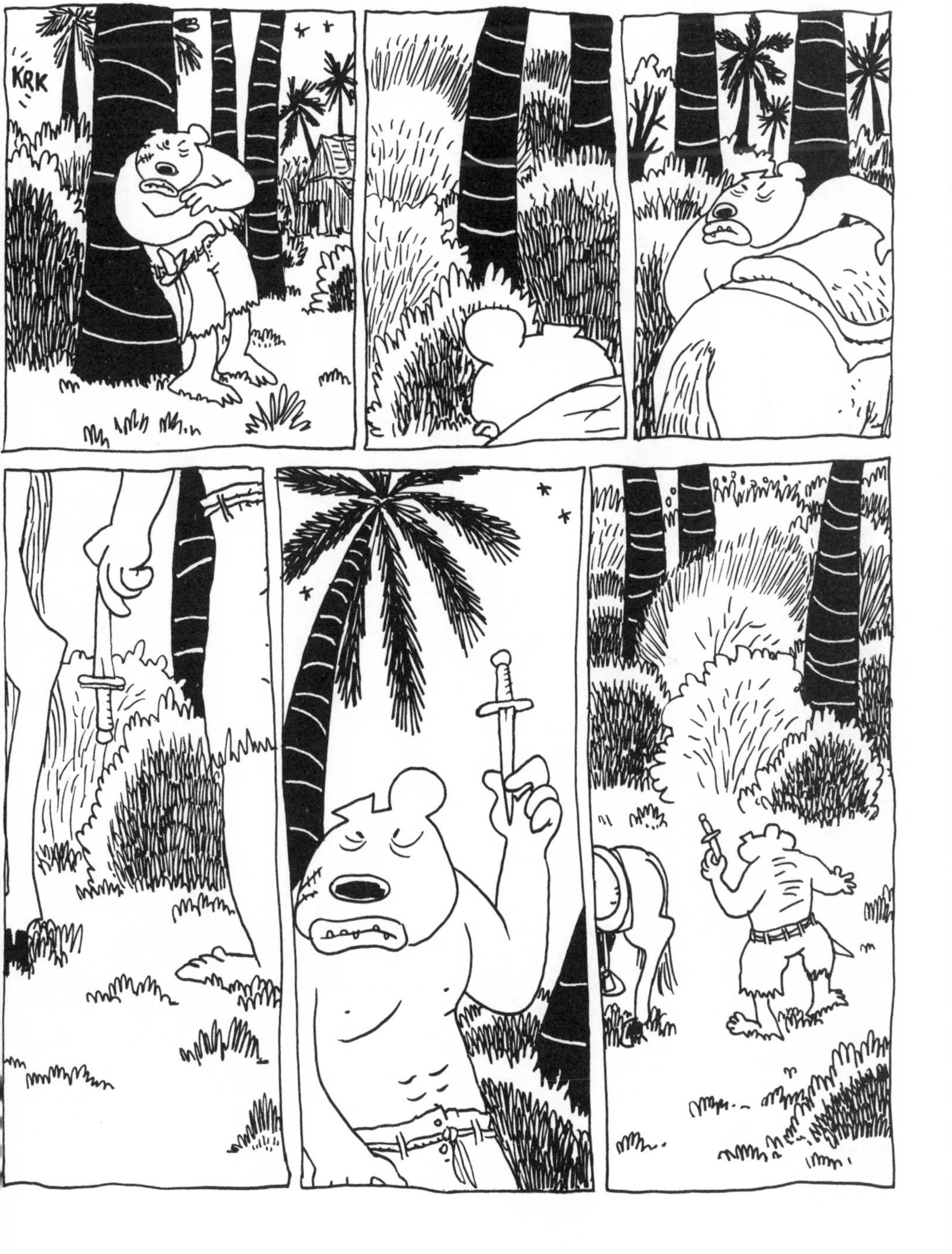
KRK

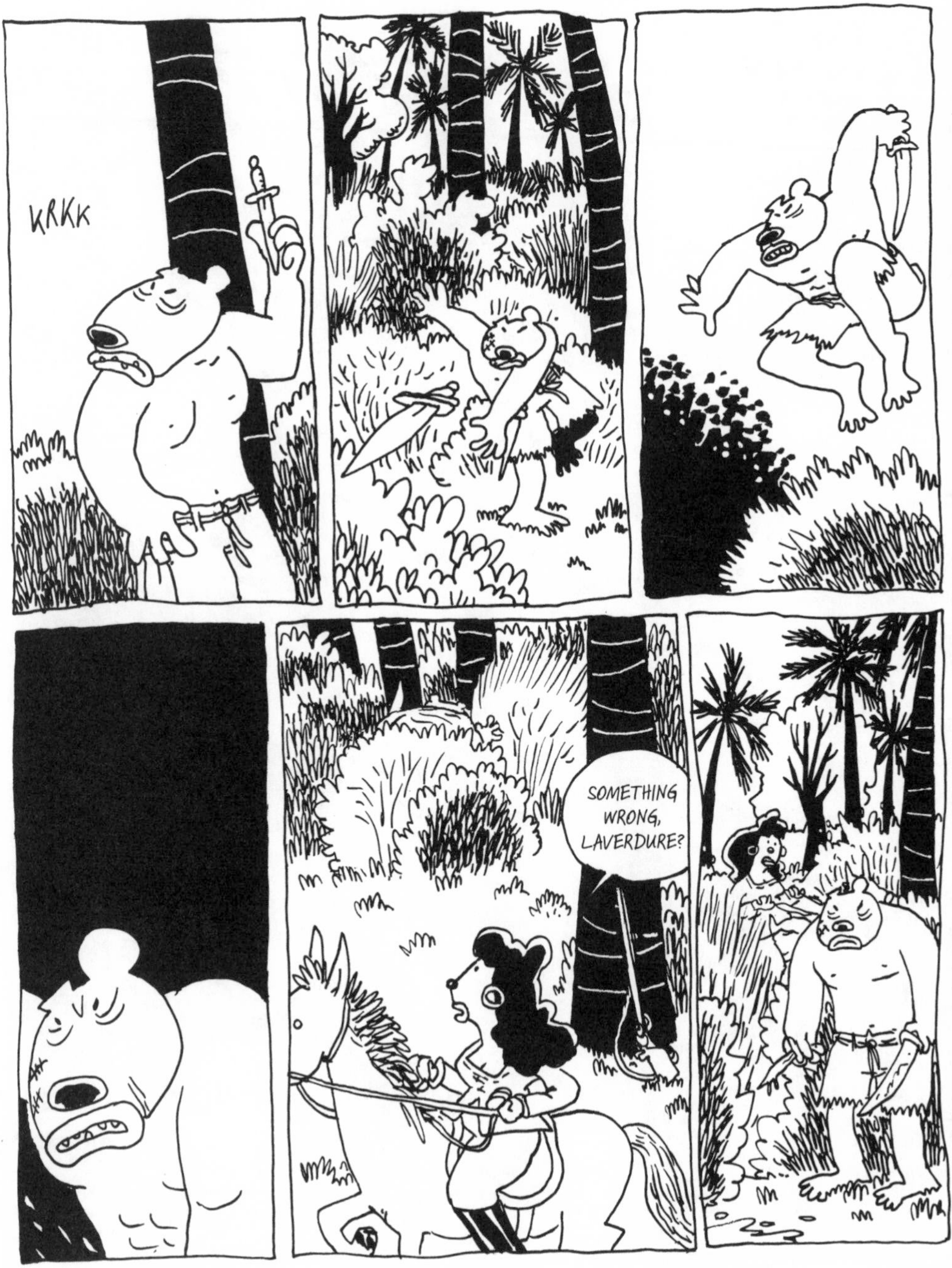
KRKK
SOMETHING WRONG, LAVERDURE?

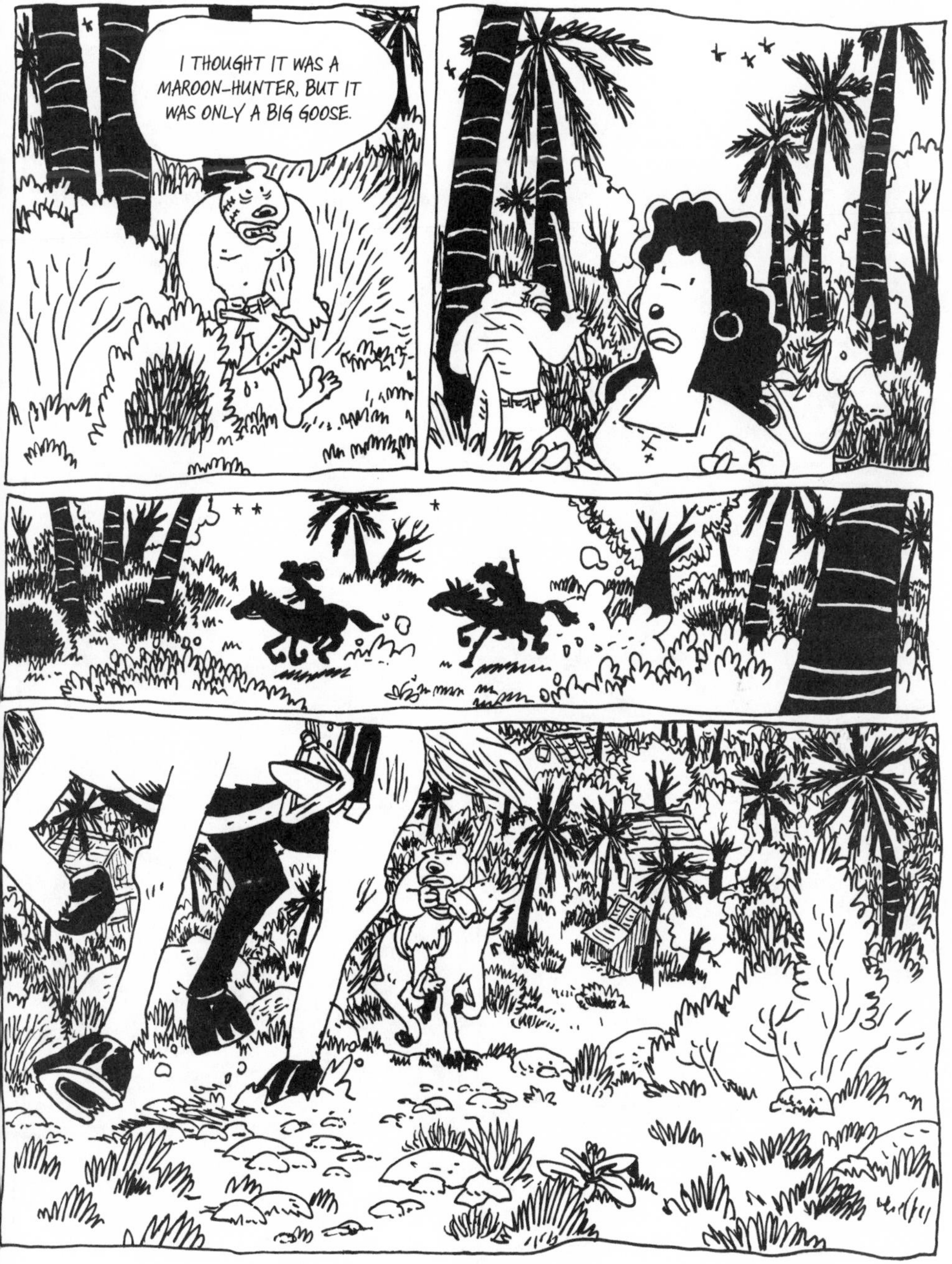
I THOUGHT IT WAS A MAROON-HUNTER, BUT IT WAS ONLY A BIG GOOSE.

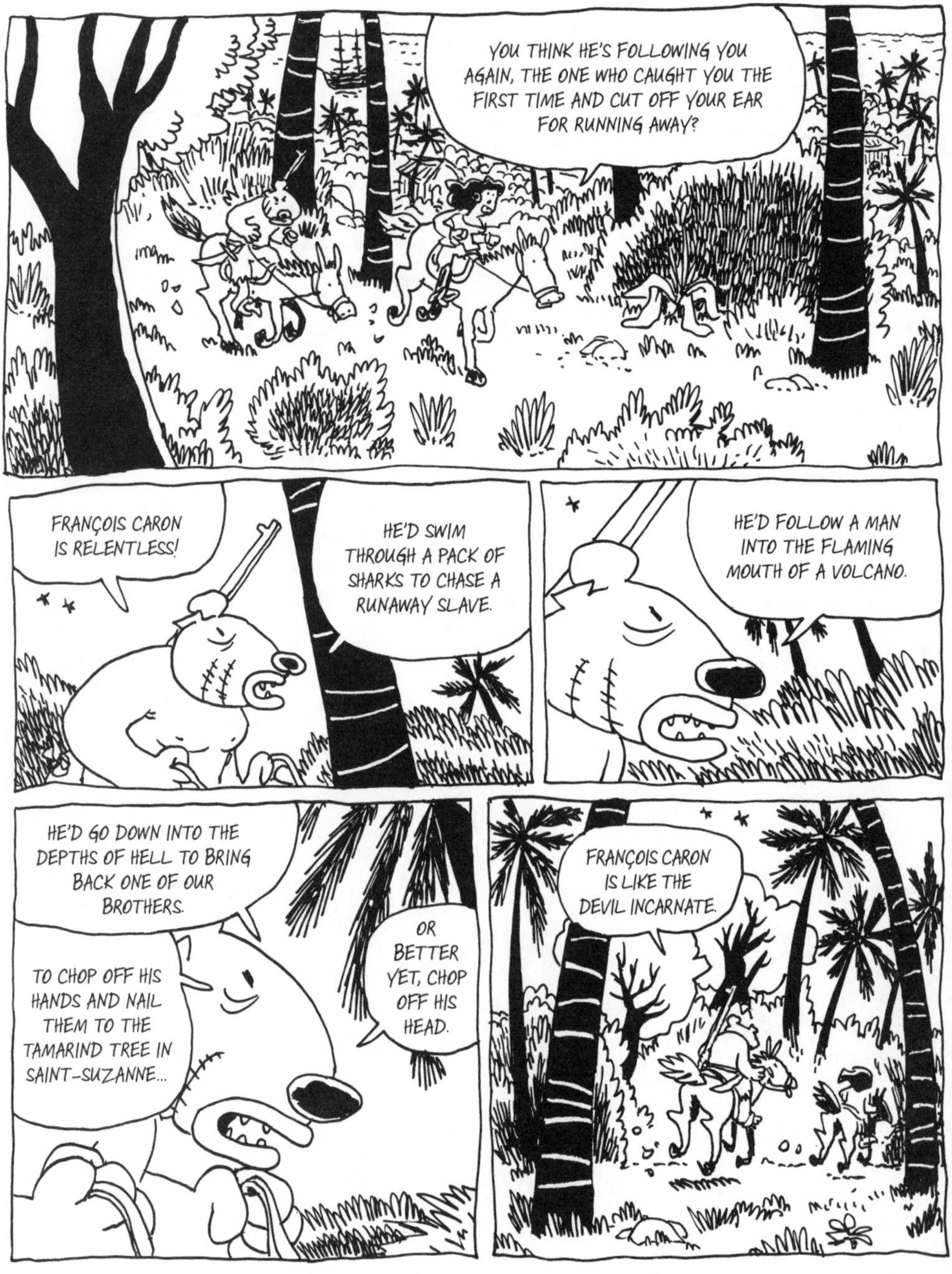
YOU THINK HE'S FOLLOWING YOU AGAIN, THE ONE WHO CAUGHT YOU THE FIRST TIME AND CUT OFF YOUR EAR FOR RUNNING AWAY?
FRANÇOIS CARON IS RELENTLESS!
HE'D SWIM THROUGH A PACK OF SHARKS TO CHASE A RUNAWAY SLAVE.
HE'D FOLLOW A MAN INTO THE FLAMING MOUTH OF A VOLCANO.
HE'D GO DOWN INTO THE DEPTHS OF HELL TO BRING BACK ONE OF OUR BROTHERS.
TO CHOP OFF HIS HANDS AND NAIL THEM TO THE TAMARIND TREE IN SAINT-SUZANNE...
OR BETTER YET, CHOP OFF HIS HEAD.
FRANÇOIS CARON IS LIKE THE DEVIL INCARNATE.

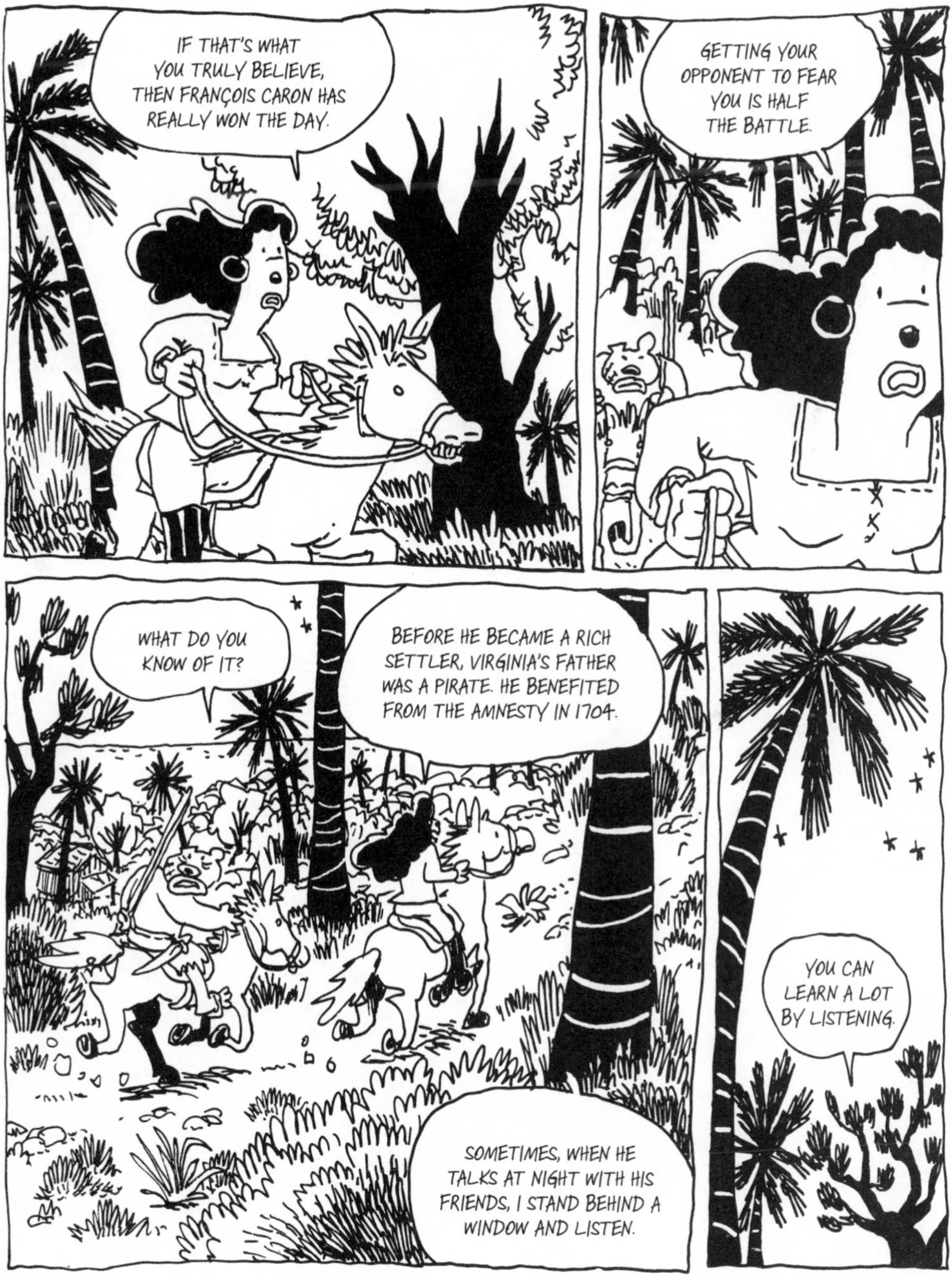
IF THAT'S WHAT YOU TRULY BELIEVE, THEN FRANÇOIS CARON HAS REALLY WON THE DAY.
GETTING YOUR OPPONENT TO FEAR YOU IS HALF THE BATTLE.
WHAT DO YOU KNOW OF IT?
BEFORE HE BECAME A RICH SETTLER, VIRGINIA'S FATHER WAS A PIRATE. HE BENEFITED FROM THE AMNESTY IN 1704.
SOMETIMES, WHEN HE TALKS AT NIGHT WITH HIS FRIENDS, I STAND BEHIND A WINDOW AND LISTEN.
YOU CAN LEARN A LOT BY LISTENING.

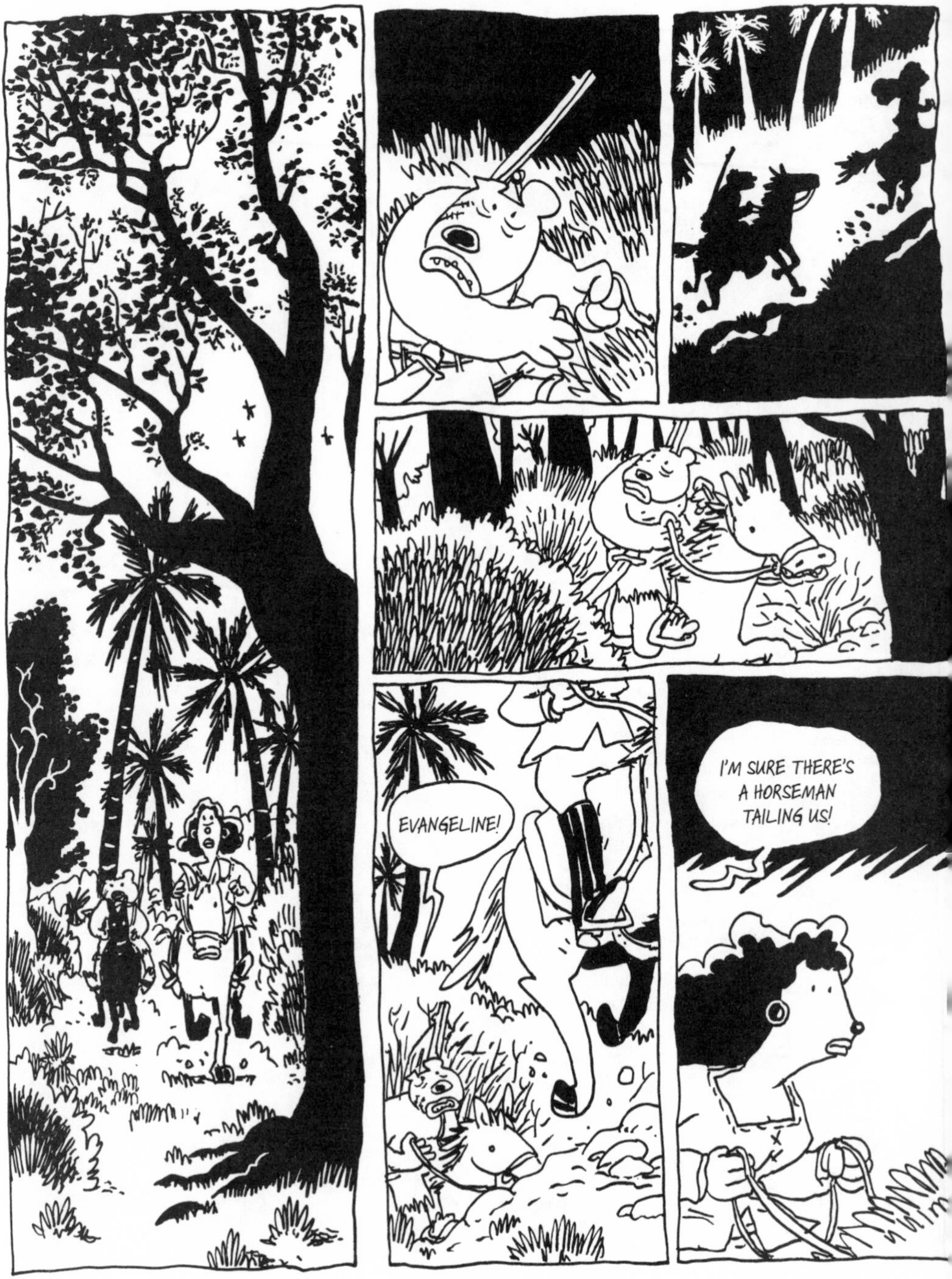
EVANGELINE!
I'M SURE THERE'S A HORSEMAN TAILING US!

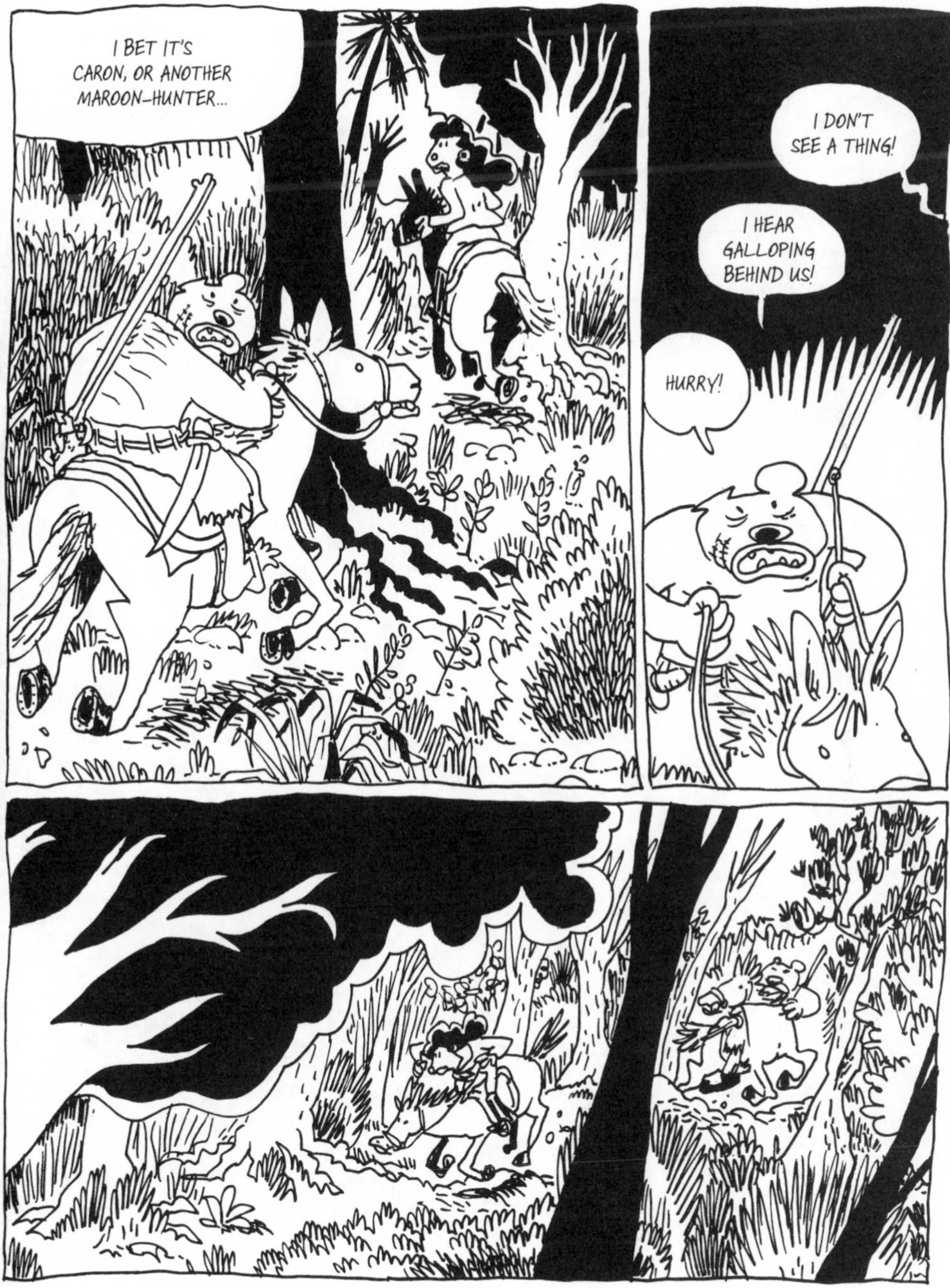
I BET IT'S CARON, OR ANOTHER MAROON-HUNTER...
I DON'T SEE A THING!
I HEAR GALLOPING BEHIND US!
HURRY!

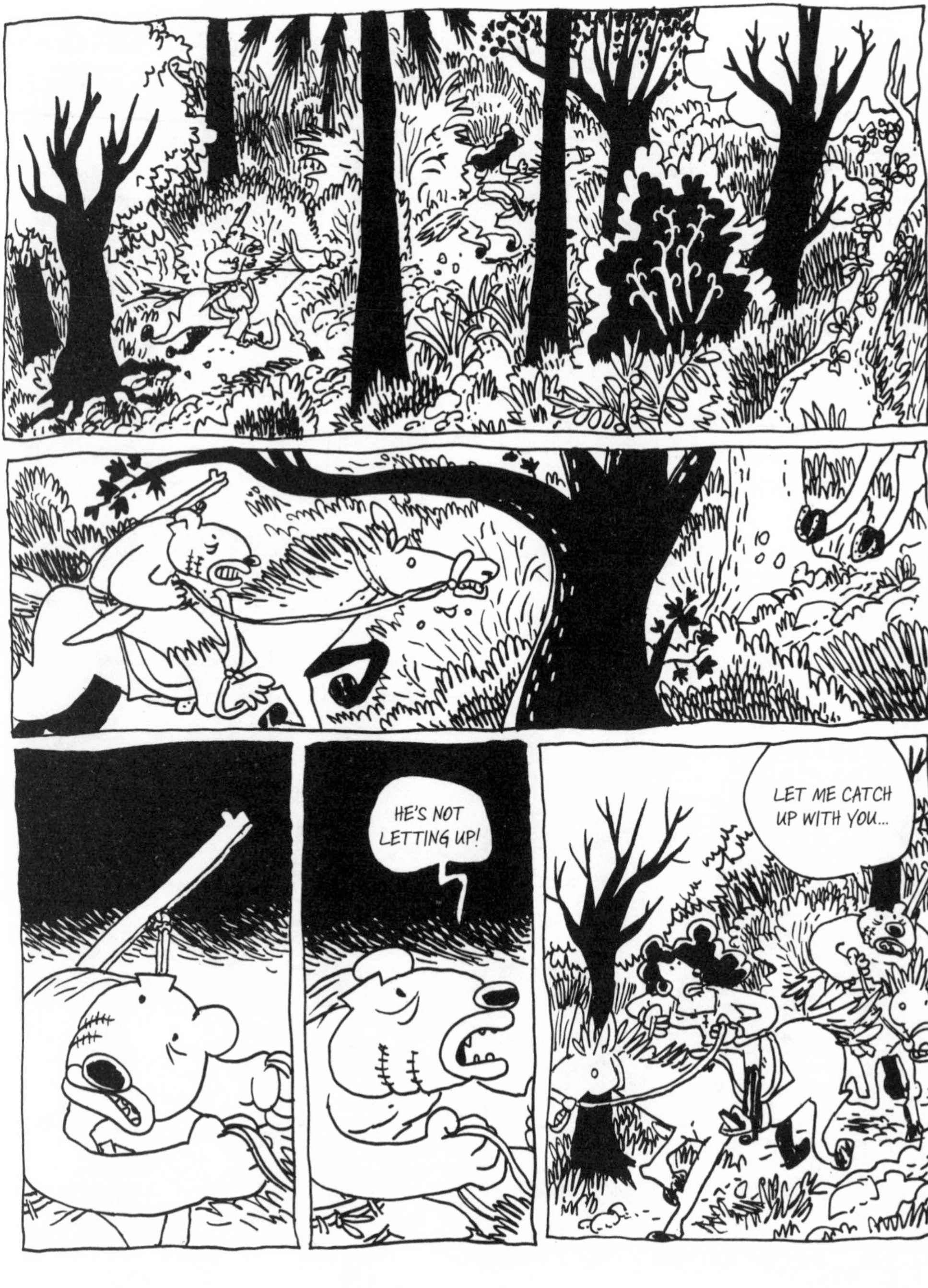
HE'S NOT LETTING UP!
LET ME CATCH UP WITH YOU...

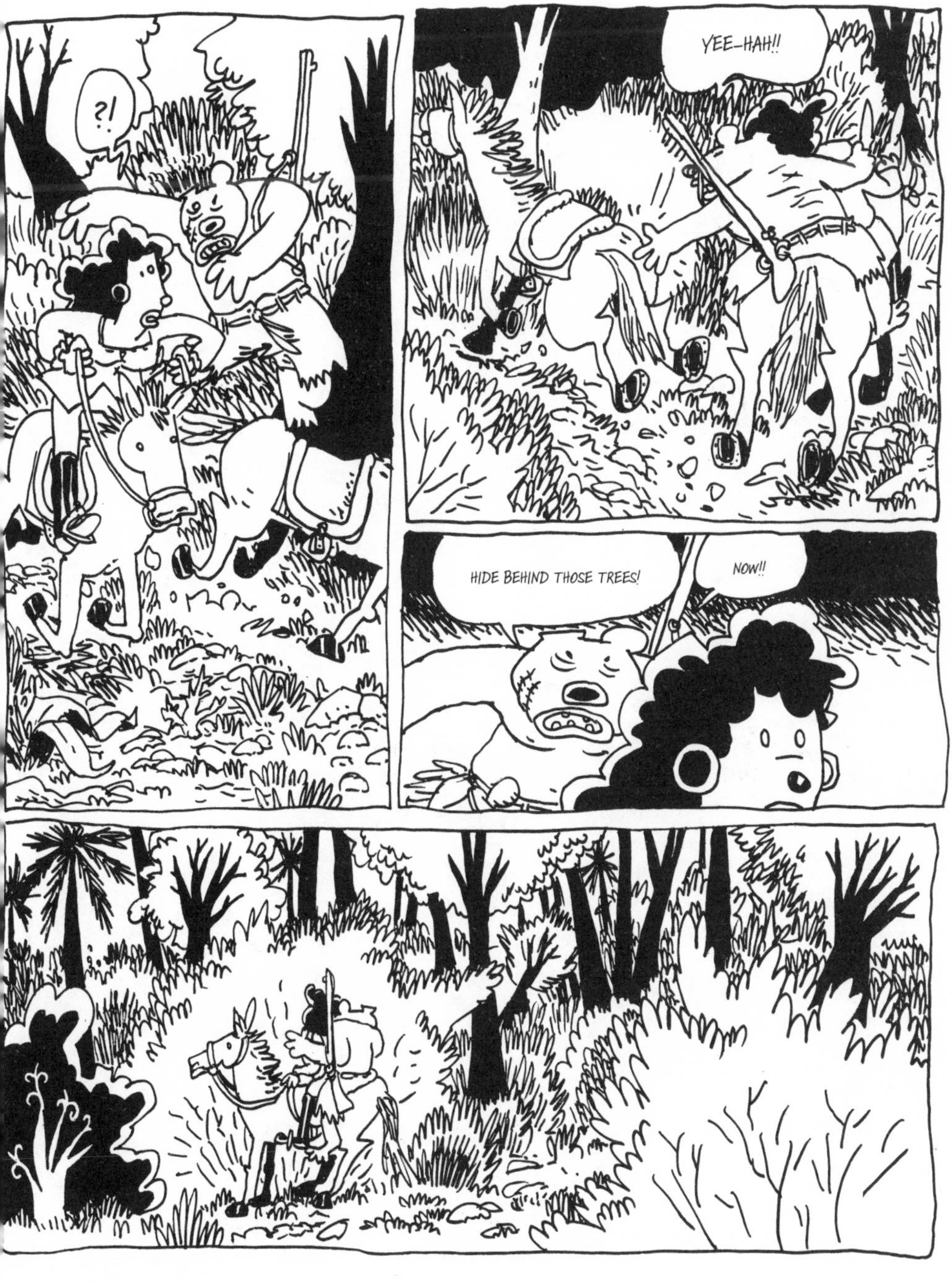
?!
YEE-HAH!!
HIDE BEHIND THOSE TREES!
NOW!!

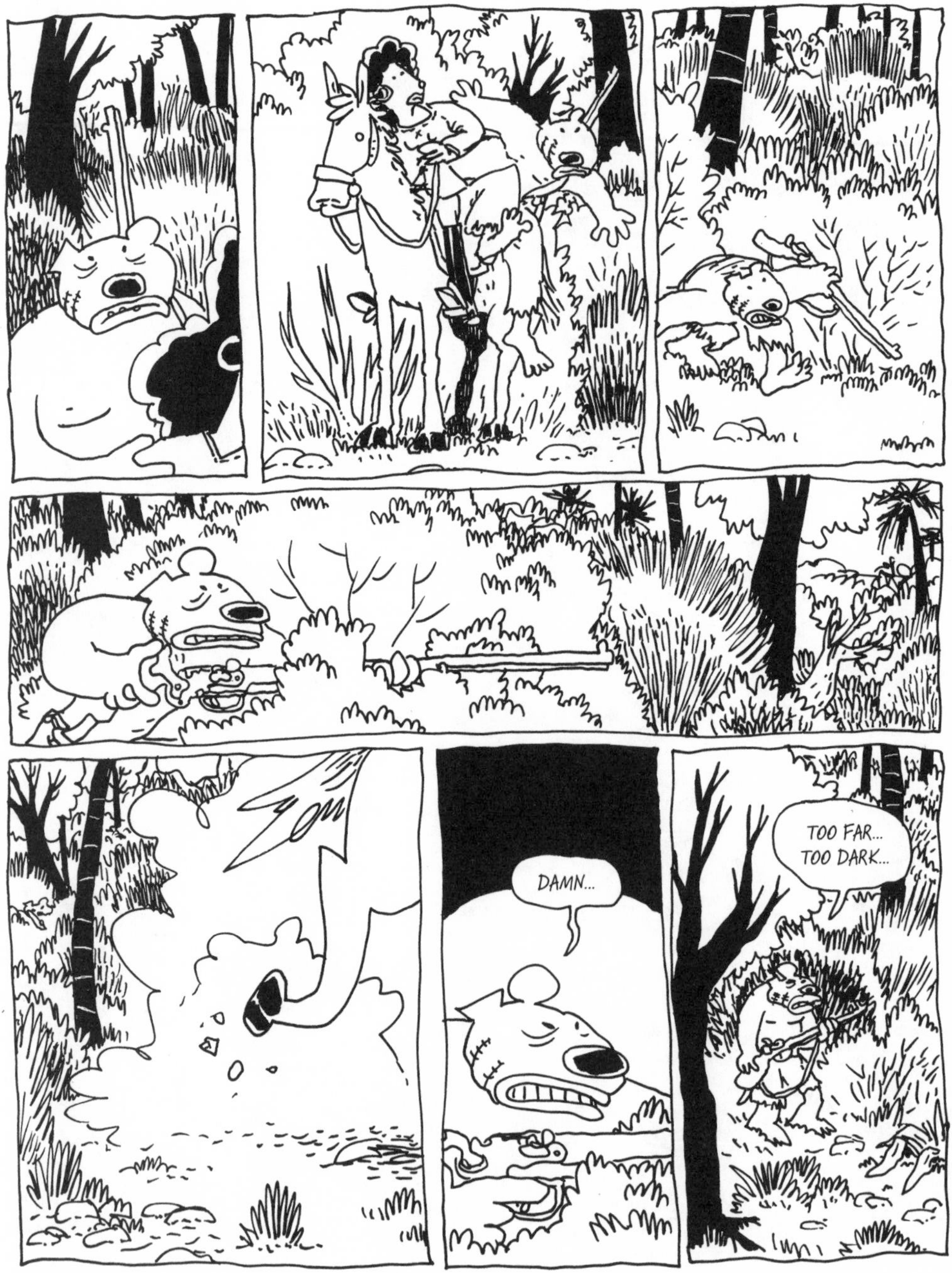
DAMN...
TOO FAR...
TOO DARK...

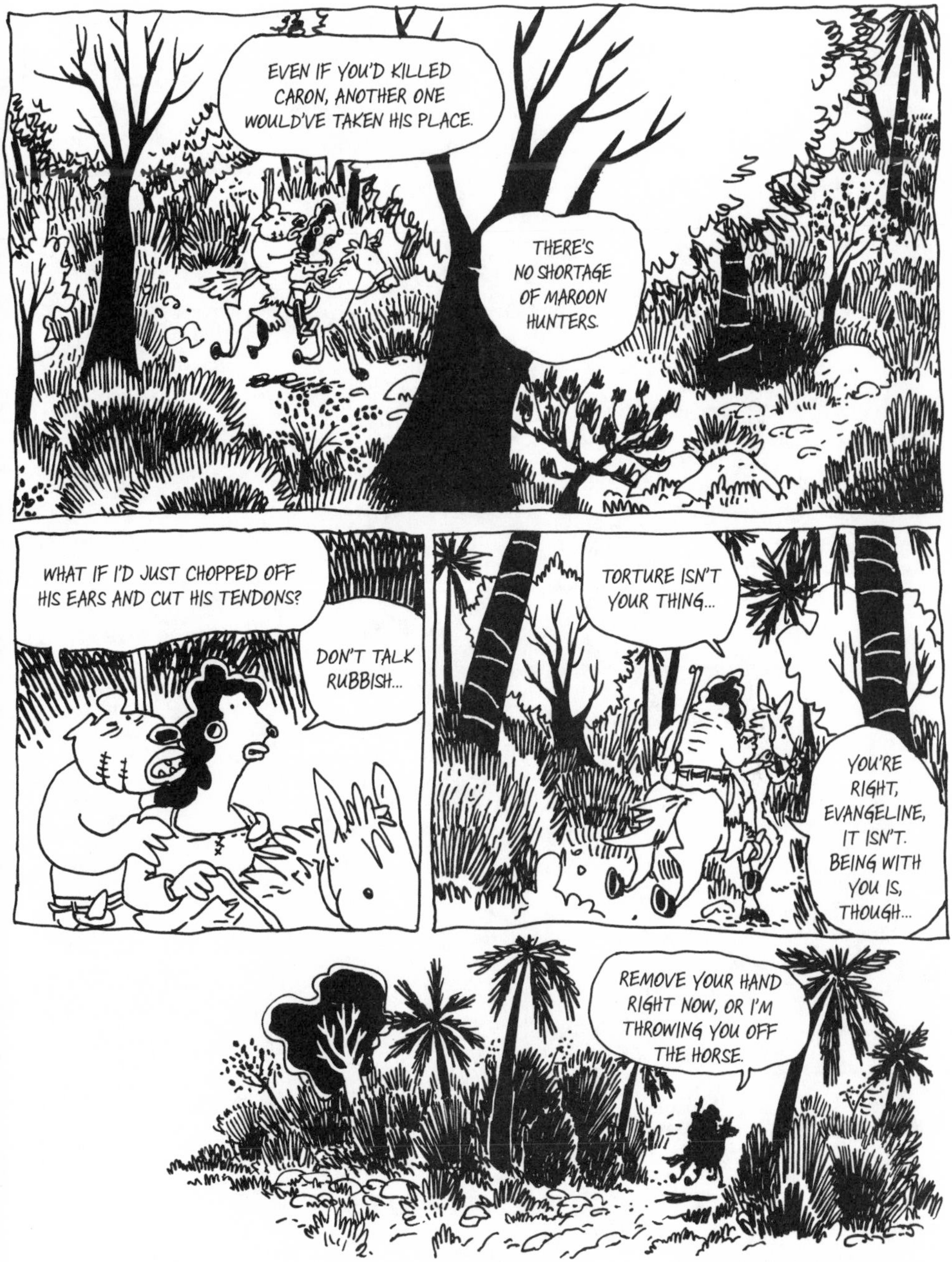
EVEN IF YOU'D KILLED CARON, ANOTHER ONE WOULD'VE TAKEN HIS PLACE.
THERE'S NO SHORTAGE OF MAROON HUNTERS.
WHAT IF I'D JUST CHOPPED OFF HIS EARS AND CUT HIS TENDONS?
DON'T TALK RUBBISH...
TORTURE ISN'T YOUR THING...
YOU'RE RIGHT, EVANGELINE, IT ISN'T. BEING WITH YOU IS, THOUGH...
REMOVE YOUR HAND RIGHT NOW, OR I'M THROWING YOU OFF THE HORSE.

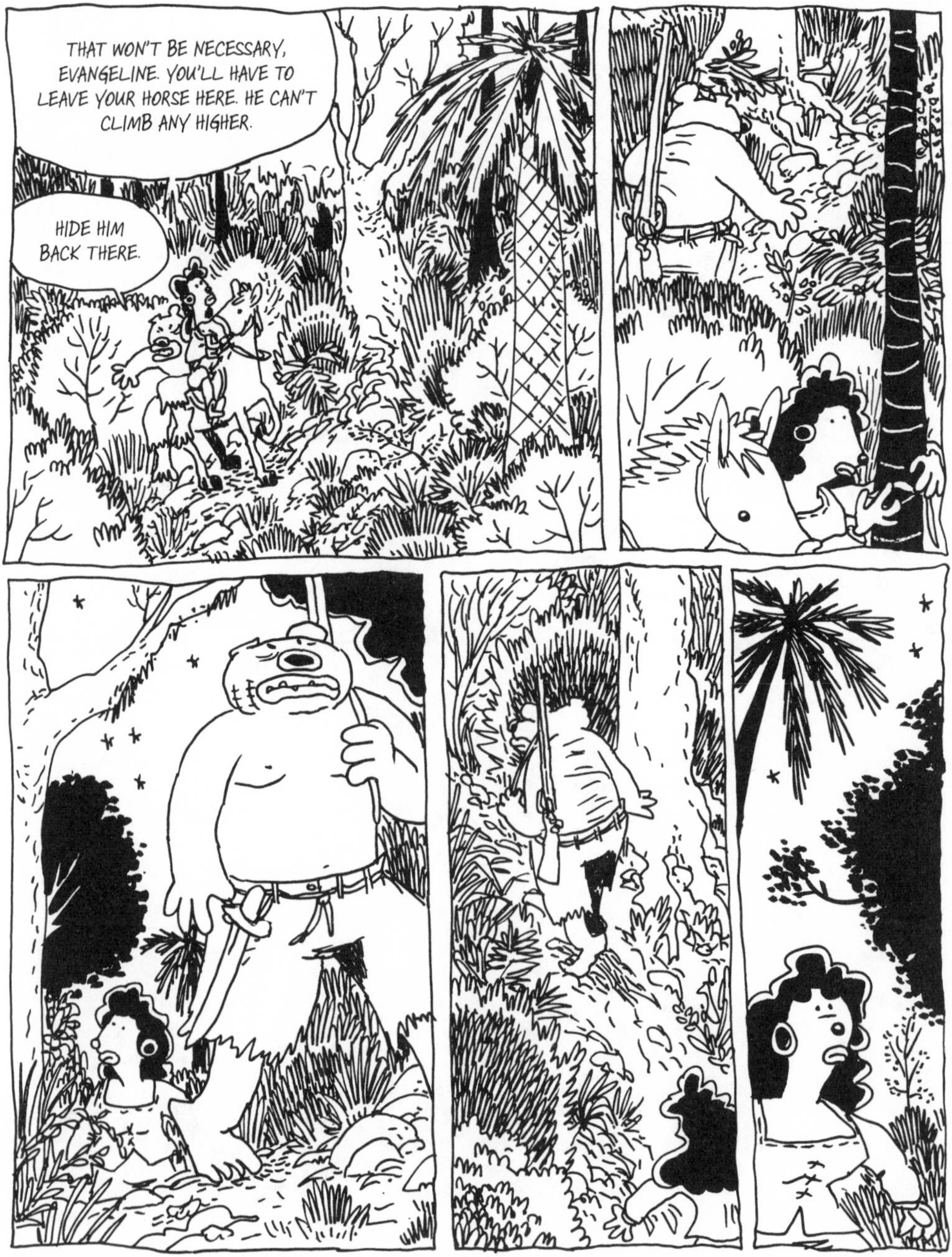
THAT WON'T BE NECESSARY, EVANGELINE. YOU'LL HAVE TO LEAVE YOUR HORSE HERE. HE CAN'T CLIMB ANY HIGHER.
HIDE HIM BACK THERE.

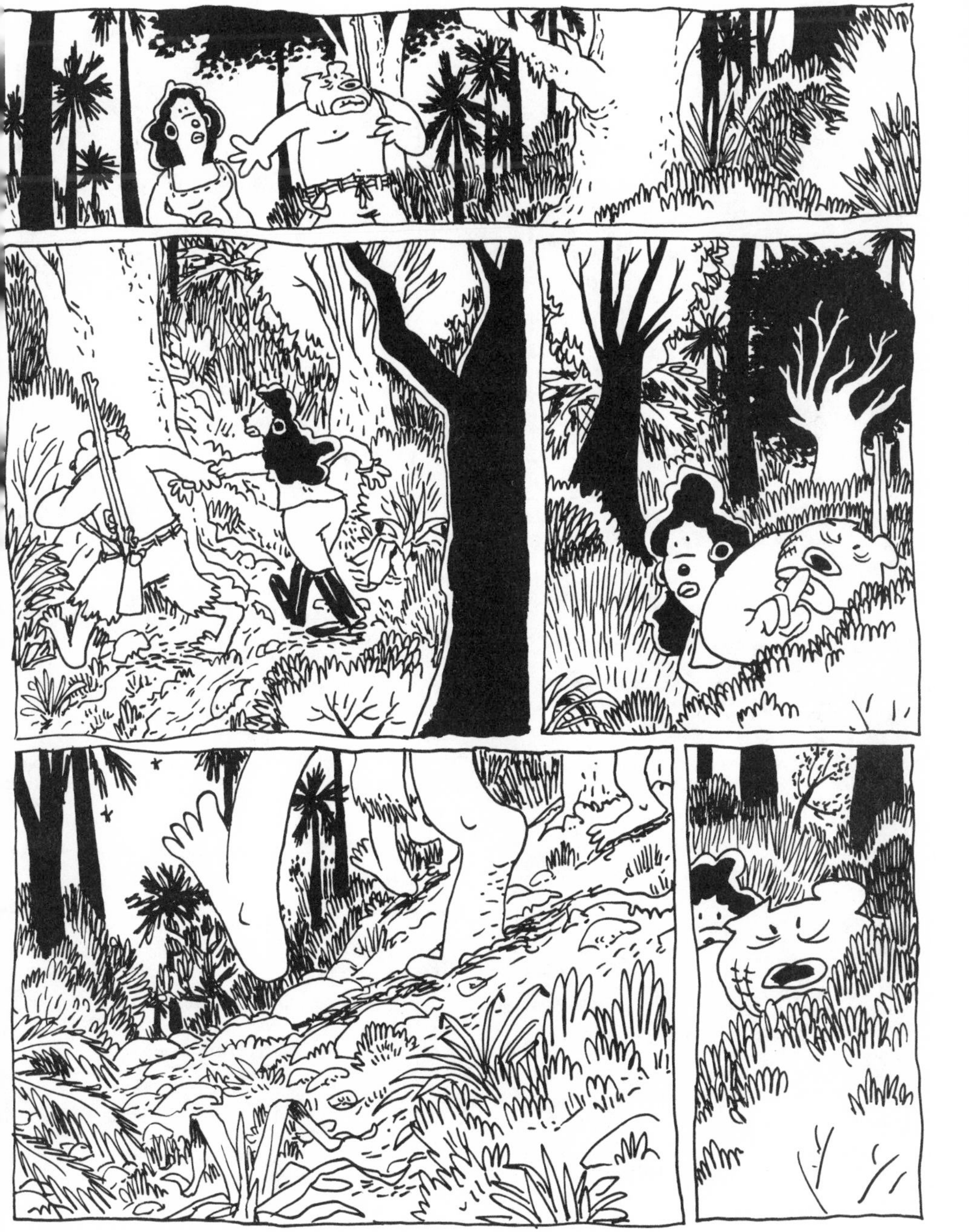

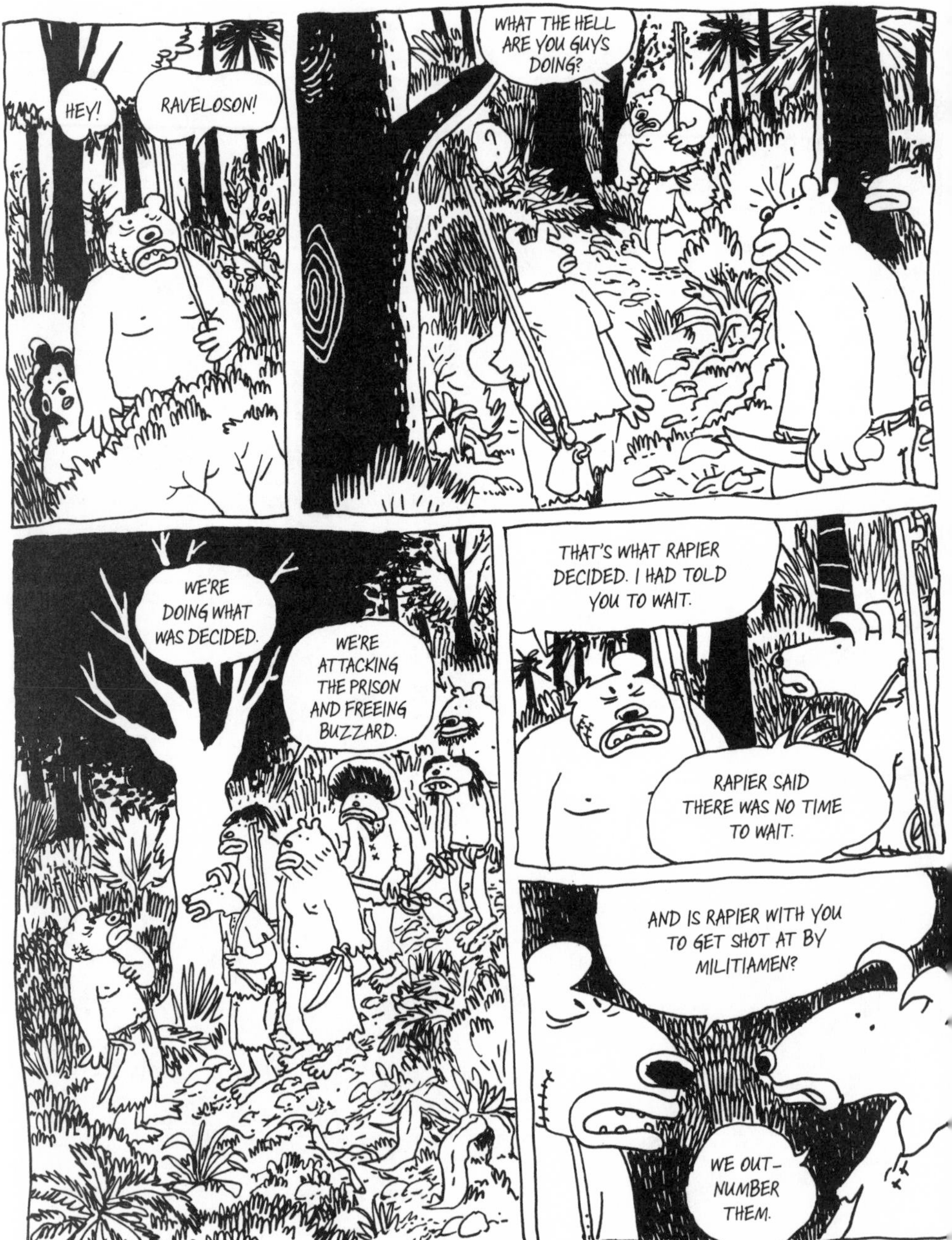
HEY!
RAVELOSON!
WHAT THE HELL ARE YOU GUYS DOING?
WE'RE DOING WHAT WAS DECIDED.
WE'RE ATTACKING THE PRISON AND FREEING BUZZARD.
THAT'S WHAT RAPIER DECIDED. I HAD TOLD YOU TO WAIT.
RAPIER SAID THERE WAS NO TIME TO WAIT.
AND IS RAPIER WITH YOU TO GET SHOT AT BY MILITIAMEN?
WE OUT-NUMBER THEM.

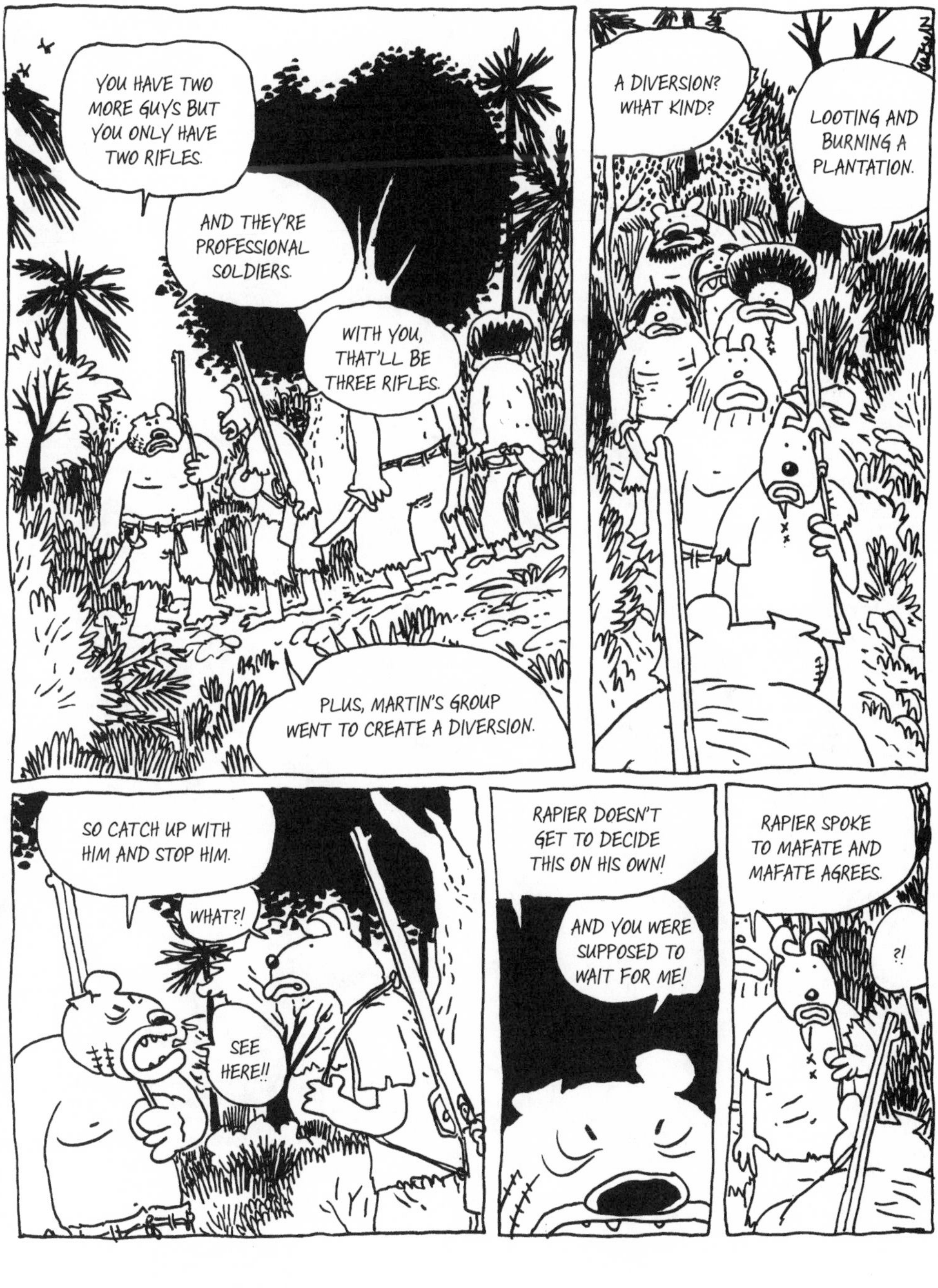
YOU HAVE TWO MORE GUYS BUT YOU ONLY HAVE TWO RIFLES.
AND THEY'RE PROFESSIONAL SOLDIERS.
WITH YOU, THAT'LL BE THREE RIFLES.
PLUS, MARTIN'S GROUP WENT TO CREATE A DIVERSION.
A DIVERSION? WHAT KIND?
LOOTING AND BURNING A PLANTATION.
SO CATCH UP WITH HIM AND STOP HIM.
WHAT?!
SEE HERE!!
RAPIER DOESN'T GET TO DECIDE THIS ON HIS OWN!
AND YOU WERE SUPPOSED TO WAIT FOR ME!
RAPIER SPOKE TO MAFATE AND MAFATE AGREES.
?!

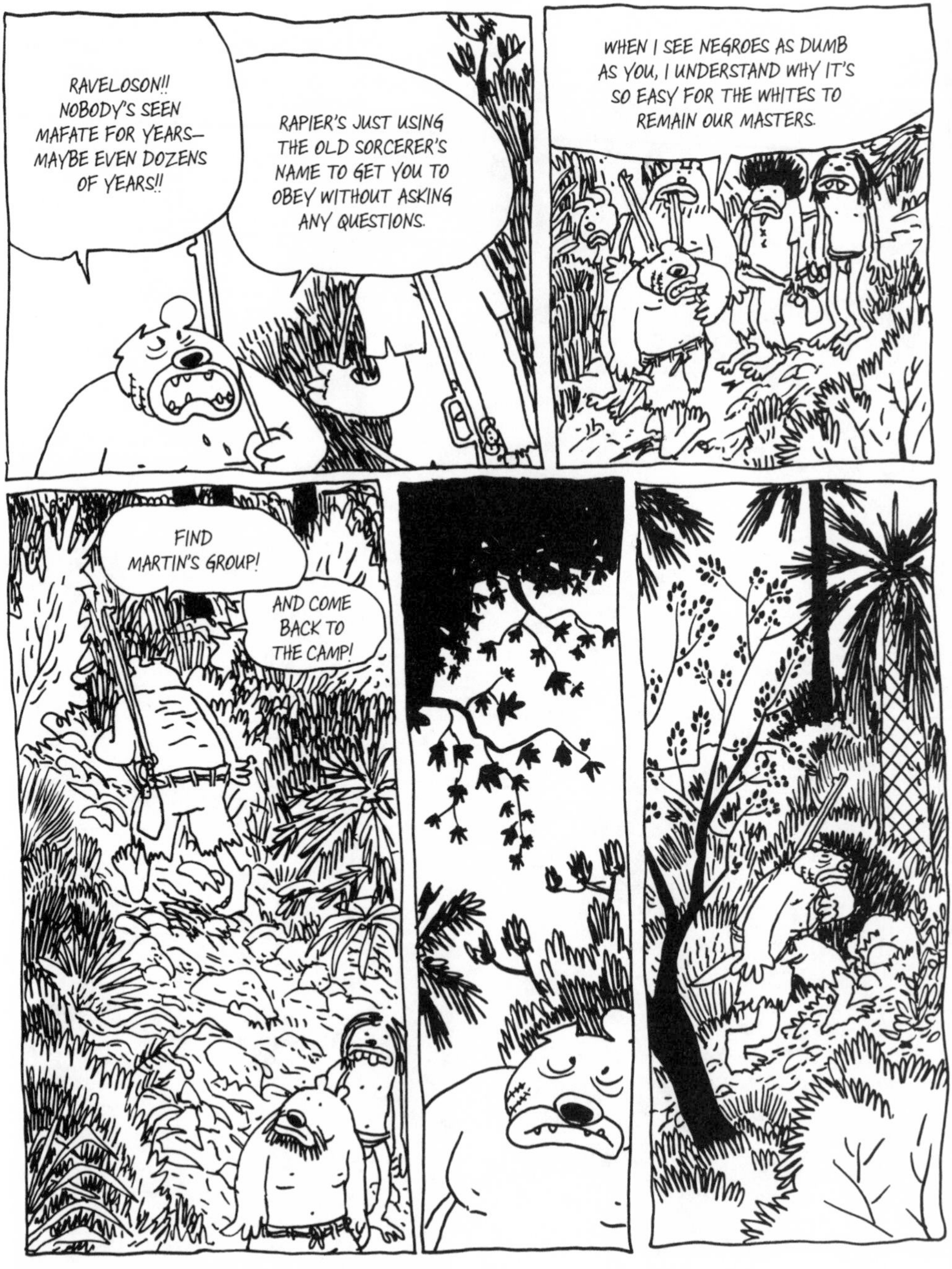
RAVELOSON!! NOBODY'S SEEN MAFATE FOR YEARS— MAYBE EVEN DOZENS OF YEARS!!
RAPIER'S JUST USING THE OLD SORCERER'S NAME TO GET YOU TO OBEY WITHOUT ASKING ANY QUESTIONS.
WHEN I SEE NEGROES AS DUMB AS YOU, I UNDERSTAND WHY IT'S SO EASY FOR THE WHITES TO REMAIN OUR MASTERS.
FIND MARTIN'S GROUP!
AND COME BACK TO THE CAMP!

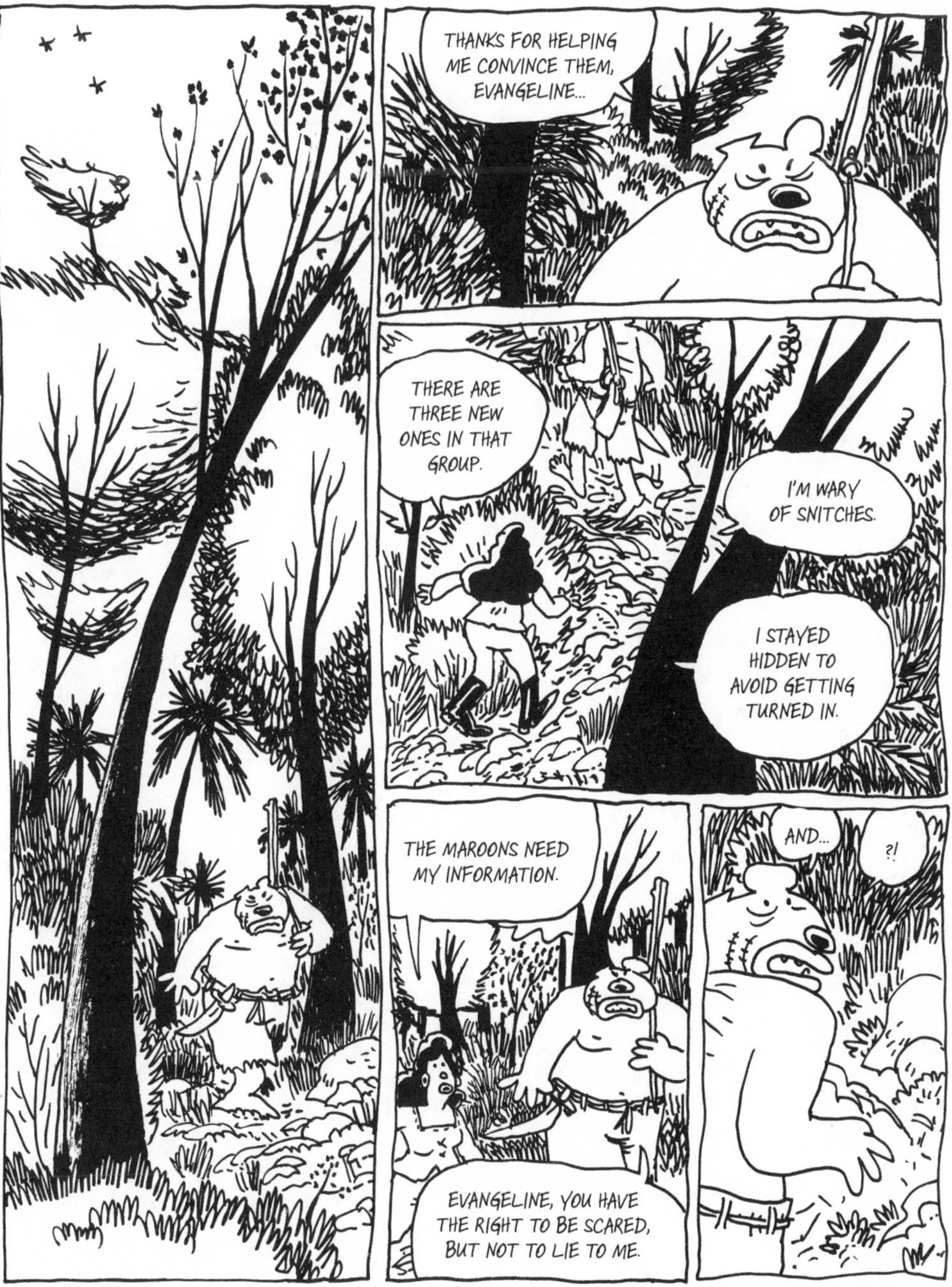
THANKS FOR HELPING ME CONVINCE THEM, EVANGELINE...
THERE ARE THREE NEW ONES IN THAT GROUP.
I'M WARY OF SNITCHES.
I STAYED HIDDEN TO AVOID GETTING TURNED IN.
THE MAROONS NEED MY INFORMATION.
EVANGELINE, YOU HAVE THE RIGHT TO BE SCARED, BUT NOT TO LIE TO ME.
AND...
?!

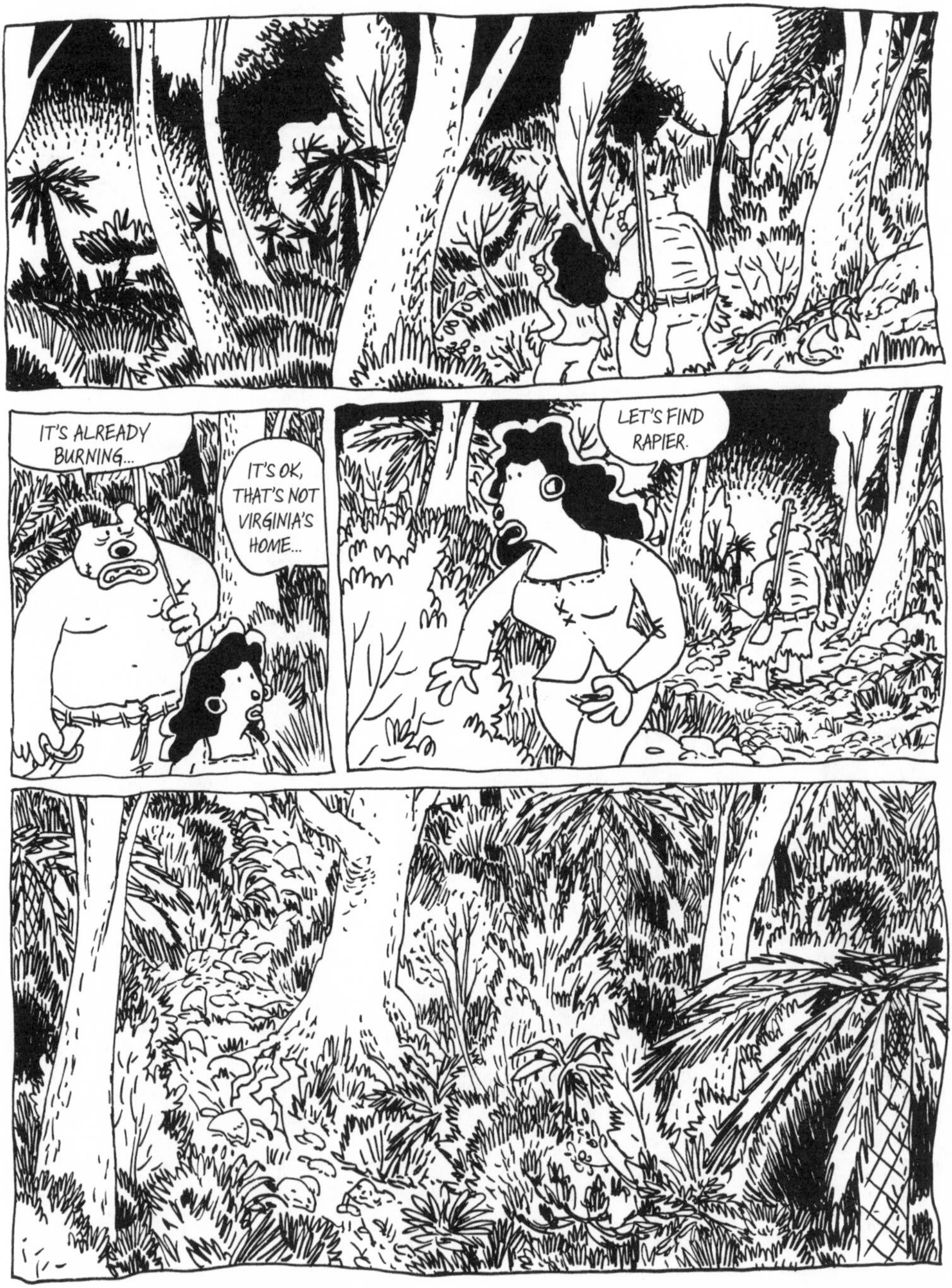
IT'S ALREADY BURNING...
IT'S OK, THAT'S NOT VIRGINIA'S HOME...
LET'S FIND RAPIER.

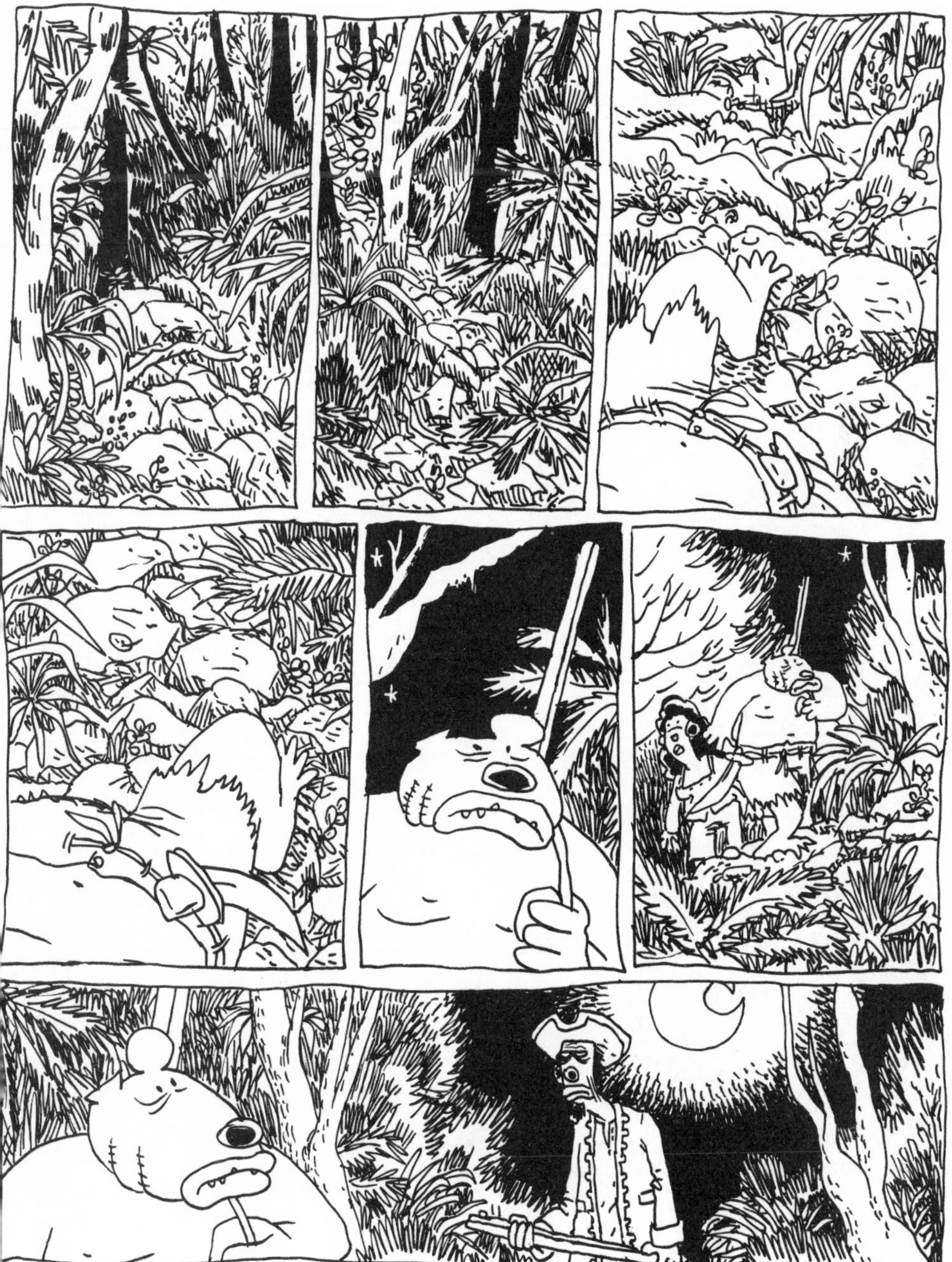

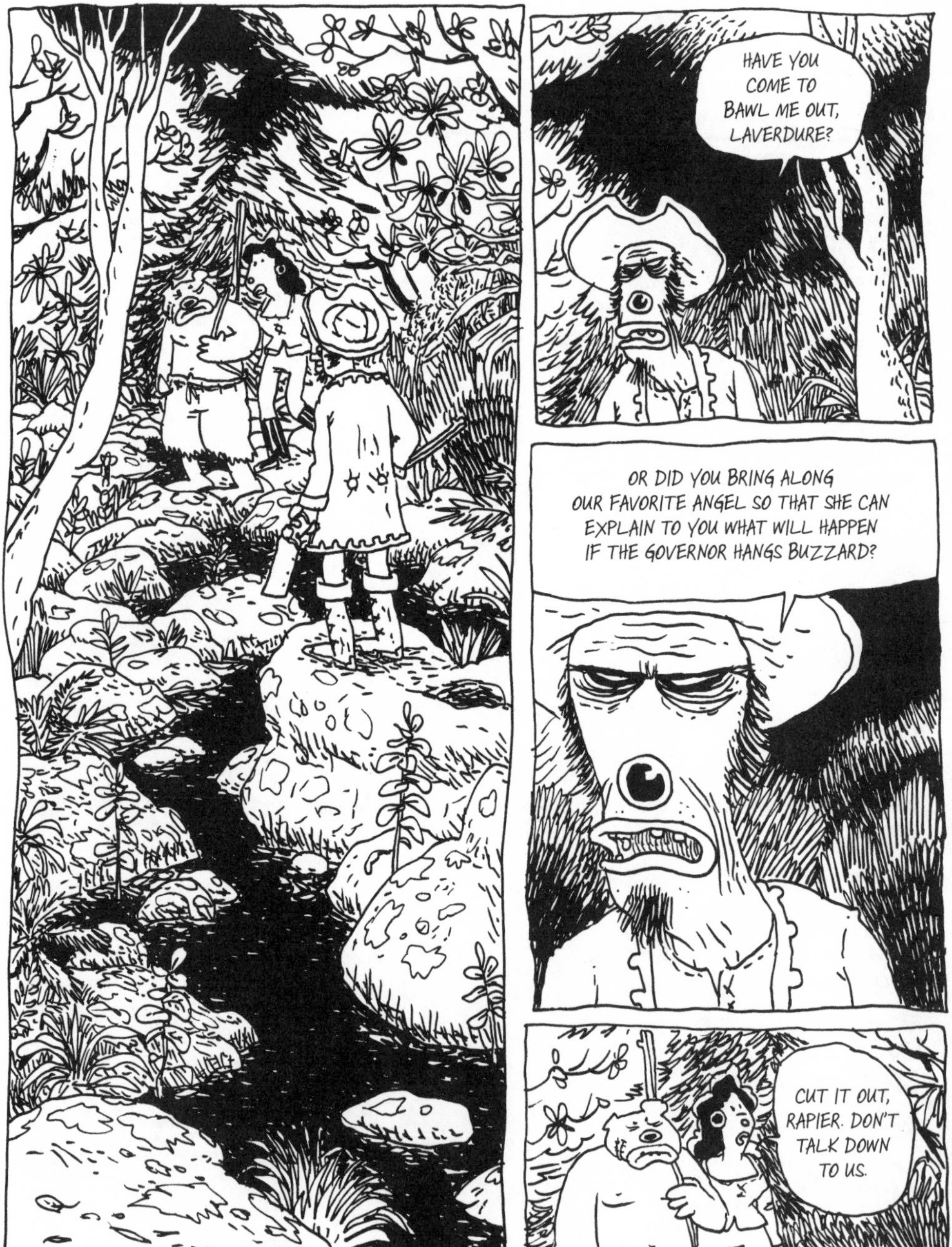
HAVE YOU COME TO BAWL ME OUT, LAVERDURE?
OR DID YOU BRING ALONG OUR FAVORITE ANGEL SO THAT SHE CAN EXPLAIN TO YOU WHAT WILL HAPPEN IF THE GOVERNOR HANGS BUZZARD?
CUT IT OUT, RAPIER. DON'T TALK DOWN TO US.

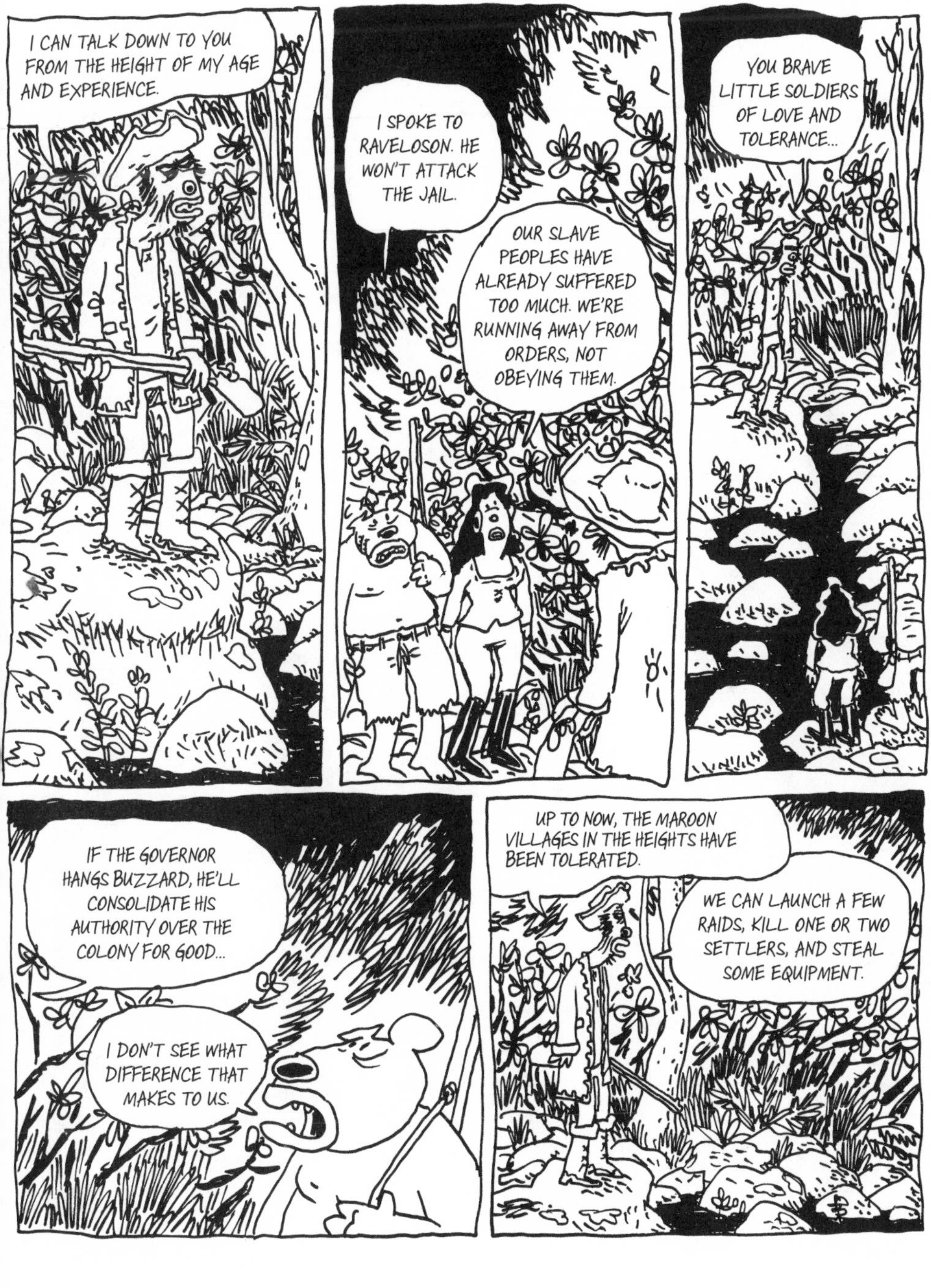
I CAN TALK DOWN TO YOU FROM THE HEIGHT OF MY AGE AND EXPERIENCE.
I SPOKE TO RAVELOSON. HE WON'T ATTACK THE JAIL.
OUR SLAVE PEOPLES HAVE ALREADY SUFFERED TOO MUCH. WE'RE RUNNING AWAY FROM ORDERS, NOT OBEYING THEM.
YOU BRAVE LITTLE SOLDIERS OF LOVE AND TOLERANCE...
IF THE GOVERNOR HANGS BUZZARD, HE'LL CONSOLIDATE HIS AUTHORITY OVER THE COLONY FOR GOOD...
I DON'T SEE WHAT DIFFERENCE THAT MAKES TO US.
UP TO NOW, THE MAROON VILLAGES IN THE HEIGHTS HAVE BEEN TOLERATED.
WE CAN LAUNCH A FEW RAIDS, KILL ONE OR TWO SETTLERS, AND STEAL SOME EQUIPMENT.

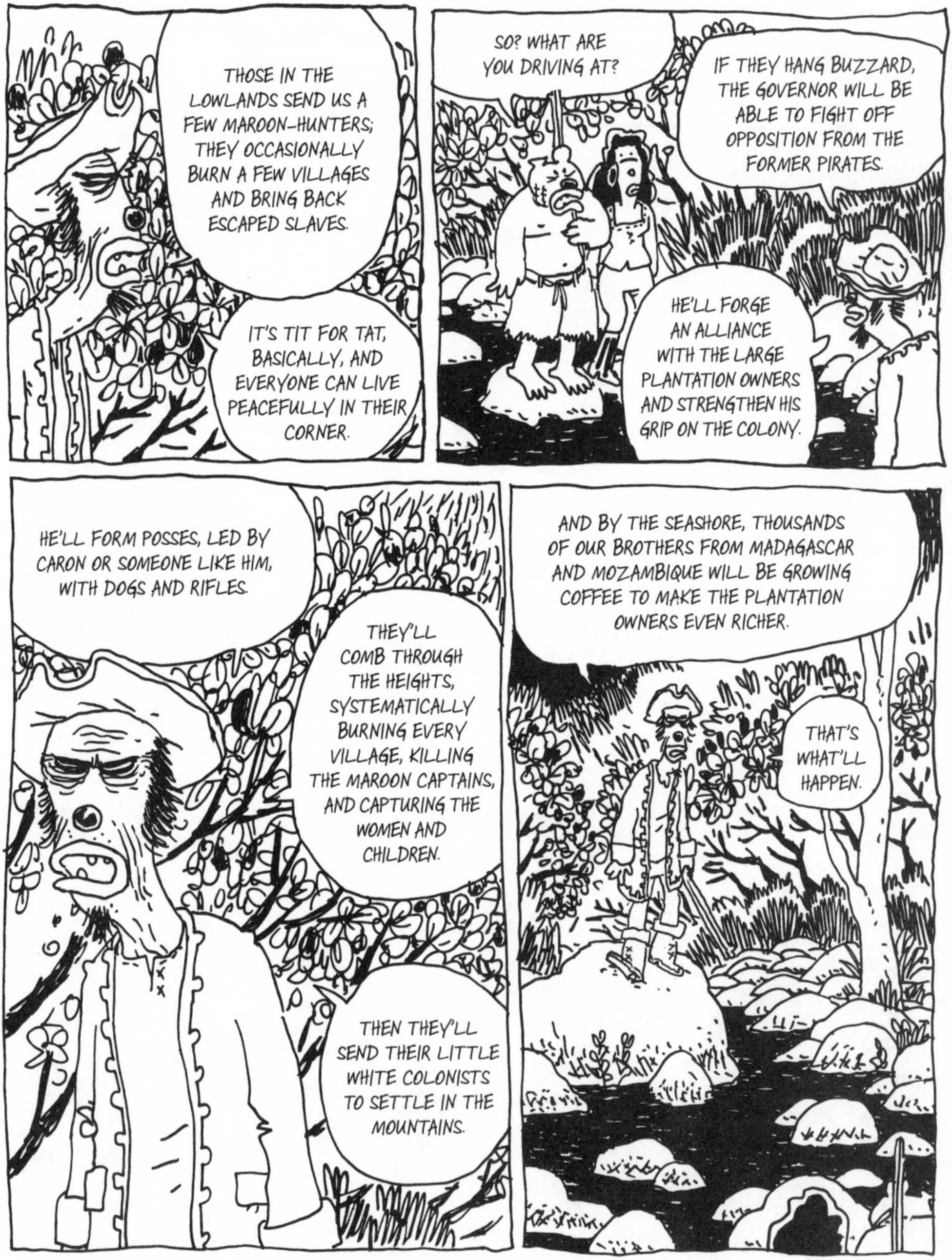
THOSE IN THE LOWLANDS SEND US A FEW MAROON-HUNTERS; THEY OCCASIONALLY BURN A FEW VILLAGES AND BRING BACK ESCAPED SLAVES.
IT'S TIT FOR TAT, BASICALLY, AND EVERYONE CAN LIVE PEACEFULLY IN THEIR CORNER.
SO? WHAT ARE YOU DRIVING AT?
IF THEY HANG BUZZARD, THE GOVERNOR WILL BE ABLE TO FIGHT OFF OPPOSITION FROM THE FORMER PIRATES.
HE'LL FORGE AN ALLIANCE WITH THE LARGE PLANTATION OWNERS AND STRENGTHEN HIS GRIP ON THE COLONY.
HE'LL FORM POSSES, LED BY CARON OR SOMEONE LIKE HIM, WITH DOGS AND RIFLES.
THEY'LL COMB THROUGH THE HEIGHTS, SYSTEMATICALLY BURNING EVERY VILLAGE, KILLING THE MAROON CAPTAINS, AND CAPTURING THE WOMEN AND CHILDREN.
THEN THEY'LL SEND THEIR LITTLE WHITE COLONISTS TO SETTLE IN THE MOUNTAINS.
AND BY THE SEASHORE, THOUSANDS OF OUR BROTHERS FROM MADAGASCAR AND MOZAMBIQUE WILL BE GROWING COFFEE TO MAKE THE PLANTATION OWNERS EVEN RICHER.
THAT'S WHAT'LL HAPPEN.

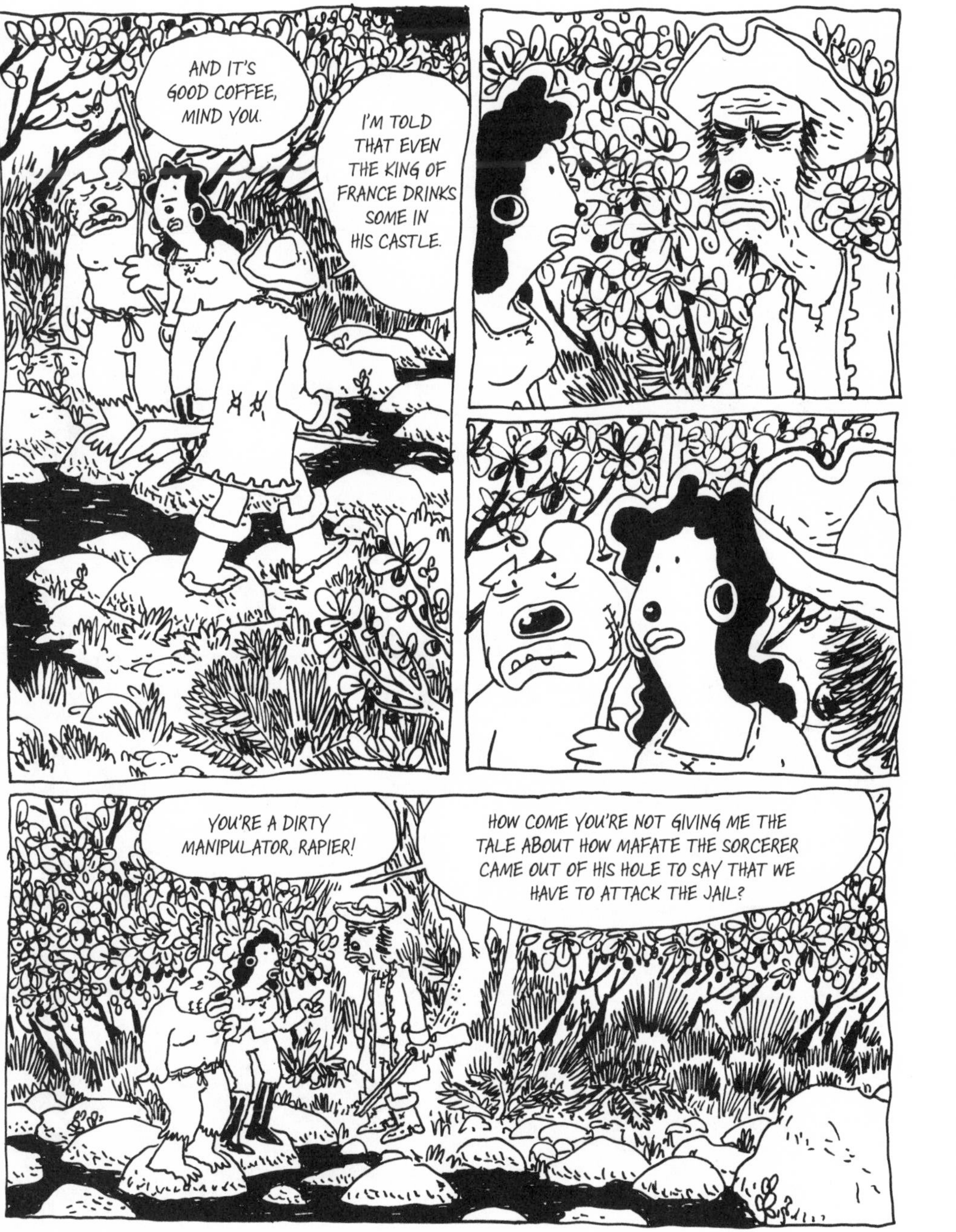
AND IT'S GOOD COFFEE, MIND YOU.
I'M TOLD THAT EVEN THE KING OF FRANCE DRINKS SOME IN HIS CASTLE.
YOU'RE A DIRTY MANIPULATOR, RAPIER!
HOW COME YOU'RE NOT GIVING ME THE TALE ABOUT HOW MAFATE THE SORCERER CAME OUT OF HIS HOLE TO SAY THAT WE HAVE TO ATTACK THE JAIL?

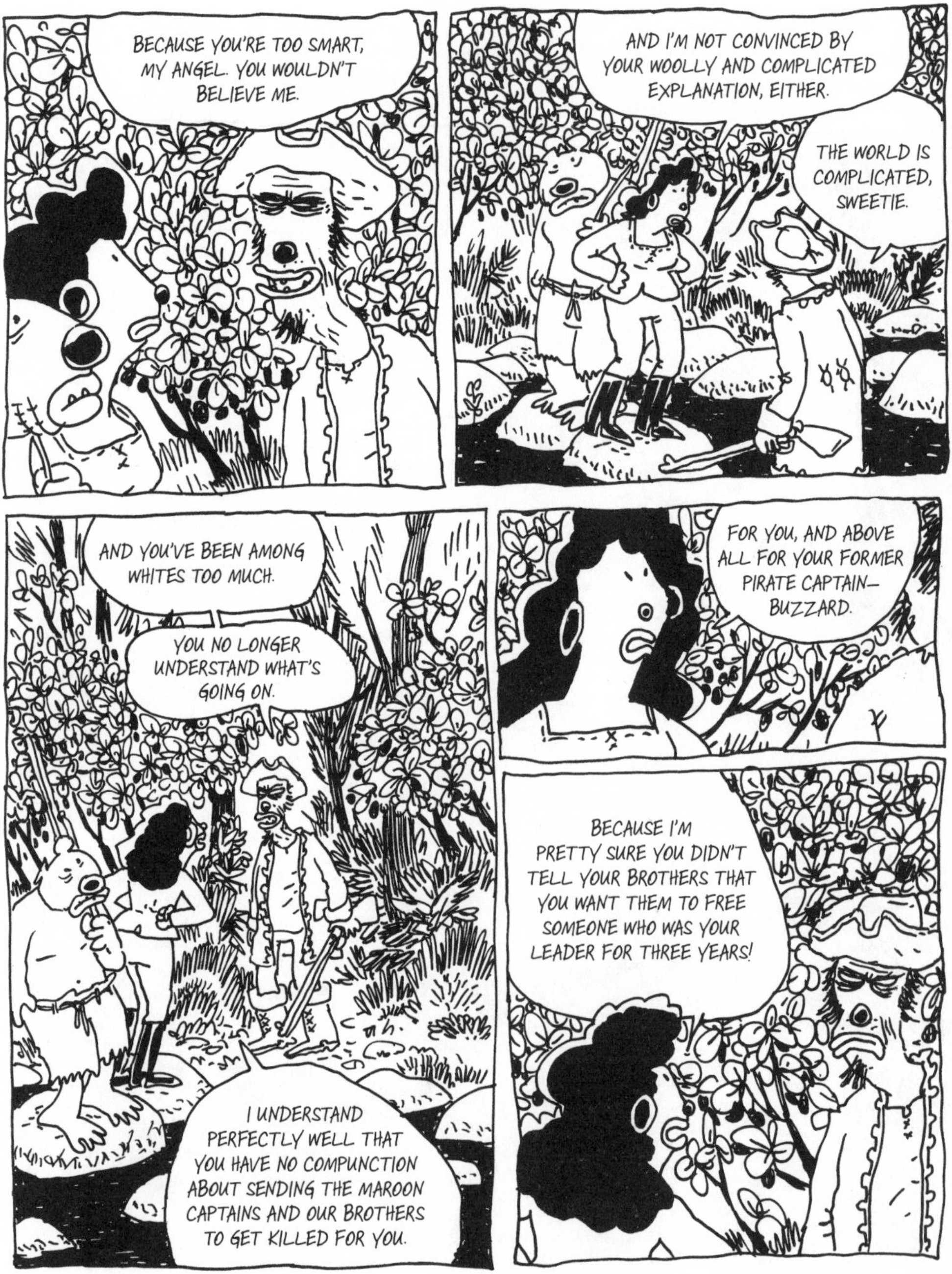
BECAUSE YOU'RE TOO SMART, MY ANGEL. YOU WOULDN'T BELIEVE ME.
AND I'M NOT CONVINCED BY YOUR WOOLLY AND COMPLICATED EXPLANATION, EITHER.
THE WORLD IS COMPLICATED, SWEETIE.
AND YOU'VE BEEN AMONG WHITES TOO MUCH.
YOU NO LONGER UNDERSTAND WHAT'S GOING ON.
I UNDERSTAND PERFECTLY WELL THAT YOU HAVE NO COMPUNCTION ABOUT SENDING THE MAROON CAPTAINS AND OUR BROTHERS TO GET KILLED FOR YOU.
FOR YOU, AND ABOVE ALL FOR YOUR FORMER PIRATE CAPTAIN—BUZZARD.
BECAUSE I'M PRETTY SURE YOU DIDN'T TELL YOUR BROTHERS THAT YOU WANT THEM TO FREE SOMEONE WHO WAS YOUR LEADER FOR THREE YEARS!

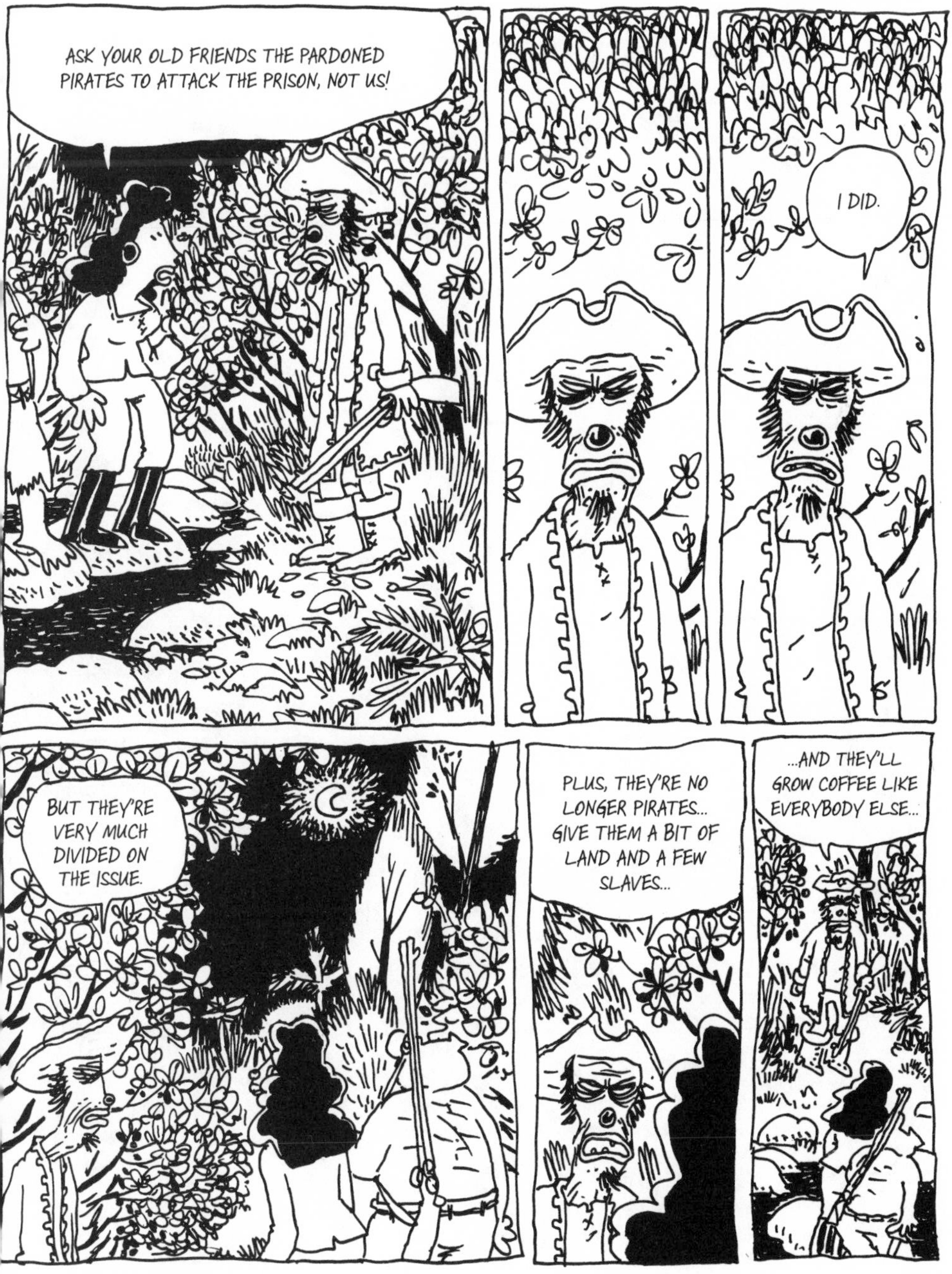
ASK YOUR OLD FRIENDS THE PARDONED PIRATES TO ATTACK THE PRISON, NOT US!
I DID.
BUT THEY'RE VERY MUCH DIVIDED ON THE ISSUE.
PLUS, THEY'RE NO LONGER PIRATES... GIVE THEM A BIT OF LAND AND A FEW SLAVES...
...AND THEY'LL GROW COFFEE LIKE EVERYBODY ELSE...

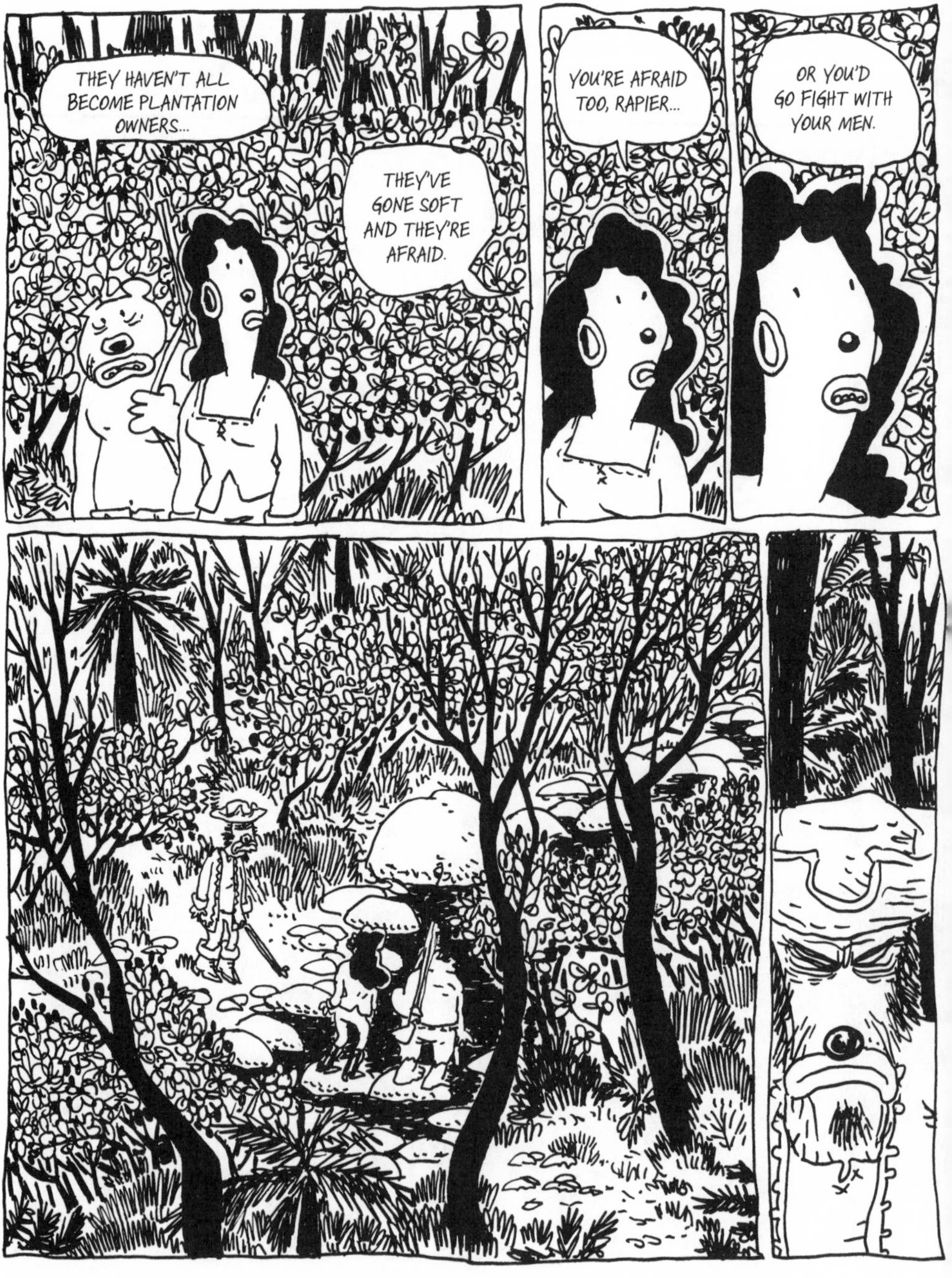
THEY HAVEN'T ALL BECOME PLANTATION OWNERS...
THEY'VE GONE SOFT AND THEY'RE AFRAID.
YOU'RE AFRAID TOO, RAPIER...
OR YOU'D GO FIGHT WITH YOUR MEN.

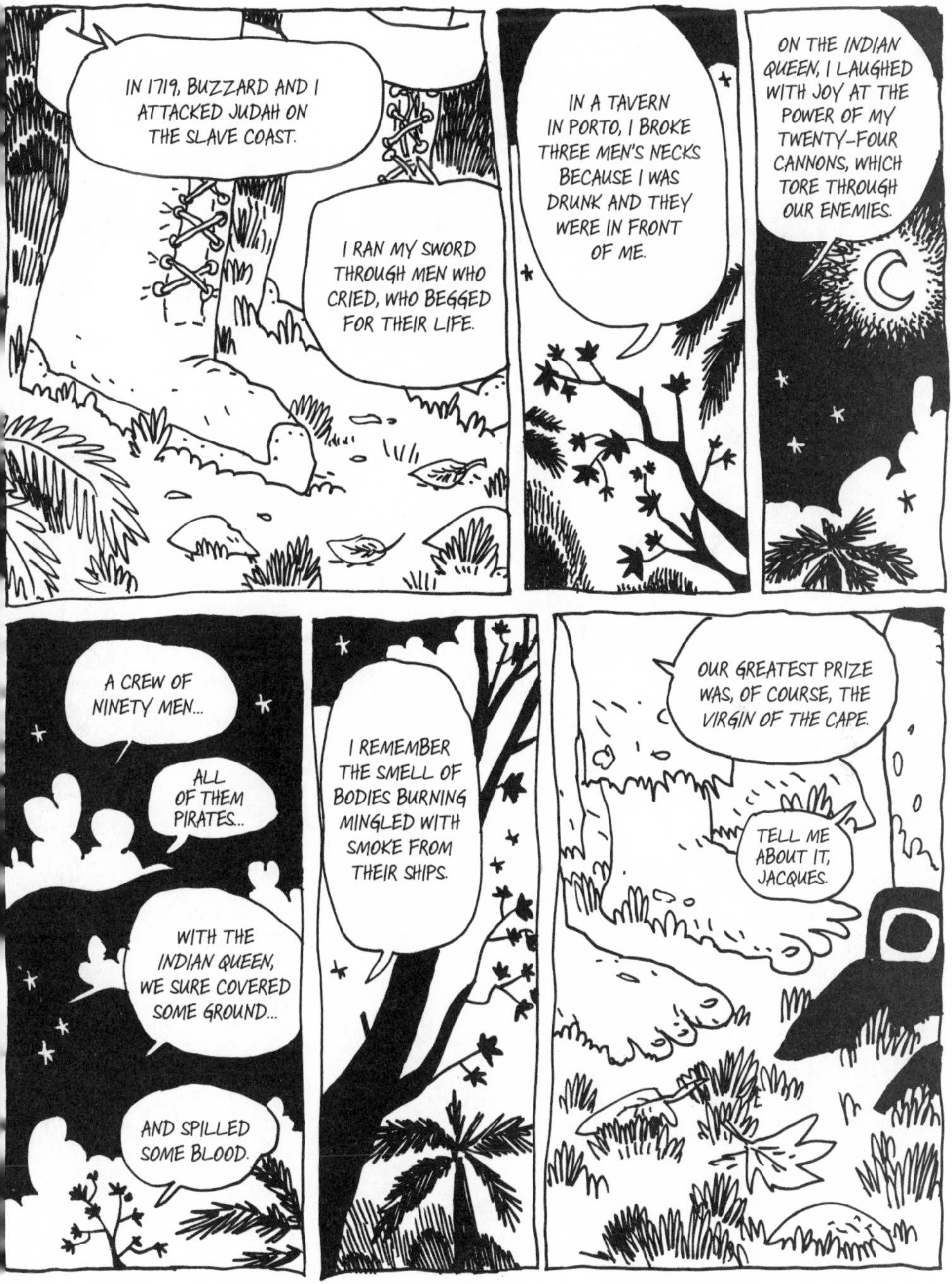
IN 1719, BUZZARD AND I ATTACKED JUDAH ON THE SLAVE COAST.
I RAN MY SWORD THROUGH MEN WHO CRIED, WHO BEGGED FOR THEIR LIFE.
IN A TAVERN IN PORTO, I BROKE THREE MEN'S NECKS BECAUSE I WAS DRUNK AND THEY WERE IN FRONT OF ME.
ON THE INDIAN QUEEN, I LAUGHED WITH JOY AT THE POWER OF MY TWENTY-FOUR CANNONS, WHICH TORE THROUGH OUR ENEMIES.
A CREW OF NINETY MEN...
ALL OF THEM PIRATES...
WITH THE INDIAN QUEEN, WE SURE COVERED SOME GROUND...
AND SPILLED SOME BLOOD.
I REMEMBER THE SMELL OF BODIES BURNING MINGLED WITH SMOKE FROM THEIR SHIPS.
OUR GREATEST PRIZE WAS, OF COURSE, THE VIRGIN OF THE CAPE.
TELL ME ABOUT IT, JACQUES.

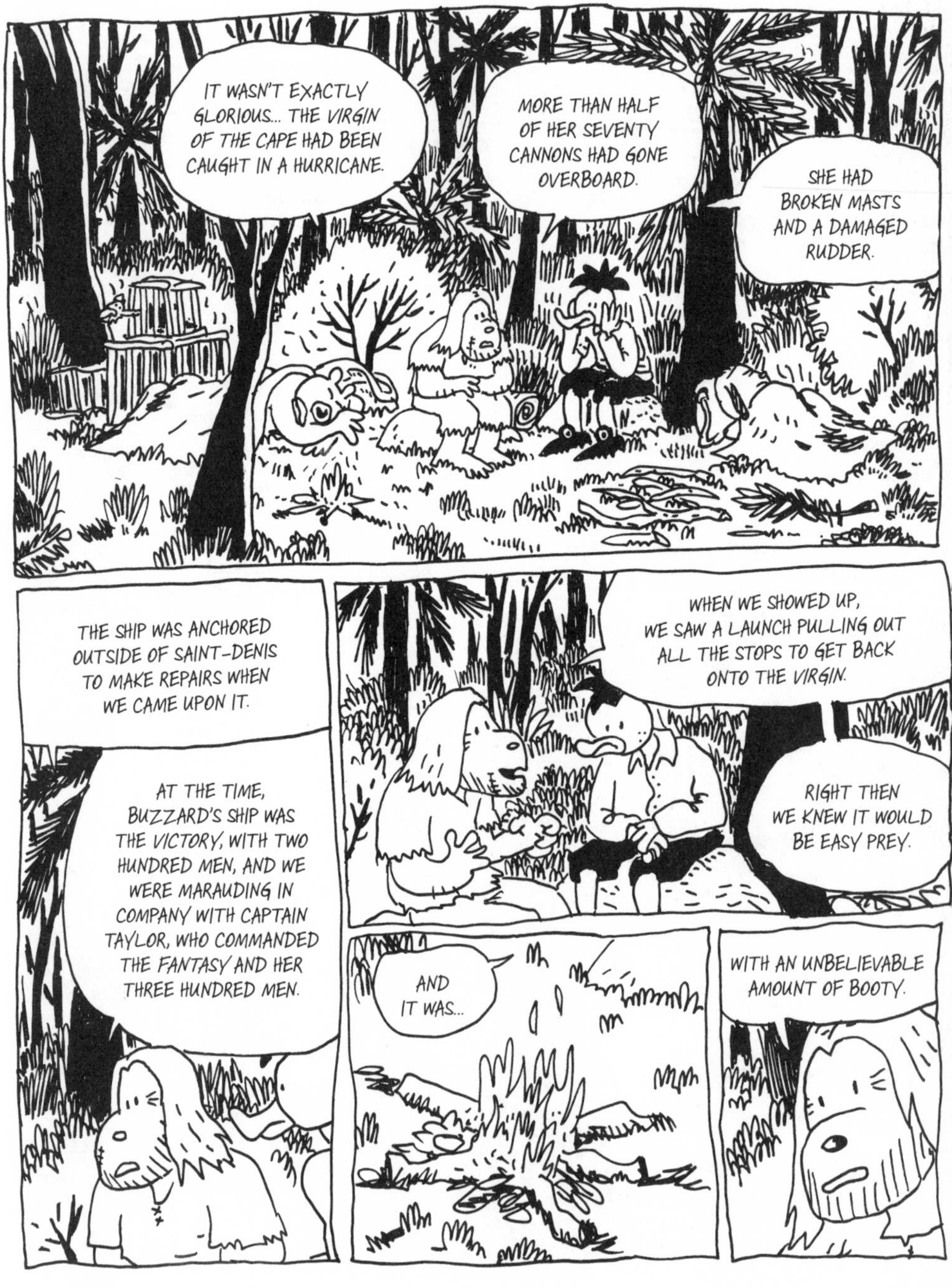
IT WASN'T EXACTLY GLORIOUS... THE VIRGIN OF THE CAPE HAD BEEN CAUGHT IN A HURRICANE.
MORE THAN HALF OF HER SEVENTY CANNONS HAD GONE OVERBOARD.
SHE HAD BROKEN MASTS AND A DAMAGED RUDDER.
THE SHIP WAS ANCHORED OUTSIDE OF SAINT-DENIS TO MAKE REPAIRS WHEN WE CAME UPON IT.
AT THE TIME, BUZZARD'S SHIP WAS THE VICTORY, WITH TWO HUNDRED MEN, AND WE WERE MARAUDING IN COMPANY WITH CAPTAIN TAYLOR, WHO COMMANDED THE FANTASY AND HER THREE HUNDRED MEN.
WHEN WE SHOWED UP, WE SAW A LAUNCH PULLING OUT ALL THE STOPS TO GET BACK ONTO THE VIRGIN.
RIGHT THEN WE KNEW IT WOULD BE EASY PREY.
AND IT WAS...
WITH AN UNBELIEVABLE AMOUNT OF BOOTY.

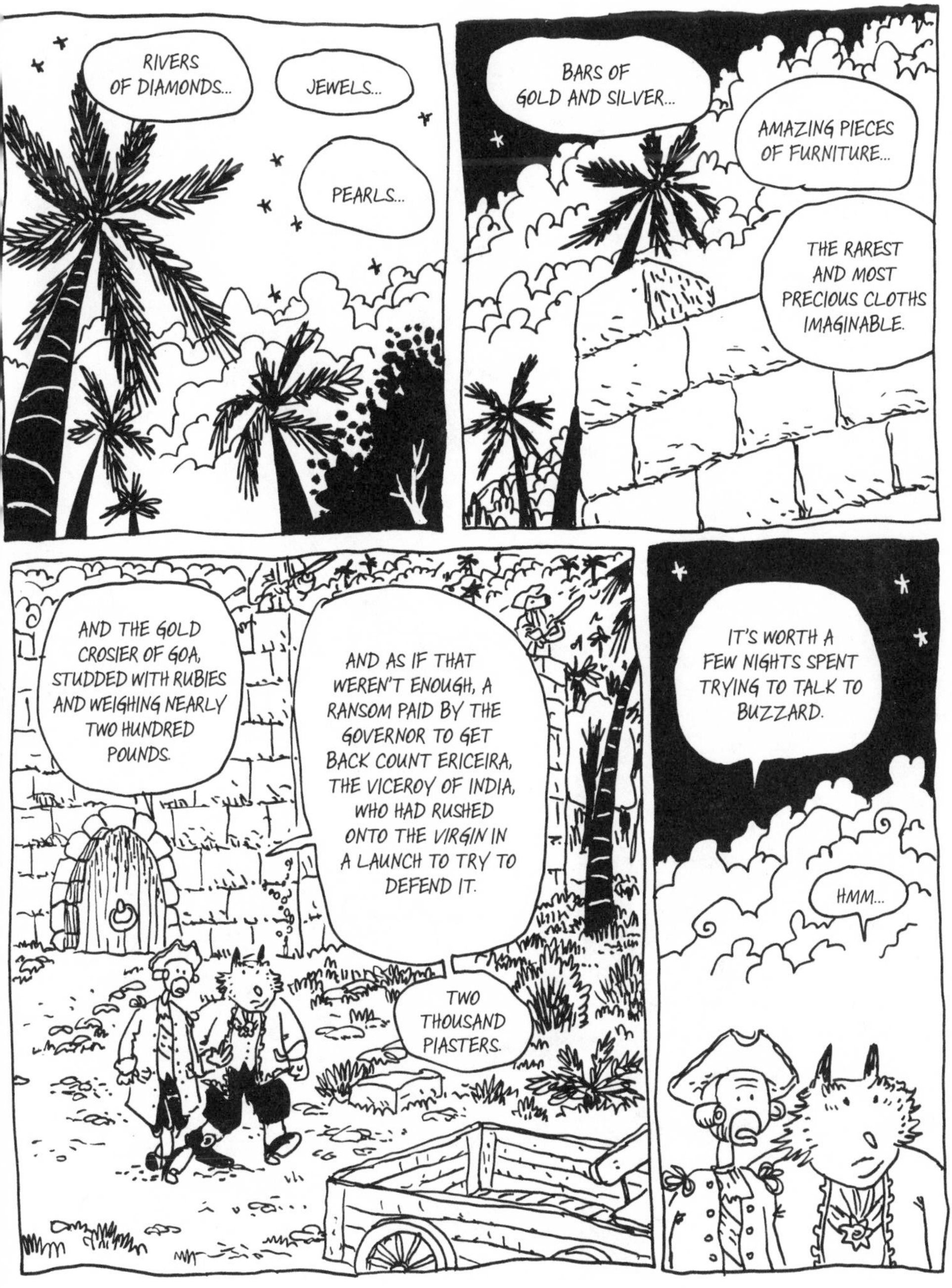
RIVERS OF DIAMONDS...
JEWELS...
PEARLS...
BARS OF GOLD AND SILVER...
AMAZING PIECES OF FURNITURE...
THE RAREST AND MOST PRECIOUS CLOTHS IMAGINABLE.
AND THE GOLD CROSIER OF GOA, STUDDED WITH RUBIES AND WEIGHING NEARLY TWO HUNDRED POUNDS.
AND AS IF THAT WEREN'T ENOUGH, A RANSOM PAID BY THE GOVERNOR TO GET BACK COUNT ERICEIRA, THE VICEROY OF INDIA, WHO HAD RUSHED ONTO THE *VIRGIN* IN A LAUNCH TO TRY TO DEFEND IT.
TWO THOUSAND PIASTERS.
IT'S WORTH A FEW NIGHTS SPENT TRYING TO TALK TO BUZZARD.
HMM...

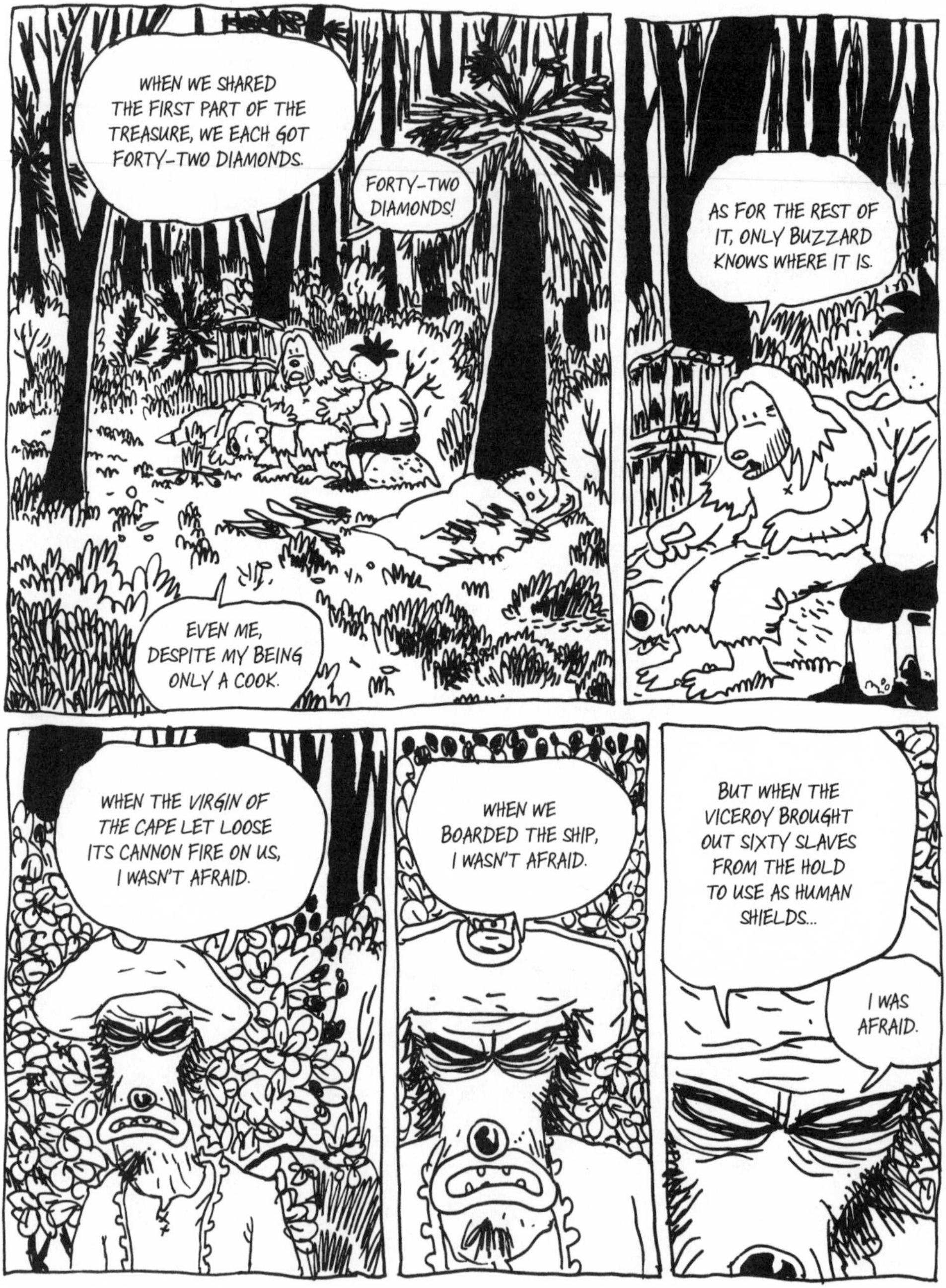
WHEN WE SHARED THE FIRST PART OF THE TREASURE, WE EACH GOT FORTY-TWO DIAMONDS.
FORTY-TWO DIAMONDS!
EVEN ME, DESPITE MY BEING ONLY A COOK.
AS FOR THE REST OF IT, ONLY BUZZARD KNOWS WHERE IT IS.
WHEN THE *VIRGIN OF THE CAPE* LET LOOSE ITS CANNON FIRE ON US, I WASN'T AFRAID.
WHEN WE BOARDED THE SHIP, I WASN'T AFRAID.
BUT WHEN THE VICEROY BROUGHT OUT SIXTY SLAVES FROM THE HOLD TO USE AS HUMAN SHIELDS...
I WAS AFRAID.

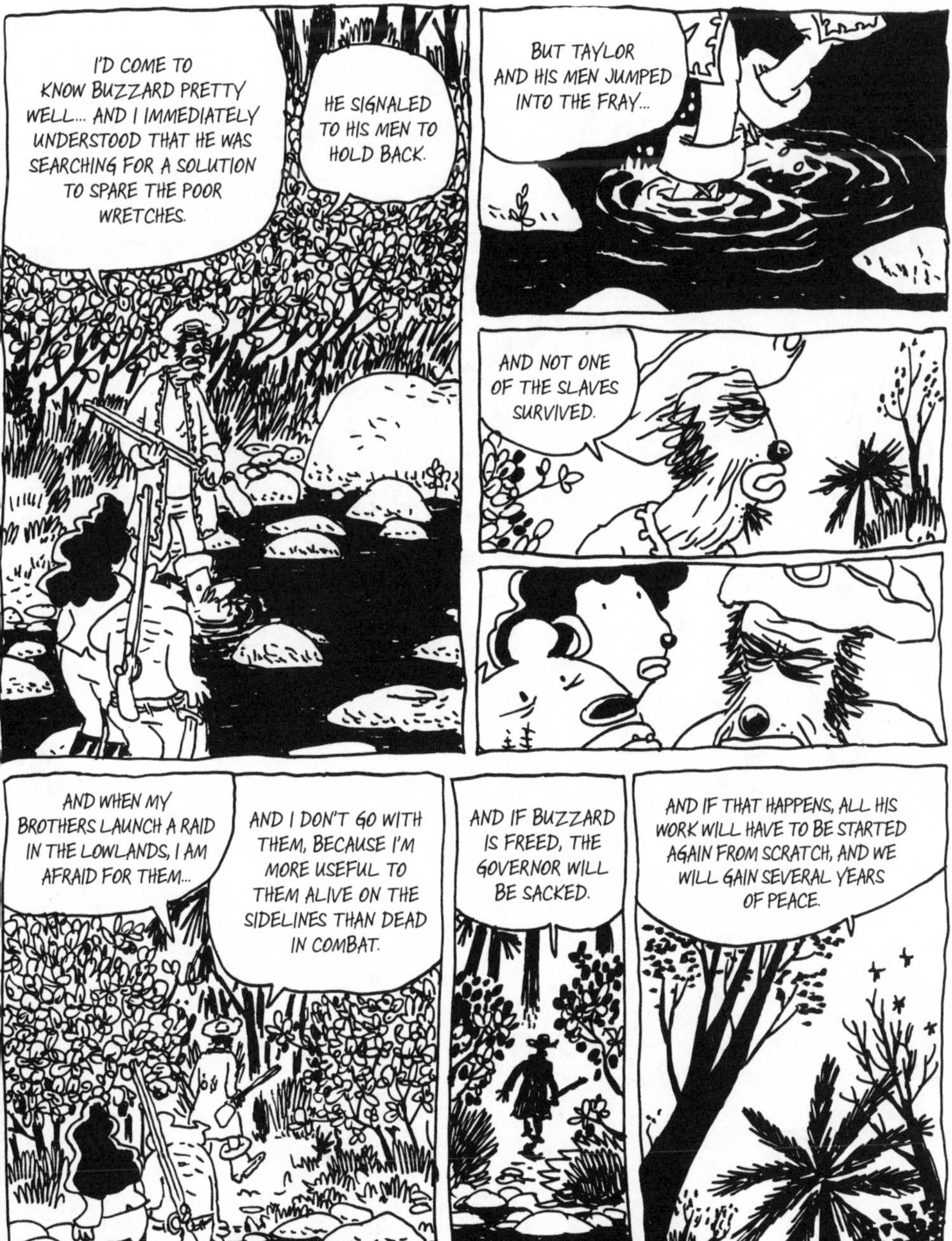
I'D COME TO KNOW BUZZARD PRETTY WELL... AND I IMMEDIATELY UNDERSTOOD THAT HE WAS SEARCHING FOR A SOLUTION TO SPARE THE POOR WRETCHES.
HE SIGNALED TO HIS MEN TO HOLD BACK.
BUT TAYLOR AND HIS MEN JUMPED INTO THE FRAY...
AND NOT ONE OF THE SLAVES SURVIVED.
AND WHEN MY BROTHERS LAUNCH A RAID IN THE LOWLANDS, I AM AFRAID FOR THEM...
AND I DON'T GO WITH THEM, BECAUSE I'M MORE USEFUL TO THEM ALIVE ON THE SIDELINES THAN DEAD IN COMBAT.
AND IF BUZZARD IS FREED, THE GOVERNOR WILL BE SACKED.
AND IF THAT HAPPENS, ALL HIS WORK WILL HAVE TO BE STARTED AGAIN FROM SCRATCH, AND WE WILL GAIN SEVERAL YEARS OF PEACE.

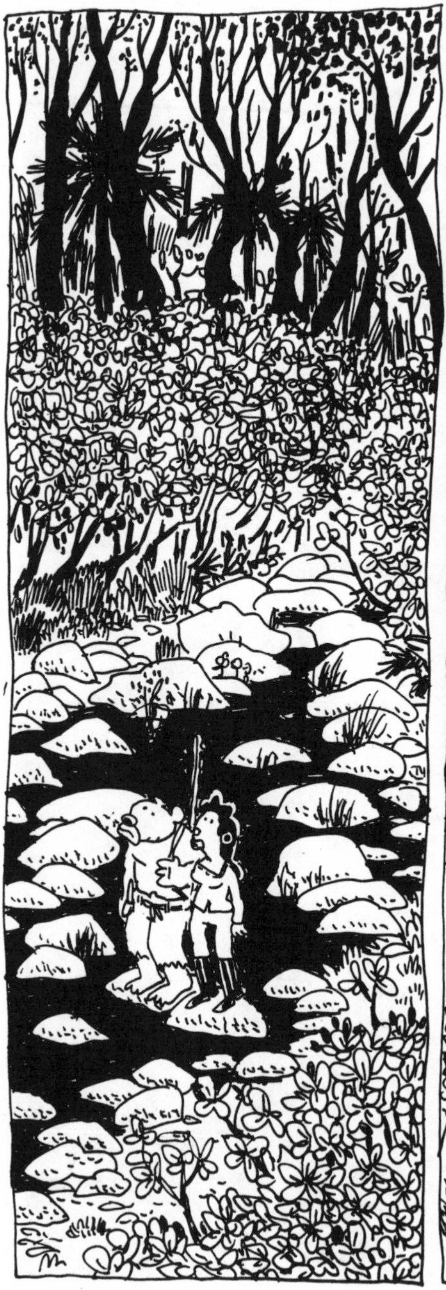

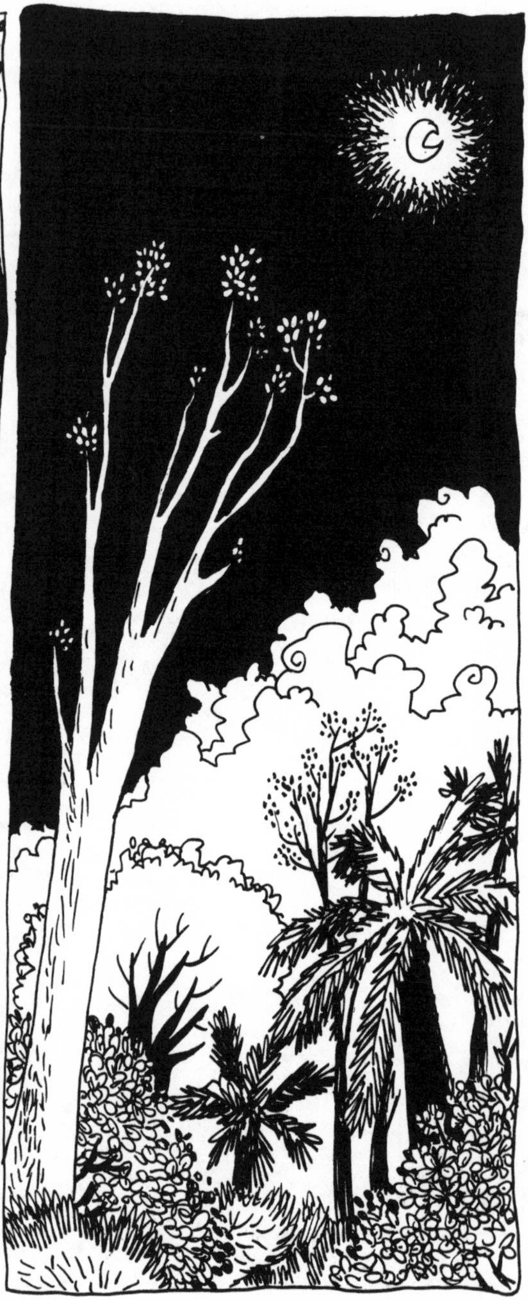

THE PARDONED ONE

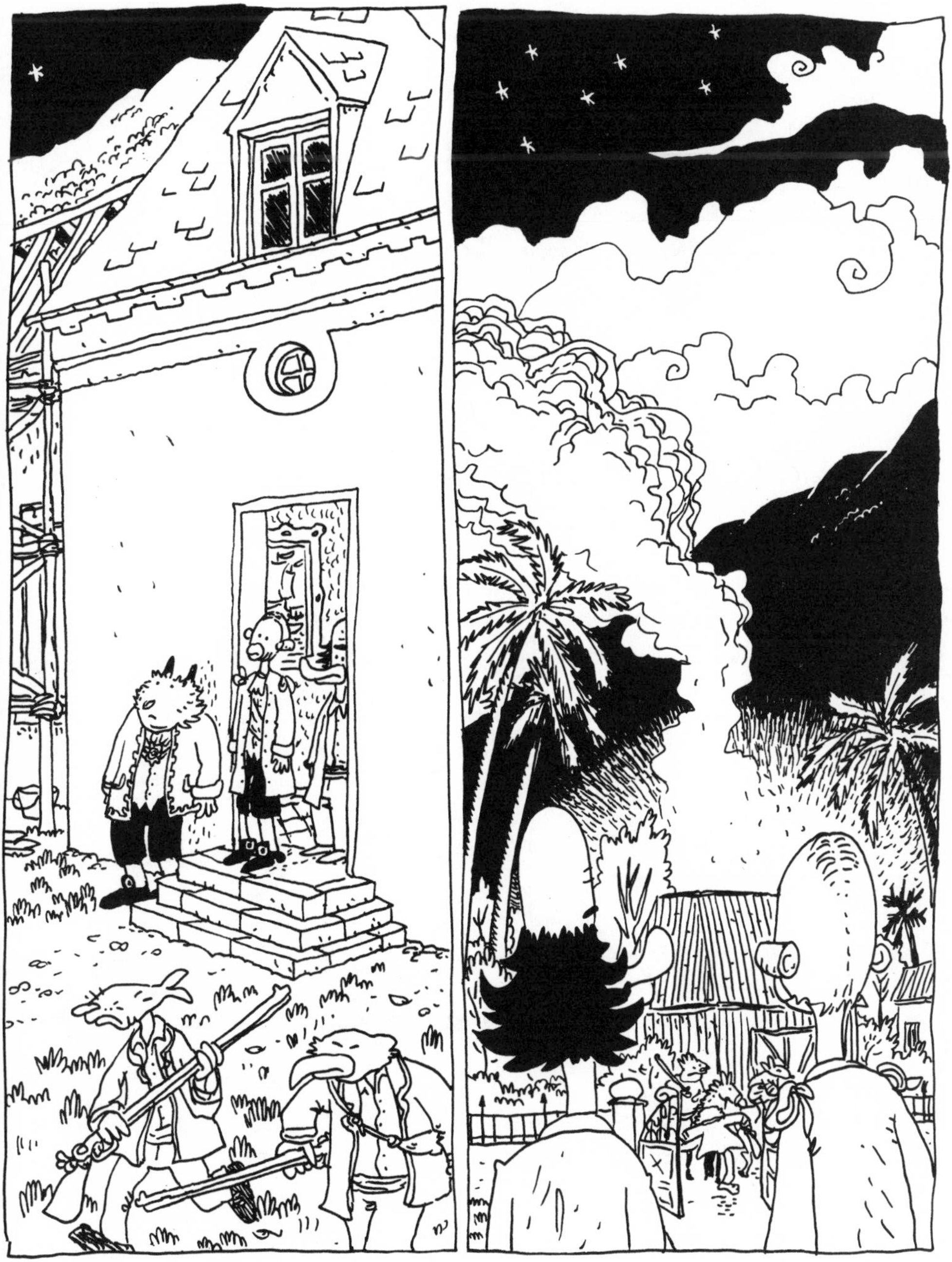

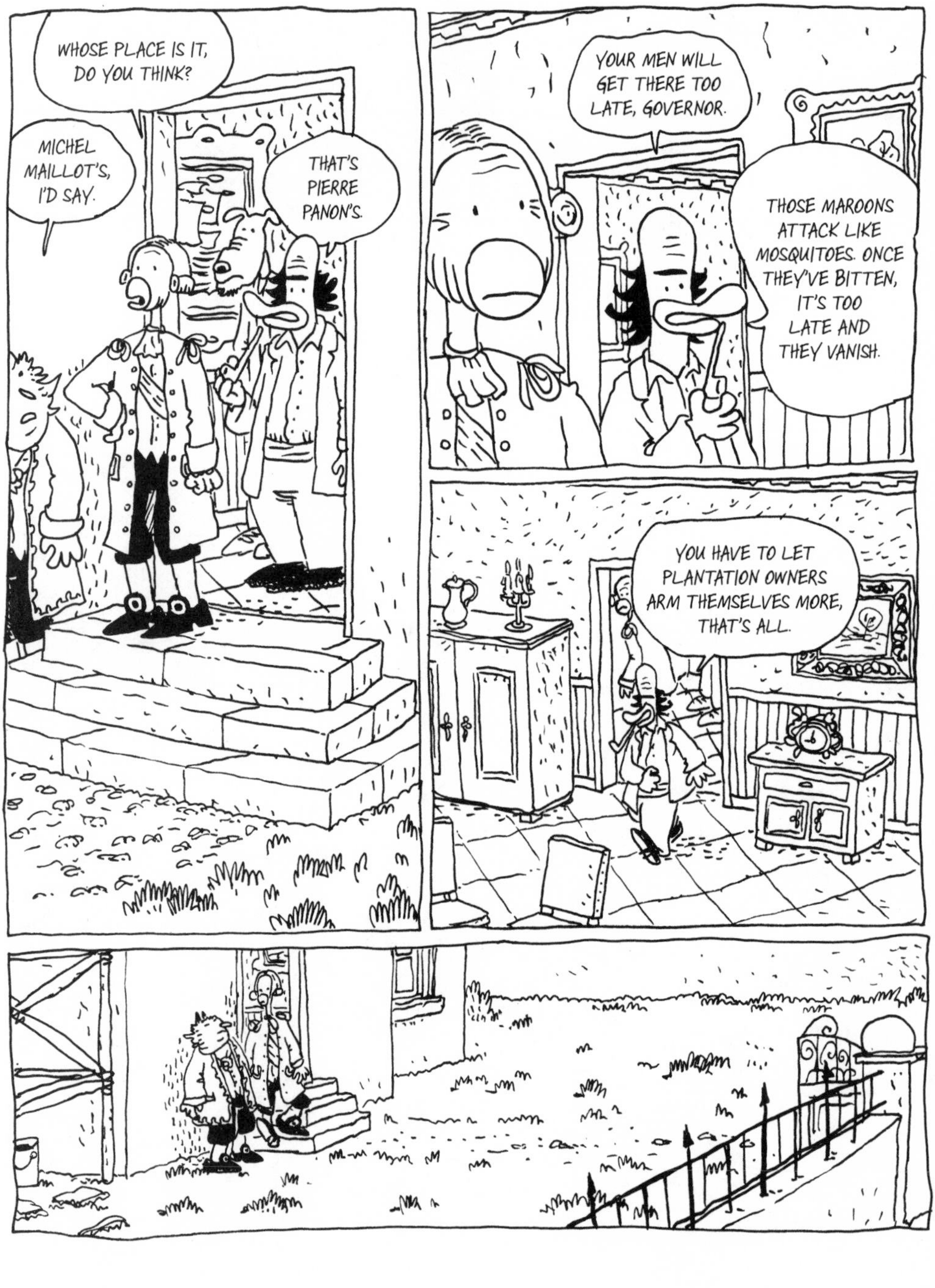
WHOSE PLACE IS IT, DO YOU THINK?
MICHEL MAILLOT'S, I'D SAY.
THAT'S PIERRE PANON'S.
YOUR MEN WILL GET THERE TOO LATE, GOVERNOR.
THOSE MAROONS ATTACK LIKE MOSQUITOES. ONCE THEY'VE BITTEN, IT'S TOO LATE AND THEY VANISH.
YOU HAVE TO LET PLANTATION OWNERS ARM THEMSELVES MORE, THAT'S ALL.

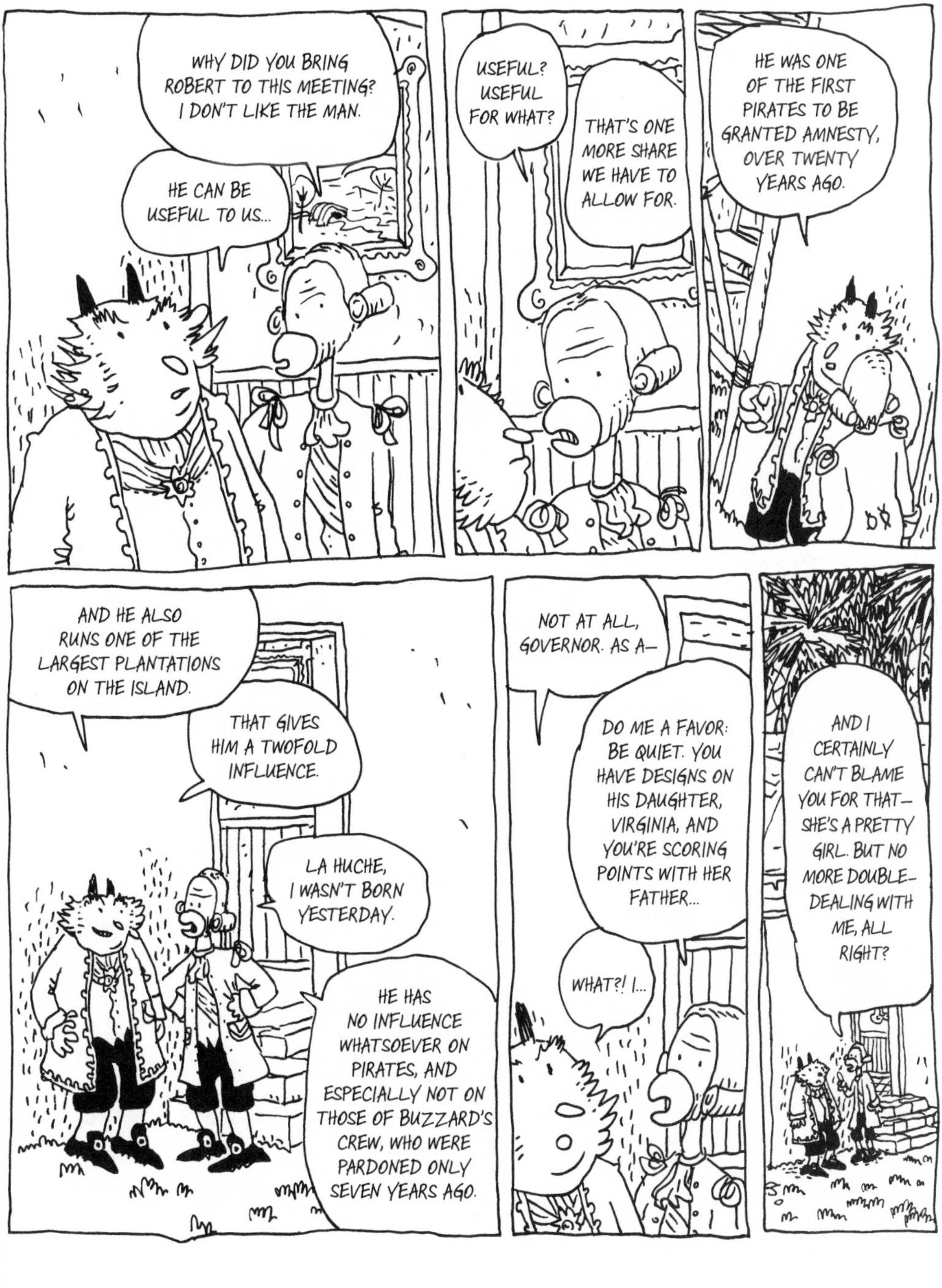

WHY DID YOU BRING ROBERT TO THIS MEETING? I DON'T LIKE THE MAN.
HE CAN BE USEFUL TO US...
USEFUL? USEFUL FOR WHAT?
THAT'S ONE MORE SHARE WE HAVE TO ALLOW FOR.
HE WAS ONE OF THE FIRST PIRATES TO BE GRANTED AMNESTY, OVER TWENTY YEARS AGO.
AND HE ALSO RUNS ONE OF THE LARGEST PLANTATIONS ON THE ISLAND.
THAT GIVES HIM A TWOFOLD INFLUENCE.
LA HUCHE, I WASN'T BORN YESTERDAY.
HE HAS NO INFLUENCE WHATSOEVER ON PIRATES, AND ESPECIALLY NOT ON THOSE OF BUZZARD'S CREW, WHO WERE PARDONED ONLY SEVEN YEARS AGO.
NOT AT ALL, GOVERNOR. AS A—
DO ME A FAVOR: BE QUIET. YOU HAVE DESIGNS ON HIS DAUGHTER, VIRGINIA, AND YOU'RE SCORING POINTS WITH HER FATHER...
WHAT?! I...
AND I CERTAINLY CAN'T BLAME YOU FOR THAT— SHE'S A PRETTY GIRL. BUT NO MORE DOUBLE-DEALING WITH ME, ALL RIGHT?

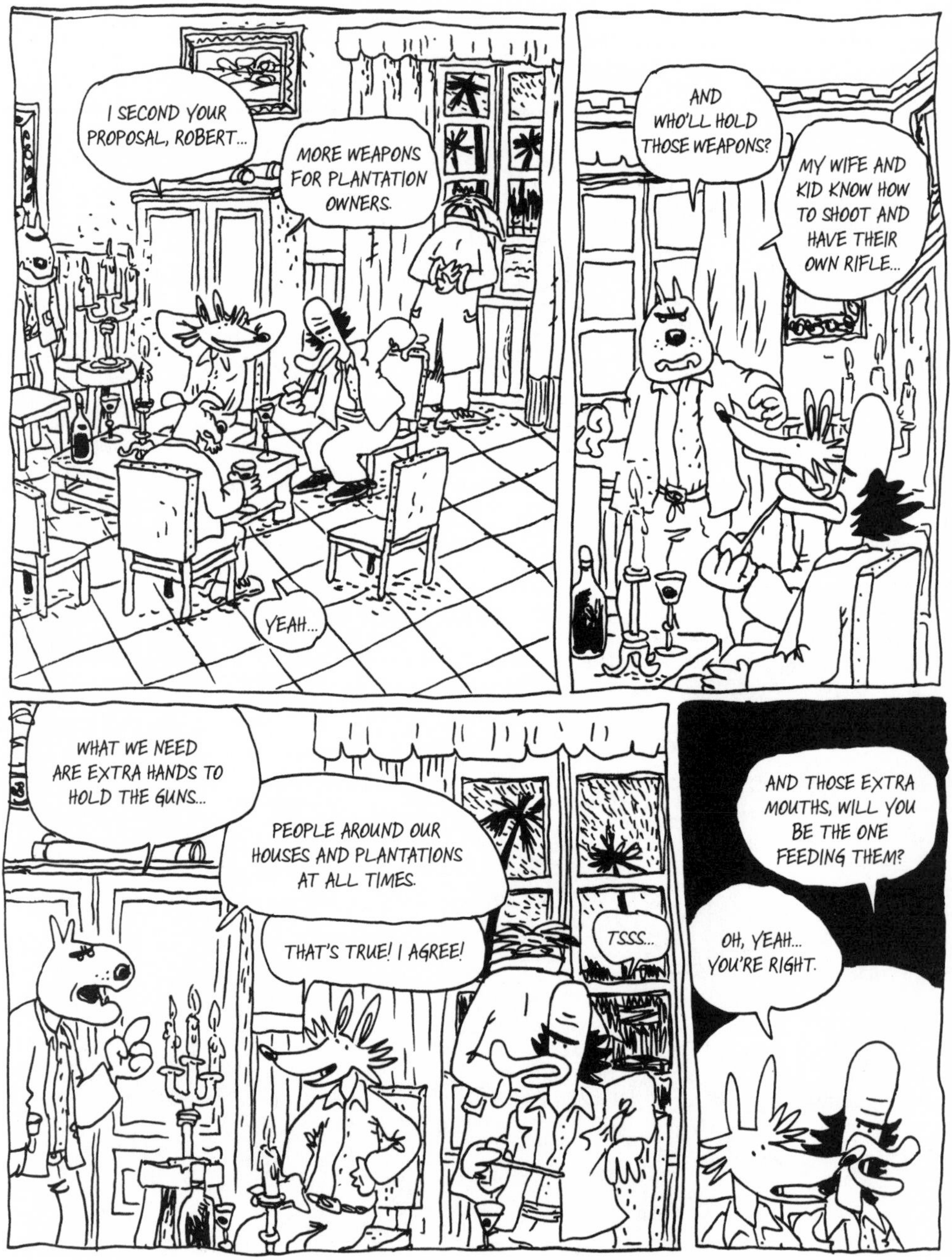
I SECOND YOUR PROPOSAL, ROBERT...
MORE WEAPONS FOR PLANTATION OWNERS.
YEAH...
AND WHO'LL HOLD THOSE WEAPONS?
MY WIFE AND KID KNOW HOW TO SHOOT AND HAVE THEIR OWN RIFLE...
WHAT WE NEED ARE EXTRA HANDS TO HOLD THE GUNS...
PEOPLE AROUND OUR HOUSES AND PLANTATIONS AT ALL TIMES.
THAT'S TRUE! I AGREE!
TSSS...
AND THOSE EXTRA MOUTHS, WILL YOU BE THE ONE FEEDING THEM?
OH, YEAH... YOU'RE RIGHT.

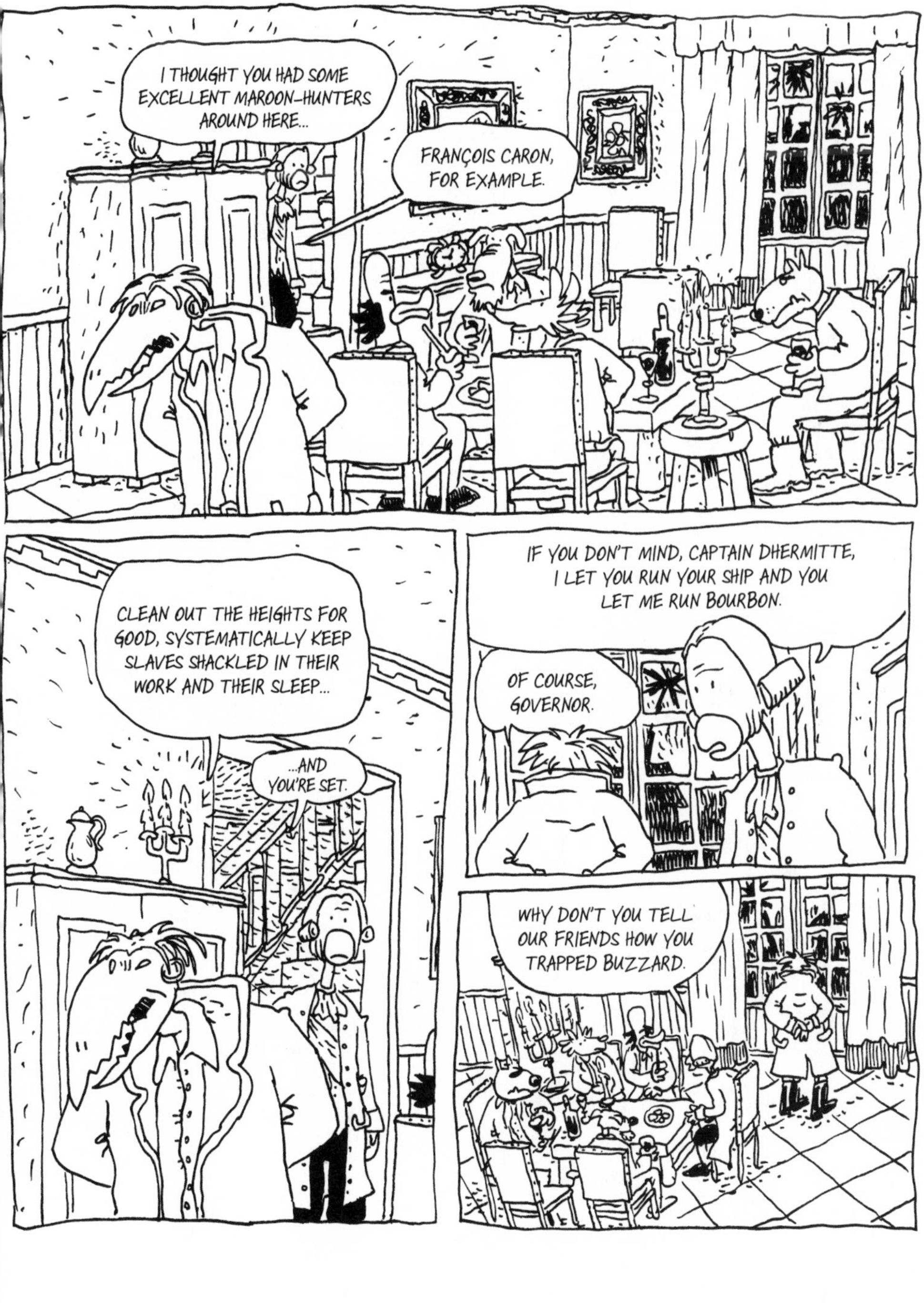
I THOUGHT YOU HAD SOME EXCELLENT MAROON-HUNTERS AROUND HERE...
FRANÇOIS CARON, FOR EXAMPLE.
CLEAN OUT THE HEIGHTS FOR GOOD, SYSTEMATICALLY KEEP SLAVES SHACKLED IN THEIR WORK AND THEIR SLEEP...
...AND YOU'RE SET.
IF YOU DON'T MIND, CAPTAIN DHERMITTE, I LET YOU RUN YOUR SHIP AND YOU LET ME RUN BOURBON.
OF COURSE, GOVERNOR.
WHY DON'T YOU TELL OUR FRIENDS HOW YOU TRAPPED BUZZARD.

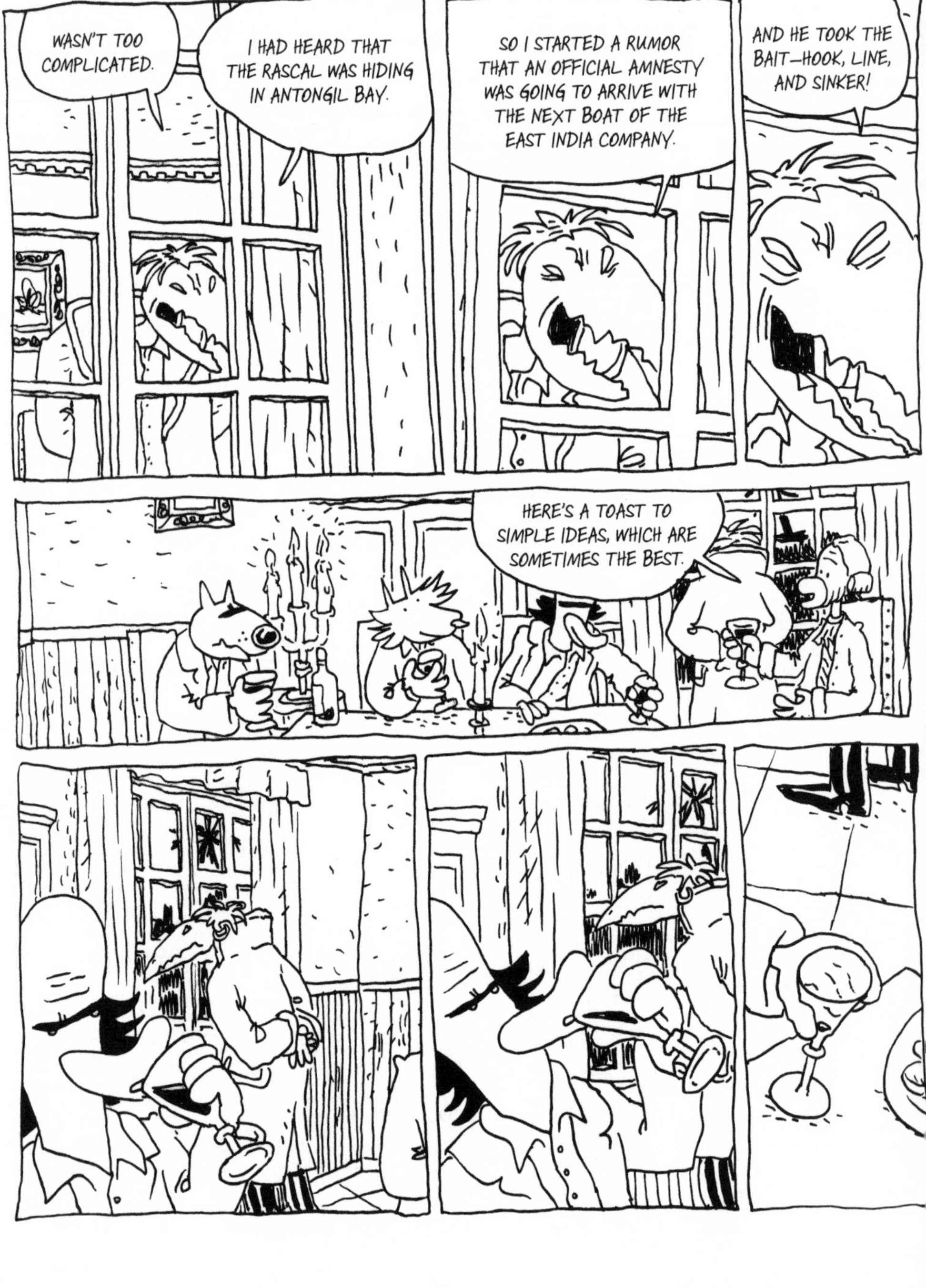
WASN'T TOO COMPLICATED.
I HAD HEARD THAT THE RASCAL WAS HIDING IN ANTONGIL BAY.
SO I STARTED A RUMOR THAT AN OFFICIAL AMNESTY WAS GOING TO ARRIVE WITH THE NEXT BOAT OF THE EAST INDIA COMPANY.
AND HE TOOK THE BAIT—HOOK, LINE, AND SINKER!
HERE'S A TOAST TO SIMPLE IDEAS, WHICH ARE SOMETIMES THE BEST.

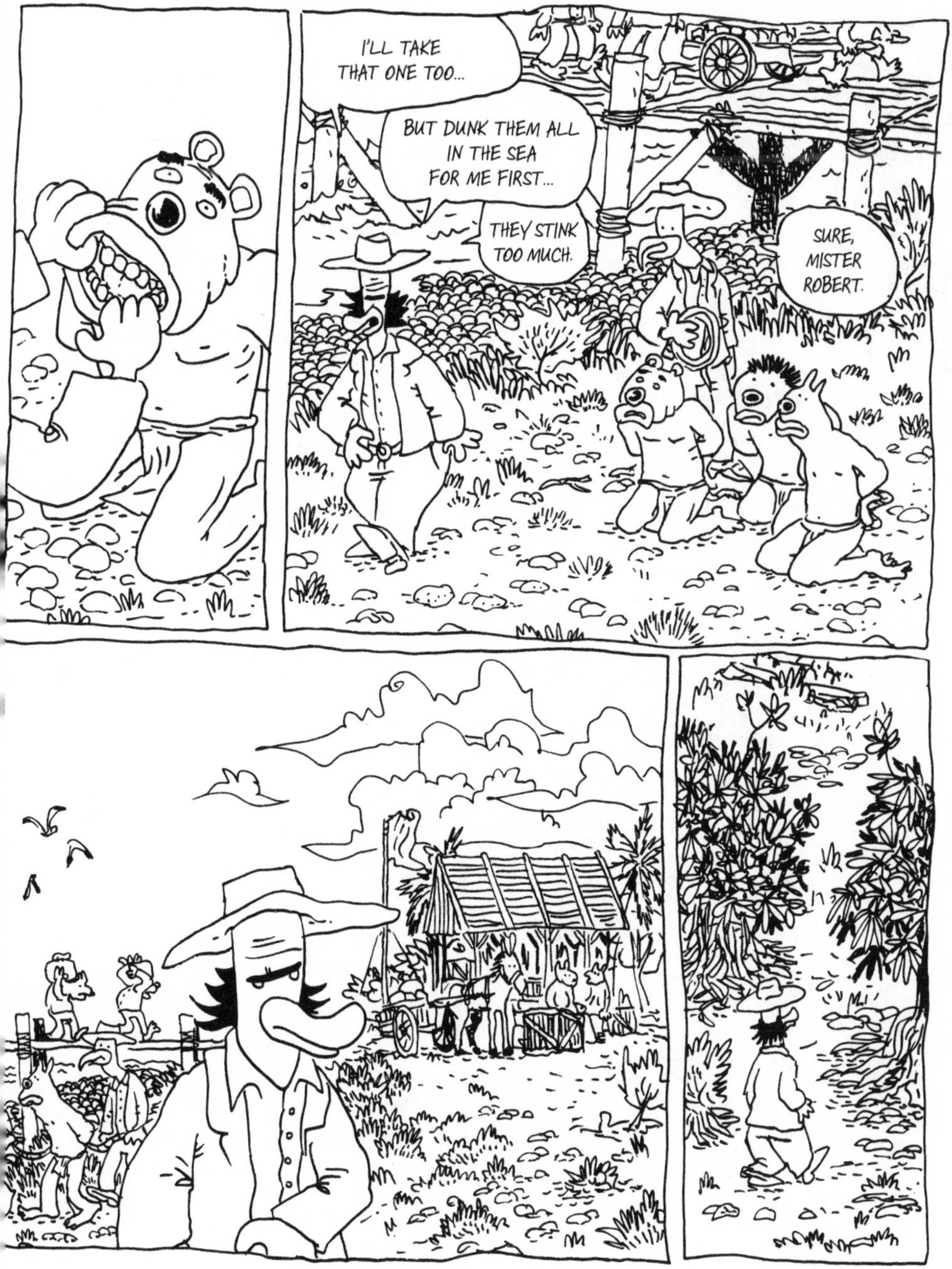
I'LL TAKE THAT ONE TOO...
BUT DUNK THEM ALL IN THE SEA FOR ME FIRST...
THEY STINK TOO MUCH.
SURE, MISTER ROBERT.

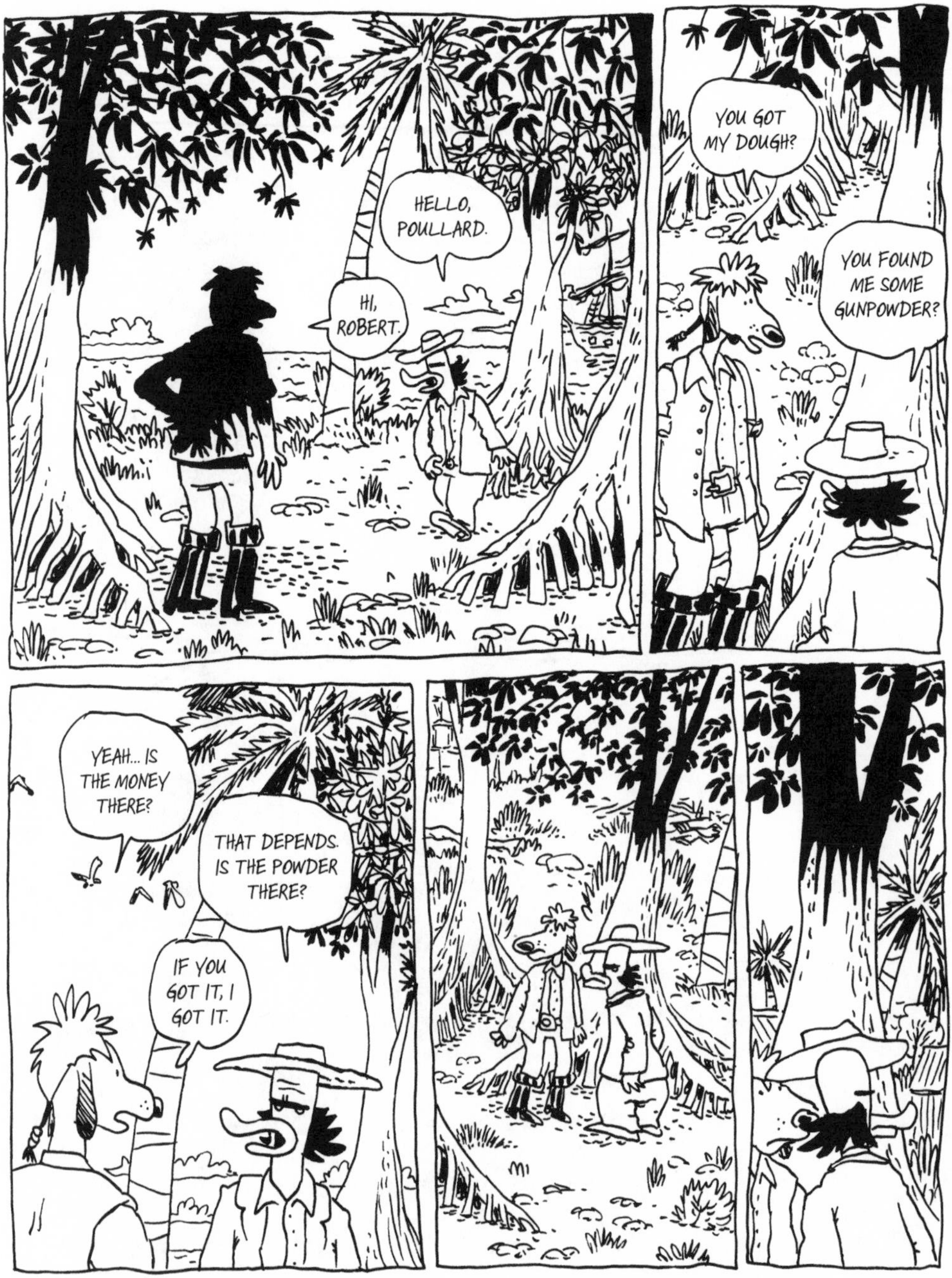
HELLO, POULLARD.
HI, ROBERT.
YOU GOT MY DOUGH?
YOU FOUND ME SOME GUNPOWDER?
YEAH... IS THE MONEY THERE?
THAT DEPENDS. IS THE POWDER THERE?
IF YOU GOT IT, I GOT IT.

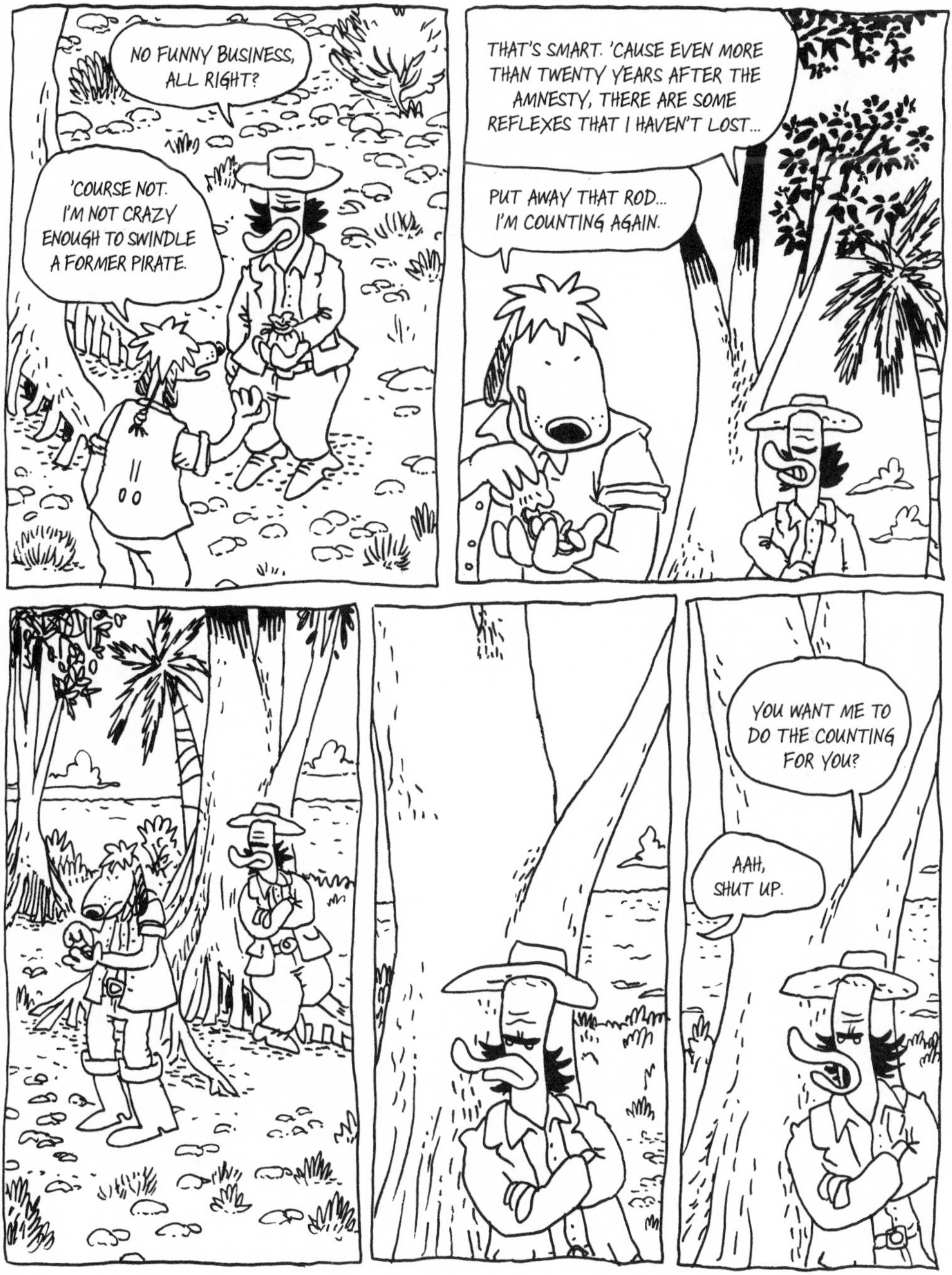
NO FUNNY BUSINESS, ALL RIGHT?
'COURSE NOT. I'M NOT CRAZY ENOUGH TO SWINDLE A FORMER PIRATE.
THAT'S SMART. 'CAUSE EVEN MORE THAN TWENTY YEARS AFTER THE AMNESTY, THERE ARE SOME REFLEXES THAT I HAVEN'T LOST...
PUT AWAY THAT ROD... I'M COUNTING AGAIN.
YOU WANT ME TO DO THE COUNTING FOR YOU?
AAH, SHUT UP.

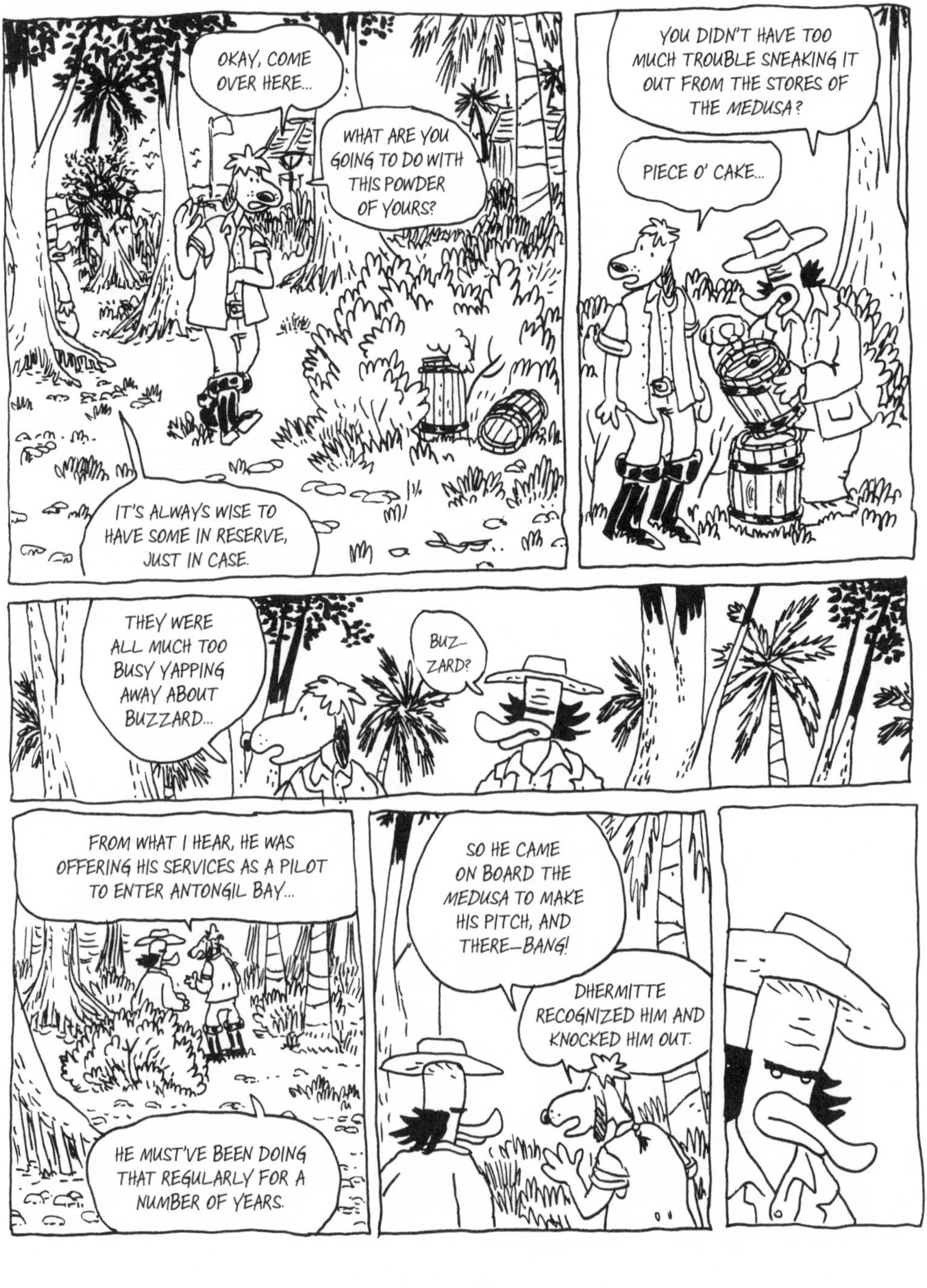
OKAY, COME OVER HERE...
WHAT ARE YOU GOING TO DO WITH THIS POWDER OF YOURS?
IT'S ALWAYS WISE TO HAVE SOME IN RESERVE, JUST IN CASE.
YOU DIDN'T HAVE TOO MUCH TROUBLE SNEAKING IT OUT FROM THE STORES OF THE *MEDUSA*?
PIECE O' CAKE...
THEY WERE ALL MUCH TOO BUSY YAPPING AWAY ABOUT BUZZARD...
BUZ-ZARD?
FROM WHAT I HEAR, HE WAS OFFERING HIS SERVICES AS A PILOT TO ENTER ANTONGIL BAY...
HE MUST'VE BEEN DOING THAT REGULARLY FOR A NUMBER OF YEARS.
SO HE CAME ON BOARD THE *MEDUSA* TO MAKE HIS PITCH, AND THERE—*BANG!*
DHERMITTE RECOGNIZED HIM AND KNOCKED HIM OUT.

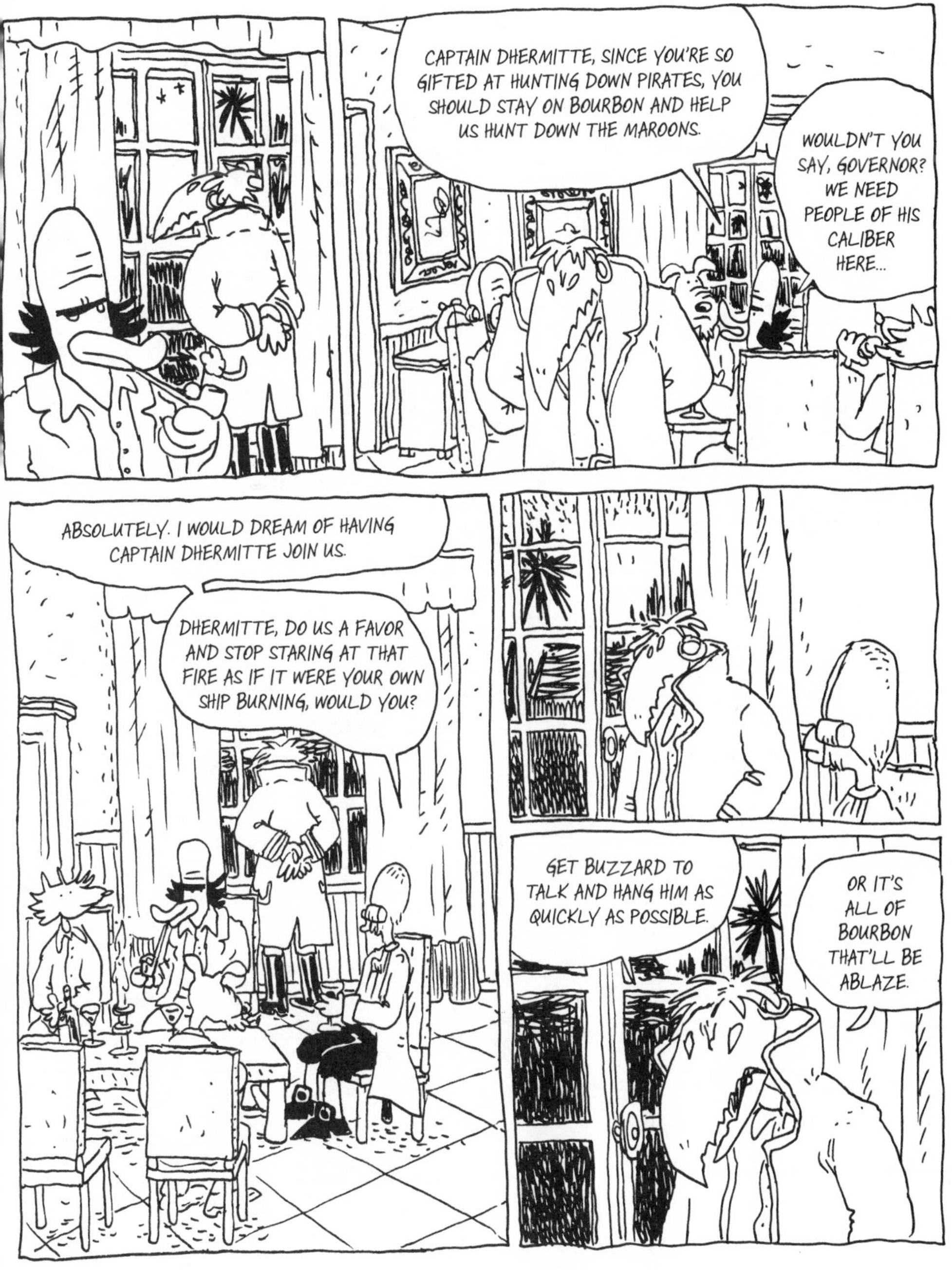
CAPTAIN DHERMITTE, SINCE YOU'RE SO GIFTED AT HUNTING DOWN PIRATES, YOU SHOULD STAY ON BOURBON AND HELP US HUNT DOWN THE MAROONS.
WOULDN'T YOU SAY, GOVERNOR? WE NEED PEOPLE OF HIS CALIBER HERE...
ABSOLUTELY. I WOULD DREAM OF HAVING CAPTAIN DHERMITTE JOIN US.
DHERMITTE, DO US A FAVOR AND STOP STARING AT THAT FIRE AS IF IT WERE YOUR OWN SHIP BURNING, WOULD YOU?
GET BUZZARD TO TALK AND HANG HIM AS QUICKLY AS POSSIBLE.
OR IT'S ALL OF BOURBON THAT'LL BE ABLAZE.

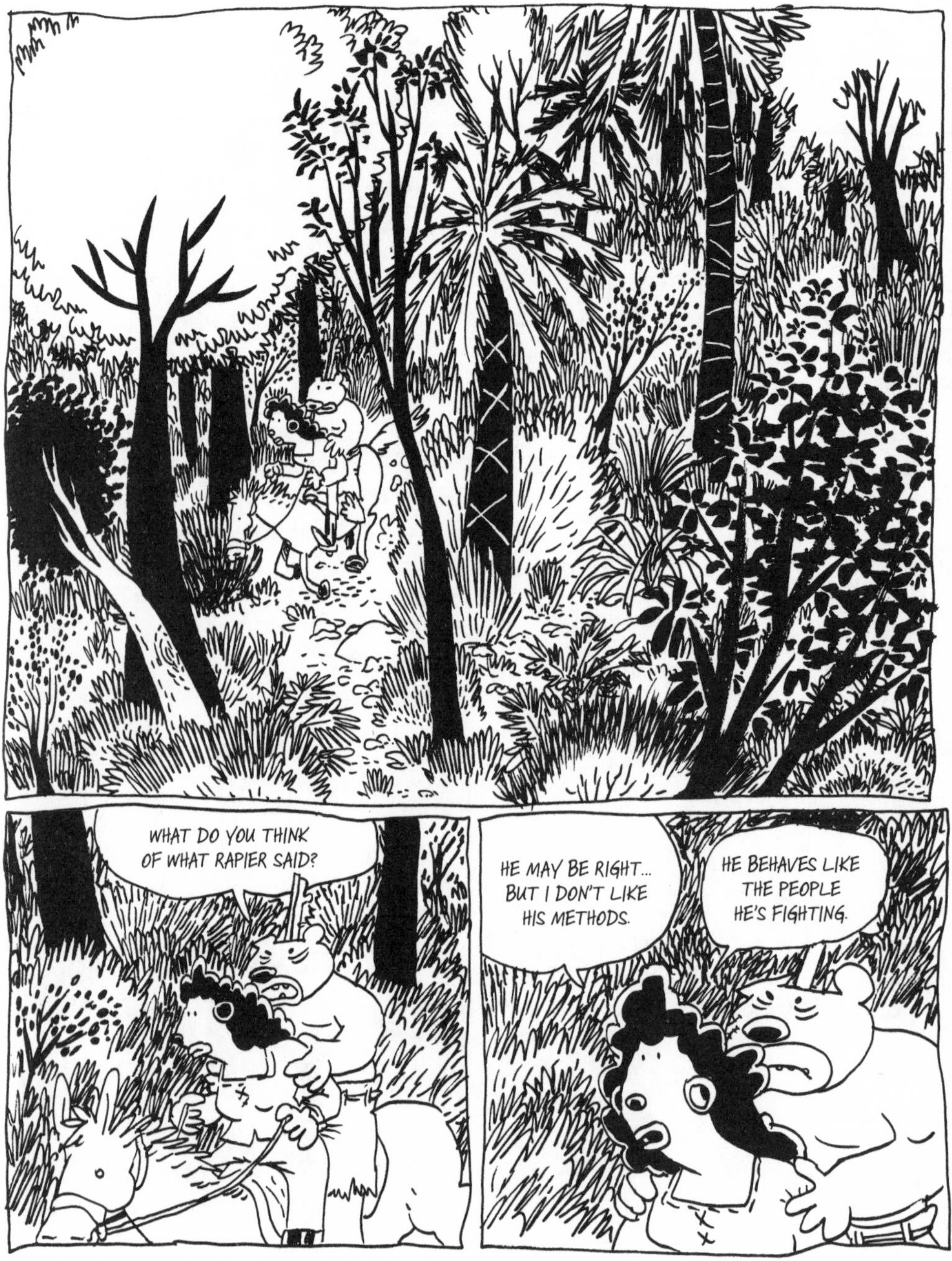
WHAT DO YOU THINK OF WHAT RAPIER SAID?
HE MAY BE RIGHT... BUT I DON'T LIKE HIS METHODS.
HE BEHAVES LIKE THE PEOPLE HE'S FIGHTING.

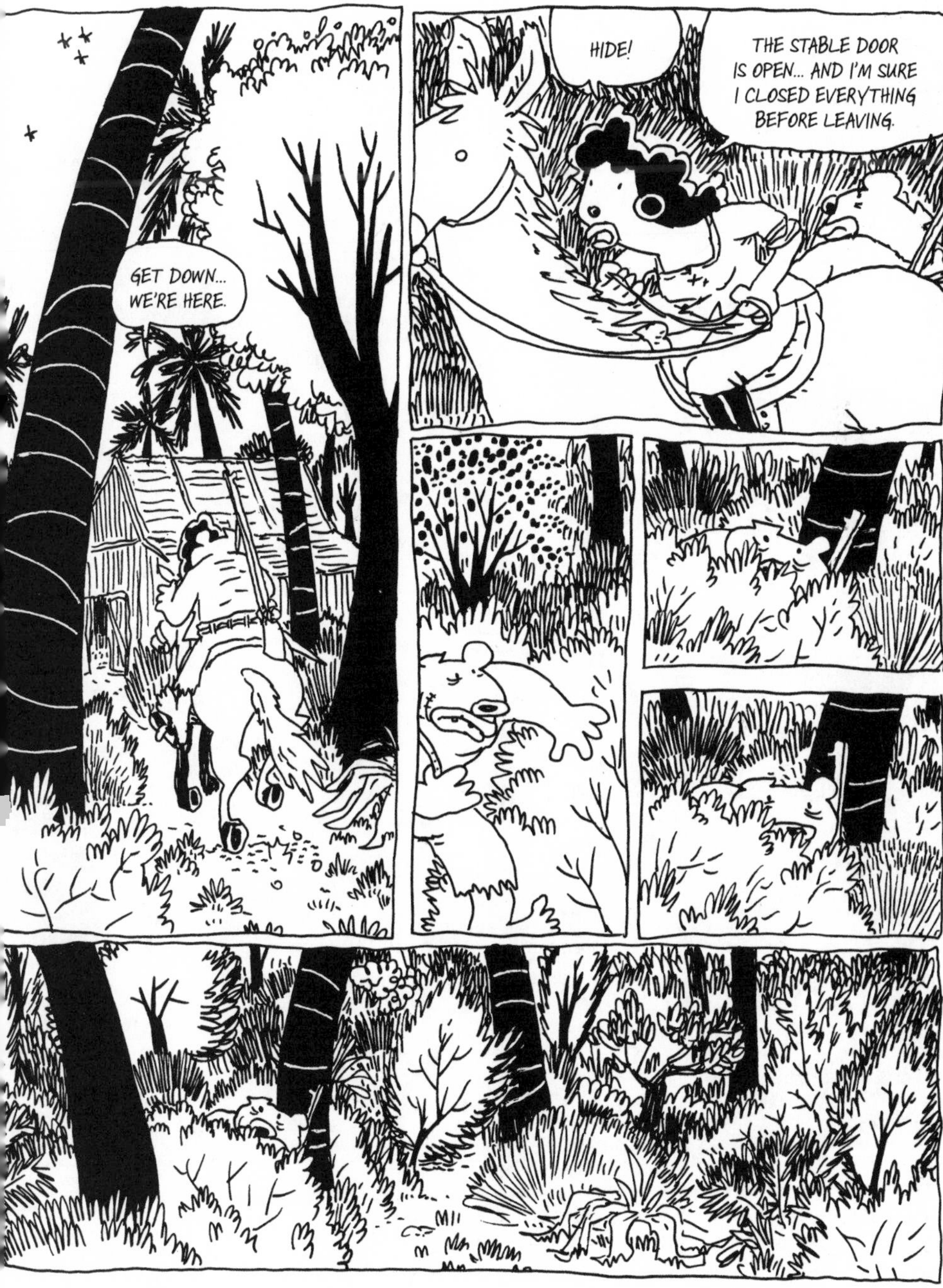
GET DOWN... WE'RE HERE.
HIDE!
THE STABLE DOOR IS OPEN... AND I'M SURE I CLOSED EVERYTHING BEFORE LEAVING.

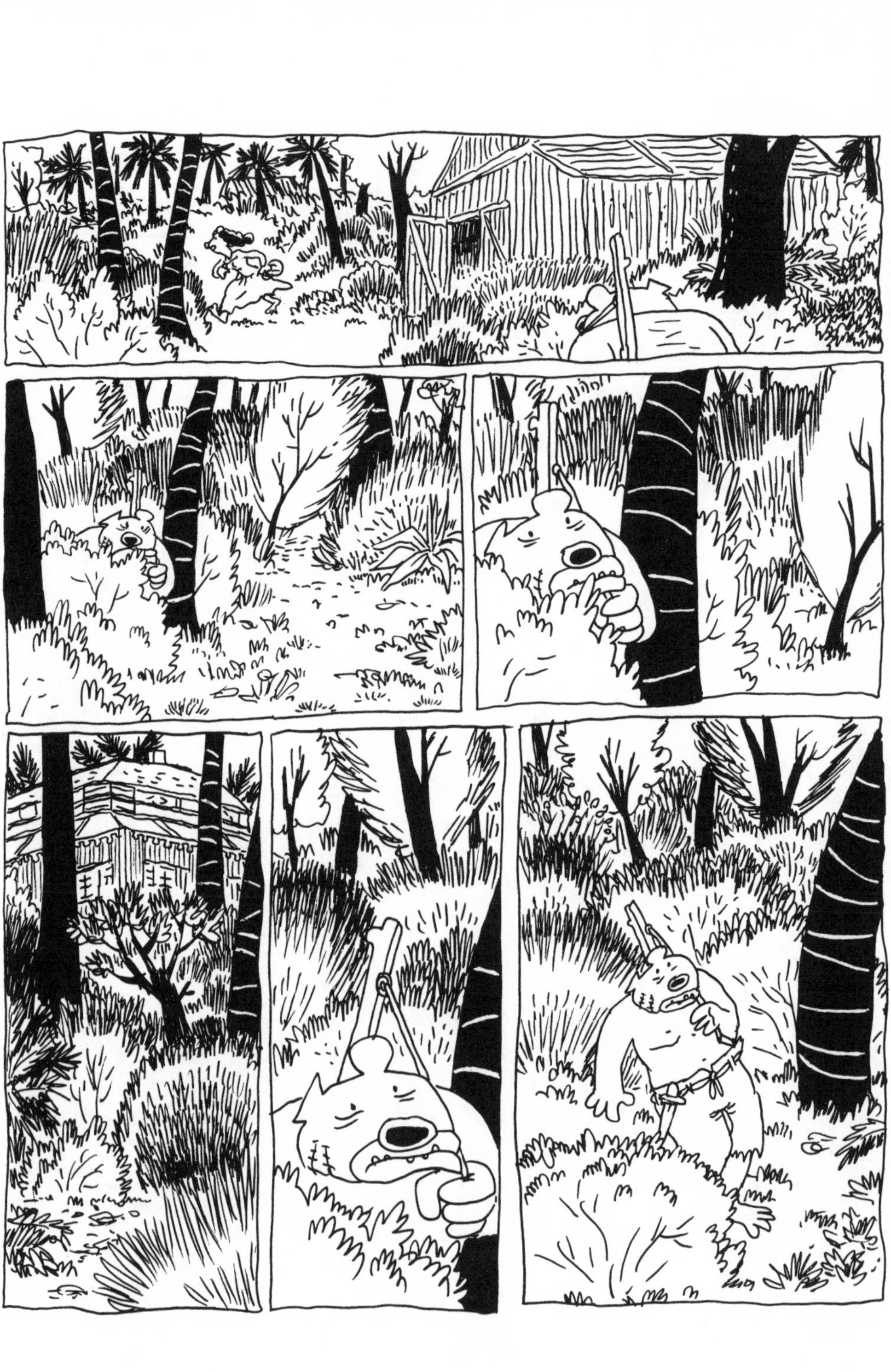

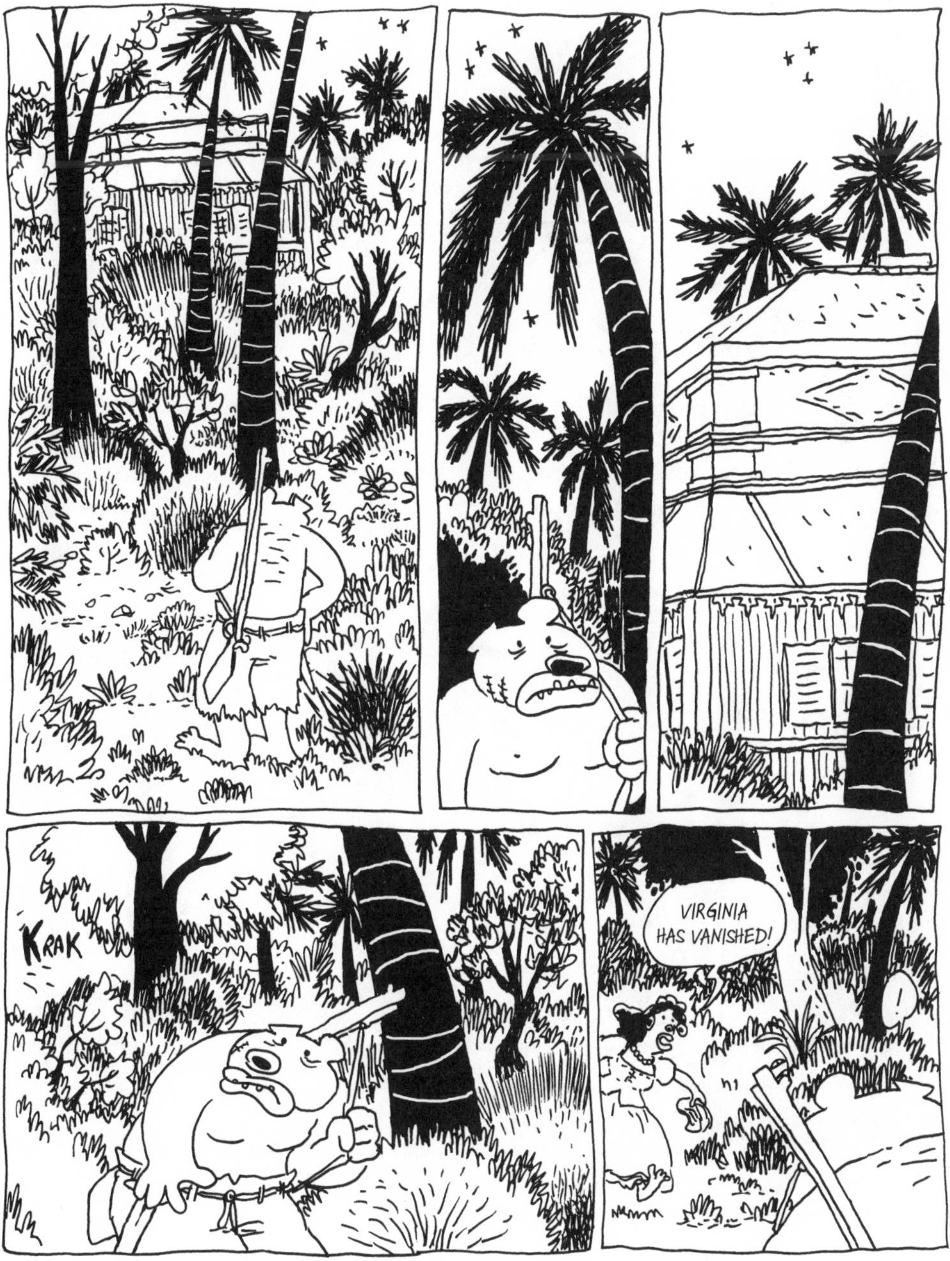
KRAK
VIRGINIA HAS VANISHED!
!

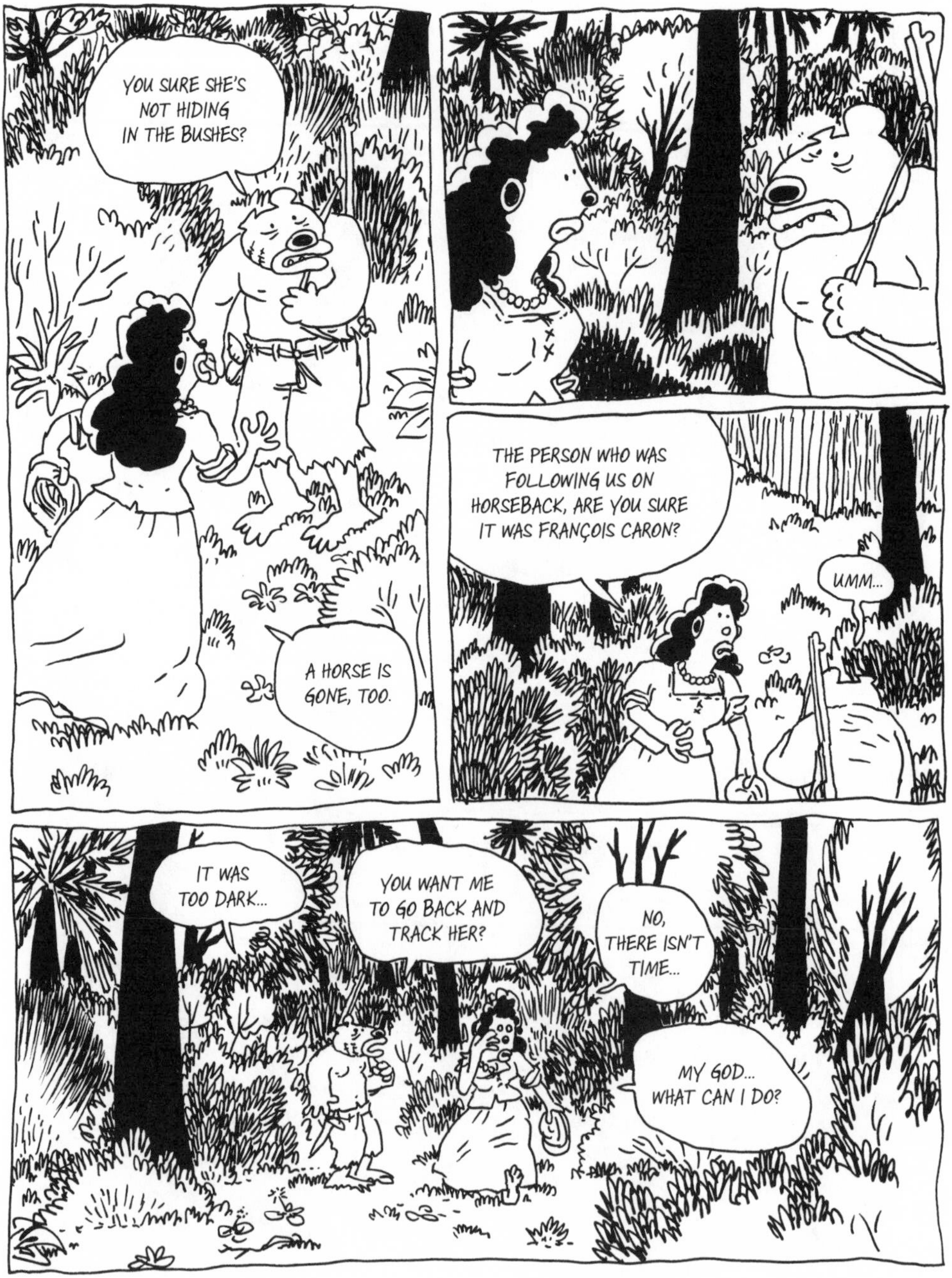
YOU SURE SHE'S NOT HIDING IN THE BUSHES?
A HORSE IS GONE, TOO.
THE PERSON WHO WAS FOLLOWING US ON HORSEBACK, ARE YOU SURE IT WAS FRANÇOIS CARON?
UMM...
IT WAS TOO DARK...
YOU WANT ME TO GO BACK AND TRACK HER?
NO, THERE ISN'T TIME...
MY GOD... WHAT CAN I DO?

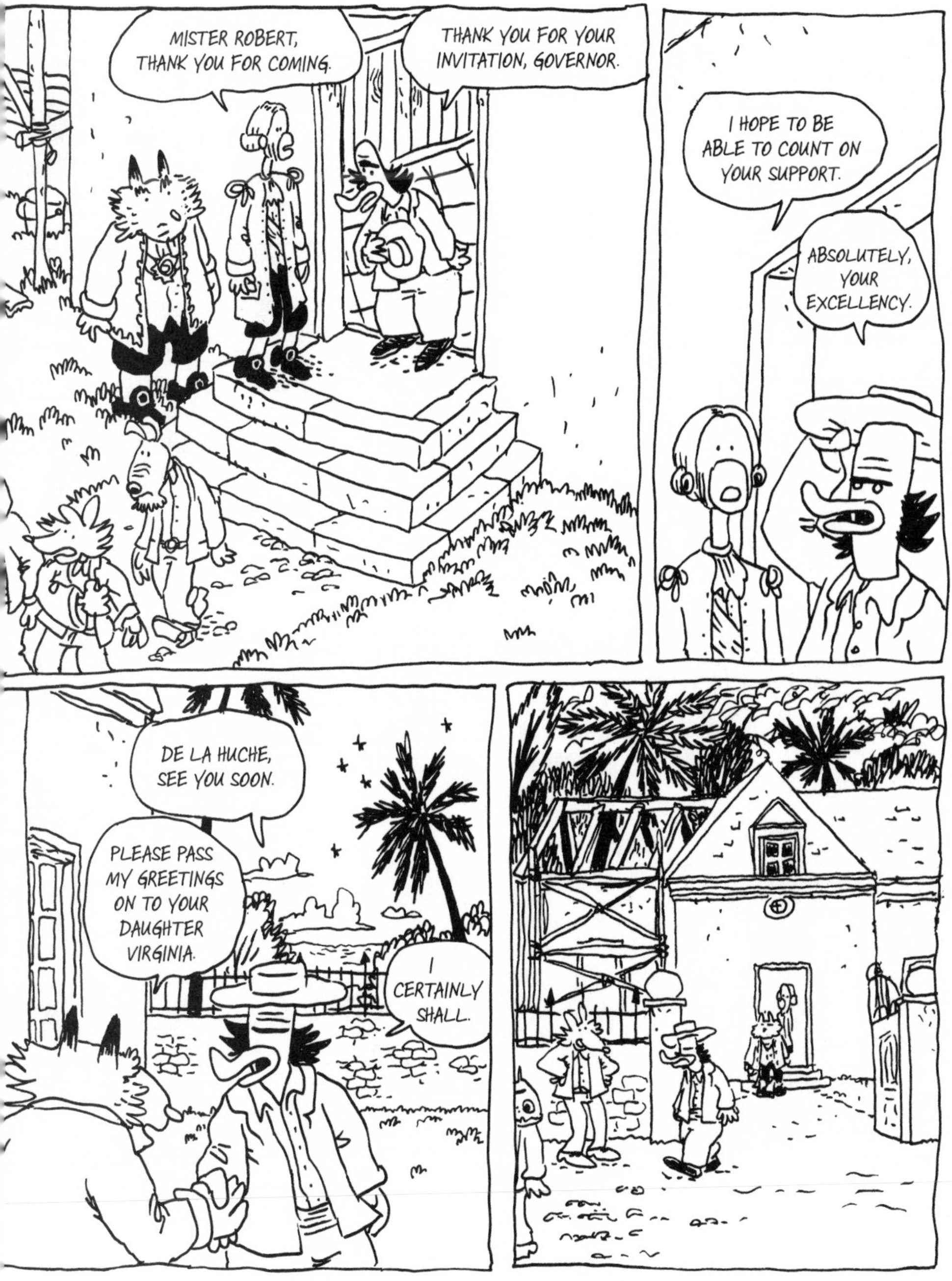
MISTER ROBERT, THANK YOU FOR COMING.
THANK YOU FOR YOUR INVITATION, GOVERNOR.
I HOPE TO BE ABLE TO COUNT ON YOUR SUPPORT.
ABSOLUTELY, YOUR EXCELLENCY.
DE LA HUCHE, SEE YOU SOON.
PLEASE PASS MY GREETINGS ON TO YOUR DAUGHTER VIRGINIA.
I CERTAINLY SHALL.

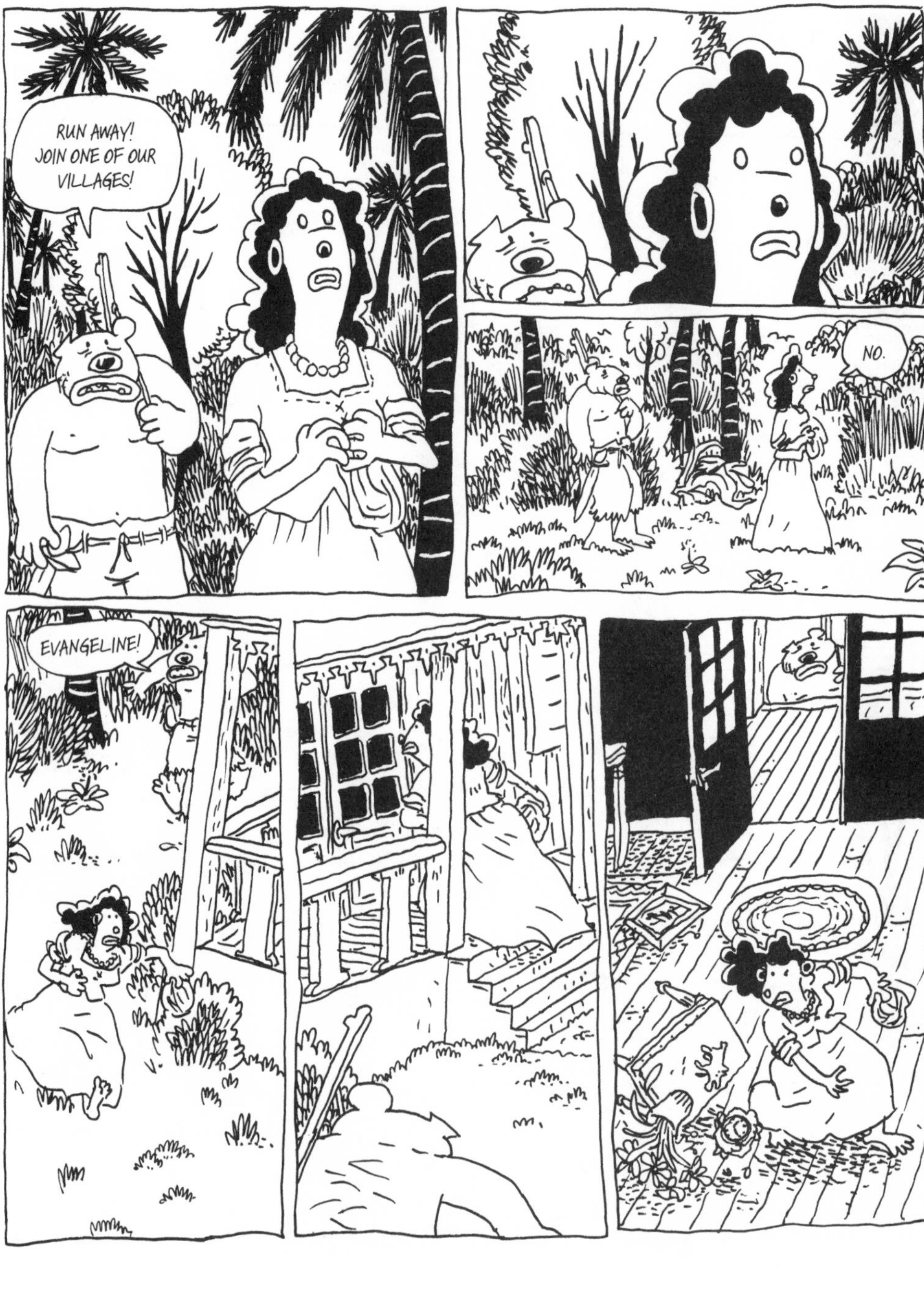
RUN AWAY! JOIN ONE OF OUR VILLAGES!
NO.
EVANGELINE!

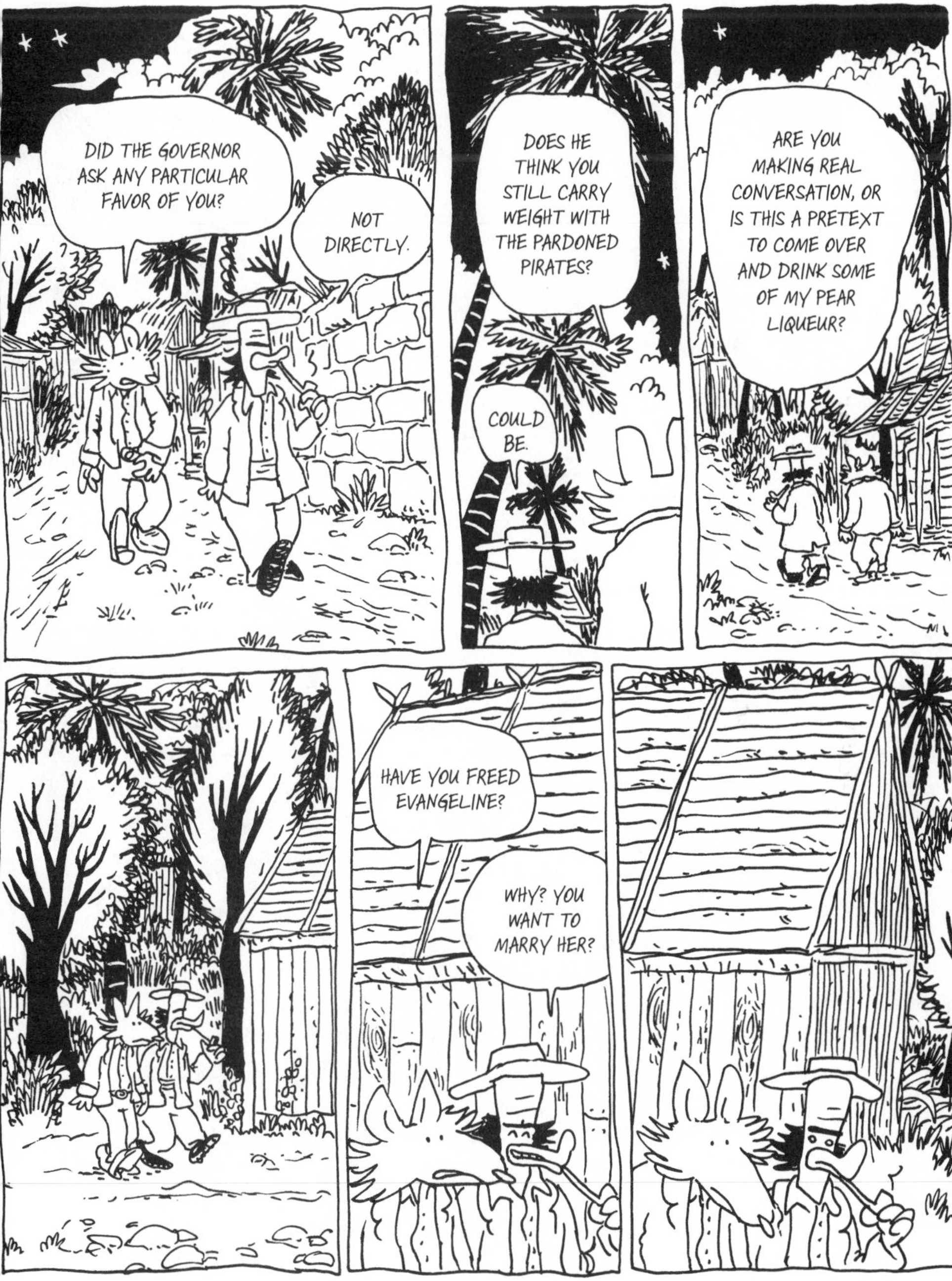
DID THE GOVERNOR ASK ANY PARTICULAR FAVOR OF YOU?
NOT DIRECTLY.
DOES HE THINK YOU STILL CARRY WEIGHT WITH THE PARDONED PIRATES?
COULD BE.
ARE YOU MAKING REAL CONVERSATION, OR IS THIS A PRETEXT TO COME OVER AND DRINK SOME OF MY PEAR LIQUEUR?
HAVE YOU FREED EVANGELINE?
WHY? YOU WANT TO MARRY HER?

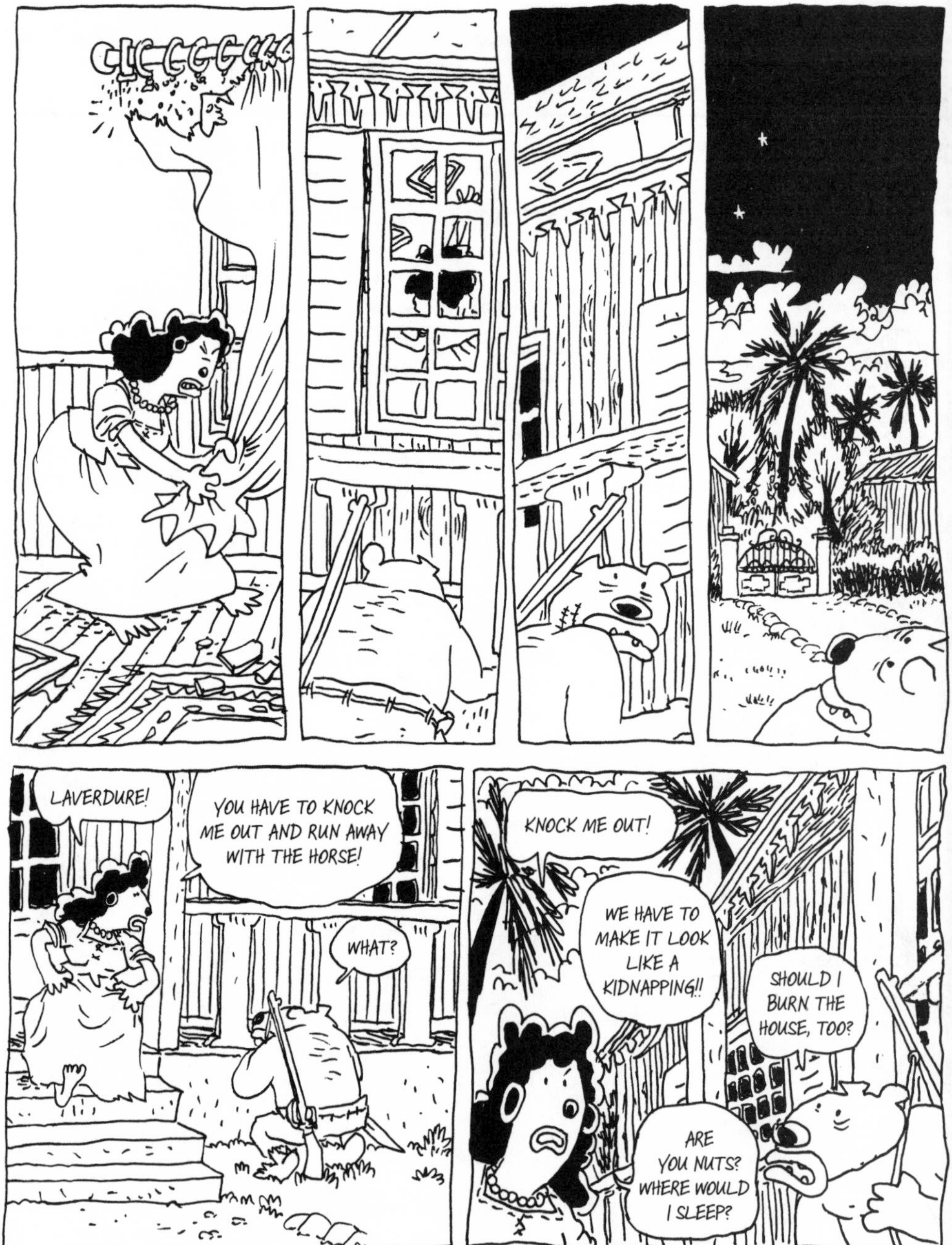
LAVERDURE!
YOU HAVE TO KNOCK ME OUT AND RUN AWAY WITH THE HORSE!
WHAT?
KNOCK ME OUT!
WE HAVE TO MAKE IT LOOK LIKE A KIDNAPPING!!
SHOULD I BURN THE HOUSE, TOO?
ARE YOU NUTS? WHERE WOULD I SLEEP?

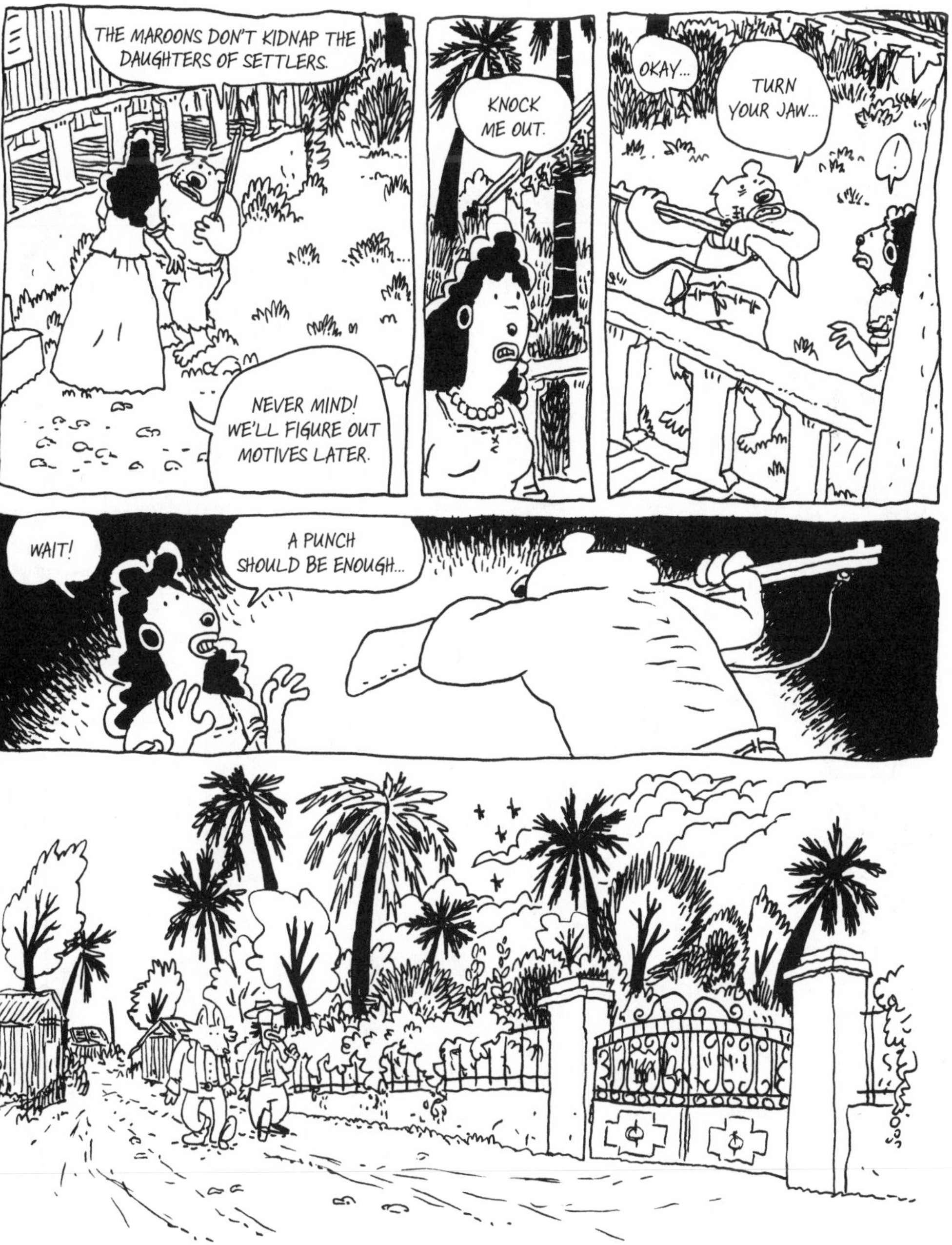
THE MAROONS DON'T KIDNAP THE DAUGHTERS OF SETTLERS.
NEVER MIND! WE'LL FIGURE OUT MOTIVES LATER.
KNOCK ME OUT.
OKAY...
TURN YOUR JAW...
!
WAIT!
A PUNCH SHOULD BE ENOUGH...

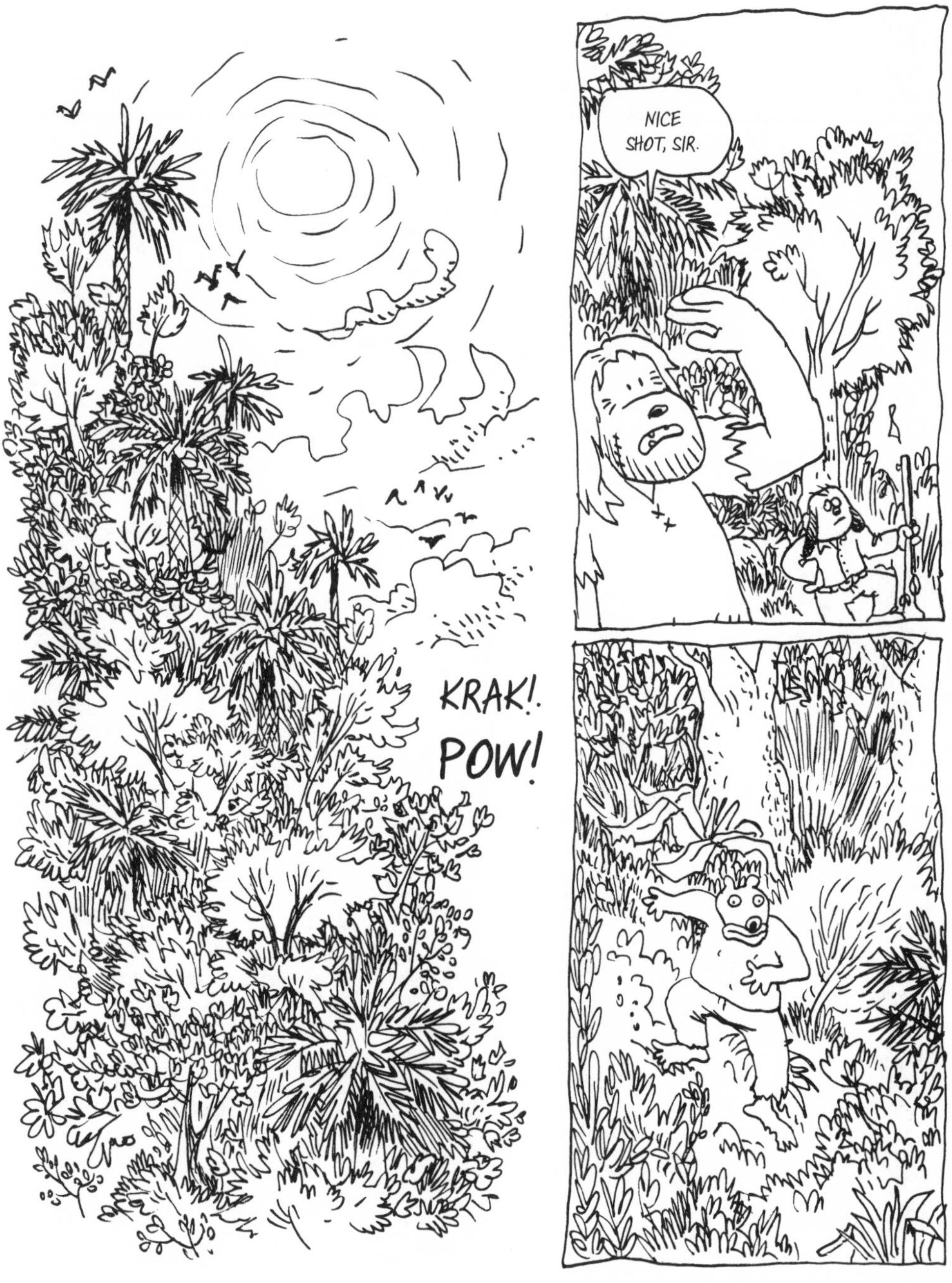
KRAK!
POW!
NICE SHOT, SIR.

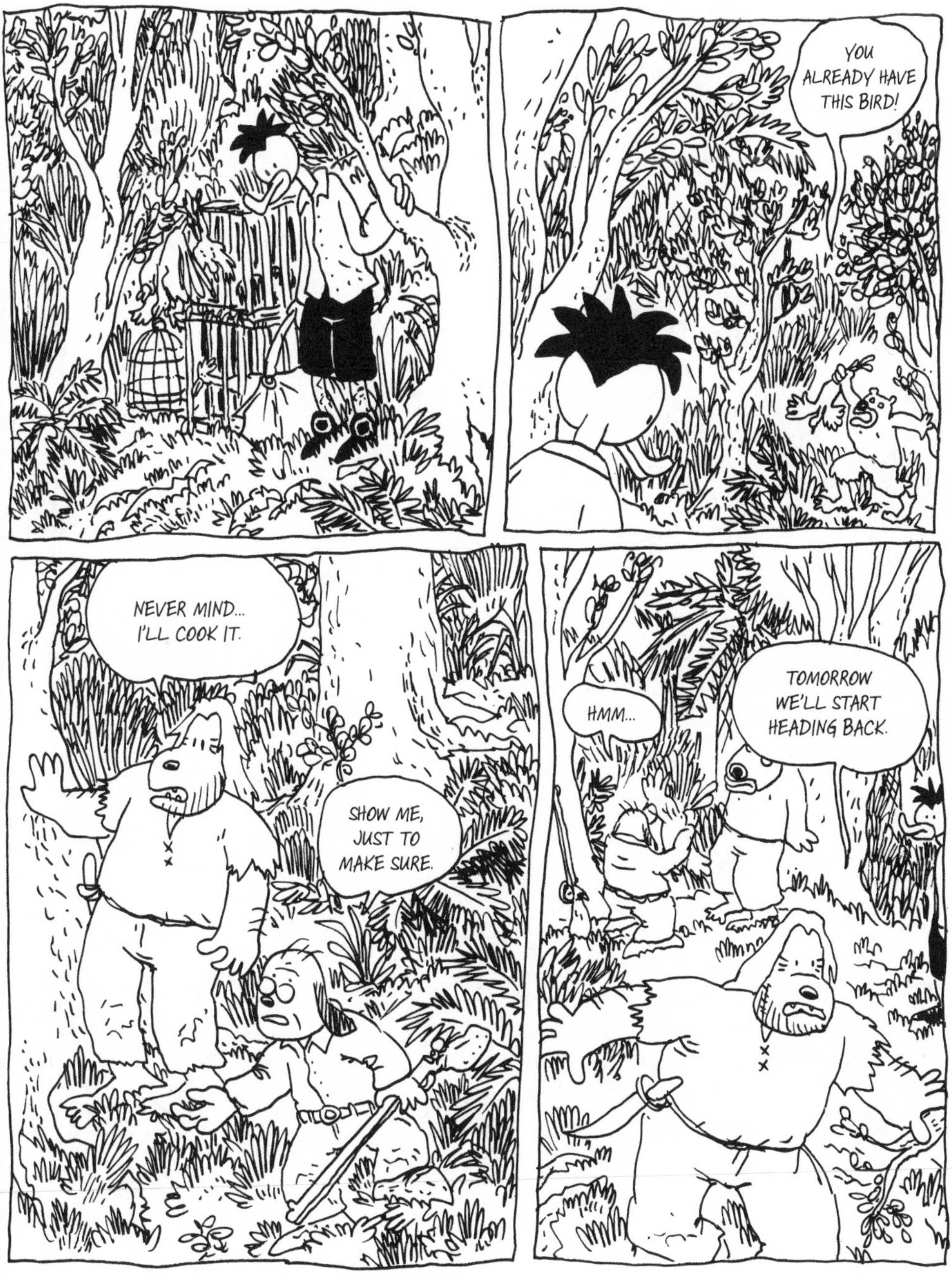
YOU ALREADY HAVE THIS BIRD!
NEVER MIND... I'LL COOK IT.
SHOW ME, JUST TO MAKE SURE.
HMM...
TOMORROW WE'LL START HEADING BACK.

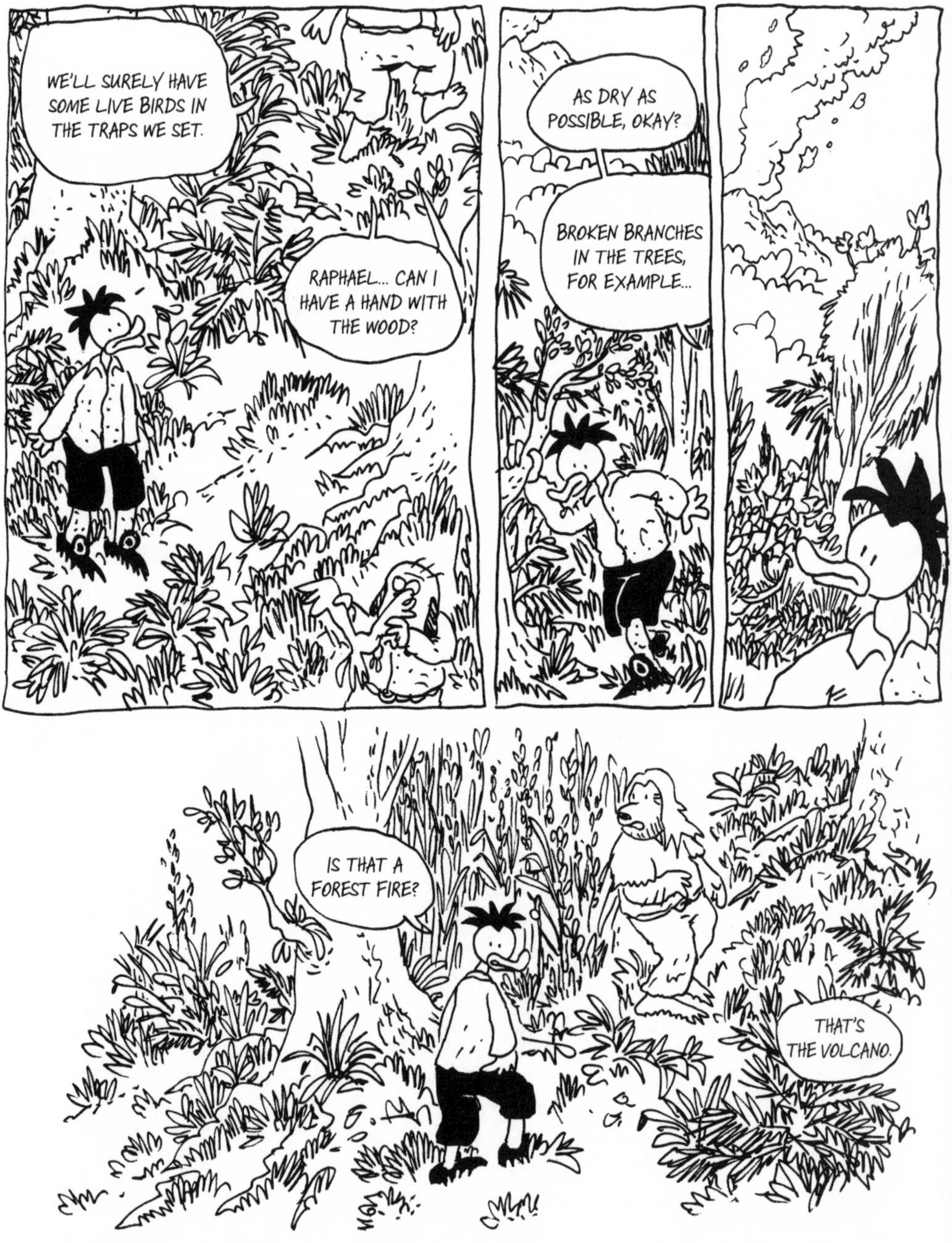
WE'LL SURELY HAVE SOME LIVE BIRDS IN THE TRAPS WE SET.
RAPHAEL... CAN I HAVE A HAND WITH THE WOOD?
AS DRY AS POSSIBLE, OKAY?
BROKEN BRANCHES IN THE TREES, FOR EXAMPLE...
IS THAT A FOREST FIRE?
THAT'S THE VOLCANO.

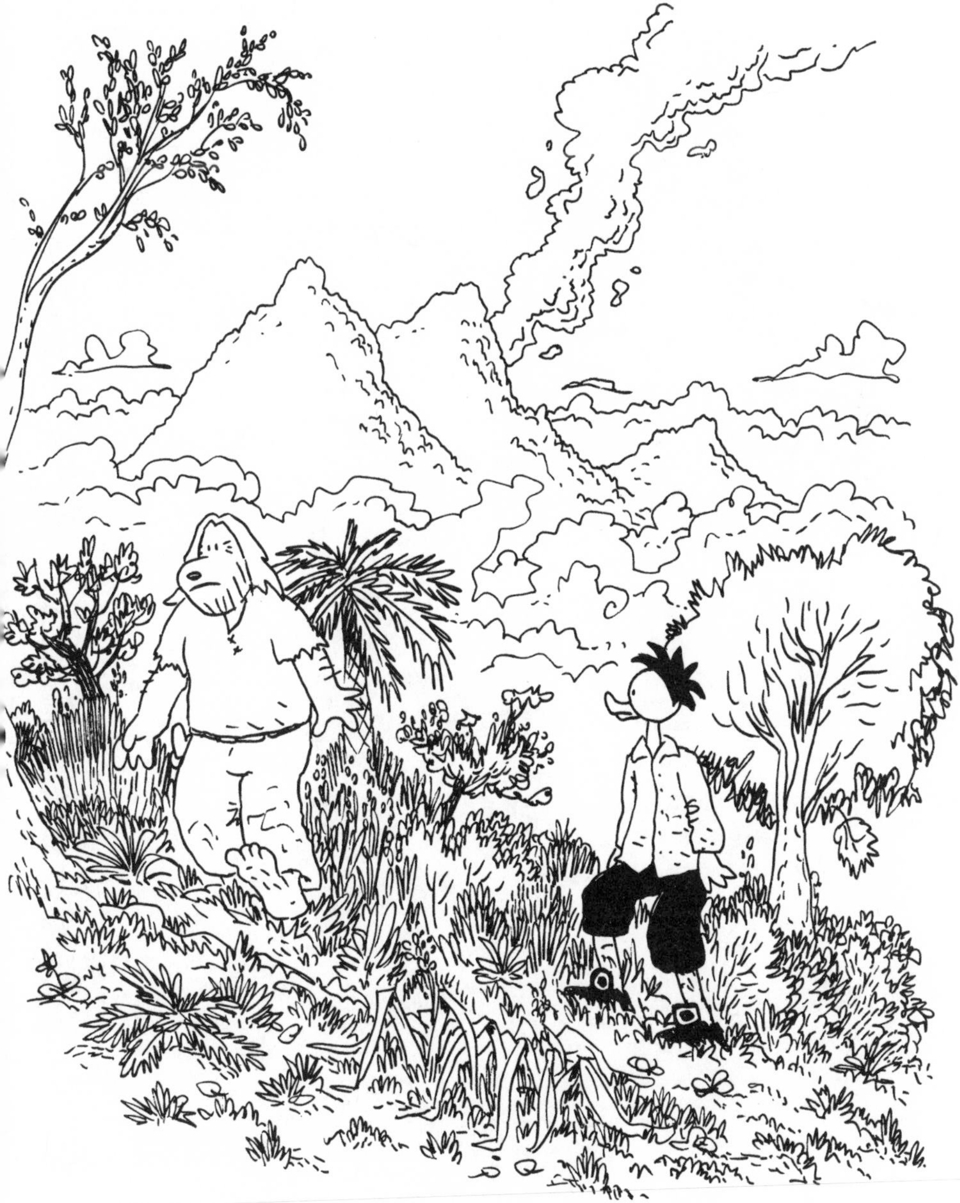

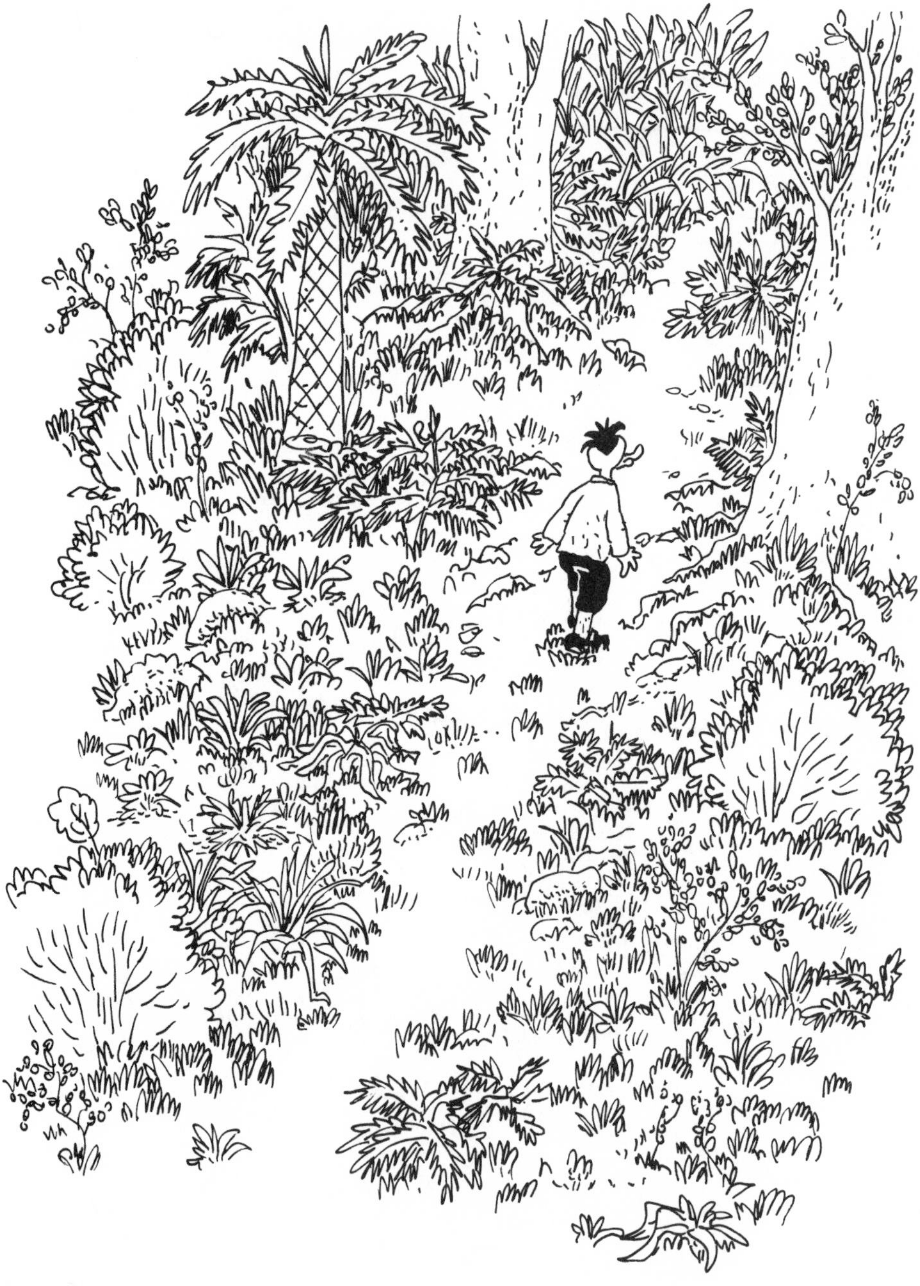

FÉNOIR

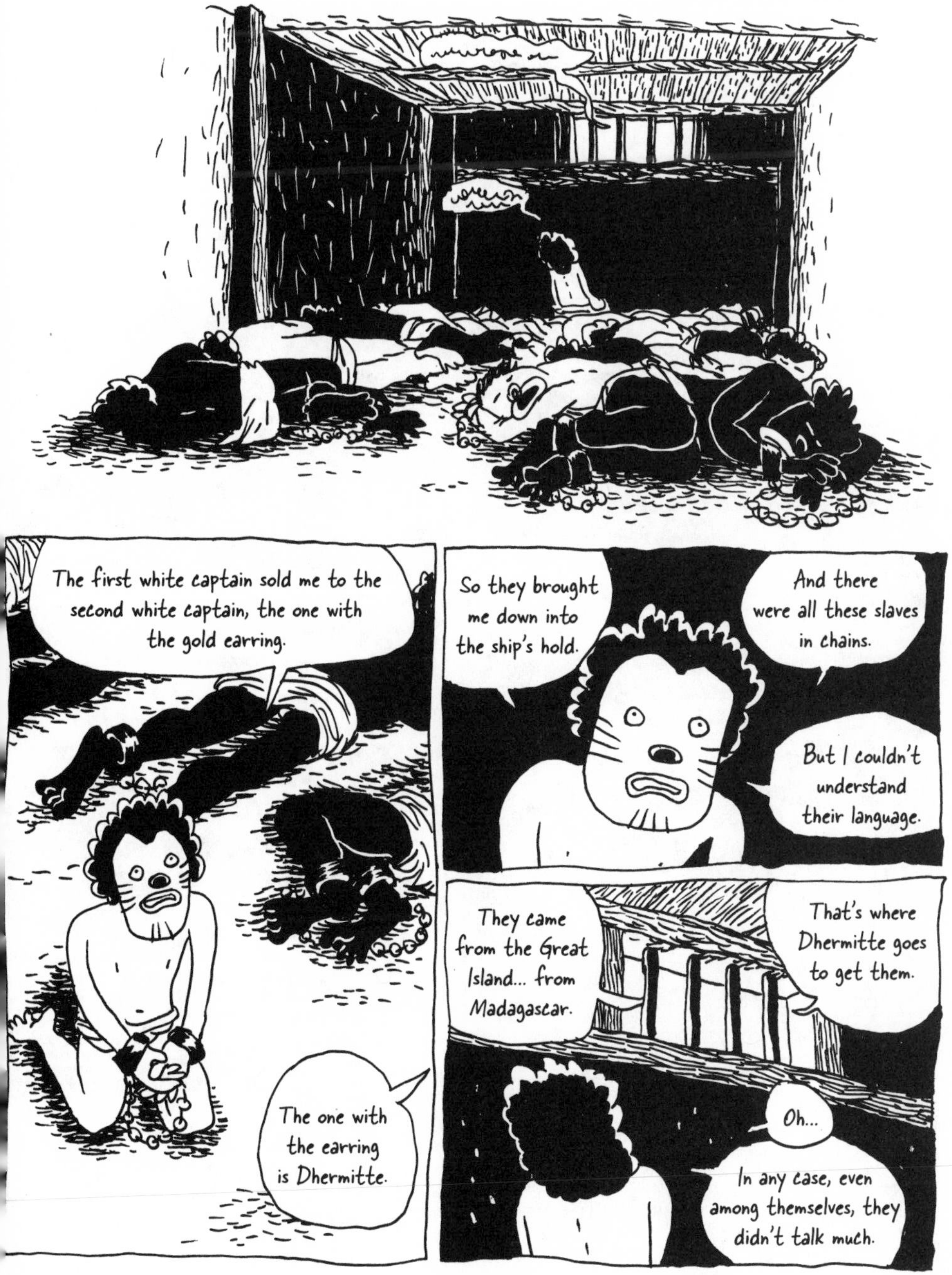

The first white captain sold me to the second white captain, the one with the gold earring.
The one with the earring is Dhermitte.
So they brought me down into the ship's hold.
And there were all these slaves in chains.
But I couldn't understand their language.
They came from the Great Island... from Madagascar.
That's where Dhermitte goes to get them.
Oh...
In any case, even among themselves, they didn't talk much.

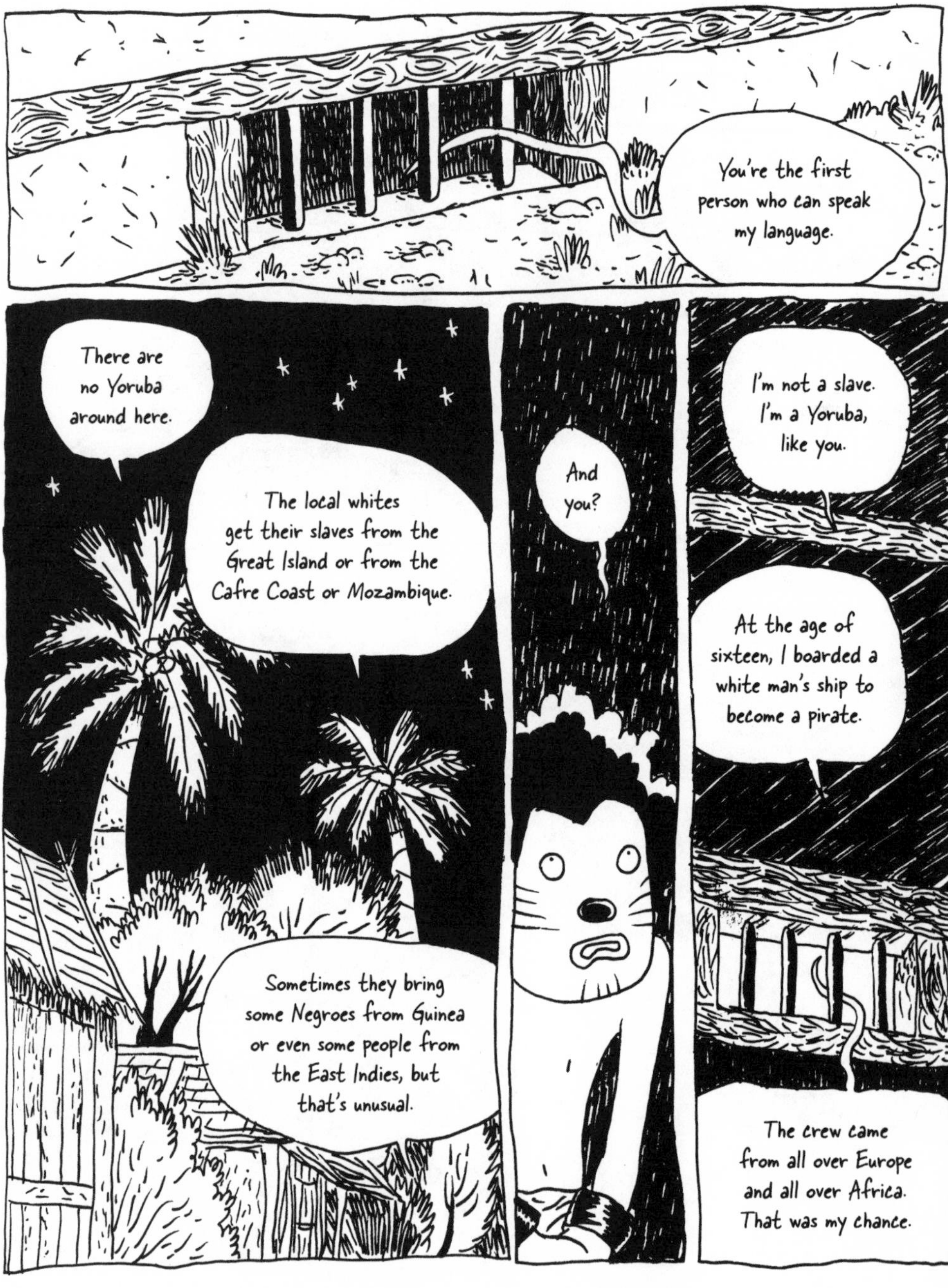
You're the first person who can speak my language.
There are no Yoruba around here.
The local whites get their slaves from the Great Island or from the Cafre Coast or Mozambique.
Sometimes they bring some Negroes from Guinea or even some people from the East Indies, but that's unusual.
And you?
I'm not a slave. I'm a Yoruba, like you.
At the age of sixteen, I boarded a white man's ship to become a pirate.
The crew came from all over Europe and all over Africa. That was my chance.

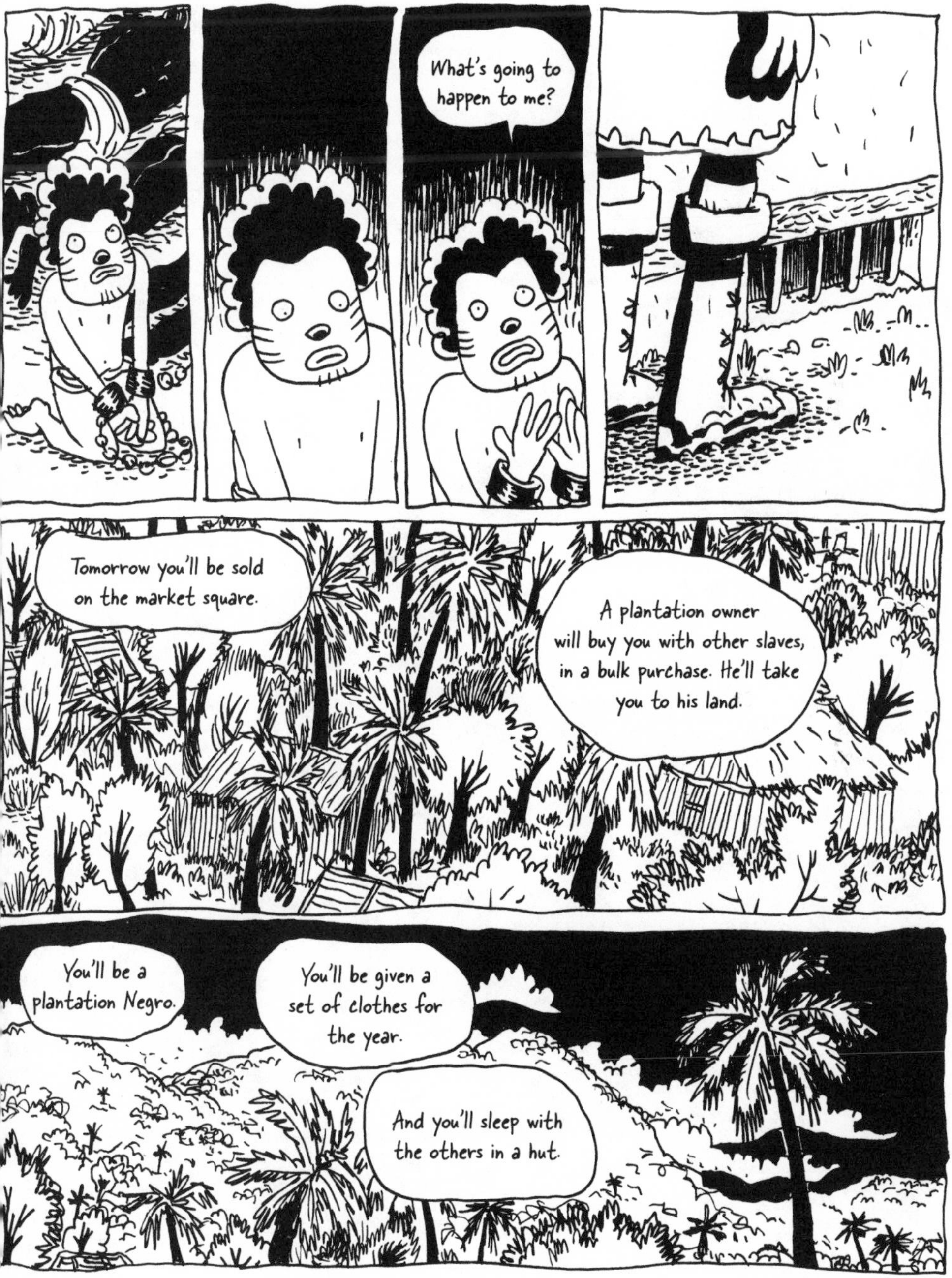
What's going to happen to me?
Tomorrow you'll be sold on the market square.
A plantation owner will buy you with other slaves, in a bulk purchase. He'll take you to his land.
You'll be a plantation Negro.
You'll be given a set of clothes for the year.
And you'll sleep with the others in a hut.

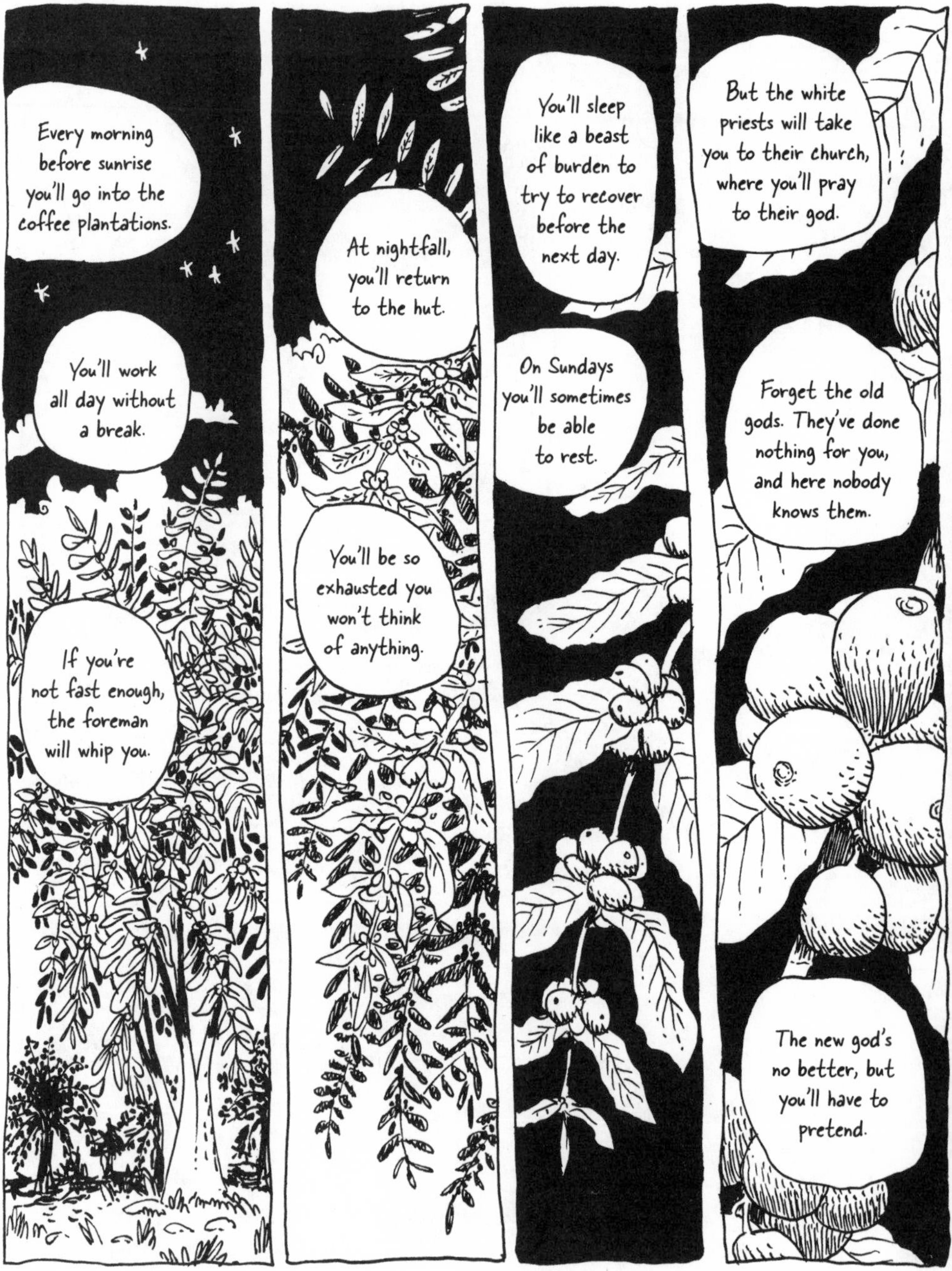
Every morning before sunrise you'll go into the coffee plantations.
You'll work all day without a break.
If you're not fast enough, the foreman will whip you.
At nightfall, you'll return to the hut.
You'll be so exhausted you won't think of anything.
You'll sleep like a beast of burden to try to recover before the next day.
On Sundays you'll sometimes be able to rest.
But the white priests will take you to their church, where you'll pray to their god.
Forget the old gods. They've done nothing for you, and here nobody knows them.
The new god's no better, but you'll have to pretend.

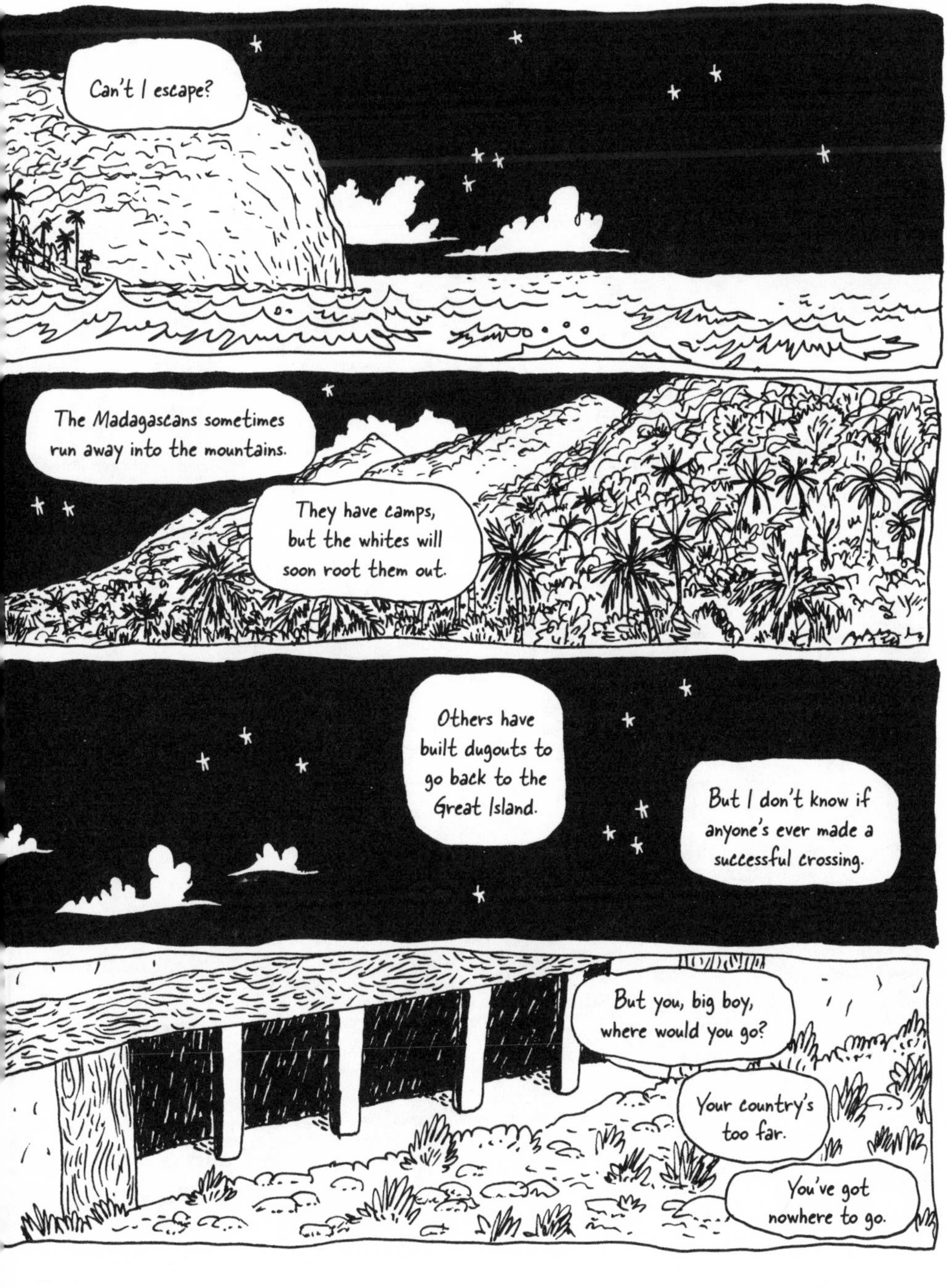
Can't I escape?
The Madagascans sometimes run away into the mountains.
They have camps, but the whites will soon root them out.
Others have built dugouts to go back to the Great Island.
But I don't know if anyone's ever made a successful crossing.
But you, big boy, where would you go?
Your country's too far.
You've got nowhere to go.

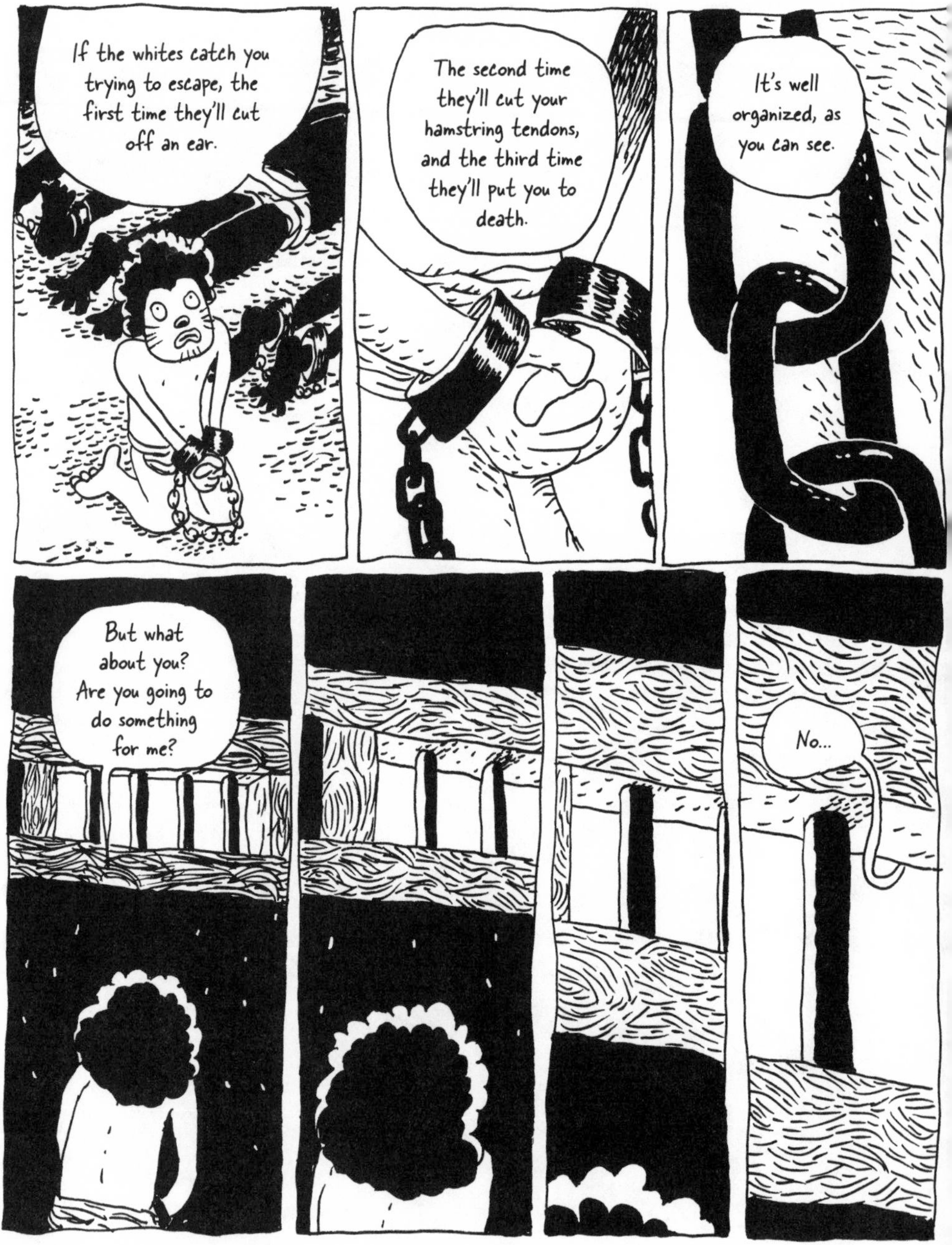
If the whites catch you trying to escape, the first time they'll cut off an ear.
The second time they'll cut your hamstring tendons, and the third time they'll put you to death.
It's well organized, as you can see.
But what about you? Are you going to do something for me?
No...

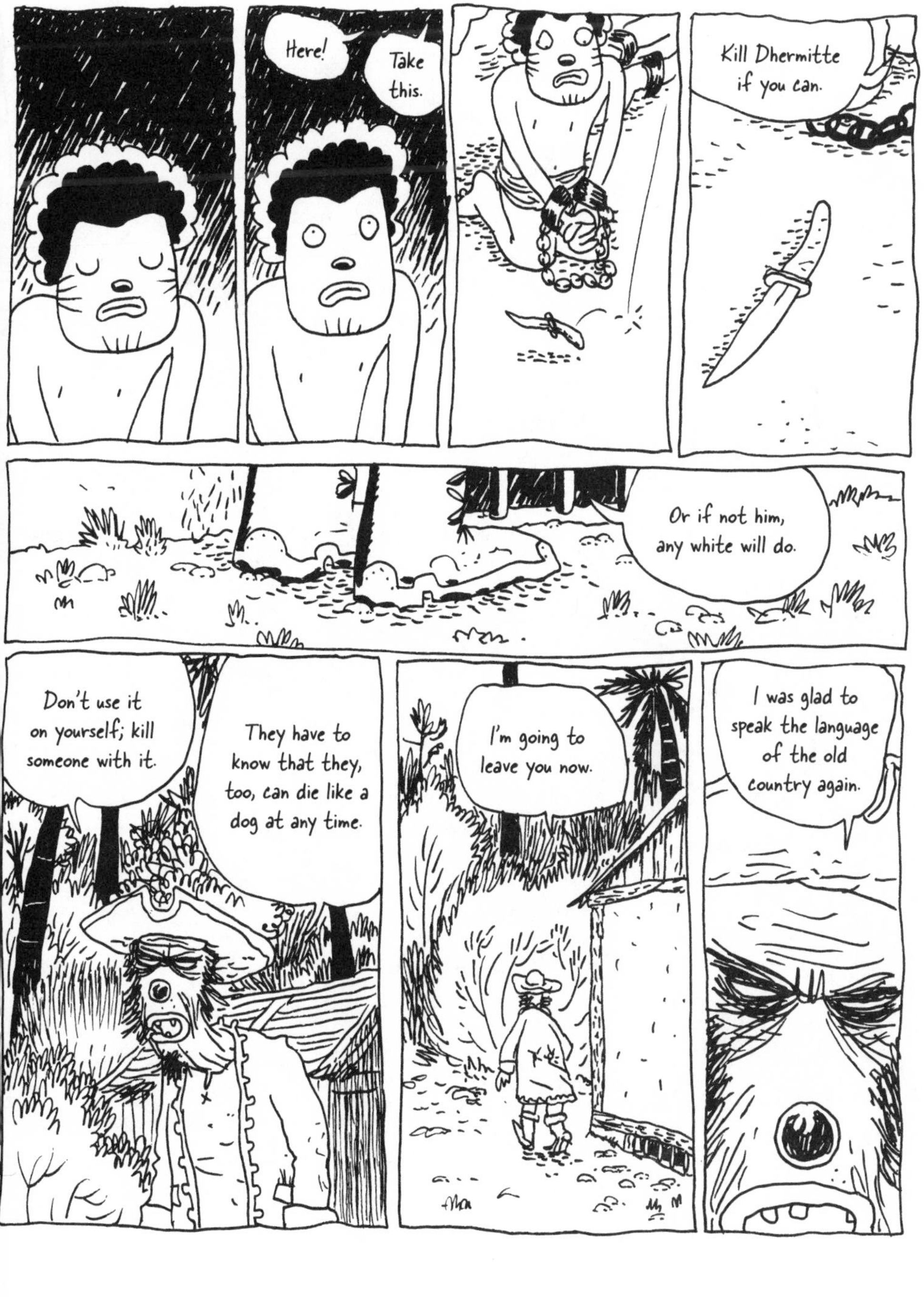
Here!
Take this.
Kill Dhermitte if you can.
Or if not him, any white will do.
Don't use it on yourself; kill someone with it.
They have to know that they, too, can die like a dog at any time.
I'm going to leave you now.
I was glad to speak the language of the old country again.

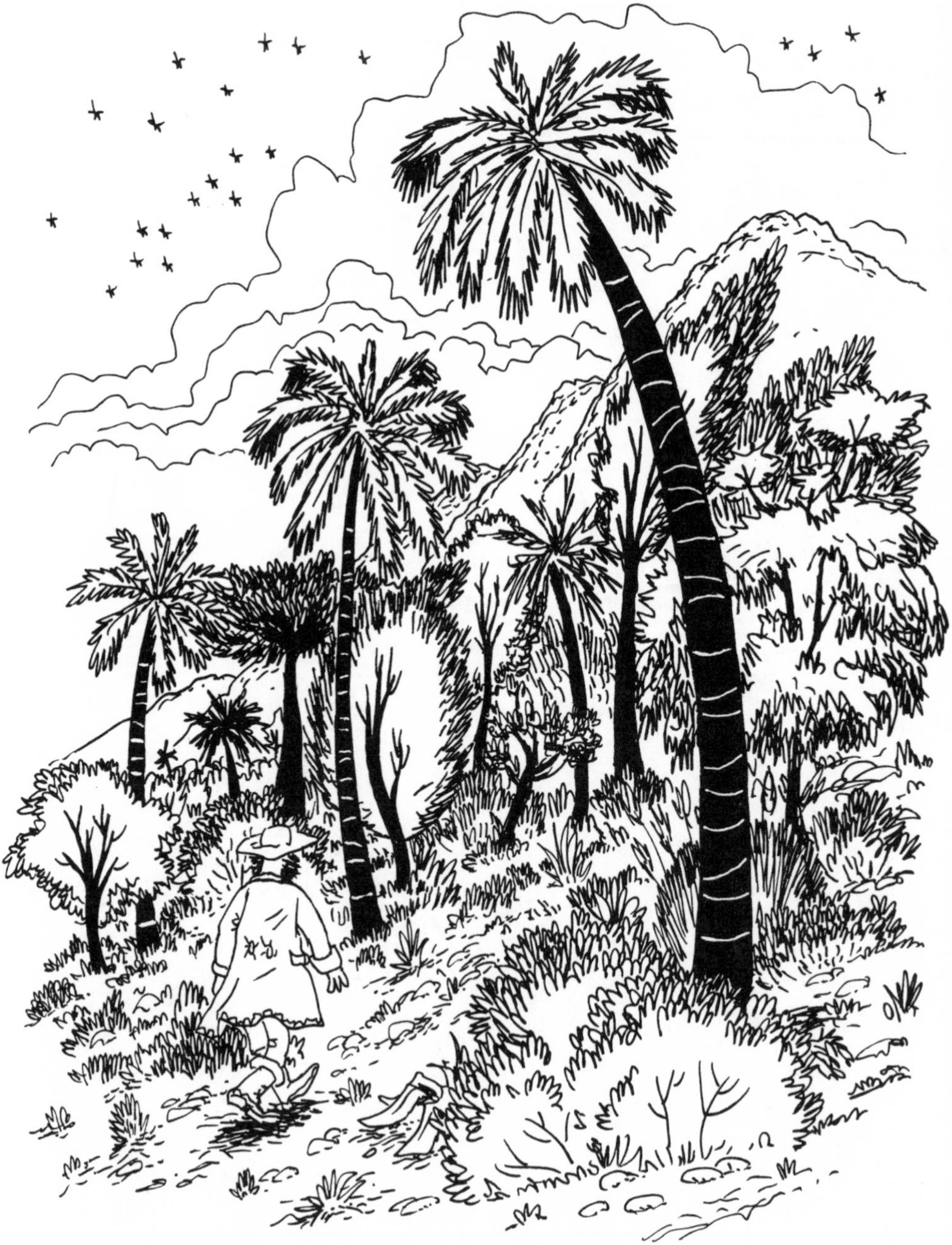

THE YOUNG LADY

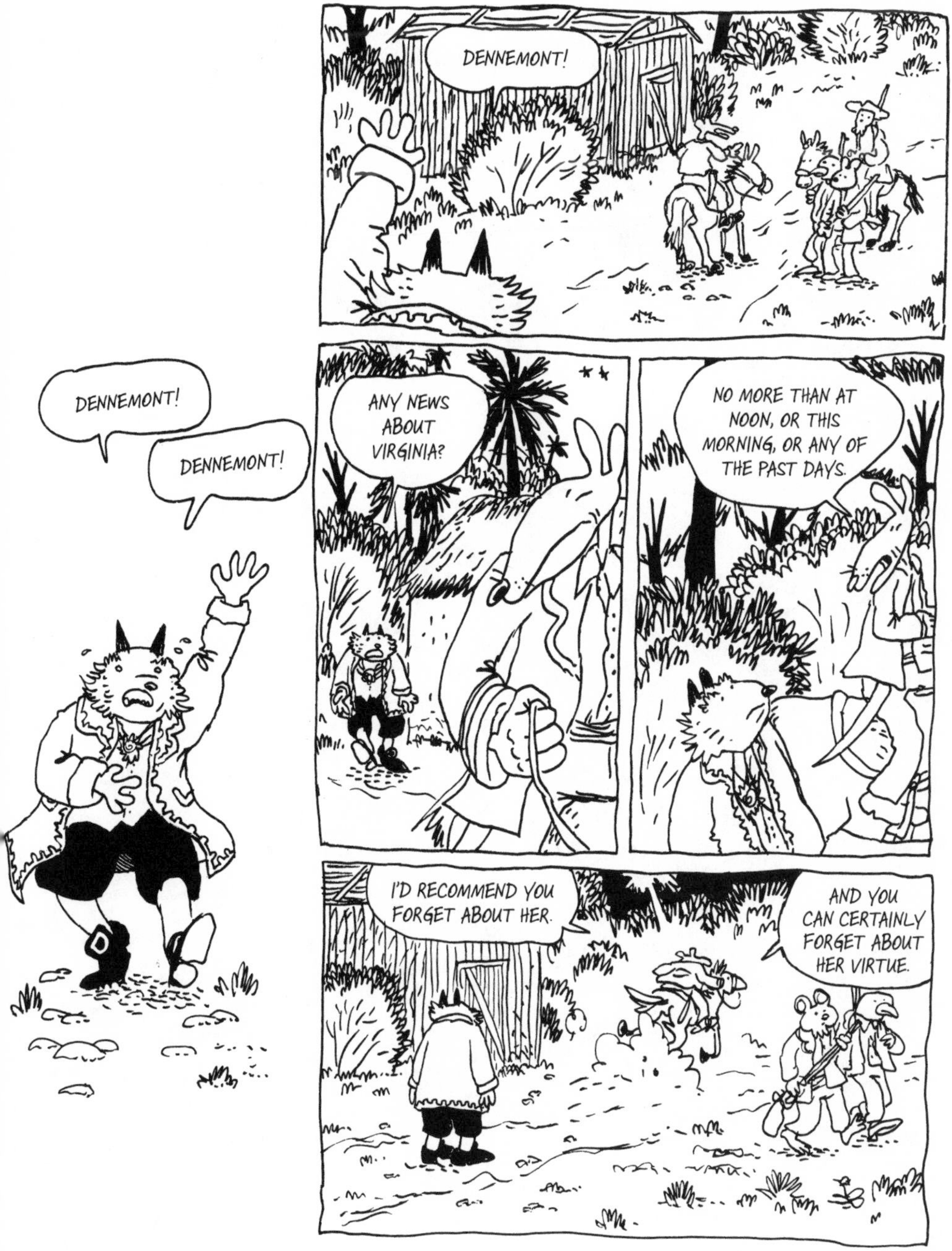

DENNEMONT!
DENNEMONT!
DENNEMONT!
ANY NEWS ABOUT VIRGINIA?
NO MORE THAN AT NOON, OR THIS MORNING, OR ANY OF THE PAST DAYS.
I'D RECOMMEND YOU FORGET ABOUT HER.
AND YOU CAN CERTAINLY FORGET ABOUT HER VIRTUE.

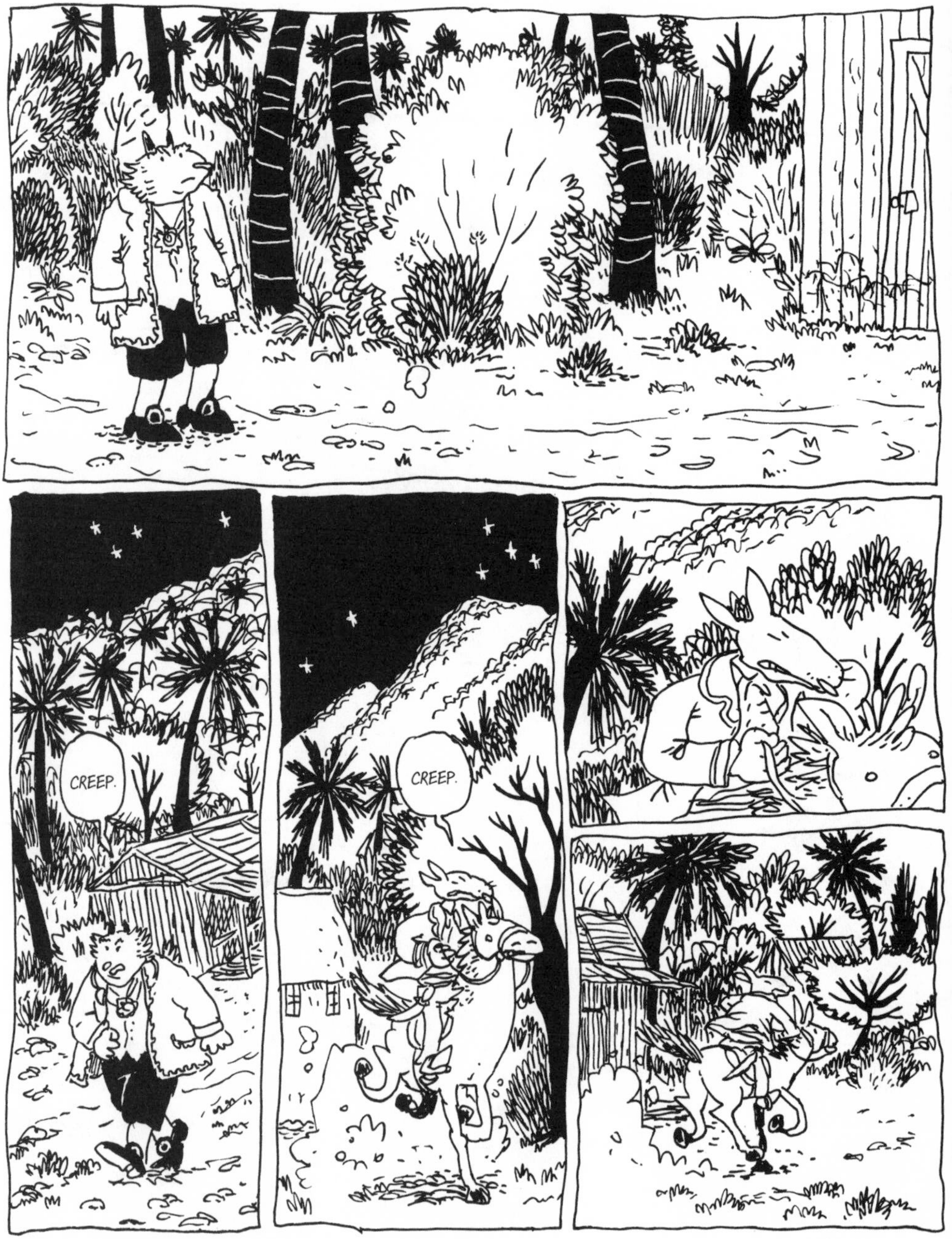
CREEP.
CREEP.

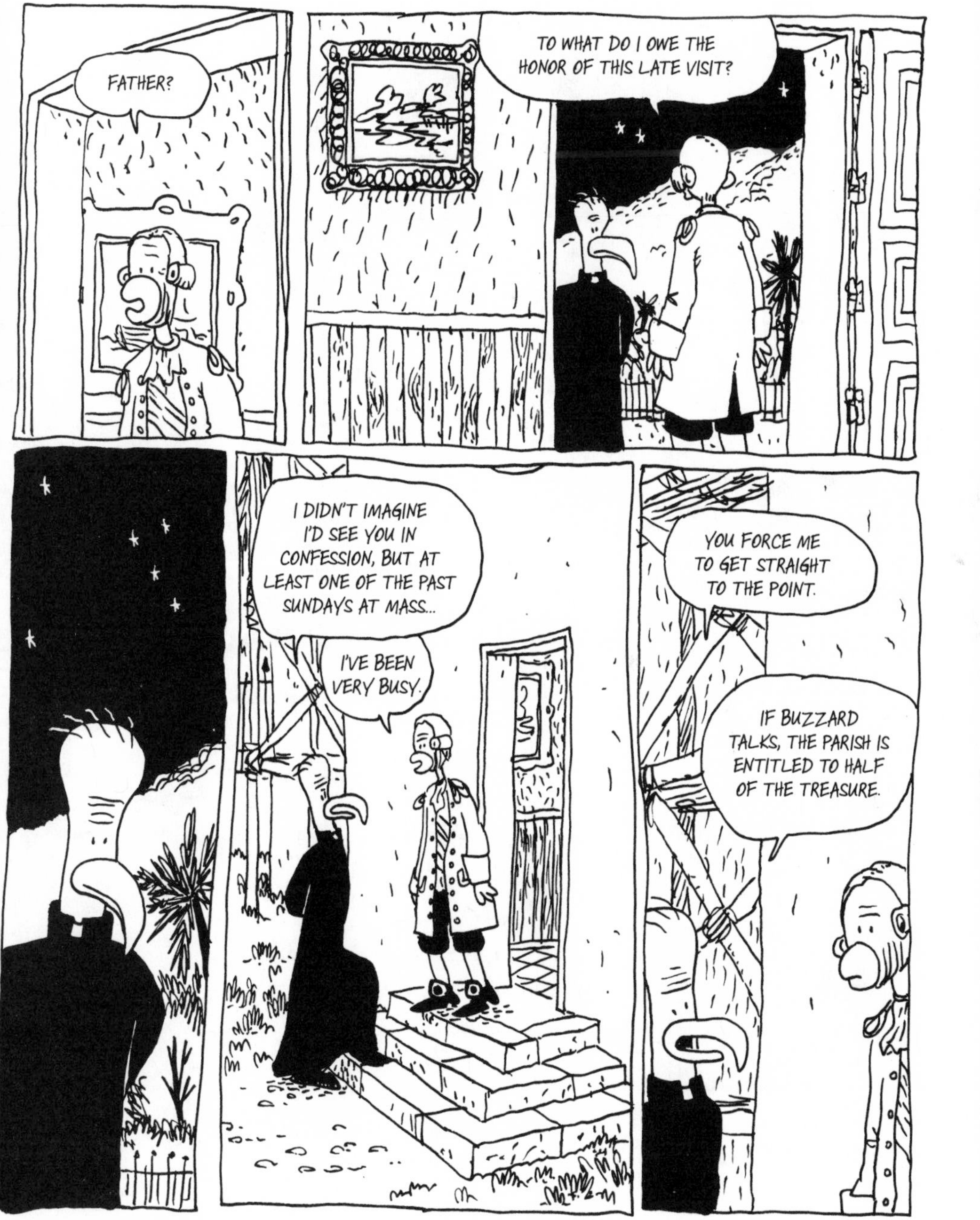
FATHER?
TO WHAT DO I OWE THE HONOR OF THIS LATE VISIT?
I DIDN'T IMAGINE I'D SEE YOU IN CONFESSION, BUT AT LEAST ONE OF THE PAST SUNDAYS AT MASS...
I'VE BEEN VERY BUSY.
YOU FORCE ME TO GET STRAIGHT TO THE POINT.
IF BUZZARD TALKS, THE PARISH IS ENTITLED TO HALF OF THE TREASURE.

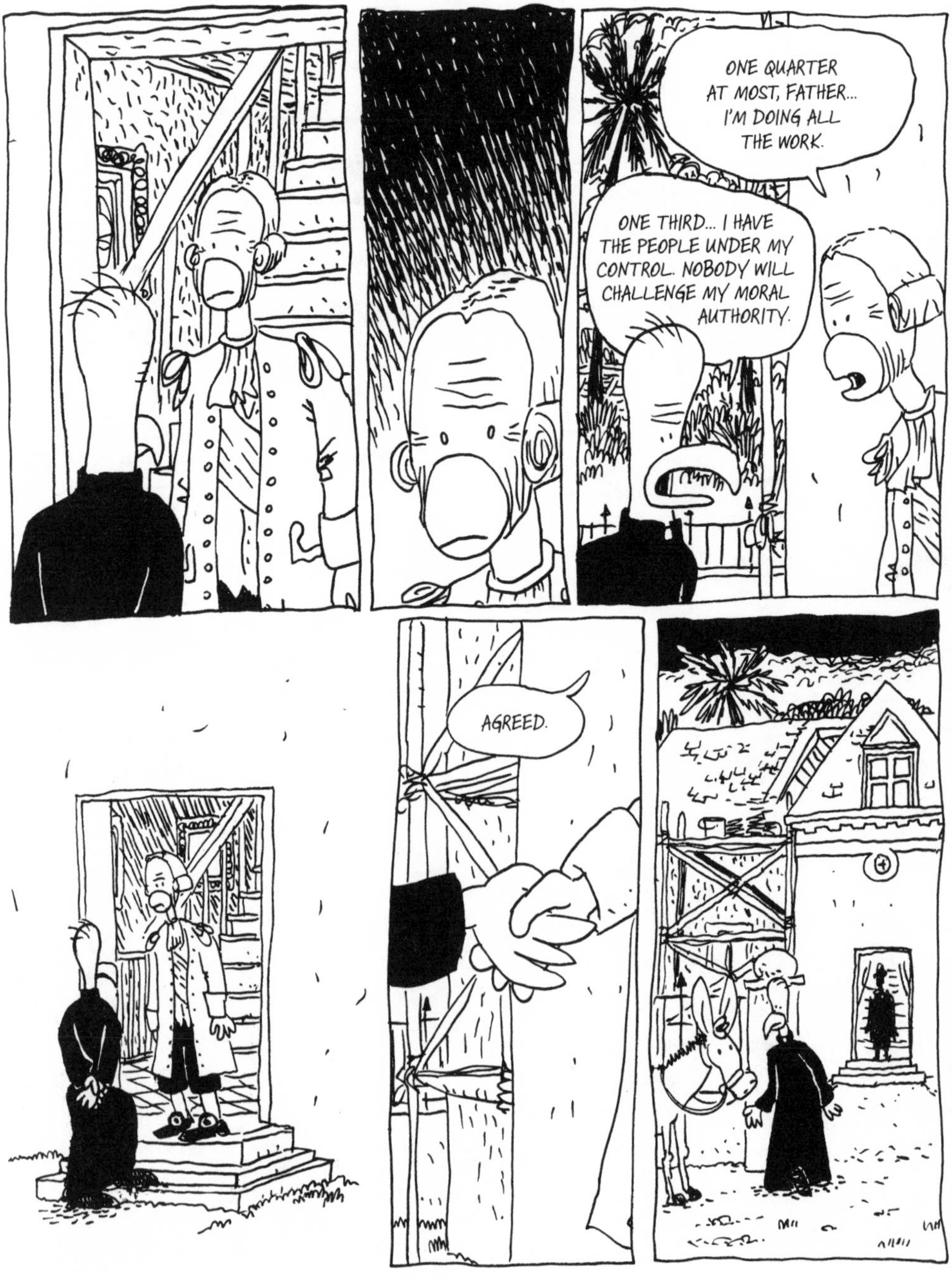
ONE QUARTER AT MOST, FATHER... I'M DOING ALL THE WORK.
ONE THIRD... I HAVE THE PEOPLE UNDER MY CONTROL. NOBODY WILL CHALLENGE MY MORAL AUTHORITY.
AGREED.

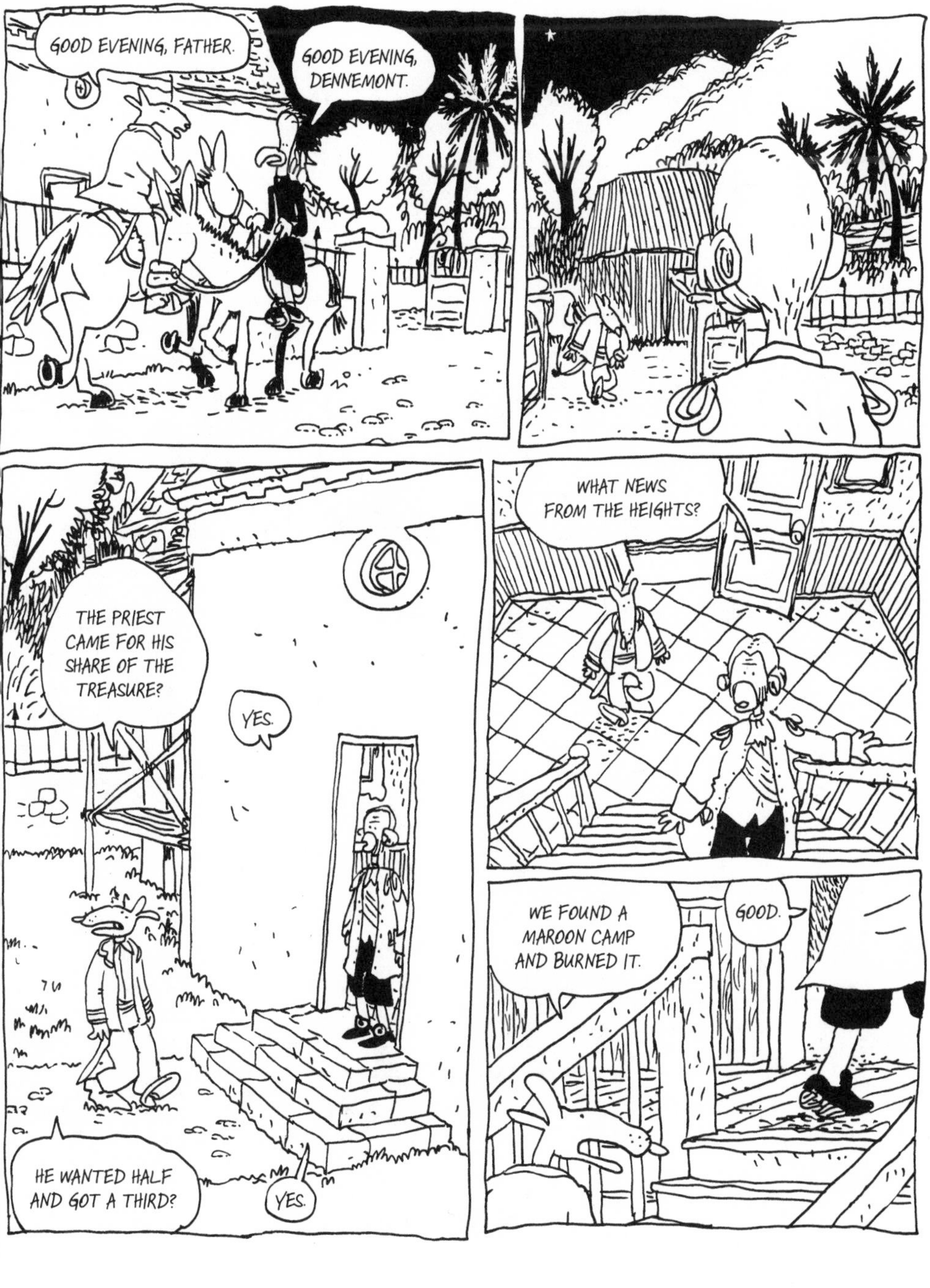
GOOD EVENING, FATHER.
GOOD EVENING, DENNEMONT.
THE PRIEST CAME FOR HIS SHARE OF THE TREASURE?
YES.
HE WANTED HALF AND GOT A THIRD?
YES.
WHAT NEWS FROM THE HEIGHTS?
WE FOUND A MAROON CAMP AND BURNED IT.
GOOD.

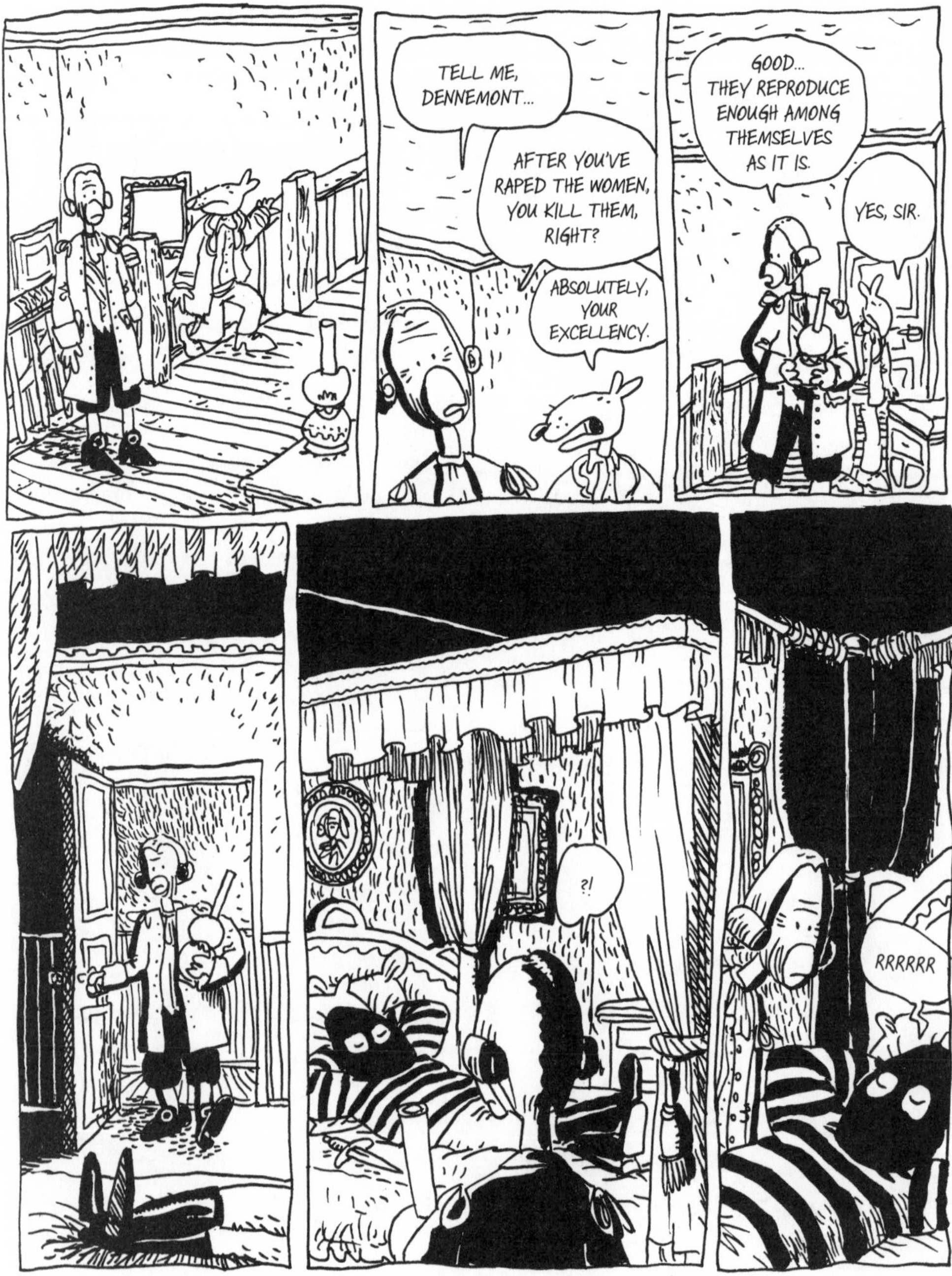
TELL ME, DENNEMONT...
AFTER YOU'VE RAPED THE WOMEN, YOU KILL THEM, RIGHT?
ABSOLUTELY, YOUR EXCELLENCY.
GOOD... THEY REPRODUCE ENOUGH AMONG THEMSELVES AS IT IS.
YES, SIR.
?!
RRRRRR

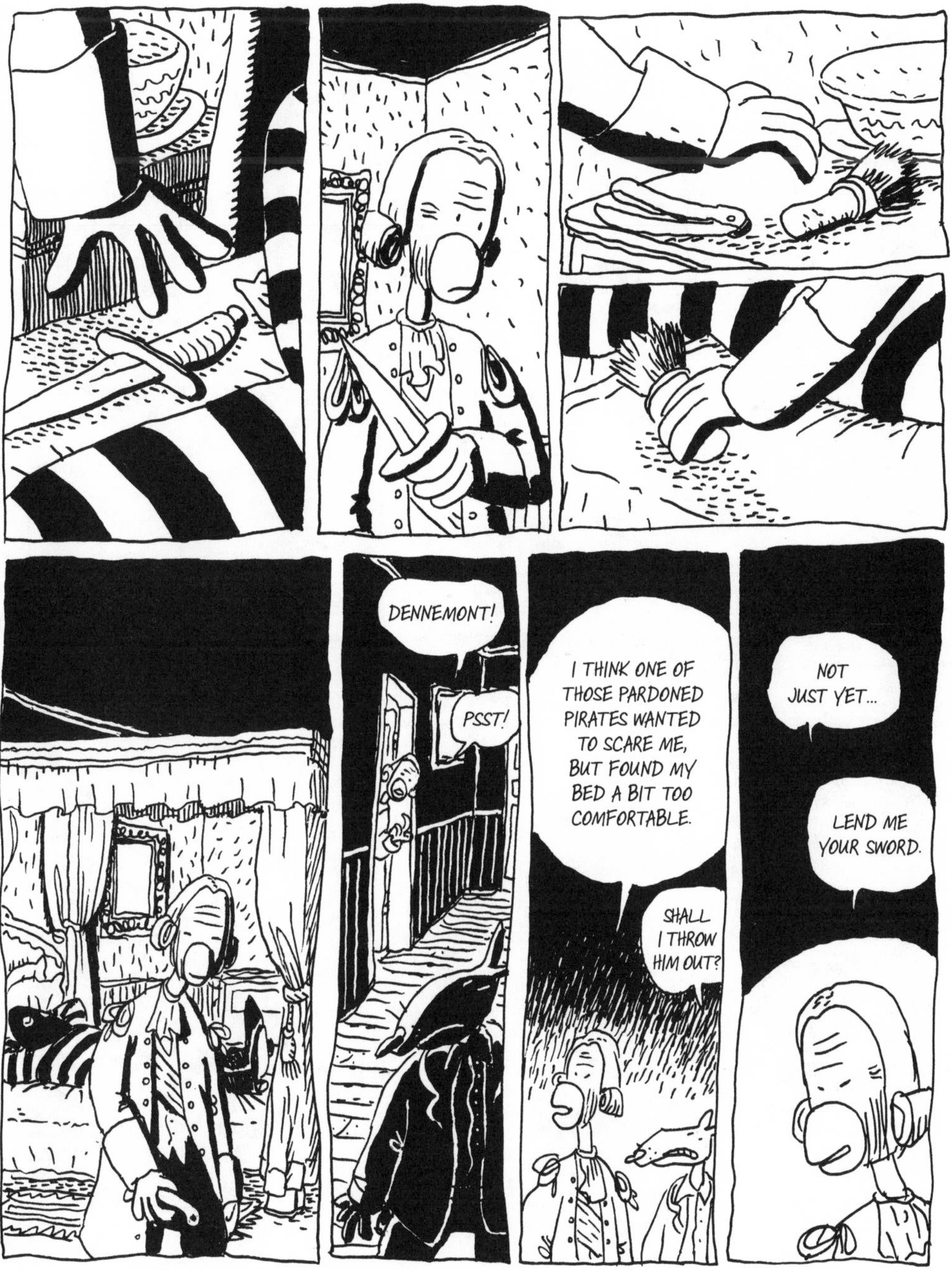
DENNEMONT!
PSST!
I THINK ONE OF THOSE PARDONED PIRATES WANTED TO SCARE ME, BUT FOUND MY BED A BIT TOO COMFORTABLE.
SHALL I THROW HIM OUT?
NOT JUST YET...
LEND ME YOUR SWORD.

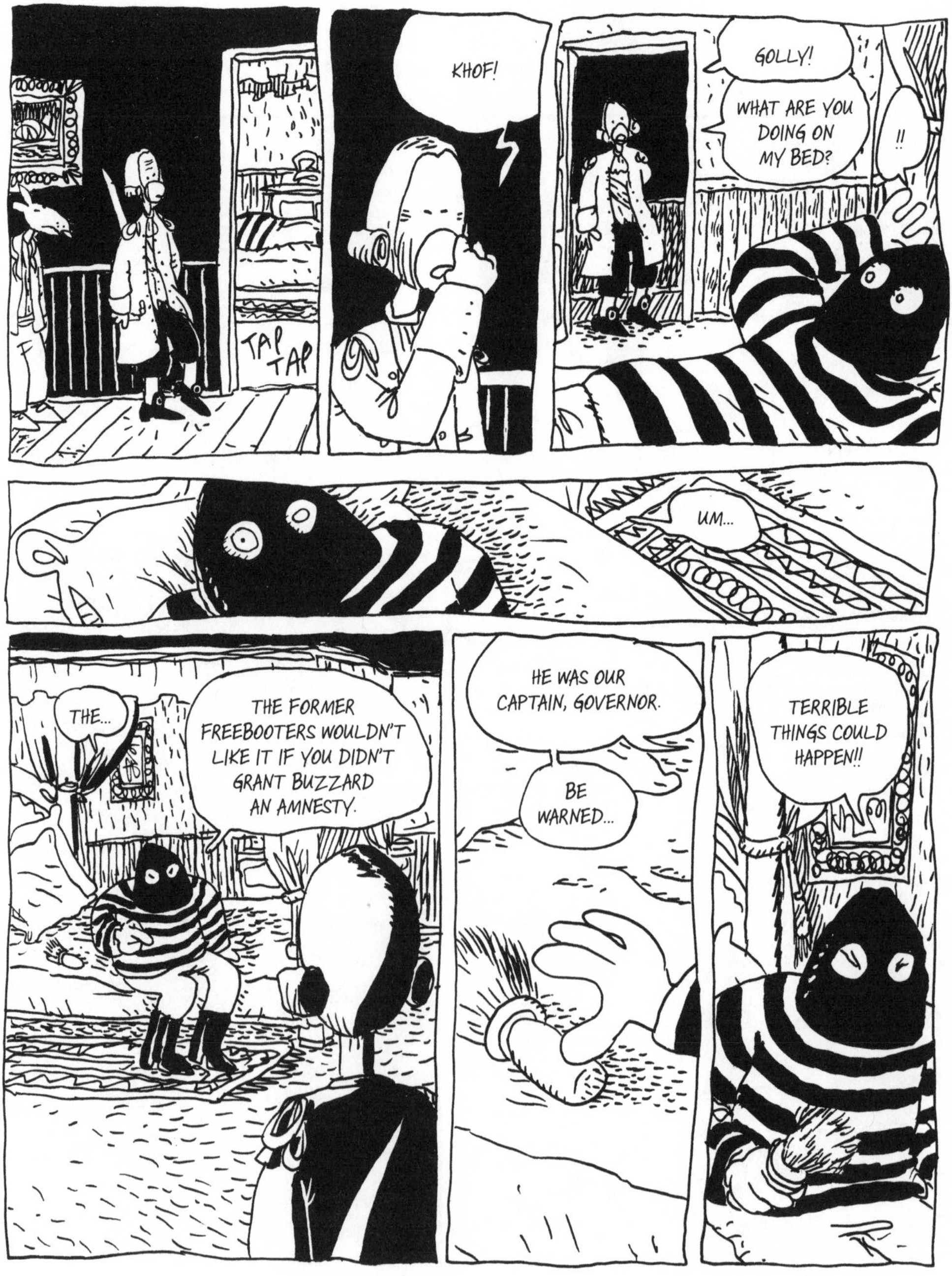
TAP TAP
KHOF!
GOLLY!
WHAT ARE YOU DOING ON MY BED?
!!
UM...
THE...
THE FORMER FREEBOOTERS WOULDN'T LIKE IT IF YOU DIDN'T GRANT BUZZARD AN AMNESTY.
HE WAS OUR CAPTAIN, GOVERNOR.
BE WARNED...
TERRIBLE THINGS COULD HAPPEN!!

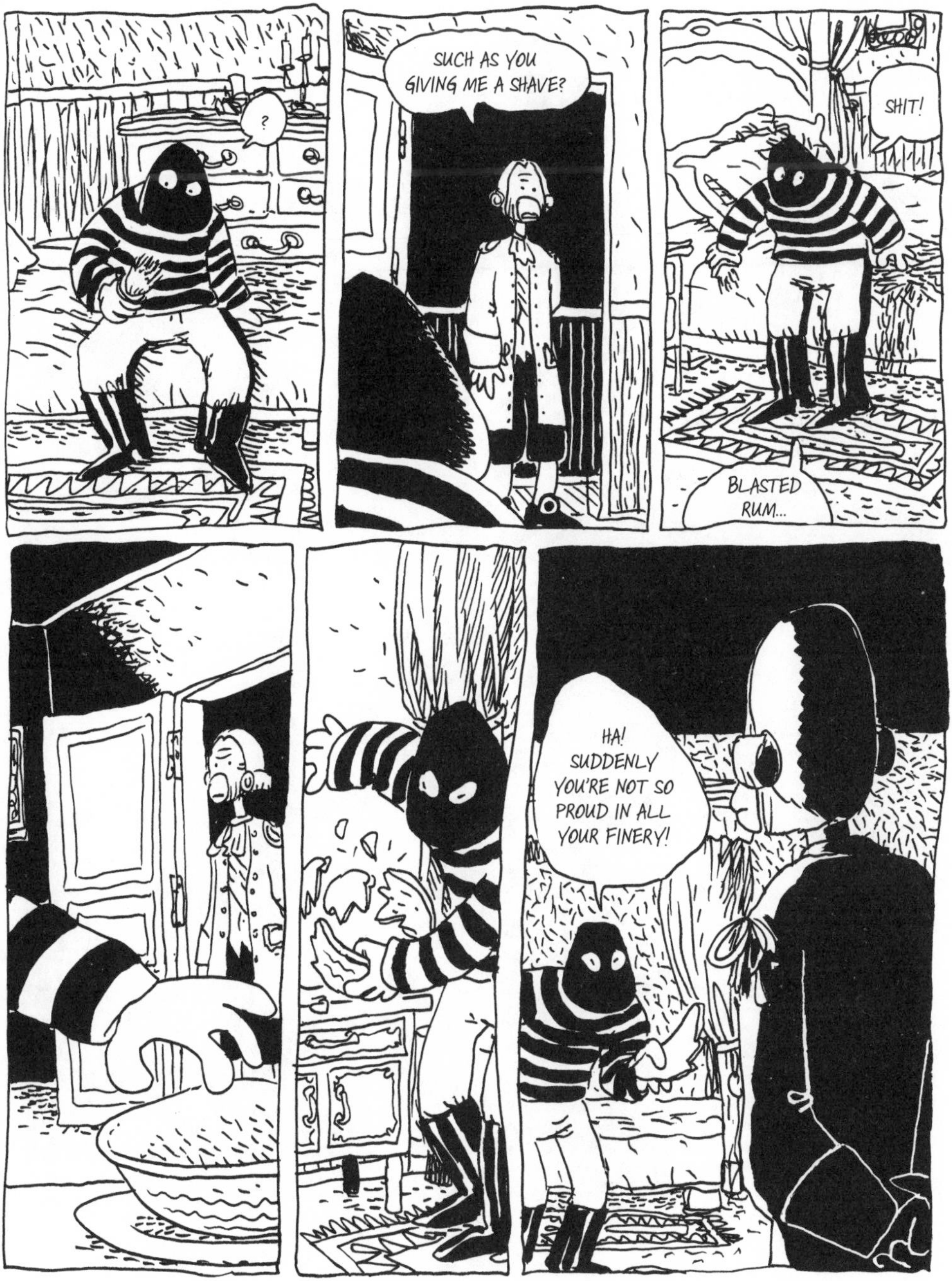
?
SUCH AS YOU GIVING ME A SHAVE?
SHIT!
BLASTED RUM...
HA! SUDDENLY YOU'RE NOT SO PROUD IN ALL YOUR FINERY!

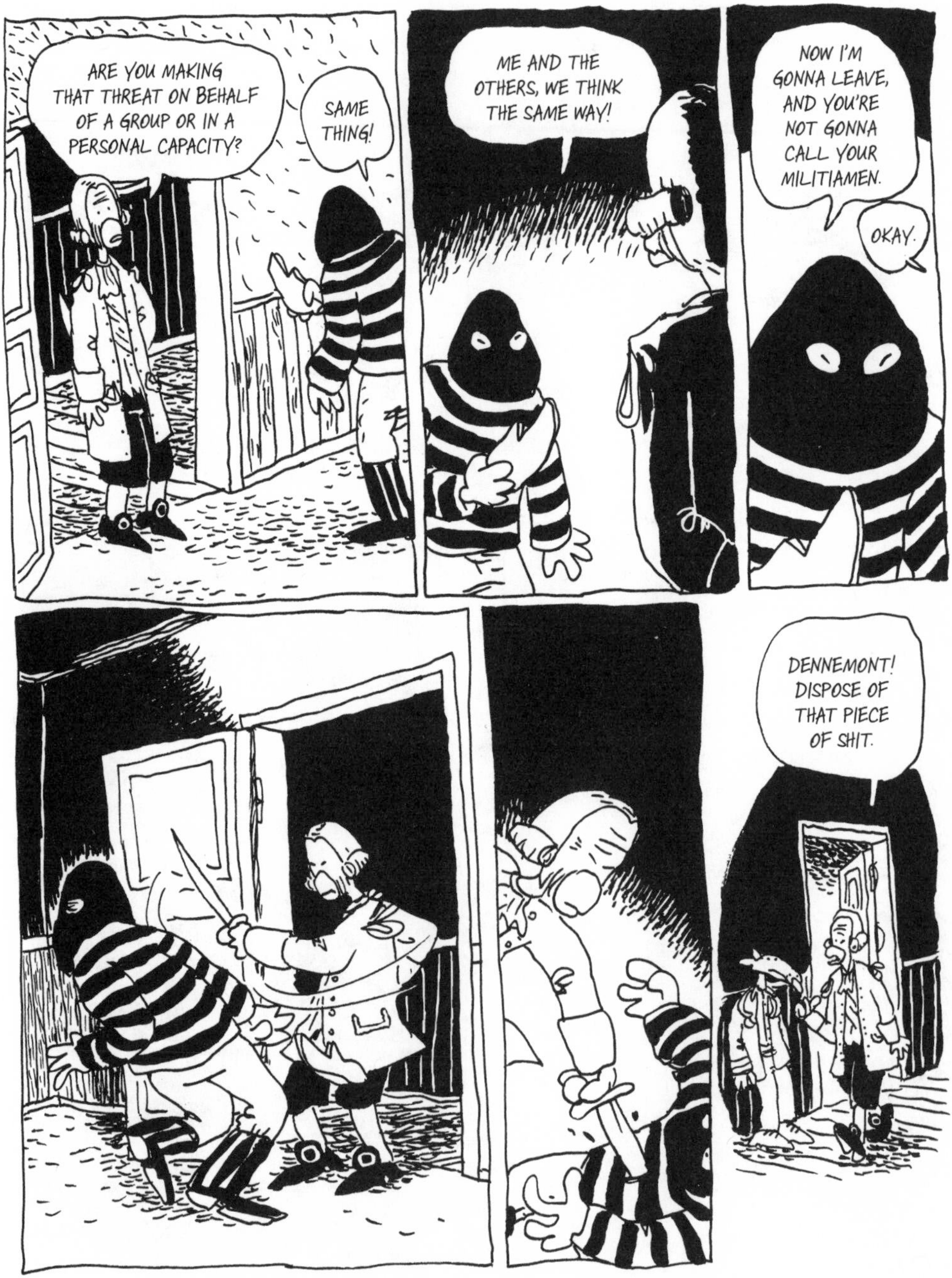
ARE YOU MAKING THAT THREAT ON BEHALF OF A GROUP OR IN A PERSONAL CAPACITY?
SAME THING!
ME AND THE OTHERS, WE THINK THE SAME WAY!
NOW I'M GONNA LEAVE, AND YOU'RE NOT GONNA CALL YOUR MILITIAMEN.
OKAY.
DENNEMONT! DISPOSE OF THAT PIECE OF SHIT.

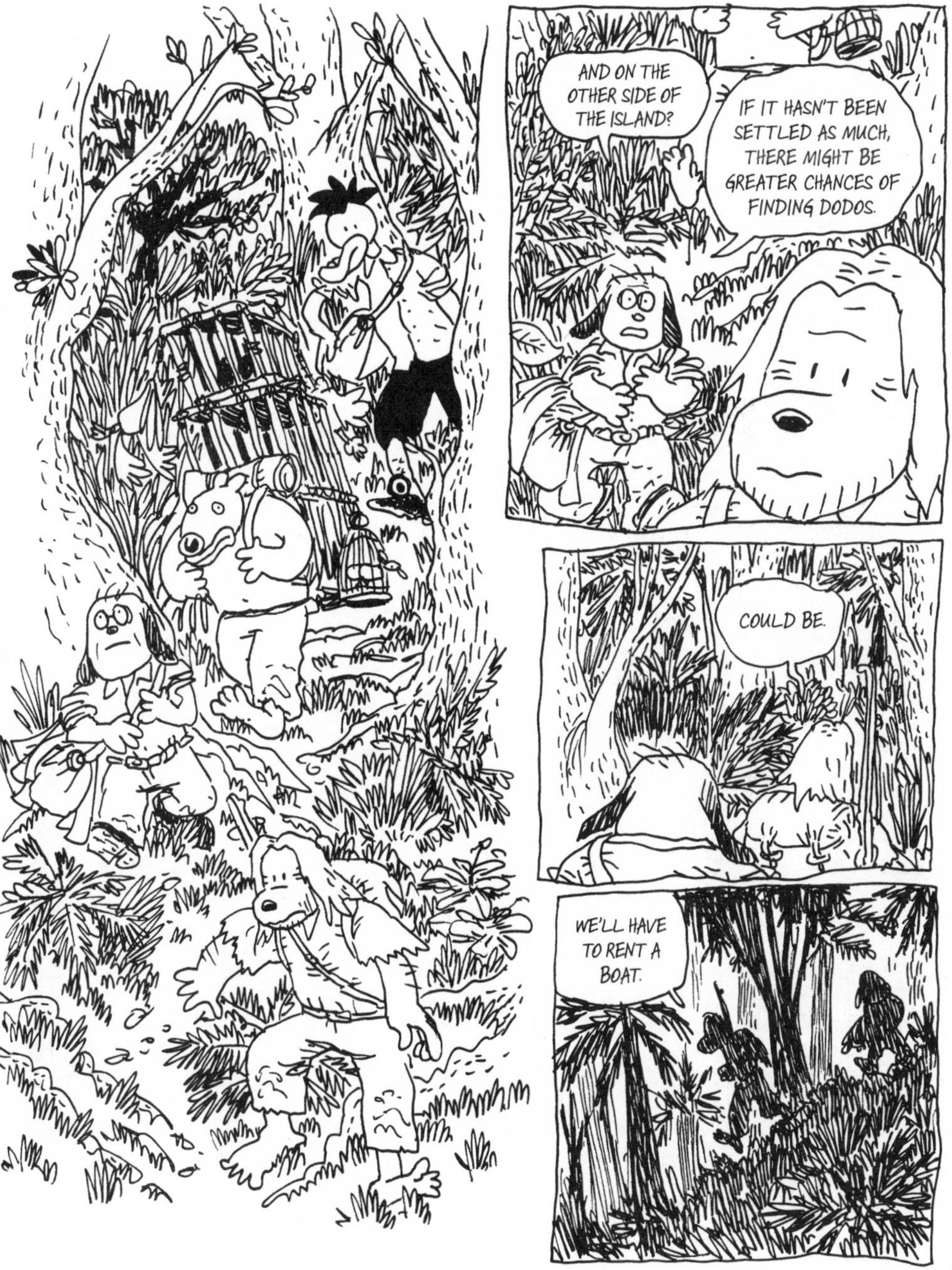
AND ON THE OTHER SIDE OF THE ISLAND?
IF IT HASN'T BEEN SETTLED AS MUCH, THERE MIGHT BE GREATER CHANCES OF FINDING DODOS.
COULD BE.
WE'LL HAVE TO RENT A BOAT.

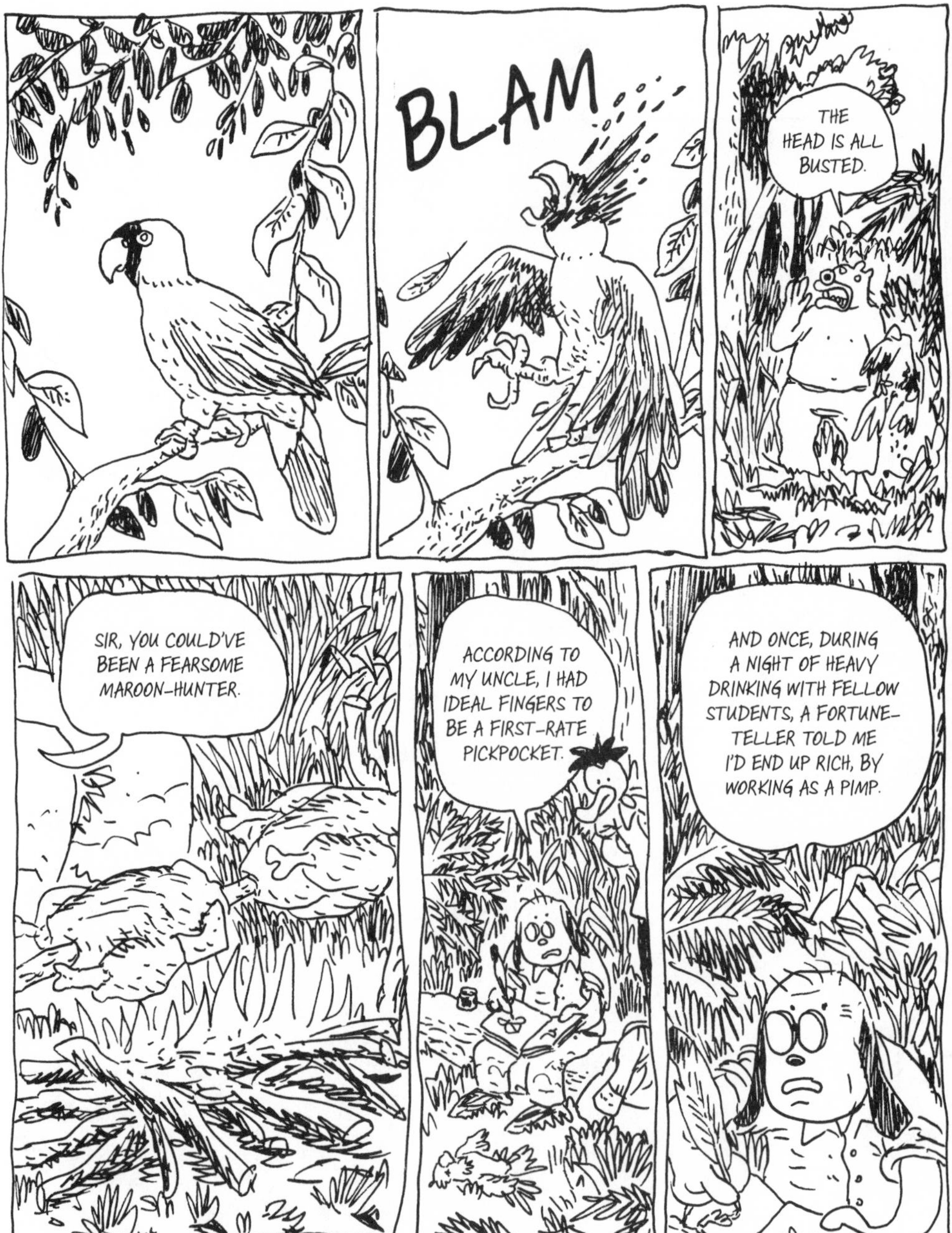
BLAM
THE HEAD IS ALL BUSTED.
SIR, YOU COULD'VE BEEN A FEARSOME MAROON-HUNTER.
ACCORDING TO MY UNCLE, I HAD IDEAL FINGERS TO BE A FIRST-RATE PICKPOCKET.
AND ONCE, DURING A NIGHT OF HEAVY DRINKING WITH FELLOW STUDENTS, A FORTUNE-TELLER TOLD ME I'D END UP RICH, BY WORKING AS A PIMP.

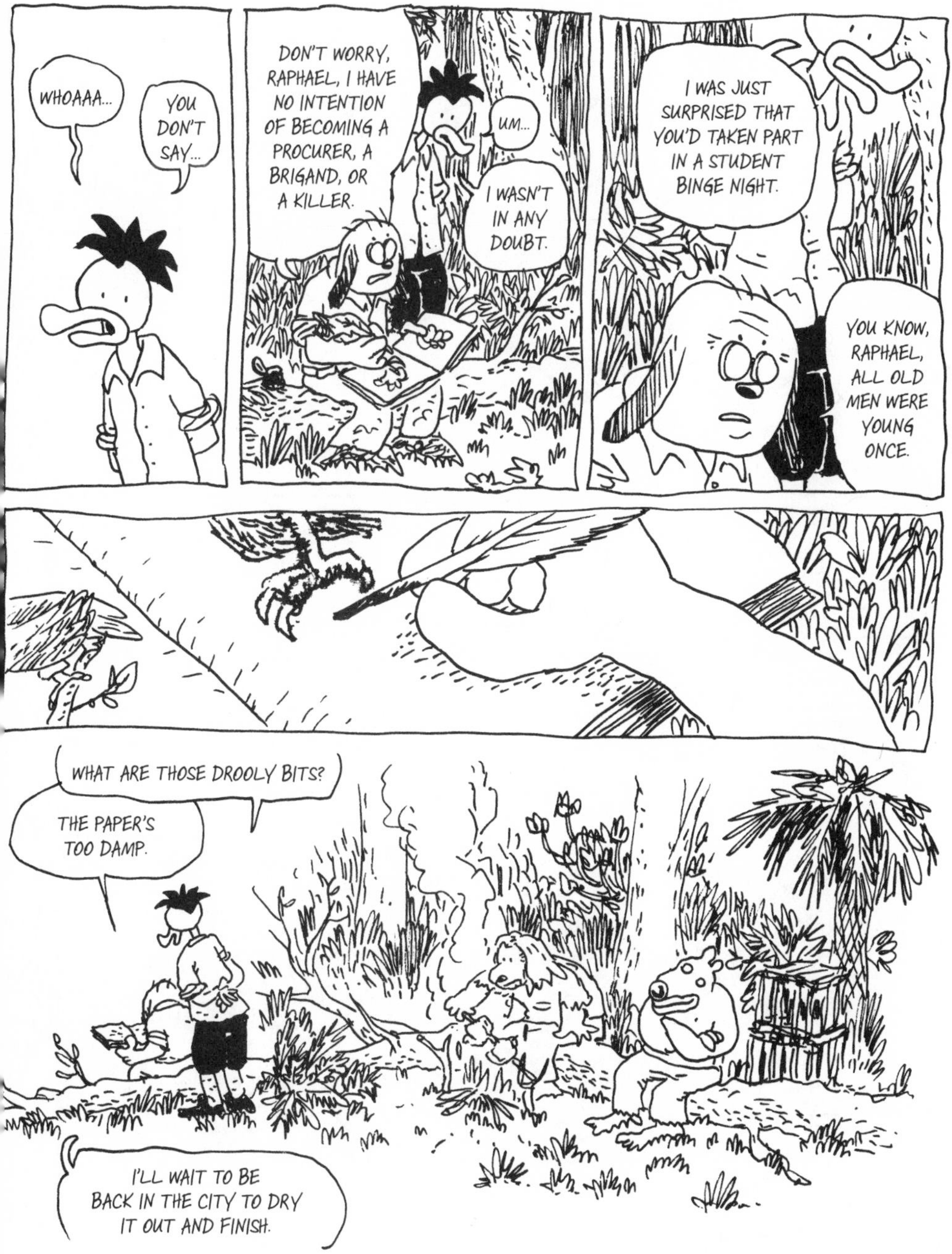
WHOAAA...
YOU DON'T SAY...
DON'T WORRY, RAPHAEL, I HAVE NO INTENTION OF BECOMING A PROCURER, A BRIGAND, OR A KILLER.
UM...
I WASN'T IN ANY DOUBT.
I WAS JUST SURPRISED THAT YOU'D TAKEN PART IN A STUDENT BINGE NIGHT.
YOU KNOW, RAPHAEL, ALL OLD MEN WERE YOUNG ONCE.
WHAT ARE THOSE DROOLY BITS?
THE PAPER'S TOO DAMP.
I'LL WAIT TO BE BACK IN THE CITY TO DRY IT OUT AND FINISH.

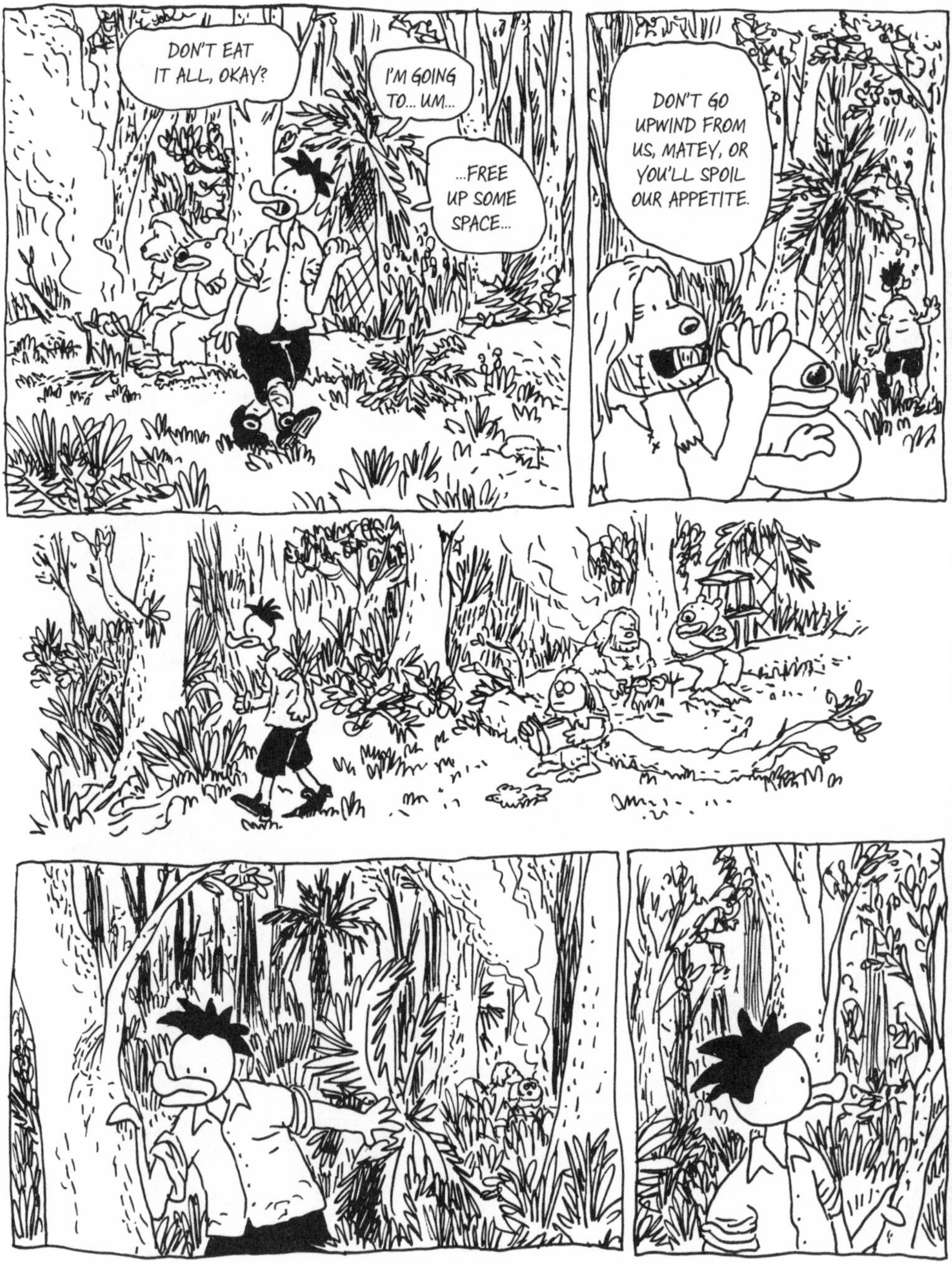
DON'T EAT IT ALL, OKAY?
I'M GOING TO... UM...
...FREE UP SOME SPACE...
DON'T GO UPWIND FROM US, MATEY, OR YOU'LL SPOIL OUR APPETITE.

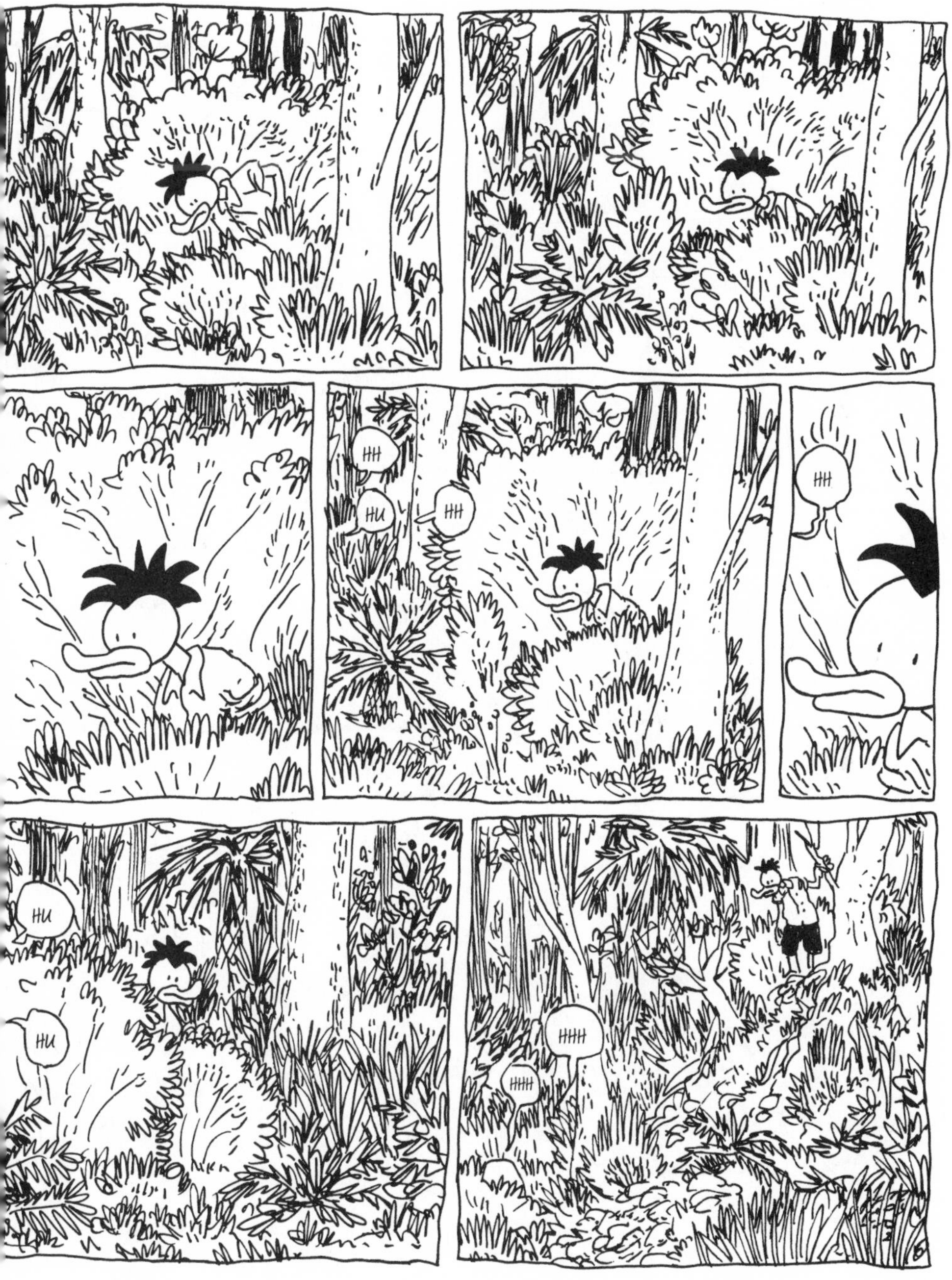
HH
HU
HH
HH
HU
HU
HHH
HHH

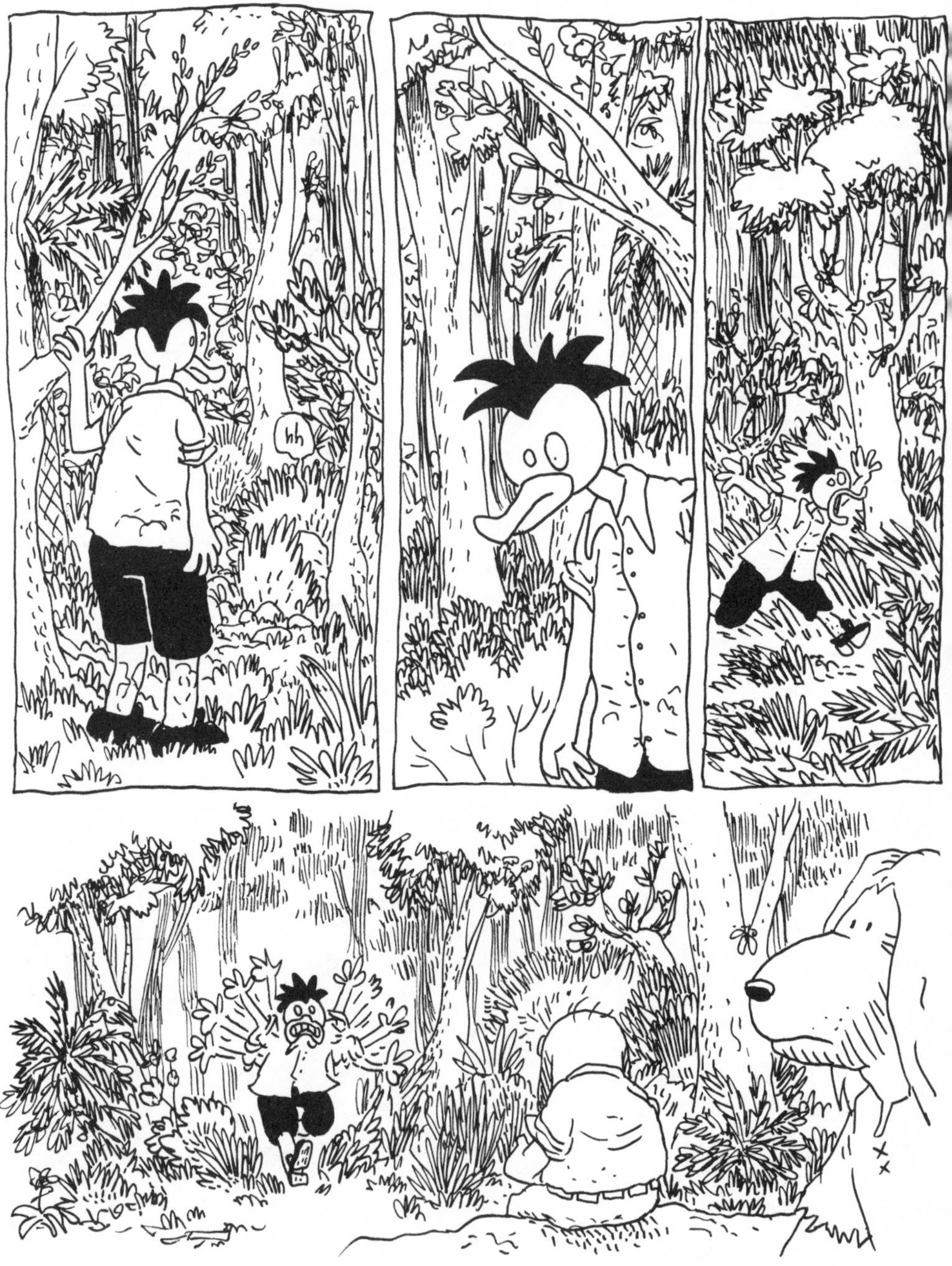
hh

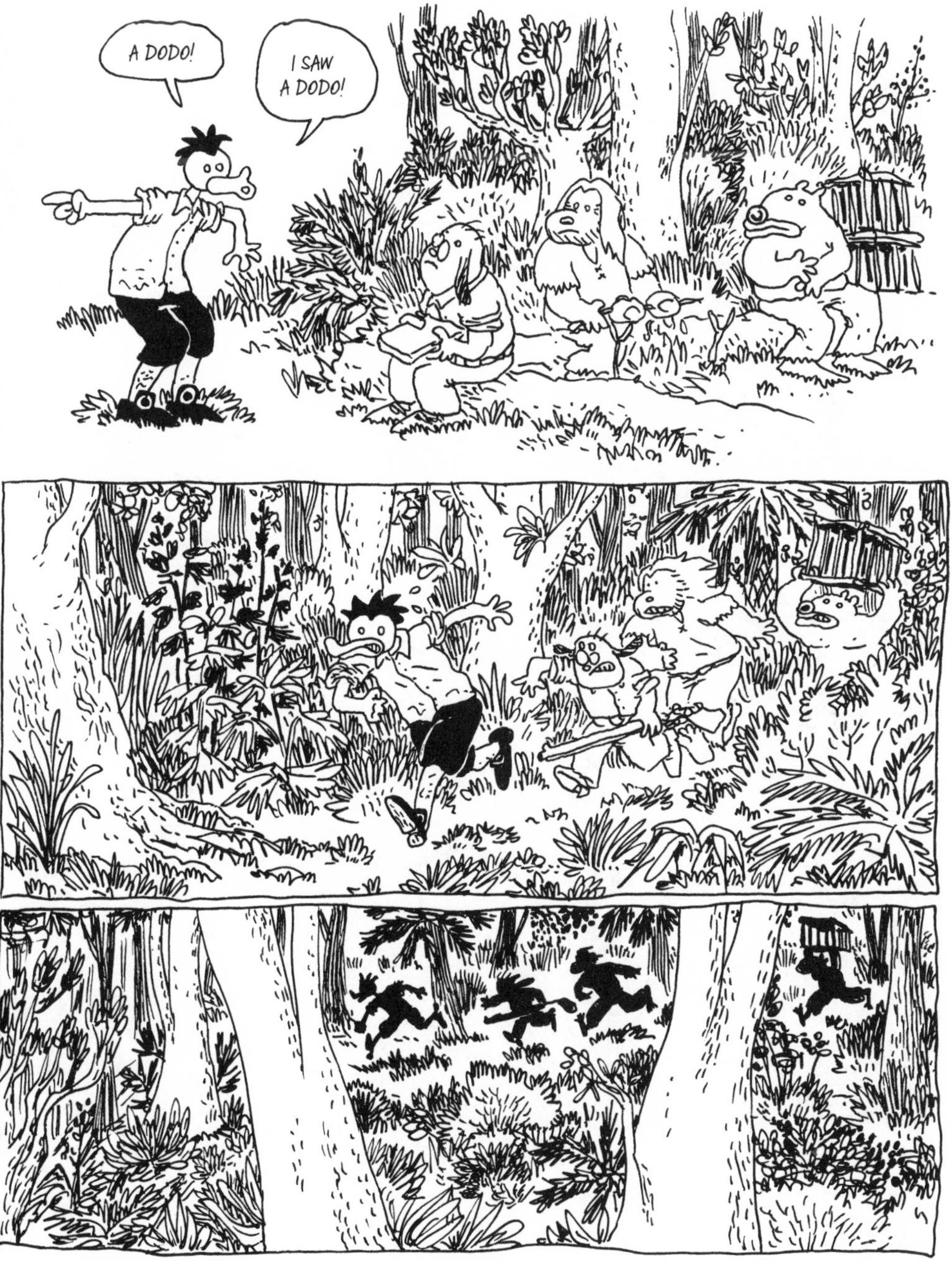
A DODO!
I SAW A DODO!

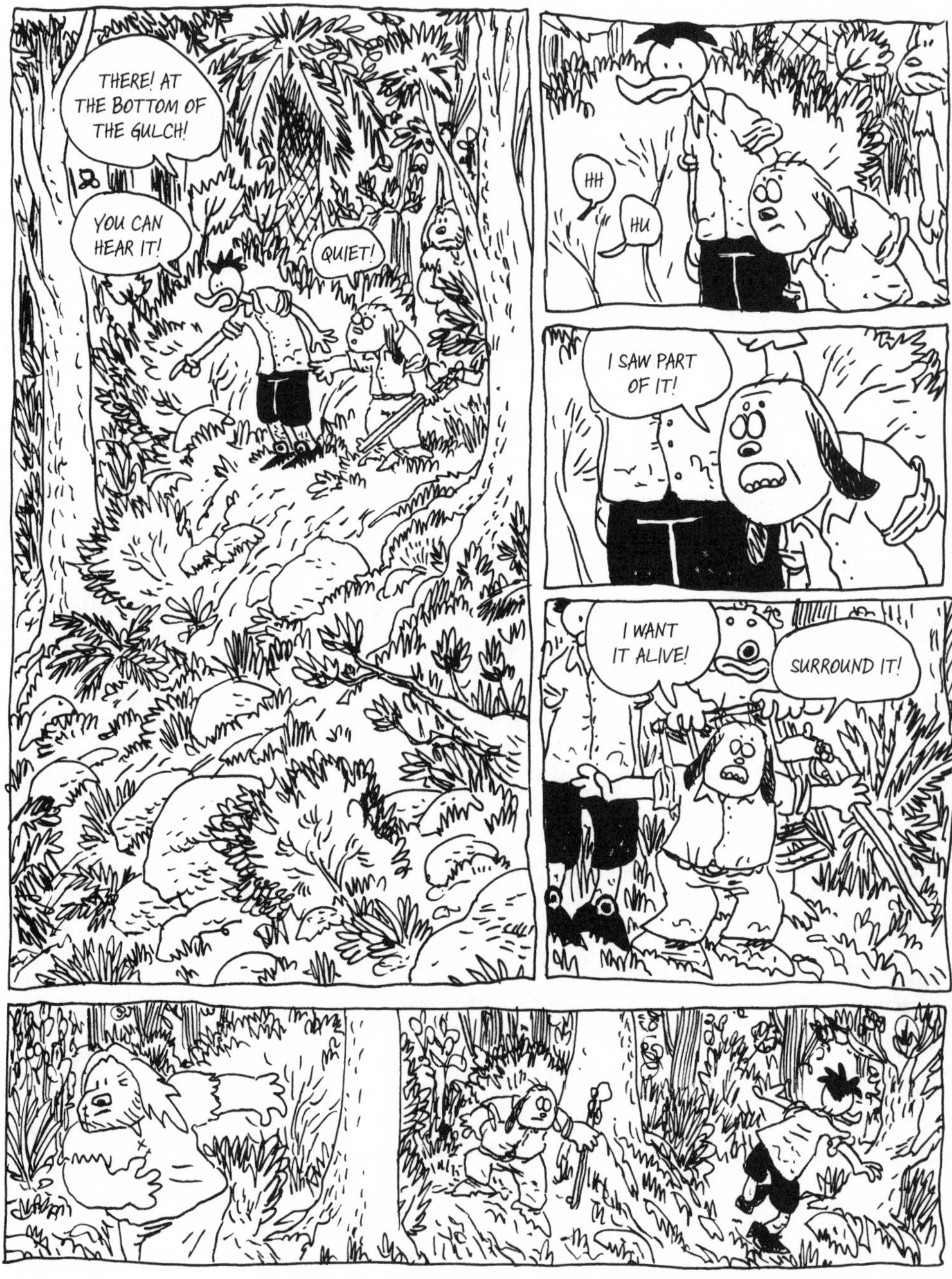
THERE! AT THE BOTTOM OF THE GULCH!
YOU CAN HEAR IT!
QUIET!
HH
HU
I SAW PART OF IT!
I WANT IT ALIVE!
SURROUND IT!

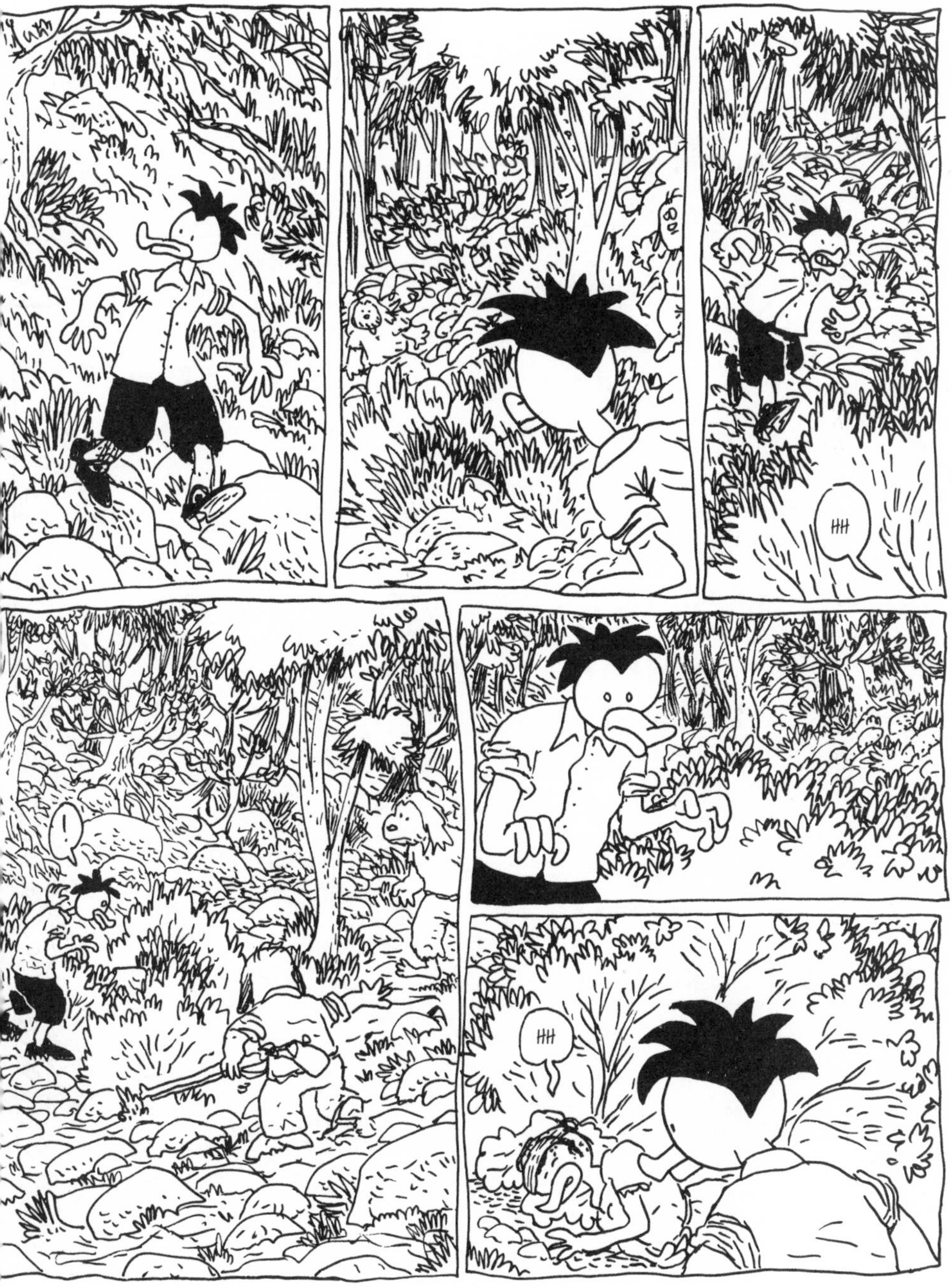
!

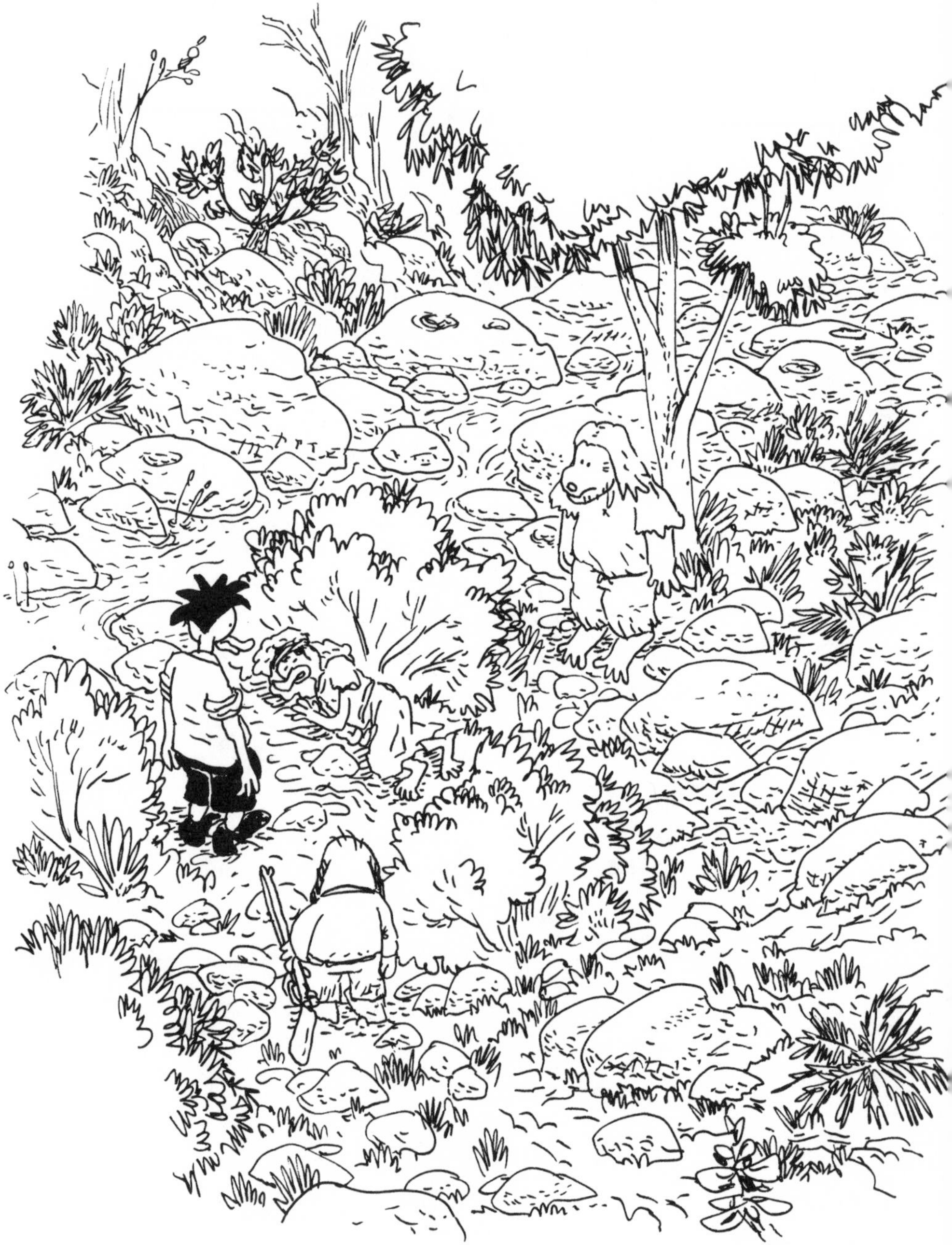

THE YOUNG 'UNS

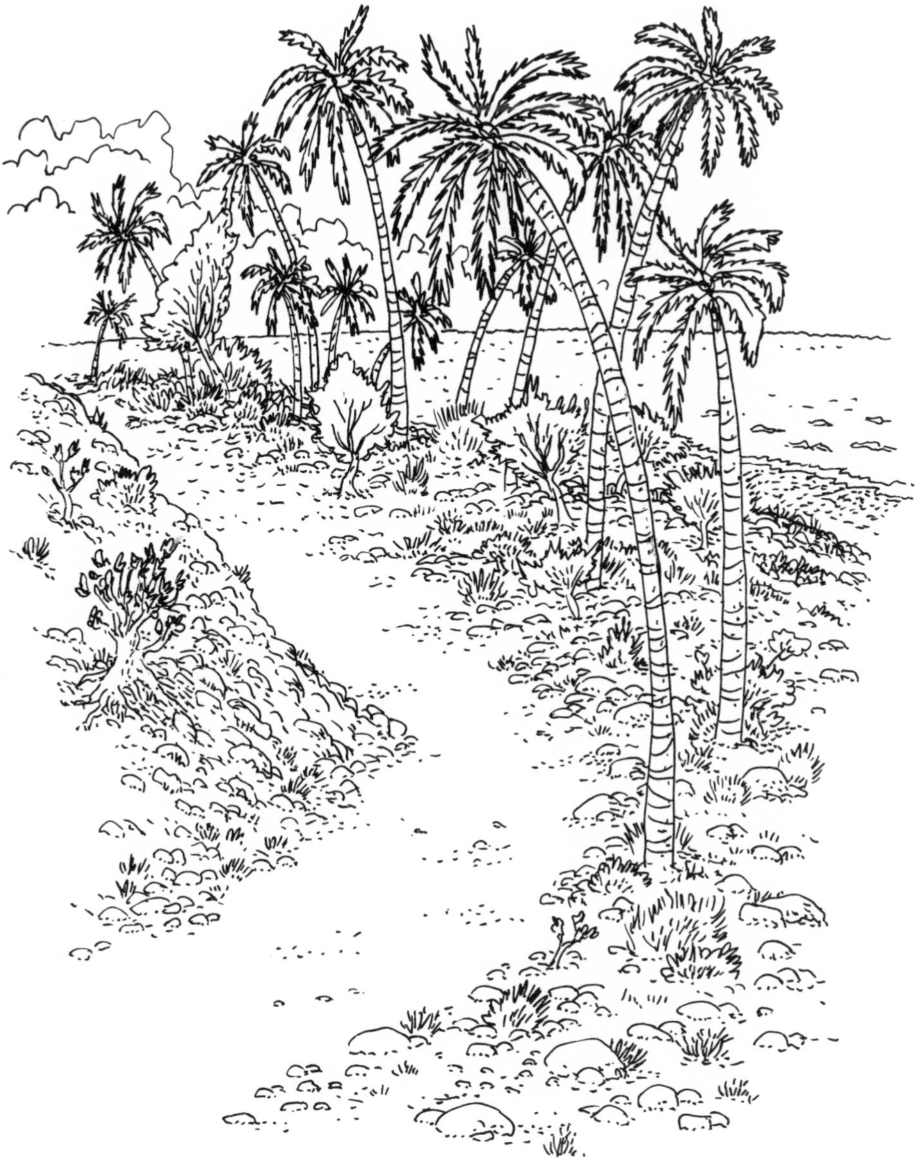

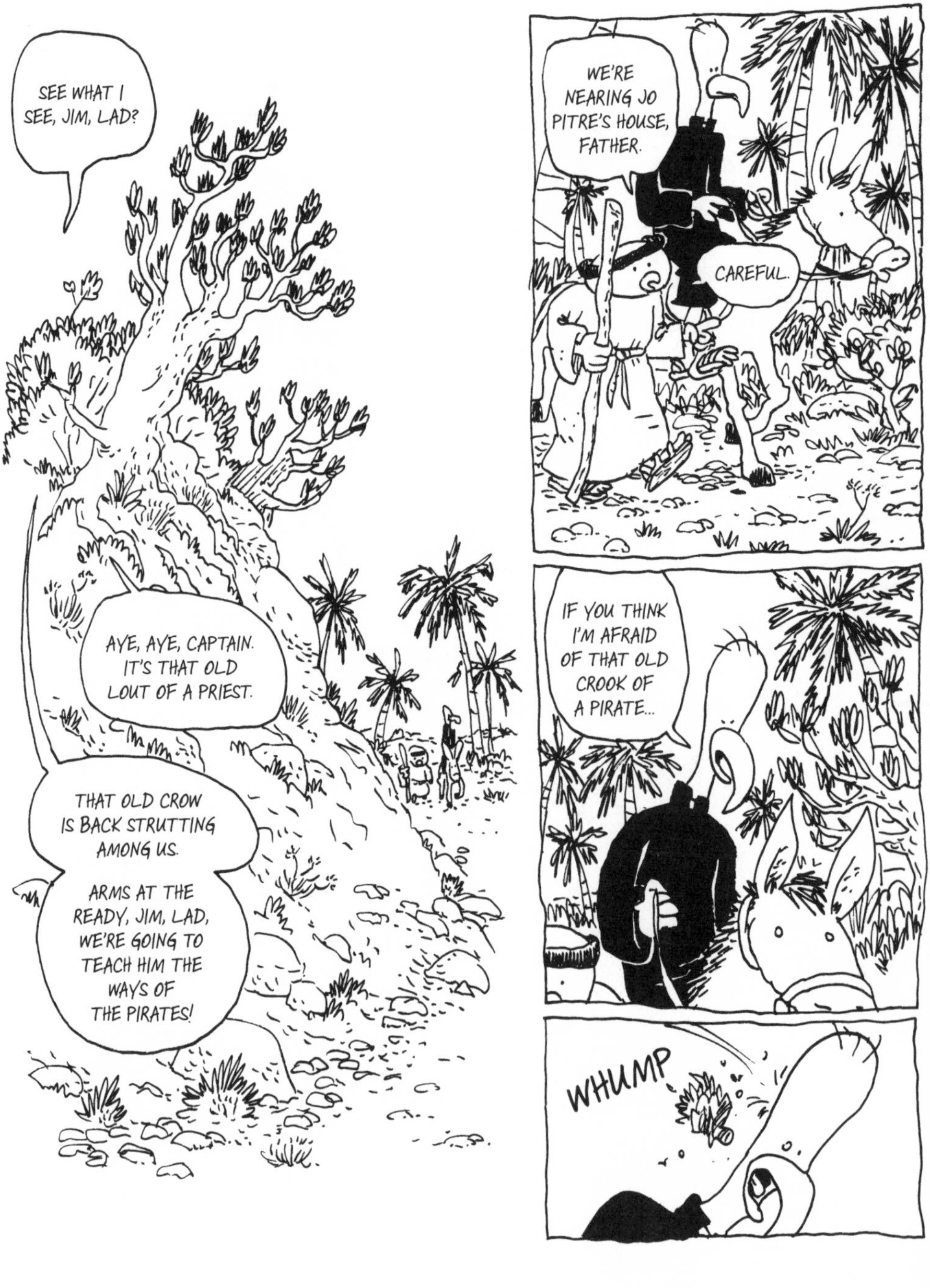
SEE WHAT I SEE, JIM, LAD?
AYE, AYE, CAPTAIN. IT'S THAT OLD LOUT OF A PRIEST.
THAT OLD CROW IS BACK STRUTTING AMONG US.
ARMS AT THE READY, JIM, LAD, WE'RE GOING TO TEACH HIM THE WAYS OF THE PIRATES!
WE'RE NEARING JO PITRE'S HOUSE, FATHER.
CAREFUL.
IF YOU THINK I'M AFRAID OF THAT OLD CROOK OF A PIRATE...
WHUMP

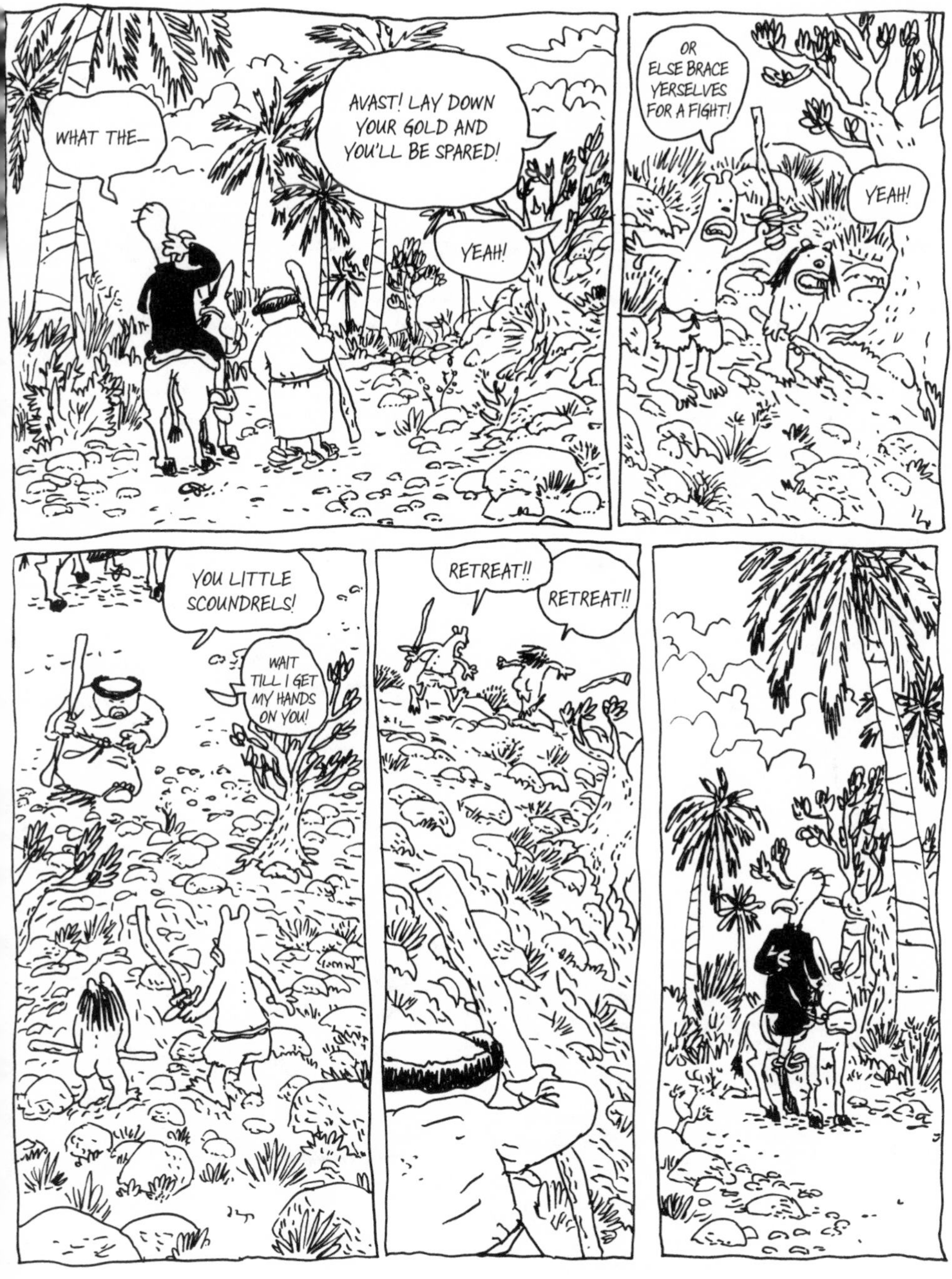
WHAT THE–
AVAST! LAY DOWN YOUR GOLD AND YOU'LL BE SPARED!
YEAH!
OR ELSE BRACE YERSELVES FOR A FIGHT!
YEAH!
YOU LITTLE SCOUNDRELS!
WAIT TILL I GET MY HANDS ON YOU!
RETREAT!!
RETREAT!!

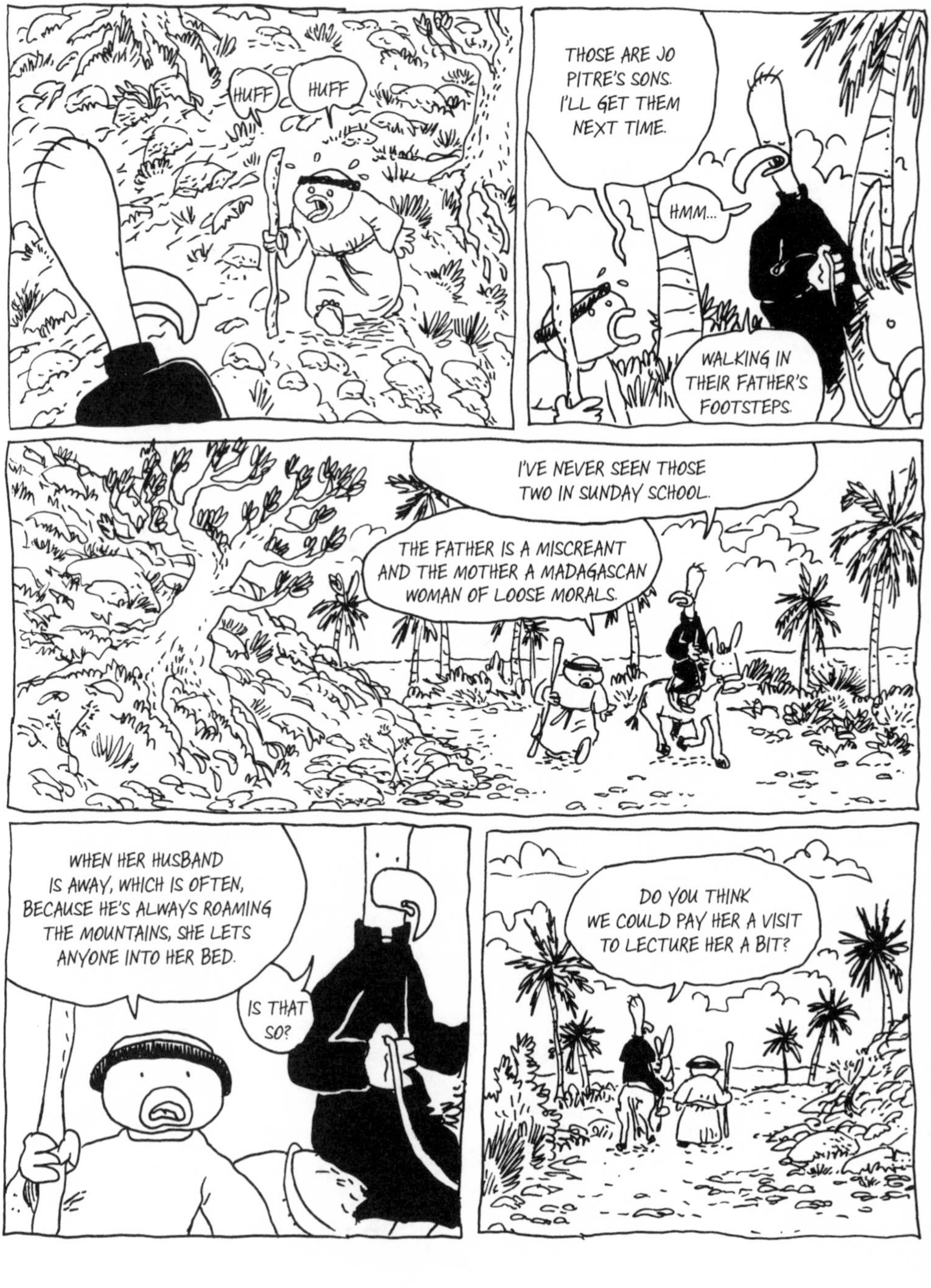
HUFF
HUFF
THOSE ARE JO PITRE'S SONS. I'LL GET THEM NEXT TIME.
HMM...
WALKING IN THEIR FATHER'S FOOTSTEPS.
I'VE NEVER SEEN THOSE TWO IN SUNDAY SCHOOL.
THE FATHER IS A MISCREANT AND THE MOTHER A MADAGASCAN WOMAN OF LOOSE MORALS.
WHEN HER HUSBAND IS AWAY, WHICH IS OFTEN, BECAUSE HE'S ALWAYS ROAMING THE MOUNTAINS, SHE LETS ANYONE INTO HER BED.
IS THAT SO?
DO YOU THINK WE COULD PAY HER A VISIT TO LECTURE HER A BIT?

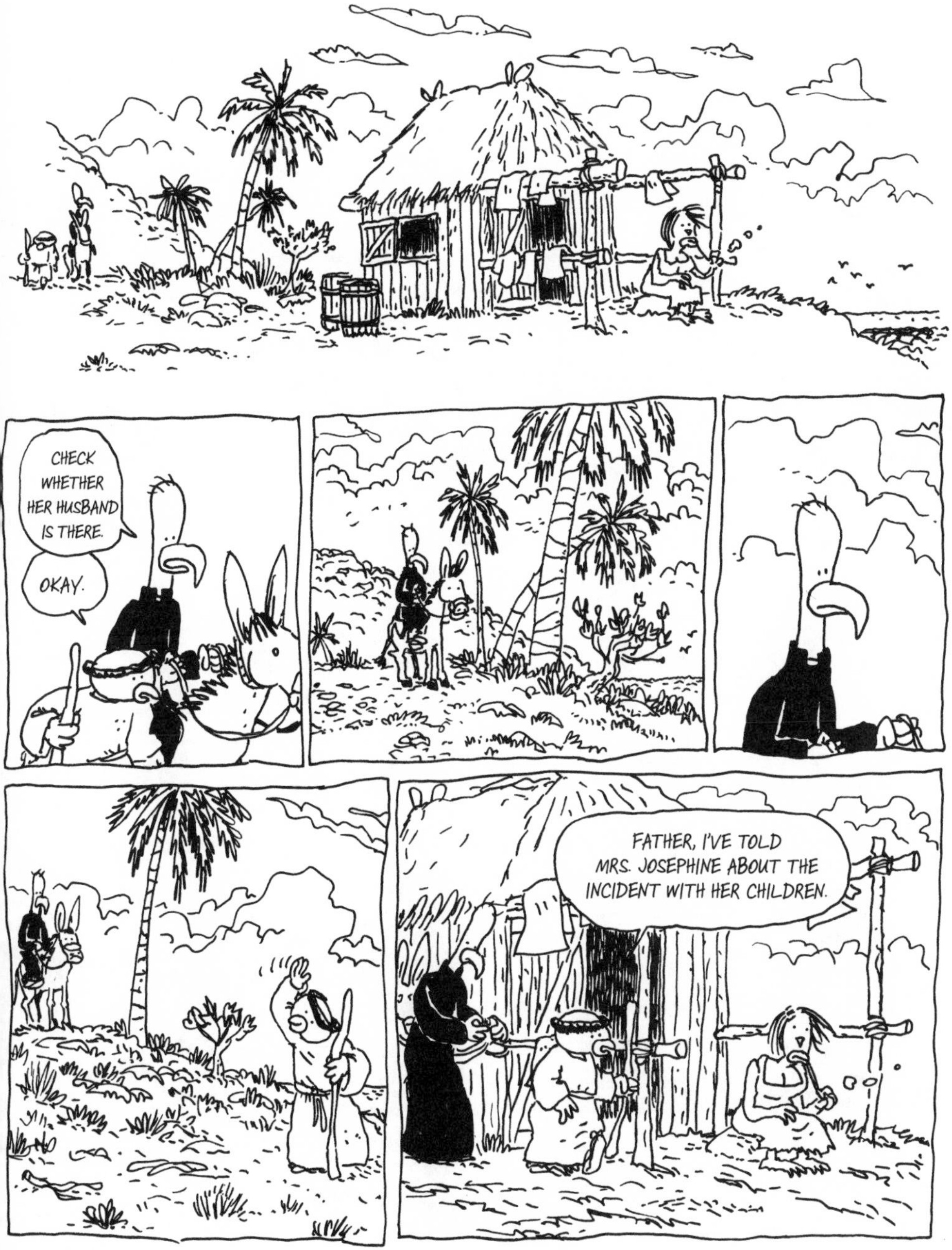
CHECK WHETHER HER HUSBAND IS THERE.
OKAY.
FATHER, I'VE TOLD MRS. JOSEPHINE ABOUT THE INCIDENT WITH HER CHILDREN.

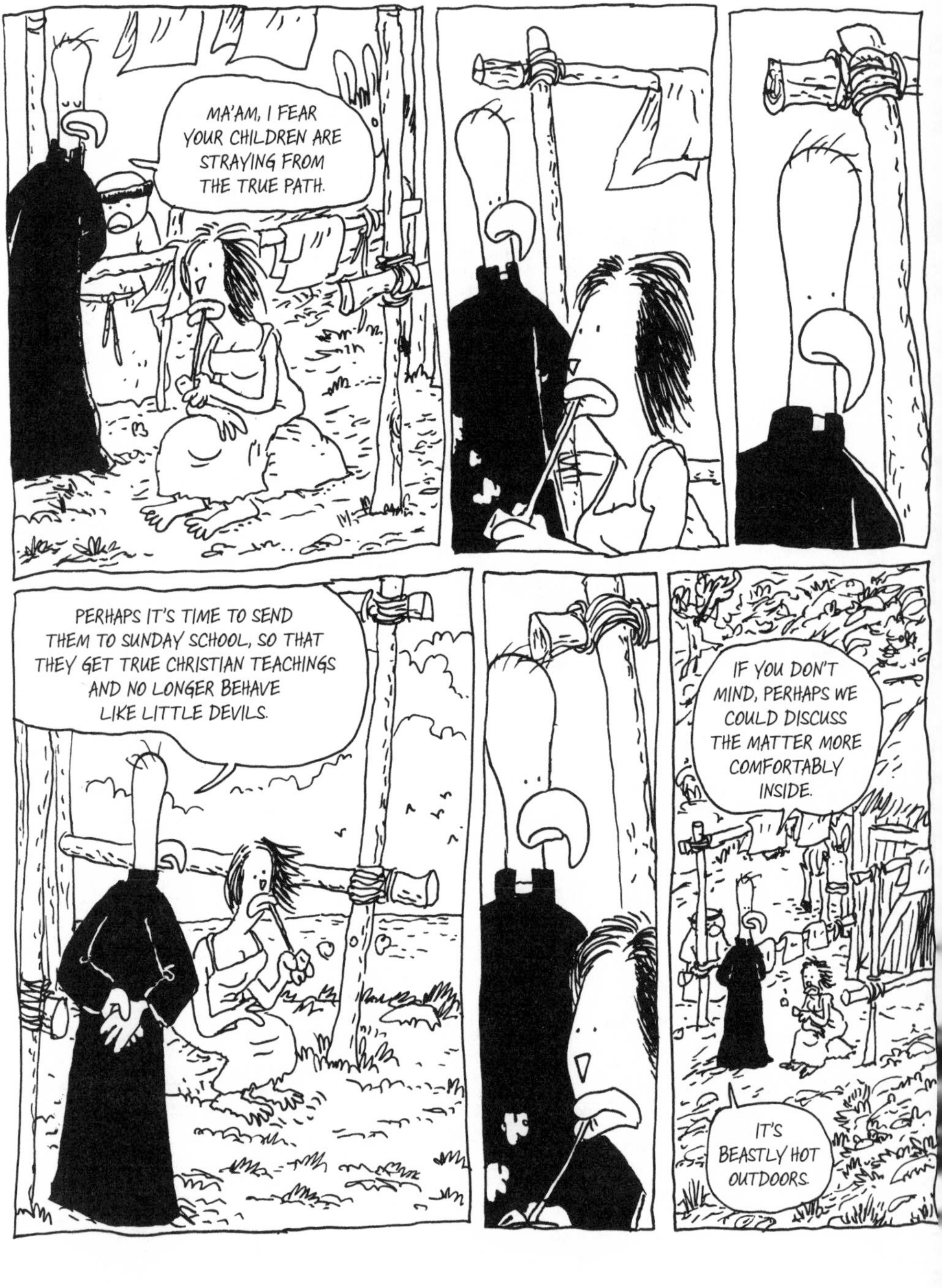
MA'AM, I FEAR YOUR CHILDREN ARE STRAYING FROM THE TRUE PATH.
PERHAPS IT'S TIME TO SEND THEM TO SUNDAY SCHOOL, SO THAT THEY GET TRUE CHRISTIAN TEACHINGS AND NO LONGER BEHAVE LIKE LITTLE DEVILS.
IF YOU DON'T MIND, PERHAPS WE COULD DISCUSS THE MATTER MORE COMFORTABLY INSIDE.
IT'S BEASTLY HOT OUTDOORS.

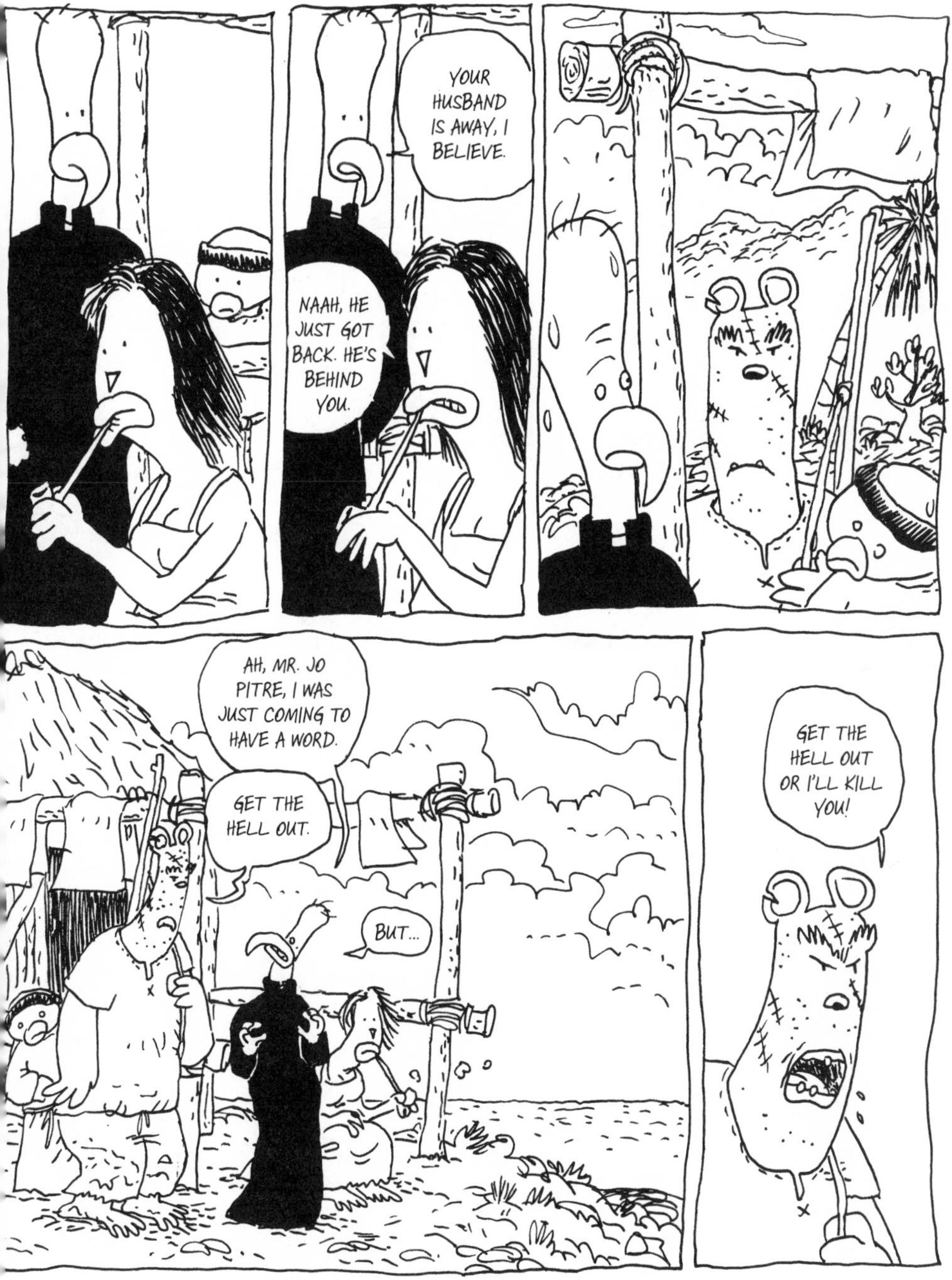
YOUR HUSBAND IS AWAY, I BELIEVE.
NAAH, HE JUST GOT BACK. HE'S BEHIND YOU.
AH, MR. JO PITRE, I WAS JUST COMING TO HAVE A WORD.
GET THE HELL OUT.
BUT...
GET THE HELL OUT OR I'LL KILL YOU!

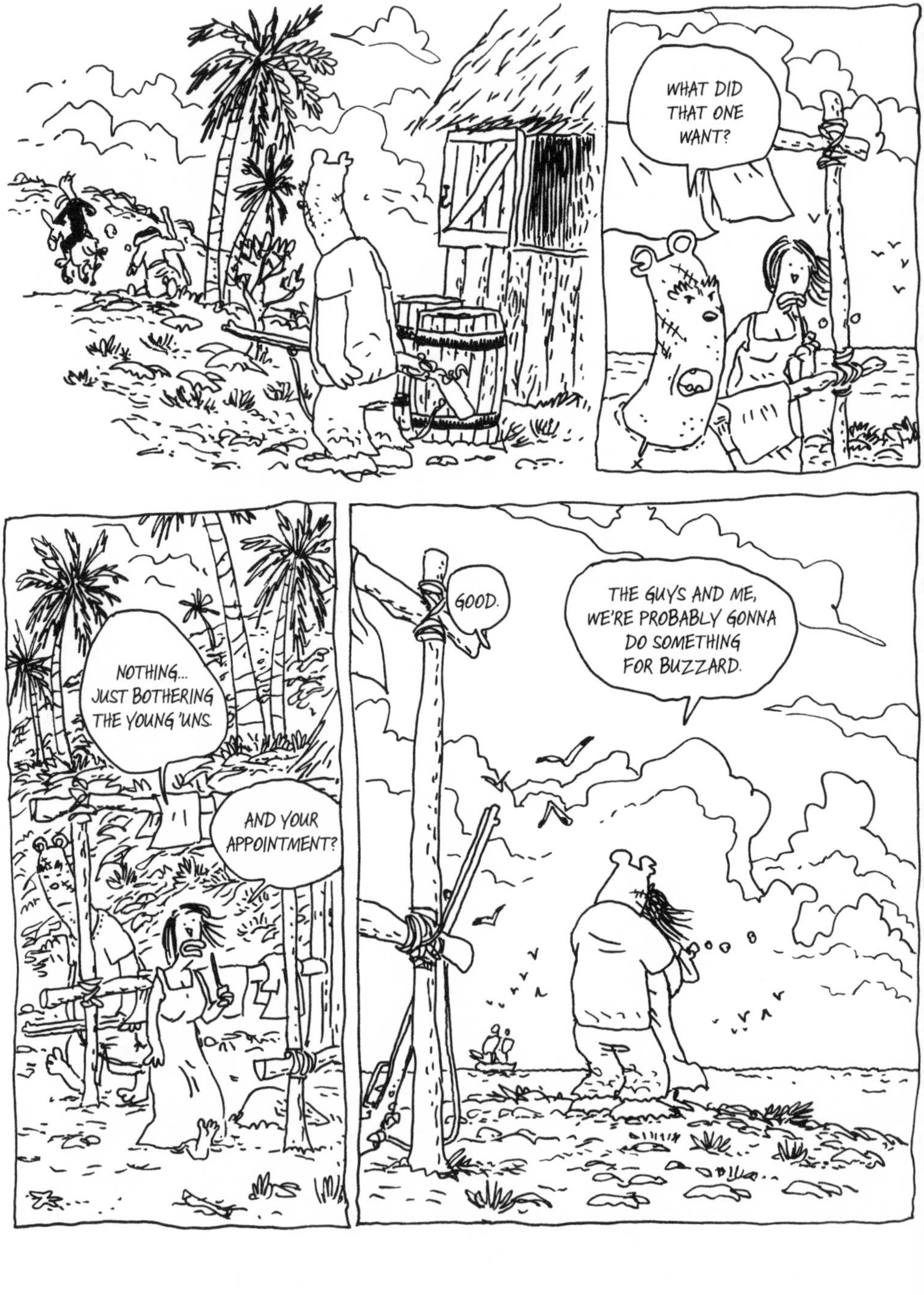
WHAT DID THAT ONE WANT?
NOTHING... JUST BOTHERING THE YOUNG 'UNS.
AND YOUR APPOINTMENT?
GOOD.
THE GUYS AND ME, WE'RE PROBABLY GONNA DO SOMETHING FOR BUZZARD.

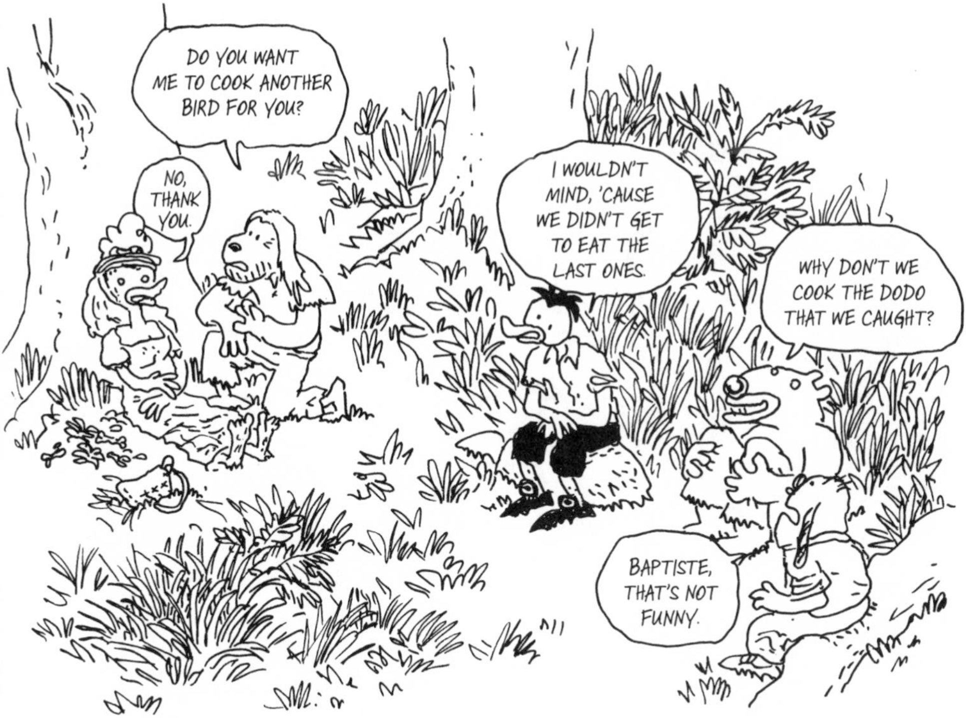
DO YOU WANT ME TO COOK ANOTHER BIRD FOR YOU?
NO, THANK YOU.
I WOULDN'T MIND, 'CAUSE WE DIDN'T GET TO EAT THE LAST ONES.
WHY DON'T WE COOK THE DODO THAT WE CAUGHT?
BAPTISTE, THAT'S NOT FUNNY.

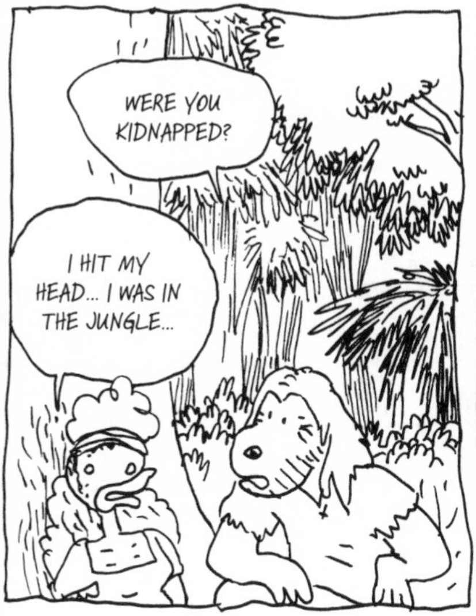
WERE YOU KIDNAPPED?
I HIT MY HEAD... I WAS IN THE JUNGLE...

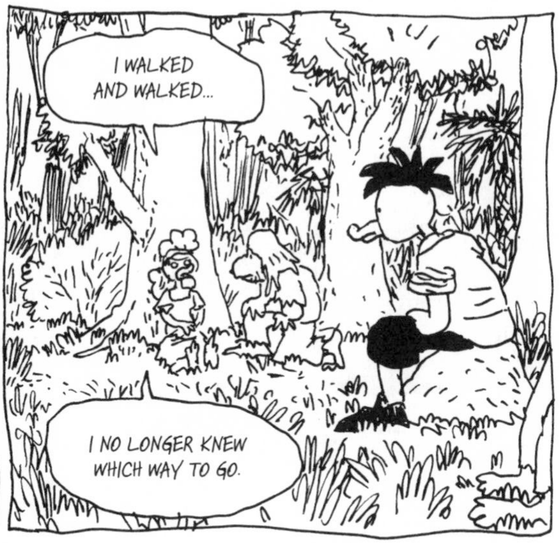
I WALKED AND WALKED...
I NO LONGER KNEW WHICH WAY TO GO.

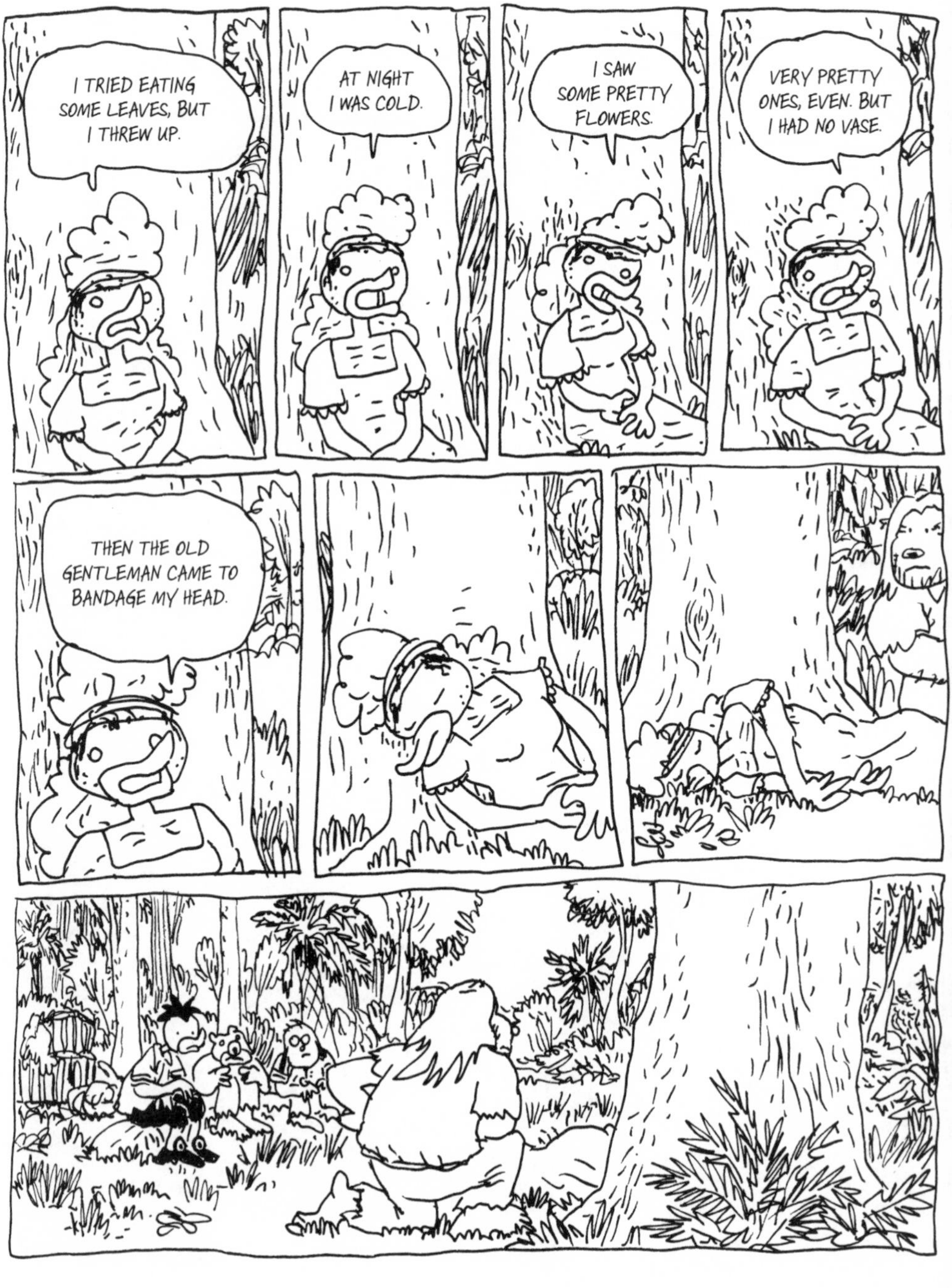
I TRIED EATING SOME LEAVES, BUT I THREW UP.
AT NIGHT I WAS COLD.
I SAW SOME PRETTY FLOWERS.
VERY PRETTY ONES, EVEN. BUT I HAD NO VASE.
THEN THE OLD GENTLEMAN CAME TO BANDAGE MY HEAD.

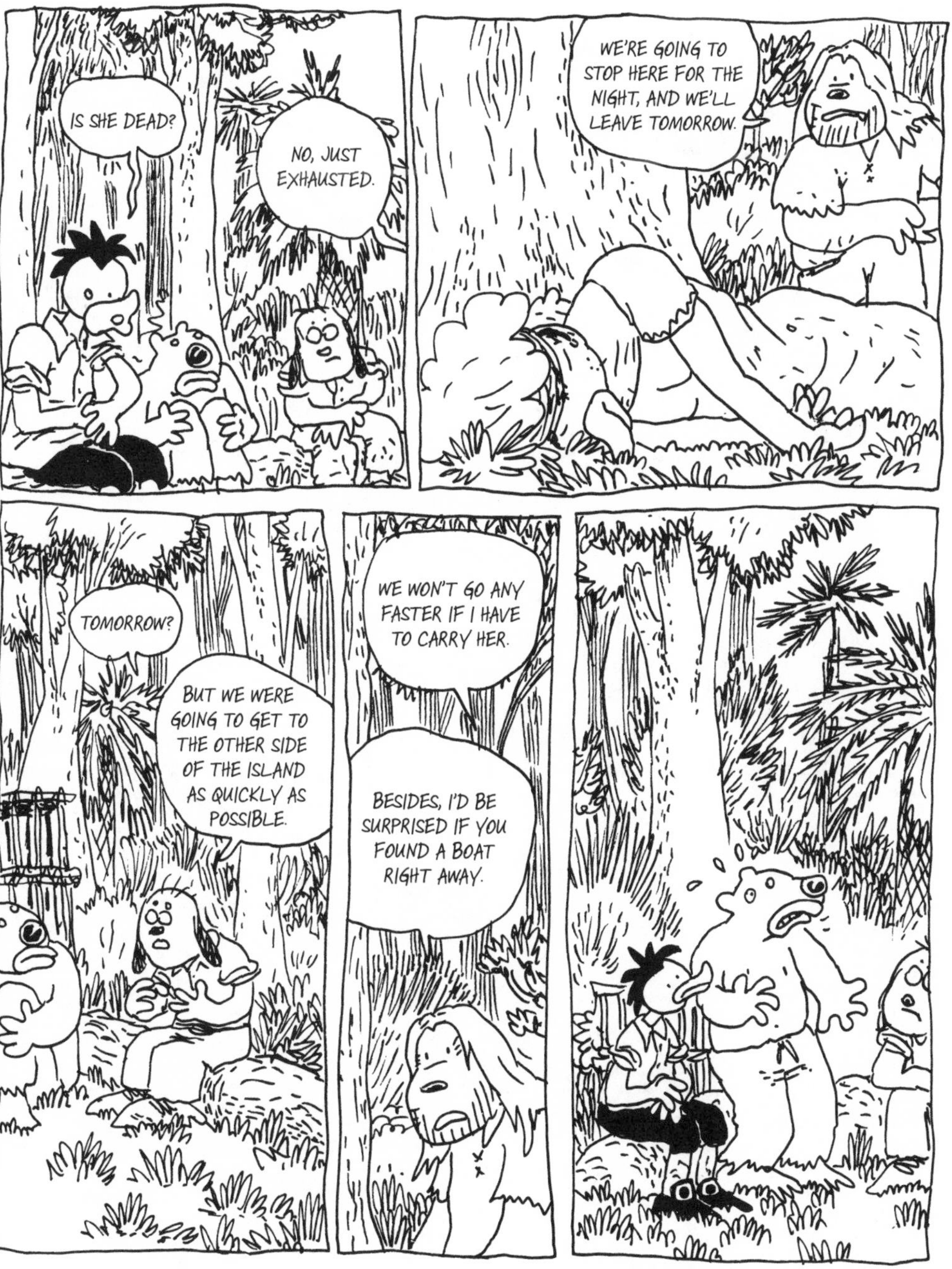
IS SHE DEAD?
NO, JUST EXHAUSTED.
WE'RE GOING TO STOP HERE FOR THE NIGHT, AND WE'LL LEAVE TOMORROW.
TOMORROW?
BUT WE WERE GOING TO GET TO THE OTHER SIDE OF THE ISLAND AS QUICKLY AS POSSIBLE.
WE WON'T GO ANY FASTER IF I HAVE TO CARRY HER.
BESIDES, I'D BE SURPRISED IF YOU FOUND A BOAT RIGHT AWAY.

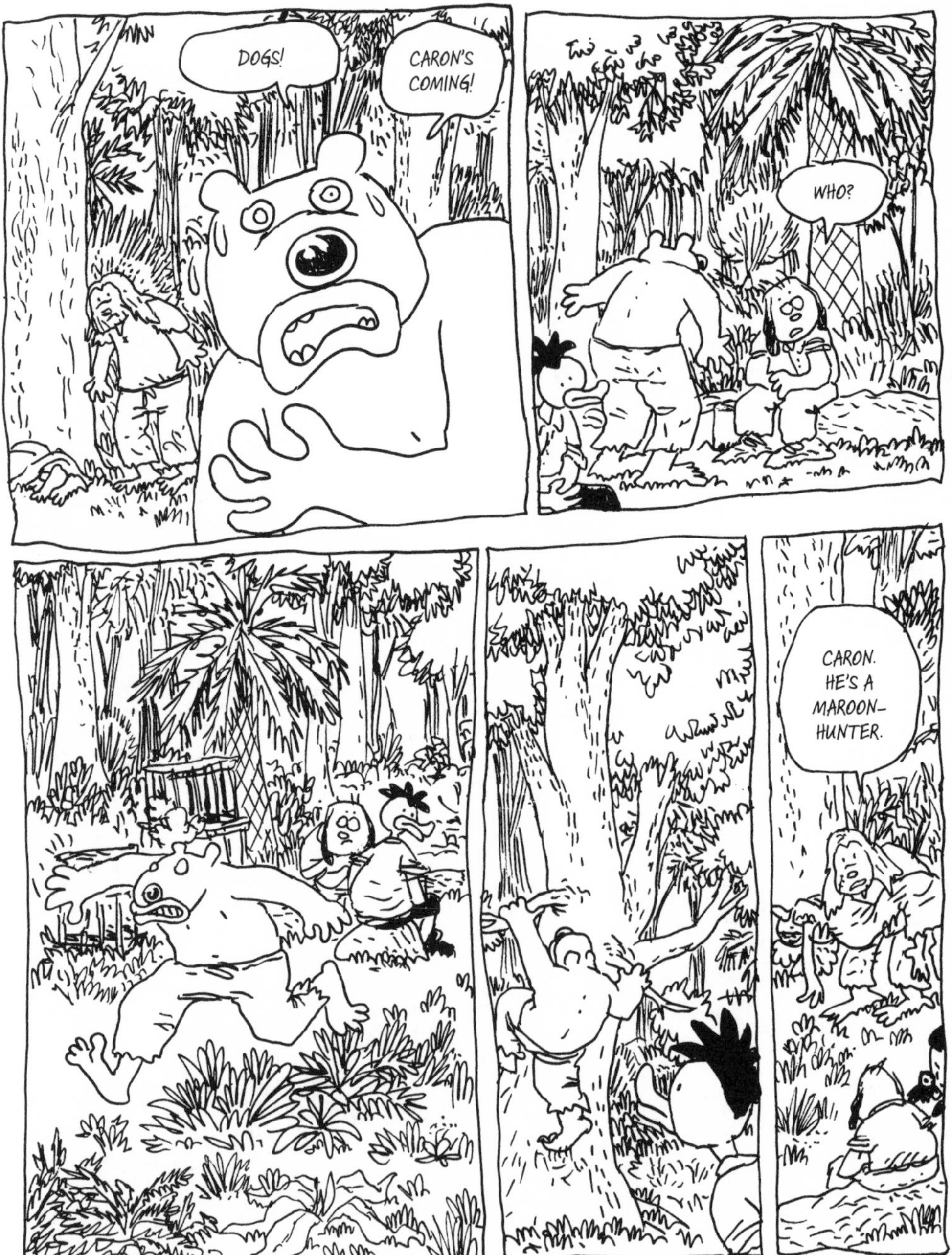
DOGS!
CARON'S COMING!
WHO?
CARON. HE'S A MAROON-HUNTER.

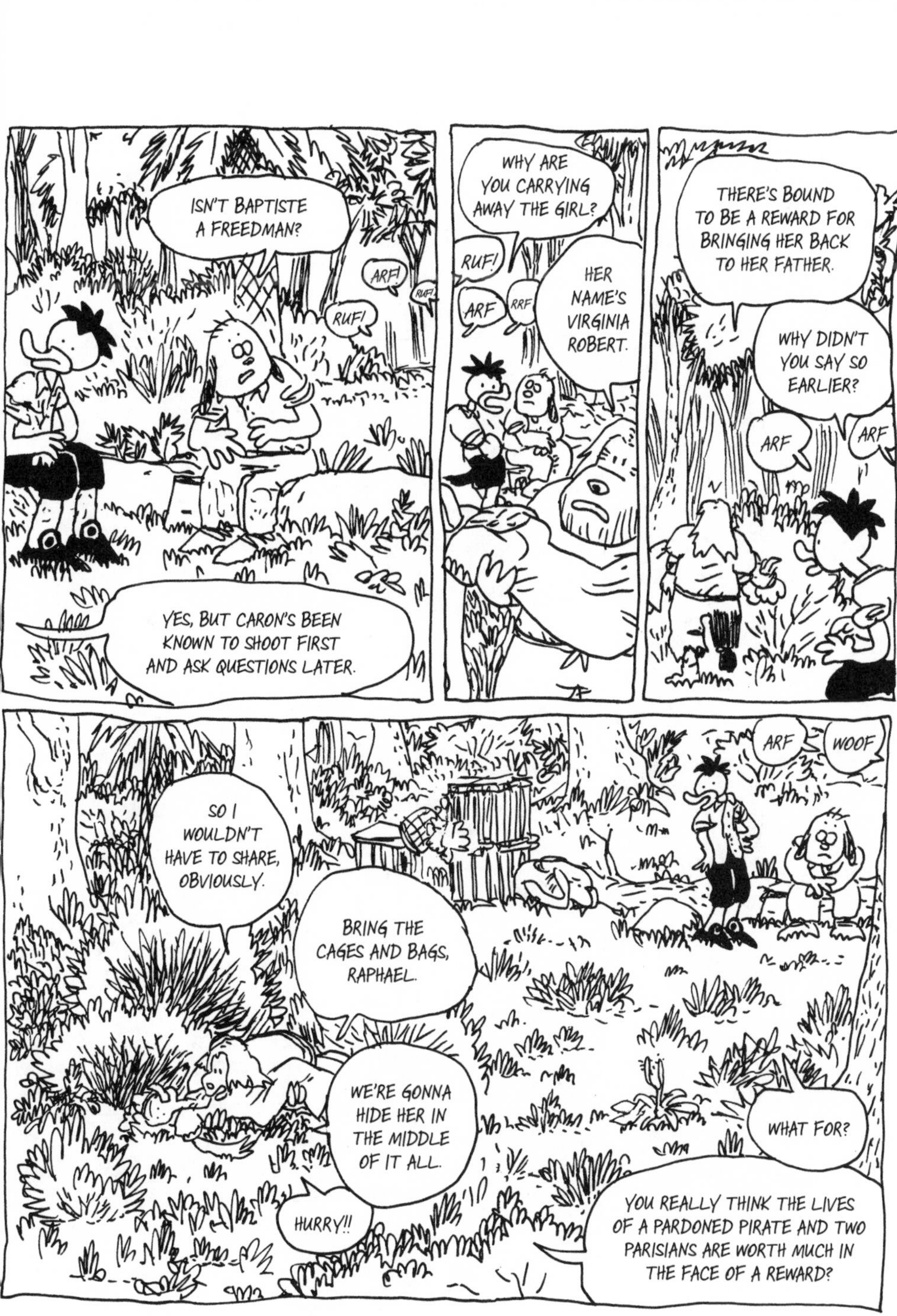
ISN'T BAPTISTE A FREEDMAN?
ARF!
RUF!
YES, BUT CARON'S BEEN KNOWN TO SHOOT FIRST AND ASK QUESTIONS LATER.
WHY ARE YOU CARRYING AWAY THE GIRL?
RUF!
ARF
RRF
HER NAME'S VIRGINIA ROBERT.
THERE'S BOUND TO BE A REWARD FOR BRINGING HER BACK TO HER FATHER.
WHY DIDN'T YOU SAY SO EARLIER?
ARF
ARF
ARF
WOOF
SO I WOULDN'T HAVE TO SHARE, OBVIOUSLY.
BRING THE CAGES AND BAGS, RAPHAEL.
WE'RE GONNA HIDE HER IN THE MIDDLE OF IT ALL.
HURRY!!
WHAT FOR?
YOU REALLY THINK THE LIVES OF A PARDONED PIRATE AND TWO PARISIANS ARE WORTH MUCH IN THE FACE OF A REWARD?

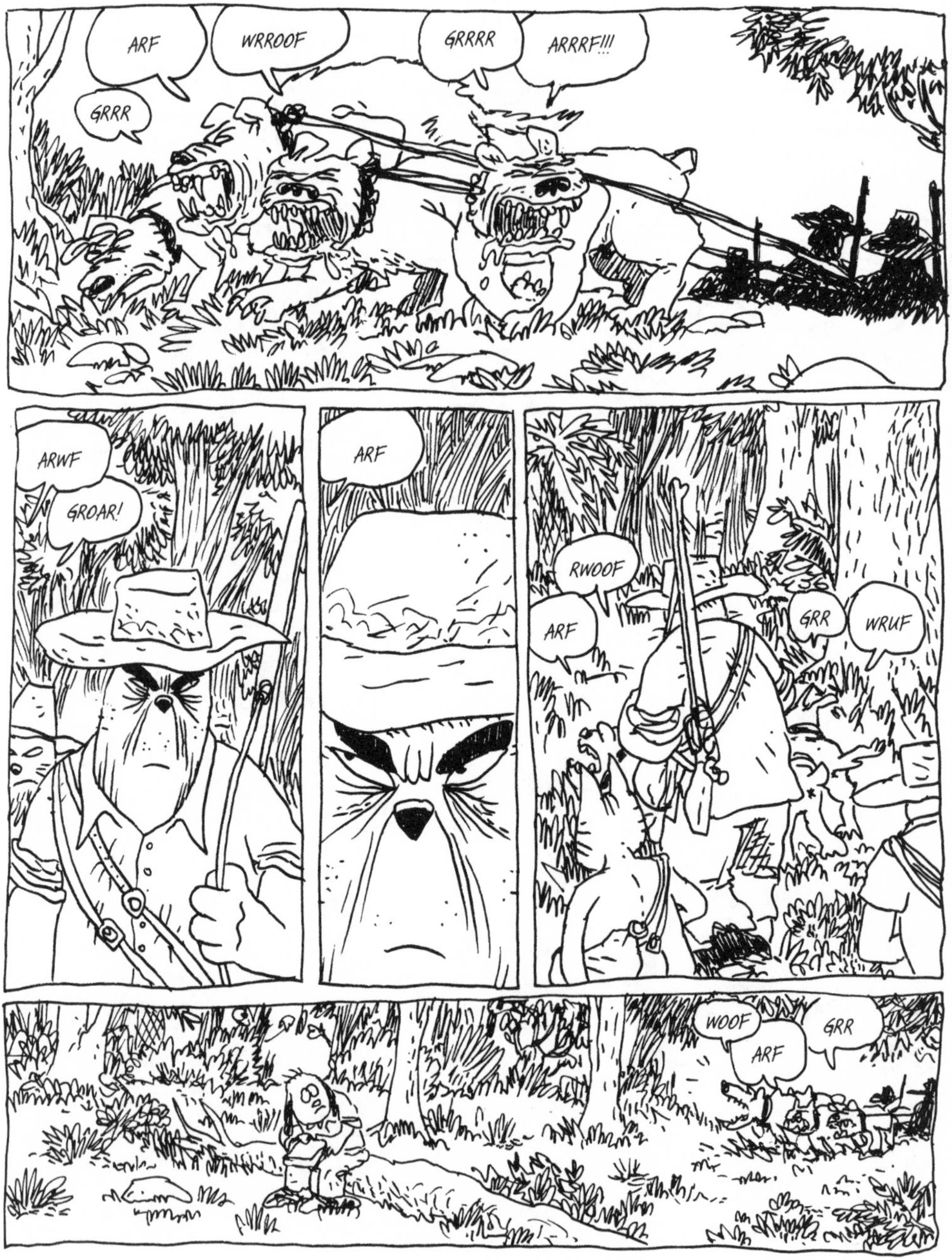
ARF
WRROOF
GRRR
GRRRR
ARRRF!!!
ARWF
GROAR!
ARF
RWOOF
ARF
GRR
WRUF
WOOF
ARF
GRR

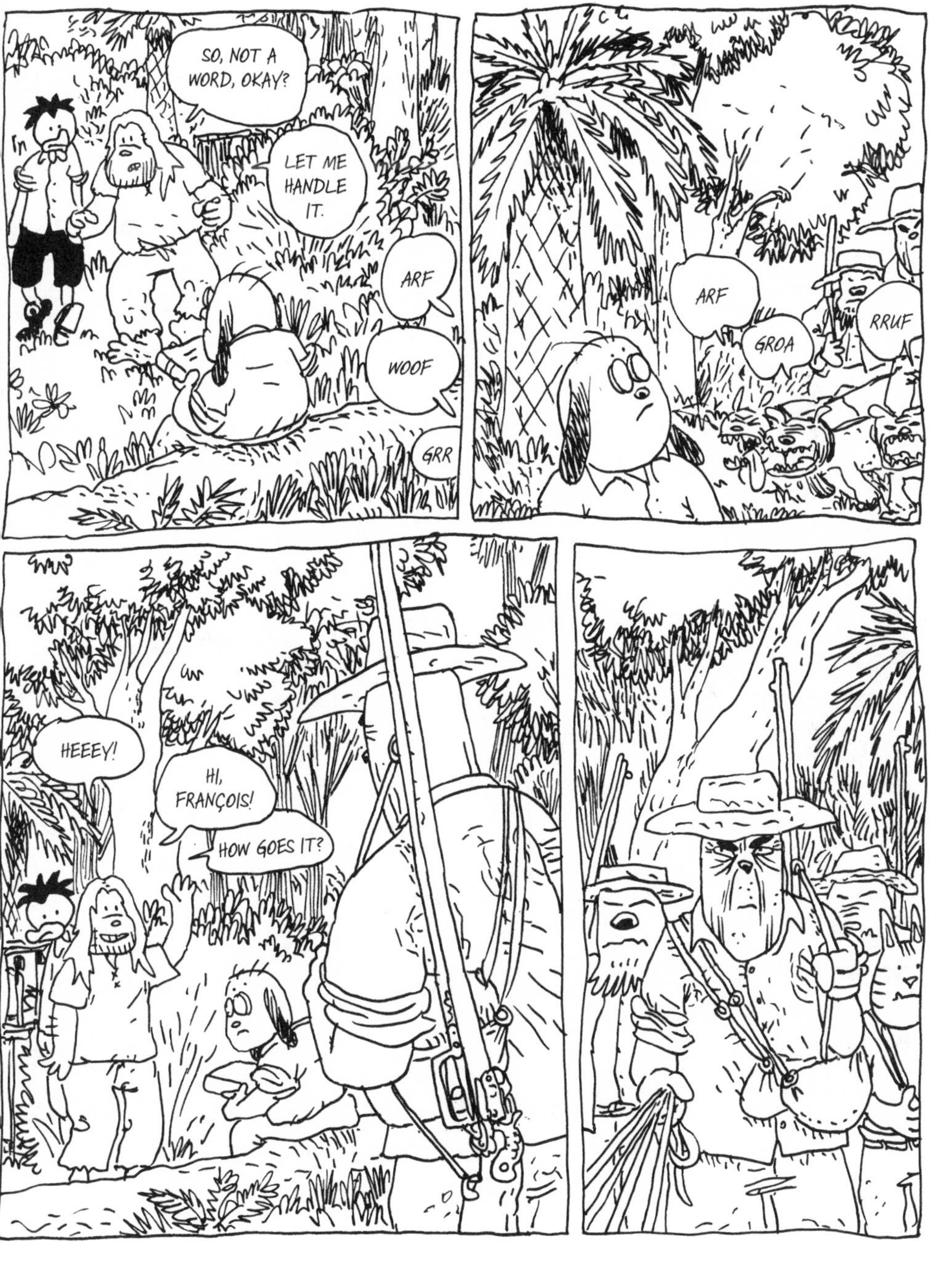
SO, NOT A WORD, OKAY?
LET ME HANDLE IT.
ARF
WOOF
GRR
ARF
GROA
RRUF
HEEEY!
HI, FRANÇOIS!
HOW GOES IT?

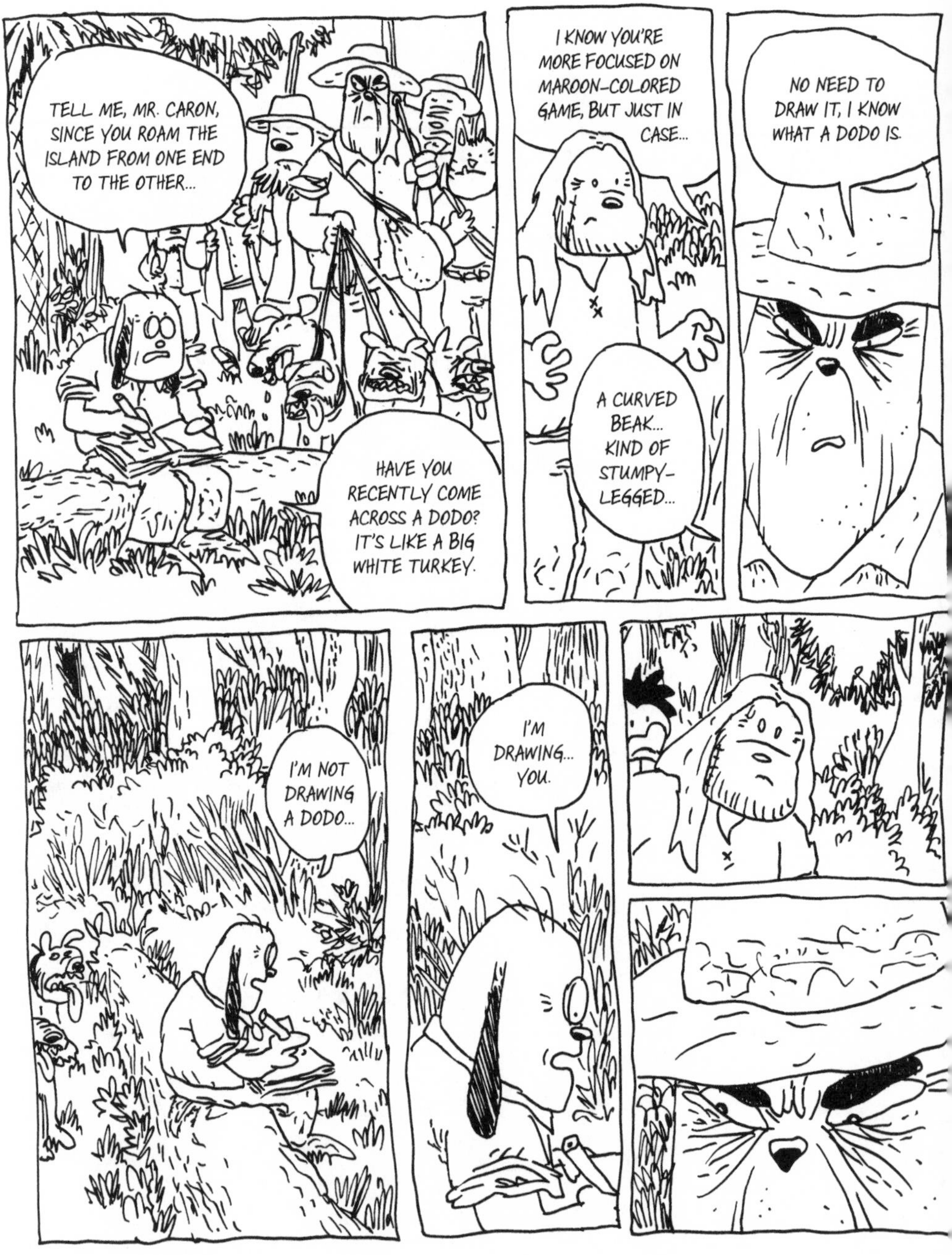
TELL ME, MR. CARON, SINCE YOU ROAM THE ISLAND FROM ONE END TO THE OTHER...
HAVE YOU RECENTLY COME ACROSS A DODO? IT'S LIKE A BIG WHITE TURKEY.
I KNOW YOU'RE MORE FOCUSED ON MAROON-COLORED GAME, BUT JUST IN CASE...
A CURVED BEAK... KIND OF STUMPY-LEGGED...
NO NEED TO DRAW IT, I KNOW WHAT A DODO IS.
I'M NOT DRAWING A DODO...
I'M DRAWING... YOU.

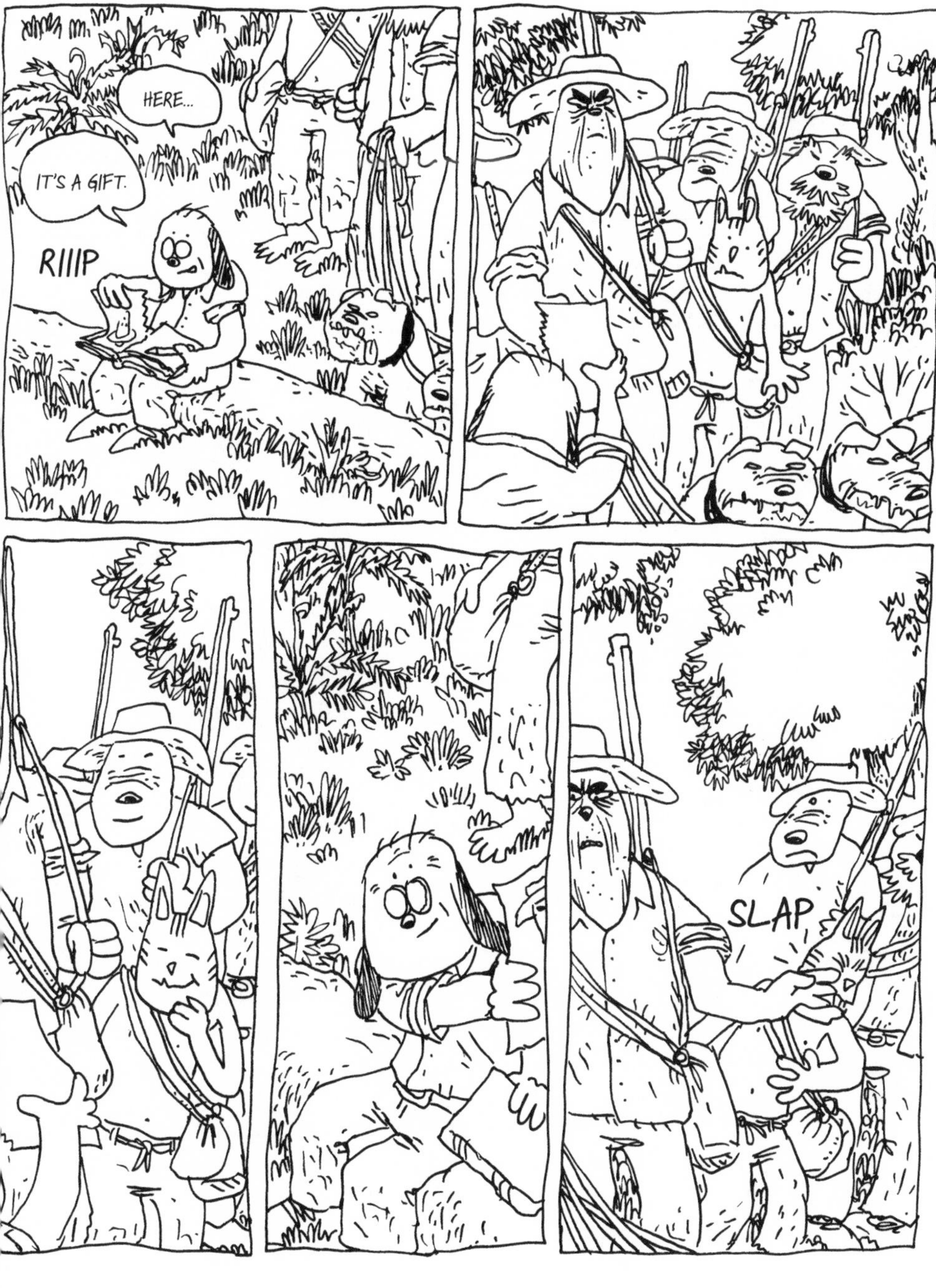
HERE...
IT'S A GIFT.
RIIIP
SLAP

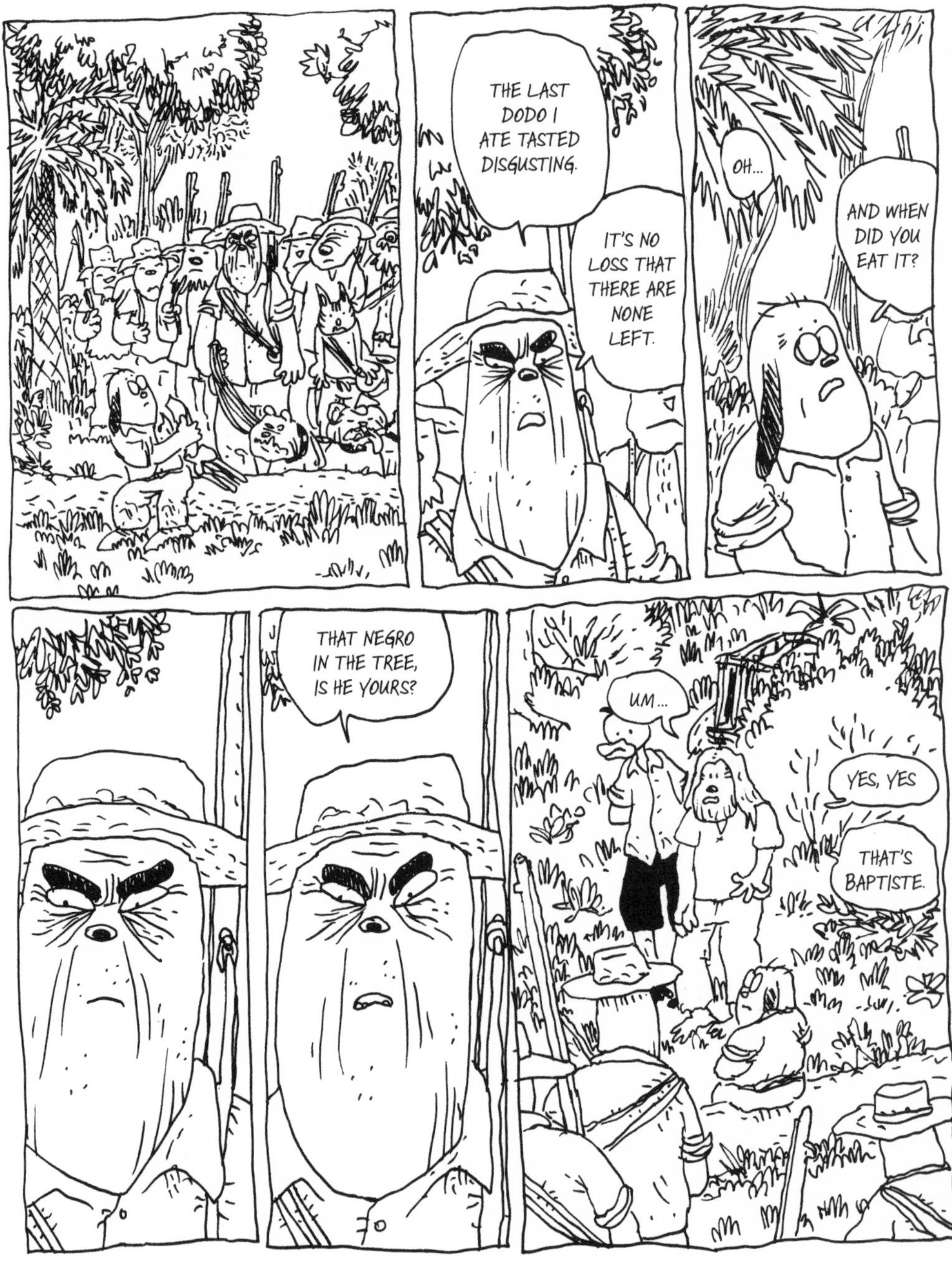
THE LAST DODO I ATE TASTED DISGUSTING.
IT'S NO LOSS THAT THERE ARE NONE LEFT.
OH...
AND WHEN DID YOU EAT IT?
THAT NEGRO IN THE TREE, IS HE YOURS?
UM...
YES, YES
THAT'S BAPTISTE.

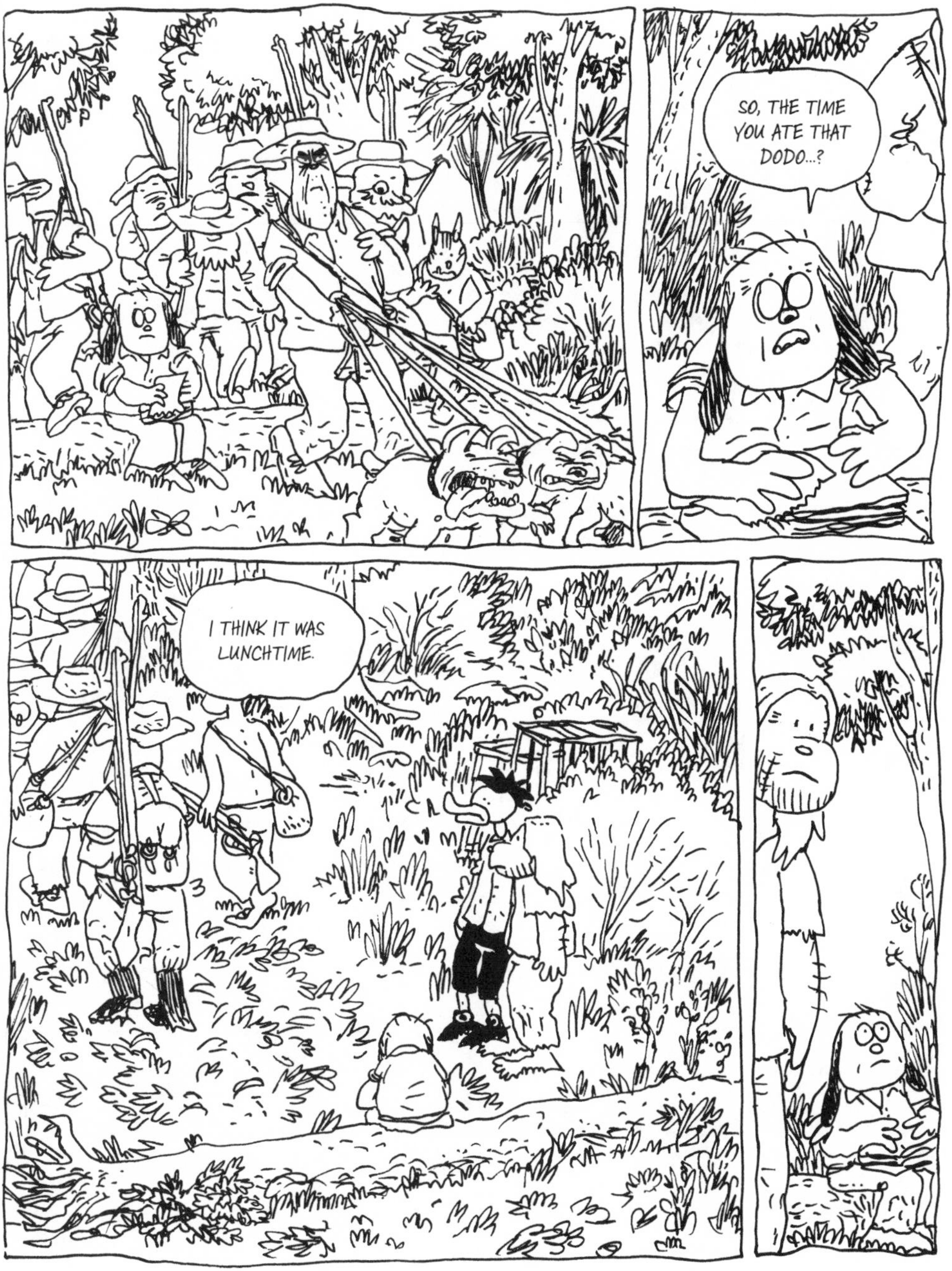
SO, THE TIME YOU ATE THAT DODO...?
I THINK IT WAS LUNCHTIME.

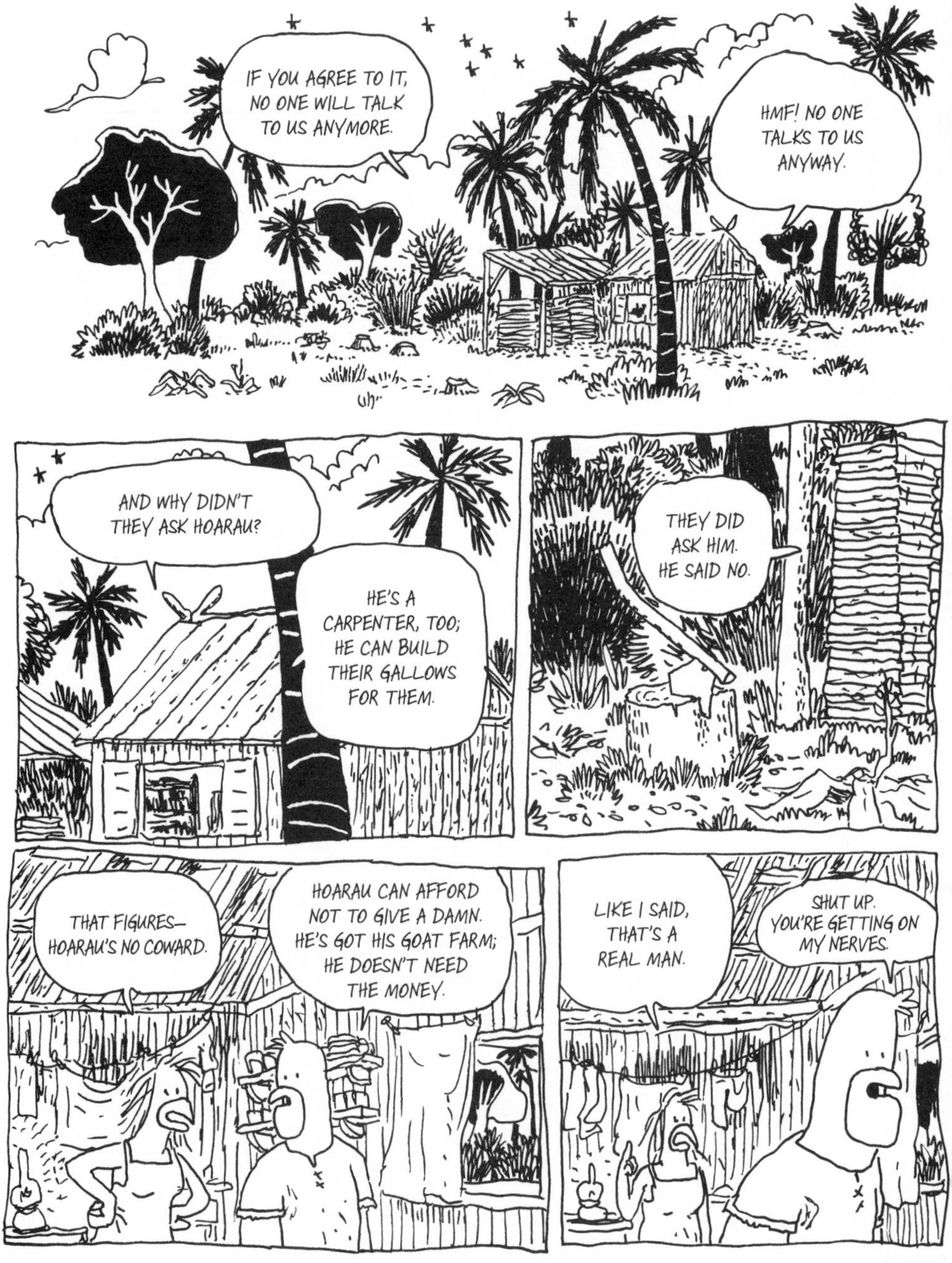
IF YOU AGREE TO IT, NO ONE WILL TALK TO US ANYMORE.
HMF! NO ONE TALKS TO US ANYWAY.
AND WHY DIDN'T THEY ASK HOARAU?
HE'S A CARPENTER, TOO; HE CAN BUILD THEIR GALLOWS FOR THEM.
THEY DID ASK HIM. HE SAID NO.
THAT FIGURES— HOARAU'S NO COWARD.
HOARAU CAN AFFORD NOT TO GIVE A DAMN. HE'S GOT HIS GOAT FARM; HE DOESN'T NEED THE MONEY.
LIKE I SAID, THAT'S A REAL MAN.
SHUT UP. YOU'RE GETTING ON MY NERVES.

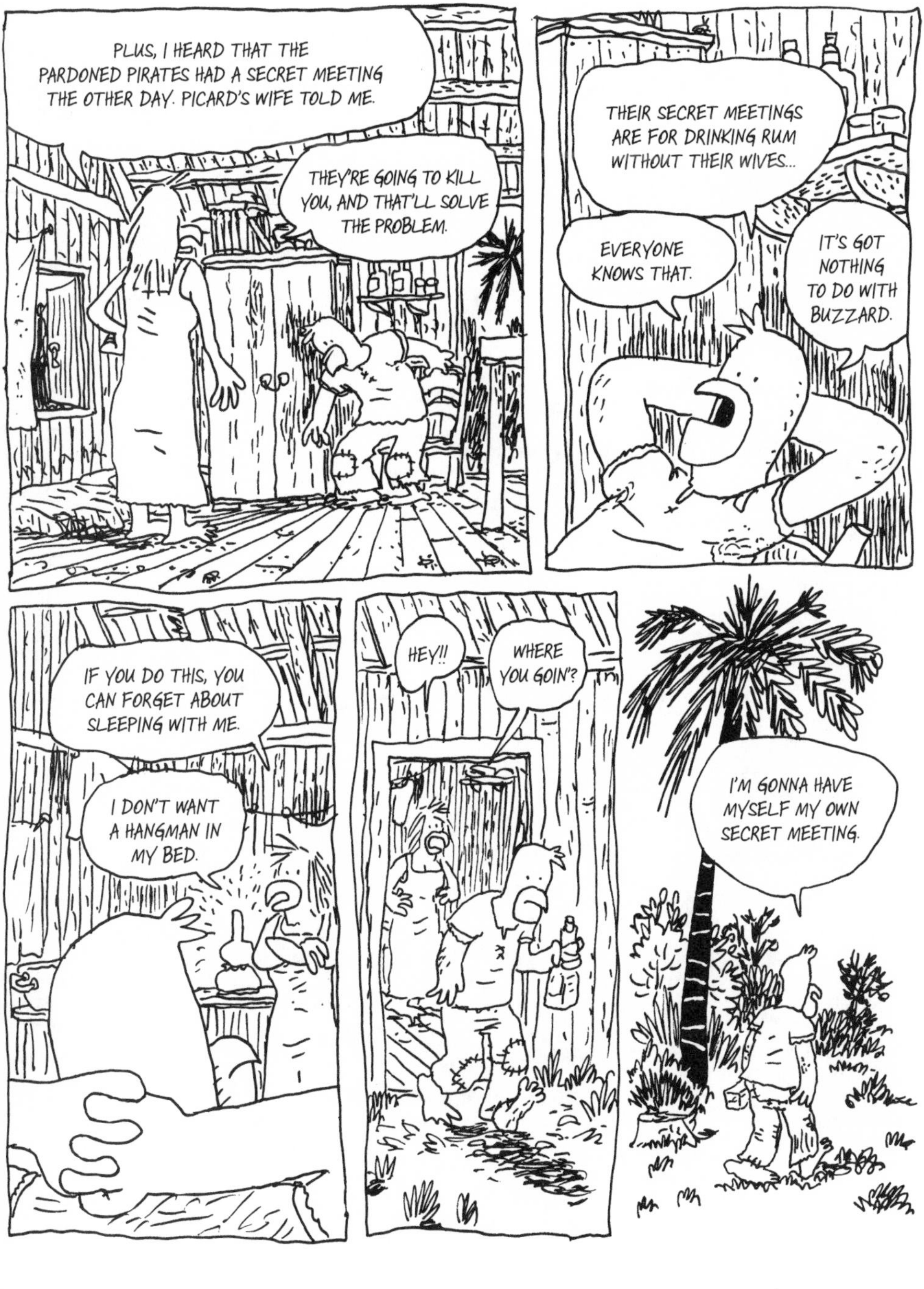

PLUS, I HEARD THAT THE PARDONED PIRATES HAD A SECRET MEETING THE OTHER DAY. PICARD'S WIFE TOLD ME.
THEY'RE GOING TO KILL YOU, AND THAT'LL SOLVE THE PROBLEM.
THEIR SECRET MEETINGS ARE FOR DRINKING RUM WITHOUT THEIR WIVES...
EVERYONE KNOWS THAT.
IT'S GOT NOTHING TO DO WITH BUZZARD.
IF YOU DO THIS, YOU CAN FORGET ABOUT SLEEPING WITH ME.
I DON'T WANT A HANGMAN IN MY BED.
HEY!!
WHERE YOU GOIN'?
I'M GONNA HAVE MYSELF MY OWN SECRET MEETING.

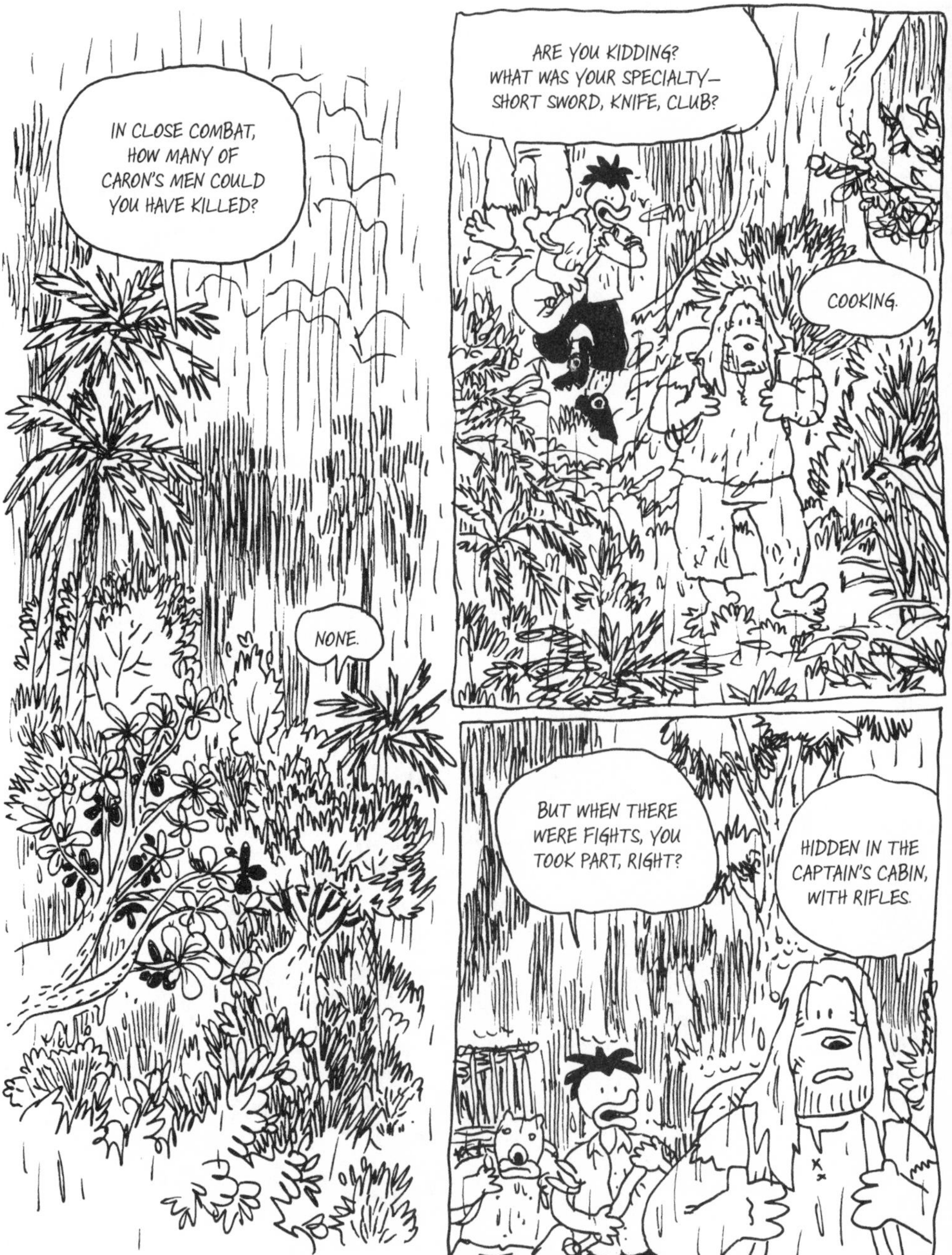
IN CLOSE COMBAT, HOW MANY OF CARON'S MEN COULD YOU HAVE KILLED?
NONE.
ARE YOU KIDDING? WHAT WAS YOUR SPECIALTY— SHORT SWORD, KNIFE, CLUB?
COOKING.
BUT WHEN THERE WERE FIGHTS, YOU TOOK PART, RIGHT?
HIDDEN IN THE CAPTAIN'S CABIN, WITH RIFLES.

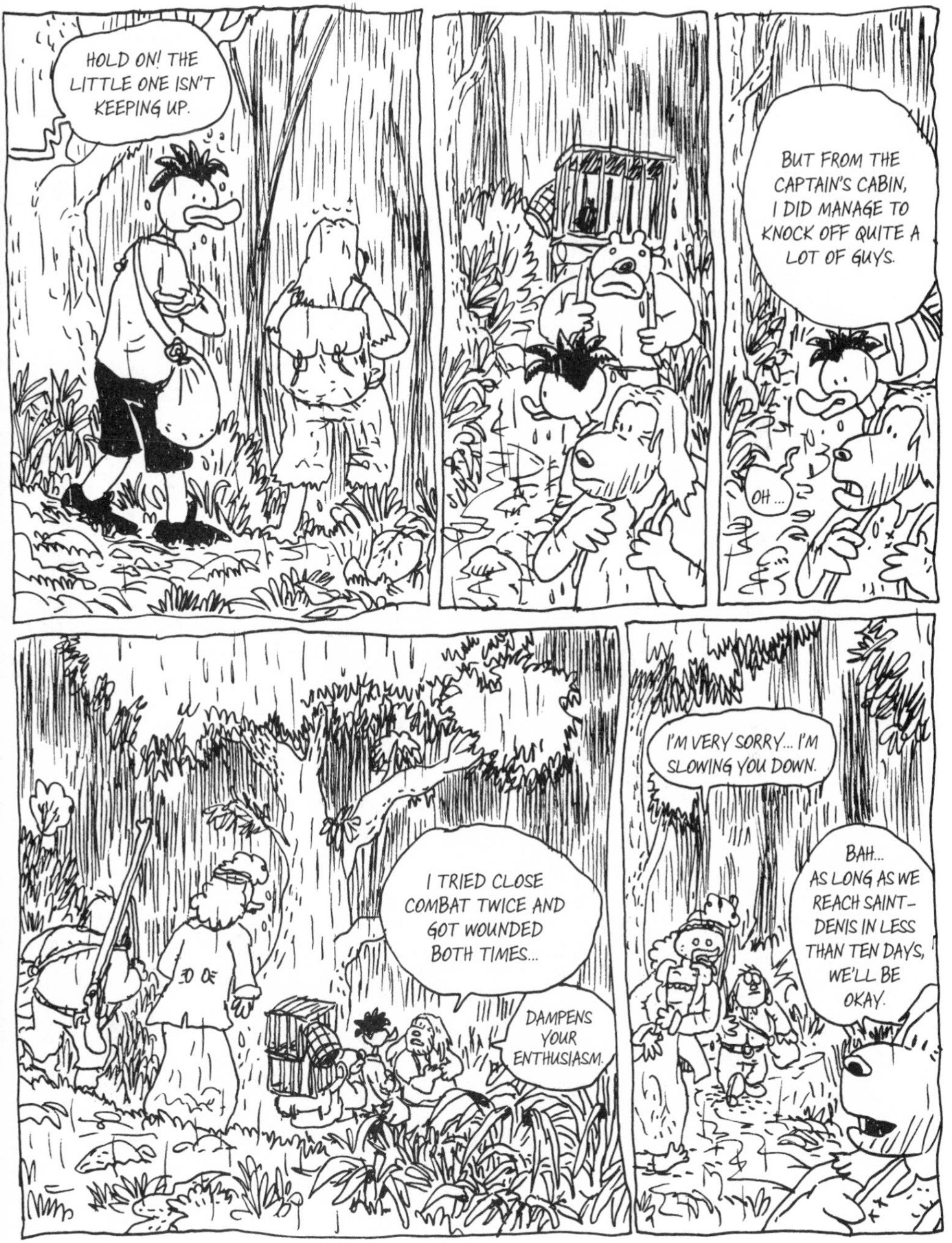
HOLD ON! THE LITTLE ONE ISN'T KEEPING UP.
BUT FROM THE CAPTAIN'S CABIN, I DID MANAGE TO KNOCK OFF QUITE A LOT OF GUYS.
OH ...
I TRIED CLOSE COMBAT TWICE AND GOT WOUNDED BOTH TIMES...
DAMPENS YOUR ENTHUSIASM.
I'M VERY SORRY... I'M SLOWING YOU DOWN.
BAH... AS LONG AS WE REACH SAINT-DENIS IN LESS THAN TEN DAYS, WE'LL BE OKAY.

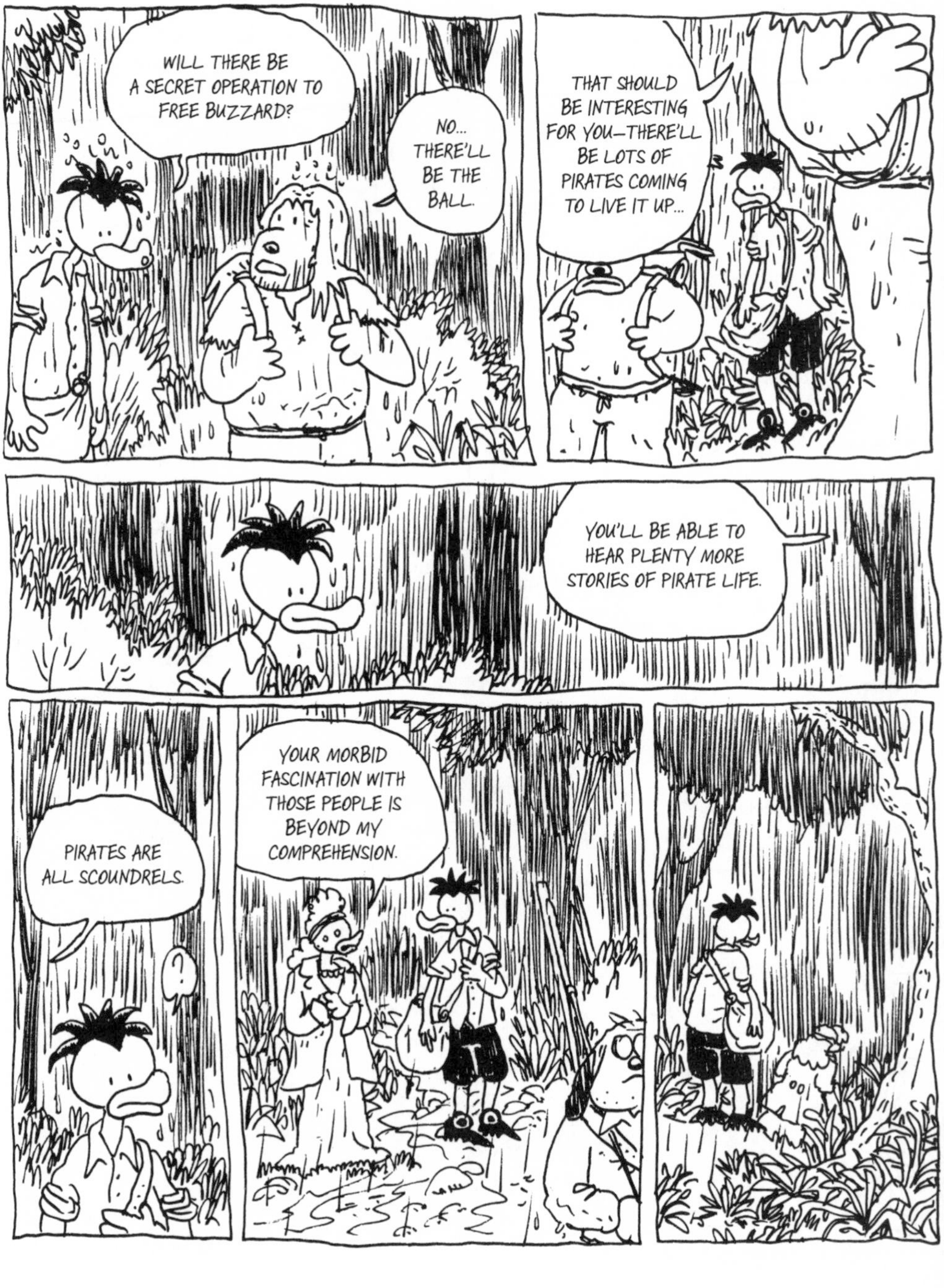
WILL THERE BE A SECRET OPERATION TO FREE BUZZARD?
NO... THERE'LL BE THE BALL.
THAT SHOULD BE INTERESTING FOR YOU—THERE'LL BE LOTS OF PIRATES COMING TO LIVE IT UP...
YOU'LL BE ABLE TO HEAR PLENTY MORE STORIES OF PIRATE LIFE.
PIRATES ARE ALL SCOUNDRELS.
?
YOUR MORBID FASCINATION WITH THOSE PEOPLE IS BEYOND MY COMPREHENSION.

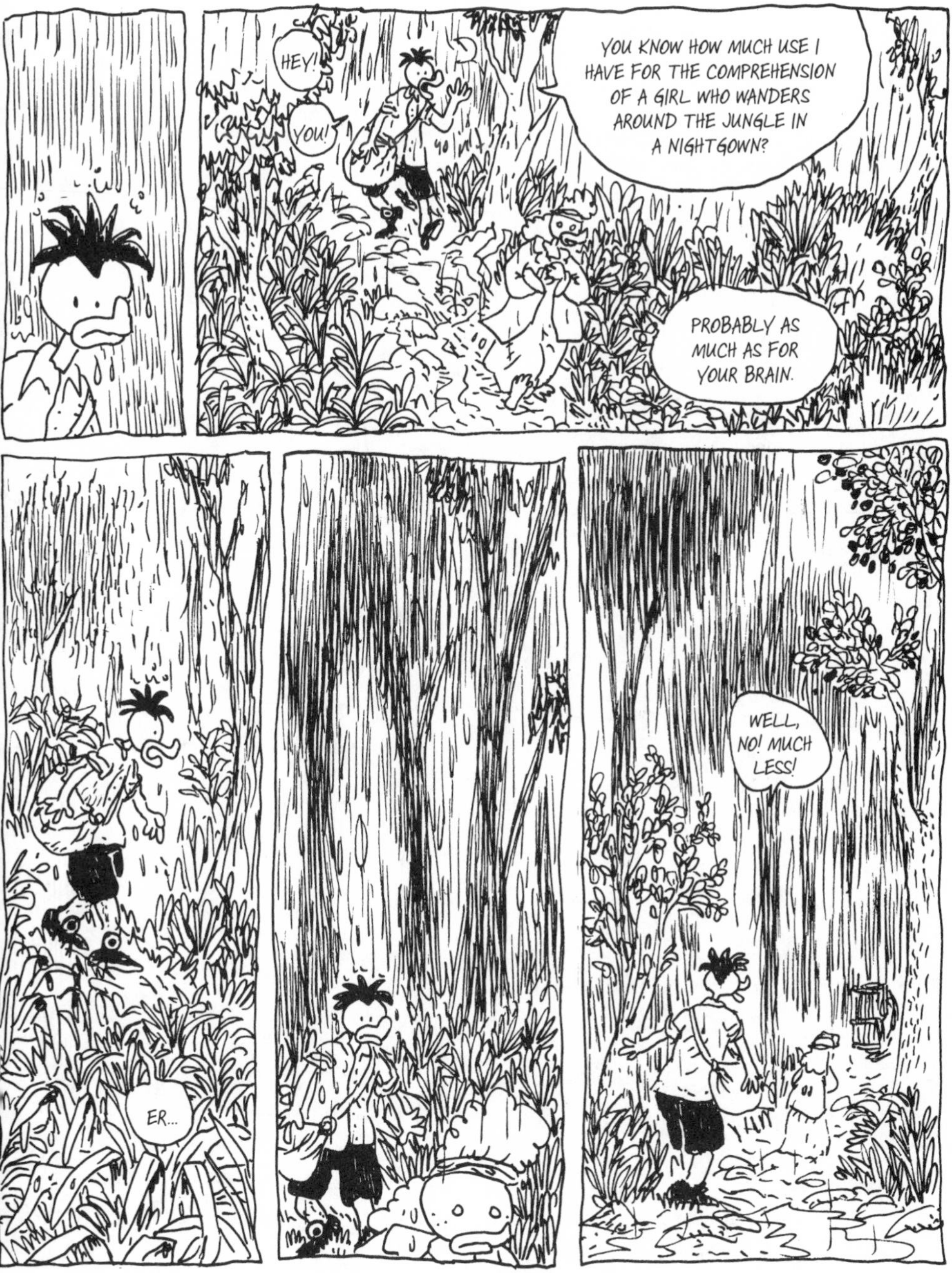
HEY!
YOU!
YOU KNOW HOW MUCH USE I HAVE FOR THE COMPREHENSION OF A GIRL WHO WANDERS AROUND THE JUNGLE IN A NIGHTGOWN?
PROBABLY AS MUCH AS FOR YOUR BRAIN.
ER...
WELL, NO! MUCH LESS!

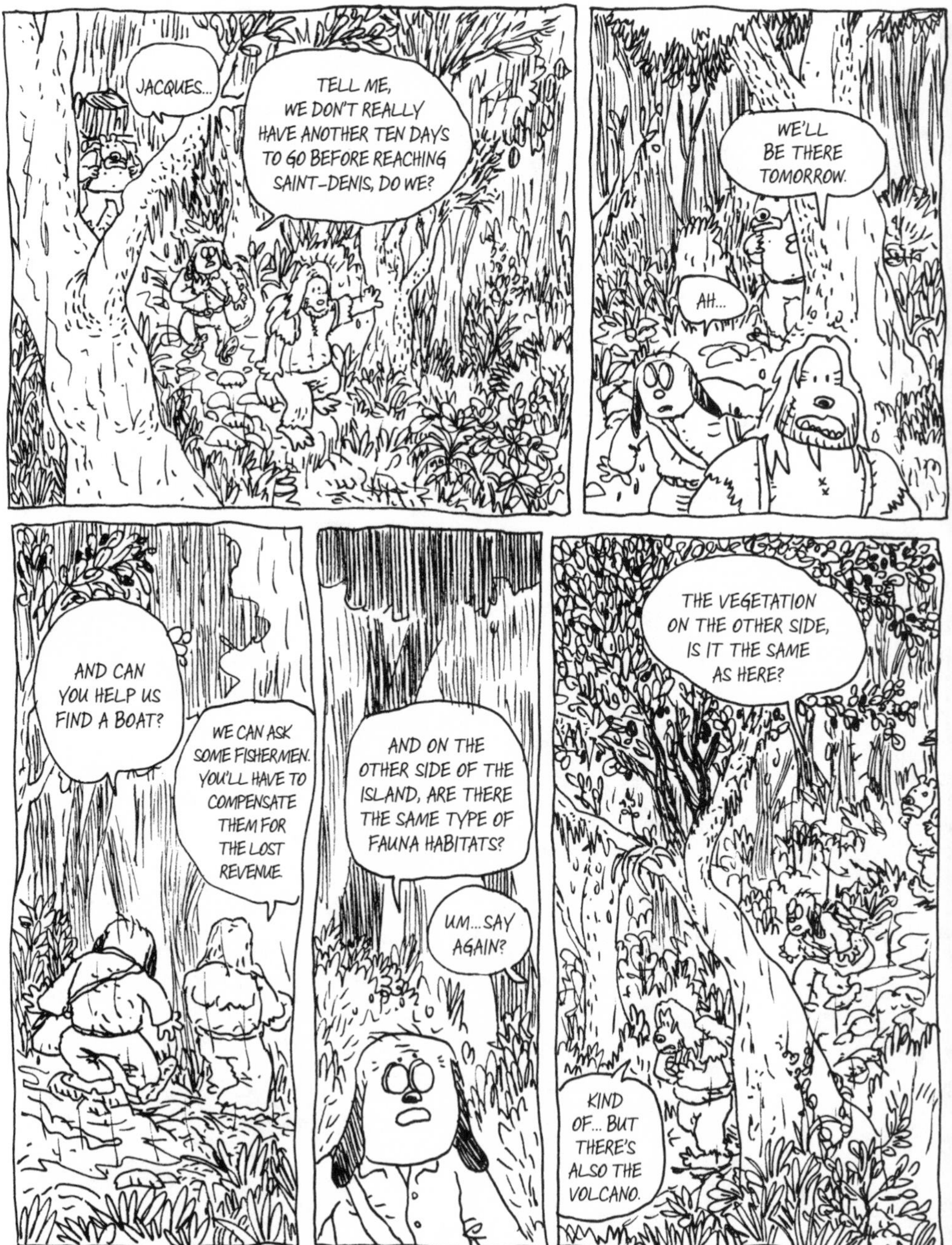
JACQUES...
TELL ME, WE DON'T REALLY HAVE ANOTHER TEN DAYS TO GO BEFORE REACHING SAINT-DENIS, DO WE?
WE'LL BE THERE TOMORROW.
AH...
AND CAN YOU HELP US FIND A BOAT?
WE CAN ASK SOME FISHERMEN. YOU'LL HAVE TO COMPENSATE THEM FOR THE LOST REVENUE.
AND ON THE OTHER SIDE OF THE ISLAND, ARE THERE THE SAME TYPE OF FAUNA HABITATS?
UM...SAY AGAIN?
THE VEGETATION ON THE OTHER SIDE, IS IT THE SAME AS HERE?
KIND OF... BUT THERE'S ALSO THE VOLCANO.

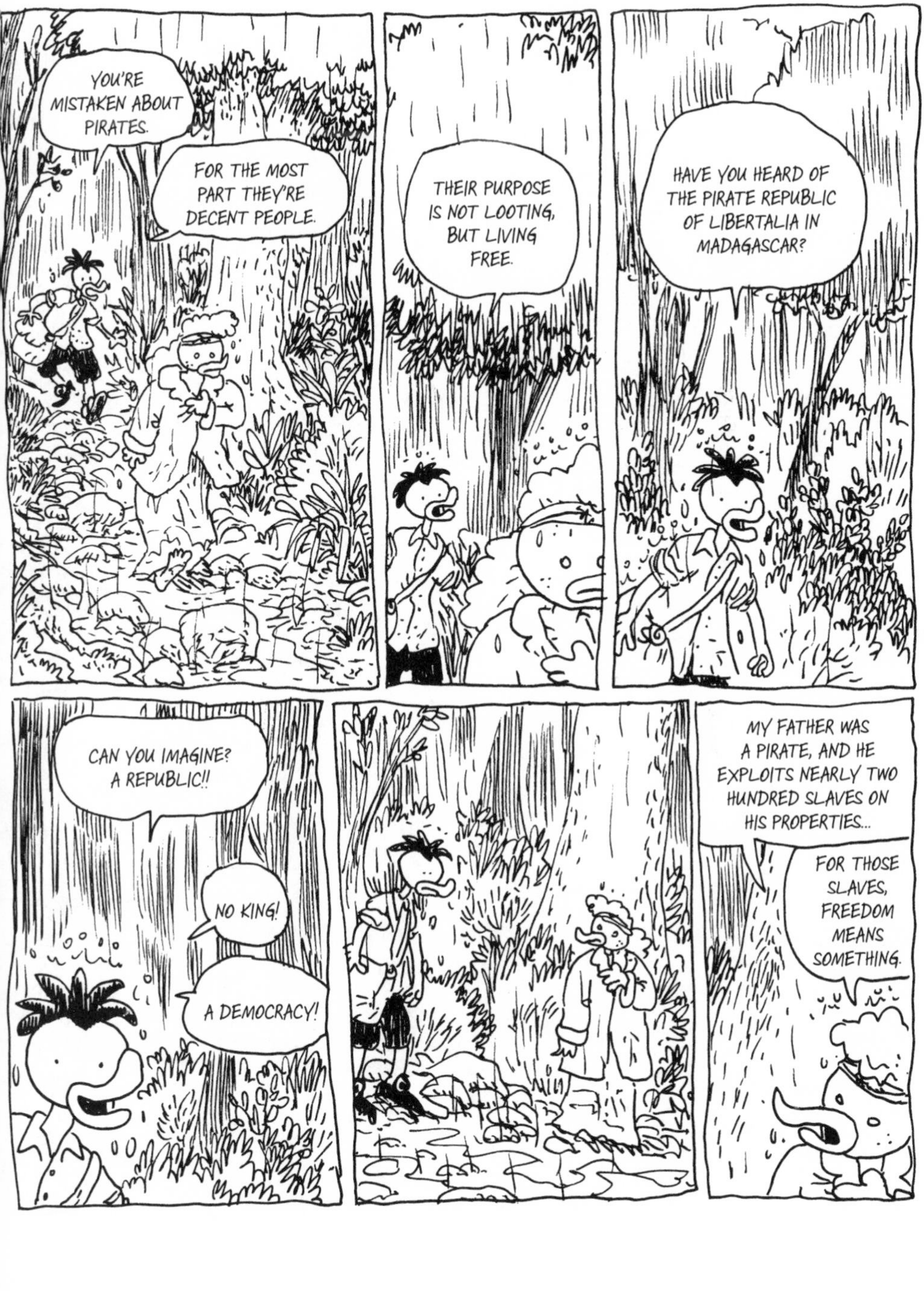
YOU'RE MISTAKEN ABOUT PIRATES.
FOR THE MOST PART THEY'RE DECENT PEOPLE.
THEIR PURPOSE IS NOT LOOTING, BUT LIVING FREE.
HAVE YOU HEARD OF THE PIRATE REPUBLIC OF LIBERTALIA IN MADAGASCAR?
CAN YOU IMAGINE? A REPUBLIC!!
NO KING!
A DEMOCRACY!
MY FATHER WAS A PIRATE, AND HE EXPLOITS NEARLY TWO HUNDRED SLAVES ON HIS PROPERTIES...
FOR THOSE SLAVES, FREEDOM MEANS SOMETHING.

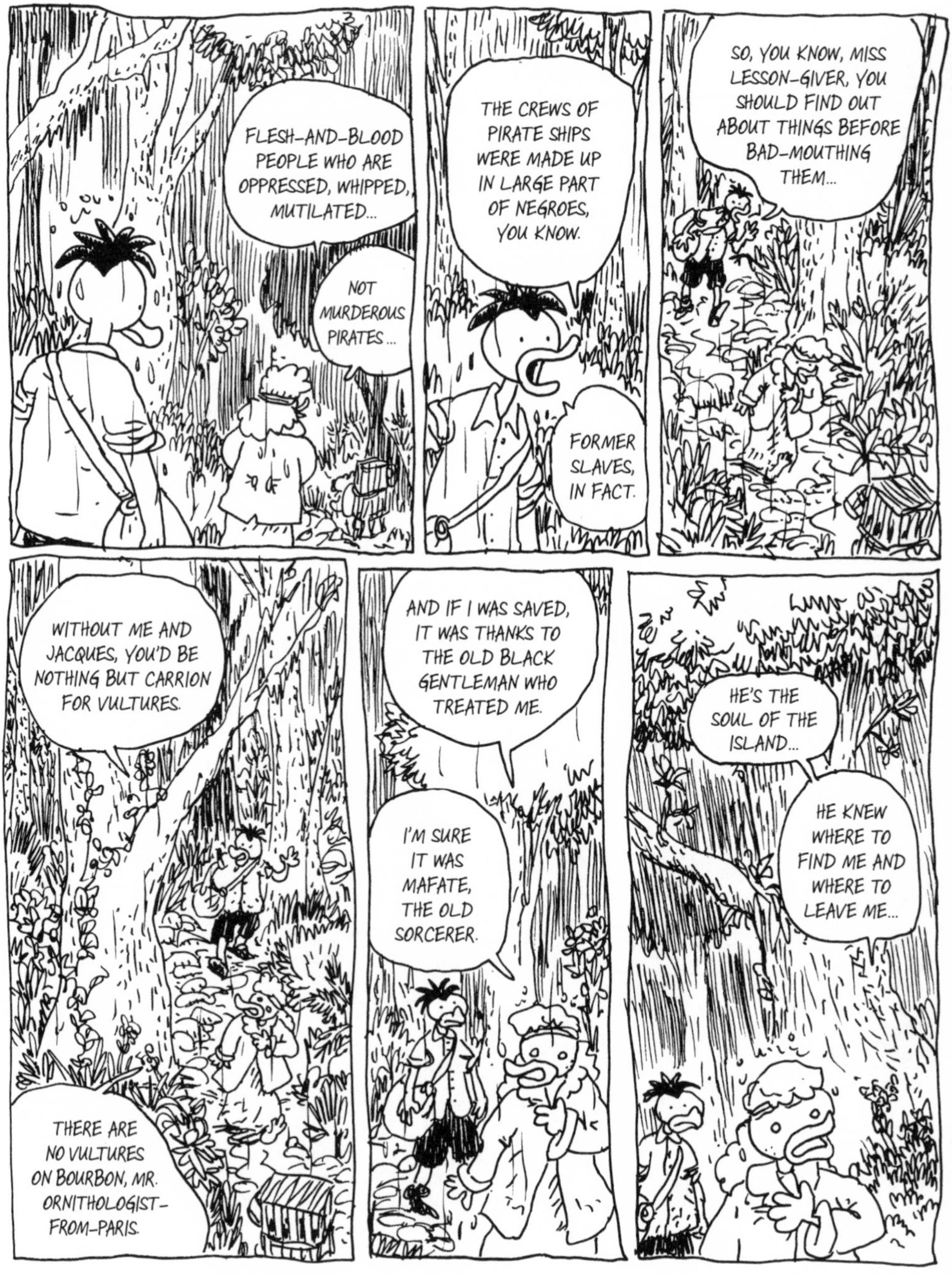
FLESH-AND-BLOOD PEOPLE WHO ARE OPPRESSED, WHIPPED, MUTILATED...
NOT MURDEROUS PIRATES...
THE CREWS OF PIRATE SHIPS WERE MADE UP IN LARGE PART OF NEGROES, YOU KNOW.
FORMER SLAVES, IN FACT.
SO, YOU KNOW, MISS LESSON-GIVER, YOU SHOULD FIND OUT ABOUT THINGS BEFORE BAD-MOUTHING THEM...
WITHOUT ME AND JACQUES, YOU'D BE NOTHING BUT CARRION FOR VULTURES.
THERE ARE NO VULTURES ON BOURBON, MR. ORNITHOLOGIST-FROM-PARIS.
AND IF I WAS SAVED, IT WAS THANKS TO THE OLD BLACK GENTLEMAN WHO TREATED ME.
I'M SURE IT WAS MAFATE, THE OLD SORCERER.
HE'S THE SOUL OF THE ISLAND...
HE KNEW WHERE TO FIND ME AND WHERE TO LEAVE ME...

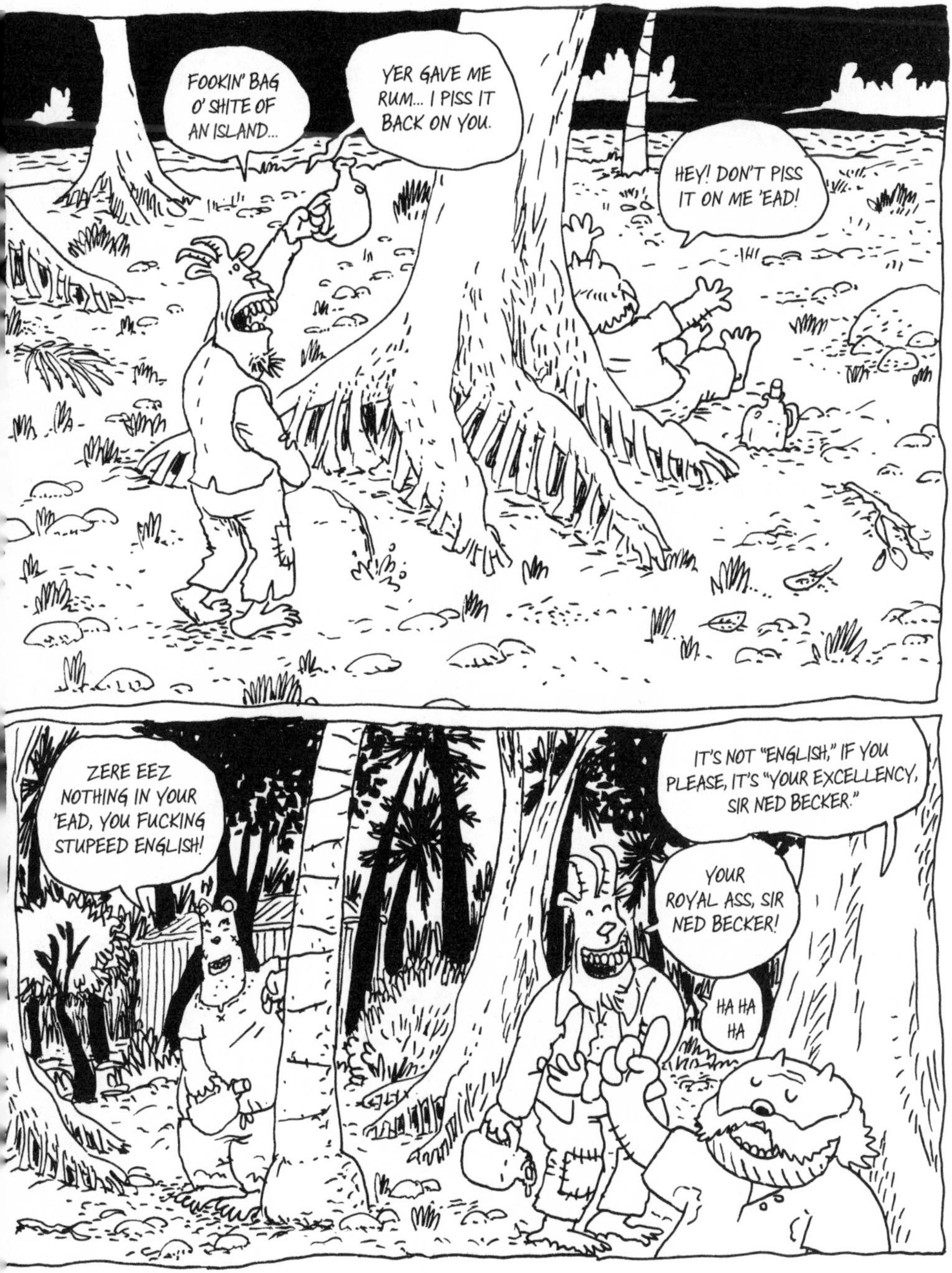
FOOKIN' BAG O' SHITE OF AN ISLAND...
YER GAVE ME RUM... I PISS IT BACK ON YOU.
HEY! DON'T PISS IT ON ME 'EAD!
ZERE EEZ NOTHING IN YOUR 'EAD, YOU FUCKING STUPEED ENGLISH!
IT'S NOT "ENGLISH," IF YOU PLEASE, IT'S "YOUR EXCELLENCY, SIR NED BECKER."
YOUR ROYAL ASS, SIR NED BECKER!
HA HA HA

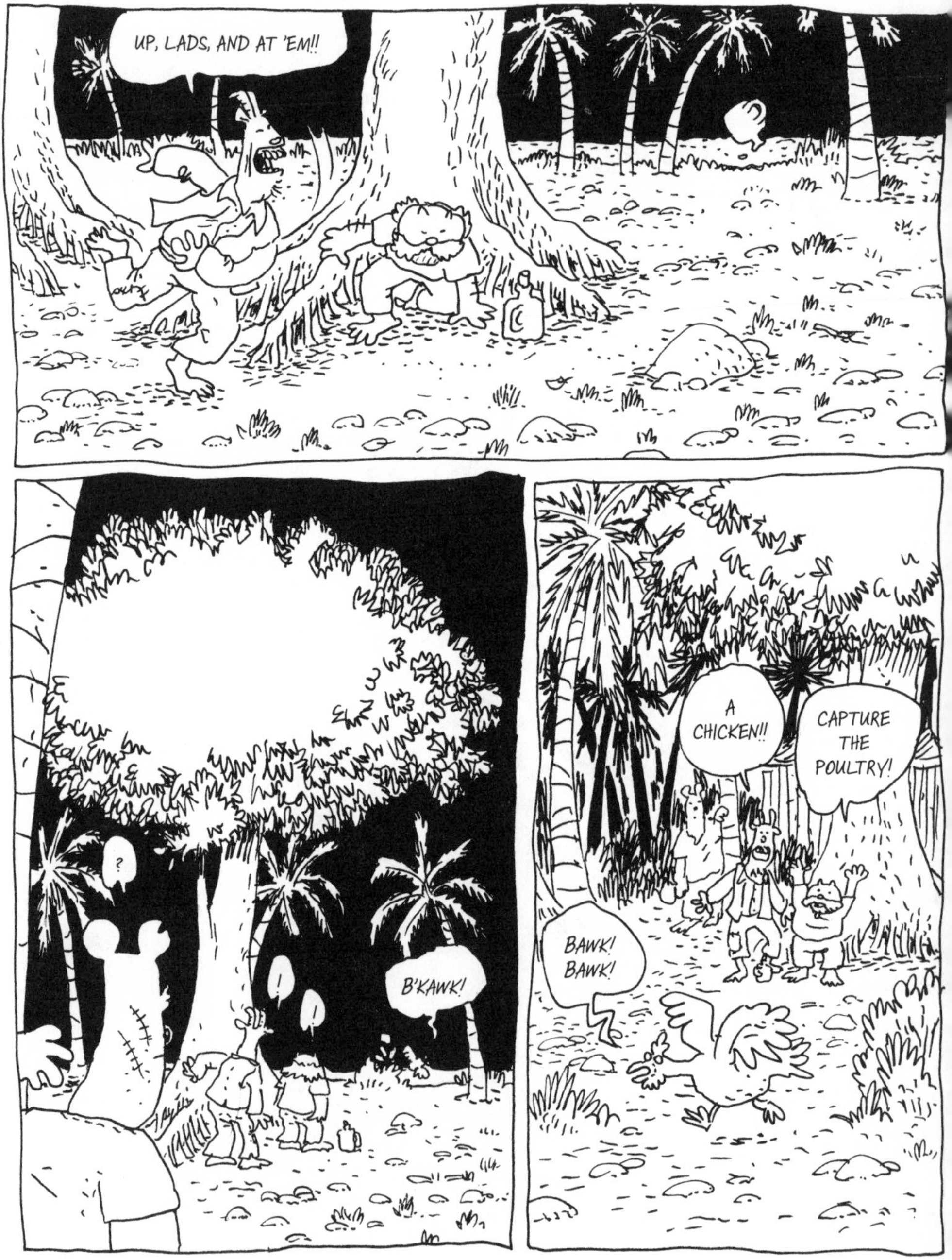
UP, LADS, AND AT 'EM!!
?
!
!
B'KAWK!
A CHICKEN!!
CAPTURE THE POULTRY!
BAWK! BAWK!

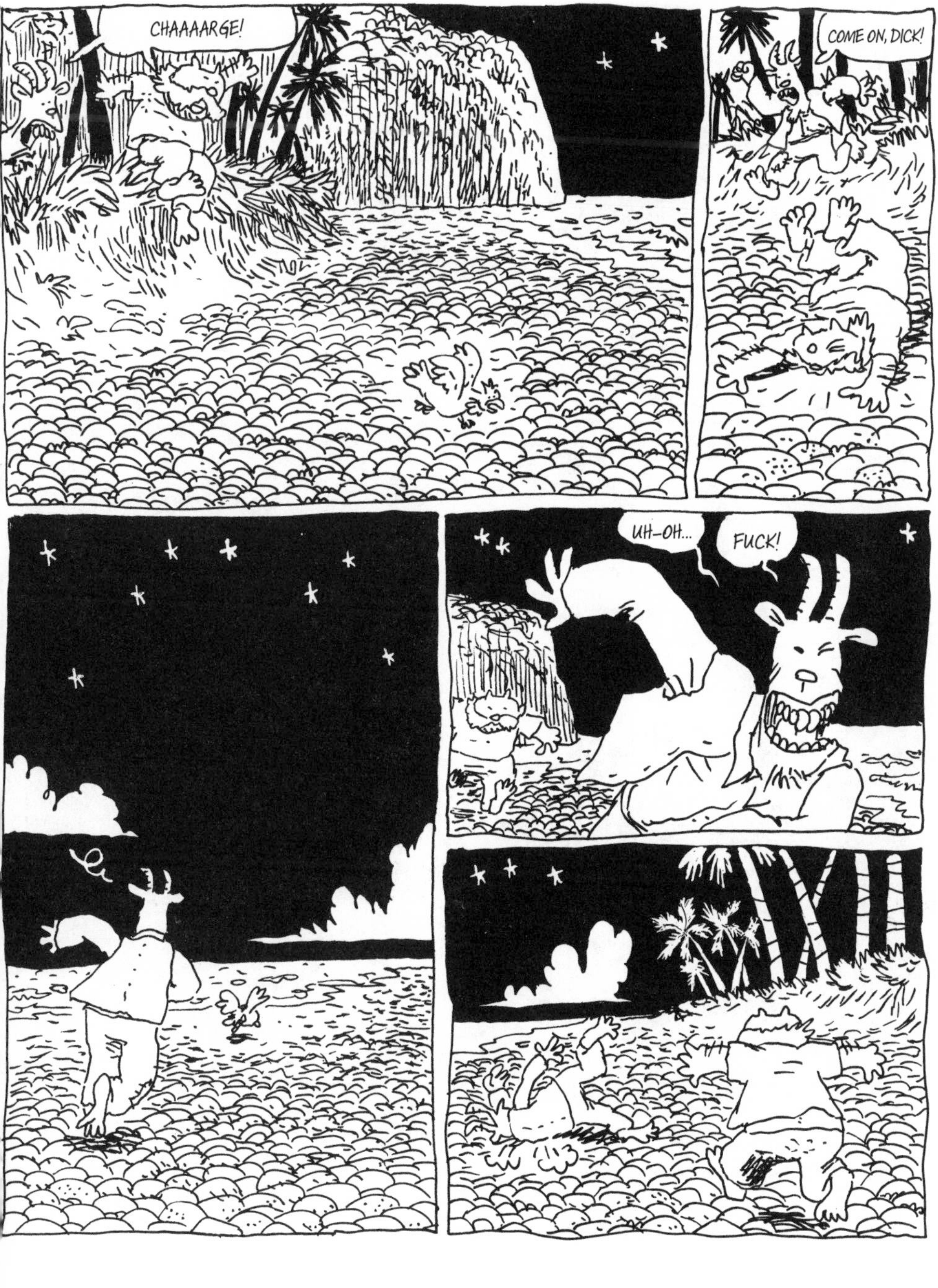
CHAAAARGE!
COME ON, DICK!
UH-OH...
FUCK!

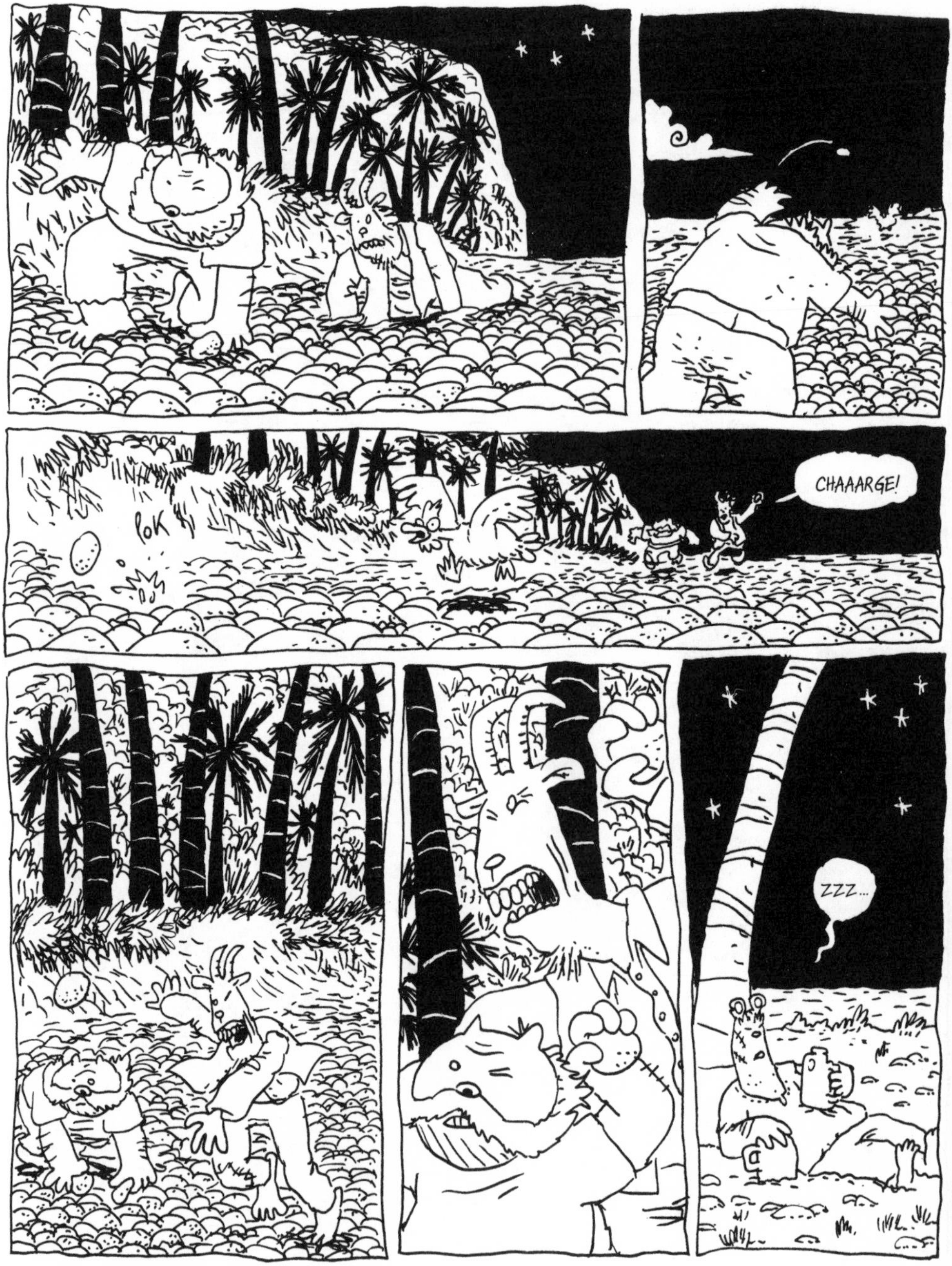
POK
CHAAARGE!
ZZZ...

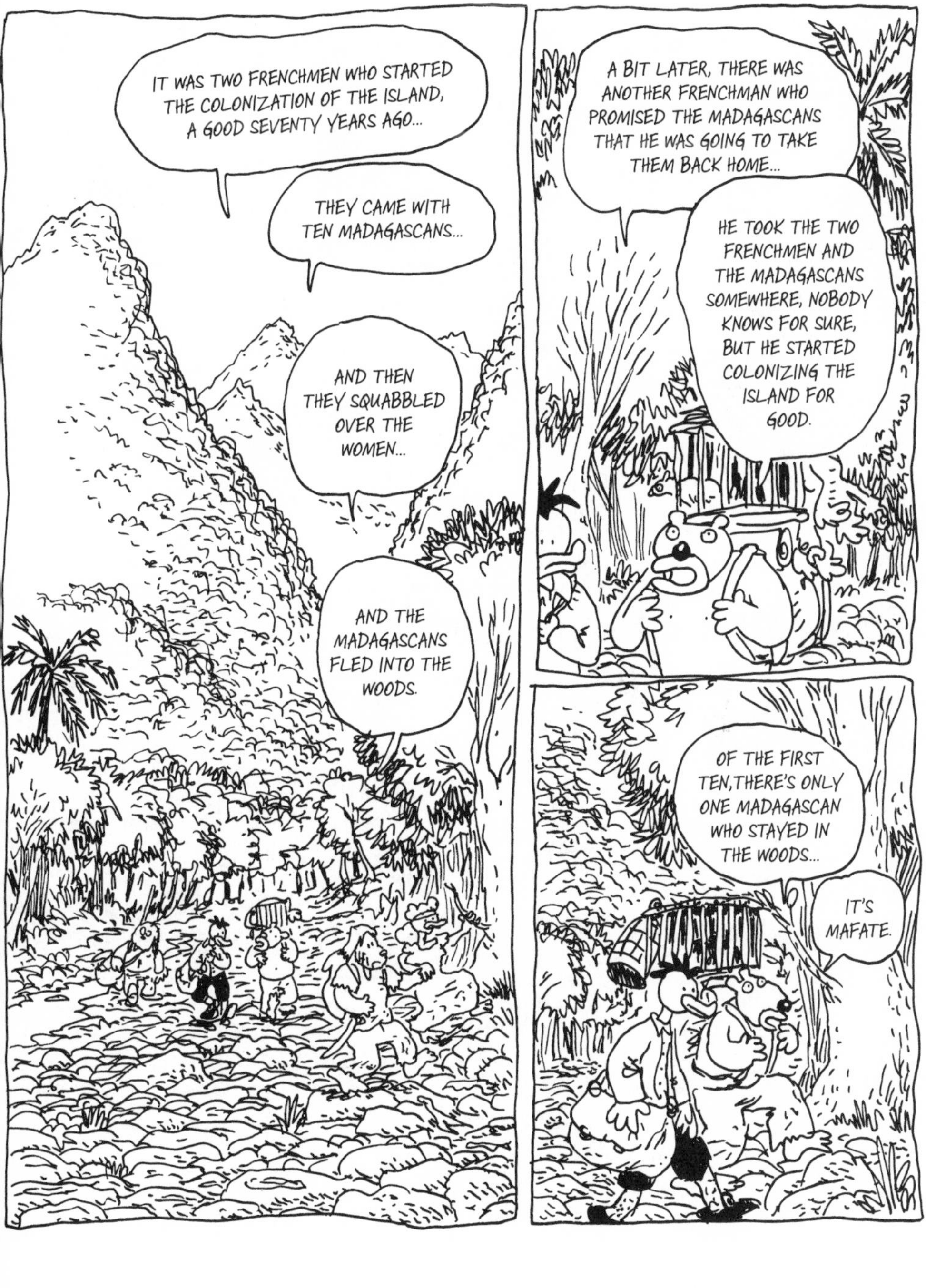
IT WAS TWO FRENCHMEN WHO STARTED THE COLONIZATION OF THE ISLAND, A GOOD SEVENTY YEARS AGO...
THEY CAME WITH TEN MADAGASCANS...
AND THEN THEY SQUABBLED OVER THE WOMEN...
AND THE MADAGASCANS FLED INTO THE WOODS.
A BIT LATER, THERE WAS ANOTHER FRENCHMAN WHO PROMISED THE MADAGASCANS THAT HE WAS GOING TO TAKE THEM BACK HOME...
HE TOOK THE TWO FRENCHMEN AND THE MADAGASCANS SOMEWHERE, NOBODY KNOWS FOR SURE, BUT HE STARTED COLONIZING THE ISLAND FOR GOOD.
OF THE FIRST TEN,THERE'S ONLY ONE MADAGASCAN WHO STAYED IN THE WOODS...
IT'S MAFATE.

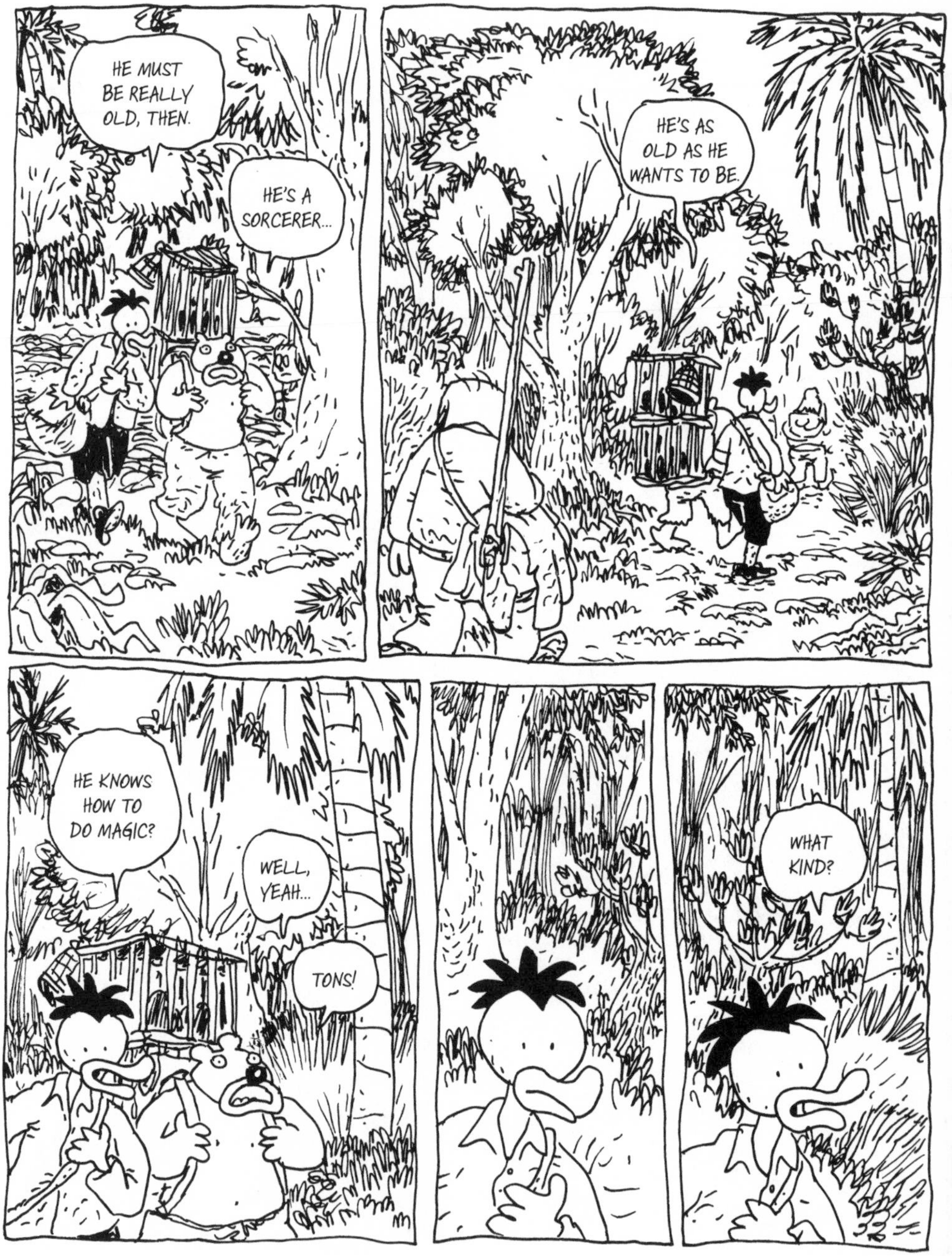
HE MUST BE REALLY OLD, THEN.
HE'S A SORCERER...
HE'S AS OLD AS HE WANTS TO BE.
HE KNOWS HOW TO DO MAGIC?
WELL, YEAH...
TONS!
WHAT KIND?

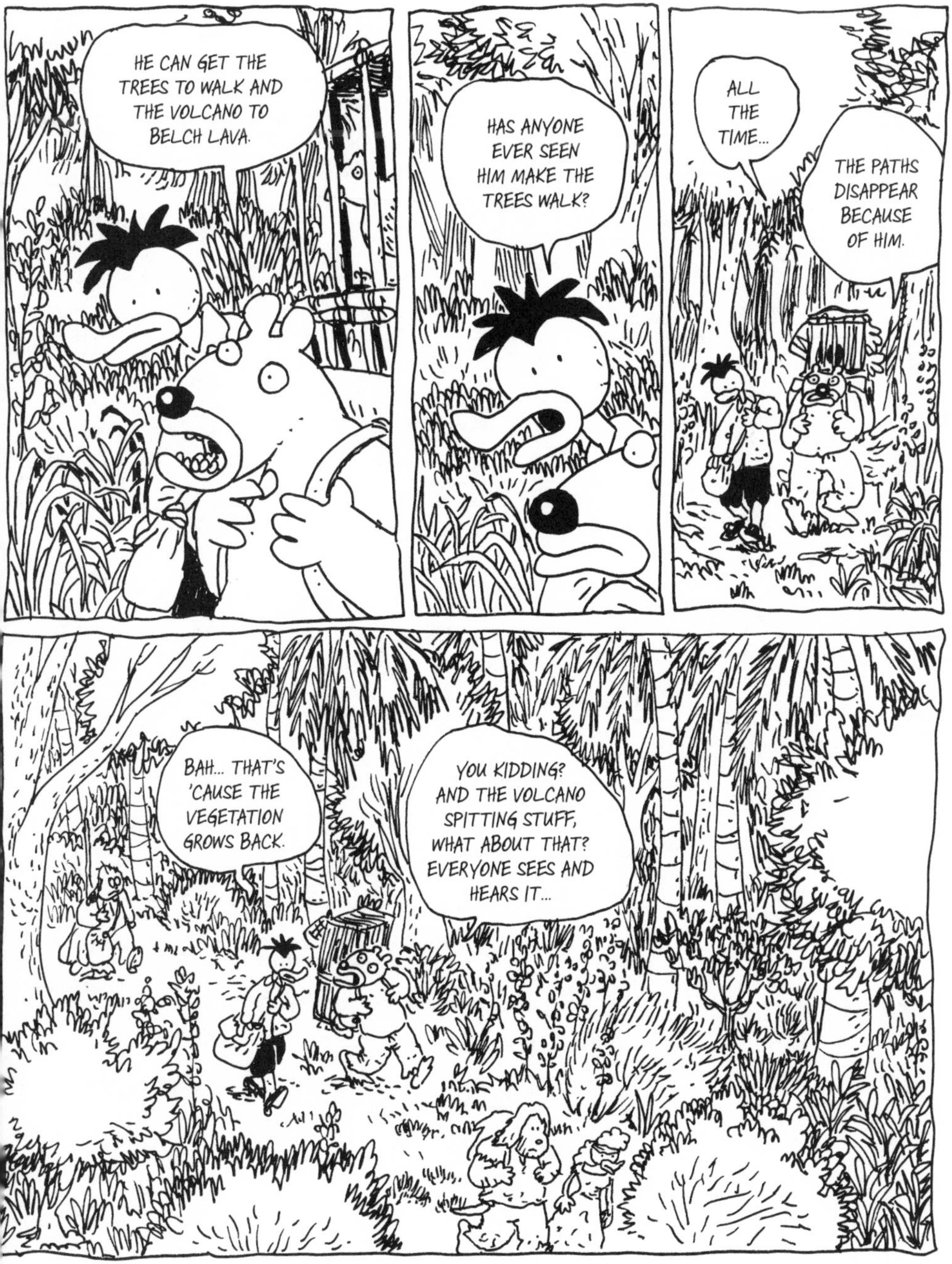

HE CAN GET THE TREES TO WALK AND THE VOLCANO TO BELCH LAVA.
HAS ANYONE EVER SEEN HIM MAKE THE TREES WALK?
ALL THE TIME...
THE PATHS DISAPPEAR BECAUSE OF HIM.
BAH... THAT'S 'CAUSE THE VEGETATION GROWS BACK.
YOU KIDDING? AND THE VOLCANO SPITTING STUFF, WHAT ABOUT THAT? EVERYONE SEES AND HEARS IT...

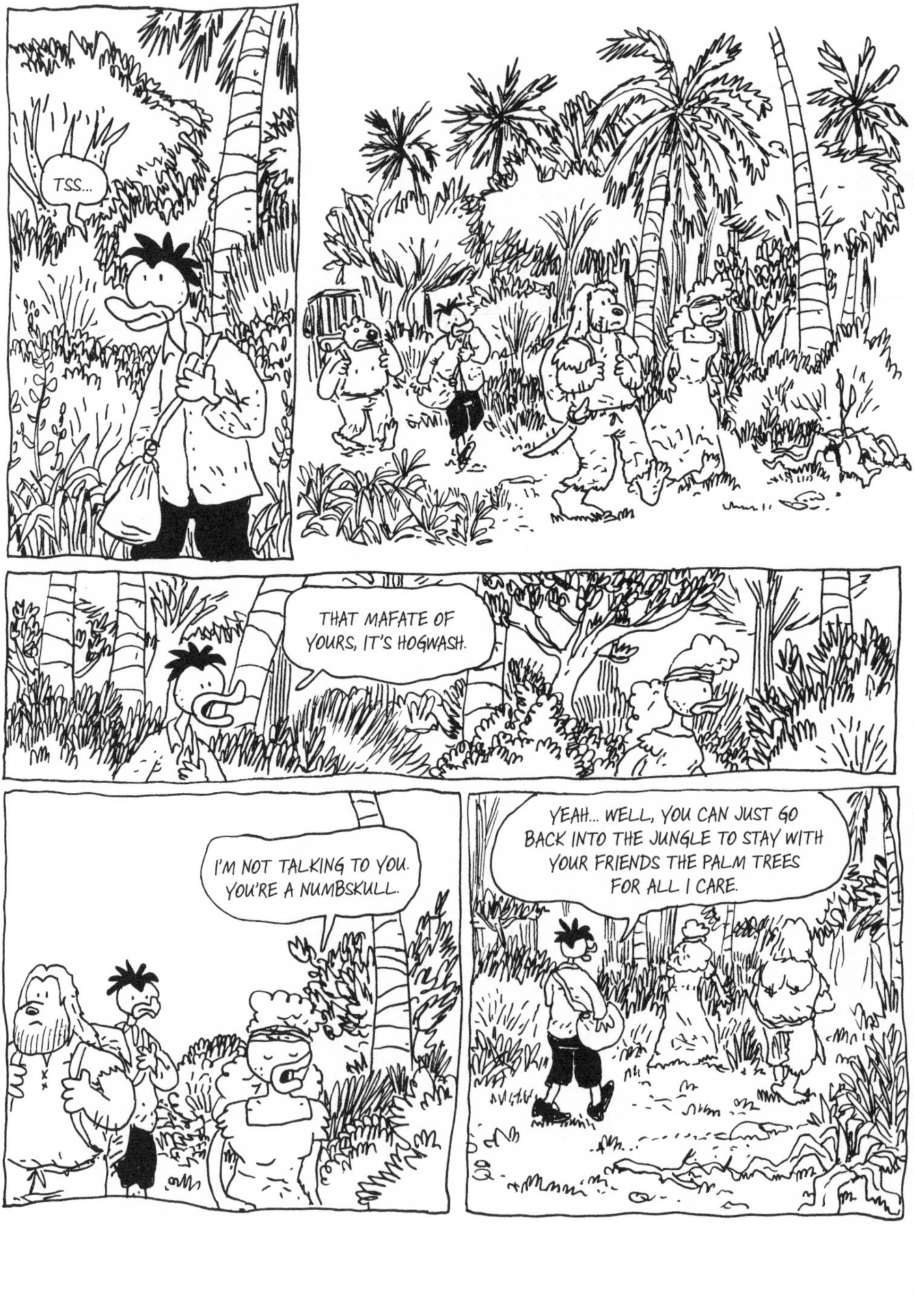

TSS...
THAT MAFATE OF YOURS, IT'S HOGWASH.
I'M NOT TALKING TO YOU. YOU'RE A NUMBSKULL.
YEAH... WELL, YOU CAN JUST GO BACK INTO THE JUNGLE TO STAY WITH YOUR FRIENDS THE PALM TREES FOR ALL I CARE.

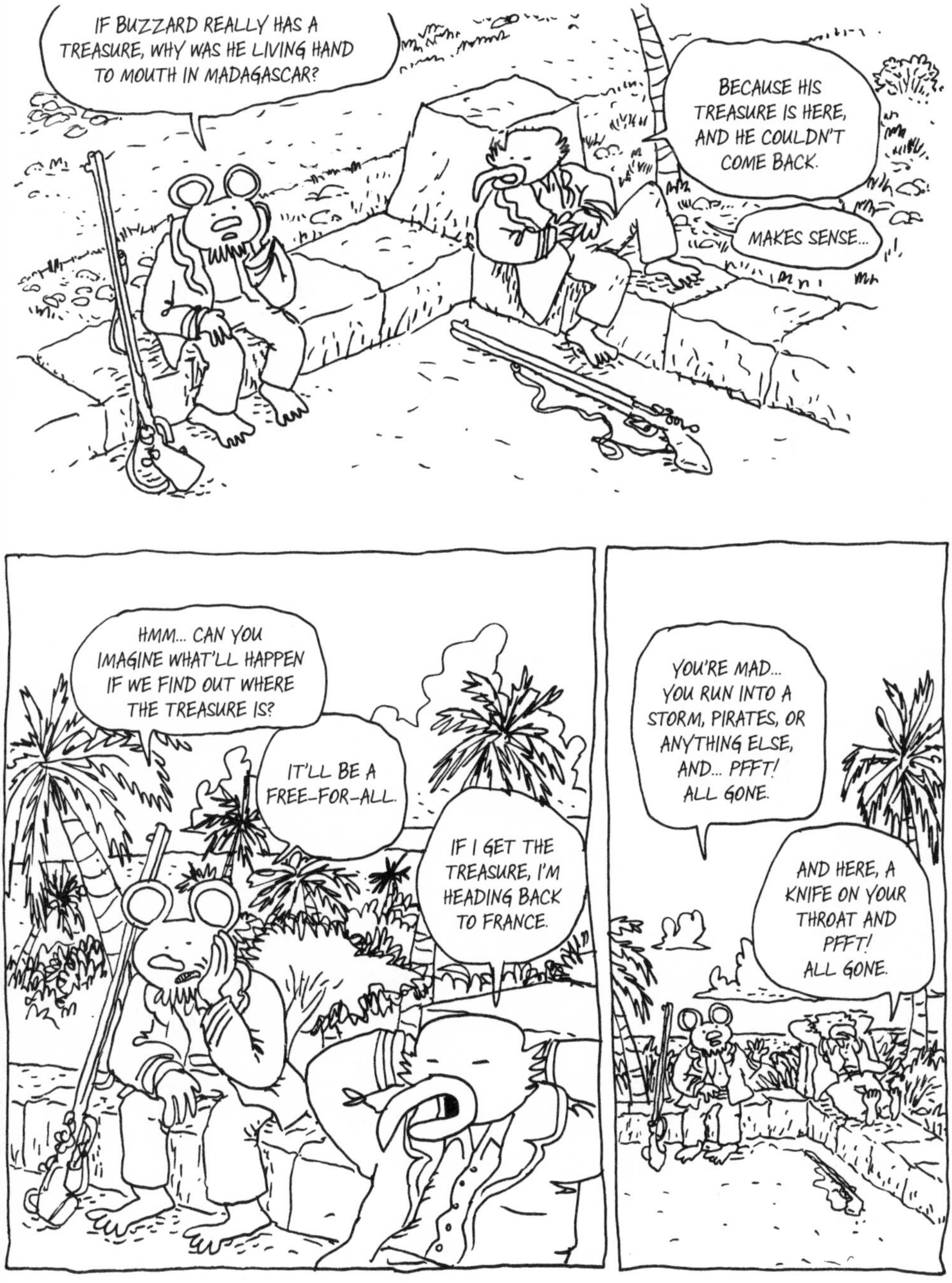
IF BUZZARD REALLY HAS A TREASURE, WHY WAS HE LIVING HAND TO MOUTH IN MADAGASCAR?
BECAUSE HIS TREASURE IS HERE, AND HE COULDN'T COME BACK.
MAKES SENSE...
HMM... CAN YOU IMAGINE WHAT'LL HAPPEN IF WE FIND OUT WHERE THE TREASURE IS?
IT'LL BE A FREE-FOR-ALL.
IF I GET THE TREASURE, I'M HEADING BACK TO FRANCE.
YOU'RE MAD... YOU RUN INTO A STORM, PIRATES, OR ANYTHING ELSE, AND... PFFT! ALL GONE.
AND HERE, A KNIFE ON YOUR THROAT AND PFFT! ALL GONE.

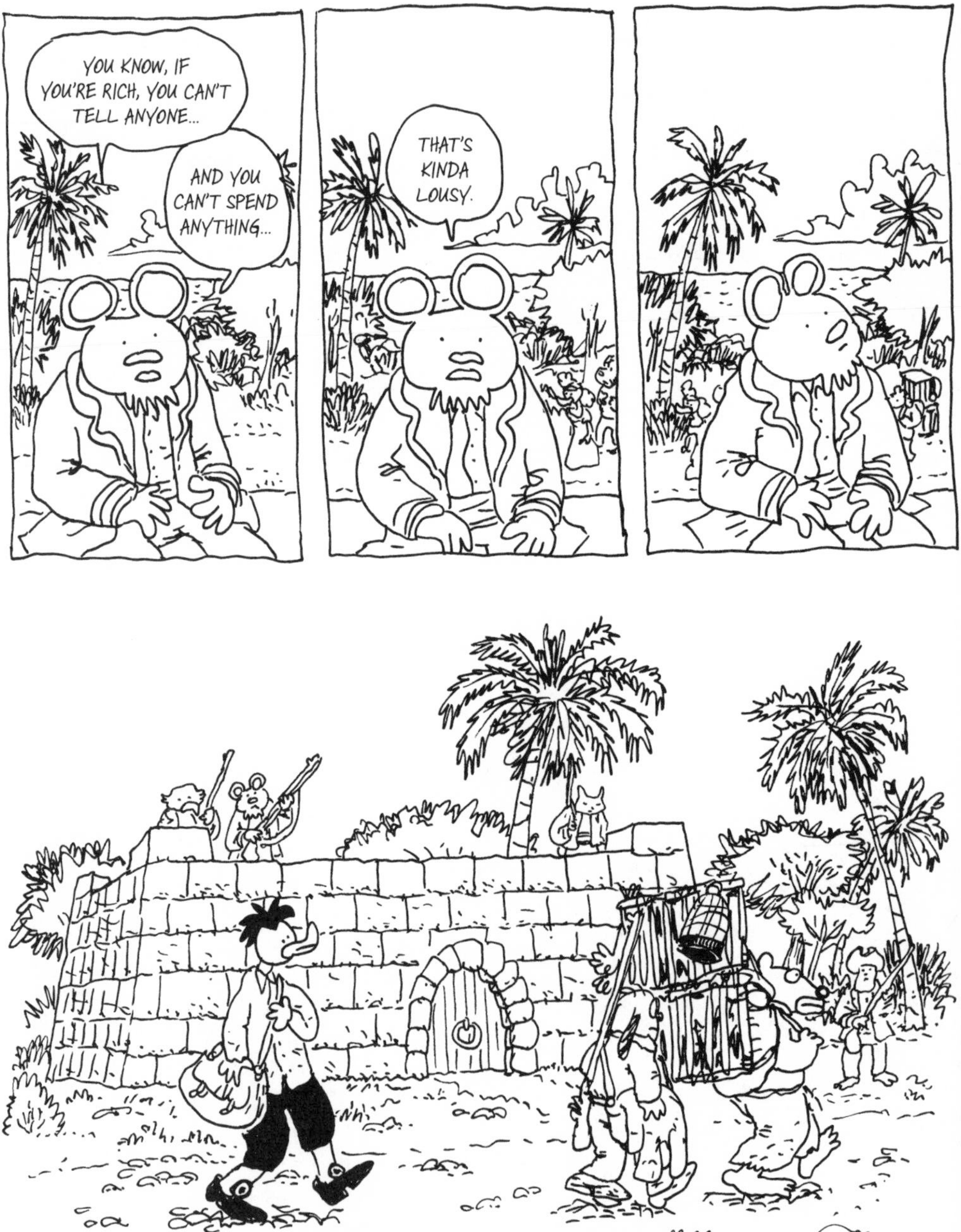
YOU KNOW, IF YOU'RE RICH, YOU CAN'T TELL ANYONE...
AND YOU CAN'T SPEND ANYTHING...
THAT'S KINDA LOUSY.

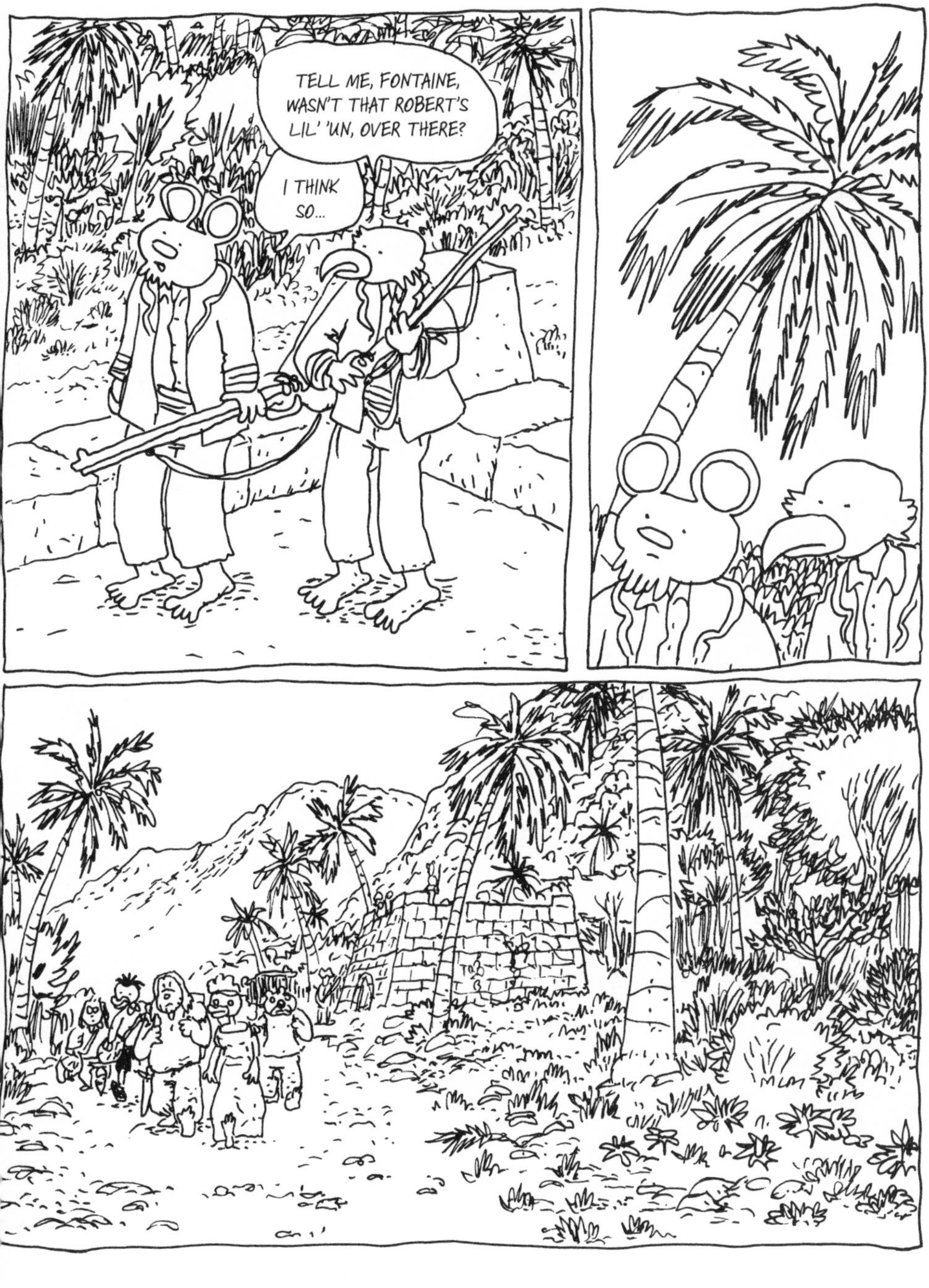
TELL ME, FONTAINE, WASN'T THAT ROBERT'S LIL' 'UN, OVER THERE?
I THINK SO...

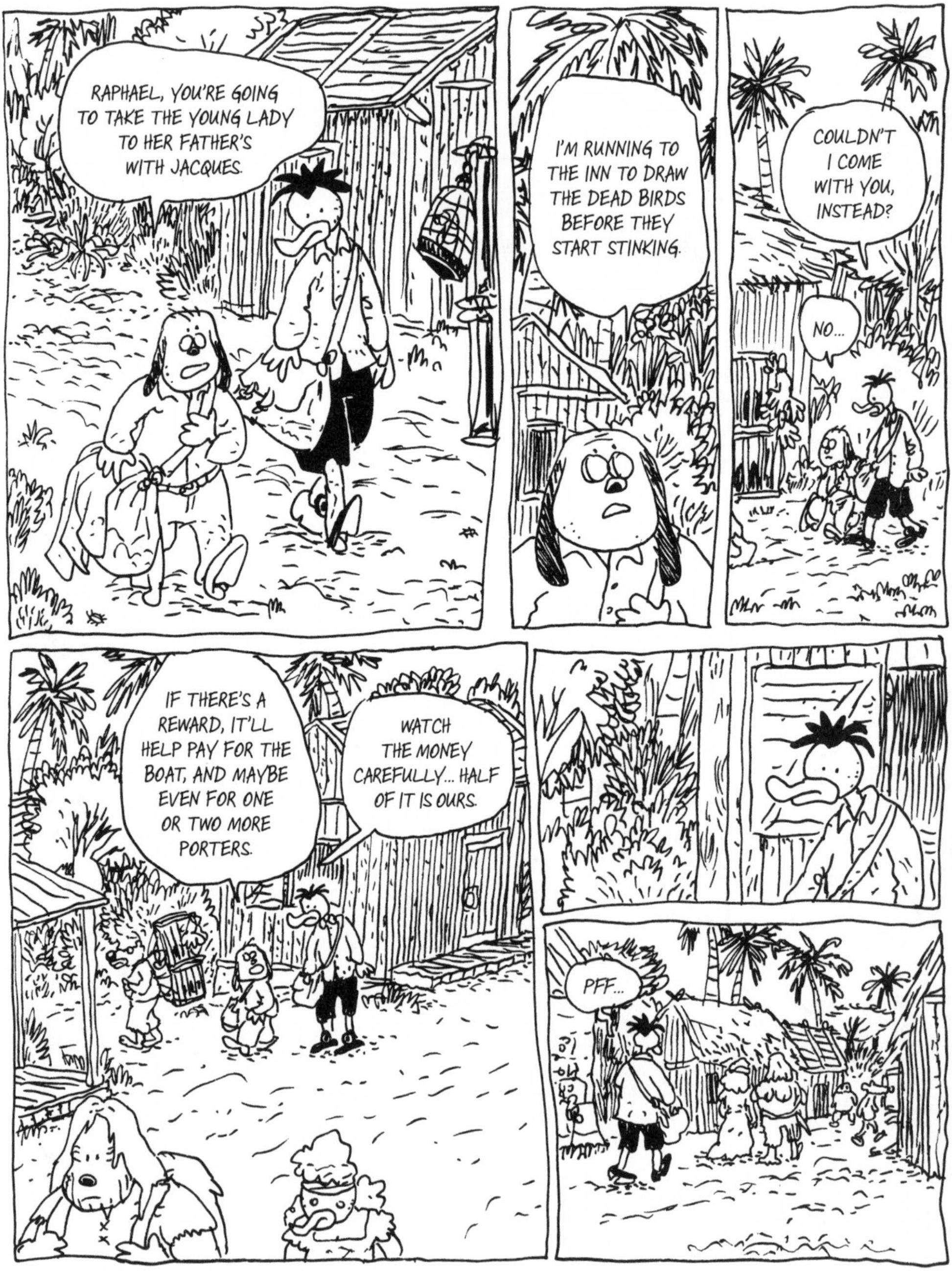
RAPHAEL, YOU'RE GOING TO TAKE THE YOUNG LADY TO HER FATHER'S WITH JACQUES.
I'M RUNNING TO THE INN TO DRAW THE DEAD BIRDS BEFORE THEY START STINKING.
COULDN'T I COME WITH YOU, INSTEAD?
NO...
IF THERE'S A REWARD, IT'LL HELP PAY FOR THE BOAT, AND MAYBE EVEN FOR ONE OR TWO MORE PORTERS.
WATCH THE MONEY CAREFULLY... HALF OF IT IS OURS.
PFF...

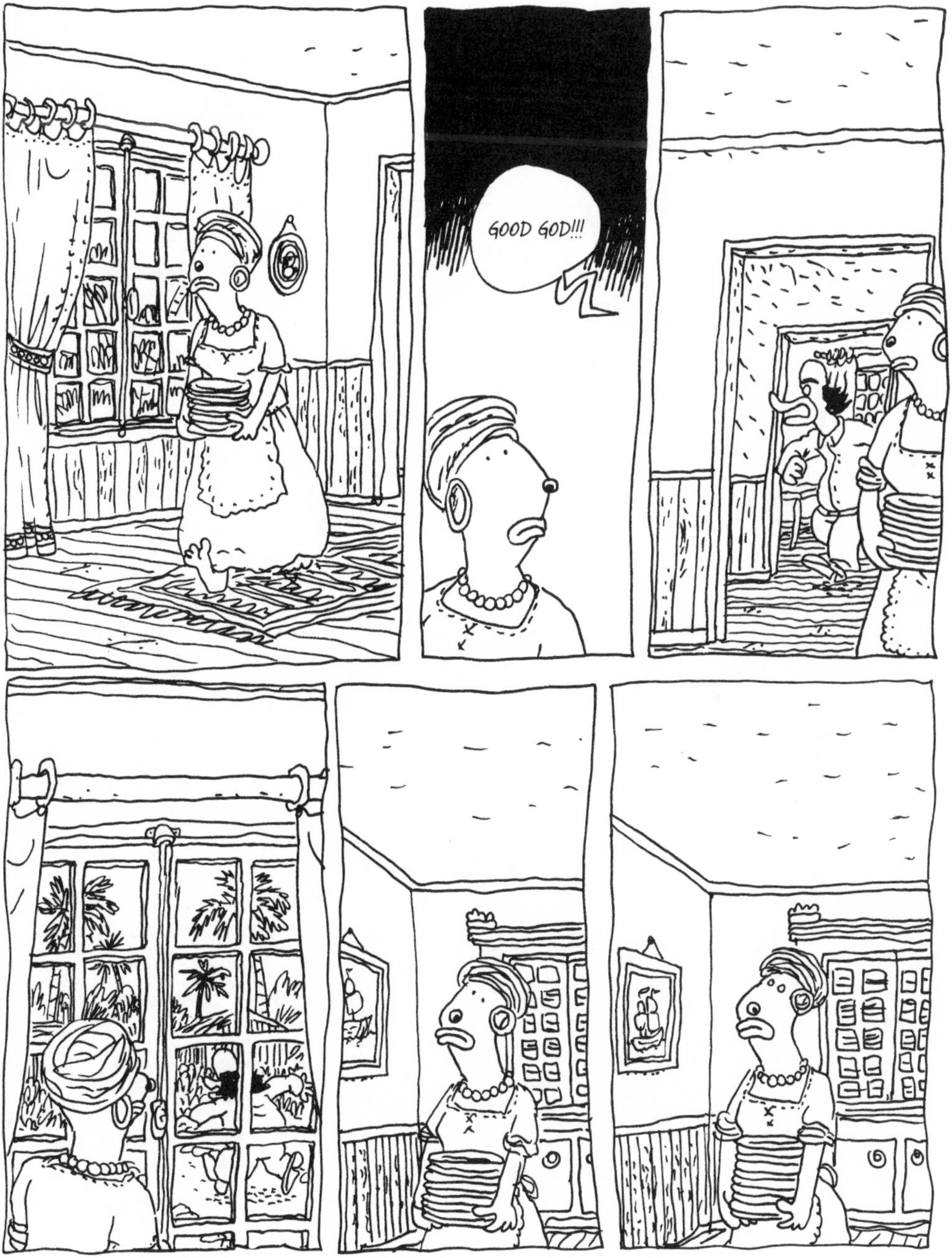
GOOD GOD!!!

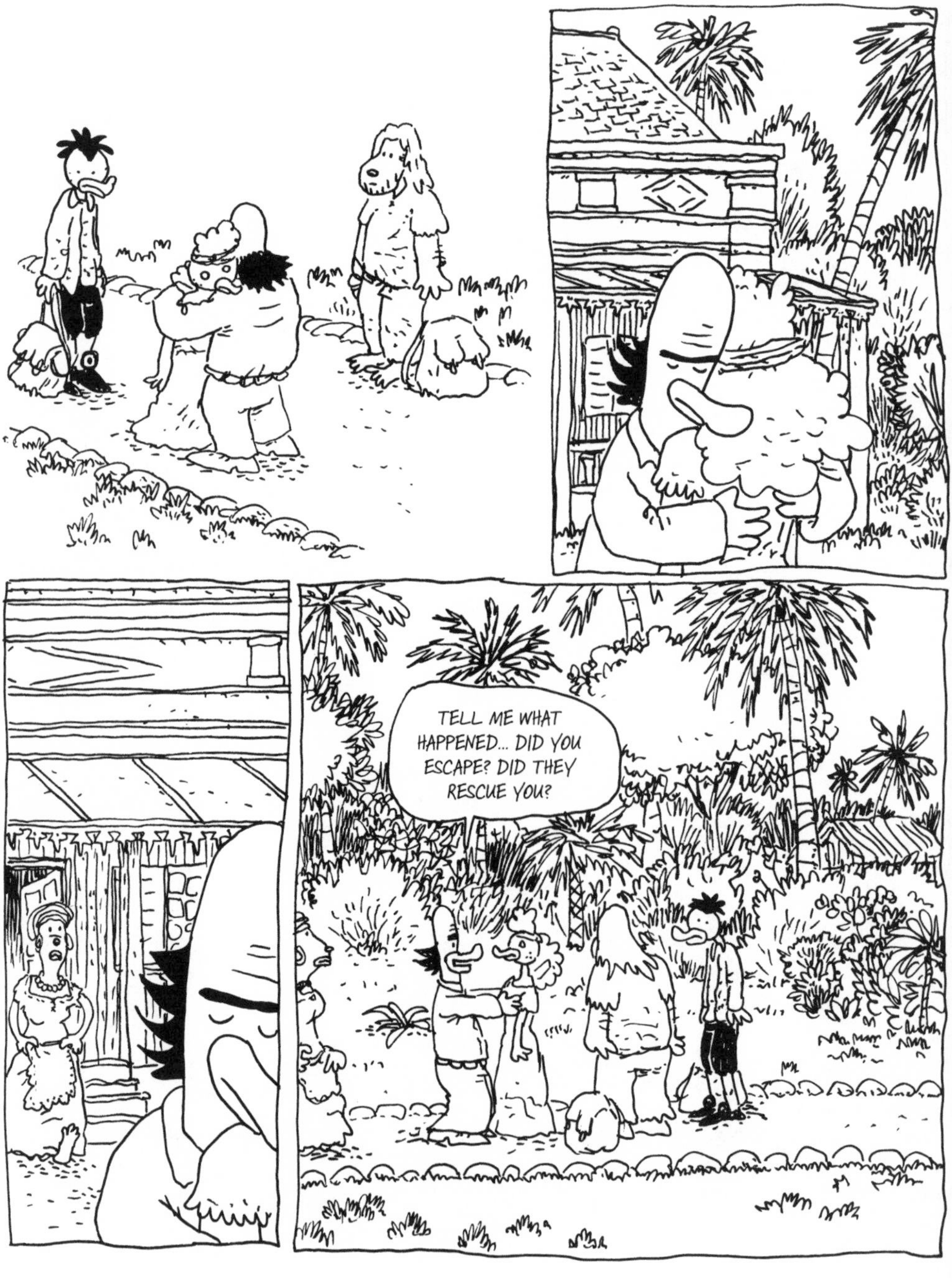
TELL ME WHAT HAPPENED... DID YOU ESCAPE? DID THEY RESCUE YOU?

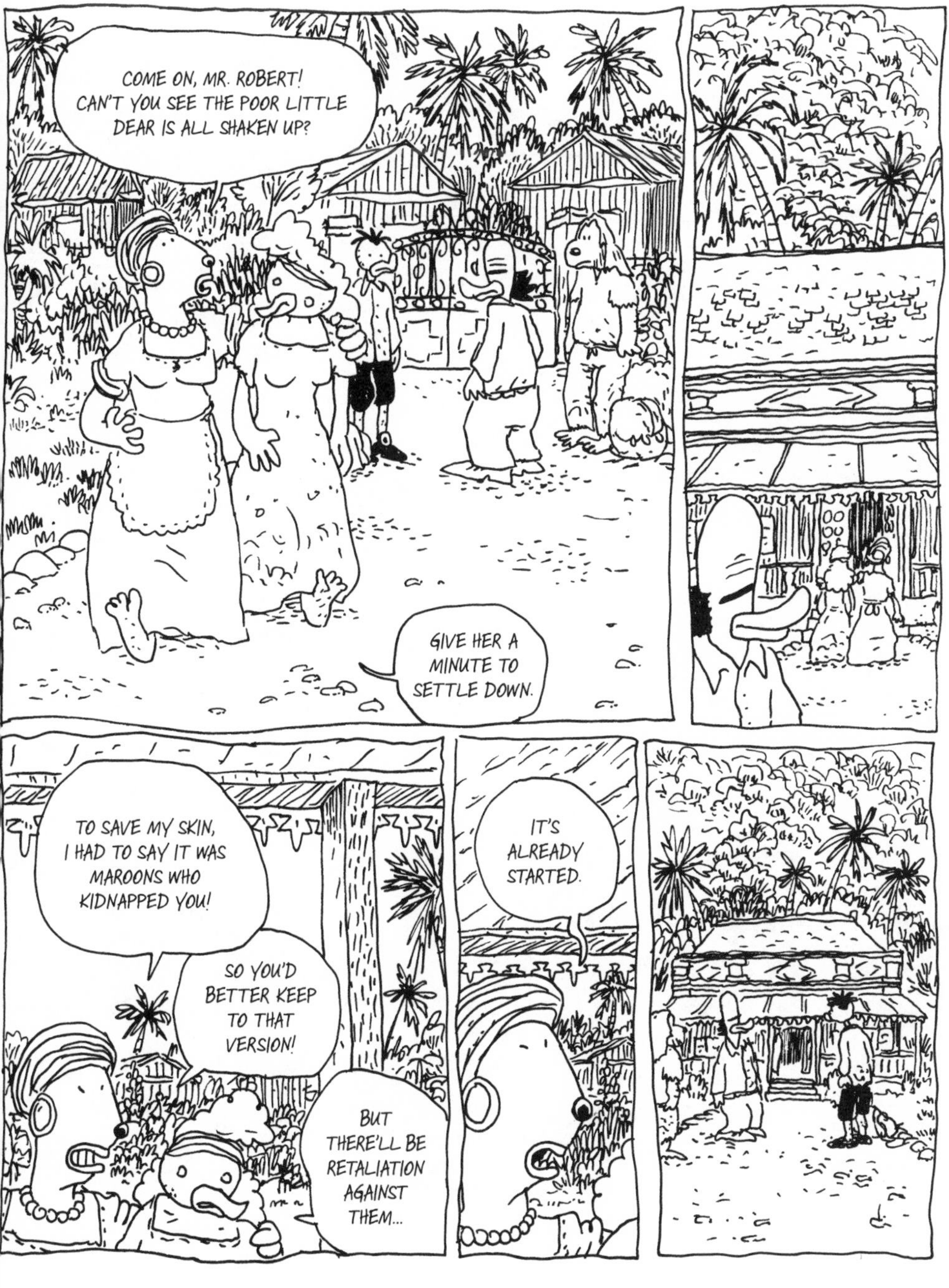

COME ON, MR. ROBERT! CAN'T YOU SEE THE POOR LITTLE DEAR IS ALL SHAKEN UP?
GIVE HER A MINUTE TO SETTLE DOWN.
TO SAVE MY SKIN, I HAD TO SAY IT WAS MAROONS WHO KIDNAPPED YOU!
SO YOU'D BETTER KEEP TO THAT VERSION!
BUT THERE'LL BE RETALIATION AGAINST THEM...
IT'S ALREADY STARTED.

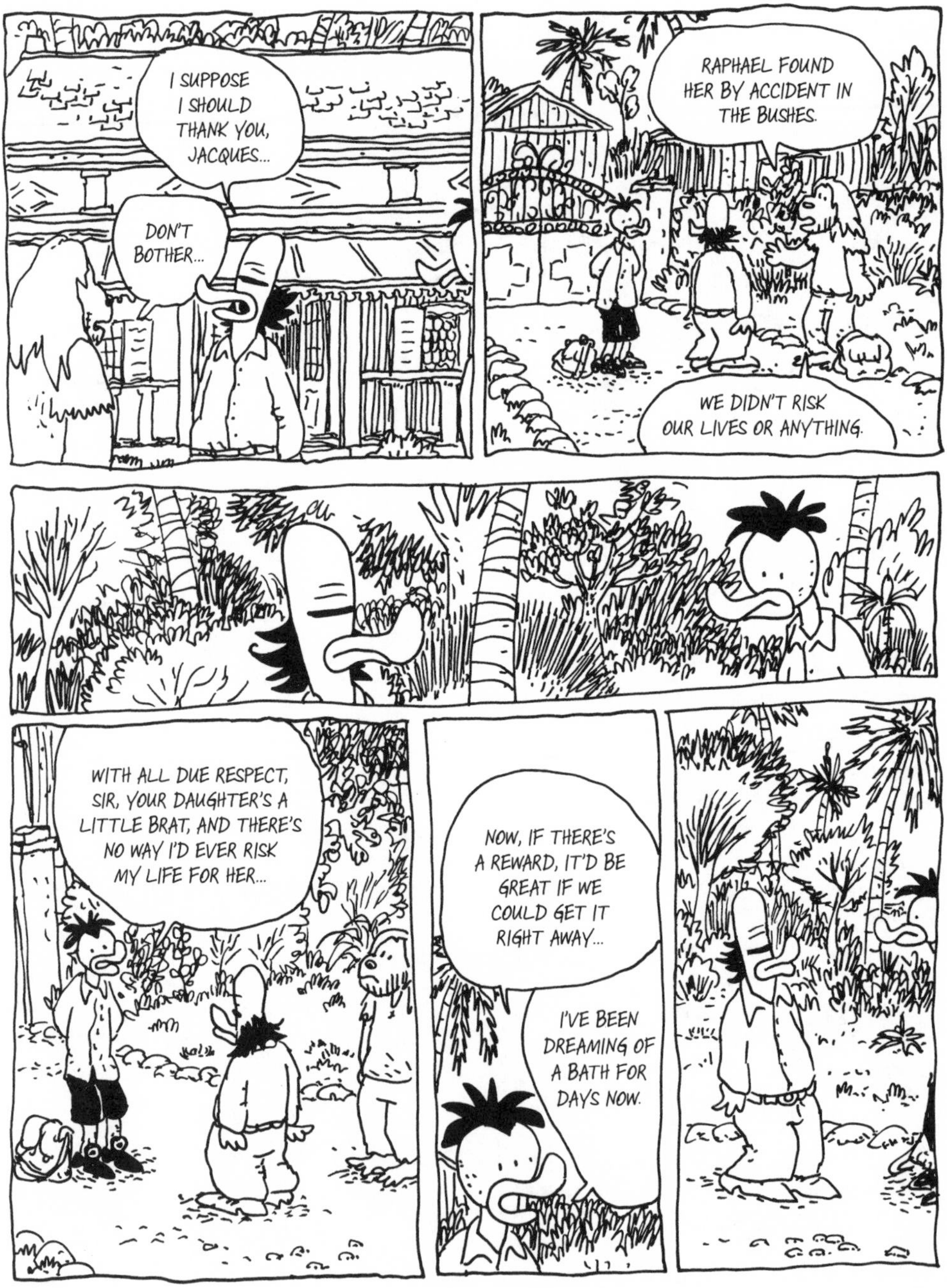
I SUPPOSE I SHOULD THANK YOU, JACQUES...
DON'T BOTHER...
RAPHAEL FOUND HER BY ACCIDENT IN THE BUSHES.
WE DIDN'T RISK OUR LIVES OR ANYTHING.
WITH ALL DUE RESPECT, SIR, YOUR DAUGHTER'S A LITTLE BRAT, AND THERE'S NO WAY I'D EVER RISK MY LIFE FOR HER...
NOW, IF THERE'S A REWARD, IT'D BE GREAT IF WE COULD GET IT RIGHT AWAY...
I'VE BEEN DREAMING OF A BATH FOR DAYS NOW.

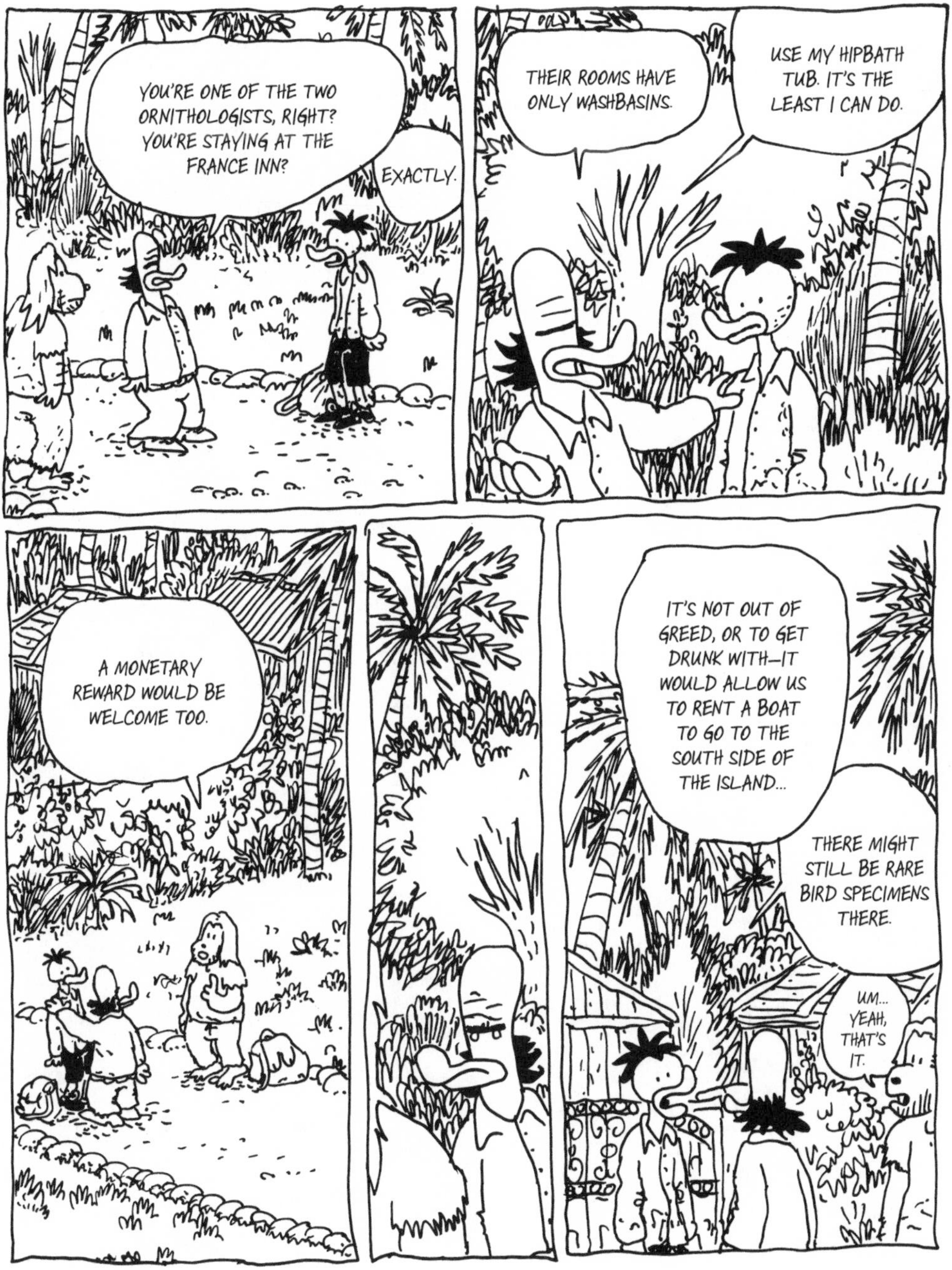
YOU'RE ONE OF THE TWO ORNITHOLOGISTS, RIGHT? YOU'RE STAYING AT THE FRANCE INN?
EXACTLY.
THEIR ROOMS HAVE ONLY WASHBASINS.
USE MY HIPBATH TUB. IT'S THE LEAST I CAN DO.
A MONETARY REWARD WOULD BE WELCOME TOO.
IT'S NOT OUT OF GREED, OR TO GET DRUNK WITH—IT WOULD ALLOW US TO RENT A BOAT TO GO TO THE SOUTH SIDE OF THE ISLAND...
THERE MIGHT STILL BE RARE BIRD SPECIMENS THERE.
UM... YEAH, THAT'S IT.

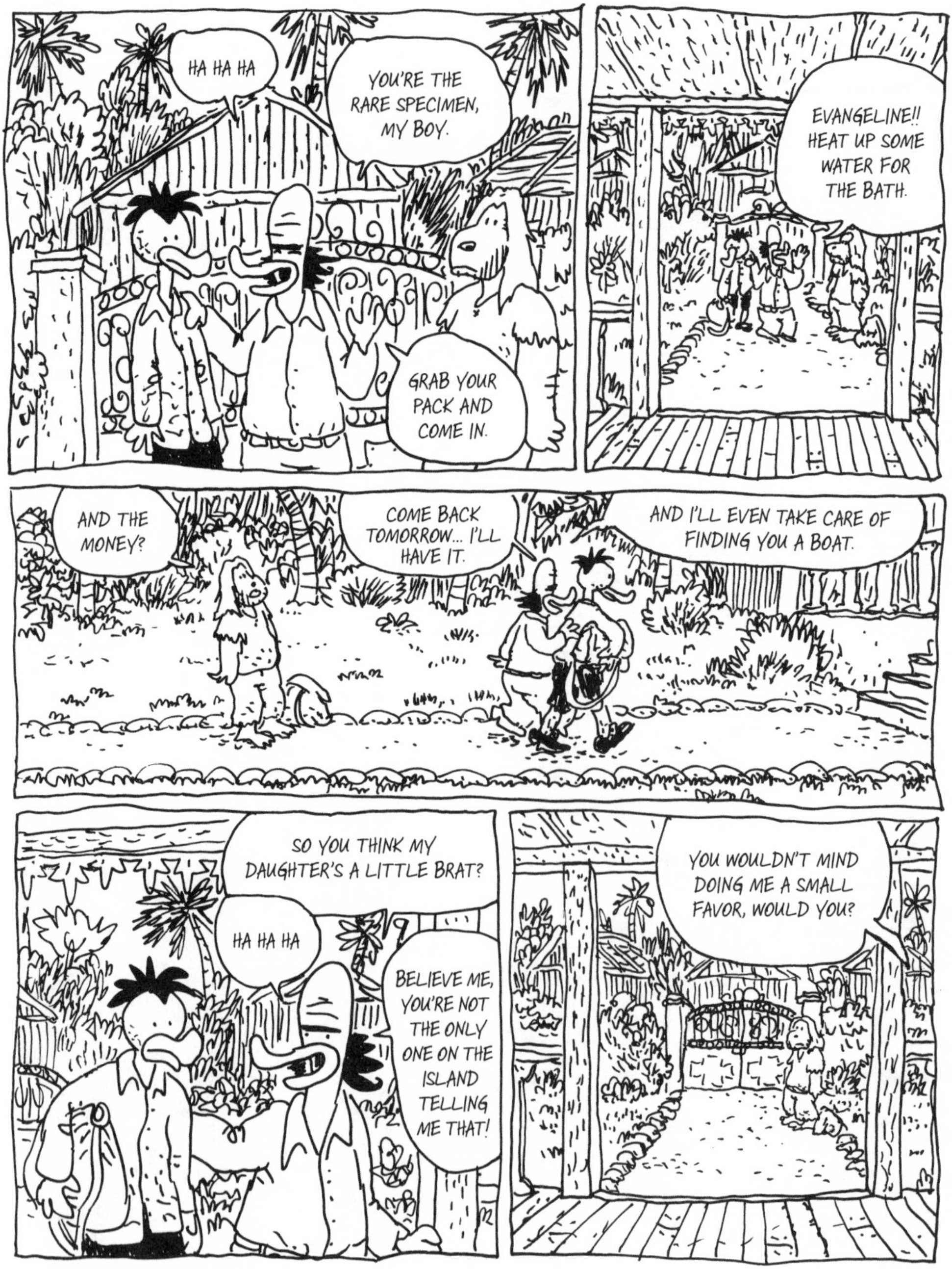
HA HA HA
YOU'RE THE RARE SPECIMEN, MY BOY.
GRAB YOUR PACK AND COME IN.
EVANGELINE!! HEAT UP SOME WATER FOR THE BATH.
AND THE MONEY?
COME BACK TOMORROW... I'LL HAVE IT.
AND I'LL EVEN TAKE CARE OF FINDING YOU A BOAT.
SO YOU THINK MY DAUGHTER'S A LITTLE BRAT?
HA HA HA
BELIEVE ME, YOU'RE NOT THE ONLY ONE ON THE ISLAND TELLING ME THAT!
YOU WOULDN'T MIND DOING ME A SMALL FAVOR, WOULD YOU?

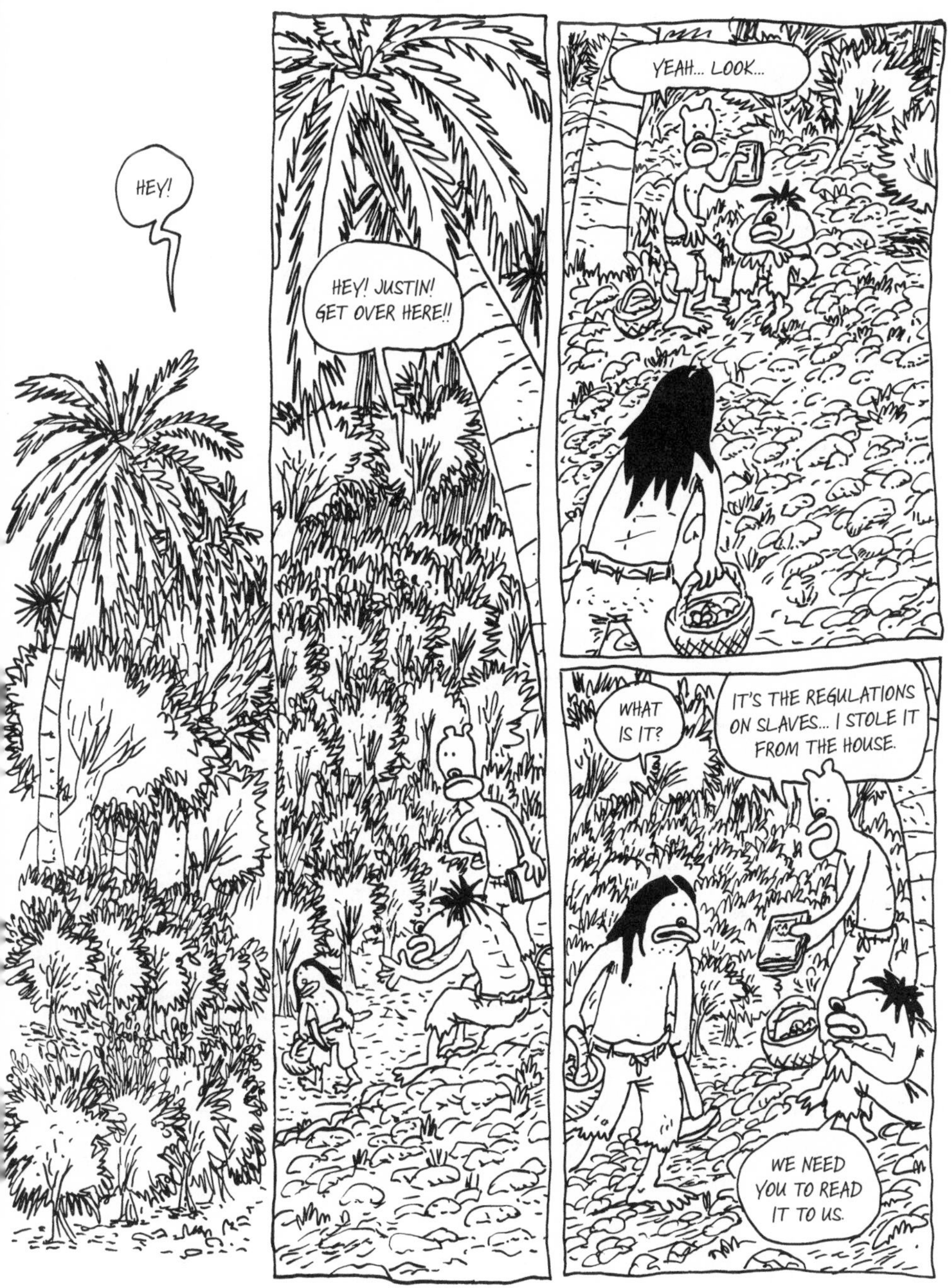
HEY!
HEY! JUSTIN! GET OVER HERE!!
YEAH... LOOK...
WHAT IS IT?
IT'S THE REGULATIONS ON SLAVES... I STOLE IT FROM THE HOUSE.
WE NEED YOU TO READ IT TO US.

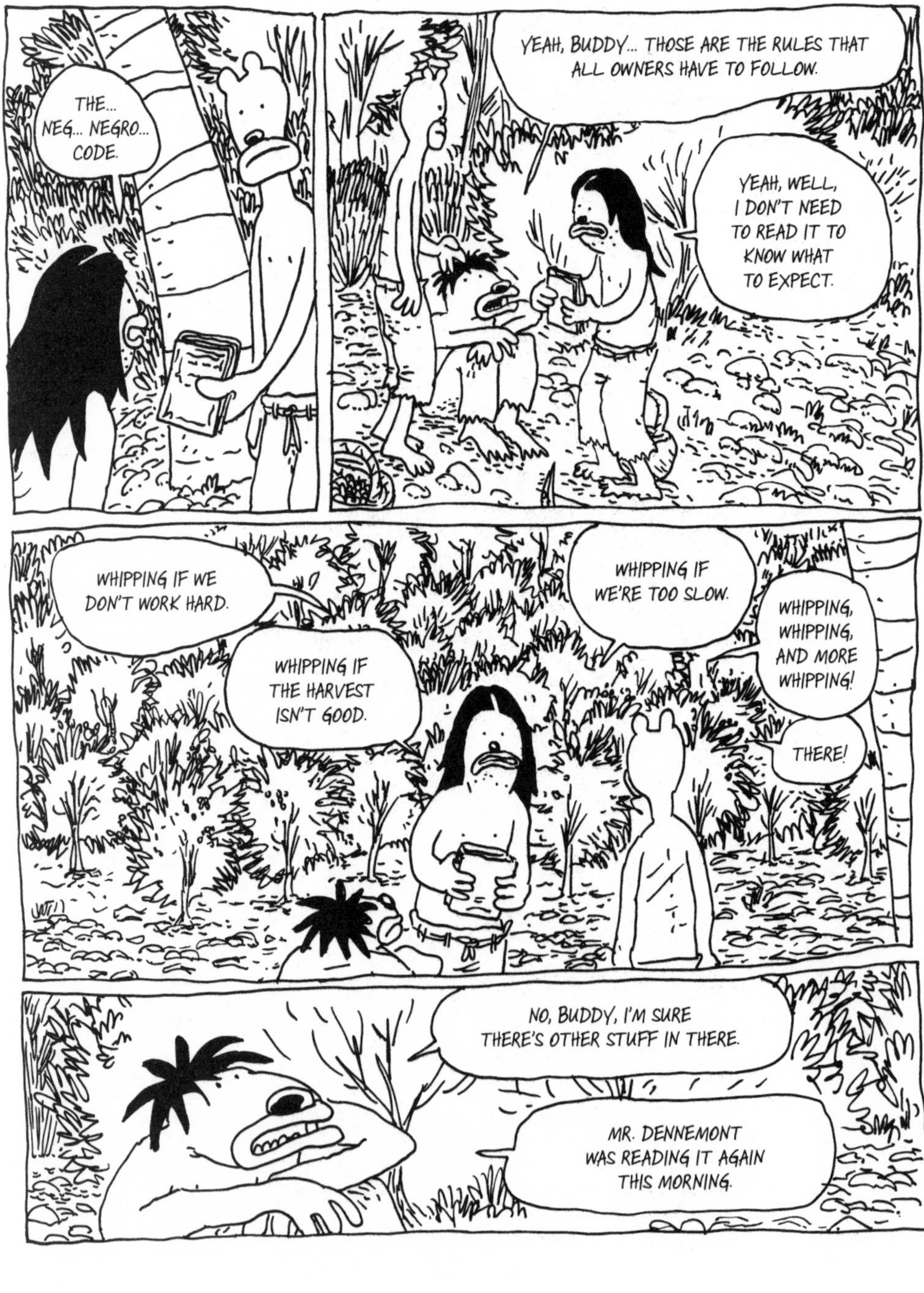

THE... NEG... NEGRO... CODE.
YEAH, BUDDY... THOSE ARE THE RULES THAT ALL OWNERS HAVE TO FOLLOW.
YEAH, WELL, I DON'T NEED TO READ IT TO KNOW WHAT TO EXPECT.
WHIPPING IF WE DON'T WORK HARD.
WHIPPING IF THE HARVEST ISN'T GOOD.
WHIPPING IF WE'RE TOO SLOW.
WHIPPING, WHIPPING, AND MORE WHIPPING!
THERE!
NO, BUDDY, I'M SURE THERE'S OTHER STUFF IN THERE.
MR. DENNEMONT WAS READING IT AGAIN THIS MORNING.

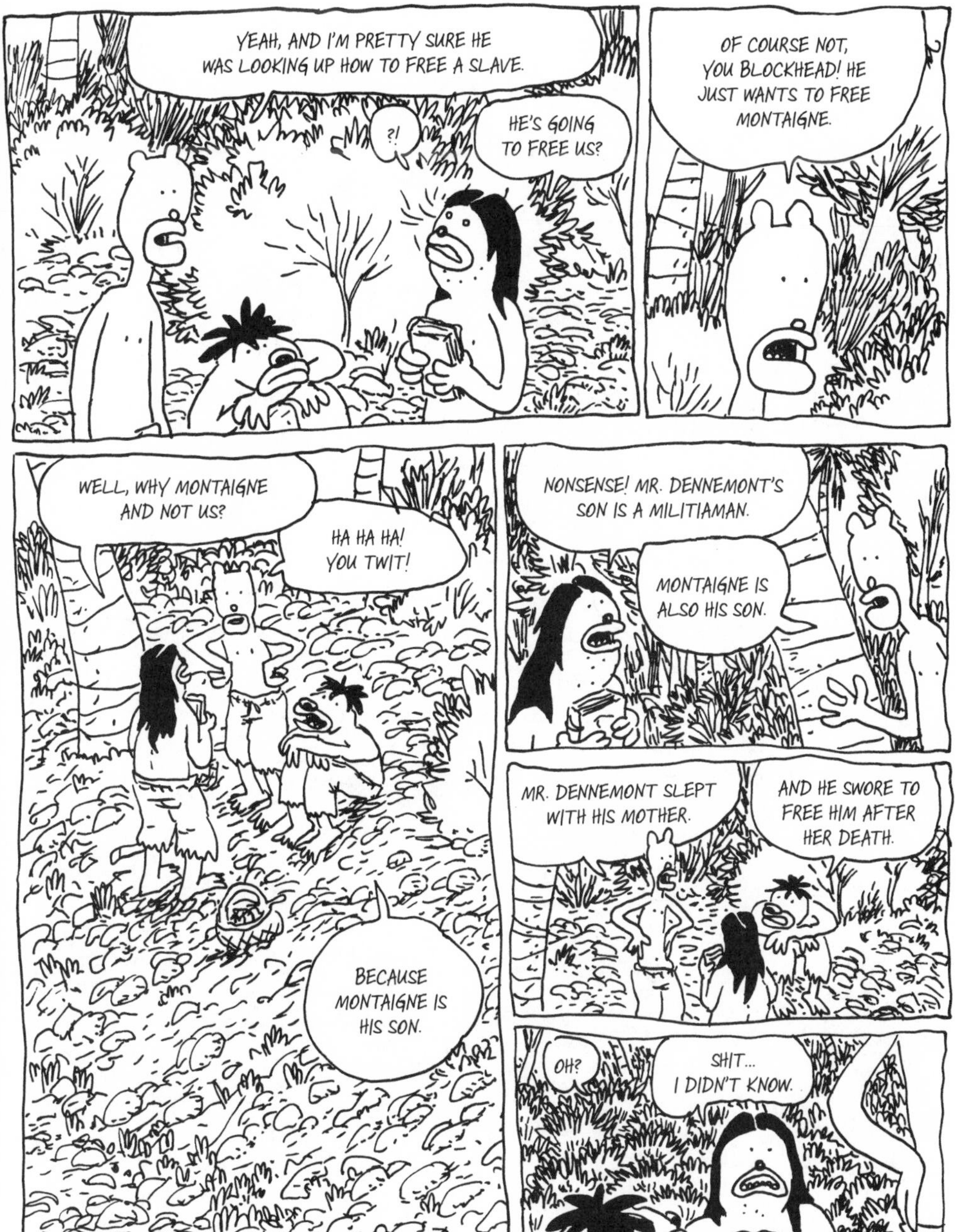
YEAH, AND I'M PRETTY SURE HE WAS LOOKING UP HOW TO FREE A SLAVE.
?!
HE'S GOING TO FREE US?
OF COURSE NOT, YOU BLOCKHEAD! HE JUST WANTS TO FREE MONTAIGNE.
WELL, WHY MONTAIGNE AND NOT US?
HA HA HA! YOU TWIT!
BECAUSE MONTAIGNE IS HIS SON.
NONSENSE! MR. DENNEMONT'S SON IS A MILITIAMAN.
MONTAIGNE IS ALSO HIS SON.
MR. DENNEMONT SLEPT WITH HIS MOTHER.
AND HE SWORE TO FREE HIM AFTER HER DEATH.
OH?
SHIT... I DIDN'T KNOW.

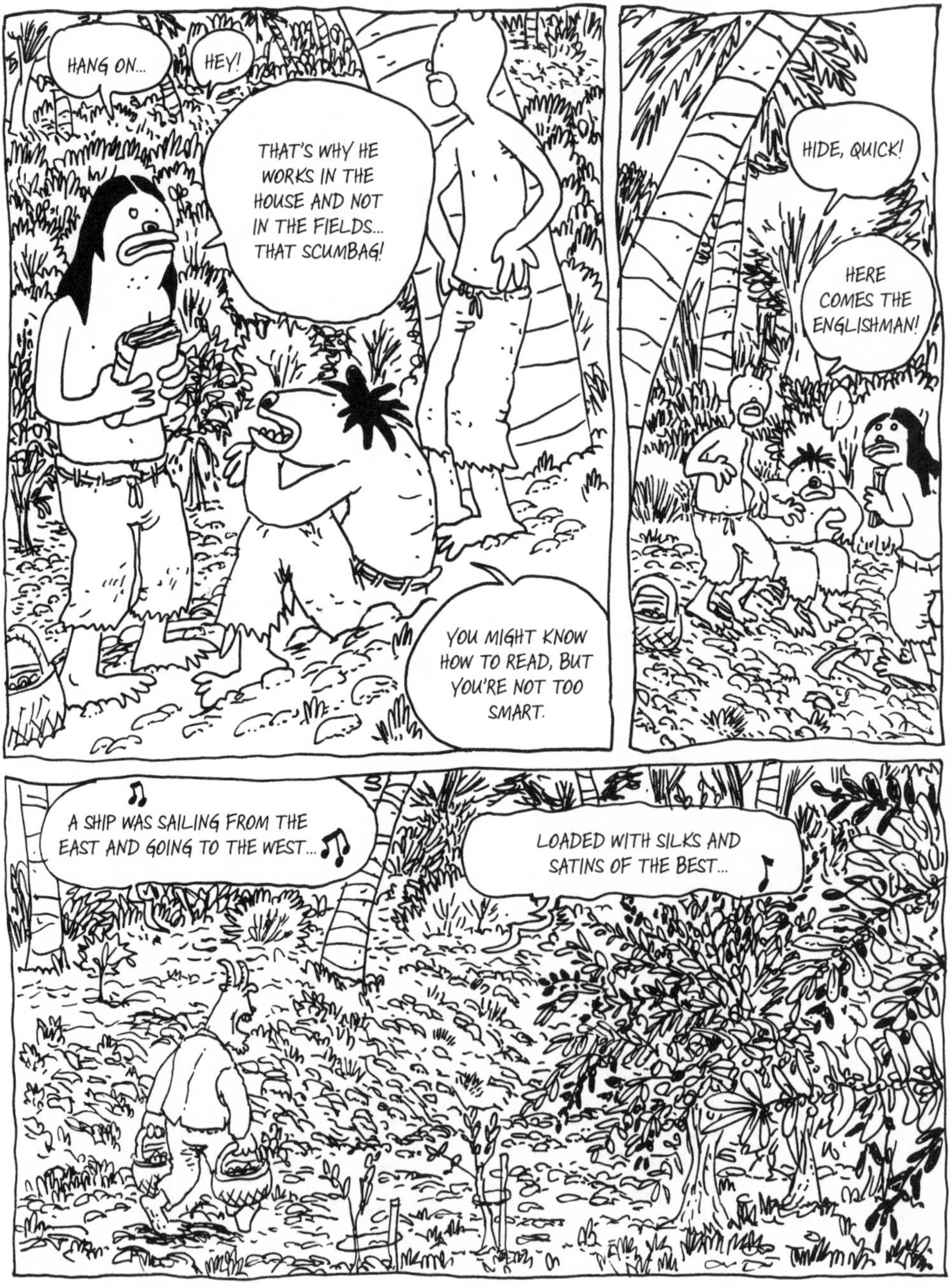
HANG ON...
HEY!
THAT'S WHY HE WORKS IN THE HOUSE AND NOT IN THE FIELDS... THAT SCUMBAG!
YOU MIGHT KNOW HOW TO READ, BUT YOU'RE NOT TOO SMART.
HIDE, QUICK!
HERE COMES THE ENGLISHMAN!
A SHIP WAS SAILING FROM THE EAST AND GOING TO THE WEST...
LOADED WITH SILKS AND SATINS OF THE BEST...

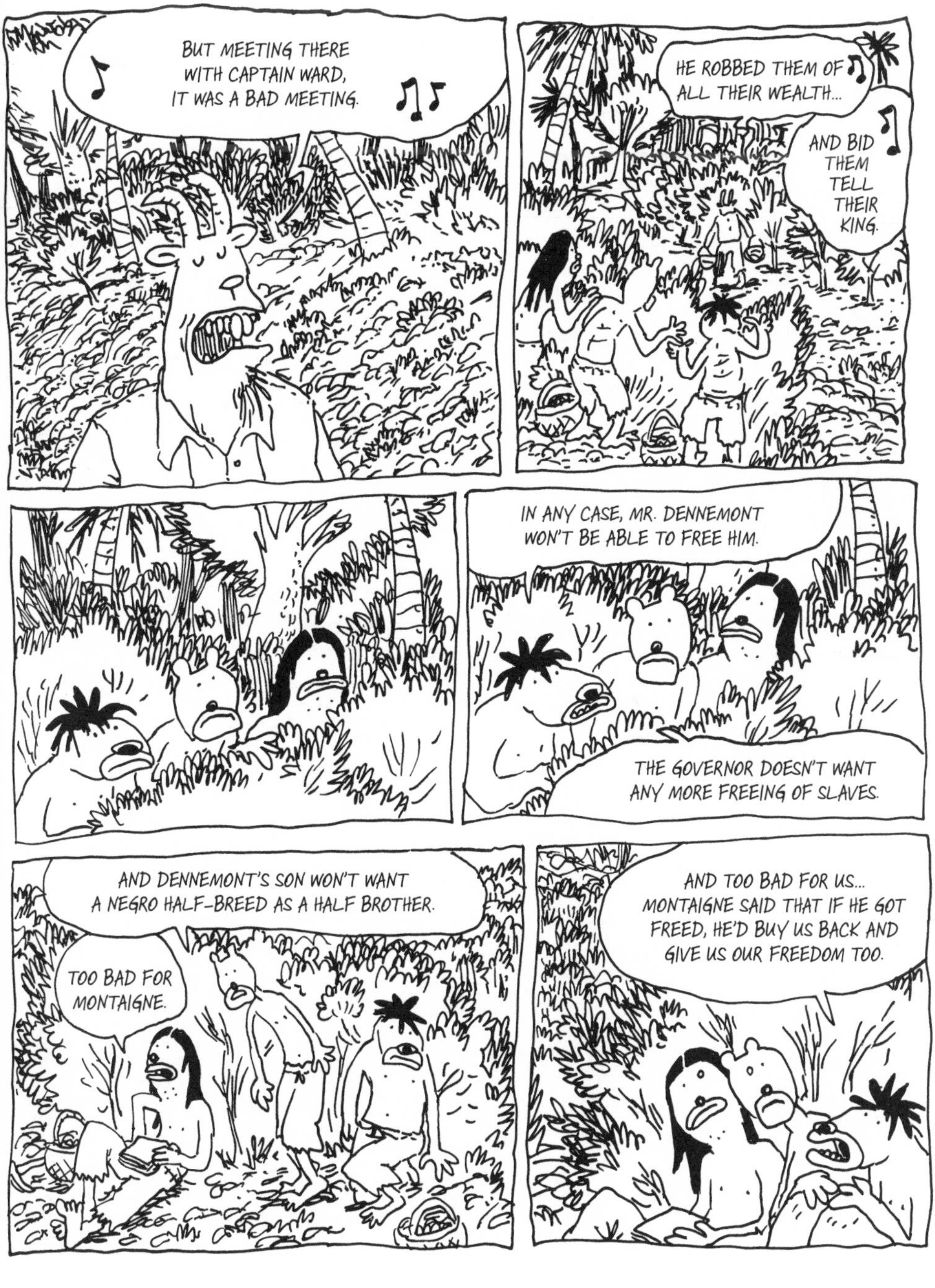
BUT MEETING THERE WITH CAPTAIN WARD, IT WAS A BAD MEETING.
HE ROBBED THEM OF ALL THEIR WEALTH...
AND BID THEM TELL THEIR KING.
IN ANY CASE, MR. DENNEMONT WON'T BE ABLE TO FREE HIM.
THE GOVERNOR DOESN'T WANT ANY MORE FREEING OF SLAVES.
AND DENNEMONT'S SON WON'T WANT A NEGRO HALF-BREED AS A HALF BROTHER.
TOO BAD FOR MONTAIGNE.
AND TOO BAD FOR US... MONTAIGNE SAID THAT IF HE GOT FREED, HE'D BUY US BACK AND GIVE US OUR FREEDOM TOO.

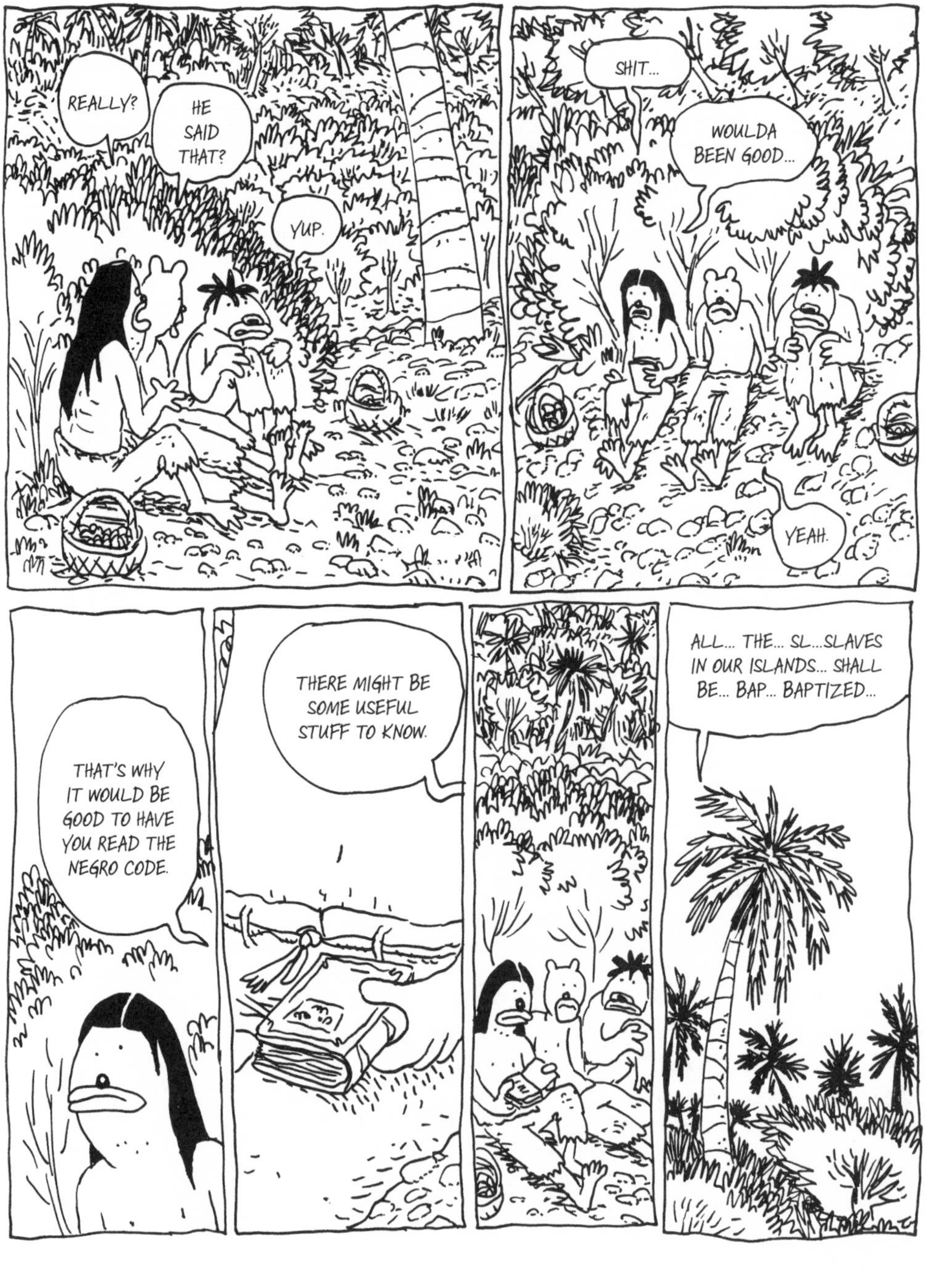
REALLY?
HE SAID THAT?
YUP.
SHIT...
WOULDA BEEN GOOD...
YEAH.
THAT'S WHY IT WOULD BE GOOD TO HAVE YOU READ THE NEGRO CODE.
THERE MIGHT BE SOME USEFUL STUFF TO KNOW.
ALL... THE... SL...SLAVES IN OUR ISLANDS... SHALL BE... BAP... BAPTIZED...

THE PIRATES' BALL

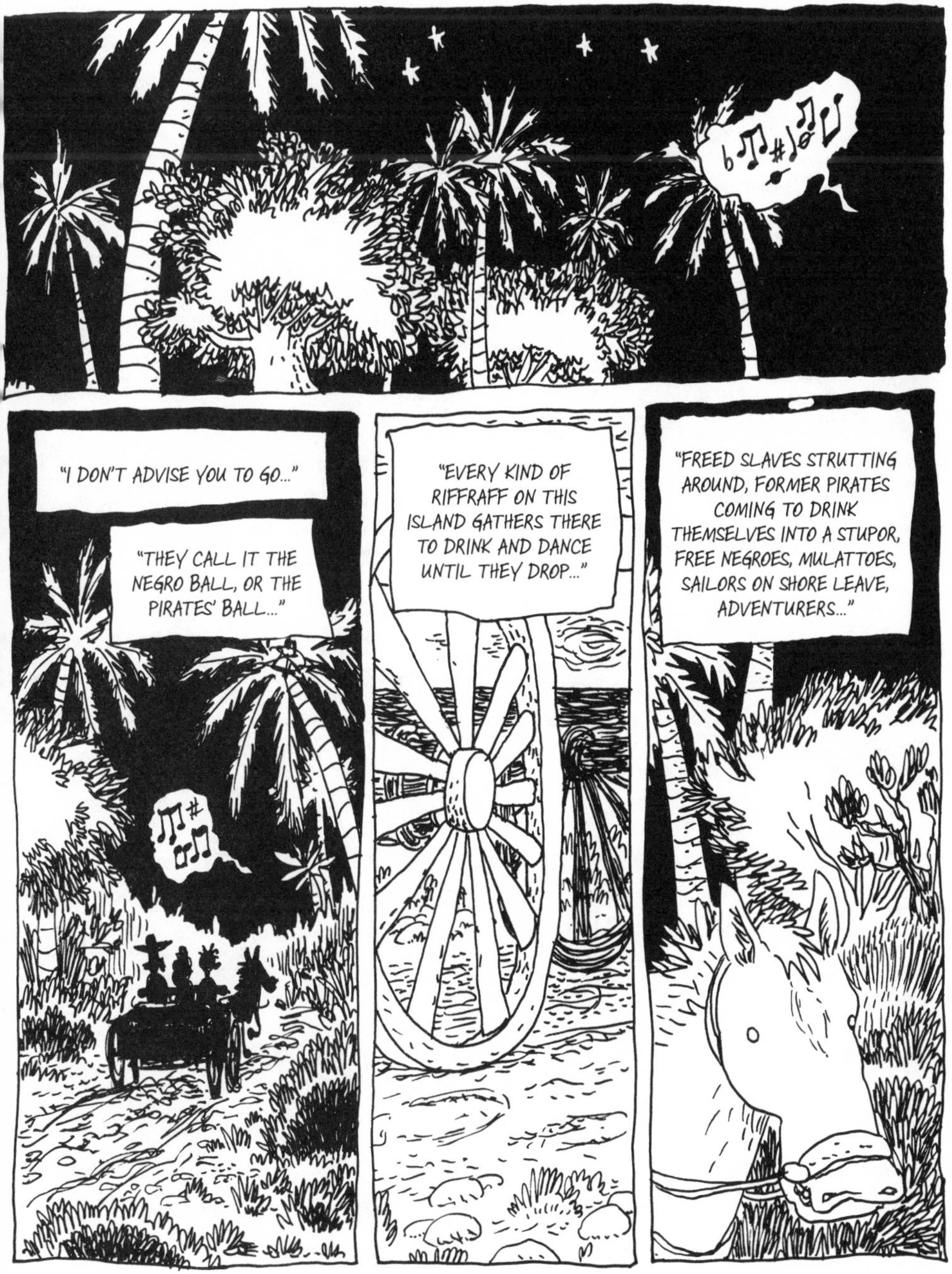
"I DON'T ADVISE YOU TO GO..."
"THEY CALL IT THE NEGRO BALL, OR THE PIRATES' BALL..."
"EVERY KIND OF RIFFRAFF ON THIS ISLAND GATHERS THERE TO DRINK AND DANCE UNTIL THEY DROP..."
"FREED SLAVES STRUTTING AROUND, FORMER PIRATES COMING TO DRINK THEMSELVES INTO A STUPOR, FREE NEGROES, MULATTOES, SAILORS ON SHORE LEAVE, ADVENTURERS..."

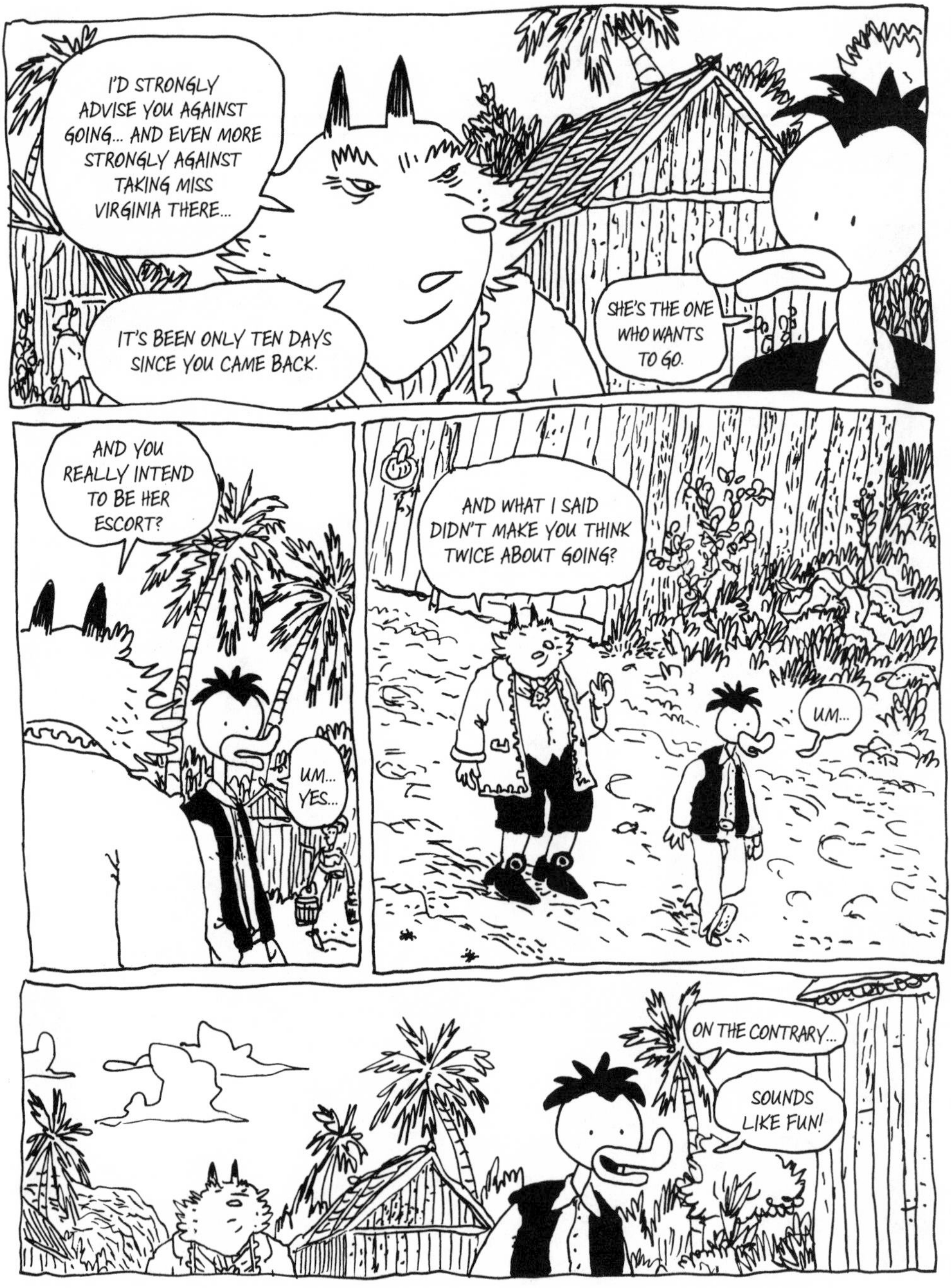
I'D STRONGLY ADVISE YOU AGAINST GOING... AND EVEN MORE STRONGLY AGAINST TAKING MISS VIRGINIA THERE...
IT'S BEEN ONLY TEN DAYS SINCE YOU CAME BACK.
SHE'S THE ONE WHO WANTS TO GO.
AND YOU REALLY INTEND TO BE HER ESCORT?
UM... YES...
AND WHAT I SAID DIDN'T MAKE YOU THINK TWICE ABOUT GOING?
UM...
ON THE CONTRARY...
SOUNDS LIKE FUN!

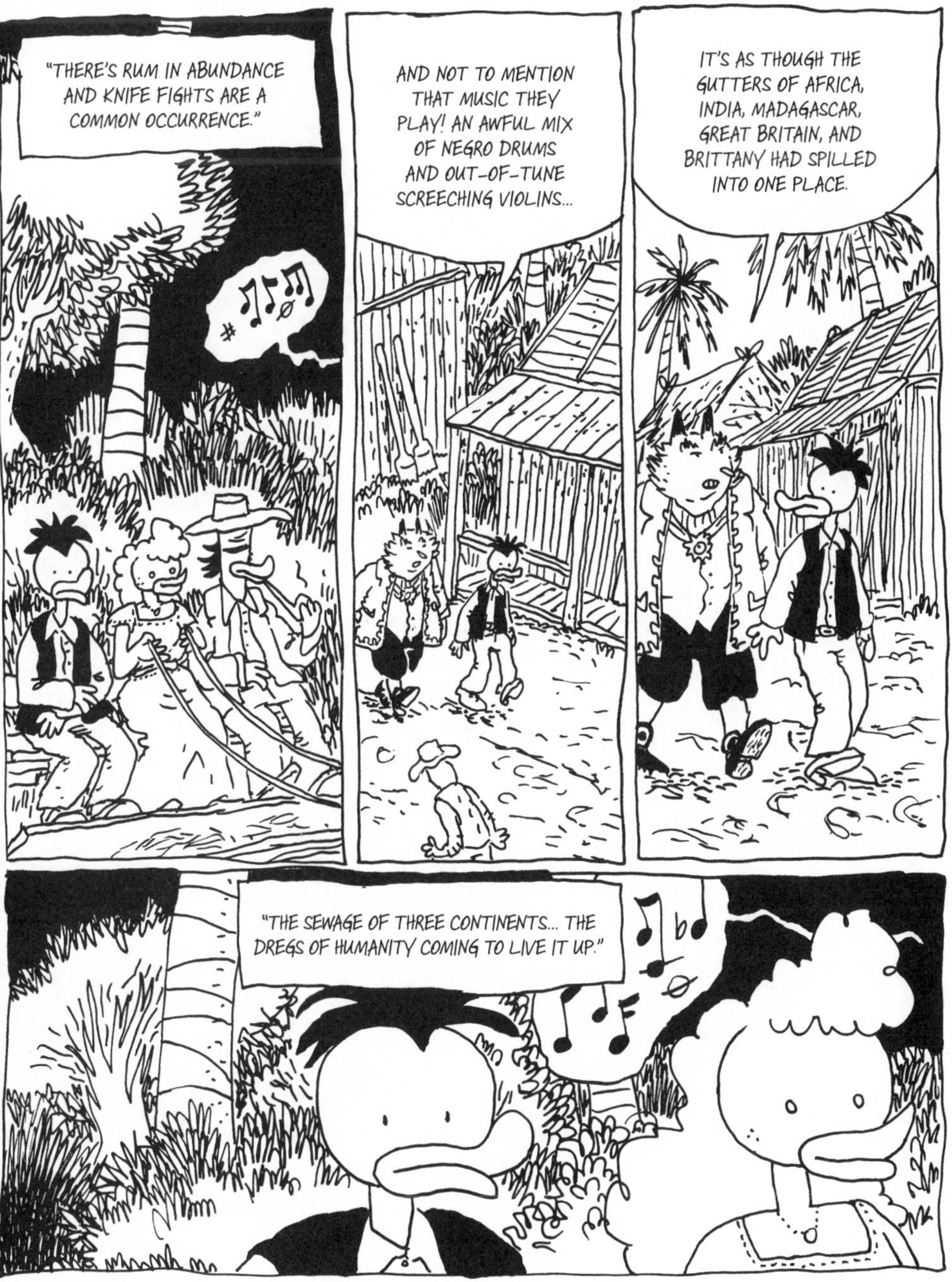
"THERE'S RUM IN ABUNDANCE AND KNIFE FIGHTS ARE A COMMON OCCURRENCE."
AND NOT TO MENTION THAT MUSIC THEY PLAY! AN AWFUL MIX OF NEGRO DRUMS AND OUT-OF-TUNE SCREECHING VIOLINS...
IT'S AS THOUGH THE GUTTERS OF AFRICA, INDIA, MADAGASCAR, GREAT BRITAIN, AND BRITTANY HAD SPILLED INTO ONE PLACE.
"THE SEWAGE OF THREE CONTINENTS... THE DREGS OF HUMANITY COMING TO LIVE IT UP."

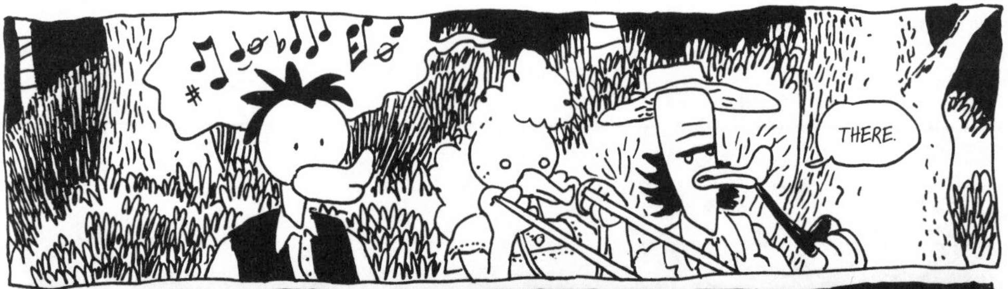
THERE.

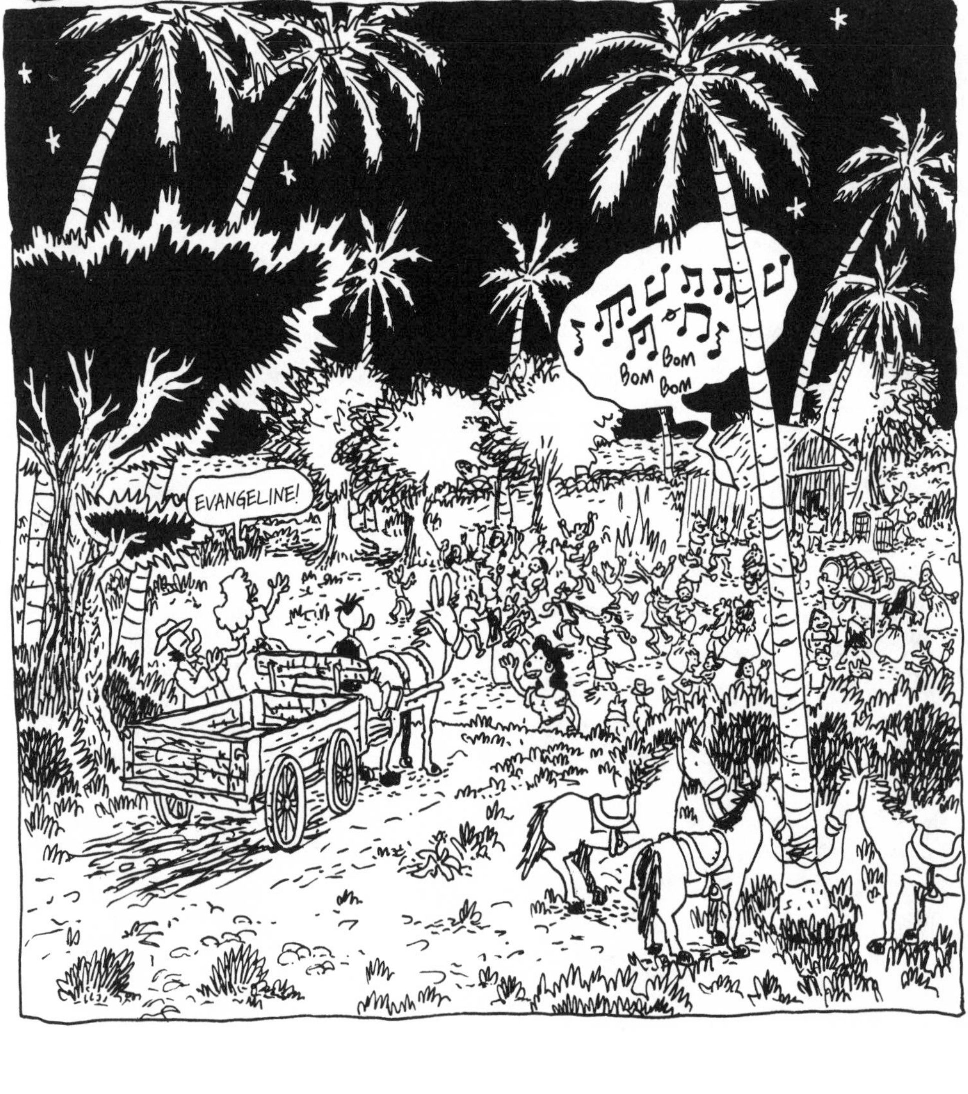
BOM BOM BOM BOM
EVANGELINE!

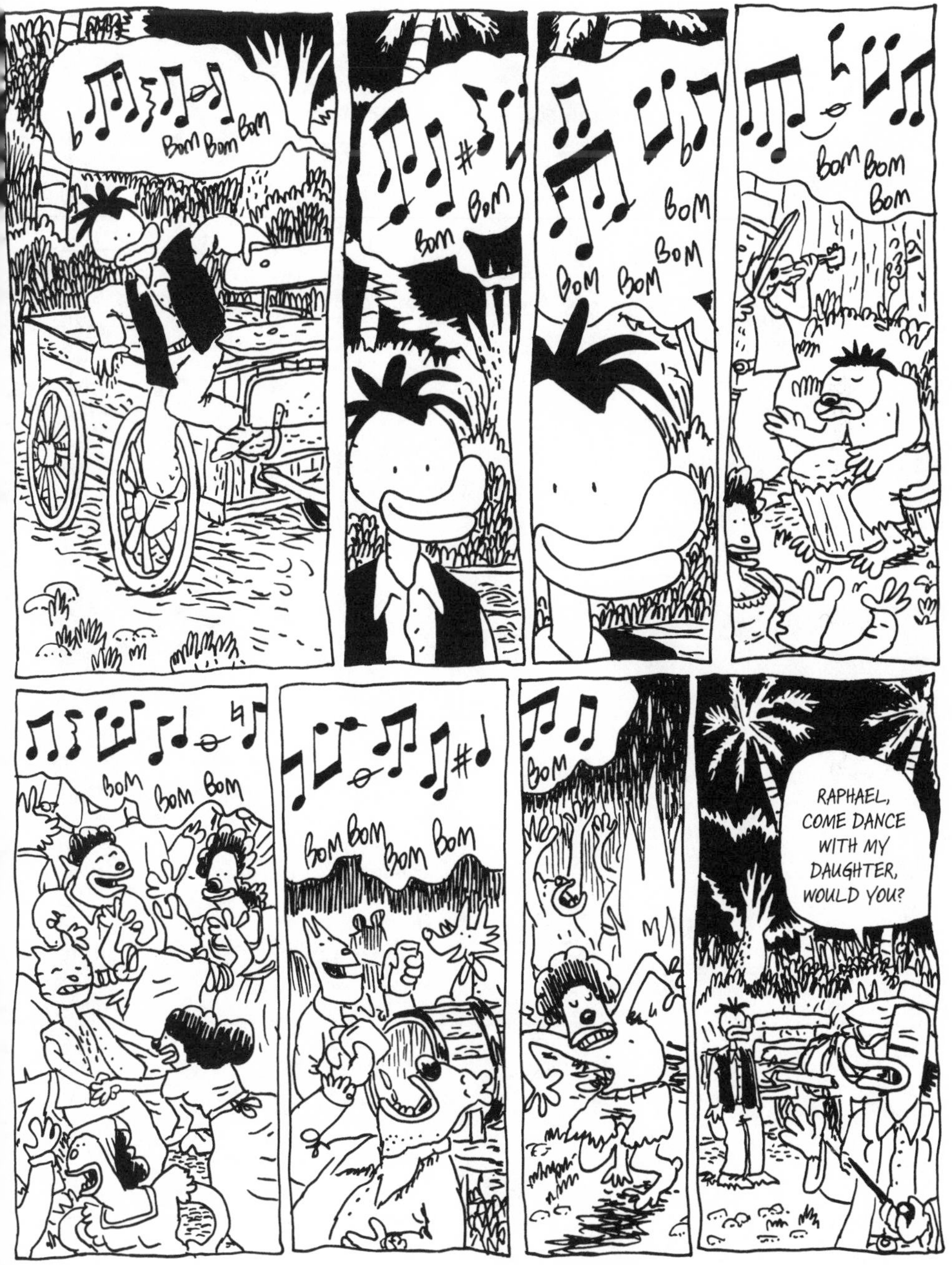

Bom Bom Bom
Bom Bom
Bom Bom
Bom Bom Bom
Bom Bom Bom
Bom Bom Bom
Bom Bom Bom Bom
Bom
RAPHAEL, COME DANCE WITH MY DAUGHTER, WOULD YOU?

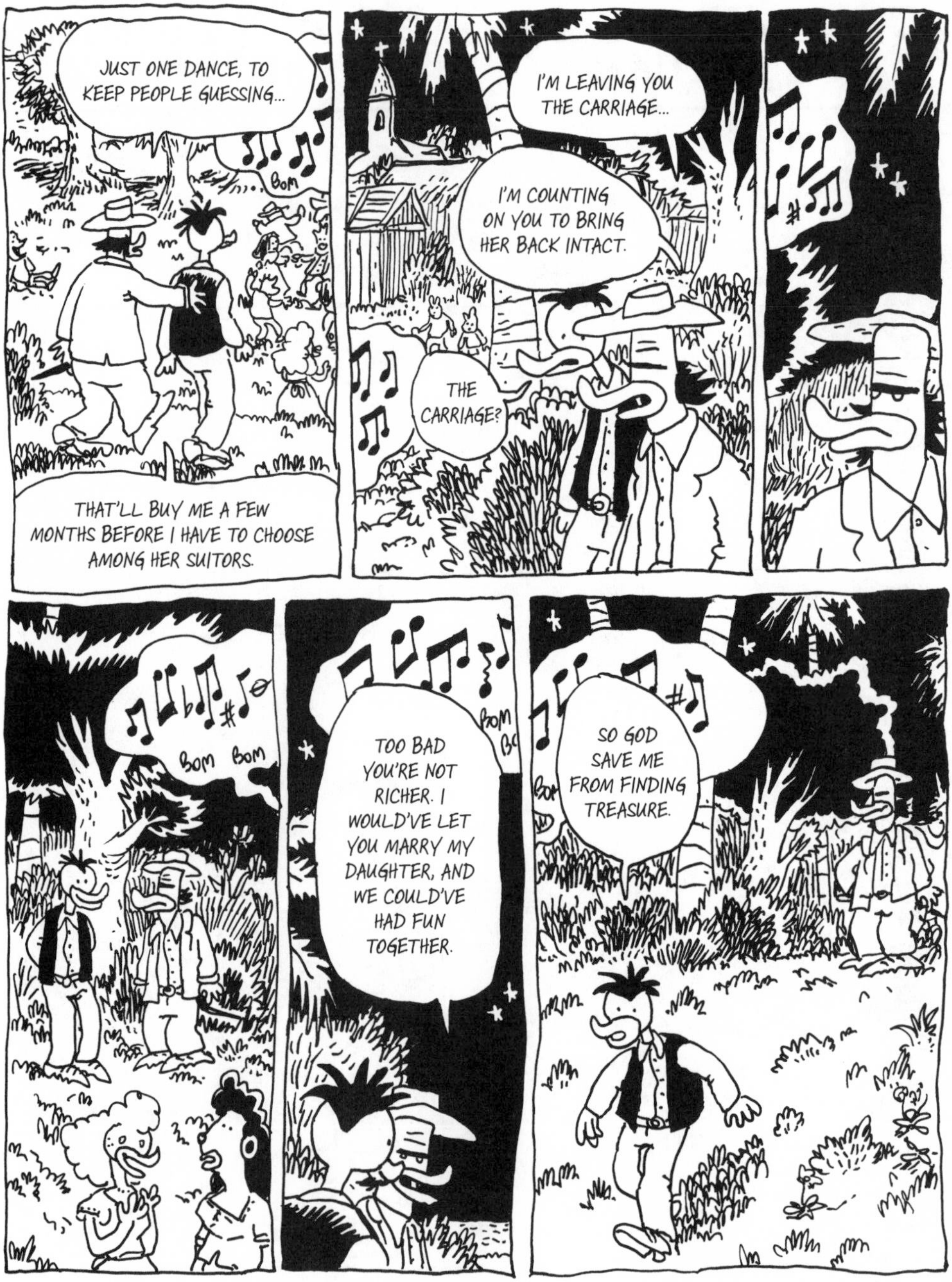
JUST ONE DANCE, TO KEEP PEOPLE GUESSING...
BOM
THAT'LL BUY ME A FEW MONTHS BEFORE I HAVE TO CHOOSE AMONG HER SUITORS.
I'M LEAVING YOU THE CARRIAGE...
I'M COUNTING ON YOU TO BRING HER BACK INTACT.
THE CARRIAGE?
BOM BOM
TOO BAD YOU'RE NOT RICHER. I WOULD'VE LET YOU MARRY MY DAUGHTER, AND WE COULD'VE HAD FUN TOGETHER.
BOM
SO GOD SAVE ME FROM FINDING TREASURE.

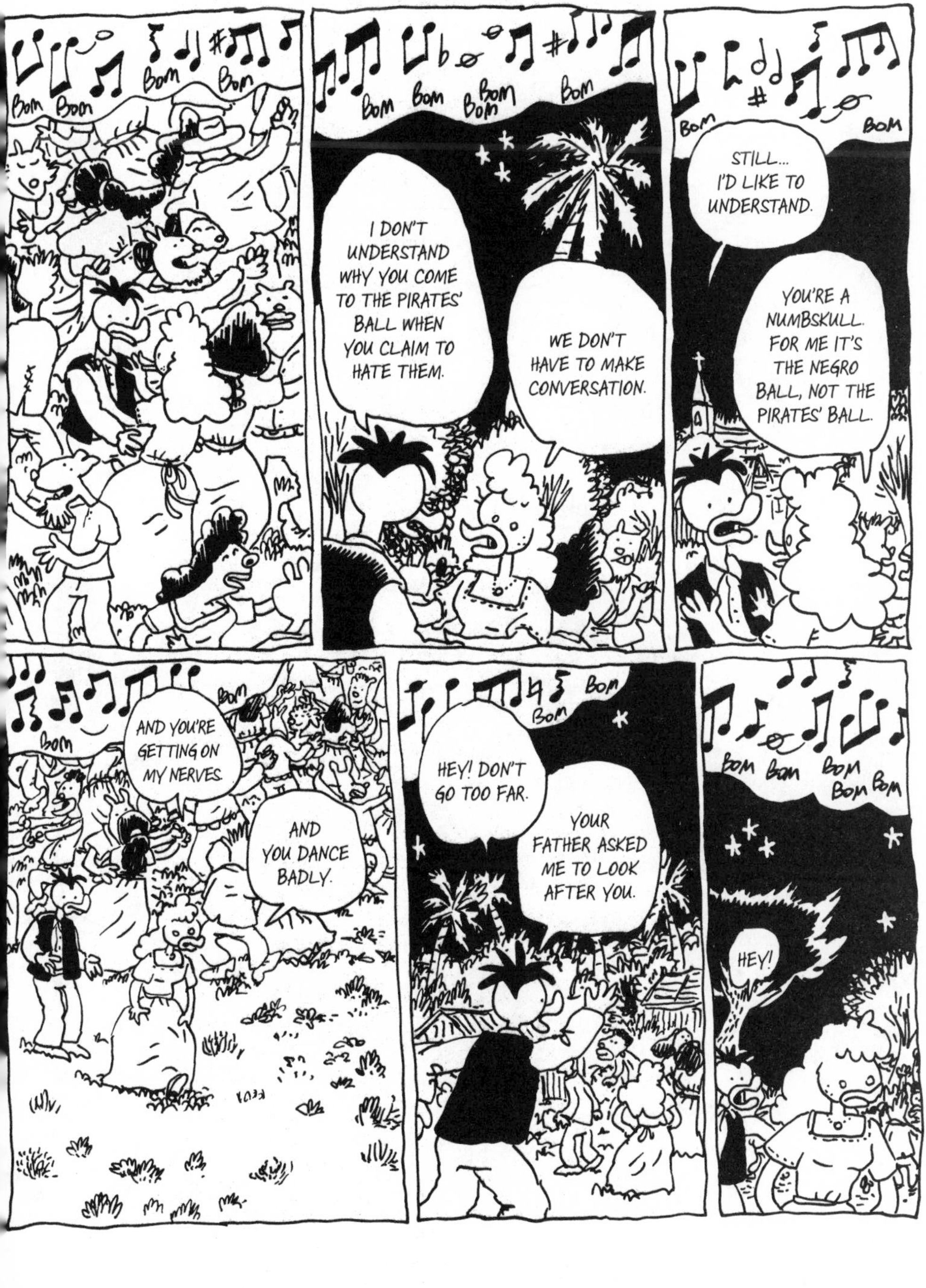
Bom Bom Bom Bom
Bom Bom Bom Bom Bom
I DON'T UNDERSTAND WHY YOU COME TO THE PIRATES' BALL WHEN YOU CLAIM TO HATE THEM.
WE DON'T HAVE TO MAKE CONVERSATION.
Bom Bom
STILL... I'D LIKE TO UNDERSTAND.
YOU'RE A NUMBSKULL. FOR ME IT'S THE NEGRO BALL, NOT THE PIRATES' BALL.
Bom Bom
AND YOU'RE GETTING ON MY NERVES.
AND YOU DANCE BADLY.
Bom Bom
HEY! DON'T GO TOO FAR.
YOUR FATHER ASKED ME TO LOOK AFTER YOU.
Bom Bom Bom Bom Bom
HEY!

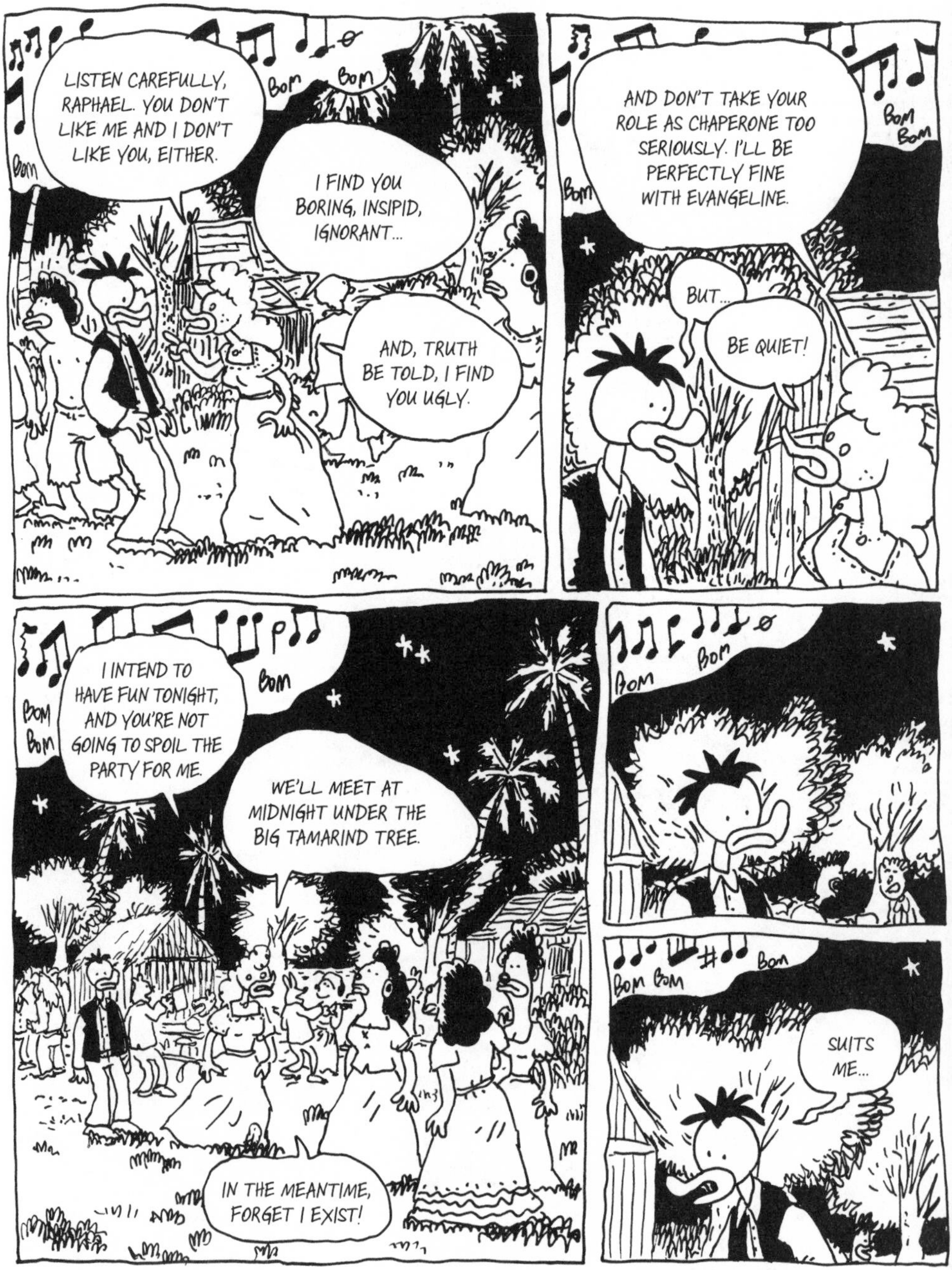
BOM
LISTEN CAREFULLY, RAPHAEL. YOU DON'T LIKE ME AND I DON'T LIKE YOU, EITHER.
BOM BOM
I FIND YOU BORING, INSIPID, IGNORANT...
AND, TRUTH BE TOLD, I FIND YOU UGLY.
AND DON'T TAKE YOUR ROLE AS CHAPERONE TOO SERIOUSLY. I'LL BE PERFECTLY FINE WITH EVANGELINE.
BOM BOM
BOM
BUT...
BE QUIET!
BOM BOM
I INTEND TO HAVE FUN TONIGHT, AND YOU'RE NOT GOING TO SPOIL THE PARTY FOR ME.
BOM
WE'LL MEET AT MIDNIGHT UNDER THE BIG TAMARIND TREE.
IN THE MEANTIME, FORGET I EXIST!
BOM BOM
BOM BOM BOM
SUITS ME...

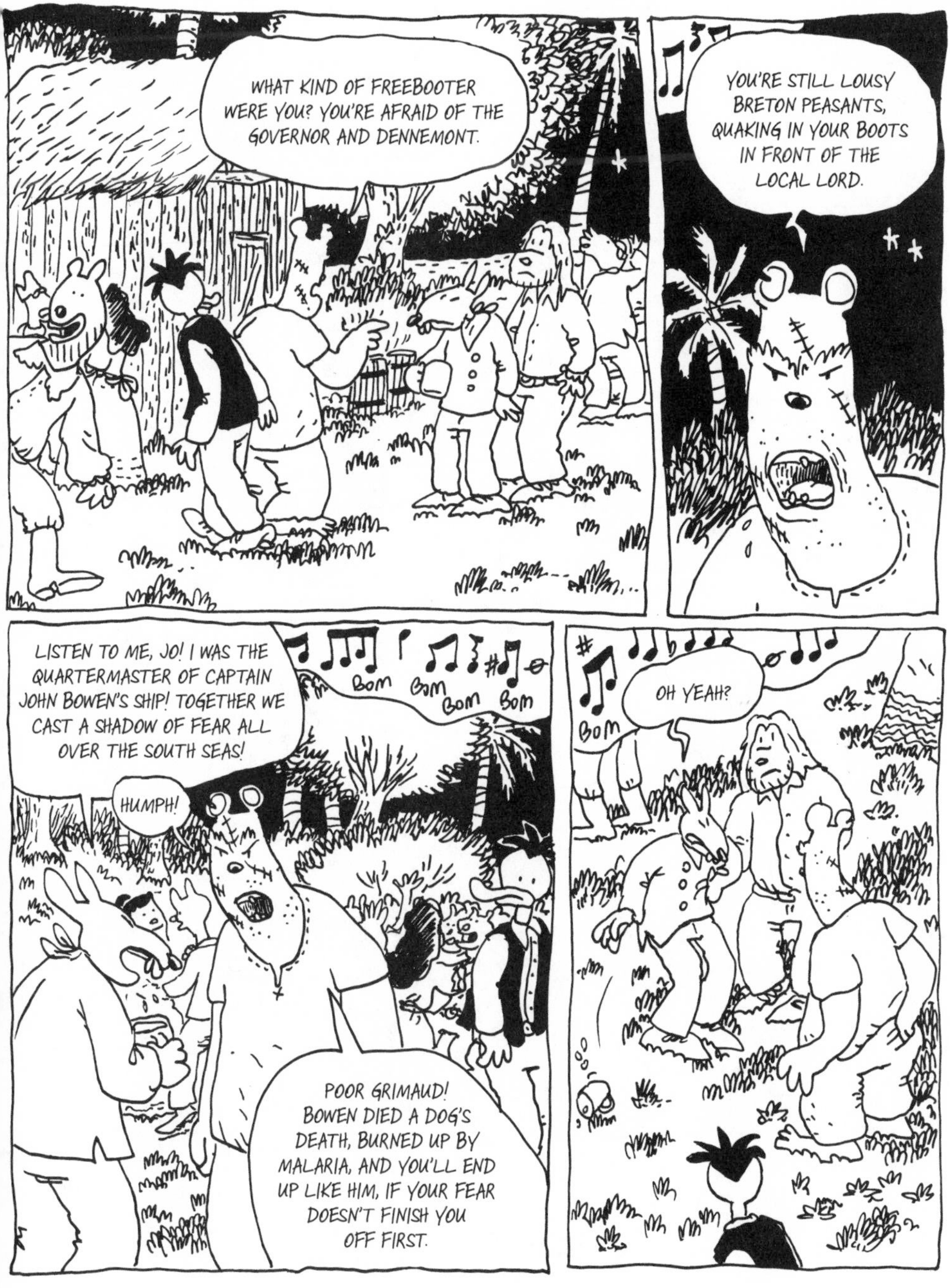
WHAT KIND OF FREEBOOTER WERE YOU? YOU'RE AFRAID OF THE GOVERNOR AND DENNEMONT.
YOU'RE STILL LOUSY BRETON PEASANTS, QUAKING IN YOUR BOOTS IN FRONT OF THE LOCAL LORD.
LISTEN TO ME, JO! I WAS THE QUARTERMASTER OF CAPTAIN JOHN BOWEN'S SHIP! TOGETHER WE CAST A SHADOW OF FEAR ALL OVER THE SOUTH SEAS!
BOM BOM BOM BOM
HUMPH!
POOR GRIMAUD! BOWEN DIED A DOG'S DEATH, BURNED UP BY MALARIA, AND YOU'LL END UP LIKE HIM, IF YOUR FEAR DOESN'T FINISH YOU OFF FIRST.
BOM
OH YEAH?

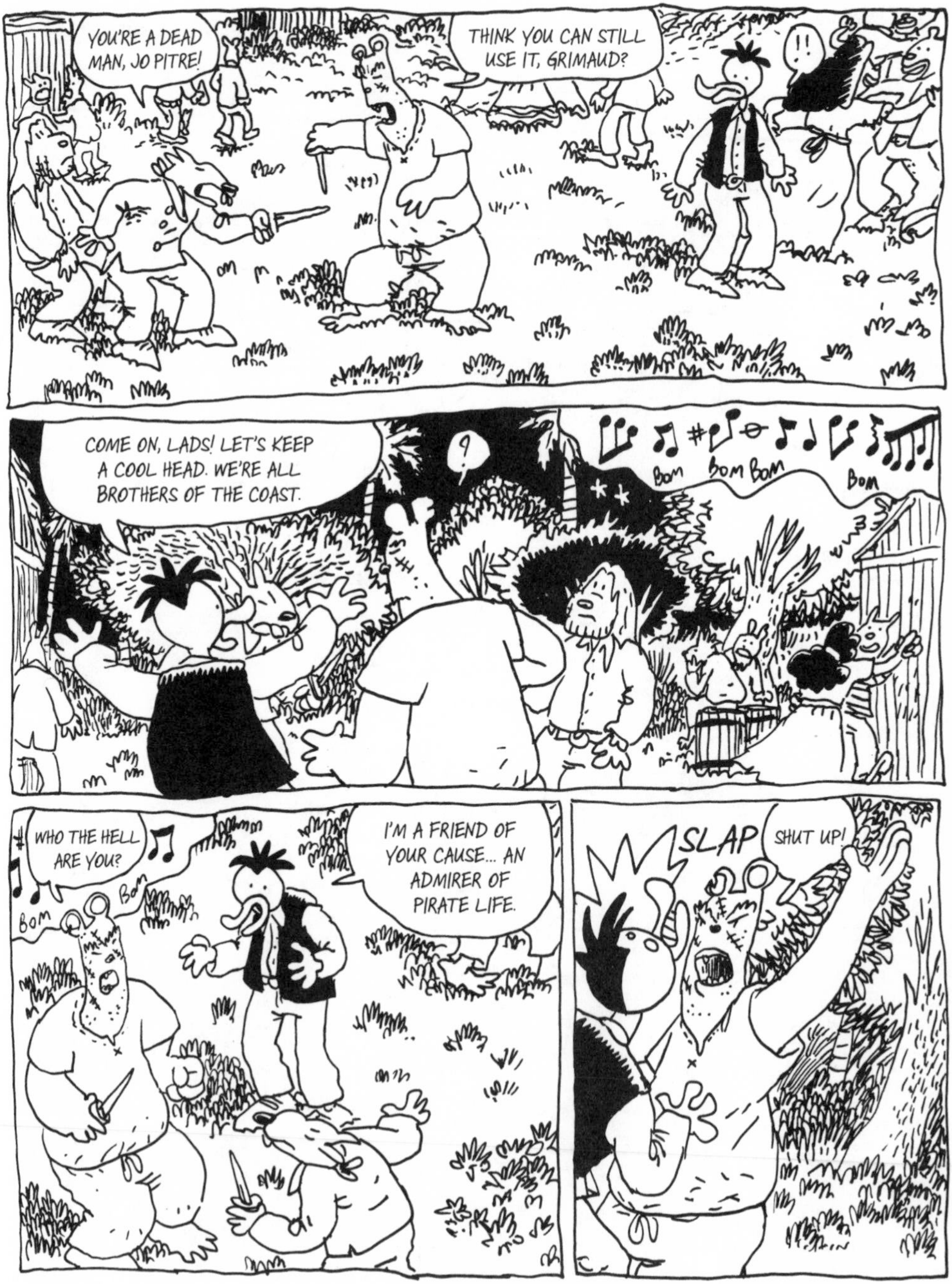

YOU'RE A DEAD MAN, JO PITRE!
THINK YOU CAN STILL USE IT, GRIMAUD?
!!
COME ON, LADS! LET'S KEEP A COOL HEAD. WE'RE ALL BROTHERS OF THE COAST.
?
BOM BOM BOM BOM
WHO THE HELL ARE YOU?
BOM BOM
I'M A FRIEND OF YOUR CAUSE... AN ADMIRER OF PIRATE LIFE.
SLAP
SHUT UP!

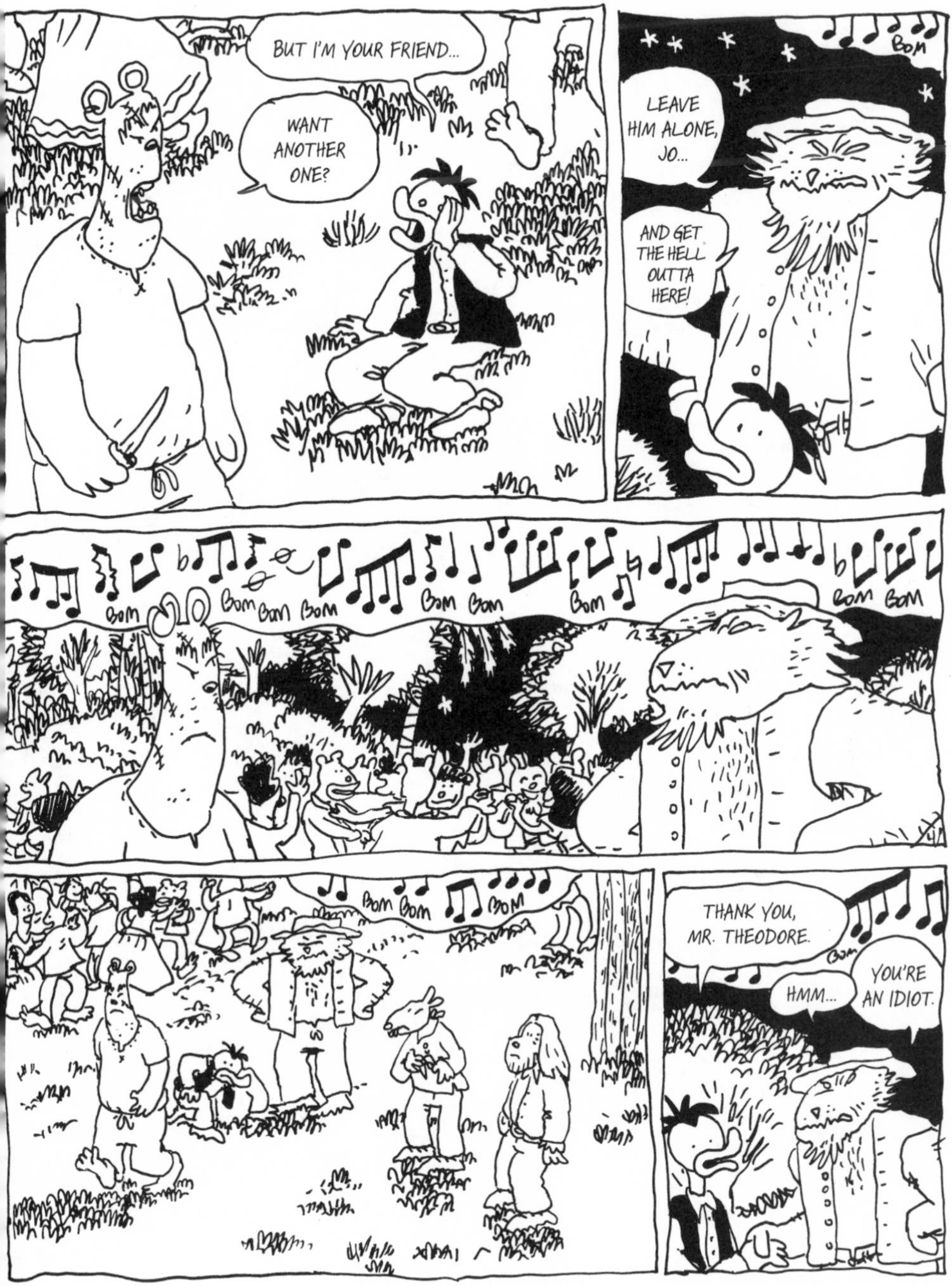
BUT I'M YOUR FRIEND...
WANT ANOTHER ONE?
BOM
LEAVE HIM ALONE, JO...
AND GET THE HELL OUTTA HERE!
BOM BOM BOM BOM BOM BOM BOM BOM BOM
BOM BOM BOM
THANK YOU, MR. THEODORE.
BOM
HMM...
YOU'RE AN IDIOT.

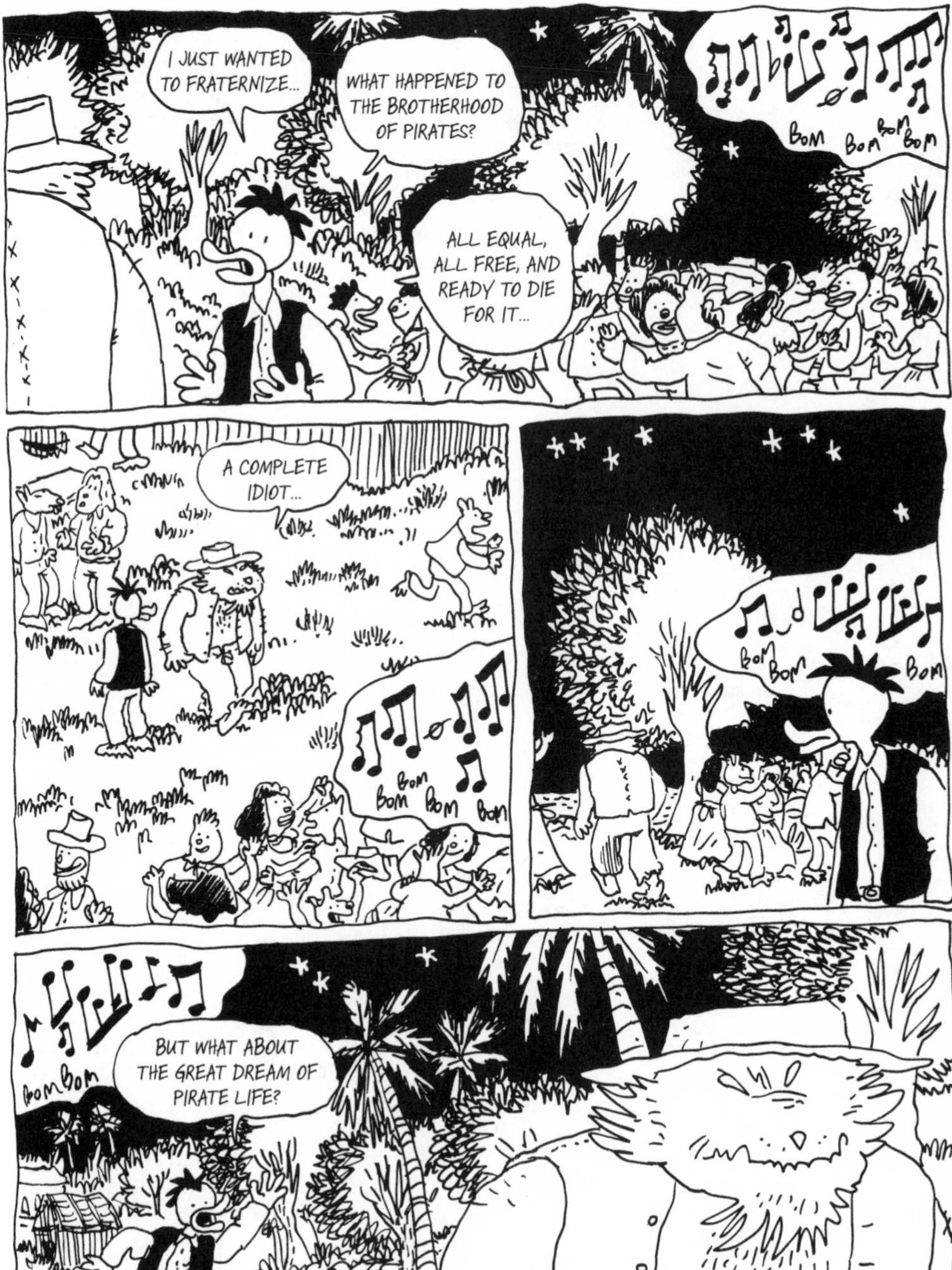
I JUST WANTED TO FRATERNIZE...
WHAT HAPPENED TO THE BROTHERHOOD OF PIRATES?
ALL EQUAL, ALL FREE, AND READY TO DIE FOR IT...
BOM BOM BOM BOM
A COMPLETE IDIOT...
BOM BOM BOM BOM
BOM BOM BOM
BOM BOM
BUT WHAT ABOUT THE GREAT DREAM OF PIRATE LIFE?

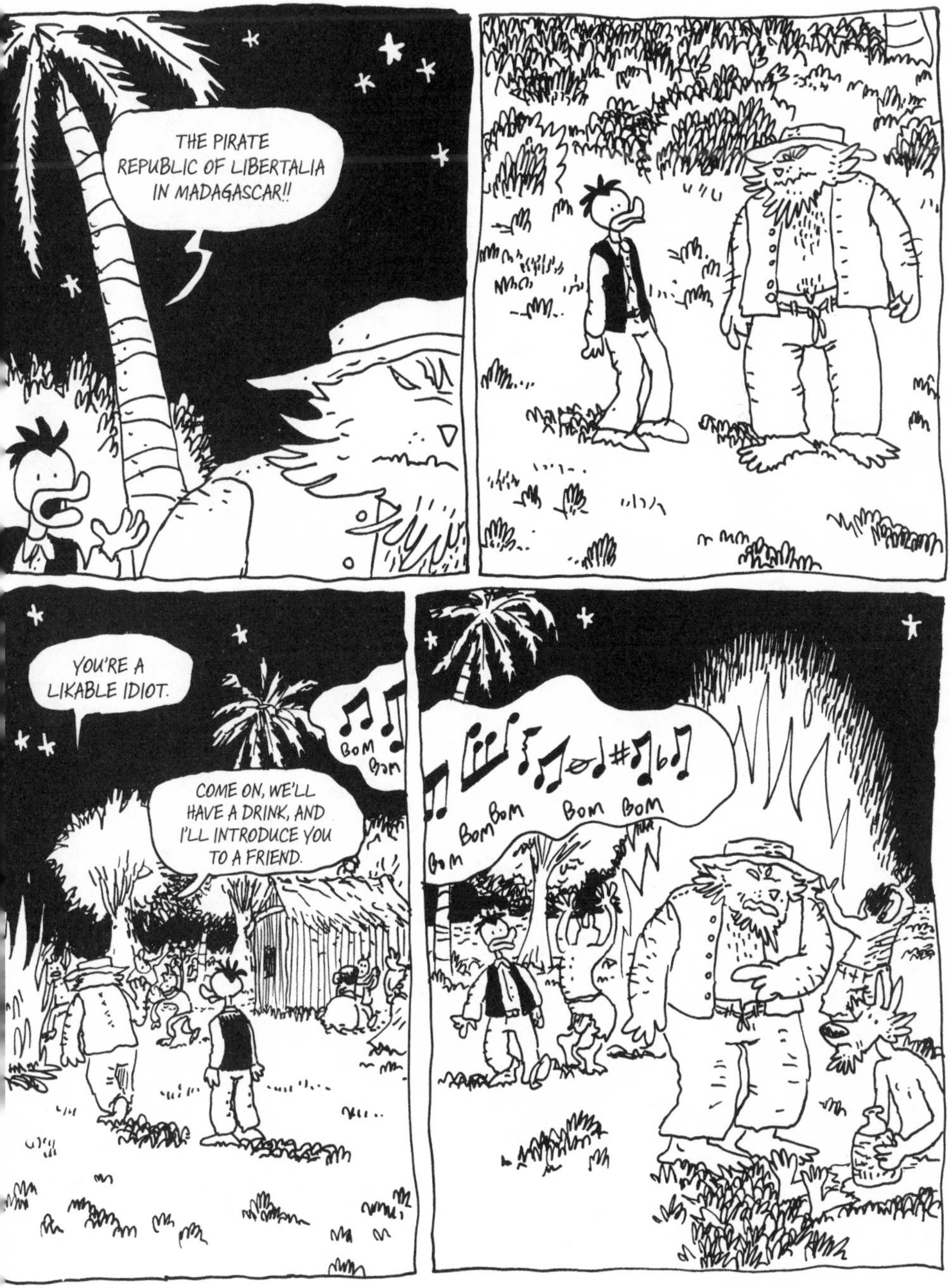
THE PIRATE REPUBLIC OF LIBERTALIA IN MADAGASCAR!!
YOU'RE A LIKABLE IDIOT.
BOM BOM
COME ON, WE'LL HAVE A DRINK, AND I'LL INTRODUCE YOU TO A FRIEND.
BOM BOM BOM BOM BOM

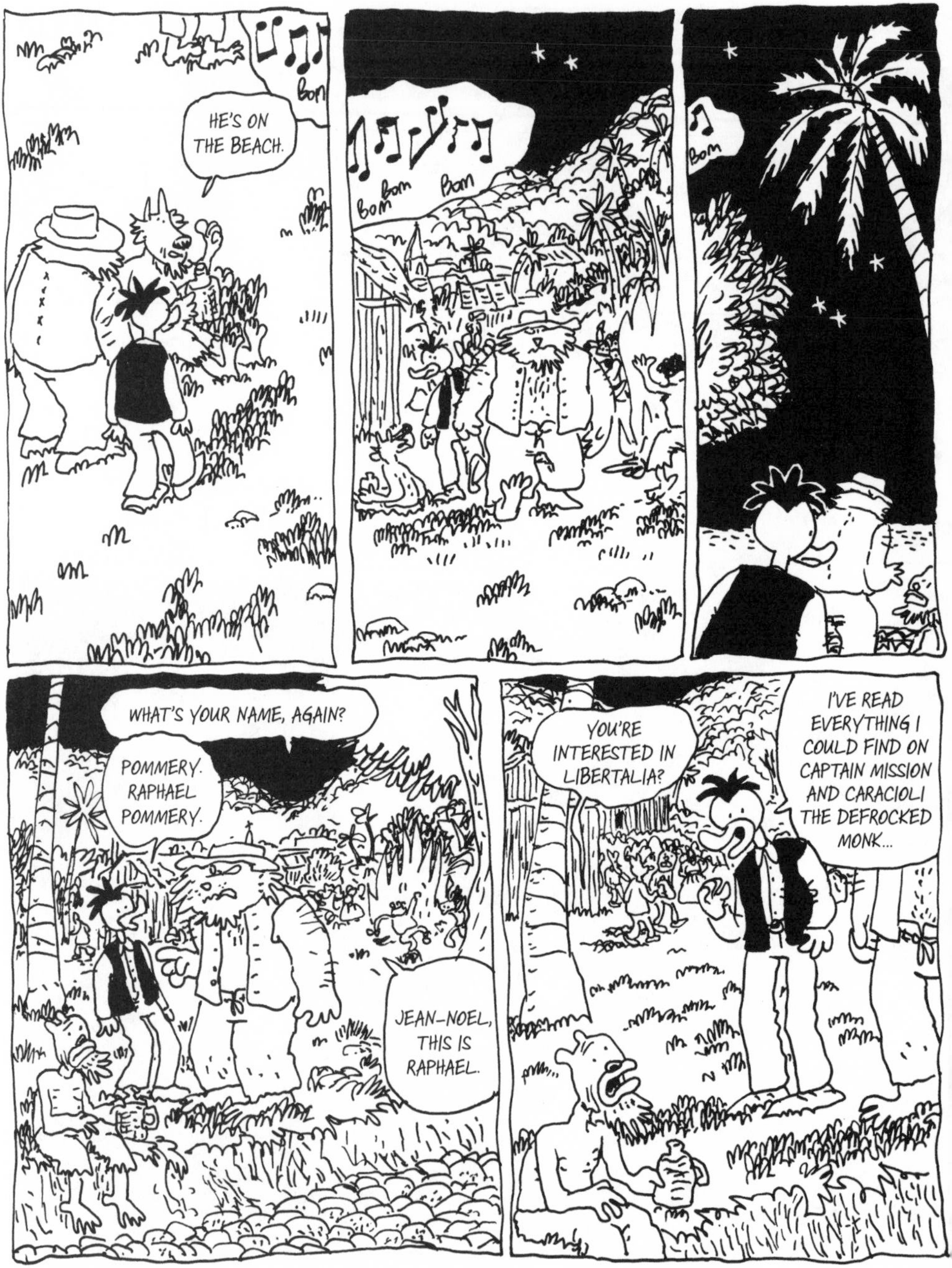

HE'S ON THE BEACH.
Bom
Bom Bom Bom Bom
Bom
WHAT'S YOUR NAME, AGAIN?
POMMERY. RAPHAEL POMMERY.
JEAN-NOEL, THIS IS RAPHAEL.
YOU'RE INTERESTED IN LIBERTALIA?
I'VE READ EVERYTHING I COULD FIND ON CAPTAIN MISSION AND CARACIOLI THE DEFROCKED MONK...

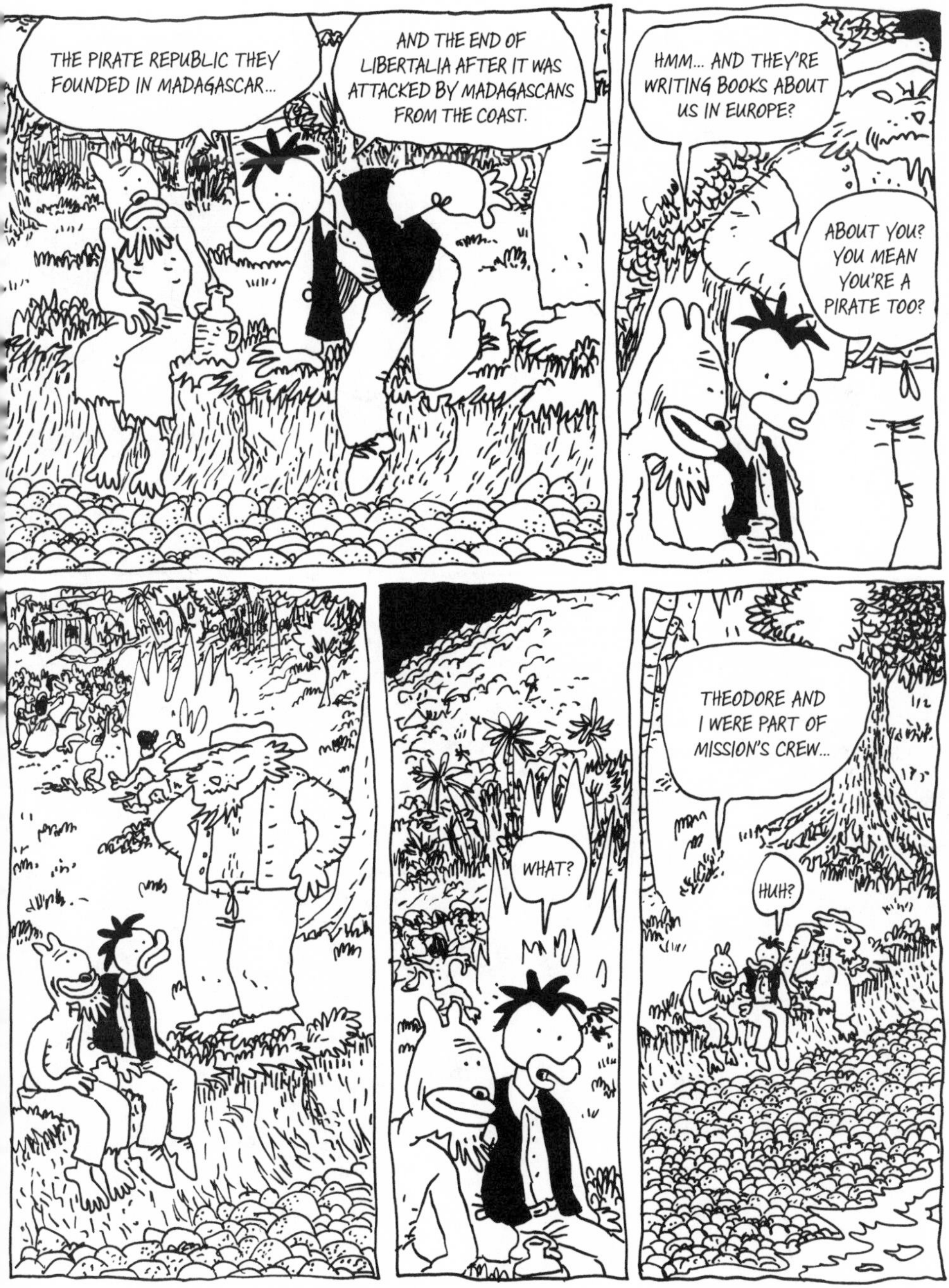
THE PIRATE REPUBLIC THEY FOUNDED IN MADAGASCAR...
AND THE END OF LIBERTALIA AFTER IT WAS ATTACKED BY MADAGASCANS FROM THE COAST.
HMM... AND THEY'RE WRITING BOOKS ABOUT US IN EUROPE?
ABOUT YOU? YOU MEAN YOU'RE A PIRATE TOO?
WHAT?
THEODORE AND I WERE PART OF MISSION'S CREW...
HUH?

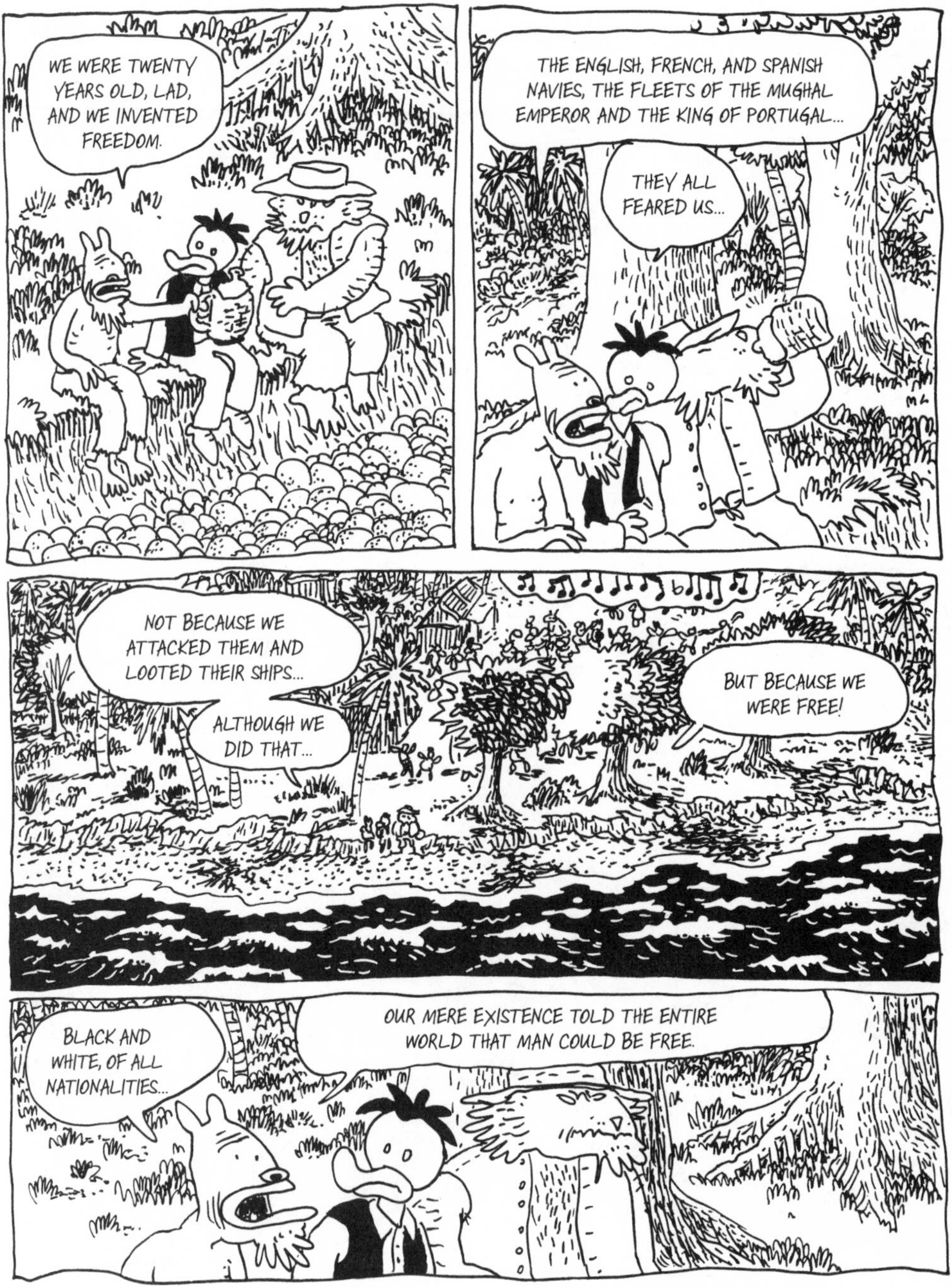
WE WERE TWENTY YEARS OLD, LAD, AND WE INVENTED FREEDOM.
THE ENGLISH, FRENCH, AND SPANISH NAVIES, THE FLEETS OF THE MUGHAL EMPEROR AND THE KING OF PORTUGAL...
THEY ALL FEARED US...
NOT BECAUSE WE ATTACKED THEM AND LOOTED THEIR SHIPS...
ALTHOUGH WE DID THAT...
BUT BECAUSE WE WERE FREE!
BLACK AND WHITE, OF ALL NATIONALITIES...
OUR MERE EXISTENCE TOLD THE ENTIRE WORLD THAT MAN COULD BE FREE.

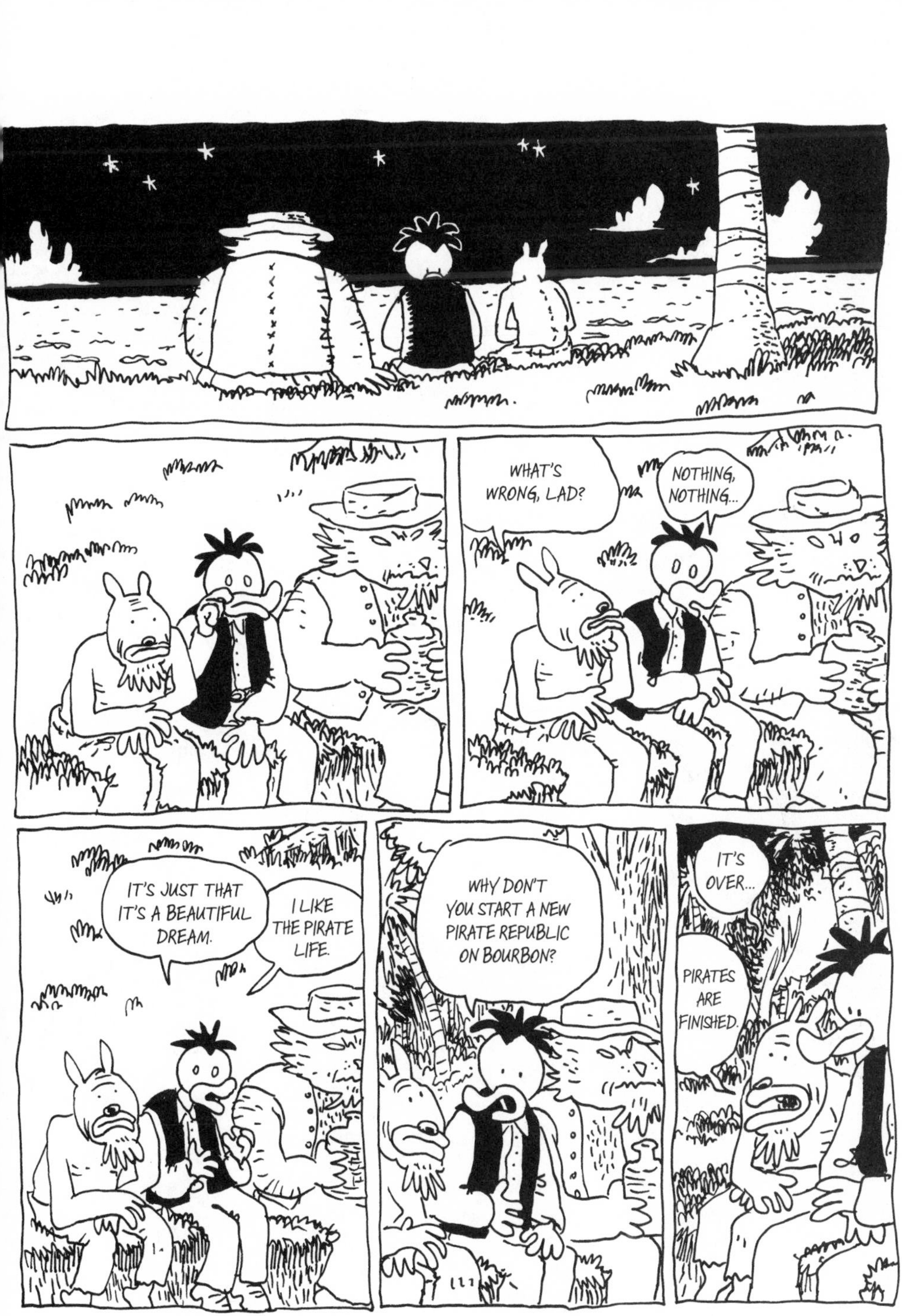
WHAT'S WRONG, LAD?
NOTHING, NOTHING...
IT'S JUST THAT IT'S A BEAUTIFUL DREAM.
I LIKE THE PIRATE LIFE.
WHY DON'T YOU START A NEW PIRATE REPUBLIC ON BOURBON?
IT'S OVER...
PIRATES ARE FINISHED.

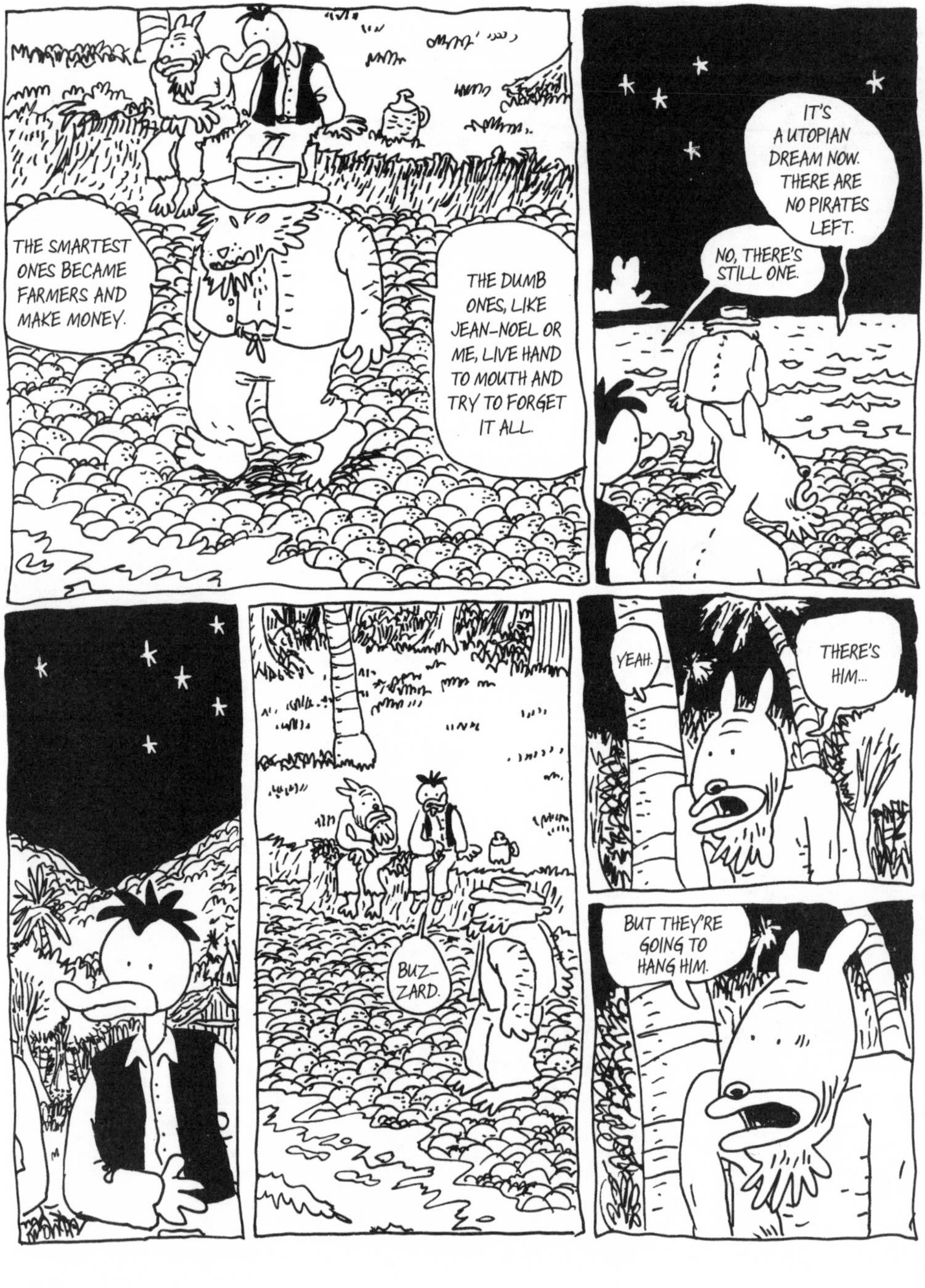
THE SMARTEST ONES BECAME FARMERS AND MAKE MONEY.
THE DUMB ONES, LIKE JEAN-NOEL OR ME, LIVE HAND TO MOUTH AND TRY TO FORGET IT ALL.
IT'S A UTOPIAN DREAM NOW. THERE ARE NO PIRATES LEFT.
NO, THERE'S STILL ONE.
BUZ-ZARD.
YEAH.
THERE'S HIM...
BUT THEY'RE GOING TO HANG HIM.

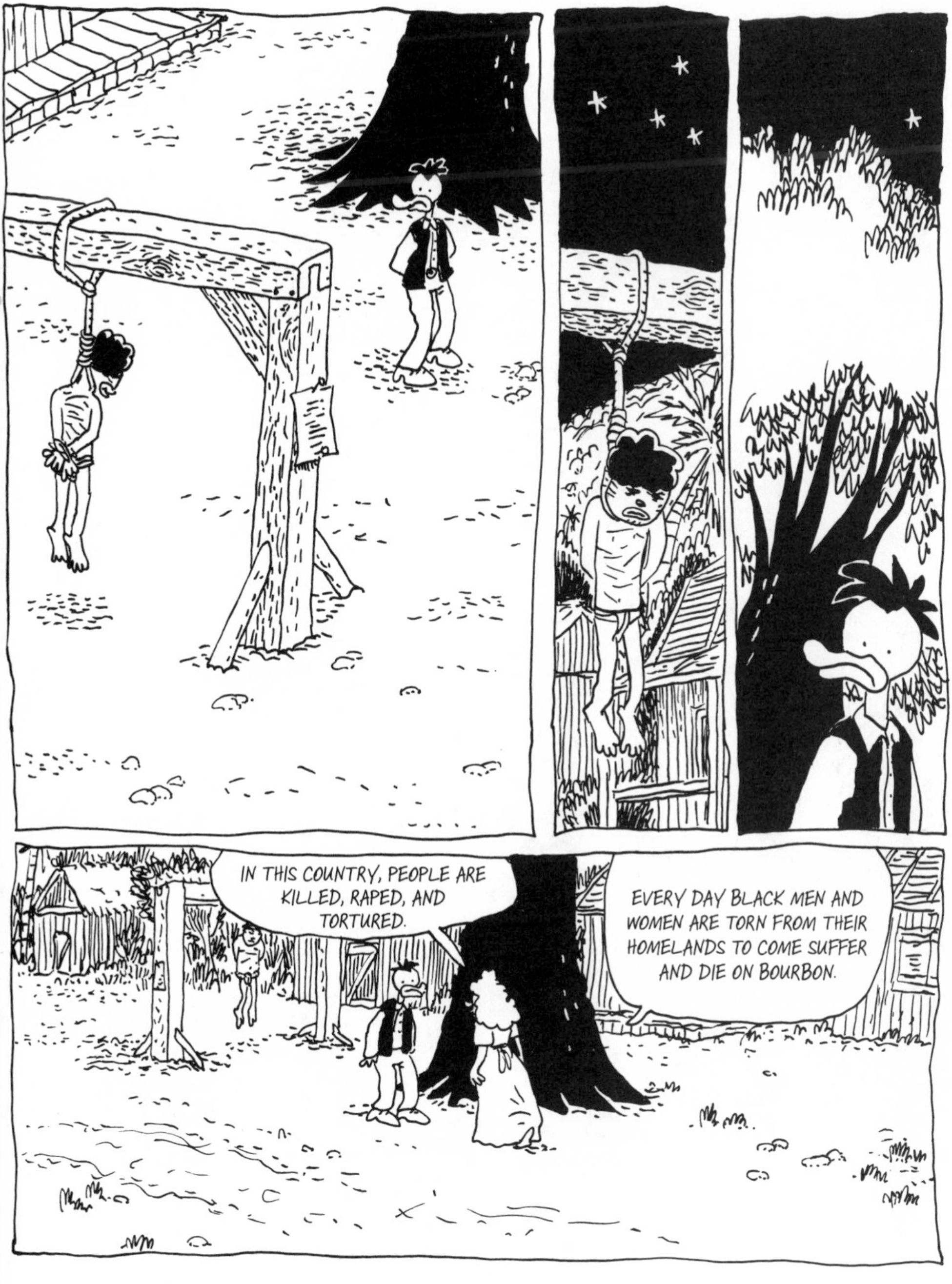
IN THIS COUNTRY, PEOPLE ARE KILLED, RAPED, AND TORTURED.
EVERY DAY BLACK MEN AND WOMEN ARE TORN FROM THEIR HOMELANDS TO COME SUFFER AND DIE ON BOURBON.

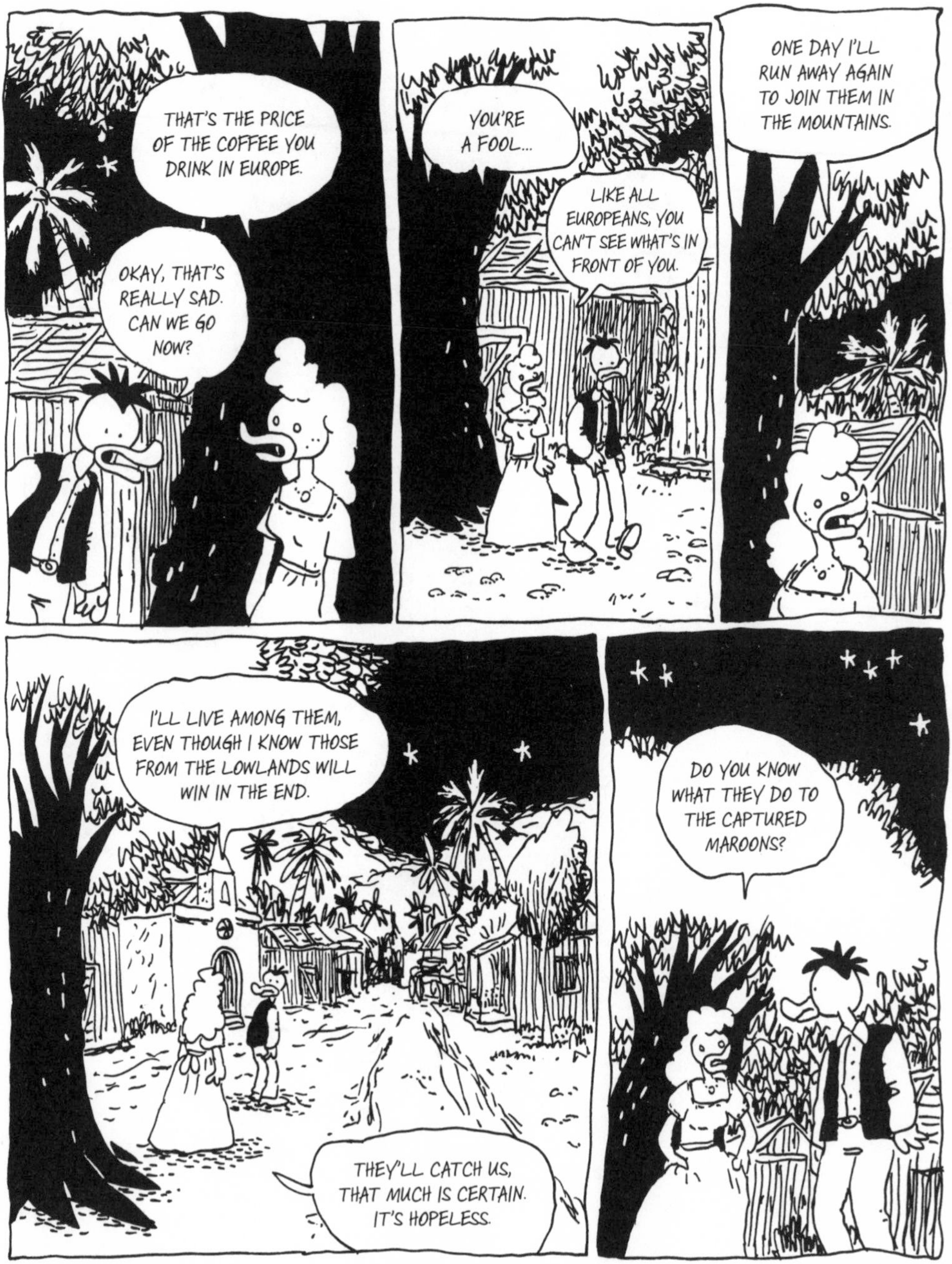
THAT'S THE PRICE OF THE COFFEE YOU DRINK IN EUROPE.
OKAY, THAT'S REALLY SAD. CAN WE GO NOW?
YOU'RE A FOOL...
LIKE ALL EUROPEANS, YOU CAN'T SEE WHAT'S IN FRONT OF YOU.
ONE DAY I'LL RUN AWAY AGAIN TO JOIN THEM IN THE MOUNTAINS.
I'LL LIVE AMONG THEM, EVEN THOUGH I KNOW THOSE FROM THE LOWLANDS WILL WIN IN THE END.
THEY'LL CATCH US, THAT MUCH IS CERTAIN. IT'S HOPELESS.
DO YOU KNOW WHAT THEY DO TO THE CAPTURED MAROONS?

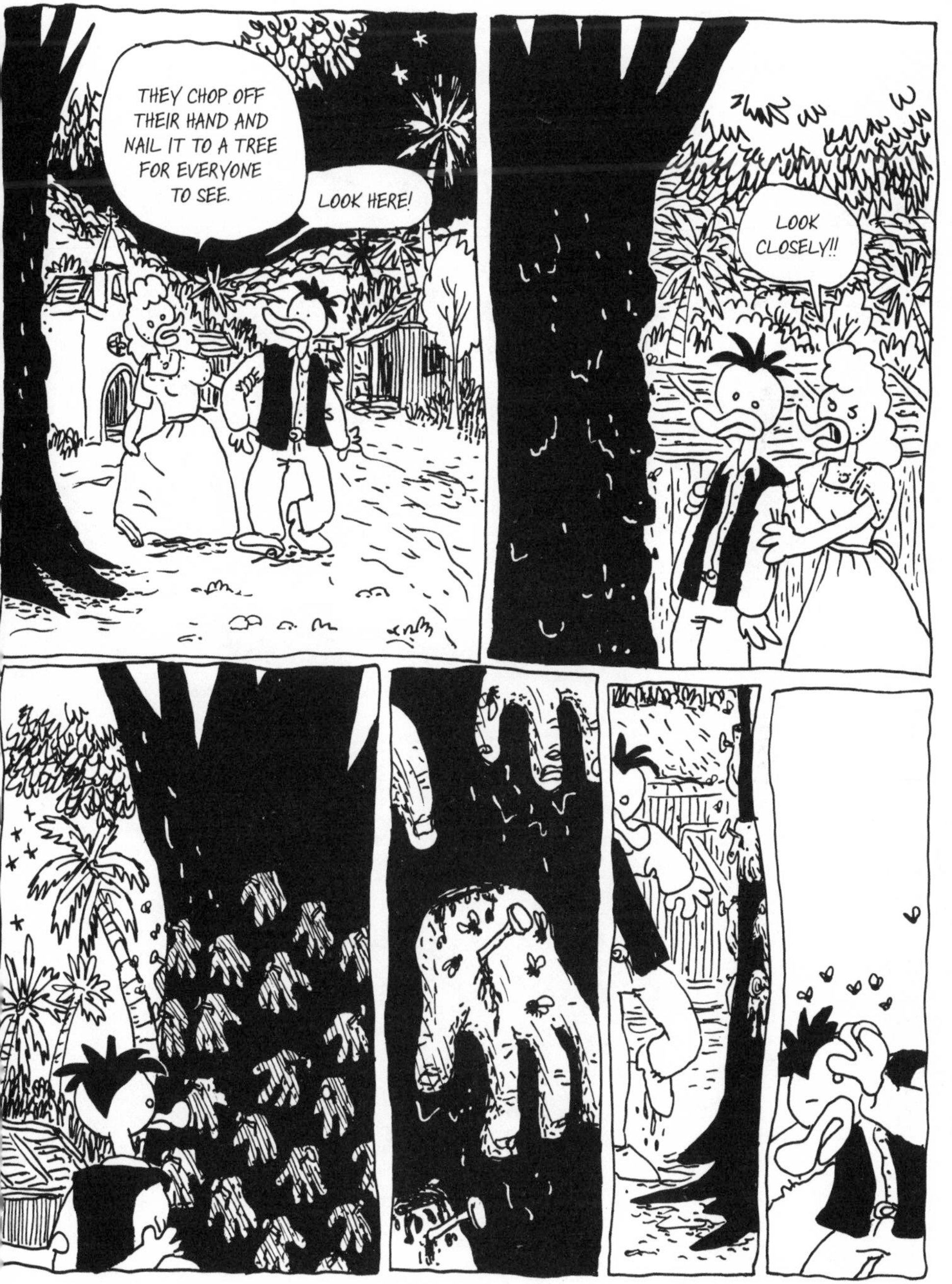
THEY CHOP OFF THEIR HAND AND NAIL IT TO A TREE FOR EVERYONE TO SEE.
LOOK HERE!
LOOK CLOSELY!!

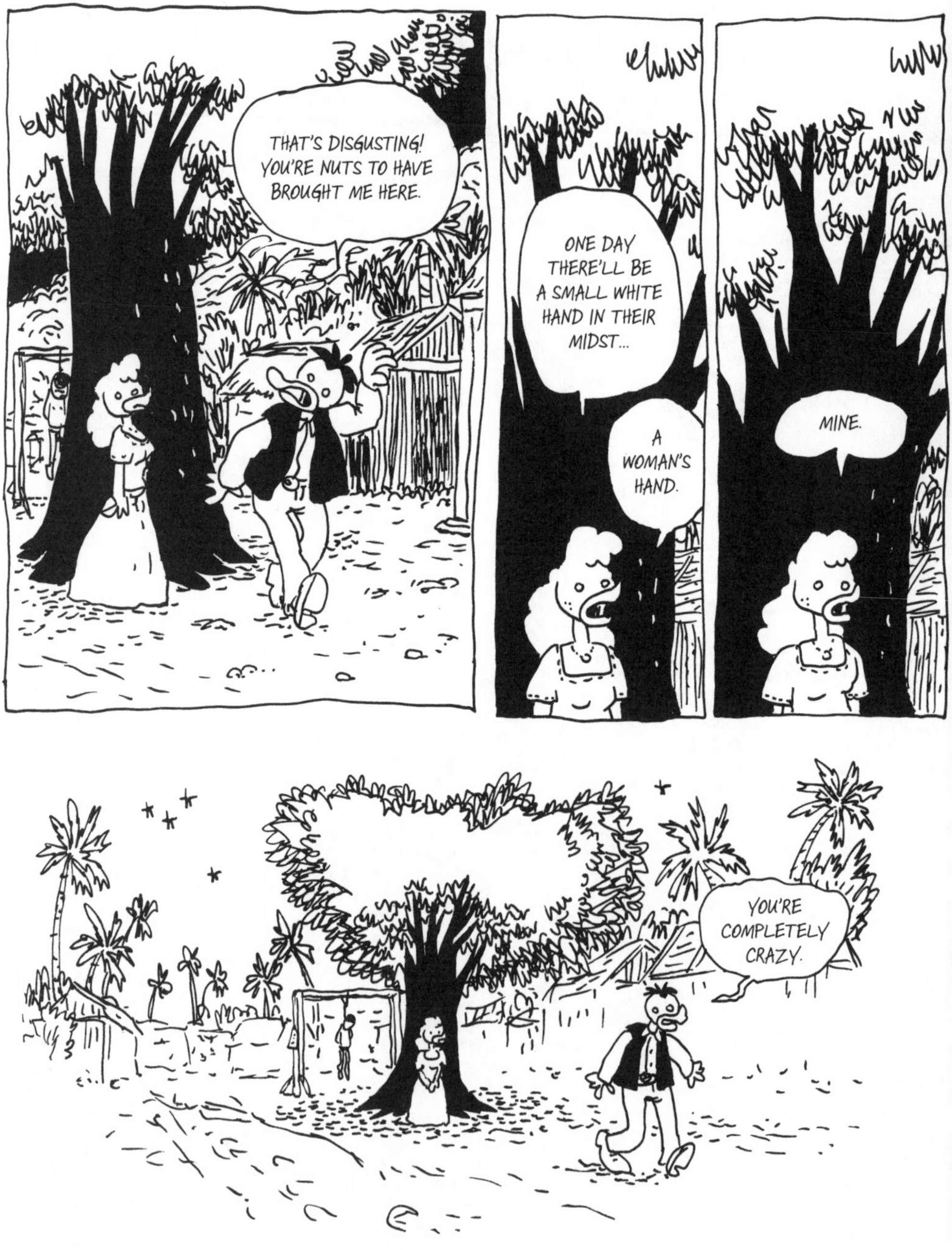
THAT'S DISGUSTING! YOU'RE NUTS TO HAVE BROUGHT ME HERE.
ONE DAY THERE'LL BE A SMALL WHITE HAND IN THEIR MIDST...
A WOMAN'S HAND.
MINE.
YOU'RE COMPLETELY CRAZY.

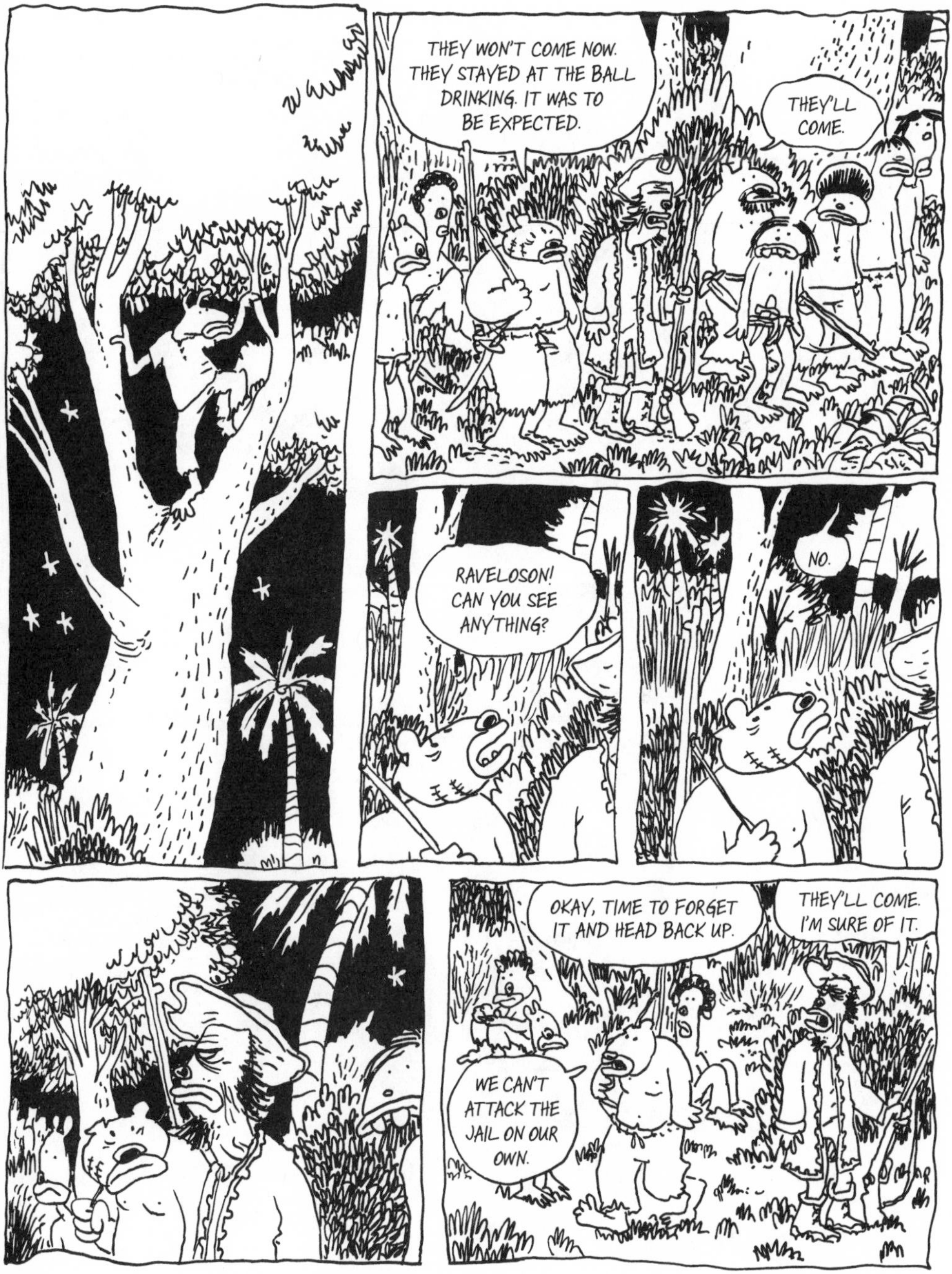

THEY WON'T COME NOW. THEY STAYED AT THE BALL DRINKING. IT WAS TO BE EXPECTED.
THEY'LL COME.
RAVELOSON! CAN YOU SEE ANYTHING?
NO.
OKAY, TIME TO FORGET IT AND HEAD BACK UP.
THEY'LL COME. I'M SURE OF IT.
WE CAN'T ATTACK THE JAIL ON OUR OWN.

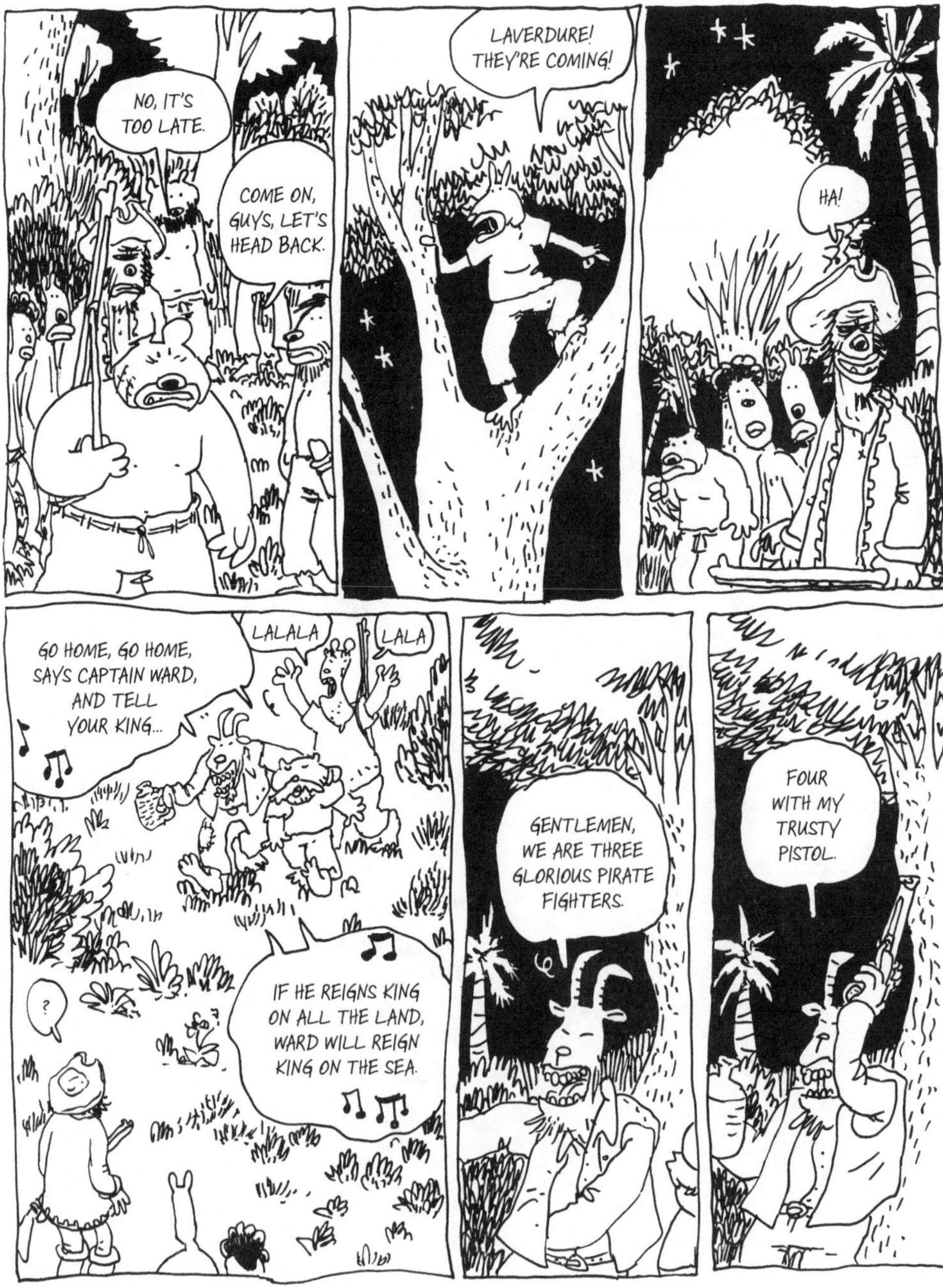
NO, IT'S TOO LATE.
COME ON, GUYS, LET'S HEAD BACK.
LAVERDURE! THEY'RE COMING!
HA!
GO HOME, GO HOME, SAYS CAPTAIN WARD, AND TELL YOUR KING...
LALALA
LALA
?
IF HE REIGNS KING ON ALL THE LAND, WARD WILL REIGN KING ON THE SEA.
GENTLEMEN, WE ARE THREE GLORIOUS PIRATE FIGHTERS.
FOUR WITH MY TRUSTY PISTOL.

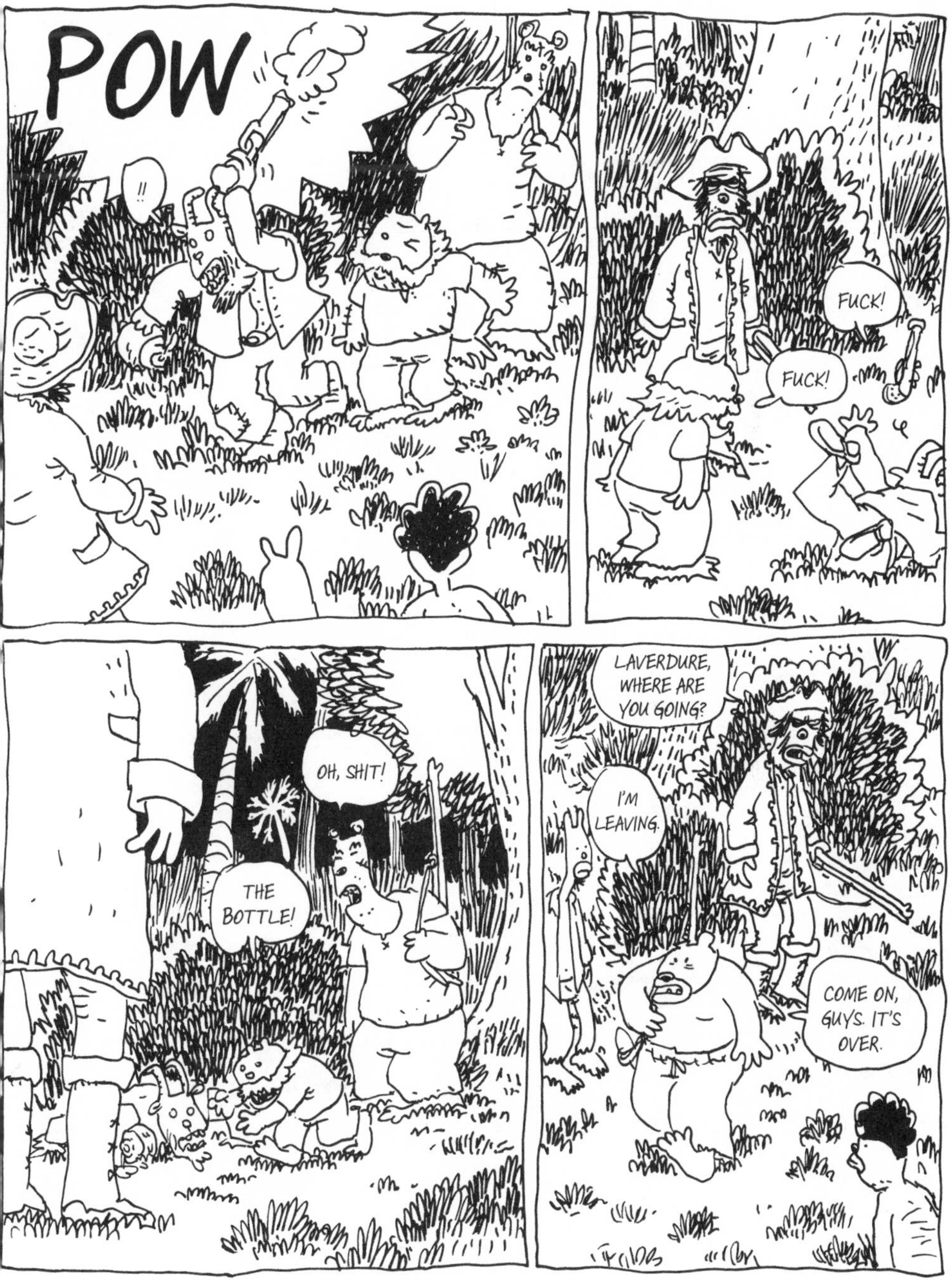
POW
!!
FUCK!
FUCK!
OH, SHIT!
THE BOTTLE!
LAVERDURE, WHERE ARE YOU GOING?
I'M LEAVING.
COME ON, GUYS. IT'S OVER.

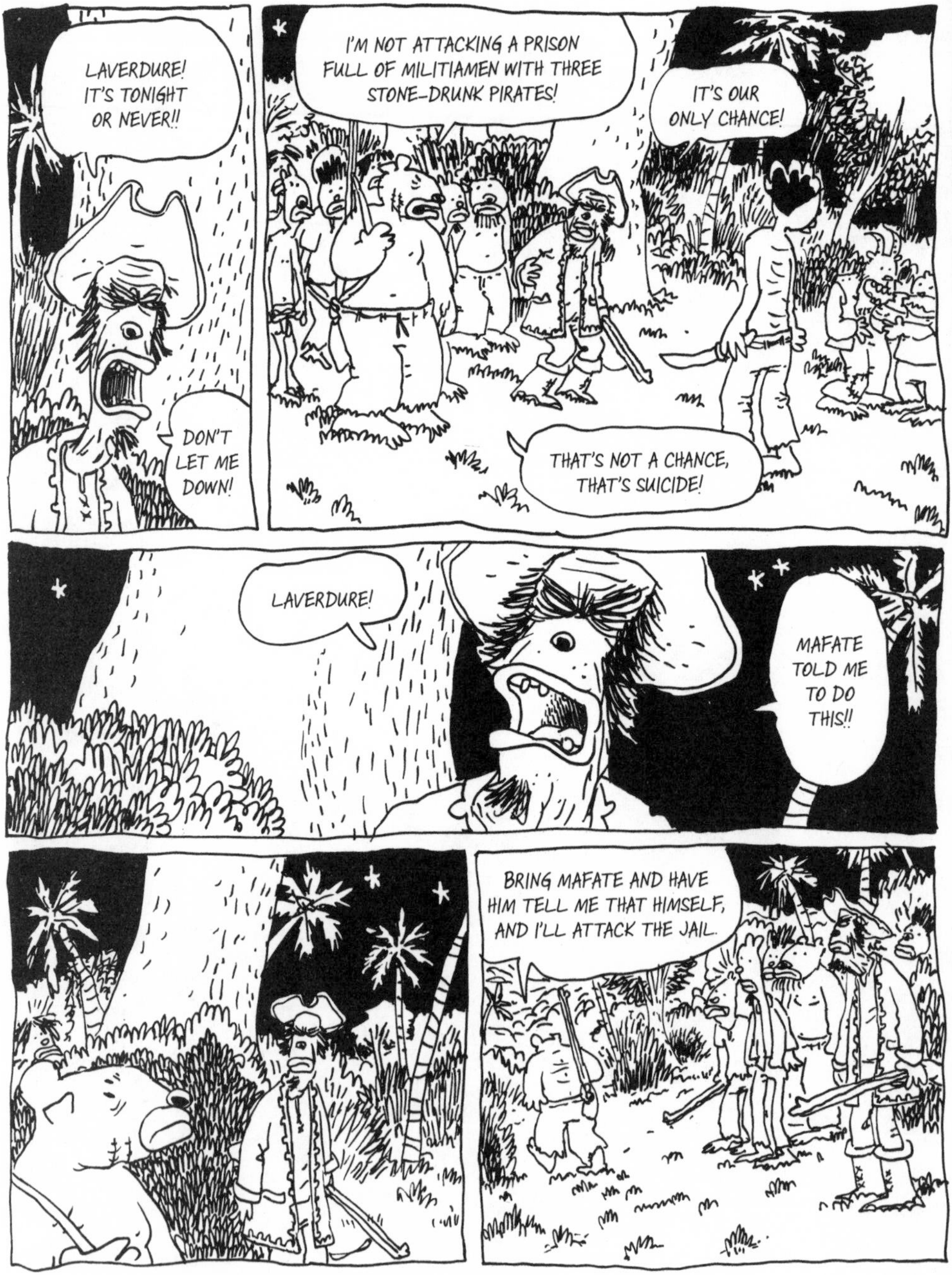
LAVERDURE! IT'S TONIGHT OR NEVER!!
DON'T LET ME DOWN!
I'M NOT ATTACKING A PRISON FULL OF MILITIAMEN WITH THREE STONE-DRUNK PIRATES!
IT'S OUR ONLY CHANCE!
THAT'S NOT A CHANCE, THAT'S SUICIDE!
LAVERDURE!
MAFATE TOLD ME TO DO THIS!!
BRING MAFATE AND HAVE HIM TELL ME THAT HIMSELF, AND I'LL ATTACK THE JAIL.

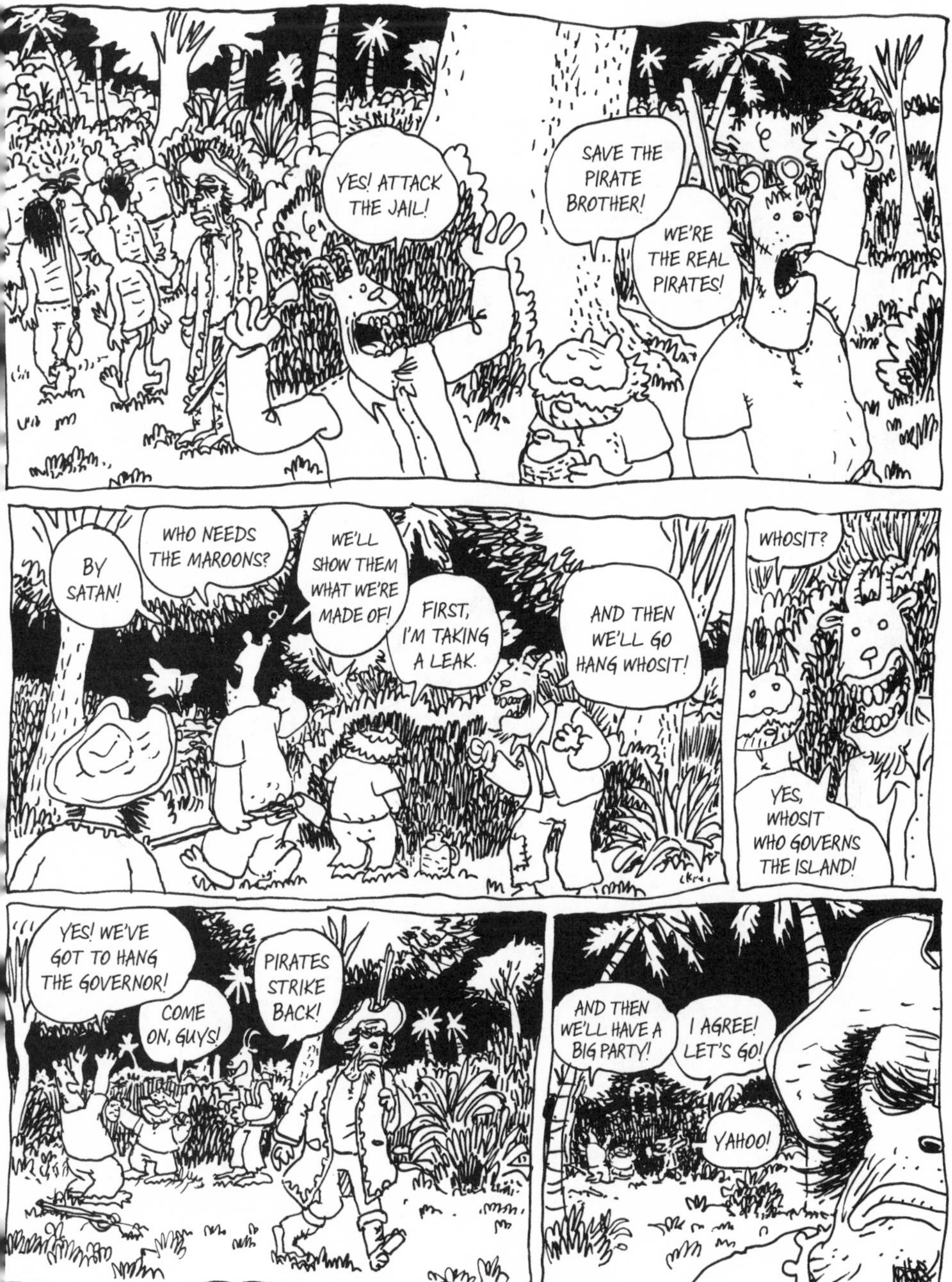
YES! ATTACK THE JAIL!
SAVE THE PIRATE BROTHER!
WE'RE THE REAL PIRATES!
BY SATAN!
WHO NEEDS THE MAROONS?
WE'LL SHOW THEM WHAT WE'RE MADE OF!
FIRST, I'M TAKING A LEAK.
AND THEN WE'LL GO HANG WHOSIT!
WHOSIT?
YES, WHOSIT WHO GOVERNS THE ISLAND!
YES! WE'VE GOT TO HANG THE GOVERNOR!
COME ON, GUYS!
PIRATES STRIKE BACK!
AND THEN WE'LL HAVE A BIG PARTY!
I AGREE! LET'S GO!
YAHOO!

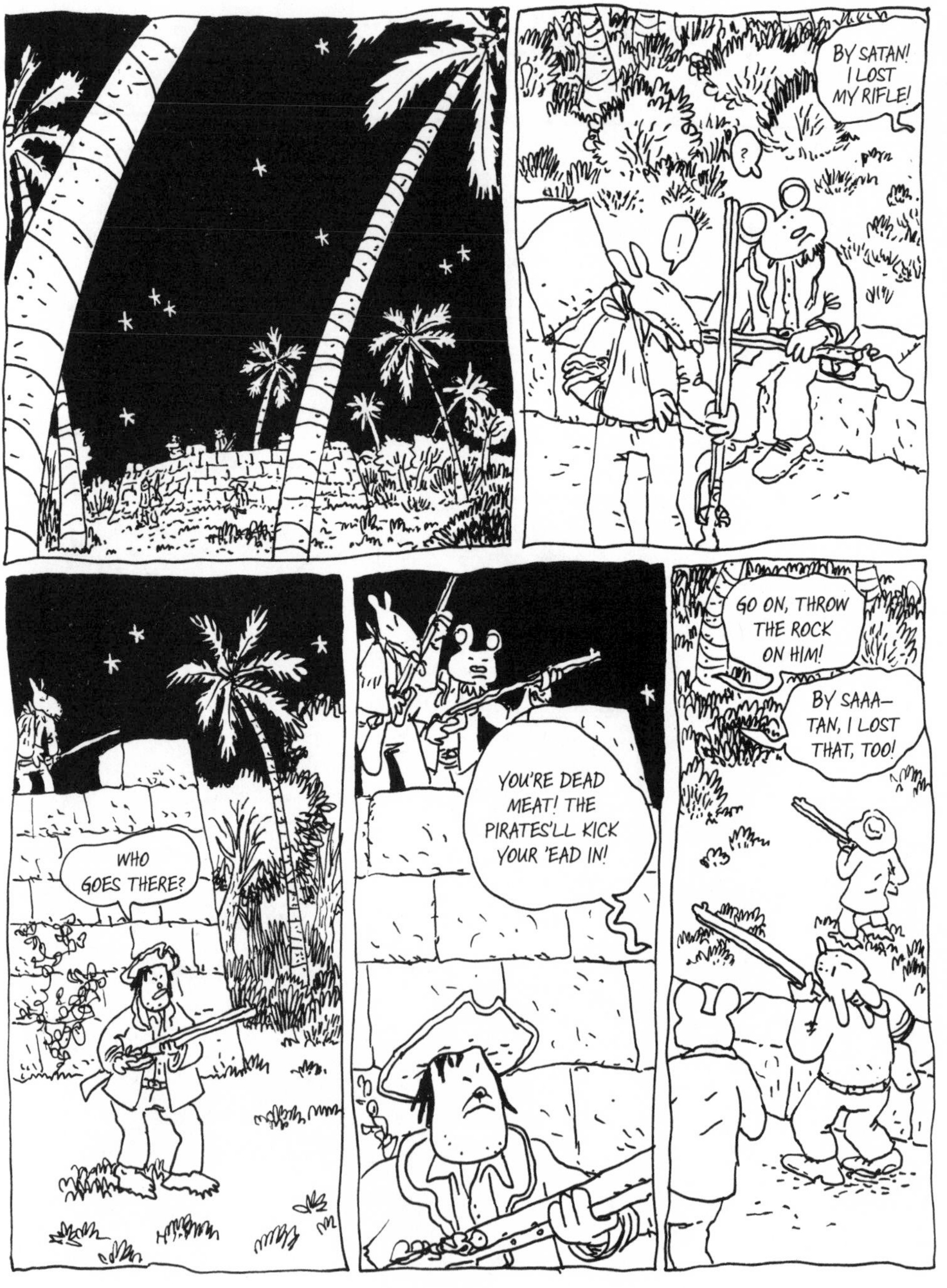
BY SATAN! I LOST MY RIFLE!
?
!
WHO GOES THERE?
YOU'RE DEAD MEAT! THE PIRATES'LL KICK YOUR 'EAD IN!
GO ON, THROW THE ROCK ON HIM!
BY SAAA-TAN, I LOST THAT, TOO!

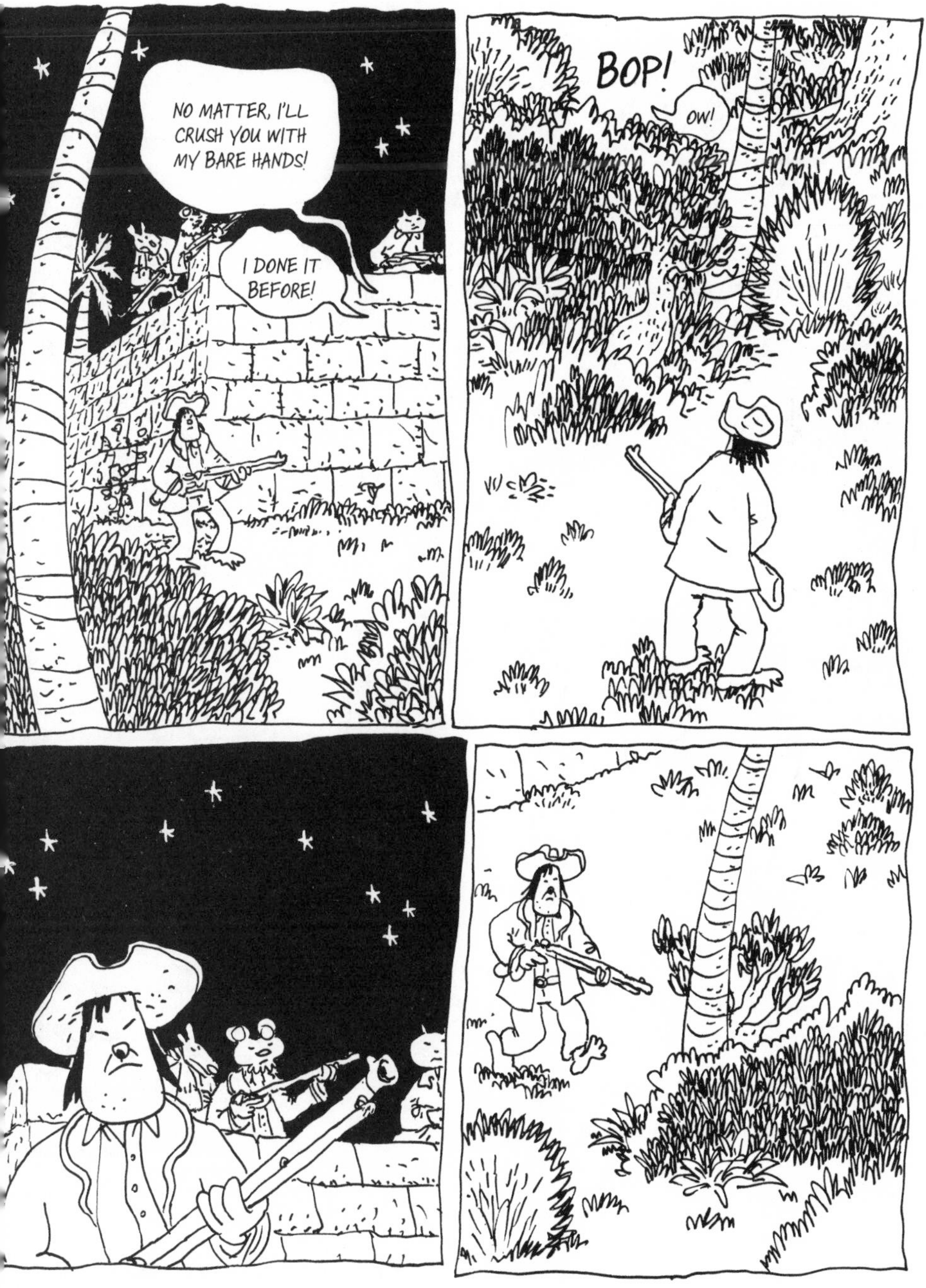
NO MATTER, I'LL CRUSH YOU WITH MY BARE HANDS!
I DONE IT BEFORE!
BOP!
OW!

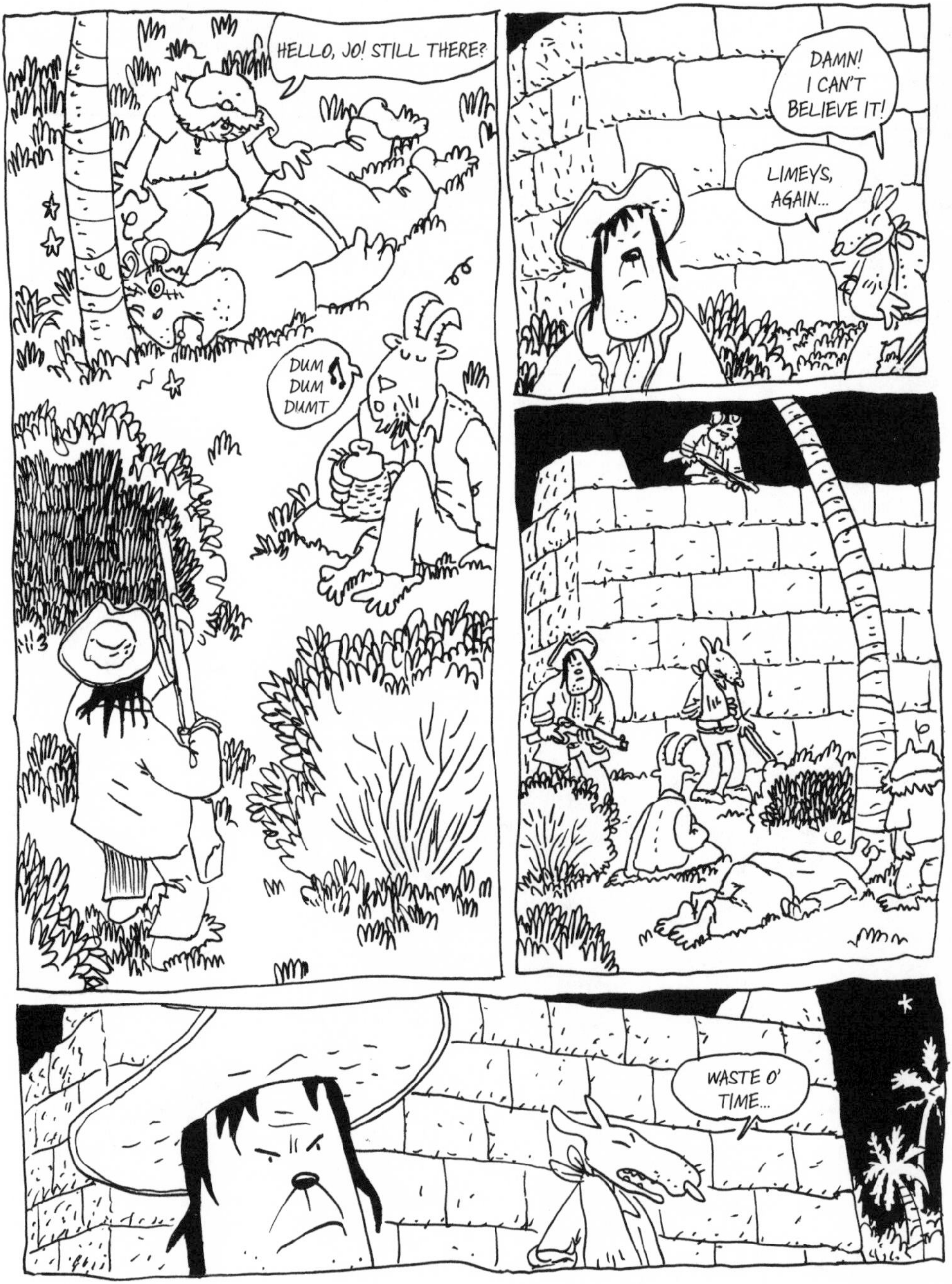
HELLO, JO! STILL THERE?
DUM DUM DUMT
DAMN! I CAN'T BELIEVE IT!
LIMEYS, AGAIN...
WASTE O' TIME...

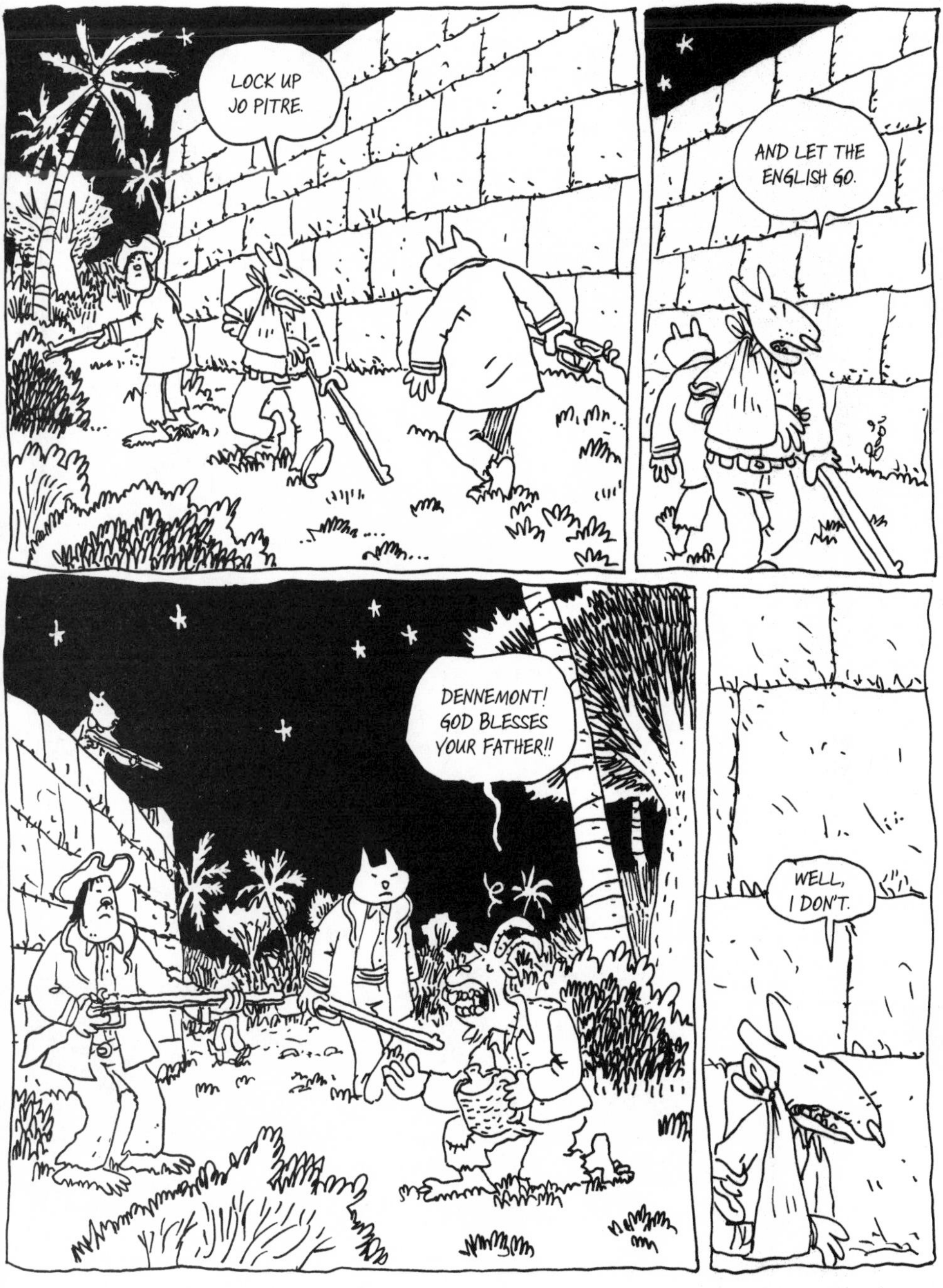
LOCK UP JO PITRE.
AND LET THE ENGLISH GO.
DENNEMONT! GOD BLESSES YOUR FATHER!!
WELL, I DON'T.

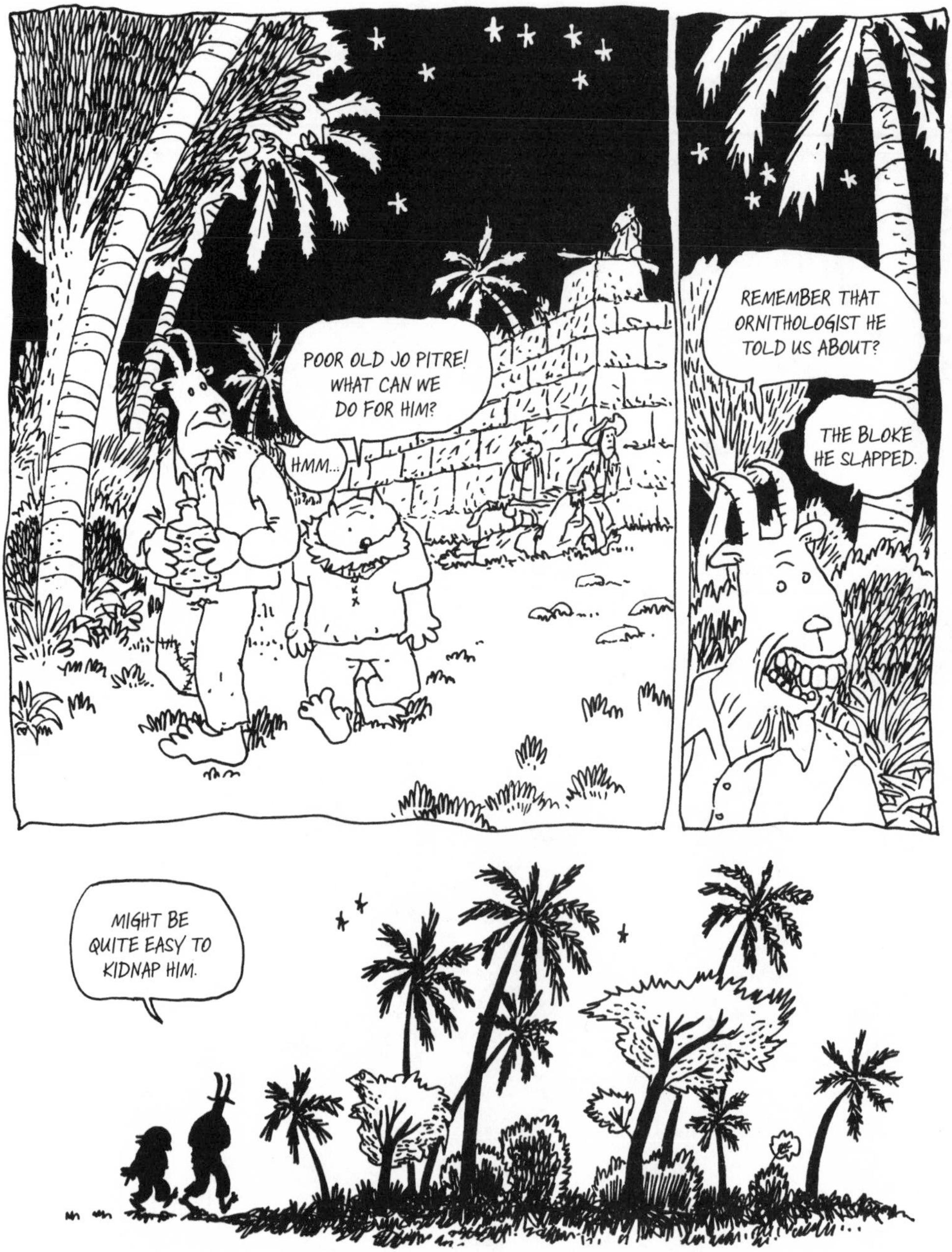
POOR OLD JO PITRE! WHAT CAN WE DO FOR HIM?
HMM...
REMEMBER THAT ORNITHOLOGIST HE TOLD US ABOUT?
THE BLOKE HE SLAPPED.
MIGHT BE QUITE EASY TO KIDNAP HIM.

MAFATE

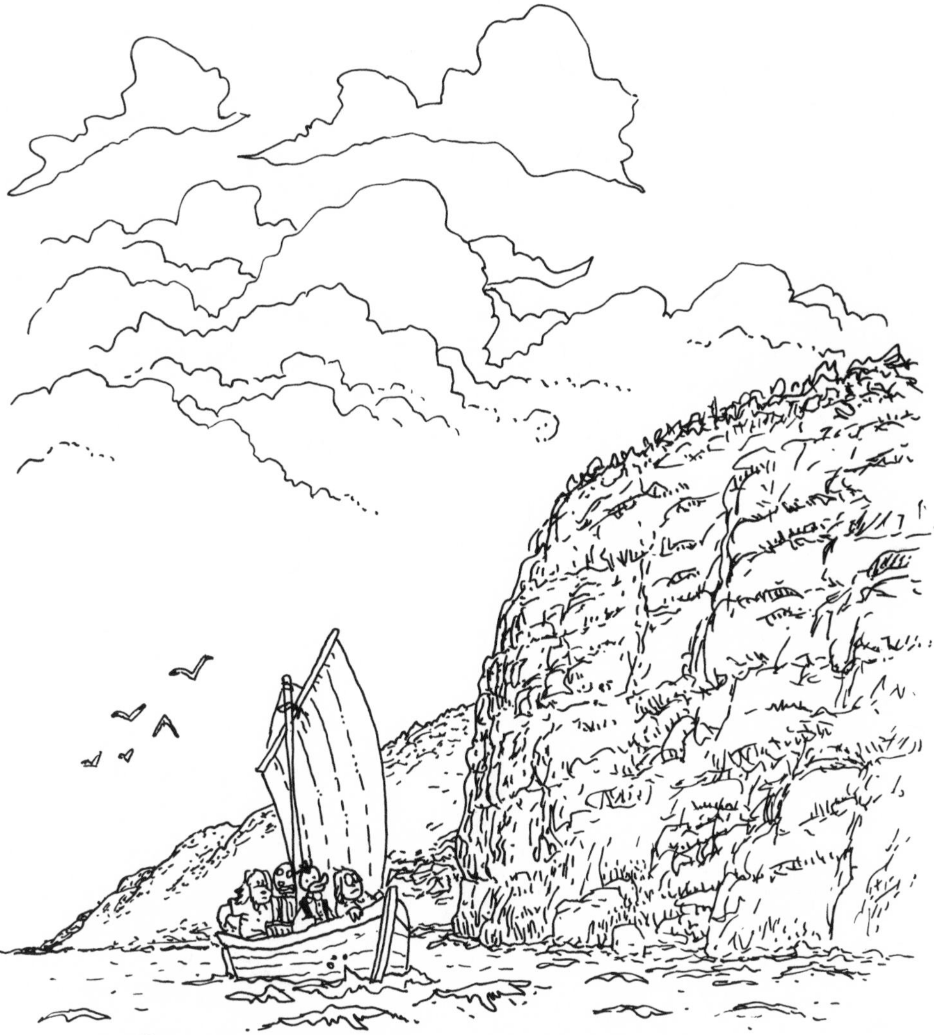

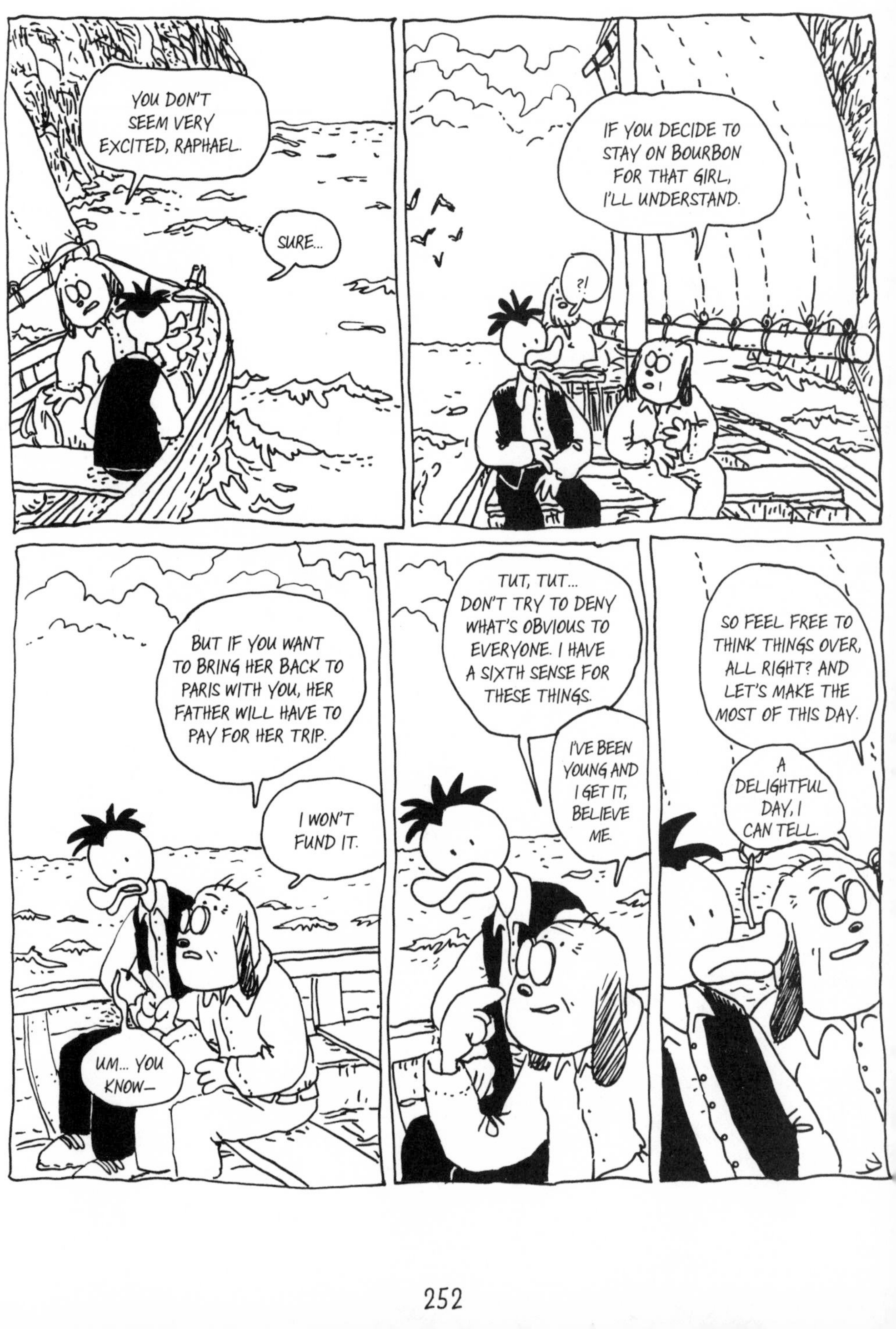
YOU DON'T SEEM VERY EXCITED, RAPHAEL.
SURE...
IF YOU DECIDE TO STAY ON BOURBON FOR THAT GIRL, I'LL UNDERSTAND.
?!
BUT IF YOU WANT TO BRING HER BACK TO PARIS WITH YOU, HER FATHER WILL HAVE TO PAY FOR HER TRIP.
I WON'T FUND IT.
UM... YOU KNOW—
TUT, TUT... DON'T TRY TO DENY WHAT'S OBVIOUS TO EVERYONE. I HAVE A SIXTH SENSE FOR THESE THINGS.
I'VE BEEN YOUNG AND I GET IT, BELIEVE ME.
SO FEEL FREE TO THINK THINGS OVER, ALL RIGHT? AND LET'S MAKE THE MOST OF THIS DAY.
A DELIGHTFUL DAY, I CAN TELL.

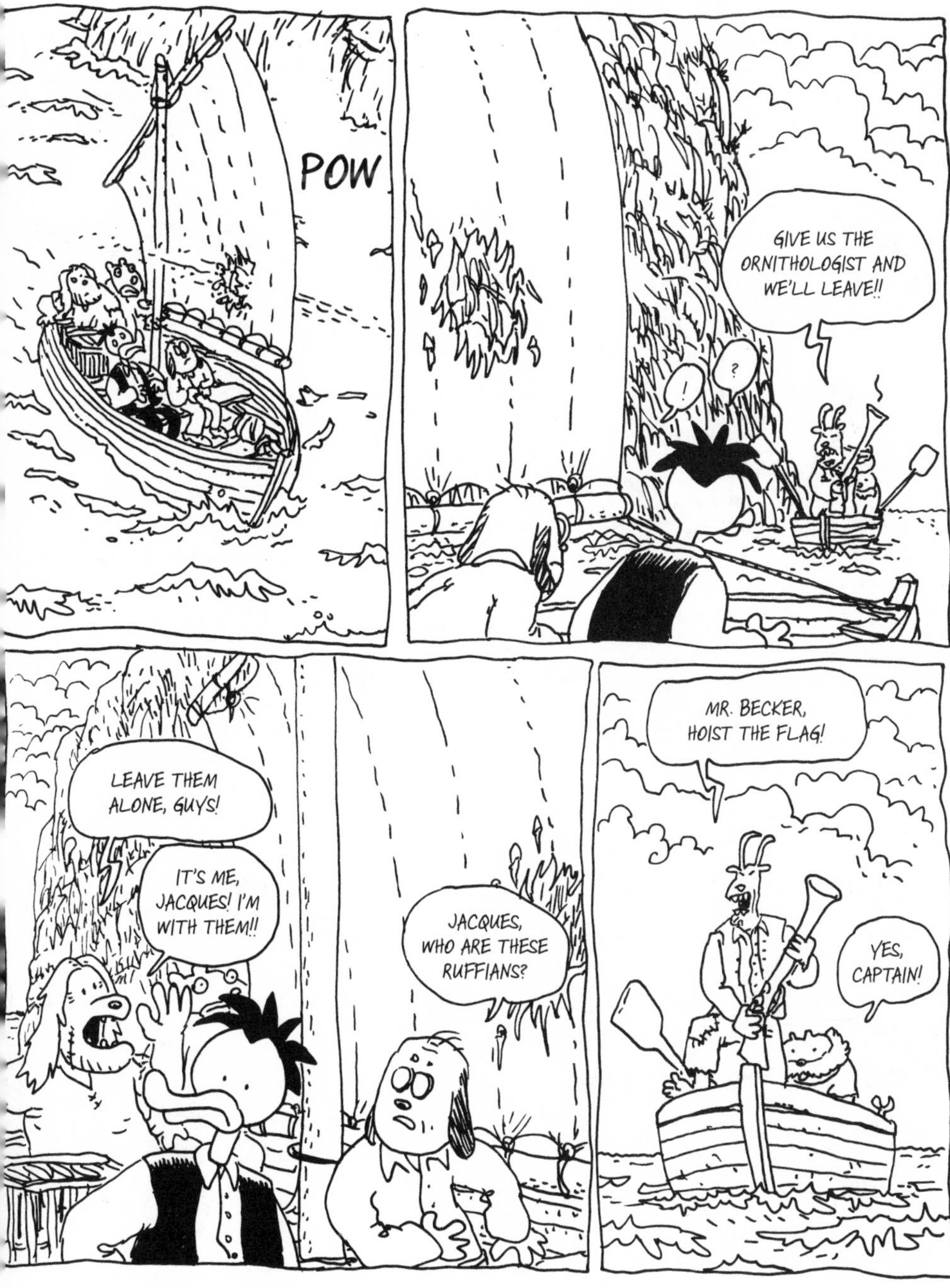
POW
!
?
GIVE US THE ORNITHOLOGIST AND WE'LL LEAVE!!
LEAVE THEM ALONE, GUYS!
IT'S ME, JACQUES! I'M WITH THEM!!
JACQUES, WHO ARE THESE RUFFIANS?
MR. BECKER, HOIST THE FLAG!
YES, CAPTAIN!

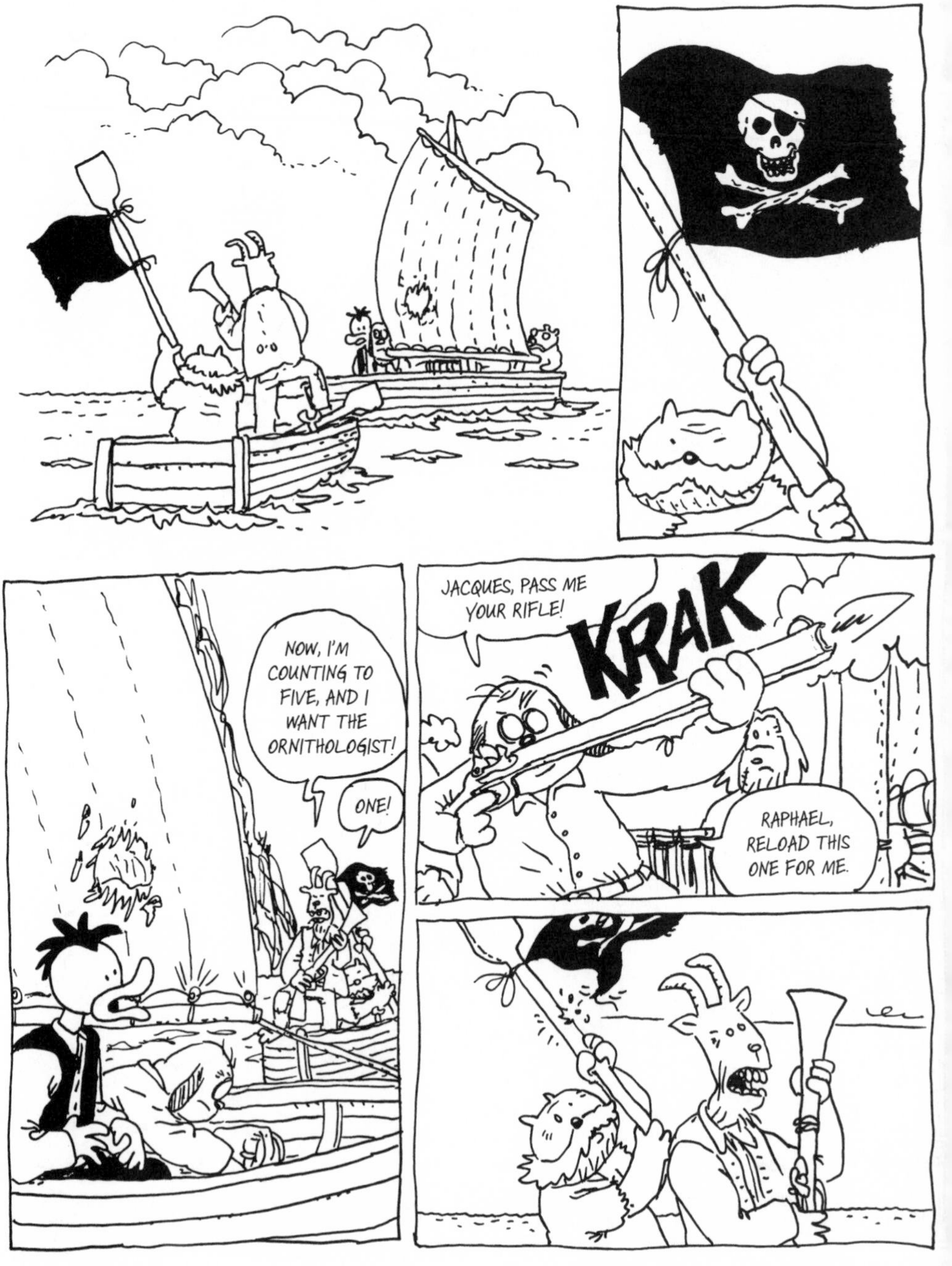
NOW, I'M COUNTING TO FIVE, AND I WANT THE ORNITHOLOGIST!
ONE!
JACQUES, PASS ME YOUR RIFLE!
KRAK
RAPHAEL, RELOAD THIS ONE FOR ME.

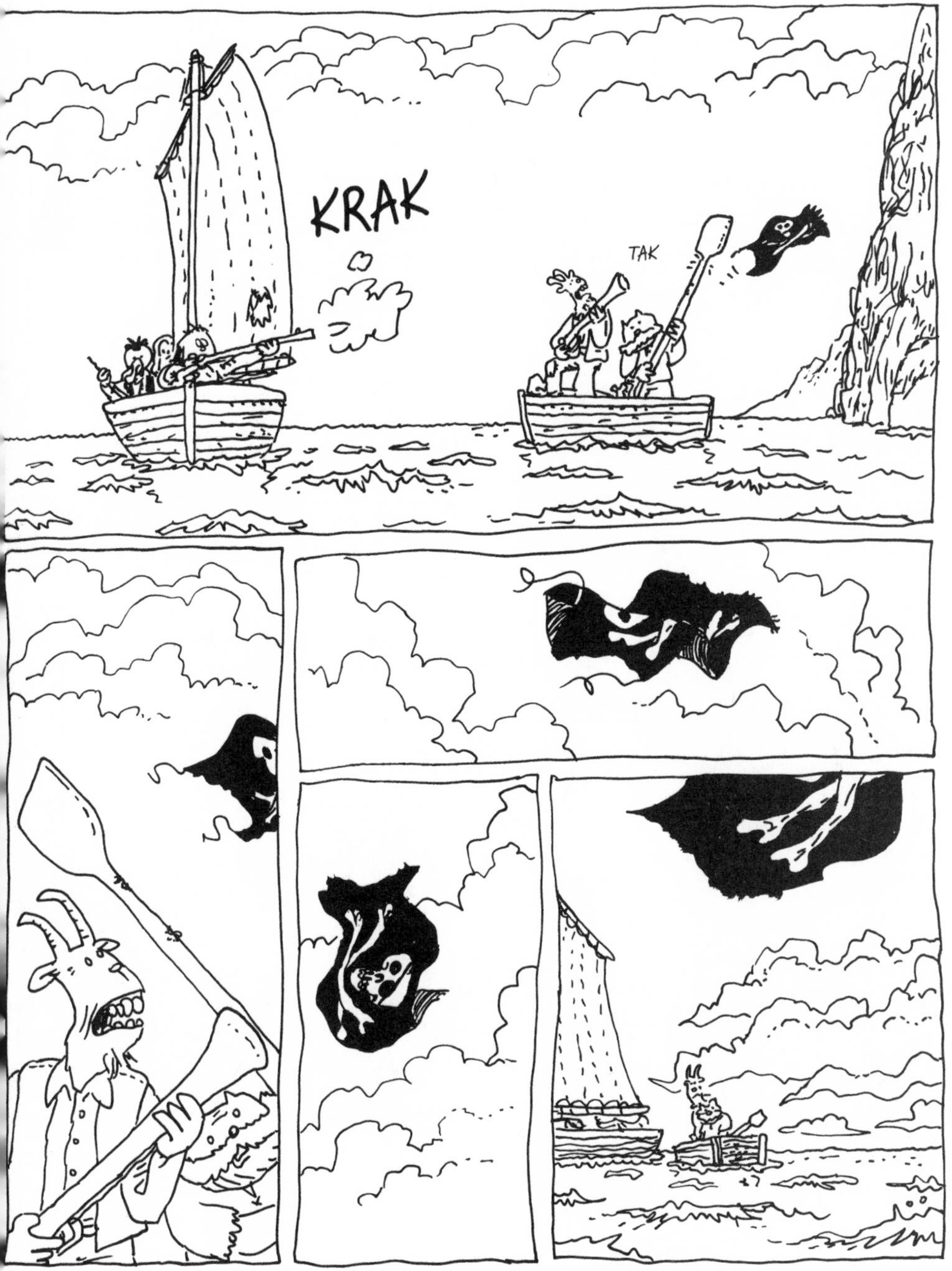
KRAK
TAK

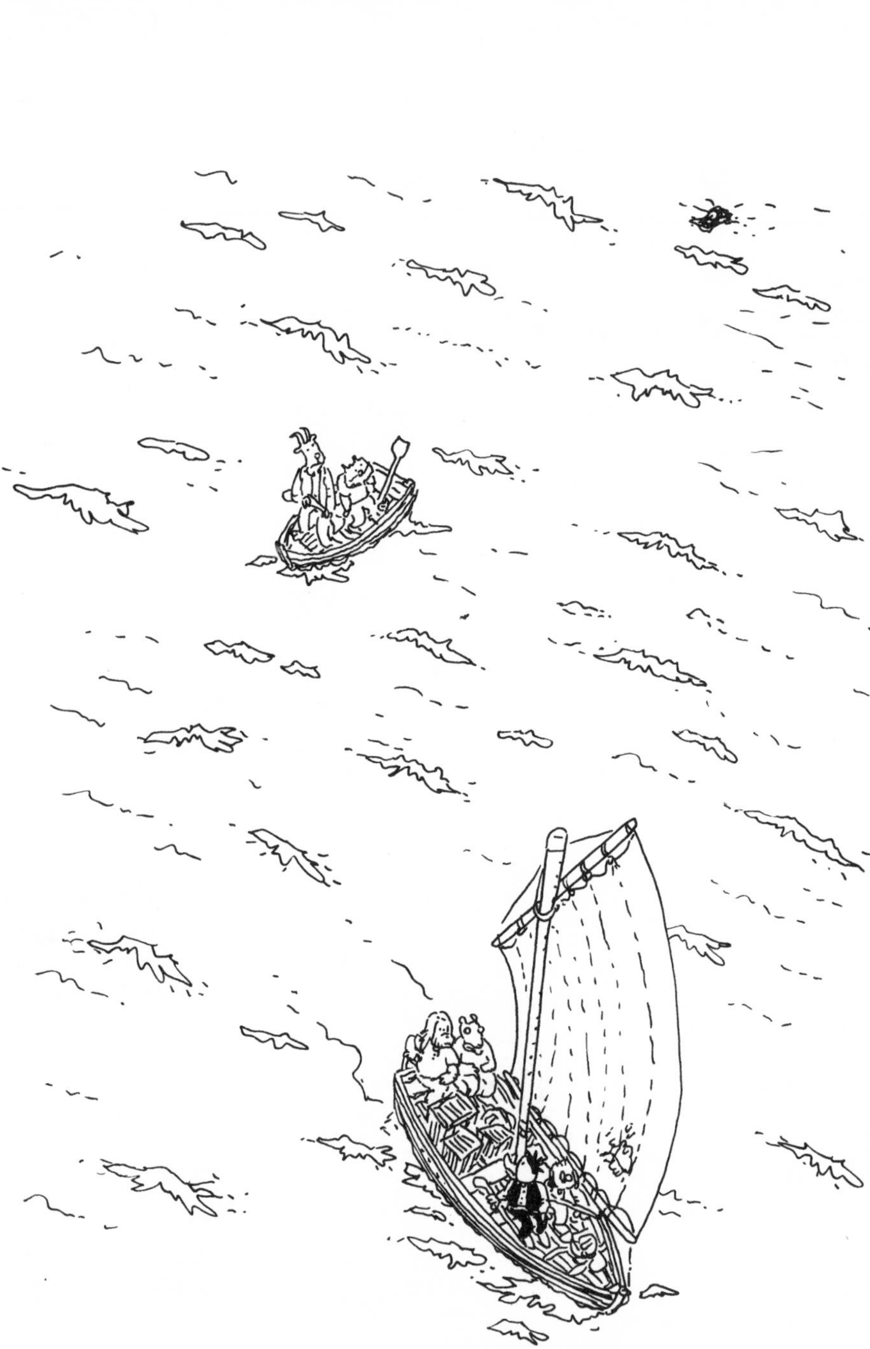

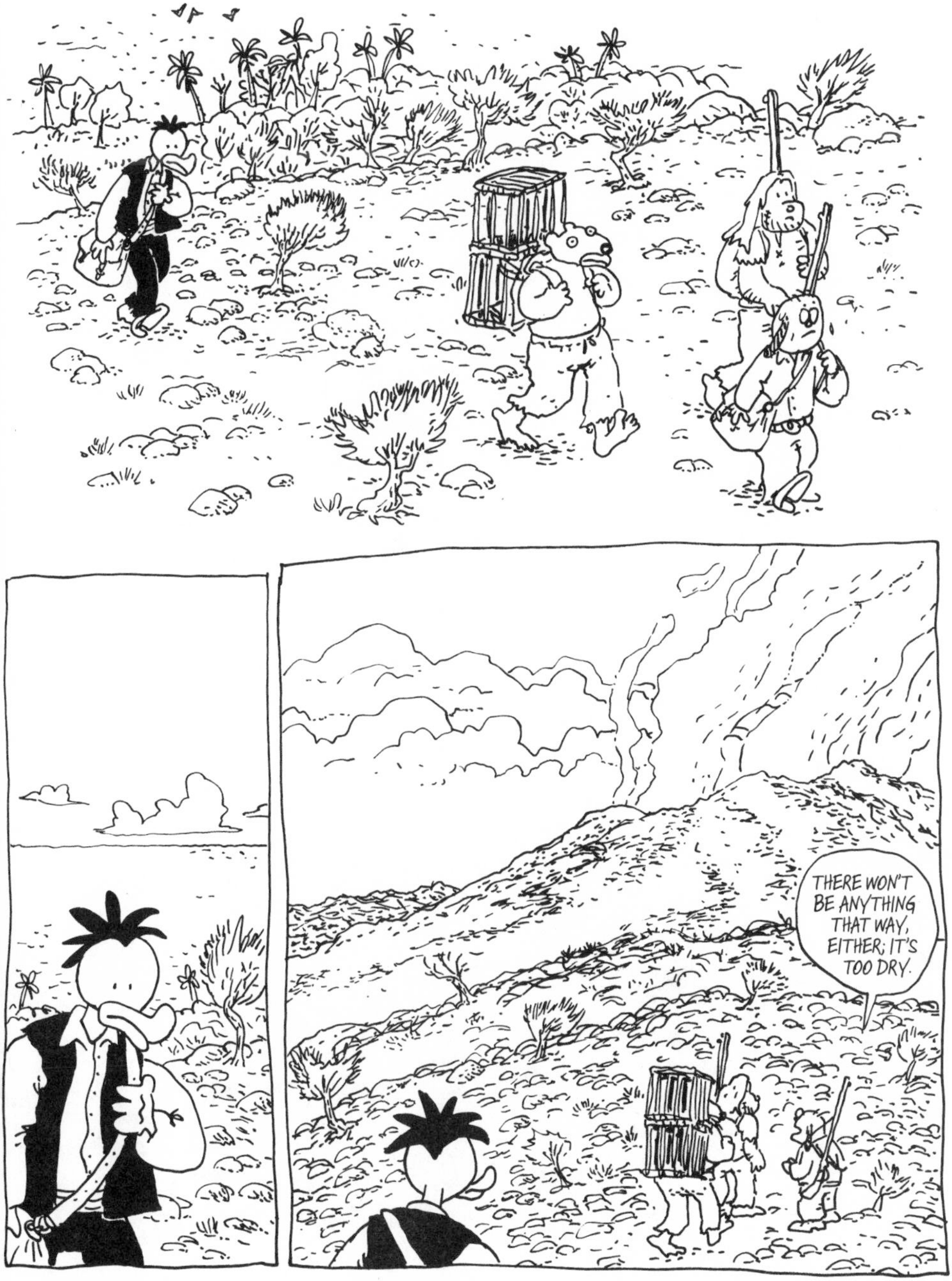
THERE WON'T BE ANYTHING THAT WAY, EITHER; IT'S TOO DRY.

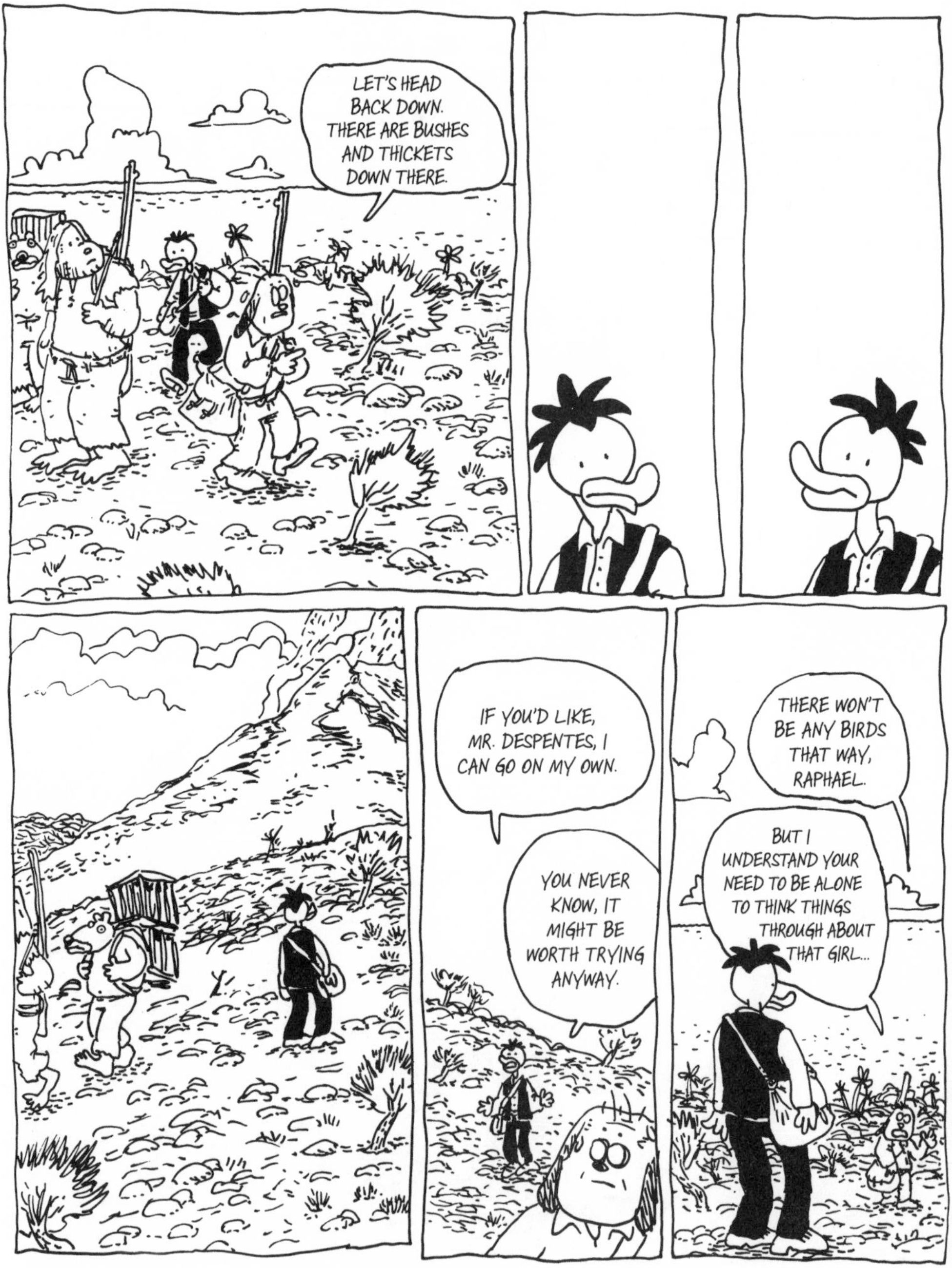
LET'S HEAD BACK DOWN. THERE ARE BUSHES AND THICKETS DOWN THERE.
IF YOU'D LIKE, MR. DESPENTES, I CAN GO ON MY OWN.
YOU NEVER KNOW, IT MIGHT BE WORTH TRYING ANYWAY.
THERE WON'T BE ANY BIRDS THAT WAY, RAPHAEL.
BUT I UNDERSTAND YOUR NEED TO BE ALONE TO THINK THINGS THROUGH ABOUT THAT GIRL...

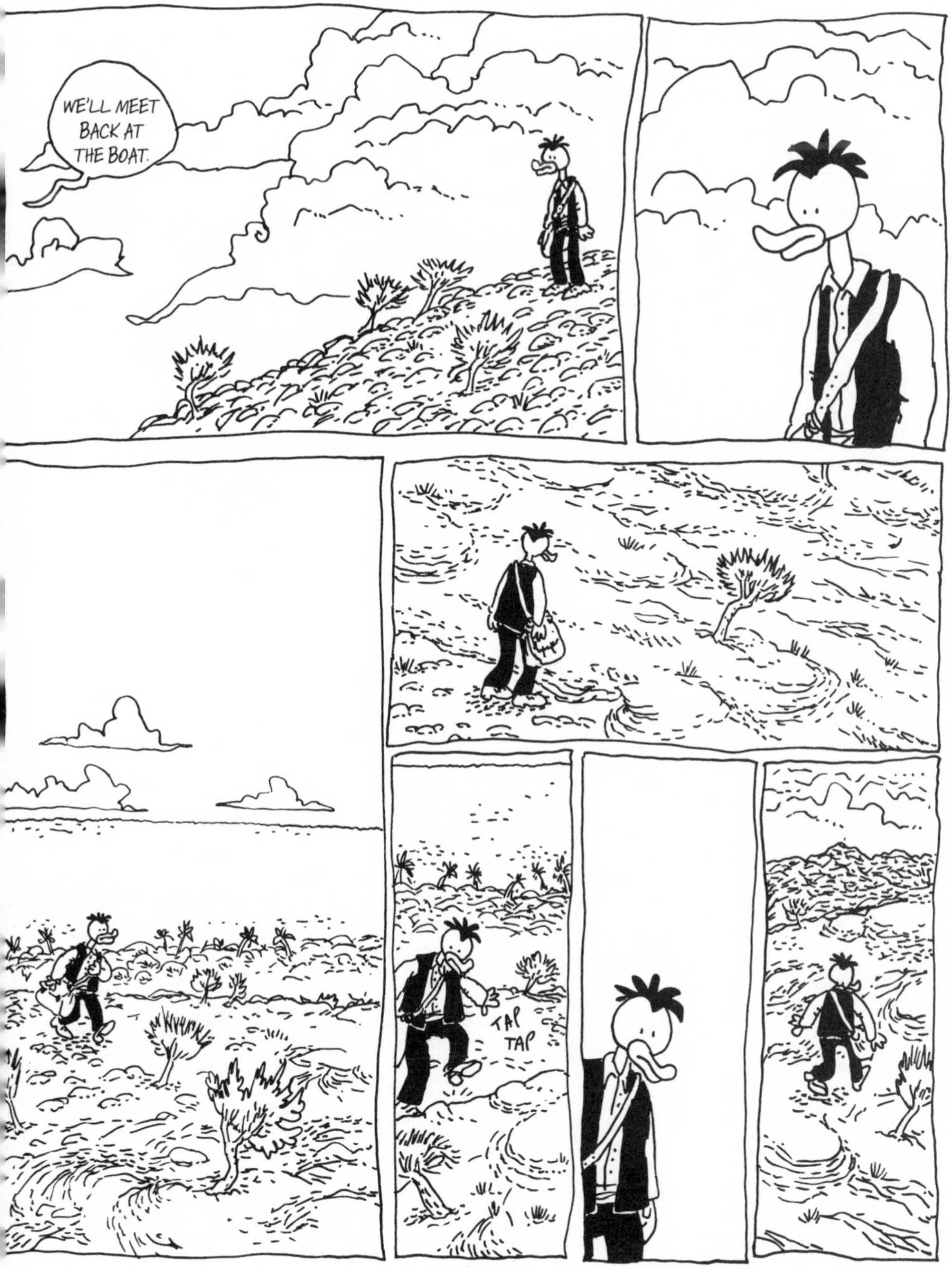
WE'LL MEET BACK AT THE BOAT.
TAP TAP

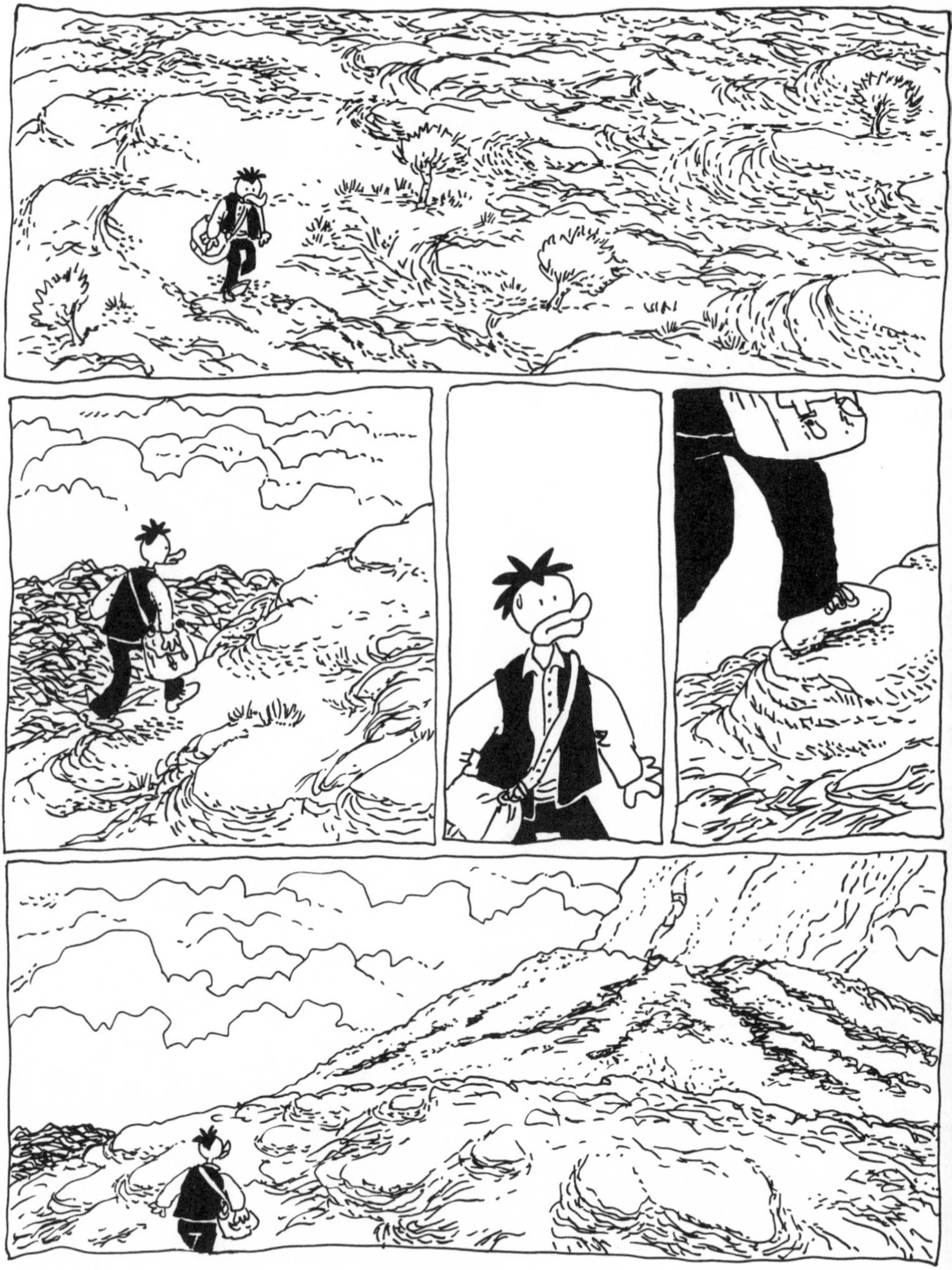

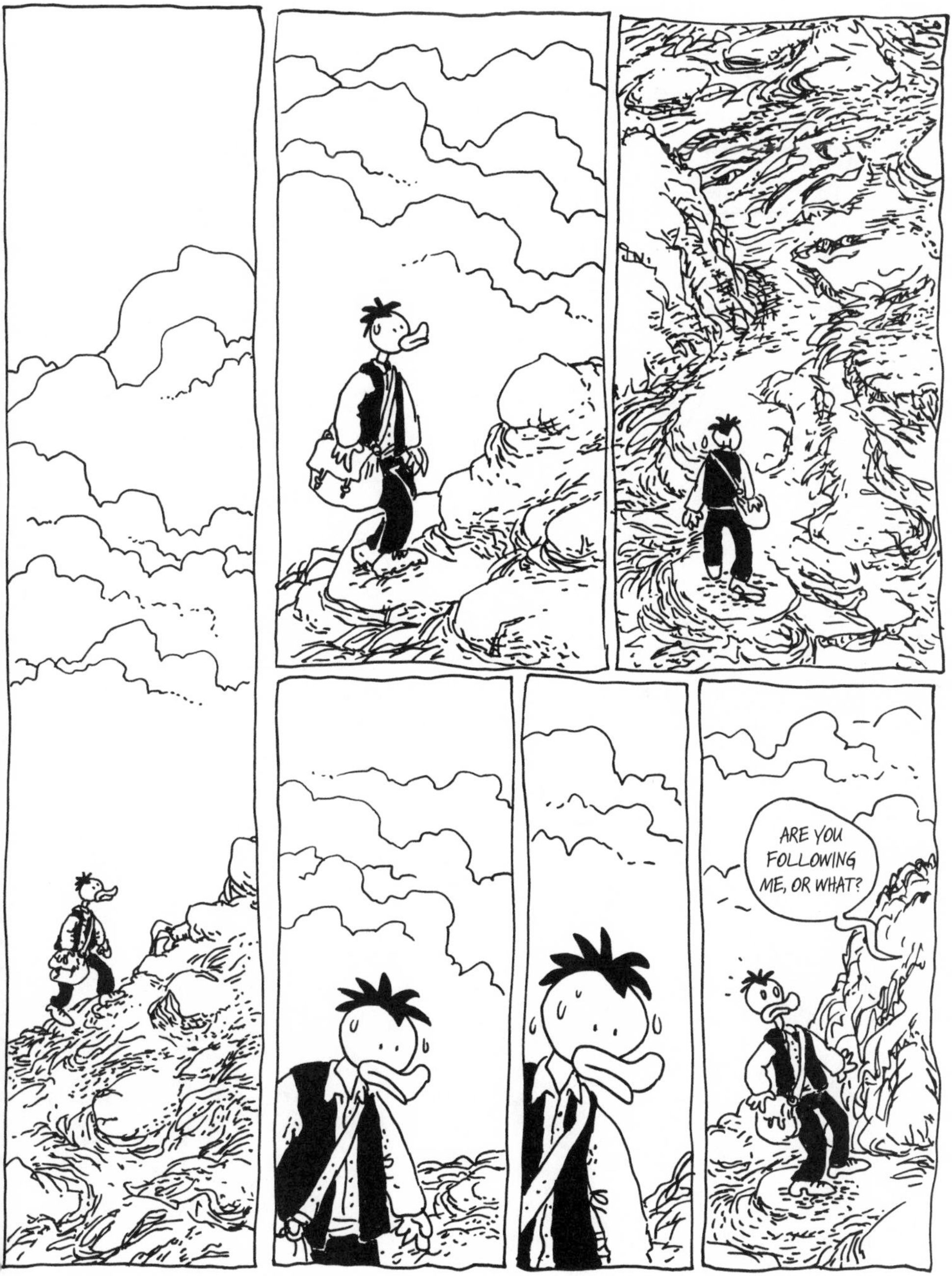
ARE YOU FOLLOWING ME, OR WHAT?

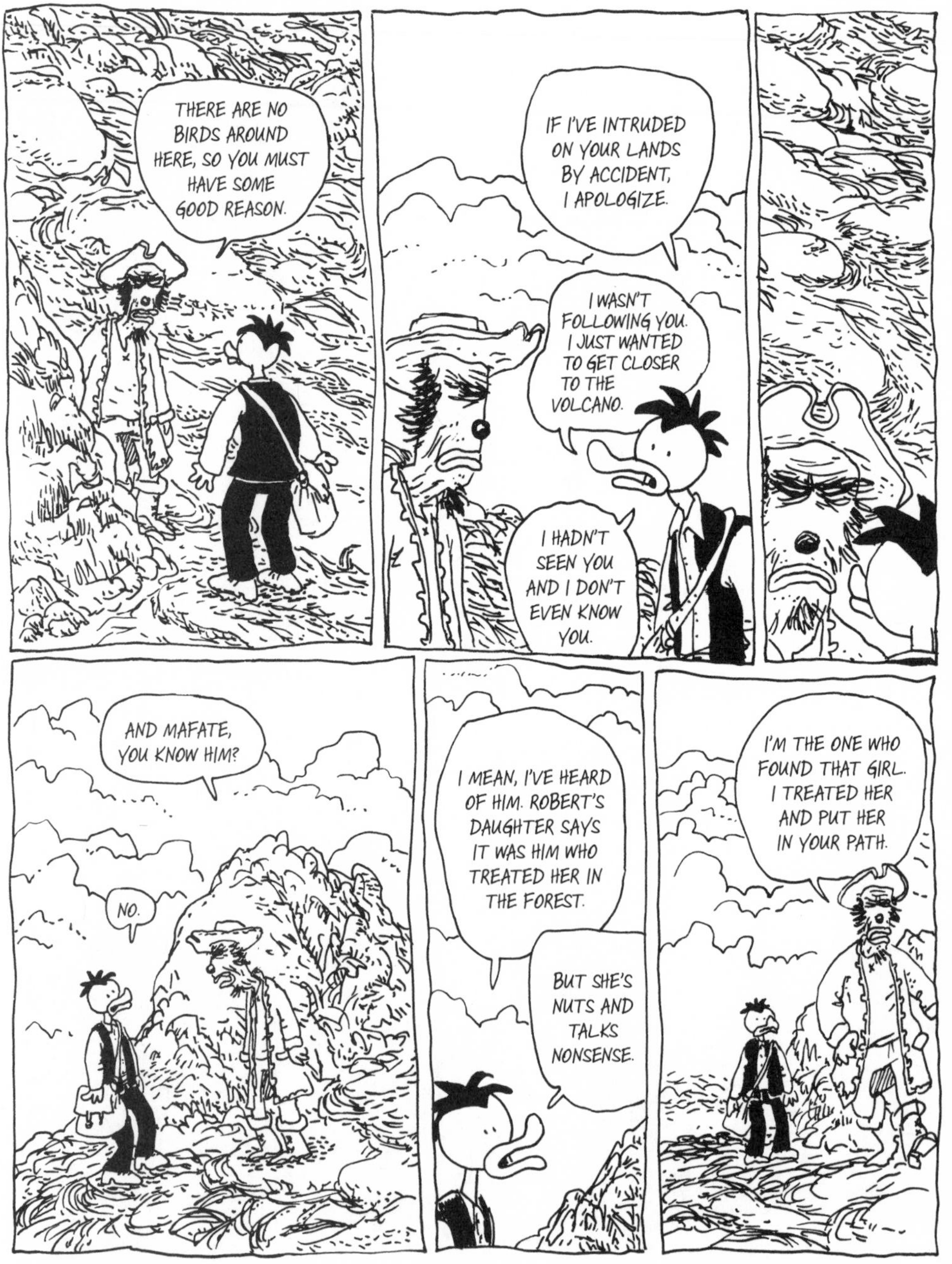
THERE ARE NO BIRDS AROUND HERE, SO YOU MUST HAVE SOME GOOD REASON.
IF I'VE INTRUDED ON YOUR LANDS BY ACCIDENT, I APOLOGIZE.
I WASN'T FOLLOWING YOU. I JUST WANTED TO GET CLOSER TO THE VOLCANO.
I HADN'T SEEN YOU AND I DON'T EVEN KNOW YOU.
AND MAFATE, YOU KNOW HIM?
NO.
I MEAN, I'VE HEARD OF HIM. ROBERT'S DAUGHTER SAYS IT WAS HIM WHO TREATED HER IN THE FOREST.
BUT SHE'S NUTS AND TALKS NONSENSE.
I'M THE ONE WHO FOUND THAT GIRL. I TREATED HER AND PUT HER IN YOUR PATH.

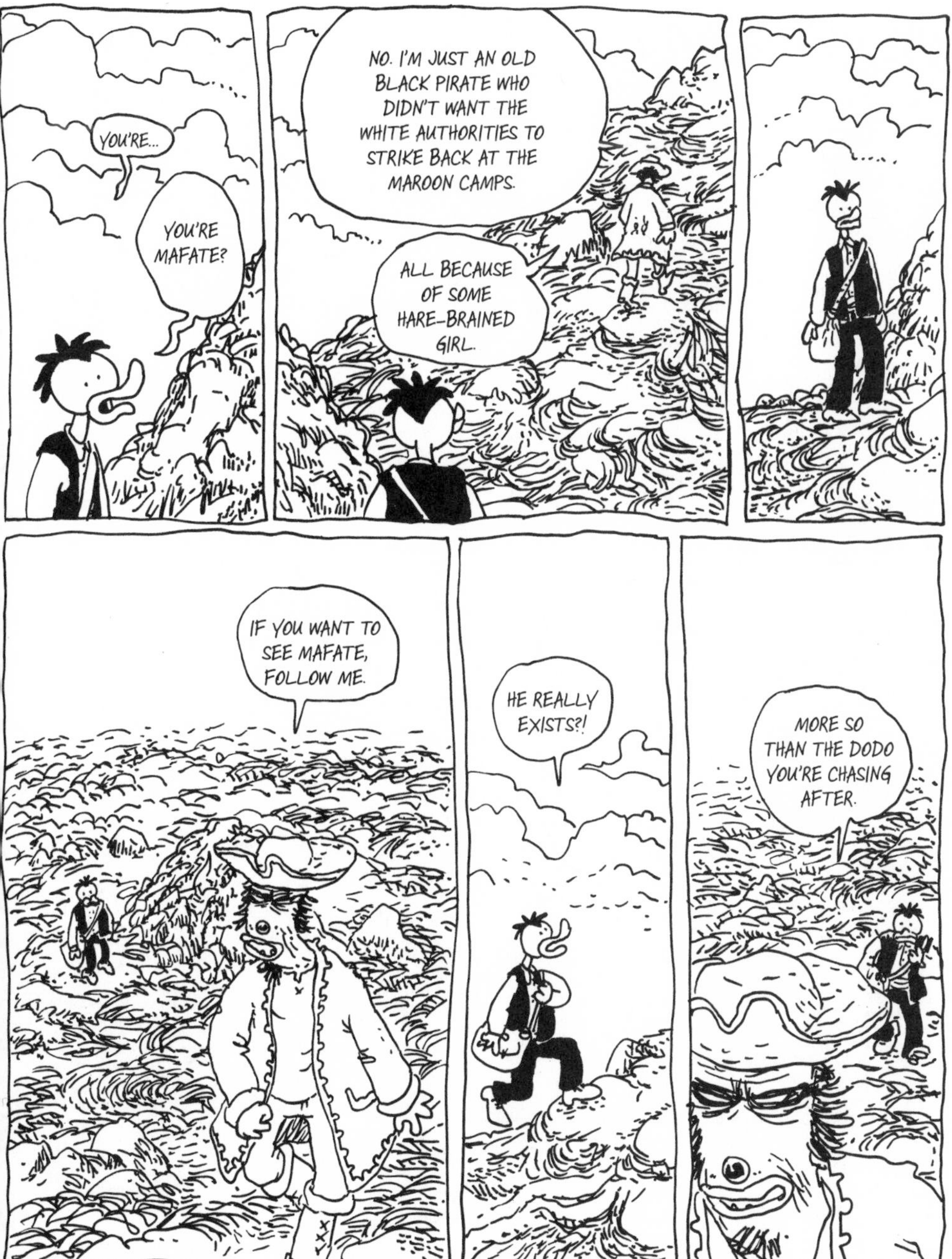
YOU'RE...
YOU'RE MAFATE?
NO. I'M JUST AN OLD BLACK PIRATE WHO DIDN'T WANT THE WHITE AUTHORITIES TO STRIKE BACK AT THE MAROON CAMPS.
ALL BECAUSE OF SOME HARE-BRAINED GIRL.
IF YOU WANT TO SEE MAFATE, FOLLOW ME.
HE REALLY EXISTS?!
MORE SO THAN THE DODO YOU'RE CHASING AFTER.

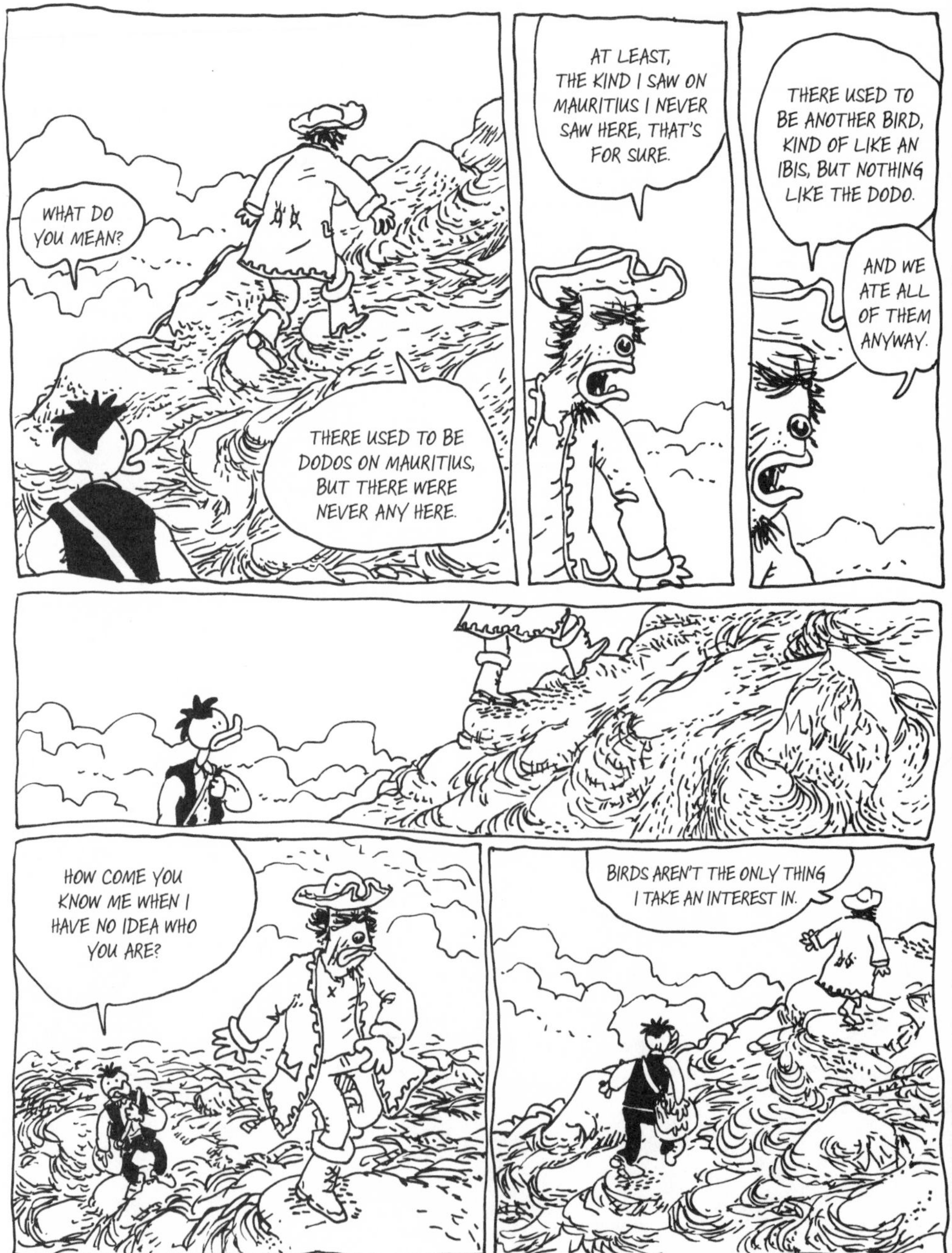
WHAT DO YOU MEAN?
THERE USED TO BE DODOS ON MAURITIUS, BUT THERE WERE NEVER ANY HERE.
AT LEAST, THE KIND I SAW ON MAURITIUS I NEVER SAW HERE, THAT'S FOR SURE.
THERE USED TO BE ANOTHER BIRD, KIND OF LIKE AN IBIS, BUT NOTHING LIKE THE DODO.
AND WE ATE ALL OF THEM ANYWAY.
HOW COME YOU KNOW ME WHEN I HAVE NO IDEA WHO YOU ARE?
BIRDS AREN'T THE ONLY THING I TAKE AN INTEREST IN.

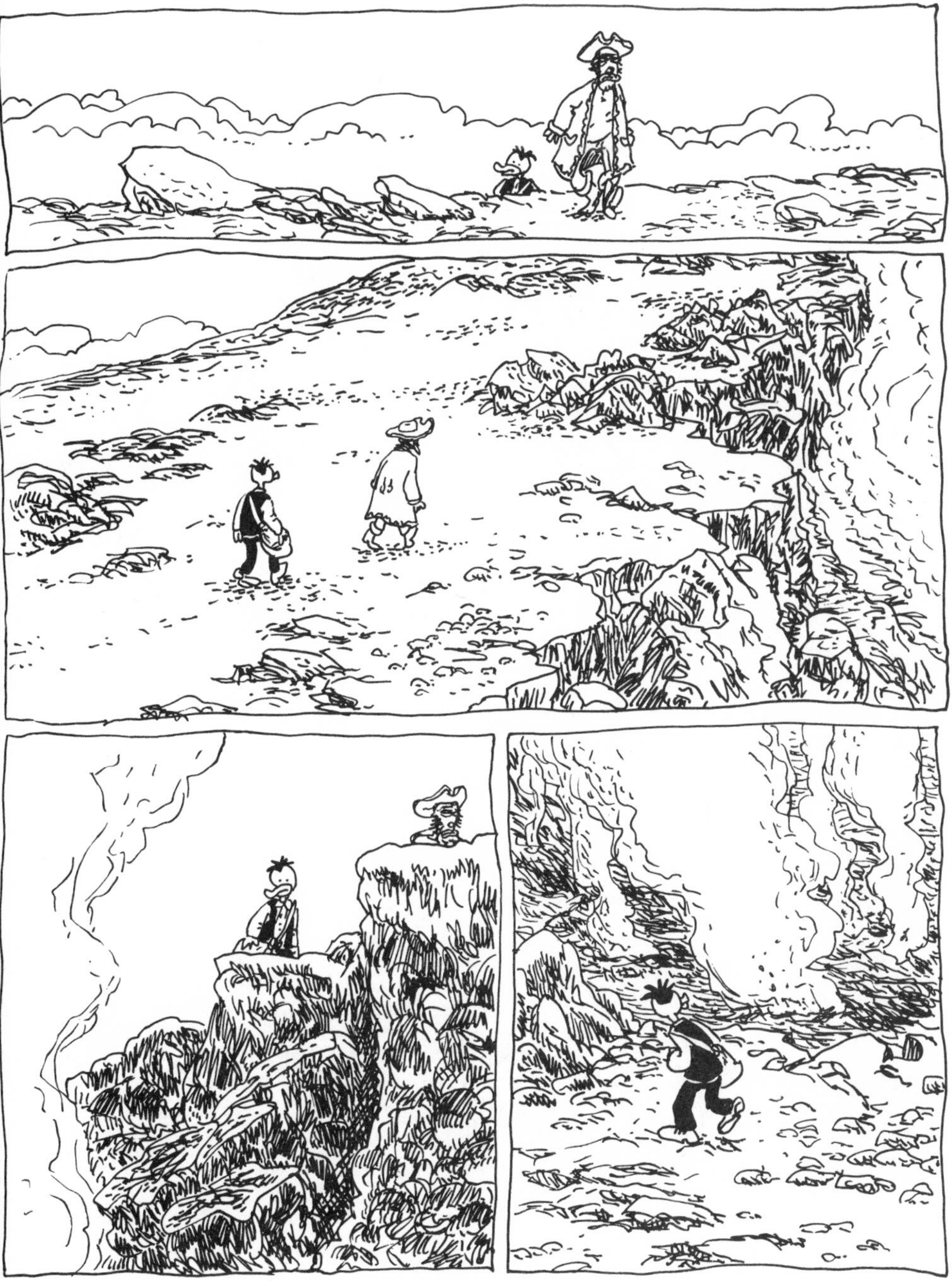

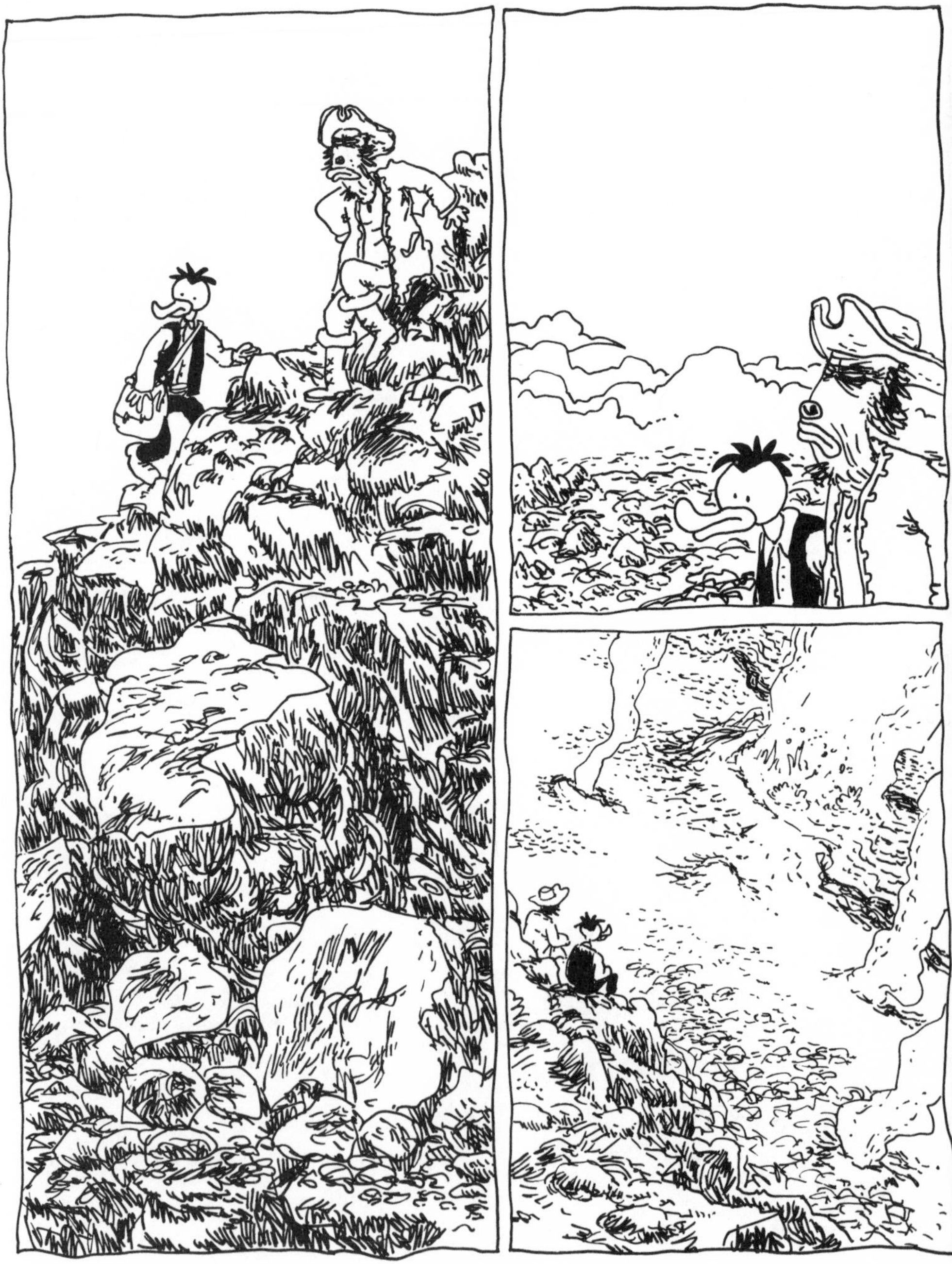

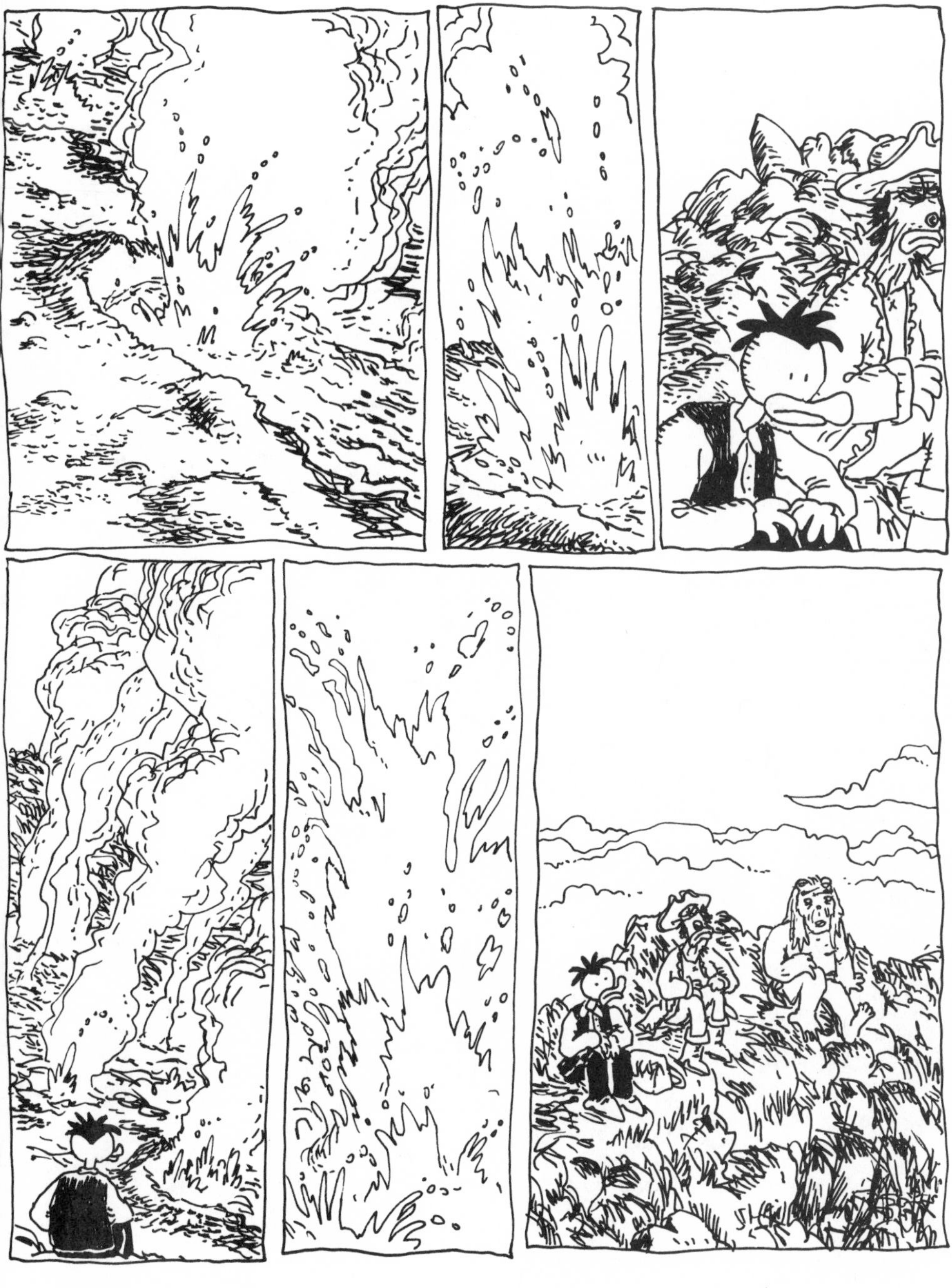

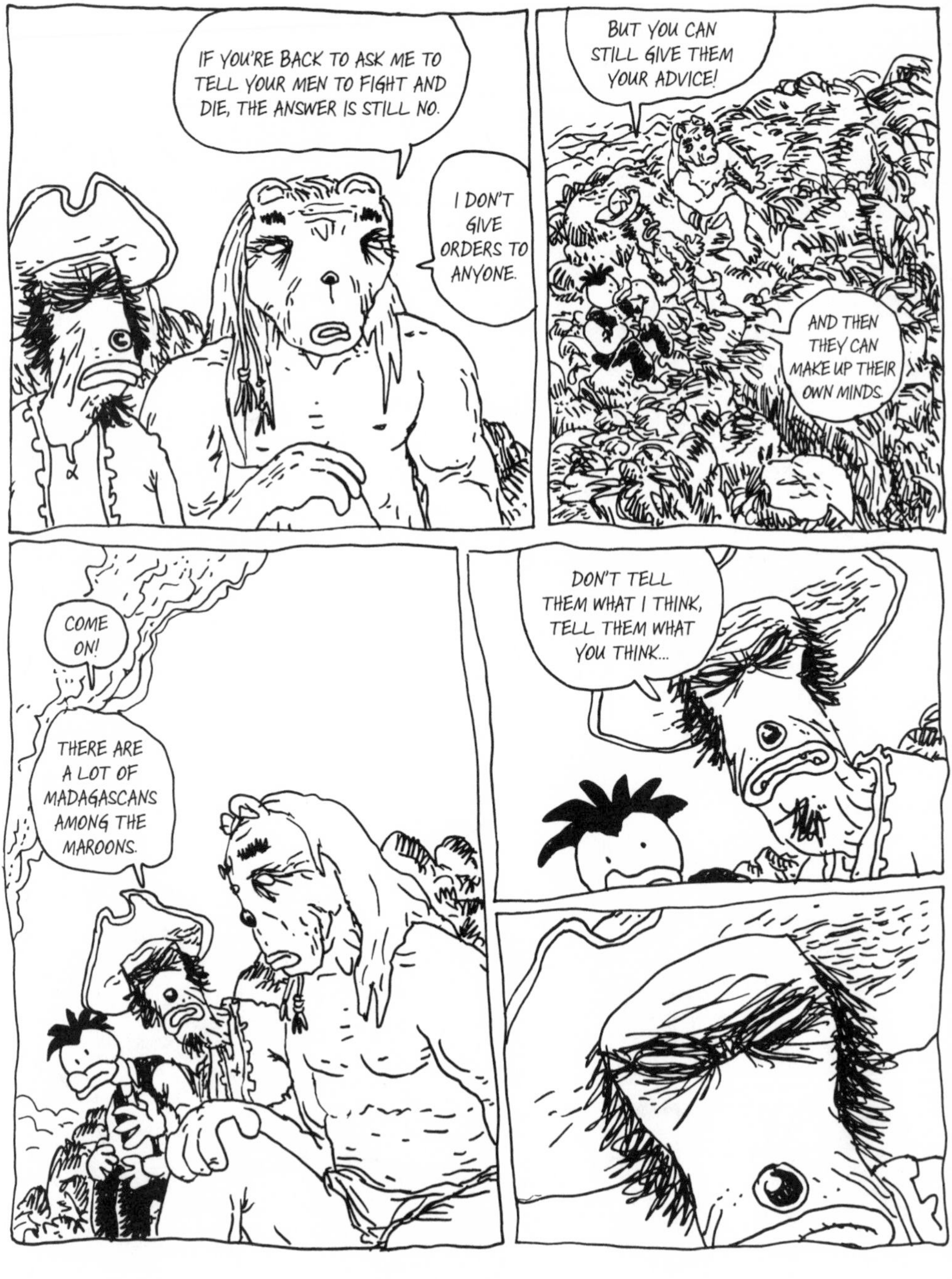
IF YOU'RE BACK TO ASK ME TO TELL YOUR MEN TO FIGHT AND DIE, THE ANSWER IS STILL NO.
I DON'T GIVE ORDERS TO ANYONE.
BUT YOU CAN STILL GIVE THEM YOUR ADVICE!
AND THEN THEY CAN MAKE UP THEIR OWN MINDS.
COME ON!
THERE ARE A LOT OF MADAGASCANS AMONG THE MAROONS.
DON'T TELL THEM WHAT I THINK, TELL THEM WHAT YOU THINK...

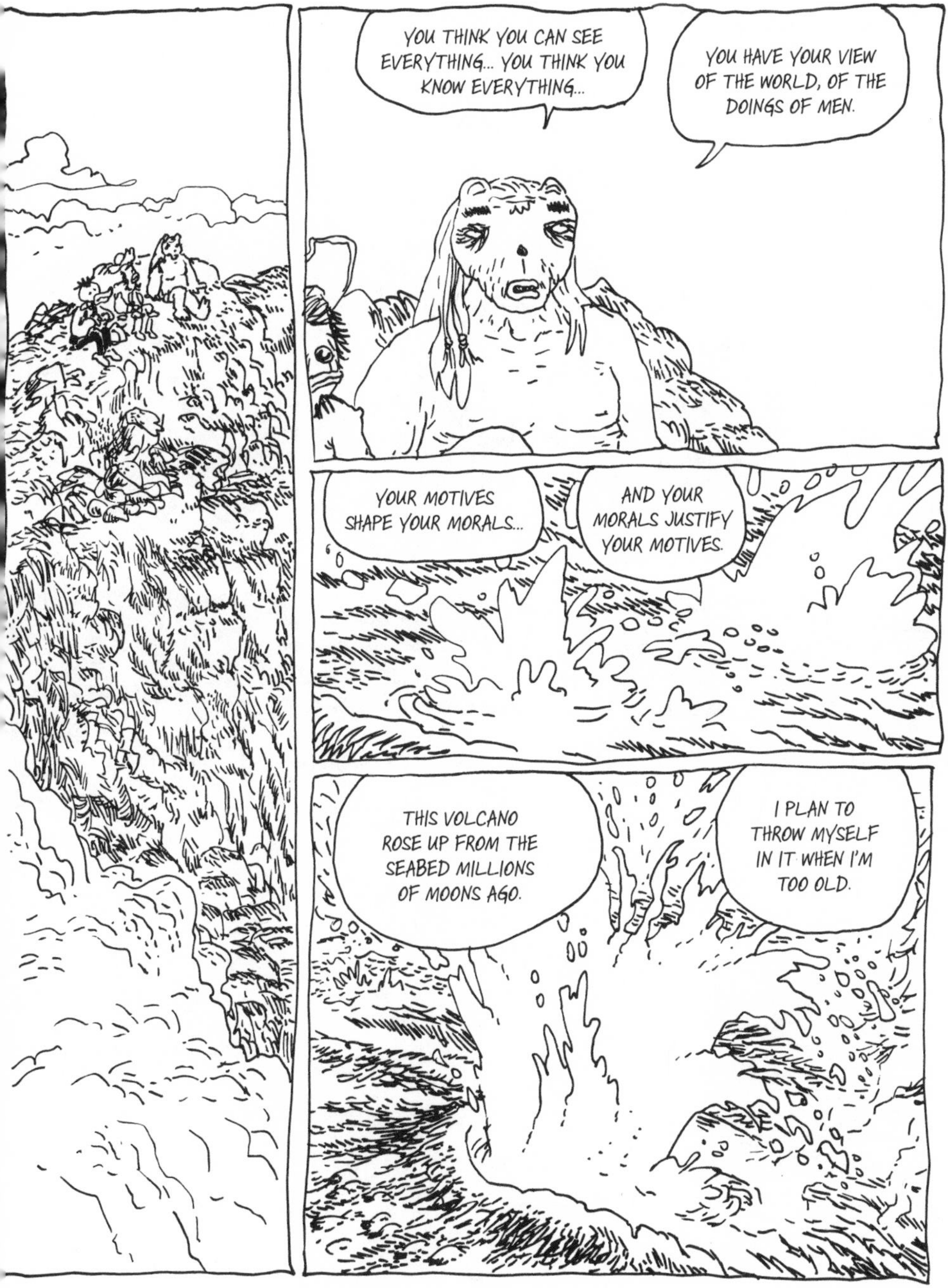
YOU THINK YOU CAN SEE EVERYTHING... YOU THINK YOU KNOW EVERYTHING...
YOU HAVE YOUR VIEW OF THE WORLD, OF THE DOINGS OF MEN.
YOUR MOTIVES SHAPE YOUR MORALS...
AND YOUR MORALS JUSTIFY YOUR MOTIVES.
THIS VOLCANO ROSE UP FROM THE SEABED MILLIONS OF MOONS AGO.
I PLAN TO THROW MYSELF IN IT WHEN I'M TOO OLD.

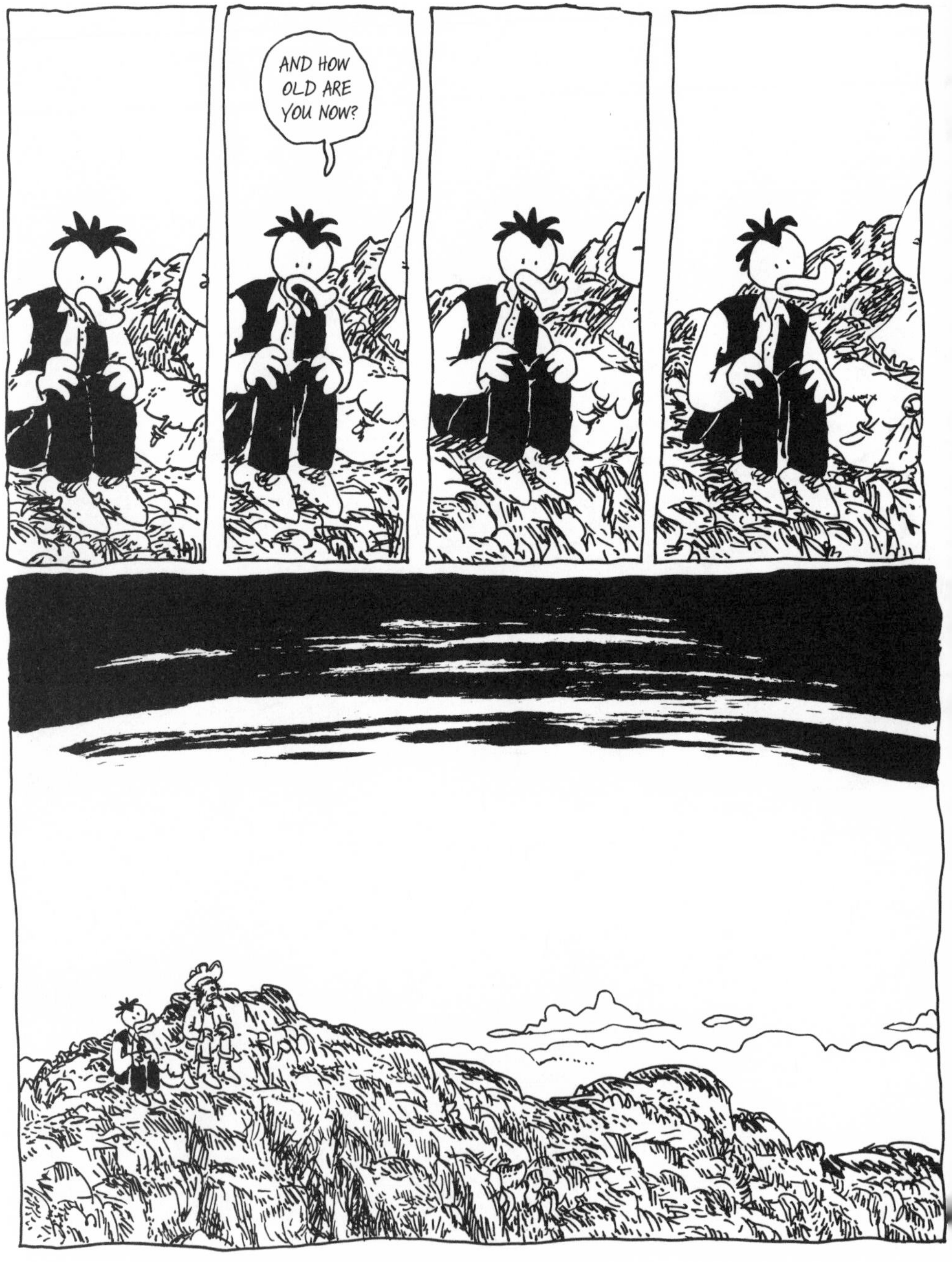
AND HOW OLD ARE YOU NOW?

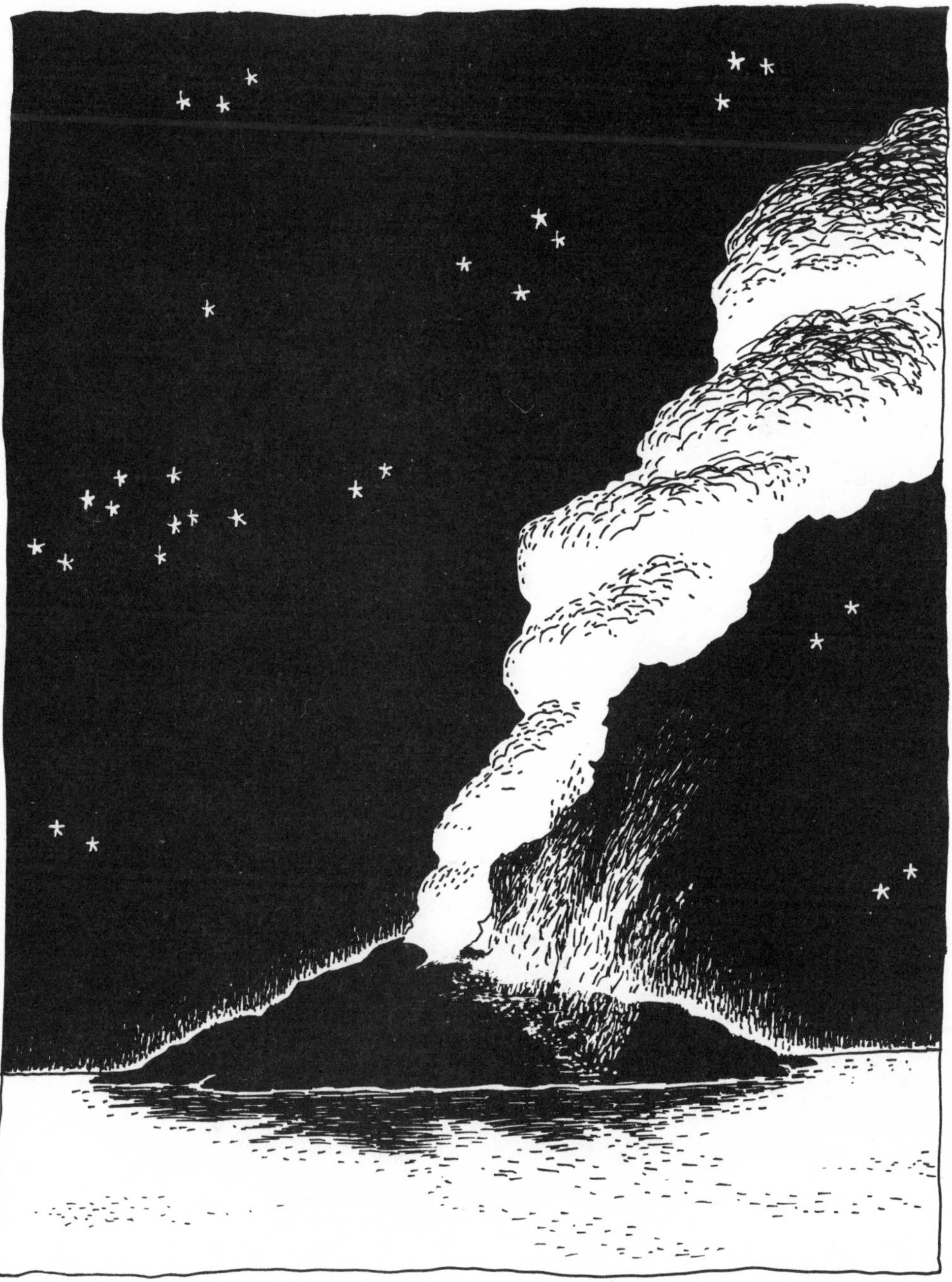

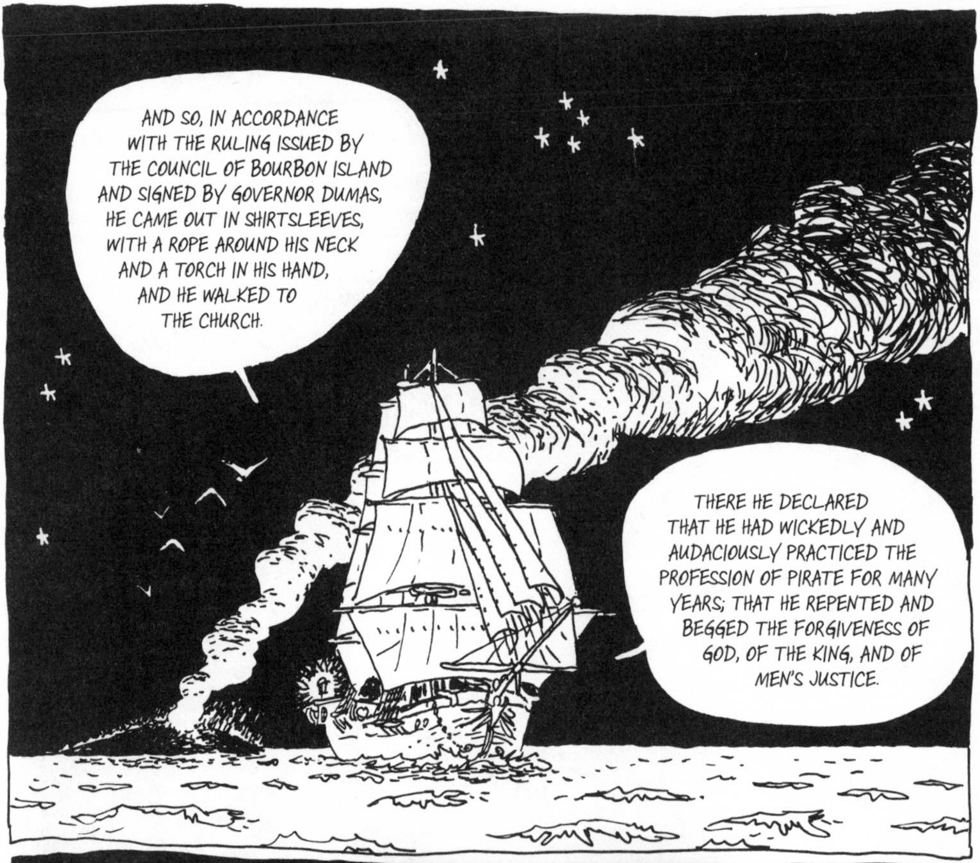
AND SO, IN ACCORDANCE WITH THE RULING ISSUED BY THE COUNCIL OF BOURBON ISLAND AND SIGNED BY GOVERNOR DUMAS, HE CAME OUT IN SHIRTSLEEVES, WITH A ROPE AROUND HIS NECK AND A TORCH IN HIS HAND, AND HE WALKED TO THE CHURCH.
THERE HE DECLARED THAT HE HAD WICKEDLY AND AUDACIOUSLY PRACTICED THE PROFESSION OF PIRATE FOR MANY YEARS; THAT HE REPENTED AND BEGGED THE FORGIVENESS OF GOD, OF THE KING, AND OF MEN'S JUSTICE.

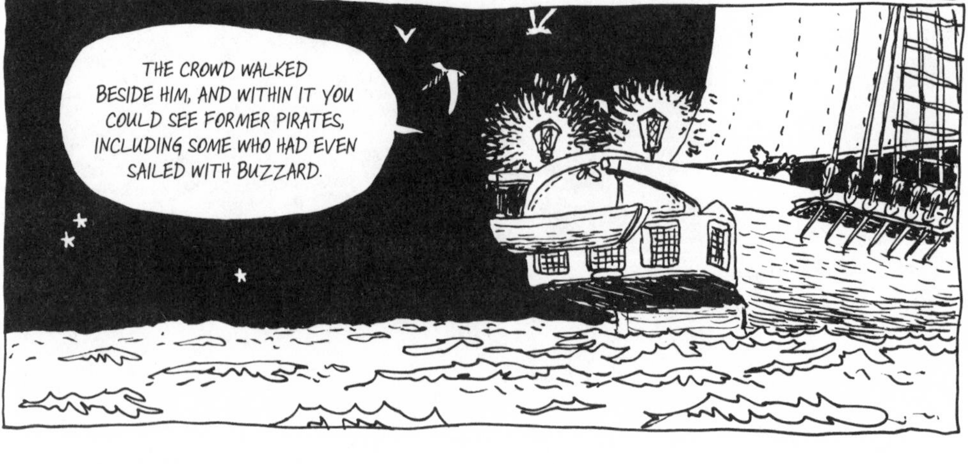
THE CROWD WALKED BESIDE HIM, AND WITHIN IT YOU COULD SEE FORMER PIRATES, INCLUDING SOME WHO HAD EVEN SAILED WITH BUZZARD.

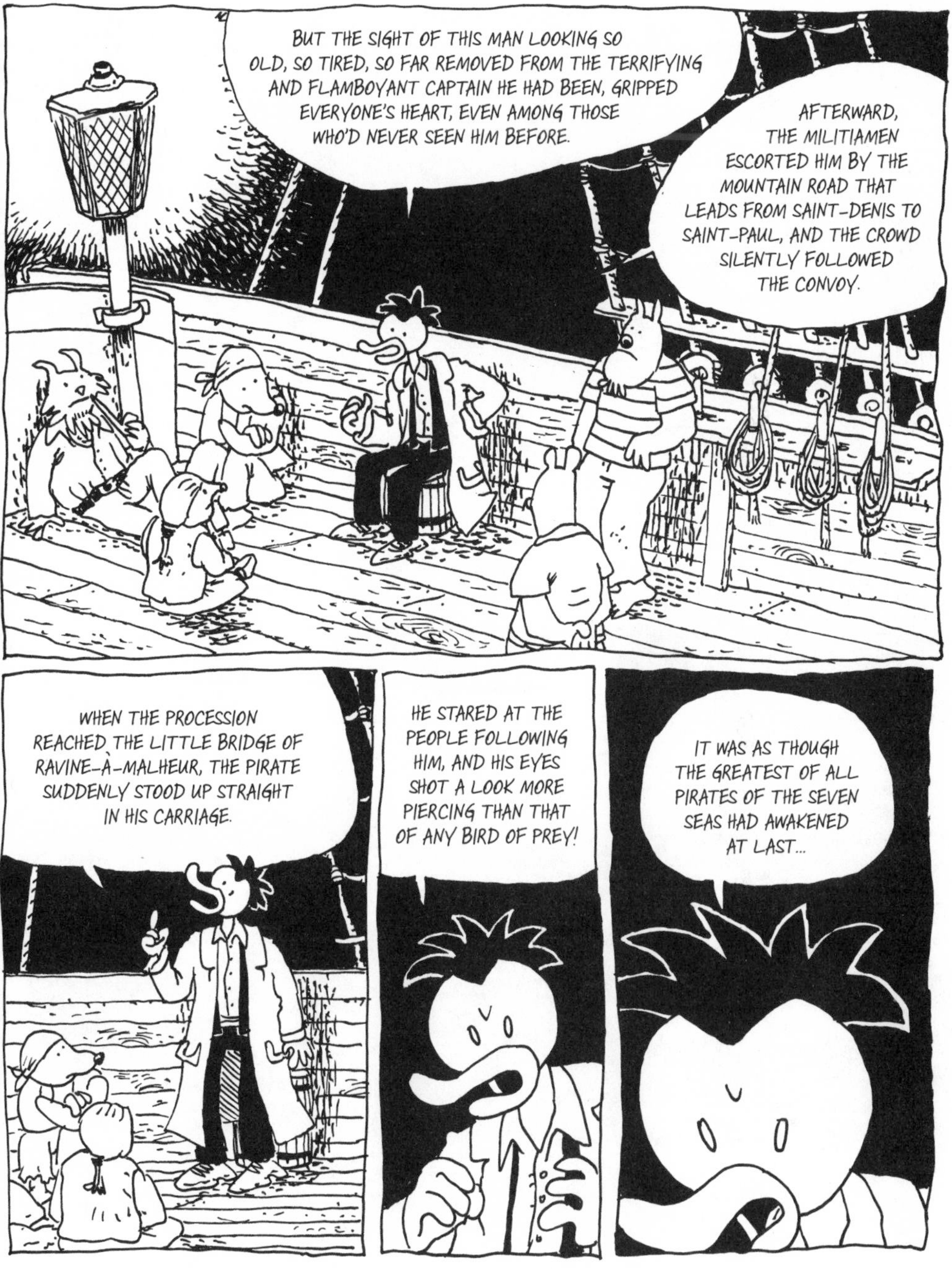
BUT THE SIGHT OF THIS MAN LOOKING SO OLD, SO TIRED, SO FAR REMOVED FROM THE TERRIFYING AND FLAMBOYANT CAPTAIN HE HAD BEEN, GRIPPED EVERYONE'S HEART, EVEN AMONG THOSE WHO'D NEVER SEEN HIM BEFORE.
AFTERWARD, THE MILITIAMEN ESCORTED HIM BY THE MOUNTAIN ROAD THAT LEADS FROM SAINT-DENIS TO SAINT-PAUL, AND THE CROWD SILENTLY FOLLOWED THE CONVOY.
WHEN THE PROCESSION REACHED THE LITTLE BRIDGE OF RAVINE-À-MALHEUR, THE PIRATE SUDDENLY STOOD UP STRAIGHT IN HIS CARRIAGE.
HE STARED AT THE PEOPLE FOLLOWING HIM, AND HIS EYES SHOT A LOOK MORE PIERCING THAN THAT OF ANY BIRD OF PREY!
IT WAS AS THOUGH THE GREATEST OF ALL PIRATES OF THE SEVEN SEAS HAD AWAKENED AT LAST...

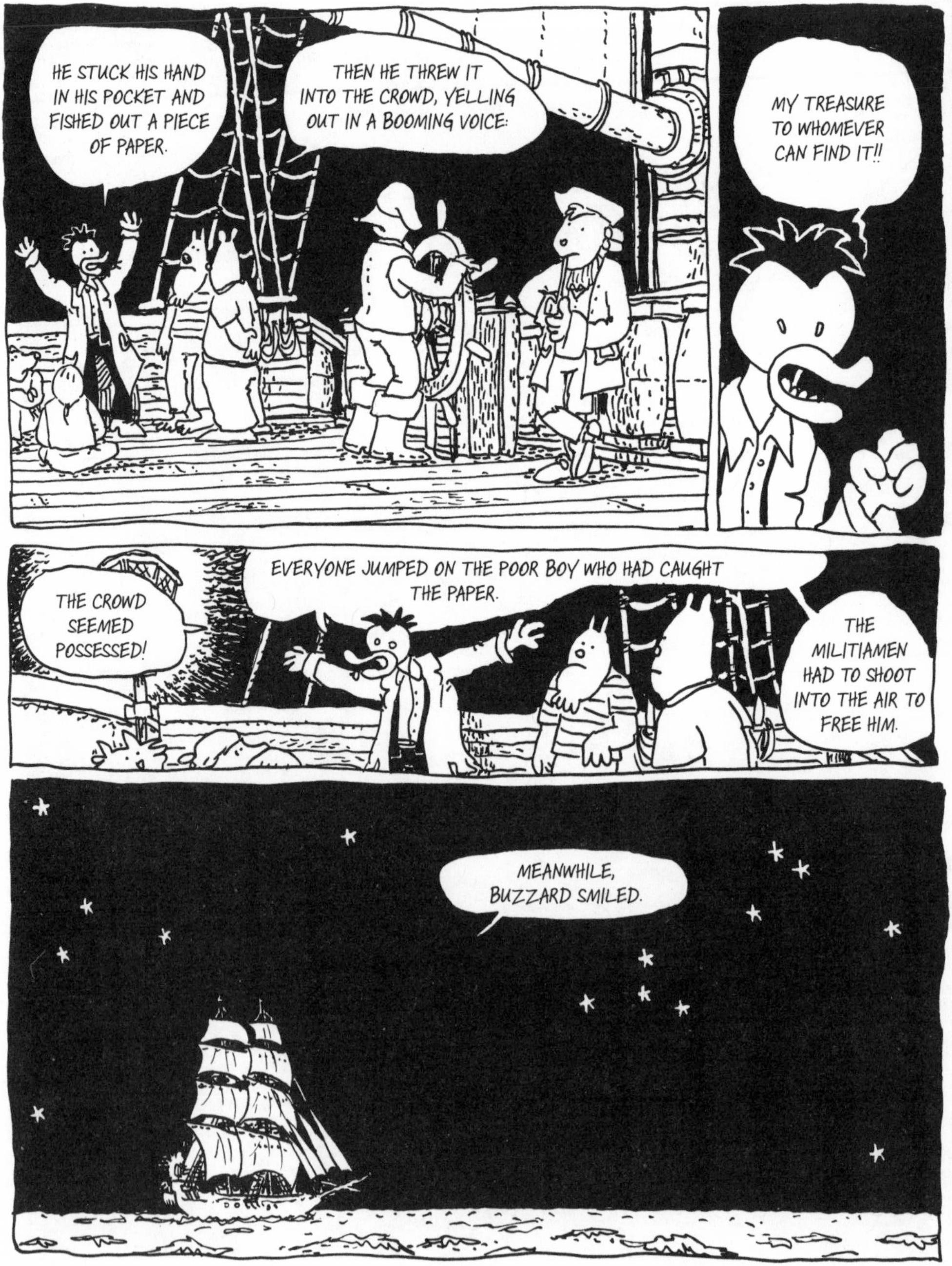
HE STUCK HIS HAND IN HIS POCKET AND FISHED OUT A PIECE OF PAPER.
THEN HE THREW IT INTO THE CROWD, YELLING OUT IN A BOOMING VOICE:
MY TREASURE TO WHOMEVER CAN FIND IT!!
THE CROWD SEEMED POSSESSED!
EVERYONE JUMPED ON THE POOR BOY WHO HAD CAUGHT THE PAPER.
THE MILITIAMEN HAD TO SHOOT INTO THE AIR TO FREE HIM.
MEANWHILE, BUZZARD SMILED.

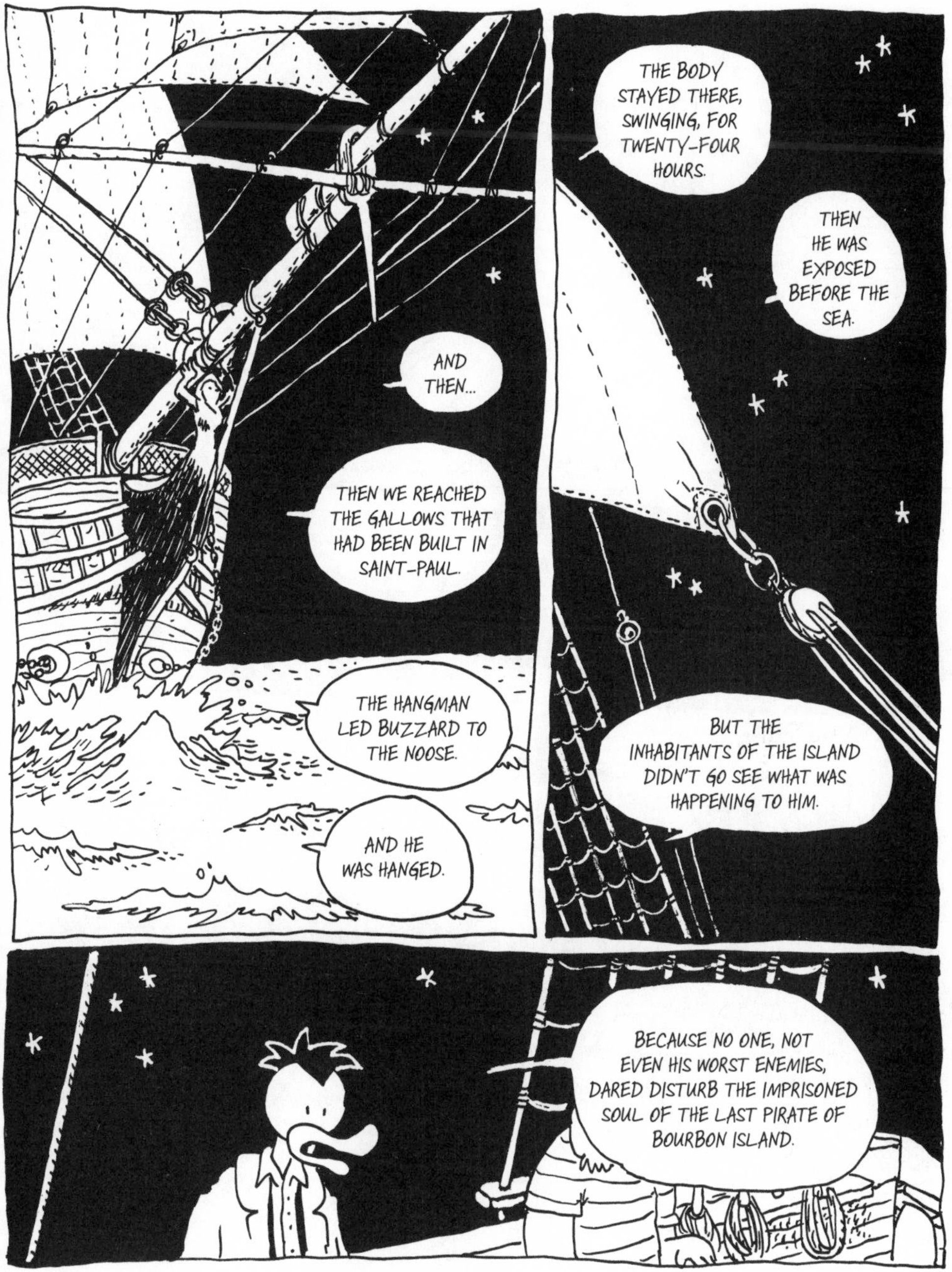
AND THEN...
THEN WE REACHED THE GALLOWS THAT HAD BEEN BUILT IN SAINT-PAUL.
THE HANGMAN LED BUZZARD TO THE NOOSE.
AND HE WAS HANGED.
THE BODY STAYED THERE, SWINGING, FOR TWENTY-FOUR HOURS.
THEN HE WAS EXPOSED BEFORE THE SEA.
BUT THE INHABITANTS OF THE ISLAND DIDN'T GO SEE WHAT WAS HAPPENING TO HIM.
BECAUSE NO ONE, NOT EVEN HIS WORST ENEMIES, DARED DISTURB THE IMPRISONED SOUL OF THE LAST PIRATE OF BOURBON ISLAND.

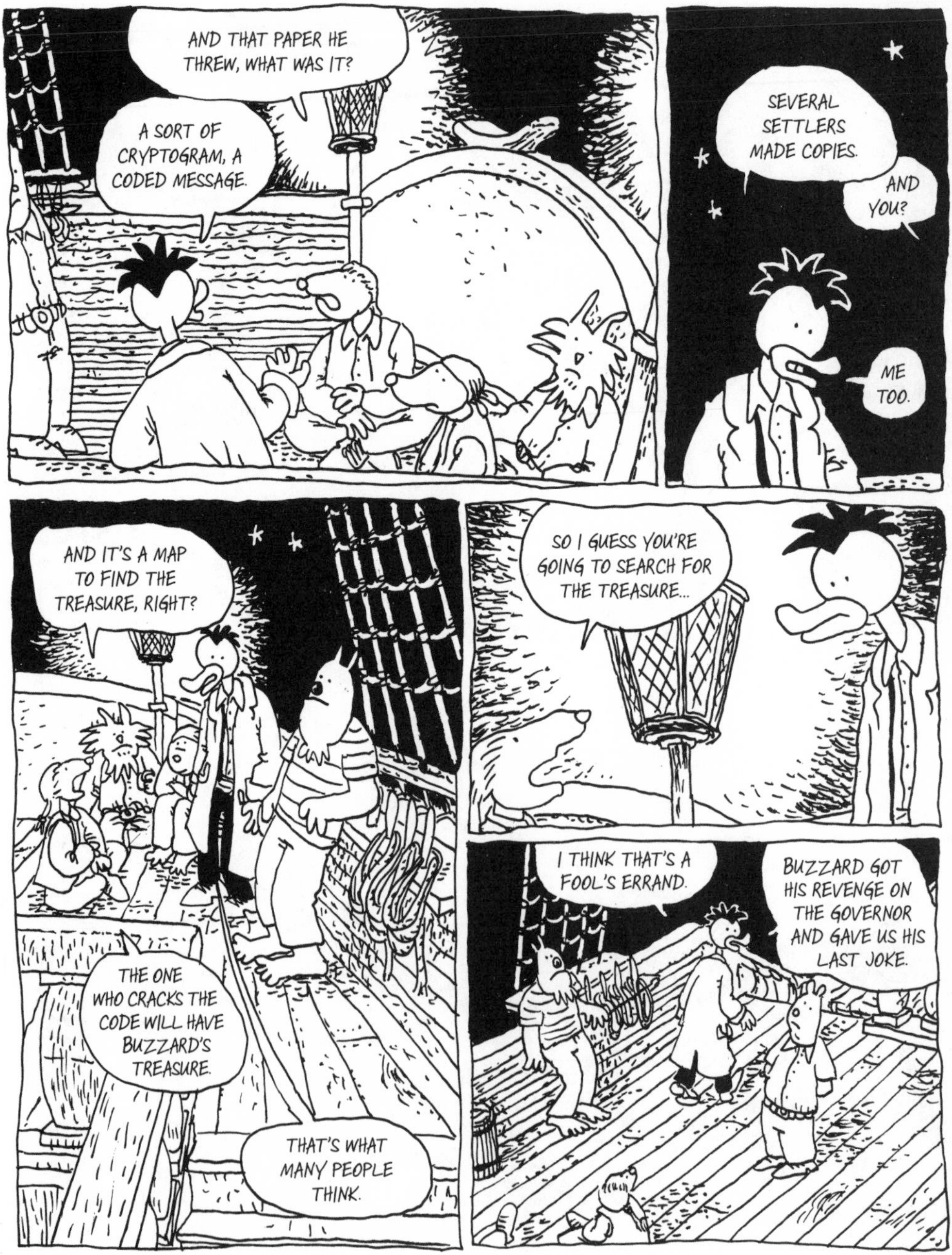
AND THAT PAPER HE THREW, WHAT WAS IT?
A SORT OF CRYPTOGRAM, A CODED MESSAGE.
SEVERAL SETTLERS MADE COPIES.
AND YOU?
ME TOO.
AND IT'S A MAP TO FIND THE TREASURE, RIGHT?
THE ONE WHO CRACKS THE CODE WILL HAVE BUZZARD'S TREASURE.
THAT'S WHAT MANY PEOPLE THINK.
SO I GUESS YOU'RE GOING TO SEARCH FOR THE TREASURE...
I THINK THAT'S A FOOL'S ERRAND.
BUZZARD GOT HIS REVENGE ON THE GOVERNOR AND GAVE US HIS LAST JOKE.

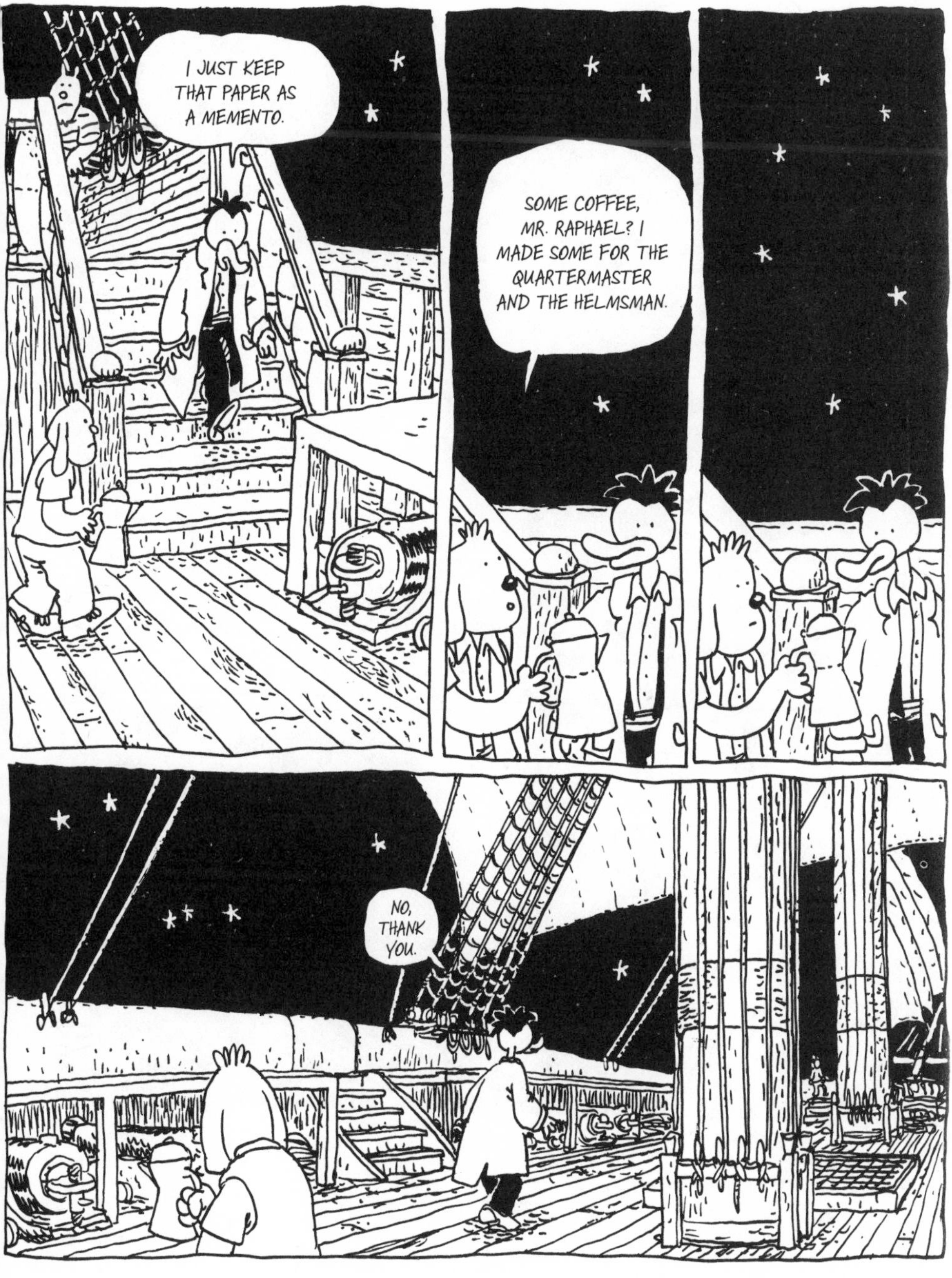
I JUST KEEP THAT PAPER AS A MEMENTO.
SOME COFFEE, MR. RAPHAEL? I MADE SOME FOR THE QUARTERMASTER AND THE HELMSMAN.
NO, THANK YOU.

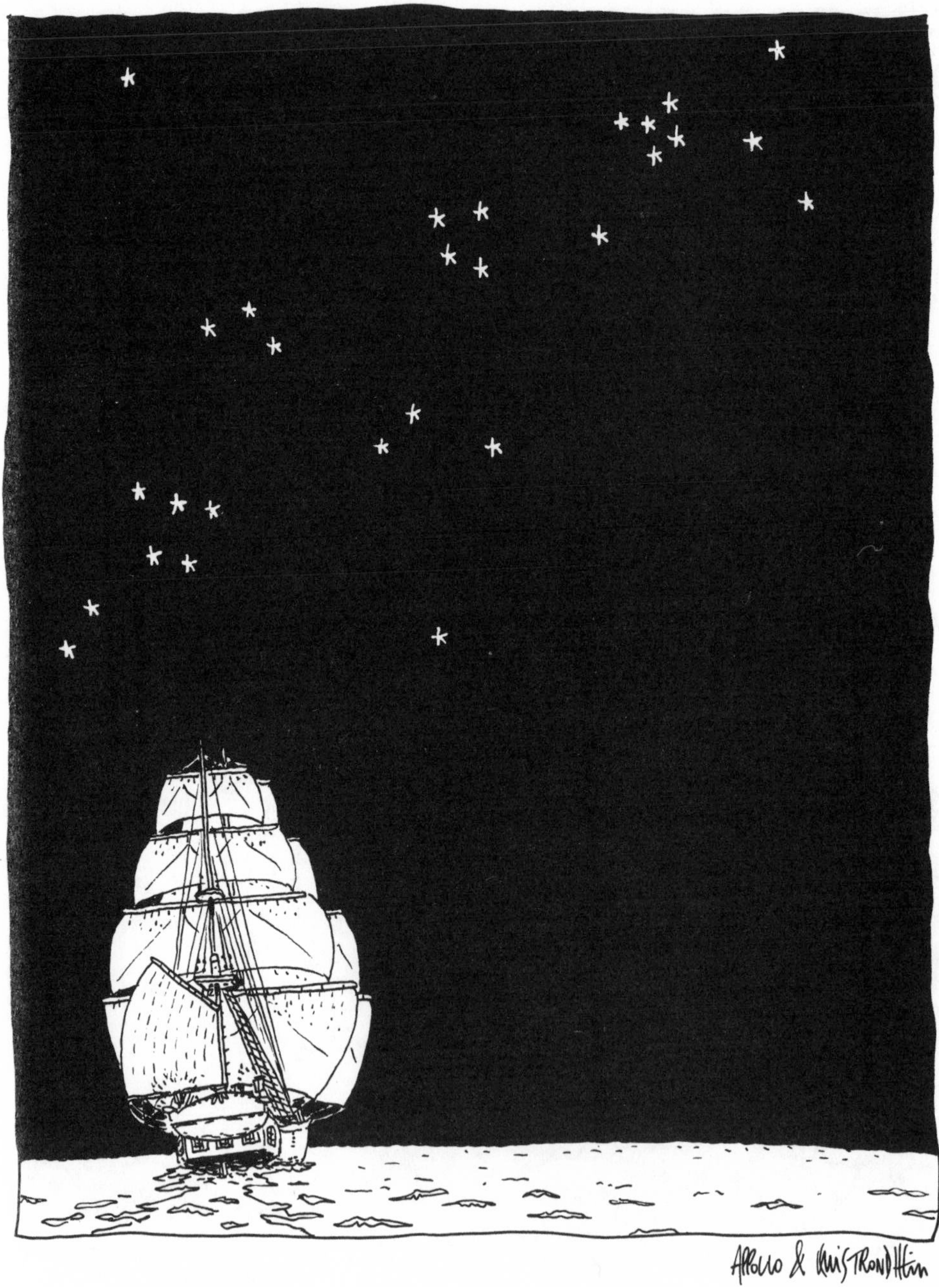
APOLLO & LEWIS TRONDHEIM

NOTES

Page 8: Bourbon Island

Bourbon is one of the ancient names given to the island of *La Réunion*, a French administrative region in the Indian Ocean, near Mauritius.

It is believed that the island, while it was still uninhabited, was sighted at the end of the Middle Ages by Arab navigators, who called it *Dina Morgabin* (Western Island). Then, in the sixteenth century, it was discovered by the Portuguese, who gave it various names, including *Santa Apollonia* (possibly because the day of its discovery was Saint Apollonia's feast day) and *Isla Mascarenha* (after the Portuguese navigator Pedro Mascarenhas). The Dutch and English (who called it "England's Forest") used it as a supply post in the seventeenth century. The French officially took possession of it in 1640, calling it Bourbon Island, after the reigning dynasty in France, but they settled it for good only from 1665 onward. The island changed names again several times after that: during the French Revolution it was renamed Reunion Island; Napoleon decided to call it Bonaparte Island; the English, who occupied it from 1810 to 1815, brought back the name of Bourbon Island. Then, after the Revolution of 1848 in France, the Second Republic again gave it the name of Reunion Island, which has remained to this day.

Page 9: Saint-Hyacinth

Most towns on Bourbon Island are named after a saint: Saint-Denis, Saint-Paul, Saint-Pierre, Saint-Suzanne, et cetera. But there is no such place as Saint-Hyacinth. That old sailor's tale seems to be completely fanciful.

Page 10: Olivier "Buzzard" Levasseur

Olivier Levasseur, aka *"La Buse"* (Buzzard), was perhaps the most famous French pirate of the eighteenth century. Not much is known about his origins—neither the place of his birth nor the circumstances by which he became a pirate—but he is mentioned as a well-known pirate captain in the famous tome *A General History of the Robberies and Murders of the Most Notorious Pyrates* by one Captain Johnson (in all likelihood an alias of novelist Daniel Defoe, who had collected, in the seediest areas of London, an impressive amount of documentation on the pirates of his time). He was one of the attendees at the meeting of Providence Island in the Bahamas, where a certain number of pirate captains decided to leave the Caribbean—which European navies were patrolling more and more closely—for the more lawless Indian Ocean.

He reappeared in the Gulf of Guinea, where he plundered alongside fellow captains Davis and Cocklyn. His whereabouts were unknown for a time, then he surfaced again on the island of Mayotte, where his ship, the *Indian Queen*, was wrecked. The pirate captain Edward England rescued him from this predicament and the two men decided to become partners. They joined up with Captain Taylor for a piracy campaign in the East Indies. Upon their return to the Mascarene Islands, England was abandoned on Mauritius, and Taylor and Buzzard set sail for Bourbon Island, which they reached on April 20, 1720, the feast day of Saint Quasimodo. In the harbor of Saint-Denis, in front of the local population and the governor who had come to watch the show, they took *La Virgen del Cabo*, an eight-hundred-ton ship, on which was the Count of Ericeira, viceroy of the Portuguese East Indies. That was and remained the largest catch by pirates in the history of piracy. A few days later, the *City of Ostend* met the same fate in the bay of Saint-Paul. Buzzard then quarreled with Taylor and slipped away with a vast amount of loot from those two catches. It is not clear what became of him after that, besides the fact that he settled in Madagascar, perhaps serving as a warlord for a local king on the coast. The slave-trading captain Dhermitte captured him a few years later, through treachery, and brought him back to Bourbon Island, where he was tried and hanged.

Page 11: The "Burnt Country"

In the southern part of the island is the *Piton de la Fournaise*, a very active volcano. The first inhabitants called the area "the burnt country" because of the many lava flows that they found there. That part of the island was not yet settled in 1730.

Page 20: Saint-Denis

The governor of Bourbon settled in Saint-Denis in 1669, and the town officially became the island's capital in 1738. At that time, the city had about two thousand inhabitants. The governor's quarters were built wher coffee warehouses had stood.

As the city does not have a natural port, the governor had a long pier built to help boats unload.

Page 21: Governor Dumas

Governor Dumas (1727–1735) was the first permanent governor of the island. He was assisted by a quartermaster, who looked after the interests of the East India Company, and by the Bourbon High Council, composed of representatives of colonists.

Dumas developed coffee production, which made the island wealthy, and boosted the importation of slaves toward this end. His administration was not always popular: he thwarted a plot by slaves, and later, the population of colonists, upset with his rule, sent emissaries to France to complain about him—to no avail.

Page 24: A Piece of Rock

Everything Raphael says on that volcanic rock is true, obviously.

Page 33: The Heights

Bourbon is very mountainous: the *Piton des Neiges* rises to 10,069 feet (3,070 m), and the colonists initially settled along the coast. The hinterland of the island long remained unexplored, except by runaway slaves (known as Maroons), who discovered, among other features, the island's three amphitheater-like valleys, or cirques—to which they gave their names (Cilaos, Salazie, and Mafate).

Page 39: Dubois

The first travelers that reached Bourbon described a heavenly island with particularly bountiful flora and fauna. One of them, Dubois, stayed there for a year, from 1671 to 1672, and produced a "Description of a few birds of Bourbon Island" that sheds light on this fauna, most of which

has since disappeared. He was the author of the description of the solitaire of Bourbon, which for a time was believed to be a cousin of the dodo of Mauritius:

Solitaires: those birds are thus named because they are always found alone. They are the size of a large goose, white-feathered except for the tips of their wings and tail, which are black. The tail has feathers that are not unlike those of an ostrich. They have a long neck, and a beak like that of a woodcock, but larger, and legs and feet like a turkey's. This bird can be chased and caught on foot, as it flies very little. It is one of the island's best game birds.

Unfortunately, Dubois left no drawing of the bird and there is no way of knowing, today, whether the solitaire of Bourbon was indeed related to the dodo of Mauritius, or if it was a variety of endemic ibis, whose bones have been found but which did not belong to the same family as the Dodo.

Page 43: "Maroon" Goats

The adjective "Maroon" probably came from the Spanish *cimarrón* (literally "mountaintop-dweller," and meaning "fugitive") and is not related to color. It describes both domesticated animals and cultivated plants that returned to the wild—there are "Maroon goats," "Maroon vines," and so on—and was applied to escaped slaves. The word also gave rise to the piracy term of *marooning*, which meant putting someone to shore in some inhospitable place and leaving them to fend for themselves and probably die there. The flight of Maroon ex-slaves (known as *marronnage*) to the heights of Bourbon Island became such a widespread phenomenon in the early part of the eighteenth century that there were full-fledged Maroon communities in the mountains.

Page 49: The Pirate Amnesty

All pirate crews stopping at Bourbon Island, or staying for varying lengths of time, received a warm welcome despite being officially undesirable. The East India Company, which was still responsible for the island, would have liked to fight both piracy at sea and the illicit trade taking place between the pirates and the population of Bourbon. However, the locals tended to be happy when a pirate ship was sighted off the island, because it meant that they would at last be able to do some trading, by selling overpriced food stuffs to sailors who were generally very rich and spent freely. So the pragmatic policy adopted by the island's governors was mostly to make friends with the pirates rather than have to contend with them as enemies. Soon there were decrees regulating the terms of amnesties and the stays of pirates.

As an example, when the pirate captain Condent (or Congdom) decided, after his miraculous capture of an Arab ship that brought him 1.3 million rupees, to retire on Bourbon Island, he and his crew of 135 men were granted very favorable amnesty terms: they were asked only to "previously hand over their weapons and munitions of war, renounce forever their disorderly ways, and remain loyal to the King of France, recognizing that they are his subjects." That done, they could retire "under the government of Bourbon, where they will enjoy the same benefits, rights, and prerogatives as the other inhabitants of this isle without distinction."

That example testifies to the successful integration of pirates on the island. Of course, they were often the only ones bringing cash into the island's economy, either by settling there after having made their fortune, or by buying provisions or weapons from the inhabitants. One contemporary observer commented that, "The truth is that most inhabitants have become so accustomed to selling on outrageous terms to the pirates that they would not relinquish the practice for any reason whatsoever, and neither the governors nor anyone else of rank in this place are strangers to this minor tyranny." As a result, pirates found Bourbon to be the ideal retirement community.

Decrees even set the terms for their temporary stays. "Each freebooter shall be required to pay 15 piasters for his lodging and food; should he have a Negro with him, he will be required to give 5 more piasters. Any inhabitant putting up one or more freebooters shall give each of them a suitable bed composed at least of a good mattress, a pillow with its case, and a blanket; such beds must be in a hut made of wood or thatch and built in such a manner as to be easily distinguished from what is known as an outhouse or ajoupa, in that the harmful elements may not enter therein."

Successive governors then offered amnesties to freebooters who gave up their trade and settled on the island. The measure enjoyed considerable success, and at the beginning of the eighteenth century, it was estimated that every fourth head of household on Bourbon was a reformed pirate. They were of many different nationalities— French, English, Dutch, even Swedish—and rapidly integrated into the island's population, even though their behavior shocked the island's elite, as the reports of Governor Desforges-Boucher attest.

Buzzard made his application for amnesty to the Bourbon High Council in 1724, from Madagascar. The amnesty was granted, but he did not come to settle in Bourbon, for unknown reasons. The offer expired in 1727, and the East India Company then forbade any new pardons and the settling of the island by pirates.

Page 55: A Wooden Hut
It's possible that the design of this hut is anachronistic and only appeared later. But it's pretty.

Page 66: One Ear Cut Off
Punishments for *marronnage* were gradual: the fugitive would have one ear cut off the first time; a repeat offender would be crippled by having his leg tendons cut; the third time was punished by death.

Page 66: Laverdure
Laverdure later became the "king of all Maroons." Two reports from Mussard, a hunter of runaway slaves, dated 1752, recount his demise:
   - Report of December 9, 1752: discovery

of the camp of Laverdure, "the King of all Malagasies," located in the valley of the Saint-Etienne river.

- Report of December 28, 1752: camp of Bras-de-la-Plaine discovered by Mussard, where lived 37 Maroons, of whom 13 were killed by the troops, including Laverdure, the king of all the Maroons, and Sarçanate, his lieutenant. Among the women killed was Sarlave, Laverdure's wife.

Page 71: Maroon-Hunters
When *marronnage* started becoming widespread, the colonial authorities initially used soldiers to fight the runaway slaves, who were establishing "kingdoms" in the heights and did not hesitate to plunder properties along the coast to resupply themselves.

As military operations proved unsuccessful, the governors called upon "Creoles"—that is, locally born whites—who knew the mountains well from having hunted wild goats there. These Maroon-hunters were very well paid, and the hunting operations grew in scale, the solitary hunter with dogs giving way to full posses. The number of Maroons brought back into the valleys or, more frequently, killed, rose markedly.

The "war" against the Maroons lasted until the 1760s, by which time large-scale *marronnage* had been utterly defeated. The hunters showed no mercy to their victims and rapidly became famous figures on the island. Caron achieved a towering reputation as a hunter of Maroons, and he was a mentor to the young Mussard, who became, a few years later, a dark legend among hunters for his murderous effectiveness. His reputation was such that neighboring Mauritius hired his services to rid itself of its own Maroons.

Page 90: The "Little Whites" of the Heights
As early as the eighteenth century, part of the island's white population became impoverished. These more and more numerous and increasingly destitute *petits blancs* (little whites) were gradually pushed back into the hinterland, which they colonized in earnest in the following century.

Page 91: Sharp Bourbon Coffee
Coffee became Bourbon Island's main crop from 1715 onward. The variety of coffee produced there was known as *Bourbon pointu* (sharp Bourbon) and was particularly popular in Europe. A decree by the Bourbon High Council made it mandatory for all colonists to grow it and even threatened with capital punishment anyone destroying coffee plants.

Page 92: Blacks with Buzzard
Half of Buzzard's crew was said to be made up of blacks from Africa and the Caribbean, the other half being Europeans of various nationalities.

Page 96: Additional Information on the Taking of the Virgin of the Cape
The taking of *La Virgen del Cabo*, as recounted by a contemporary observer, Garnier du Fougeray:

On the 3rd of November, I anchored off Bourbon Island, in the harbor of Saint-Paul. On the previous day I had lost my launch in an unforeseen accident.

I learned upon reaching land on the 20th of April 1721 that captains Siguer and La Bouce [La Buse; i.e., Buzzard], freebooters, had come to Bourbon Island, on the strength of information they had gathered, hoping to catch by surprise two vessels of your Company.

These two vessels were fortunately not present on Bourbon Island; but there was then a Portuguese ship of 30 cannon at anchor in Saint-Denis and one Ostendese at anchor in Saint-Paul. The first came from Goa and had well-nigh perished in a storm that had left her completely bereft of rigging. His Excellency the Count of Ericeira the Younger, Viceroy of the Indies, had embarked on this vessel for the purpose of returning to Portugal. He was on land when the pirates appeared, but immediately gathered those of his people whom he could find and returned onto his vessel, though unprepared as he was. He defended himself extraordinarily against the freebooters, were it not for the abandonment by his own that forced him to surrender. He continued to fight despite the hail of shot that the pirates themselves admitted having unleashed on his person, being able to distinguish him from the others. Having finally boarded the ship, they captured His Excellency arms in hand.

From there the freebooters proceeded to Saint-Paul and took the Ostendese ship without any resistance. They then landed and forced the inhabitants to supply them with provisions. Three days after their expedition they left, taking their booty with them and leaving the prisoners from the two ships on the island, which caused much shortage of food there.

Another witness, Jacob de Bucquoy, gave more details concerning the booty:

... but they obtained abundant booty; for in addition to the shipment, they shared the treasures of the Viceroy and those of the priests and other passengers. I was more than once assured that, based on the declarations and estimates of the parties concerned, the value of that capture had exceeded sixty million francs.

The same source describes the sharing of the treasure as follows:

The pirates then put their affairs in order, disarmed the prisoners, kept watch on them, admitted those who volunteered, opened with levers the coffers and strong-boxes and delivered to the quartermaster all they contained in the way of diamonds and gold or silver, whether minted or as bullion.

These various pursuits completed, they began to drink and it would have been unwise to venture among them at that time. After the sharing of the booty came the sharing of the ships: Taylor became the commander of La Défense and the leader of the squadron; Captain La Bouze had the large vessel with 72 cannon, a vessel which had previously belonged to the Dutch Government under the name of Galderland and which had been sold to the King of Portugal.

Page 108: Dhermitte

Dhermitte, Captain of La Méduse (The Medusa), had a reputation for violence and cruelty. Not only was he a slave trader—who brought, at the same time as Buzzard, four hundred slaves from Madagascar—but as a commander, he was also hated by his men and officers, several of whom lodged complaints against him for brutality.

Page 131: Slaves

The first French colonists that arrived on Bourbon Island were accompanied by Malagasy "servants." Initially, there was officially no slavery on Bourbon, and the white population quickly mixed with the black population—especially given the severe shortage of women on the island in the first years of settlement. As a result, French colonists married women from Madagascar, the Comoros, or the Portuguese Indies. Slavery was officially instituted on Bourbon only from 1687, and interracial marriages were then prohibited.

The main source of slaves was initially Mada-

gascar, but the proximity of the two islands helped drive attempts to escape by sea and marronnage. Slave drivers then turned toward the Cafre Coast, in present-day Mozambique, which became the leading provider of slaves, but there were also slaves from the coast of Guinea, from the Congo, and even from India.

Page 152: Mascarene Parrot

The Mascarene parrot (Psittacus mascarin) was one of the endemic birds of Bourbon Island. The species became extinct in the wild around 1770, but there are claims that the last specimen died in captivity in the menagerie of the king of Bavaria, in 1834.

Page 171: Report of Desforges-Boucher

Governer Desforges-Boucher (1723-1725) bequeathed to posterity a memoir titled "To Serve for the Particular Knowledge of each of the Residents of Bourbon Island" (Pour servir à la connoissance particulière de chacun des habitans de l'isle de Bourbon). The governor, who had previously been the island's quartermaster for many years, clearly knew the various inhabitants of the island very well and painted a portrait of them that was exceptionally mean—as well as remarkably funny. The character of Jo Pitre was inspired by several portraits, including that of Robert Tardy. The following was Desforges-Boucher's account of Robert Tardy:

Is a Scotsman, aged thirty-three. He stayed on Bourbon Island in 1704, in April, off a freebooter ship; the man is as much of a drunkard as can be, so much so that it has made him lame, adding to some other foul malady that has spread sores all over his body. He is much given to swearing, as are nearly all buccaneers, since it seems that among these persons that is a most desirable quality, without which one would not be horrid enough. He shows little attachment to the Roman religion, which he has not been professing for very long at all; it was on the Island that he renounced the Protestant one, into which he claimed to have been born; though the very meager education he has suggests that he knew none.

As for a profession, he has none whatsoever, other than that of seaman, which he can no longer practice now that he is lame.

He resides in Sainte-Marie, where he has far more

land than he will ever farm and has a great deal of difficulty making a living, even with that amount of land, for he farms it poorly, though he does have 2 Negroes and 3 Negresses, some of whom, it must be said, are young. He is as badly decked out as can be, and expends not much effort trying to amass what would allow him to dress better. He has beasts—4 bulls, 3 pigs, 8 goats, and 4 horses, but no cash whatsoever.

He additionally has the unfortunate trait of being quarrelsome and obeying only reluctantly. He has as wife one Anne Du Guain, a very ugly mulatta: a tall coiffed beast with no education whatsoever, whose virtue offers precious little resistance to any other men, save those who are afraid of paying too much for that brutish pleasure. He has had from that marriage 2 girls, who are still very young, and one cannot but wonder what education those children will have, being led and educated by such a father and mother.

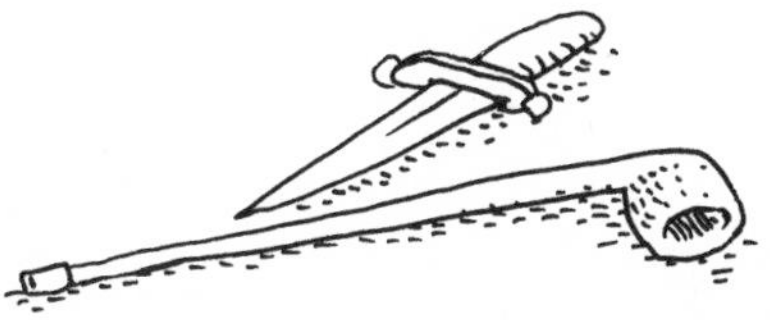

Page 166: Interracial Mixing

From the beginning, the population of Bourbon Island intermarried across races. The first French colonists married Malagasy, Indian, or African women. Even after such marriages were prohibited, the population—particularly in its poorest categories—took no notice and eagerly continued to intermarry.

Page 191: Net and Dick

Note from Governor Desforges-Boucher concerning Net Bequer and Dick:

Are two Englishmen who, having been put to shore on Rodrigues Island, made a small canoe 12 feet long and a foot and a half wide from a single tree-trunk that they dug out with a piece of iron they found by chance, after having spent a full 2 years on that island. With that raft they reached Mauritius, though there be 100 leagues of high seas to cross from one to the other of these islands. Being in Mauritius, they remained in the woods, until they chanced upon an opportunity to steal the launch of an English vessel that had put into port on that island, and with that launch they came to Bourbon, where they are presently.

Those two men are true rascals, as thoroughly depraved as can be, and complete drunkards, constantly caught up in some row, and awaiting only the opportunity of a pirate ship to flee therein. One lives at the property of Thomas Elgar, and the other at Gilles Dennemont's, where they work for their food. Those people are only fit to be chased off the island, as they debauch the young Creoles, who are only too prone to it of their own account; moreover, it is to be feared that they may abscond with a few launches and take away all the Negroes of some inhabitant, which would leave him destitute, and they may not leave without causing some commotion.

Page 210: The Negro Code

The *Code noir*, or Negro Code, was a compendium of regulations concerning the status of slaves in French colonies. It was issued in 1685 under the reign of Louis XIV; Bourbon Island had its own in 1723. It detailed the legal status of slaves, the punishments that they were subject to, as well as all the prohibitions that applied to them.

Page 225: Great Pirate Captains on Reunion Island

The oldest account of the passage of a freebooter on the island dates from 1687. After the hanging of Buzzard, in 1730, European piracy ceased to exist in the Indian Ocean or anywhere else in the world, at least in the unusual form it had taken until then—as freebooting. But between those two dates, many pirate ships called at the island. Though most of them remained anonymous, a few famous ones can be identified.

In November 1695, a freebooter ship called at Bourbon and off it came "70 freebooters flush with gold and silver." That ship probably belonged to the famous captain Avery, who could not stop in Madagascar because he had already abandoned some of his companions there to avoid having to share booty into too many portions. Some of the pirates left on Bourbon by Avery decided to settle on the island, while others decided to leave. The latter began building a small boat, but on July 2, 1696, a French squadron commanded by the Count of Serquigny destroyed it and took about twenty of the pirates back to France as prisoners.

It is believed that around 1710, Caraccioli, a one-legged former Dominican monk serving as the secretary of state of the pirate Republic of Libertalia, called at Bourbon Island to hire pirate citizens—or so Johnson's *A General History of the Robberies and Murders of the Most Notorious Pyrates* suggests.

John Bowen—known to the French as Jean Bouin—a famous pirate of the West Indies mentioned by Johnson, stopped over several times in Bourbon Island and even settled there for good in April 1704, following a campaign with Nathaniel North, another famous pirate. Bowen died there a few months later, but the whereabouts of his tomb remain unknown.

Thomas White called at the island several times, left a few of his men there, and, according to Robert Drury, died during a stopover in Saint-Paul in 1719.

Lastly, Buzzard, Taylor, and perhaps England called at the island in 1720 or 1721 (accounts differ).

Page 230: Libertalia

The story of the pirate republic of Libertalia is one of the most enigmatic in the history of piracy. Once again, it was told by Johnson, in his *General History of the Robberies and Murders of the Most Notorious Pyrates*, published in 1726. A Protestant aristocrat from Provence, Misson, and a defrocked Dominican monk, Caraccioli, having become a pirate, decided to found an egalitarian republic in Madagascar.

They called it Libertalia, and set it up in a protected bay, perhaps the Bay of Antongil in the north of the main island. In Libertalia, all citizens, both European pirates and freed slaves, were equal. A universal language was even invented, and individual freedom was the guiding principle, as was collective ownership of property. The motto of the Republic was "For God and Freedom."

As the pirate republic got organized, it attracted many freebooters from around the Indian Ocean, who enjoyed a quiet retirement there. To defend its small city from European navies, the Republic built a fort to guard against any attack from the sea.

But the utopian experiment was cut short when a Malagasy tribe from the interior attacked and destroyed the small community. Caracioli was killed, as were a large number of the Liberi. Captains Misson and Tew escaped, but the first perished in a storm at sea, and the second was killed several years later in an attempt to board a ship. With their deaths disappeared the last witnesses to this unique adventure.

The story of this first republic of the modern era captured the imagination of many who heard it, but recent research has cast doubt on its reality and suggests that Daniel Defoe—who was the author hiding behind the pseudonym of Captain Johnson—may have completely invented this story and woven it into his compilation of authentic stories about piracy.

Page 233: A Republic on Bourbon

There had been an attempted revolt by the colonists of Bourbon against their governor. On November 26, 1690, a certain number of colonists, exasperated with Governor Vauboulon's abuses of authority and violence, burst into a mass that the governor was attending, arrested him, and threw him into a dungeon, where he died shortly thereafter, probably from poisoning.

The inhabitants then elected representatives, and the island governed itself, not without difficulty, for several years. In July 1696, a French navy squadron commanded by the Count of Serquigny fortuitously arrived on the island. Serquigny reestablished order through military force and had the rebel leaders arrested (they were tried and executed the following year in Rennes, France) before appointing a new governor.

That was the end of the Republic of Bourbon.

Page 274: Buzzard's Cryptogram

The cryptogram of La Buse (Buzzard) was apparently found in the National Archives in Paris, by Charles de la Roncière, in the early part of the twentieth century. Its authenticity has not been proven.

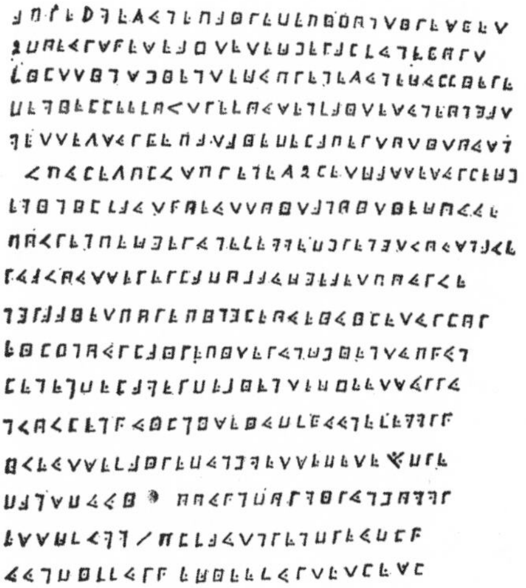

Since that find, droves of treasure-hunters have po red over it and have tried to use it to locate the treasure. Some of them believed that the cryptogram used the alphabet of the Knights Templar and claimed that it could only be translated using the *Clavicles of Solomon*, a Kabalistic work. However, this has not yielded any truly usable result:

APREJME TO A PAIR OF PIJONTIRE SKET 2 HARD QU SE AJHEAD HORSE FUNE KORT FITT IN SHIENTOO PREEN TO A STRAP HALF THE E FO VTE CRAZY N MADE S A ONGAT PUT ONGAT OL VS PREEN TO 2 LEYT BREAK ON THE WAY MUST QCEUTTOIT TO NOITE COVER FOR ENPECGE A WOMAN DH RENGT YOU NAVE RVA YOU CLOSE THE DORRAUC GEA AND FOR VENGRAAI AND POUR PINGLE OR EIUI THE TURLORE IT J NOUR LAIRE PITER A DOGTURQ_A THE BEG QAMER OF GOODTE CJE AND ON R A VOV THE NQUIL NOR SEIUD FKU INE FEMMR HOO WANT THE MAKE HIMELF ANY NH PUT HIM DTE SOUTH RE IN ANY UI OR O QN SLEEP A MAN SSCVFMM/PL MUST N RETURN UDL QU A DIF FURK

Some people thought they had located Buzzard's treasure on Rodrigues Island, in the Seychelles (on Mahé Island), or on Reunion Island. For decades, treasure-hunters of various stripes, some more eccentric than others, have conducted digs in those various islands. Unsuccessfully, so far.

First Second

New York & London

Text copyright © 2008 by Appollo and Lewis Trondheim
Art copyright © 2008 by Lewis Trondheim
English translation copyright © 2008 by First Second

Published by First Second
First Second is an imprint of Roaring Brook Press,
a division of Holtzbrinck Publishing Holdings Limited Partnership
175 Fifth Avenue, New York, NY 10010

Distributed in Canada by H. B. Fenn and Company Ltd.
Distributed in the United Kingdom by Macmillan Children's Books, a division of Pan Macmillan.

Design by Nicole Concepción

Library of Congress Cataloging-in-Publication Data
Trondheim, Lewis.
[L'île Bourbon 1730. English]
Bourbon Island 1730 / by Appollo and Lewis Trondheim; English translation by Alexis Siegel.—1st ed.
p. cm.
Summary: On Bourbon Island off the coast of Madagascar, a French ornithologist and his assistant are
caught up in an adventure involving slavery, colonialism, and the last days of the great pirates.
ISBN-13: 978-1-59643-258-1
ISBN-10: 1-59643-258-6
1. Graphic novels. [1. Graphic novels. 2. Pirates--Fiction. 3. Ornithologists--Fiction. 4. Slavery--
Fiction. 5. Réunion--History--18th century--Fiction.] I. Appollo, 1969- II. Siegel, Alexis. III. Title.
IV. Title: Bourbon Island seventeen hundred thirty.
PZ7.7.T76Bou 2008
[Fic]--dc22
2007046138

First Second books are available for special promotions and premiums.
For details, contact: Director of Special Markets, Holtzbrinck Publishers.

FIRST
EDITION

First Edition November 2008
Printed in the United States of America
1 3 5 7 9 10 8 6 4 2

BY ART
WE LIVE